VISUAL QUICKSTART GUIDE

Microsoft Office

FOR MACINTOSH

- **Word 6.0**
- **Excel 5.0**
- **PowerPoint 4.0**
- **Mail 3.1**

Steve Sagman

Adaptation for the Mac by
Dan Henderson

Peachpit Press

Visual QuickStart Guide

Microsoft Office for Macintosh

Steve Sagman
Adaptation for the Mac by Dan Henderson

Peachpit Press
2414 Sixth Street
Berkeley, CA 94710
(510) 548-4393
(510) 548-5991 (fax)

Peachpit Press is a division of
Addison-Wesley Publishing Company.

Cover design: The Visual Group.

ISBN: 0-201-48599-0

0 9 8 7 6 5 4 3 2 1

Printed and bound in the United States.

Printed on recycled paper

Thank You

To **Roslyn Bullas** at Peachpit Press for guidance, flexibility, and patience.

To **Ted Nace** and the folks at Peachpit Press for producing such outstanding books and for giving me this opportunity.

To **Elaine Weinmann** for allowing me to employ her superb book design.

To **Pat** for her patience, support, and love.

To **Josephine Bacon** at Chanterelle Books in London for introducing us to each other.

To **Eric** and **Lola** for their patience and love.

Book Design
Elaine Weinmann

Additional Design
Milton Zelman

About the Authors

Steve Sagman

Half a million readers know Steve Sagman's books on PC software, including his best-sellers on Harvard Graphics and Microsoft PowerPoint.

He gives classes and seminars nationwide on application software, presentation graphics, desktop publishing, and online services. His technical communications company, The Water Mill Group, provides training, courseware, user documentation, and user interface consulting.

He welcomes comments, questions, and suggestions and can be reached at:

Net: steves@msn.com
CompuServe: 72456,3325

or at: Steve Sagman
The Water Mill Group
570 Mecox Road
Water Mill, NY 11976

Dan Henderson

Dan Henderson has worked in software development, support, and training since the early 1970s, focusing on helping Macintosh users since the early days of the original 128K Mac. Consulting assignments have taken him to such varied locations as Hawaii and Sweden, where he has worked with Macintosh and PC owners of every skill level, from computer phobics to power users.

In his consulting work, he specializes in helping people improve their relationships with their computers and with each other. In addition to his computer-oriented skills, he is also a licensed psychotherapist.

Until he began his collaboration with Steve Sagman on this book, most of his writing was for user group and private organization newsletters. He welcomes comments, questions, and suggestions, and can be reached at:

Net: dh@tyrell.net
CompuServe: 72106,1460
AOL, eWorld: DHenderson

or at: Dan Henderson
206 NE 58th St. #14
Gladstone, MO 64118-4290

Other Books by Steve Sagman

Using Harvard Graphics

1-2-3 Graphics Techniques

*Getting Your Start in Hollywood***

Using Windows Draw

*Mastering CorelDraw 3** **

Using Freelance Graphics 2

*Using 1-2-3 for Windows Release 4**

*Mastering CorelDraw 4** **

*The PC Bible** **

Running PowerPoint 4

*Harvard Graphics for Windows 2: Visual QuickStart Guide***

Traveling the Microsoft Network

* Contributor.

** Also published by Peachpit Press.

Table of Contents

Common Office Techniques

1. Basic Macintosh Procedures

2. Essential Office Techniques

Word 6.0 Word Processing

3. About Word

4. Entering and Editing the Text

5. Font Formatting

6. Paragraph Formatting

7. Automatic Text Formatting

8. Page Formatting

9. Creating Tables

10. Special Word Techniques

Excel 5.0 Number Crunching

11. About Excel

12. Entering Headings and Data

Mail 3.1 Communicating

30. About Mail

31. Reading Messages

32. Sending Messages

33. Managing Your Mail

Combining the Office Applications

34. Basic Techniques

35. Combining Applications

Common Office Techniques

Common Office Techniques

Basic Macintosh Procedures

Essential Office Techniques

Basic Macintosh Procedures

1

What is Macintosh?

The Macintosh is a personal computer system that provides both picture and text controls you can use to run *applications* (programs that perform specific tasks, such as word processing). These controls are menus, buttons, scroll bars, and other onscreen items that you operate with a mouse, trackball, or trackpad.

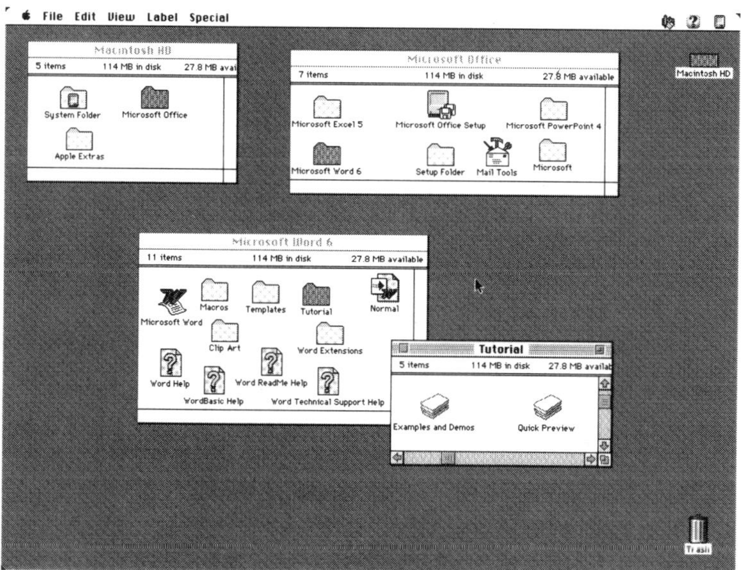

Figure 1. *The Mac desktop.*

All Macintosh applications run in windows on the screen and sport nearly identical menus, buttons, scroll bars, dialog boxes, and other controls that work alike in every program. This makes it easy to learn and use one program and transfer your knowledge to many other programs.

The Macintosh also features "plug and play" simplicity for installing a wide variety of peripheral devices, such as printers, modems, CD-ROM drives, scanners, and removable cartridge drives

Starting the Macintosh

Depending on your model of Macintosh, you may start the computer one of three ways:

- Press the large triangle key on the keyboard.

  or
- Push the front panel button.

  or
- Flip a switch or push a button on the back panel.

If the Macintosh passes its internal self tests, you will hear a musical chord. If it then finds a disk containing a valid System Folder, you will see the "Happy Mac" icon followed by the "Welcome to Macintosh" screen.

If the Macintosh does not find a disk with a valid System Folder, you will see a disk icon with a flashing question mark.

During normal start-up, you will see icons for any Extensions or Control Panels you have installed in the System Folder. These appear one by one across the bottom of the screen. When your system software is completed loaded, you will see the Macintosh Desktop, including the menu bar of the Finder, the icons of any available storage devices, and the Trash icon. **(Figure 2)** You may also see one or more windows open showing the contents of storage devices.

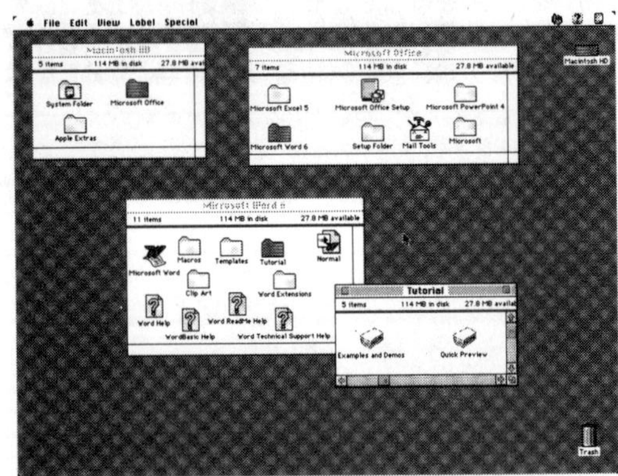

Figure 2. *The Macintosh desktop.*

Shutting Down the Macintosh

You should *always* shut down the Macintosh by returning to the Finder, pulling down the Special menu, and choosing Shut Down. **(Figure 3)**

If any documents are open and changes have not been saved, you will get the opportunity to save or discard them properly.

Figure 3. *The Special menu.*

Using the Pointing Device

Moving the mouse on the desktop moves the pointer on the screen. Rolling the ball on a trackball or moving your finger across a trackpad also moves the mouse pointer. Here are the three basic mouse techniques:

Click

Place the pointer on something and click the mouse button once. Click on an icon to select it, or click on an onscreen button to press it.

Double-click

Place the pointer on something and then click the mouse button twice in quick succession. Double-click a storage device or folder to show its contents, double-click an icon to launch an application, or double-click a word to select the word.

Drag

Place the pointer on something, press and hold down the mouse button, move the mouse, and then release the mouse button. Drag to highlight text, or to move an object or window.

Terminology

Select

Click on an object on the screen. Your next action will affect the selected object. To select a menu, click its name and hold down the mouse button. To select text, place the pointer at the beginning of the text and then drag across the text. Selected text is highlighted.

Press

Press a key on the keyboard.

Drop-down list

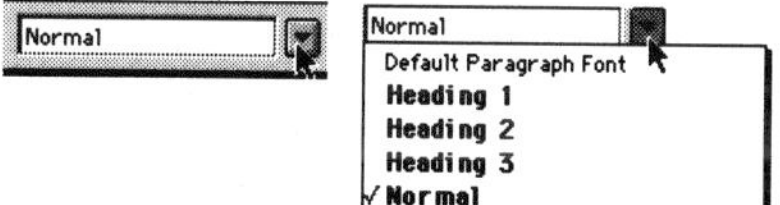

Click the drop-down arrow at the right end of a text box to pull down a list of alternatives. Drag through the list until an item is highlighted and then release the mouse button.

Check/ Uncheck

Click the checkbox next to an option to turn it on or off. A checked box indicates that the option is turned on.

Scroll

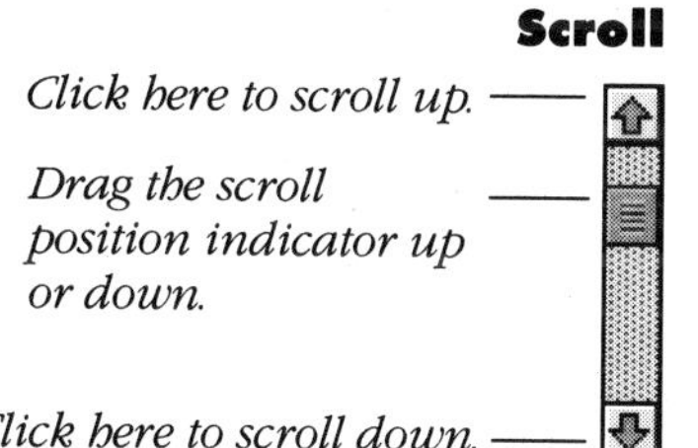

Use the scroll bar to the right of a list to move up or down through the list. Drag the scroll position indicator along the scroll bar or click the up or down arrow buttons at the ends of the scroll bar. You may also click in the gray area between the scroll button and an arrow button to scroll a window-full at a time. Horizontal scroll bars at the bottom of windows work in similar ways.

The Desktop

1 Apple menu icon
2 Menu bar
3 Window
4 Microsoft Office Folder window
5 Application menu icon
6 Apple Guide menu icon
7 Storage device icon
File Edit View Label Special
Macintosh HD
5 items 114 MB in disk 27.8 MB avai
System Folder
Microsoft Office
Apple Extras
Microsoft Office
7 items 114 MB in disk 27.8 MB available
Microsoft Excel 5
Microsoft Office Setup
Microsoft PowerPoint 4
Microsoft Word 6
Setup Folder
Mail Tools
Microsoft
Macintosh HD
Microsoft Word 6
11 items 114 MB in disk 27.8 MB available
Microsoft Word
Macros
Templates
Tutorial
Normal
Clip Art
Word Extensions
Word Help
Word ReadMe Help
WordBasic Help
Word Technical Support Help
Tutorial
5 items 114 MB in disk 27.8 MB availab
Examples and Demos
Quick Preview
Trash
8 Title bar
9 Close box
11 Zoom box
12 Resize box
10 Active window
13 Trash can icon

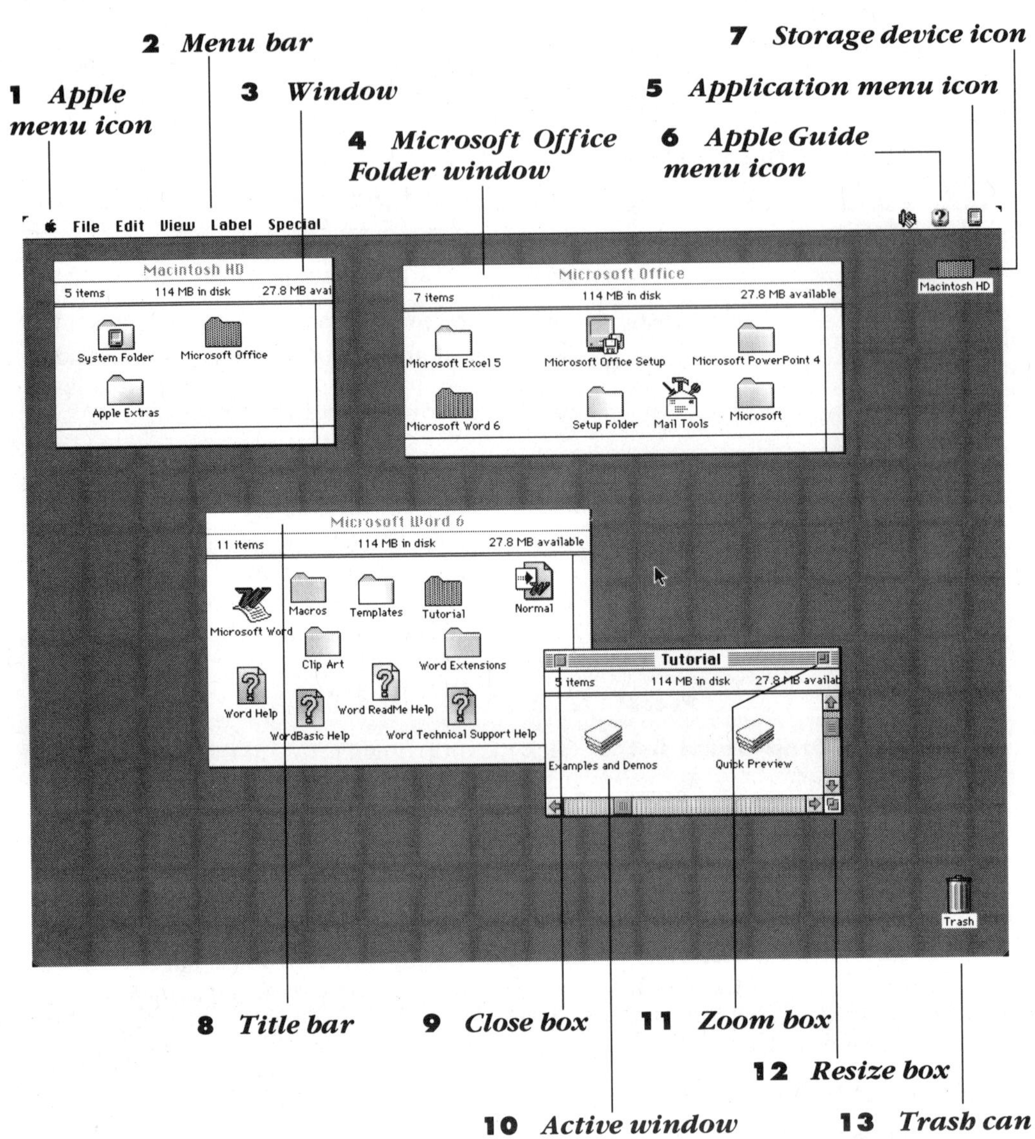

Key to the Desktop

1 *Apple menu icon*

Click this icon to open a menu of items you have placed in the Apple Menu Items folder inside the System Folder on the disk used to start up your Macintosh.

2 *Menu bar*

Each word or icon represents a menu. Use the pointing device to place the pointer on one of the words or icons, then click and hold down the button to see the menu. Continue to hold down the button and drag the pointer down the menu until a selection is highlighted. Release the button.

3 *Window*

Shows the contents of a storage device or folder.

4 *Microsoft Office Folder window*

This window contains icons for the Microsoft Office applications and utilities.

5 *Application menu icon*

Click this icon to open a menu of application programs that are currently running. Select an application from this menu to bring it to the front of all other windows. To hide the other windows, choose Hide Others from this menu.

7 *Apple Guide menu icon*

Click this icon to open a menu which activates the Apple Guide online help feature of Macintosh System 7.5.

7 *Storage device icon*

To see the files and folders contained in a storage device, place the pointer on the storage device icon and double-click.

8 *Title bar*

Names the window. Drag the title bar to move a window.

9 *Close box*

Click here to close a window. To close all windows, hold down the Option key and click in the close box of the active window.

10 *Active window*

The window that displays horizontal lines in its title bar. The active window can be moved or resized. To make a window the active window, click in any portion of the window.

11 *Zoom box*

Click in the zoom box to resize a window so it shows as many files and folders as possible. Click in the zoom box again to restore the window's size and shape.

12 *Resize box*

Click in this box, hold down the mouse button, and drag to move the lower right corner of a window. The upper left corner of the window stays anchored in place.

13 *Trash can icon*

Drag a file or folder to the trash can and release the button when the trash can is highlighted. To permanently delete the items in the trash, choose Empty Trash from the Special menu. To retrieve an item from the trash, double-click the trash can icon to open its window and drag the item to be rescued to another window or click on the item to select it, pull down the File menu, and choose Put Away. Drag the icon of a floppy disk to the trash to eject it. This does *not* delete the information on the disk.

An Application Layout

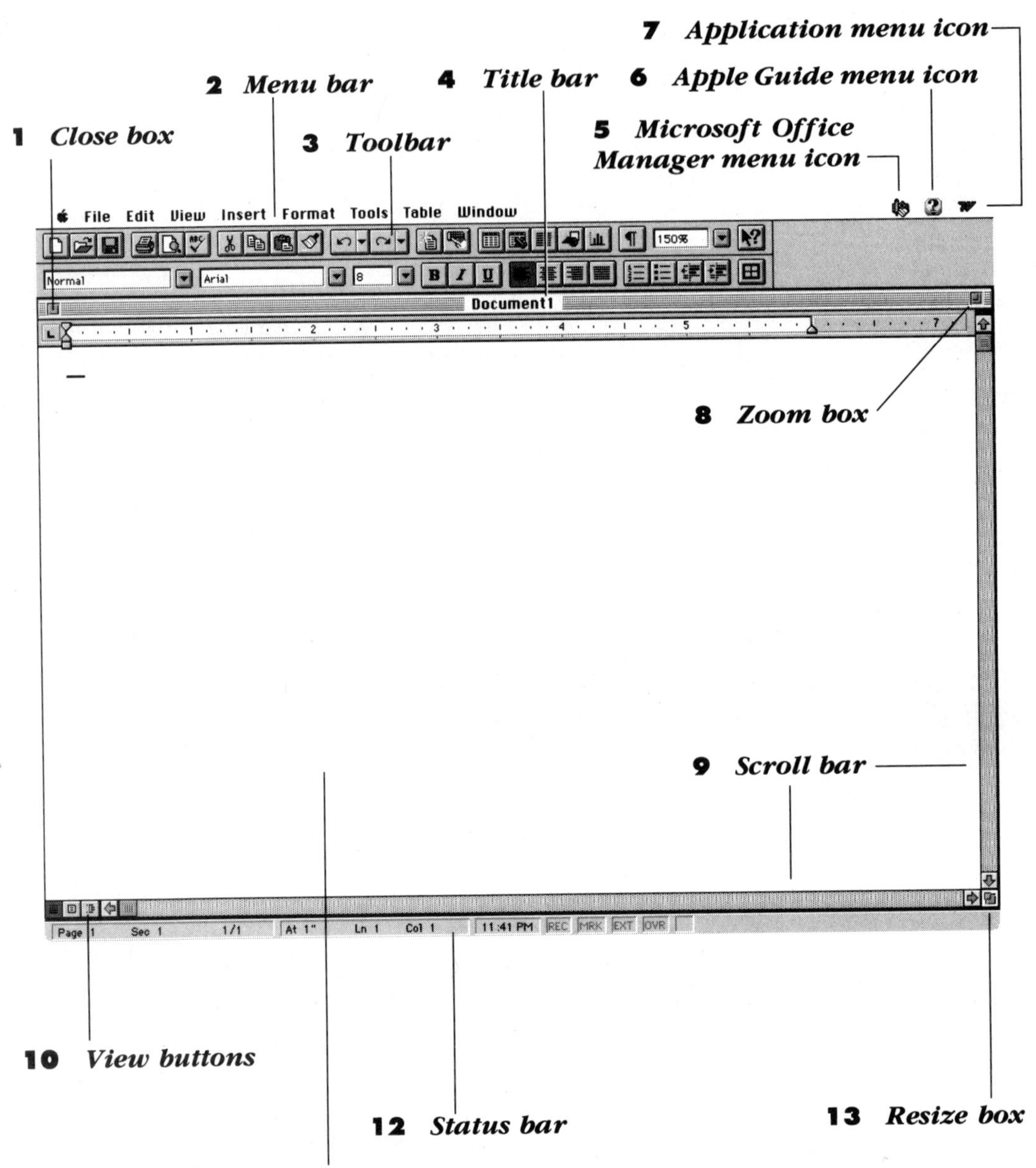

Key to the Application Layout

1 *Close box*

Click in the close box to close the window. This closes the currently active document and leaves the application running.

2 *Menu bar*

Place the pointer on a menu name, then click and hold down the mouse button to pull down a menu. Keep the button held down and drag the pointer down the list until the item you want to select is highlighted. Release the mouse button.

3 *Toolbar*

Click a tool to perform a frequently needed task. Place the pointer on a tool without clicking and pause to see a description of the tool in a tooltip.

4 *Title bar*

Displays the document name. Drag the title bar to move the document window.

5 *Microsoft Office Manager menu icon*

Click this icon to open a menu of Microsoft Office applications and utilities.

6 *Apple Guide menu icon*

Click this icon to open a menu which activates the Apple Guide online help feature of Macintosh System 7.5.

7 *Application menu icon*

Click this icon to open a menu of applications currently running. Select an application on the menu to move the application in front of other applications.

8 *Zoom box*

Click in this box to resize a document window to fill the screen. Click in the zoom box again to restore a window to its previous size and shape.

9 *Scroll bar*

Click the arrows at either ends of a scroll bar or drag the scroll button to see more of a document than shows in the current window. Click in the gray areas to move a window-full at a time.

10 *View buttons*

Click these buttons to switch among alternate views of the document.

11 *Document window*

Shows contents of the currently active document.

12 *Status bar*

Displays the current status of the document.

13 *Resize box*

Drag the resize box to resize or reshape the document window.

Choosing From Menus

Every application has a menu bar that crosses the top of the screen. Each menu name and icon on the menu bar represents a group of commands or options on a menu that drops down when you click the menu name.

1. Place the pointer on a menu name and press and hold the mouse button. **(Figure 4)**

2. Keep the mouse button down and drag down the list of items on the menu. **(Figure 5)**

3. Release the mouse button when the item you want is highlighted.

✔ Tips

- Many menu options have keyboard equivalents indicated to the right of the option. These keyboard alternatives allow you to invoke an action without removing your hands from the keyboard.
- Items that are shown in gray text cannot be performed at the time the menu is pulled down.

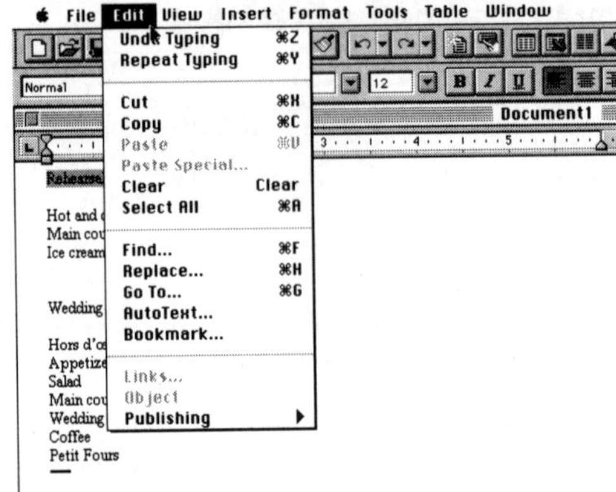

Figure 4. *Click a menu name.*

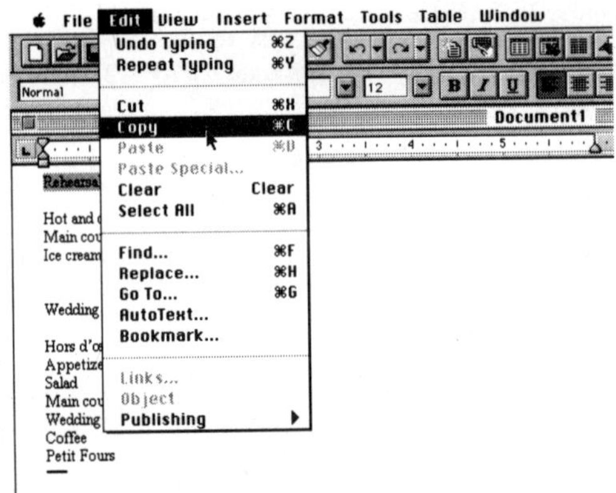

Figure 5. *A menu.*

Selecting Options in Dialog Boxes

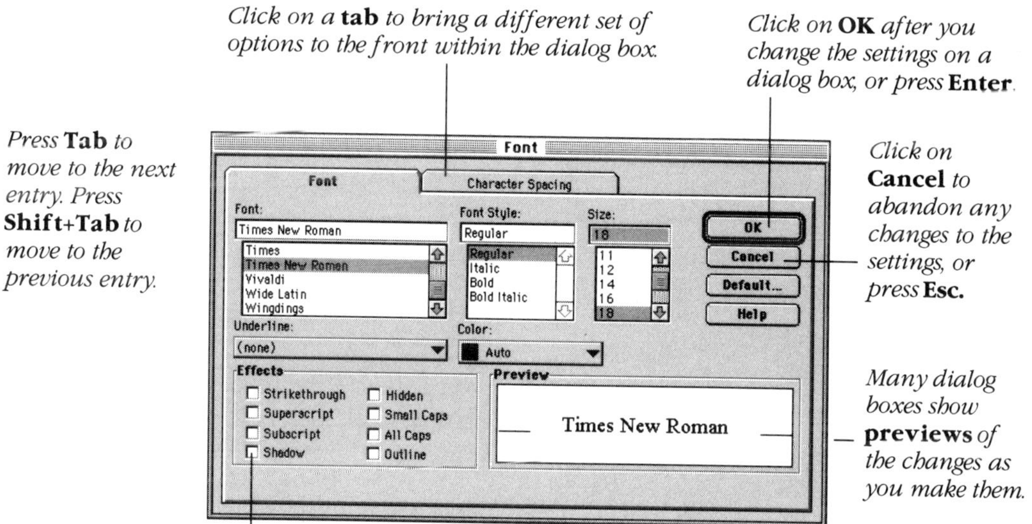

Click on a **checkbox** to turn the option on or off. When a checkbox is checked with an "x", the option is on.

Figure 6. *The Font dialog box.*

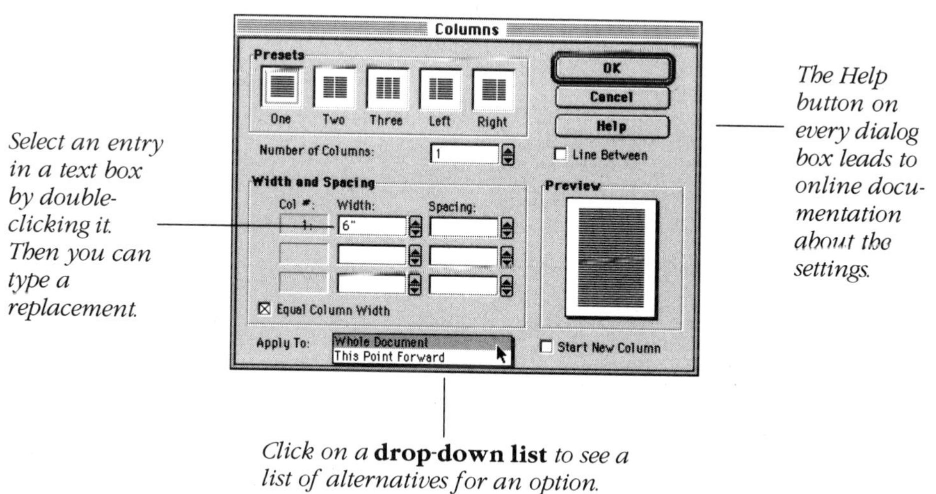

Figure 7. *The Columns dialog box.*

Using the Toolbars

Click any toolbar button to perform an action. **(Figure 8)**

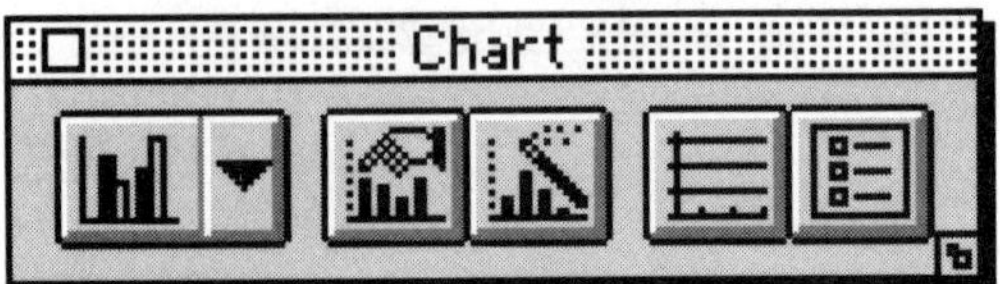

Figure 8. *The Chart toolbar for Excel.*

✓ Tip

- To see a description of a button, place the pointer on the button and pause for a moment without clicking. **(Figure 9)**

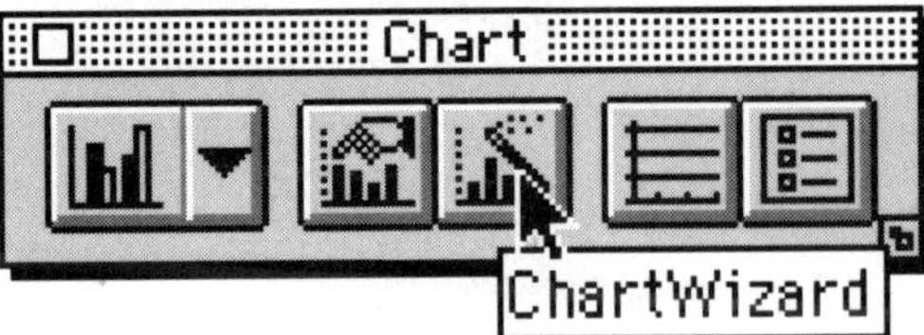

Figure 9. *Pause on a button to get a descriptive Tooltip.*

Starting Applications

1. In the Microsoft Office folder, double-click the icon of an application's folder. Then, in the window that opens, double-click the icon of the application. **(Figure 10)**

   or

   Pull down the Microsoft Office Manager menu and choose the program you want to launch. **(Figure 11)**

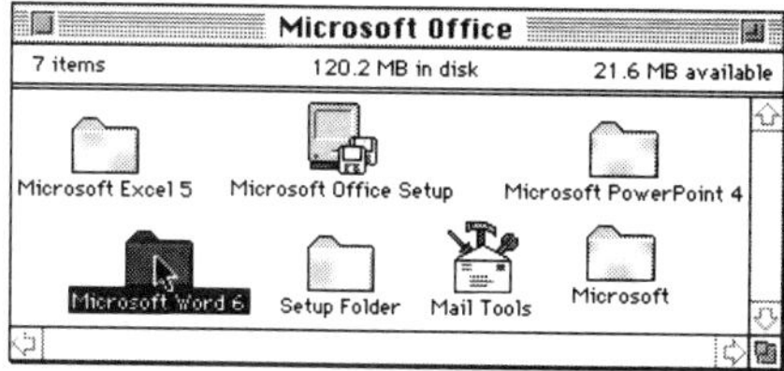

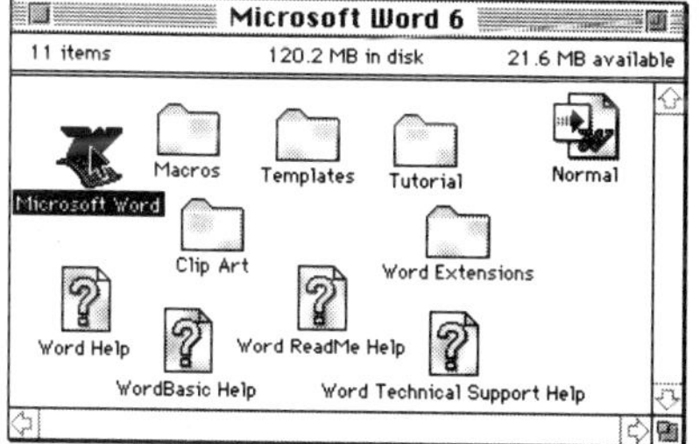

Figure 10. *The Microsoft Office and Microsoft Word folders.*

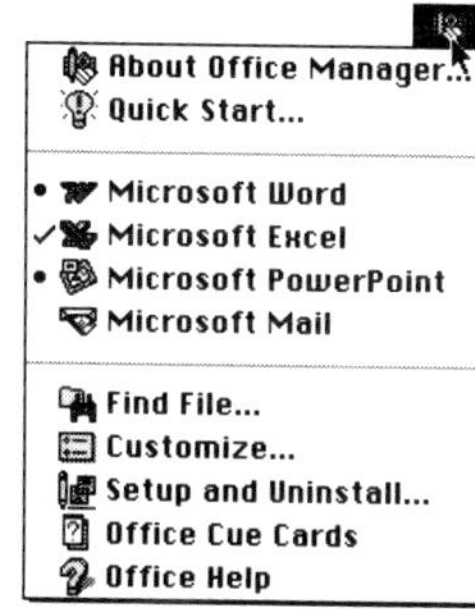

Figure 11. *Drag down to the icon of the application to open and release the mouse button.*

Quitting Applications

1. Pull down the File menu and choose Quit. **(Figure 12)**

   or

   Use the keyboard equivalent for the Quit command. (⌘+Q)

✔ Tip

- If you have changed any of the documents that are open in an application, the system will ask if you want to save the changes, so you need not worry about losing work by quitting prematurely.

Figure 12. *The File menu.*

About Manipulating Windows

As you work in an application, you might want to move one of its windows or zoom a window to the fill the screen. You might also want to switch among the windows that are already open on the screen.

Moving, zooming, and switching among windows are all indispensable tasks while working on the Macintosh.

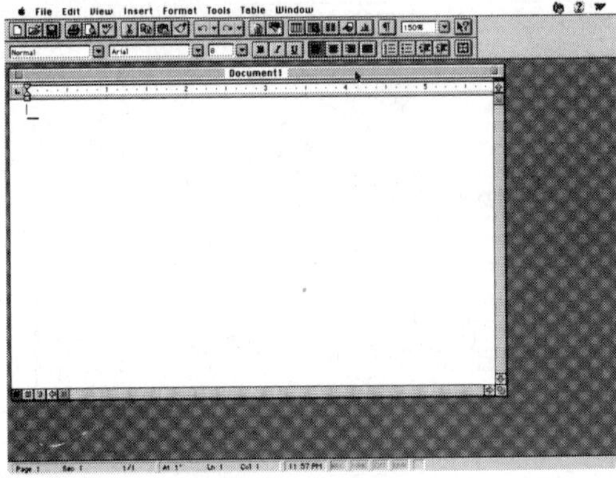

Figure 13. *Point to the title bar.*

Moving a Window

1. Place the mouse pointer on the window's title bar. **(Figure 13)**
2. Press and hold the mouse button.
3. Move the mouse to drag the window. **(Figure 14)**
4. Release the mouse button. **(Figure 15)**

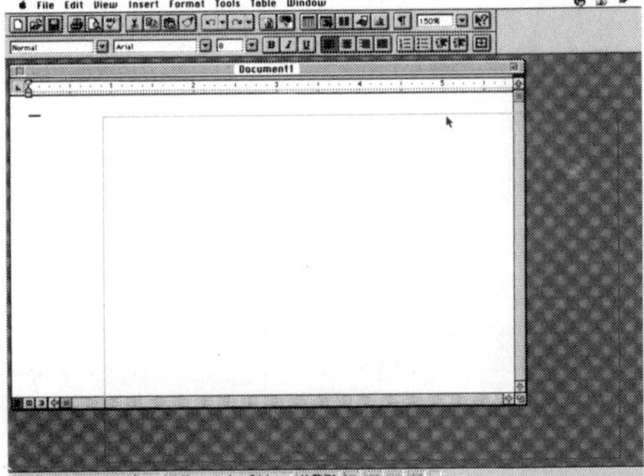

Figure 14. *Hold down the mouse button and move the mouse.*

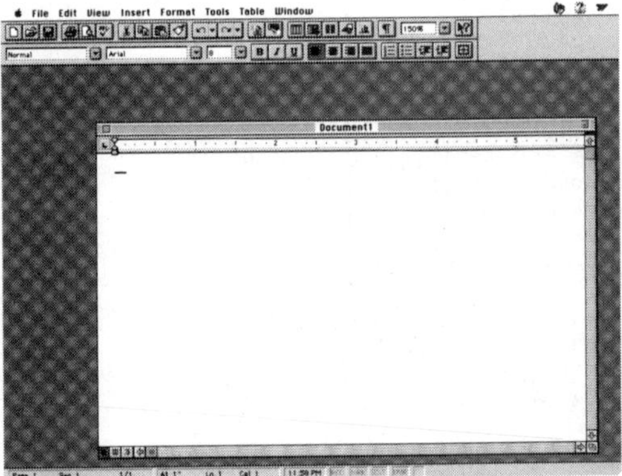

Figure 15. *The window after it has been moved.*

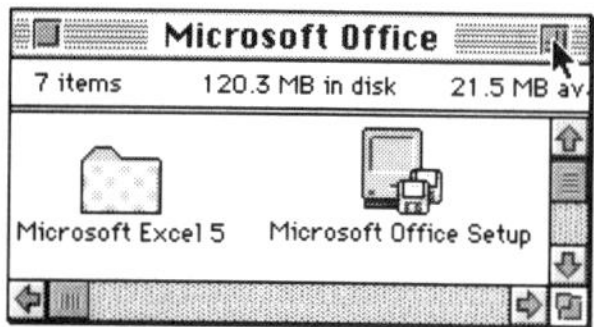

Figure 16. *The Zoom button on a standard window.*

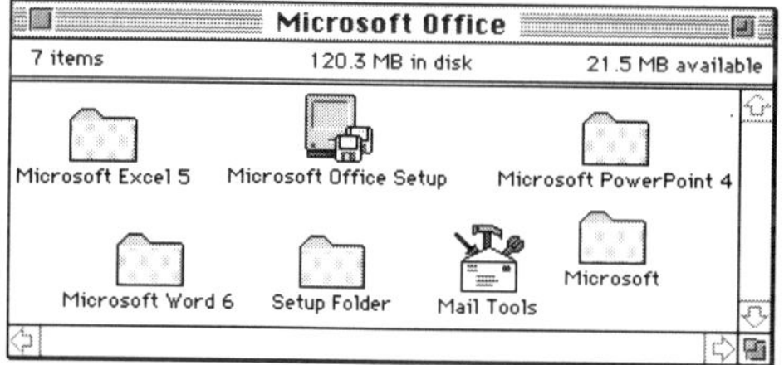

Figure 17. *The window after it has been zoomed.*

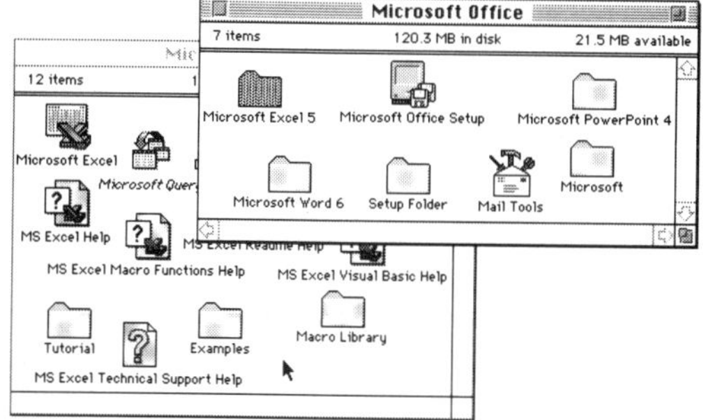

Figure 18. *Place the pointer on any visible part of a window.*

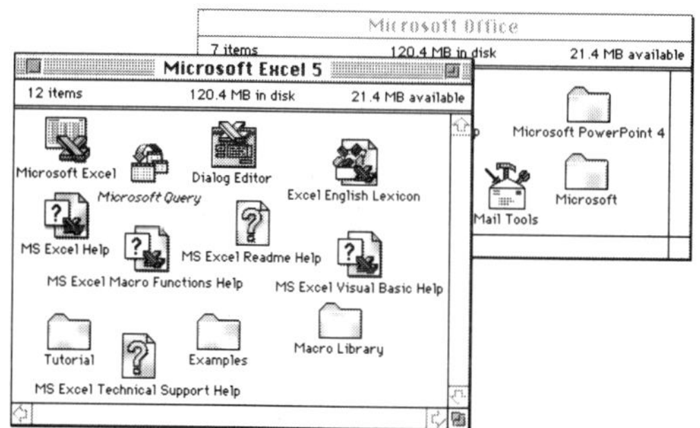

Figure 19. *The window comes to the front when you click the mouse button.*

Zooming a Window

The active window has a zoom box that you can click to make the window larger. Zooming a window allows you to see more of its contents. You can zoom a window that contains the contents of a folder, for example, to show more of the files inside.

1. Place the pointer on the zoom box and click. **(Figures 16 17)**

✔ Tips

- Click the zoom button again to return the window to its previous size and shape.
- Scroll bars are active only when there is more to see in a window than is currently visible.

Switching Windows

You can work in only one window at a time, even though you may have several windows open on the screen.

1. Place the pointer on any visible part of the window. **(Figure 18)**
2. Click the mouse button. **(Figure 19)**

✔ Tip

- If one window fills the screen, you may have to click the window's zoom box or use its resize box to restore it to a normal size. Then, you will be able to see and click in other windows.

Opening a File on the Desktop

When you double-click a file's icon, the application in which the file was originally created is automatically opened. If the application was already open, the file becomes the active file in the application.

1. Open the folder that contains the file's icon. **(Figure 20)**
2. Double-click the file's icon. **(Figure 21)**

✔ Tips

- Because you can simply double-click a file to open it, you don't have to worry about which application to use to open the file.
- If you want to try to open a file in a program other than the one that created it, use the Open command on the program's File menu instead of double-clicking the file.
  See Opening a File in an Application, page 17.

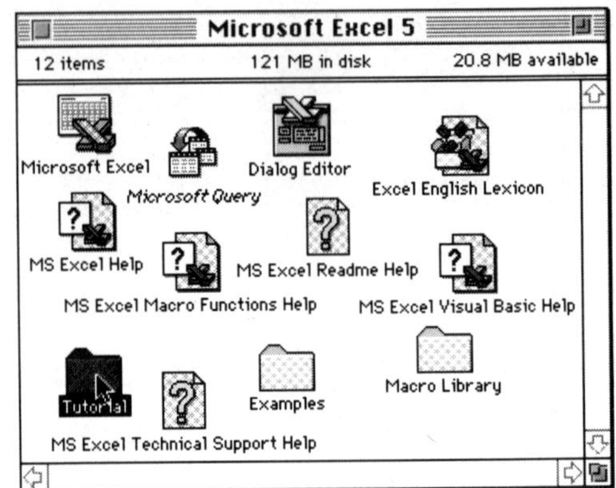

Figure 20. *The Microsoft Excel 5 window.*

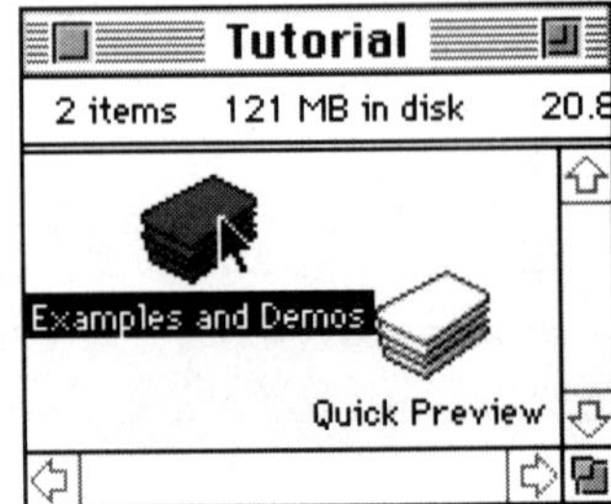

Figure 21. *Double-click a file's icon to open the file.*

Figure 22. *The File menu.*

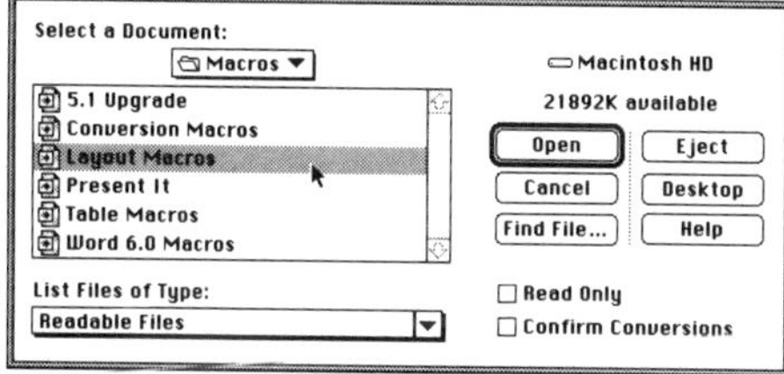

Figure 23. *Double-click a filename.*

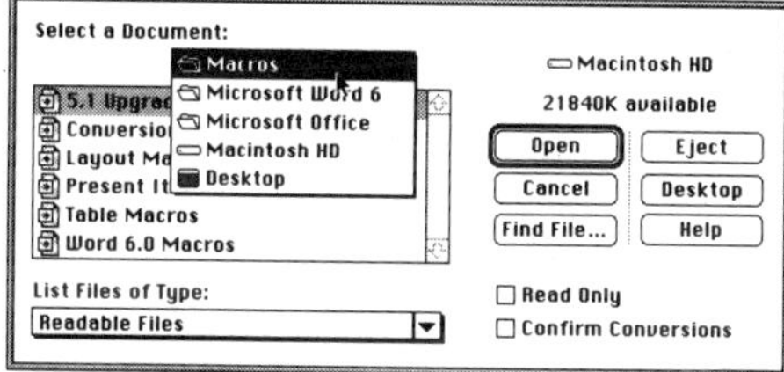

Figure 24. *Place the mouse pointer on the name of the current folder and release the mouse button.*

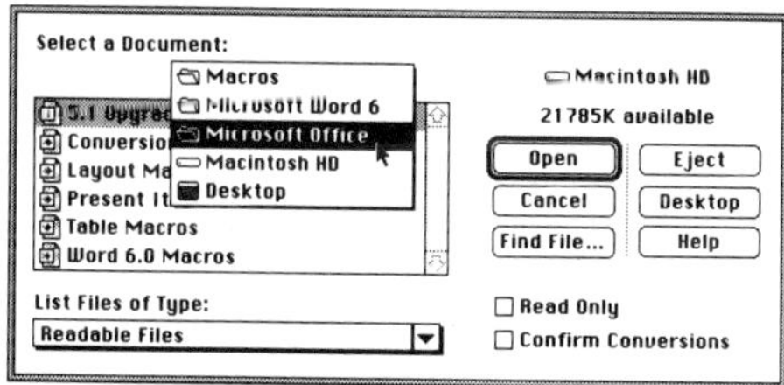

Figure 25. *Choose a folder from this list.*

Opening a File in an Application

If you have already opened an application, you can use the application's File menu to open a file.

1. From the File menu, choose Open. **(Figure 22)**
2. Double-click the name of a file to open. **(Figure 23)**

   or, if the file you want is not visible on the list

   Double-click any other folder on the list. Then double-click on one of the files inside.

   If you still don't see the file you want
3. Click on the name of the current folder or disk. **(Figure 24)**
4. Select one of the items on the list that opens so you can look inside that folder or disk for your file. **(Figure 25)**

✔ Tips

- If you click the name of the current folder, you will see the levels of storage organization from your current folder, to the disk that contains the folder, to the desktop. You can select any item on this list to open it.
- When you pull down the File menu, the file you want to open may appear on a list of recently used files. If so, simply choose the file you want to open.

Opening a File with Drag and Drop

Another technique you can use to open a file, if your Macintosh supports Drag and Drop, is to drag the file's icon on top of an icon for an application.

1. Place the pointer on the icon for the file you want to open. **(Figure 26)**
2. Press and hold the mouse button.
3. Drag the icon on top of the icon for an application. **(Figure 27)**
4. When the application's icon is highlighted, release the mouse button.

✔ **Tip**

- Because Microsoft Office applications can open files created in some other applications, you might want to try dragging an icon for a file to a Microsoft Office application icon even if you didn't create the file in the Microsoft Office application. This technique can be handy when you get a file from someone and you do not own the original application used to create the file.

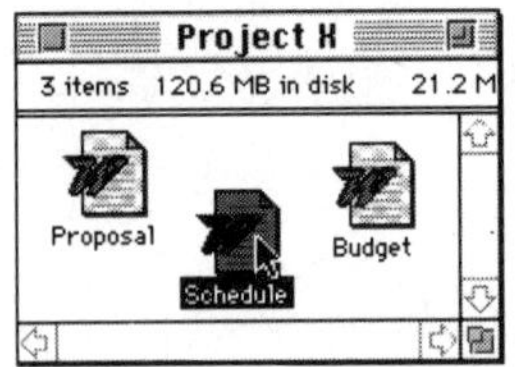

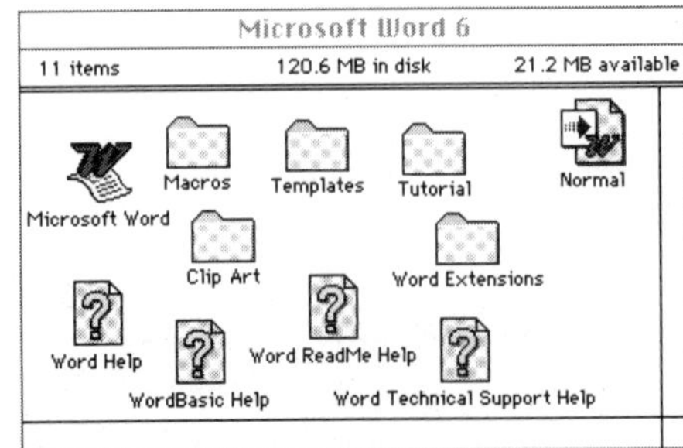

Figure 26. *Place the pointer on the icon for a file..*

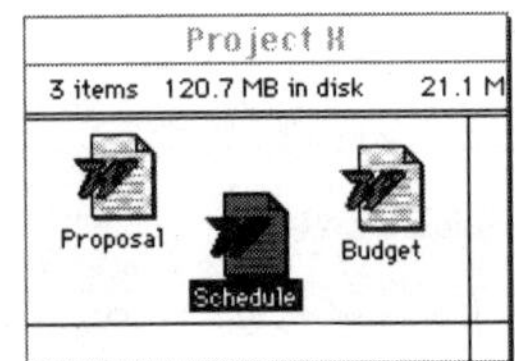

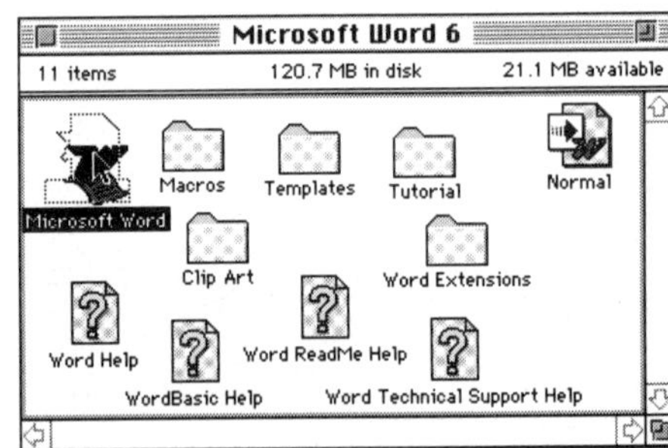

Figure 27. *Drag the file icon to the icon for an application.*

Essential Office Techniques

Figure 1. *The Undo button.*

Edit
Undo Clear ⌘Z
Repeat Clear ⌘Y
Cut ⌘X
Copy ⌘C
Paste ⌘V
Paste Special...
Clear Clear
Select All ⌘A
Find... ⌘F
Replace... ⌘H
Go To... ⌘G
AutoText...
Bookmark...
Links...
Object
Publishing

Figure 2. *The Edit menu.*

Click here to pull down the undo list...

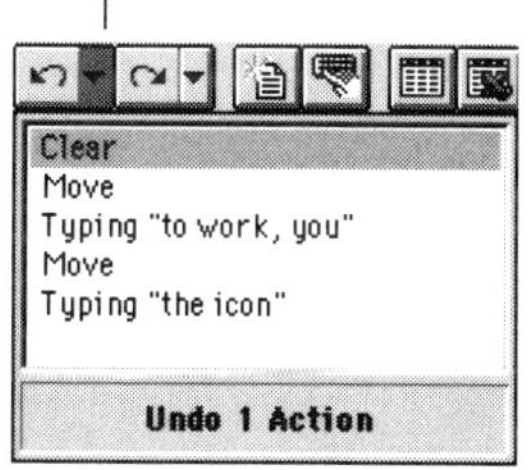

...then select an item on the list.

Figure 3. *The undo list.*

Figure 4. *The Redo button.*

About Office Techniques

One advantage of working in Microsoft Office is the body of procedures that the applications share in common. If something works a certain way in one application, it almost always works identically in all the other applications.

Become acquainted with these common techniques early and try them in any application. You'll be using them constantly.

Undoing Any Change

Remember Undo! You can undo just about any error as long as you undo it right away. If you do something else before you undo, you won't be able to undo anything you did before (except in **Word** where you can choose from a list of recent actions to undo).

1. Click the Undo button on the Standard toolbar. **(Figure 1)**

   or

   Press ⌘+Z.

   or

   From the Edit menu, choose Undo *action*. **(Figure 2)**

✔ Tips

- In **Word**, click the pull-down button next to the Undo button to choose from a list of recent actions that you can undo. **(Figure 3)**
- To redo something you've undone, click the Redo button. Redo undoes an undo. **(Figure 4)**

Entering Text

Whenever an application is ready for you to type text, a blinking insertion point appears. Whatever you type appears at the insertion point. **(Figures 5-6)**

1. Simply begin typing to insert text at the insertion point.

✔ **Tip**

- To type over existing text that is to the right of the insertion point, press the Insert key to switch from Insert to Overwrite mode. **(Figure 7)**

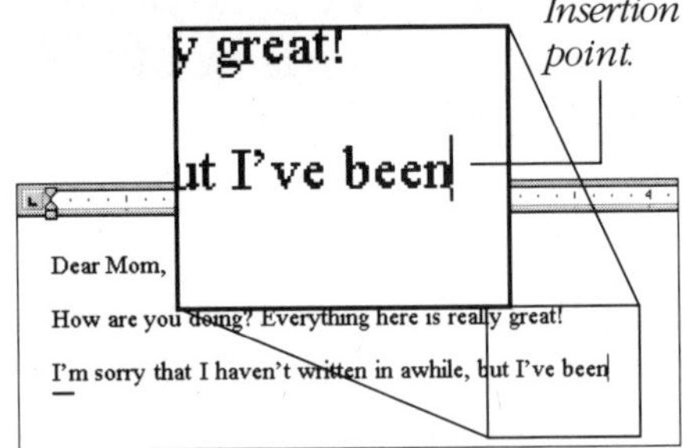

Figure 5. *The insertion point.*

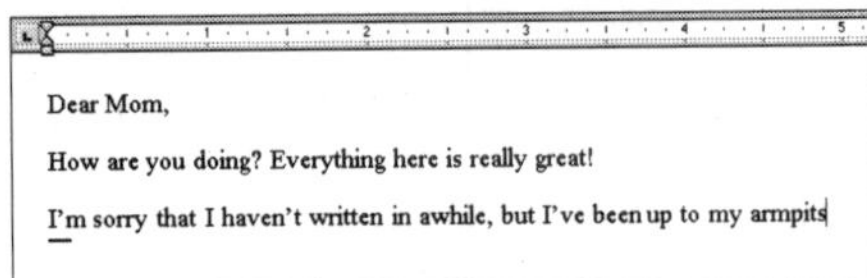

Figure 6. *Anything you type is inserted at the insertion point.*

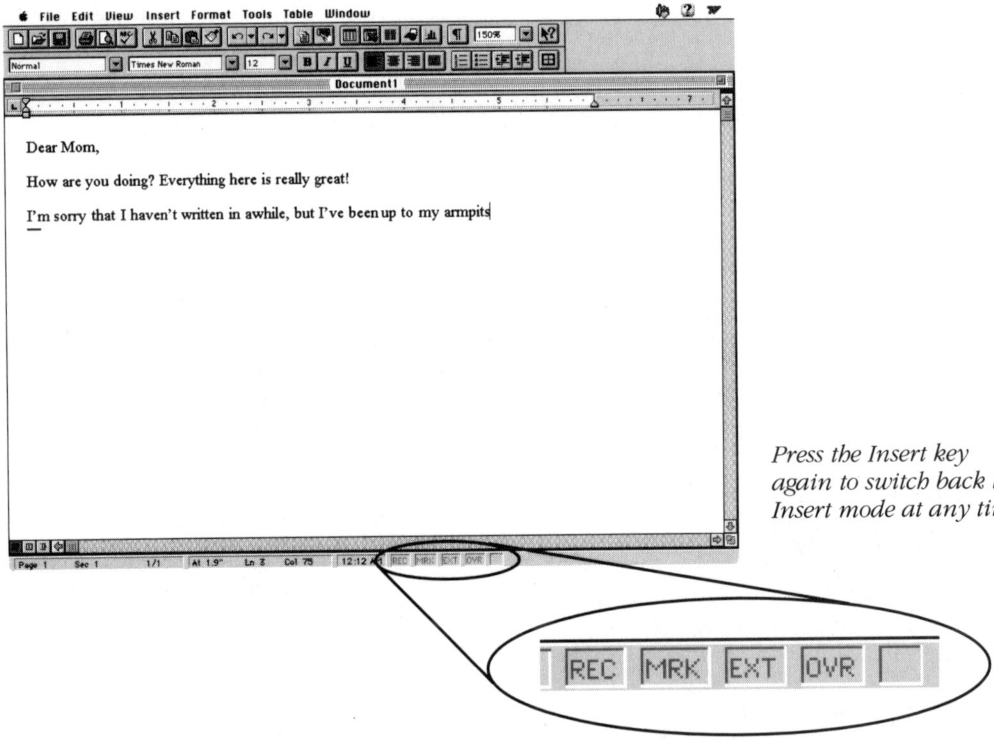

Press the Insert key again to switch back to Insert mode at any time.

Figure 7. *An OVR indicator appears when Word is in Overwrite mode.*

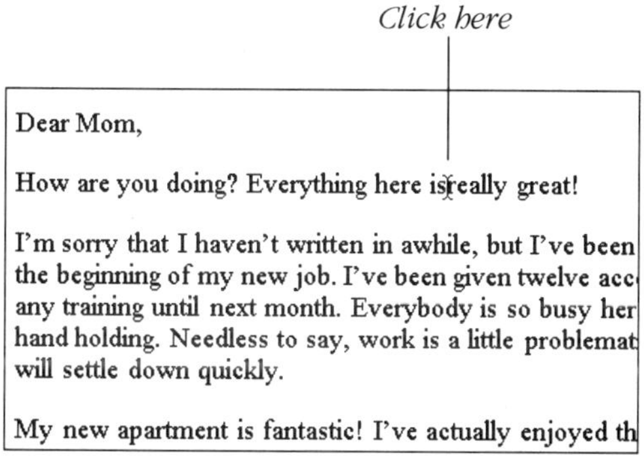

Click here

Dear Mom,

How are you doing? Everything here is really great!

I'm sorry that I haven't written in awhile, but I've been
the beginning of my new job. I've been given twelve acc
any training until next month. Everybody is so busy her
hand holding. Needless to say, work is a little problemat
will settle down quickly.

My new apartment is fantastic! I've actually enjoyed th

Figure 8. *Click at the spot to insert new text.*

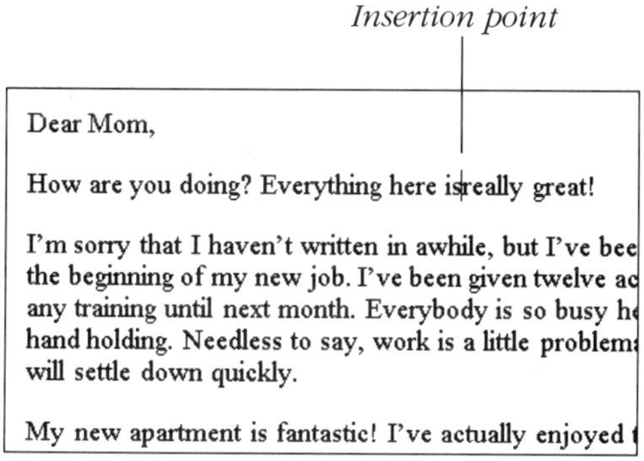

Insertion point

Dear Mom,

How are you doing? Everything here is really great!

I'm sorry that I haven't written in awhile, but I've bee
the beginning of my new job. I've been given twelve ac
any training until next month. Everybody is so busy h
hand holding. Needless to say, work is a little problem
will settle down quickly.

My new apartment is fantastic! I've actually enjoyed

Figure 9. *An insertion point appears.*

Moving the Insertion Point

To revise or add to existing text, you must move the insertion point to the spot for editing.

1. Click once in the existing text where you'd like to add or edit text. **(Figures 8-9)**

   or

   Press the arrow keys on the keyboard to move the insertion point.

✔ Tips

- Hold down ⌘ while pressing the right- or left-arrow key to move the insertion point a whole word to the right or left. **(Figure 10)**
- Hold down ⌘ while pressing the up- or down-arrow keys to move paragraph by paragraph.
- In **Excel**, the insertion point appears on the Edit Line.

Table 2-1. ***Other Keyboard Shortcuts***

Home	Beginning of a line.
End	End of a line.
⌘+Home	Top of document.
⌘+End	Bottom of document.

My new apartment is fantastic! I've actually enjoyed the renovations.

Figure 10. *Hold down ⌘ and press the right-arrow key to move the insertion point a whole word.*

Using the Scroll Bars

The scroll bars show the current vertical or horizontal location in a document. They also provide a quick method for jumping to a position along the length or width of a document. **(Figure 11)**

The span of each scroll bar represents the entire length or width of the document. The position of the *scroll button* along the *scroll bar* shows your extent through the document. To use the scroll bars:

1. Click an arrow button at the end of a scroll bar to move a single increment in one direction.

   or

2. Drag the scroll button along the scroll bar to move to a particular location. **(Figure 12)**

   or

3. Press and hold the mouse button at the spot along the scroll bar that represents the extent in the document to jump to. For example, press and hold halfway down the vertical scroll bar to jump to a point halfway through a file. **(Figure 13)**

✔ Tip

- Scroll bars appear only when you can move to a point that does not show on the screen.

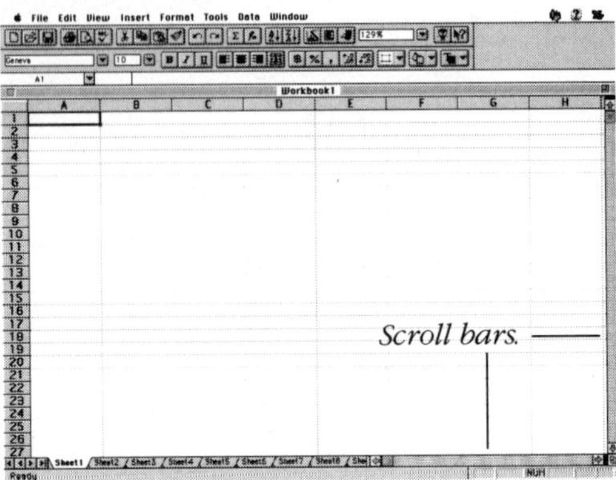

Figure 11. *The scroll bars.*

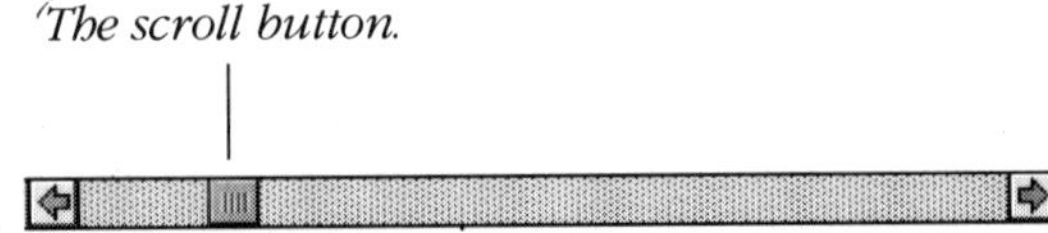

Figure 12. *Drag the scroll button to move to a new spot on the screen or in a document.*

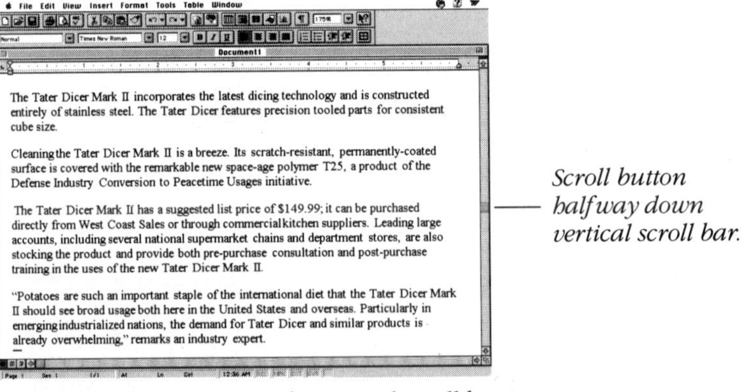

Figure 13. *Halfway down the vertical scroll bar represents halfway through the length of the entire document.*

The I-beam pointer.

I've been up to my armpits in work
welve accounts to handle and I don't

Figure 14. *Place the pointer on the first word...*

I've been up to my armpits in work
welve accounts to handle and I don't

Figure 15. *...then drag across the text to select.*

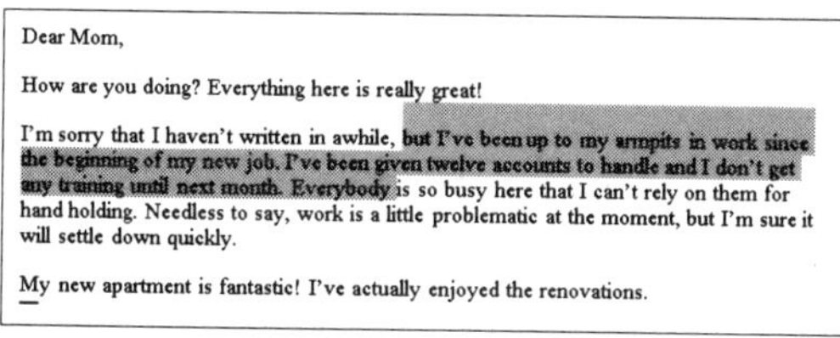

Dear Mom,

How are you doing? Everything here is really great!

I'm sorry that I haven't written in awhile, but I've been up to my armpits in work since the beginning of my new job. I've been given twelve accounts to handle and I don't get any training until next month. Everybody is so busy here that I can't rely on them for hand holding. Needless to say, work is a little problematic at the moment, but I'm sure it will settle down quickly.

My new apartment is fantastic! I've actually enjoyed the renovations.

Figure 16. *Drag down to select several lines.*

Selecting Text with the Mouse: Part I

Knowing how to select text is critically important as you must **always** select text **before** you can format, copy, move, or delete it.

1. Place the I-beam pointer at one end of the text you want to select. **(Figure 14)**
2. **Hold down** the mouse button and drag to the other end of the text to select. **(Figure 15)**

   or, to select text on multiple lines

   Hold down the mouse button and drag down through the document to highlight multiple lines. **(Figure 16)**
3. Release the mouse button.

✔ Tips

- The Automatic Word Selection option guarantees that the entire first and last word of the selection are highlighted.
- In **Excel**, you must select text on the Edit Line. **(Figure 17)**
- **Mouse shortcut**: Click to place an insertion point at the beginning of the text, release the mouse button, press and hold the Shift key, and click at the end of the text.

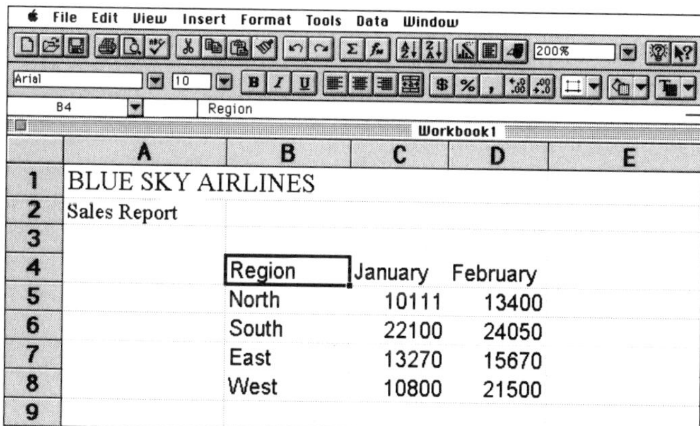

Figure 17. *The Edit Line in Excel.*

Selecting Text with the Mouse: Part II

To select a word	Double-click the word. **(Figure 18)**
To select a paragraph	Triple-click the paragraph. **(Figure 19)**

✔ Tips

- **Word tip**: To select an entire line of text, click in the left margin next to the line. **(Figure 20)**
- **Word tip**: To select multiple entire lines, click to the left of a line and then drag down through the left margin.

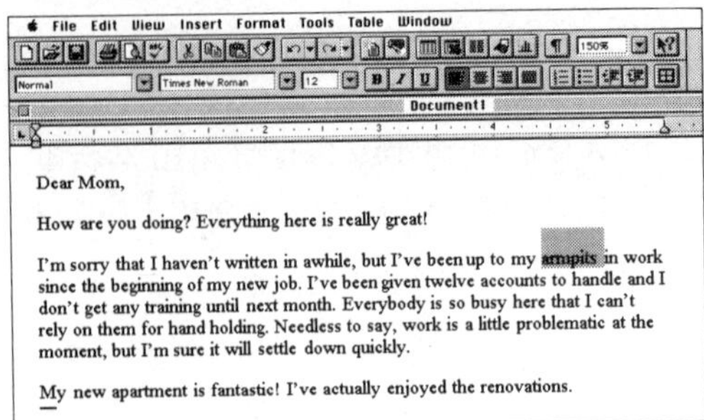

Figure 18. *Select a word by double-clicking it.*

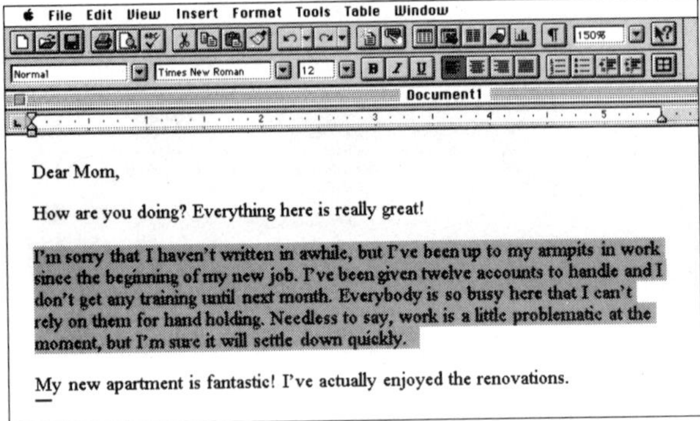

Figure 19. *Triple-click to select a paragraph.*

Click in left margin.

I'm sorry that I haven't written in awhile, but I've been up to my armpits in work since the beginning of my new job. I've been given twelve accounts to handle and I don't get any training until next month. Everybody is so busy here that I can't rely on them for hand holding. Needless to say, work is a little problematic at the moment, but I'm sure it will settle down quickly.

Figure 20. *In Word, click in the left margin to select a line.*

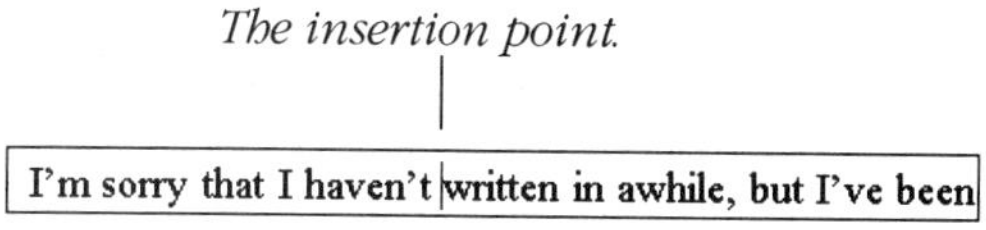

The insertion point.

I'm sorry that I haven't written in awhile, but I've been

Figure 21. *The insertion point.*

I'm sorry that I haven't written in awhile, but I've been

Figure 22. *Hold Shift and move to the last character to select.*

Figure 23. *Press ⌘+Shift+arrow key to select text word by word.*

Selecting Text with the Keyboard

1. Use the arrow keys to position the insertion point in front of the first character. **(Figure 21)**
2. Press and hold the Shift key and use the arrow keys to move the insertion point to the end of the last word to select. **(Figure 22)**

✔ Tips

- Press and hold Shift and press the down arrow key to select multiple lines of text.
- Press the ⌘ and Shift keys along with the left or right arrow keys to select a word at a time. **(Figure 23)**

Selecting and Replacing Text

To replace text in a document or in a text box on a dialog box, you can always select the text and simply type over it. The characters that are selected will be replaced when you begin typing.

1. Select the text to replace. **(Figure 24)**
2. Type replacement text. **(Figures 25)**

✔ Tip

- To quickly replace an entry in a text box, double-click the entry and then type a replacement. **(Figures 26–27)**

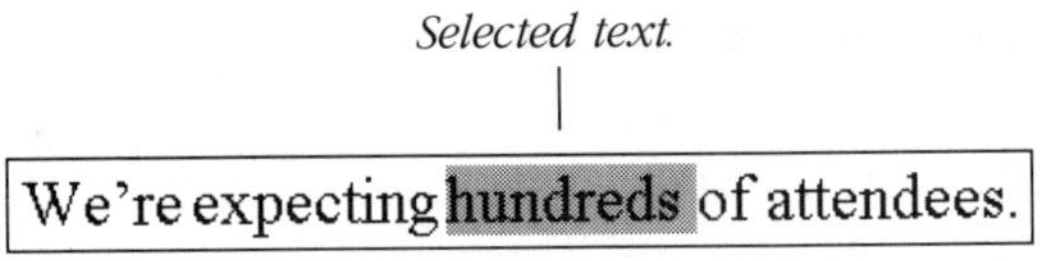

Selected text.

We're expecting hundreds of attendees.

Figure 24. *Selecting text in a document.*

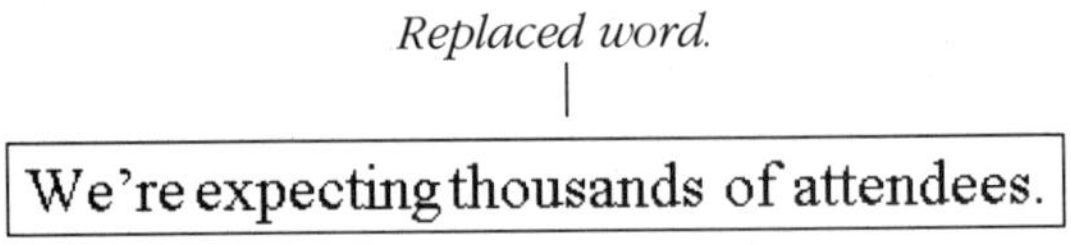

Replaced word.

We're expecting thousands of attendees.

Figure 25. *Typed text replaces selected text.*

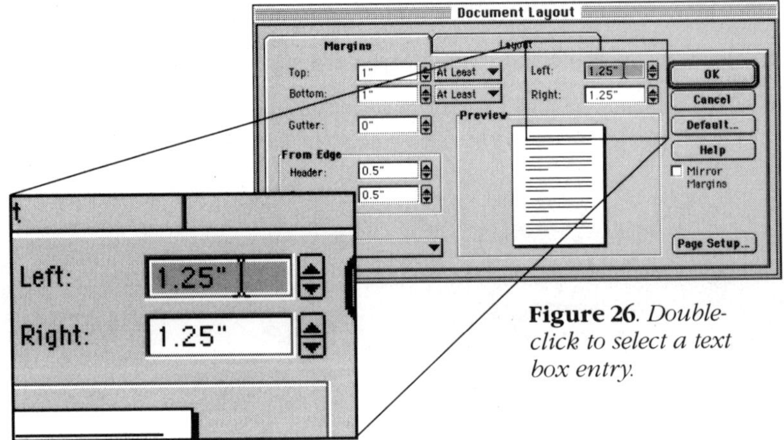

Figure 26. *Double-click to select a text box entry.*

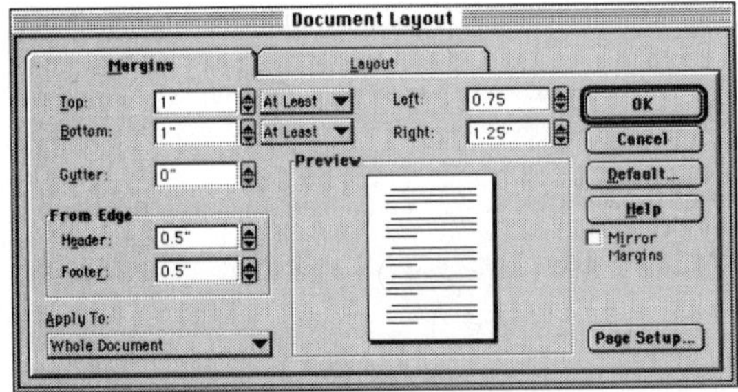

Figure 27. *A new typed entry replaces a selected entry.*

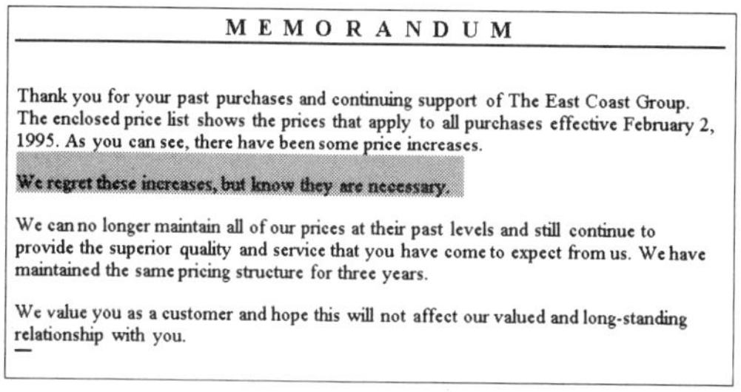

Dragging and Dropping Text

To move text in a document, you can always select the text and then drag it to a new location. You can even drag text from one document to another or from one application window to another.

1. Select the text to move. **(Figure 28)**
2. Place the mouse pointer on the selected text. The mouse pointer becomes an arrow. **(Figure 29)**
3. Press and hold the mouse button and drag the pointer to the destination for the text. A gray insertion point indicates the exact spot the text will reappear. **(Figure 30)**
4. Release the mouse button to drop the text at the new location. **(Figure 31)**

✔ Tips

- To **copy** rather than **move** the text, (leaving the original intact) press and hold the Option key while you drag.
- **Excel**, **PowerPoint**, and **Mail** have other types of objects you can drag and drop using similar techniques.

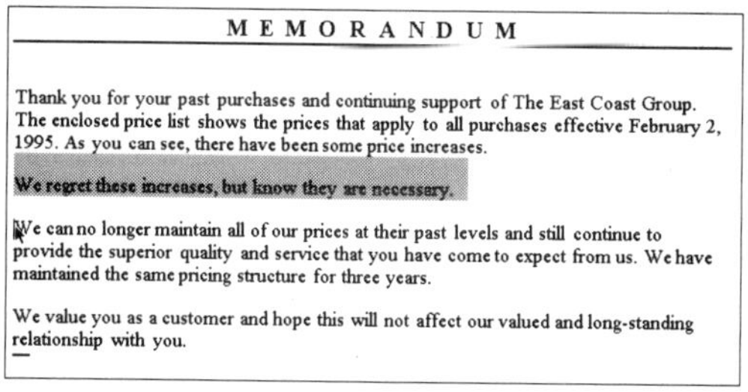

MEMORANDUM

Thank you for your past purchases and continuing support of The East Coast Group. The enclosed price list shows the prices that apply to all purchases effective February 2, 1995. As you can see, there have been some price increases.

We regret these increases, but know they are necessary.

We can no longer maintain all of our prices at their past levels and still continue to provide the superior quality and service that you have come to expect from us. We have maintained the same pricing structure for three years.

We value you as a customer and hope this will not affect our valued and long-standing relationship with you.

Figure 28. *Select the text to move.*

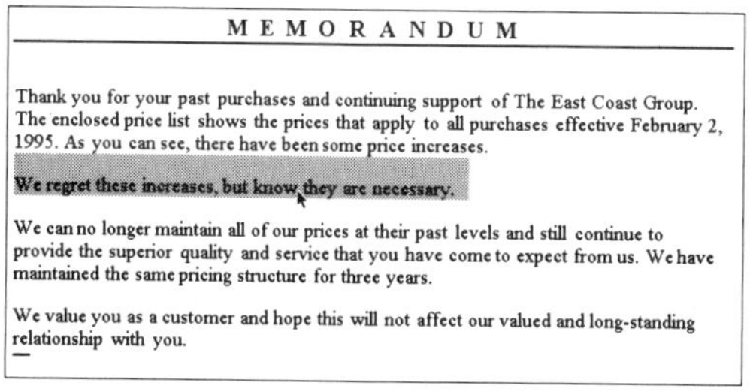

MEMORANDUM

Thank you for your past purchases and continuing support of The East Coast Group. The enclosed price list shows the prices that apply to all purchases effective February 2, 1995. As you can see, there have been some price increases.

We regret these increases, but know they are necessary.

We can no longer maintain all of our prices at their past levels and still continue to provide the superior quality and service that you have come to expect from us. We have maintained the same pricing structure for three years.

We value you as a customer and hope this will not affect our valued and long-standing relationship with you.

Figure 29. *Place the mouse pointer on the text.*

MEMORANDUM

Thank you for your past purchases and continuing support of The East Coast Group. The enclosed price list shows the prices that apply to all purchases effective February 2, 1995. As you can see, there have been some price increases.

We regret these increases, but know they are necessary.

We can no longer maintain all of our prices at their past levels and still continue to provide the superior quality and service that you have come to expect from us. We have maintained the same pricing structure for three years.

We value you as a customer and hope this will not affect our valued and long-standing relationship with you.

Figure 30. *Drag the gray insertion point to the destination.*

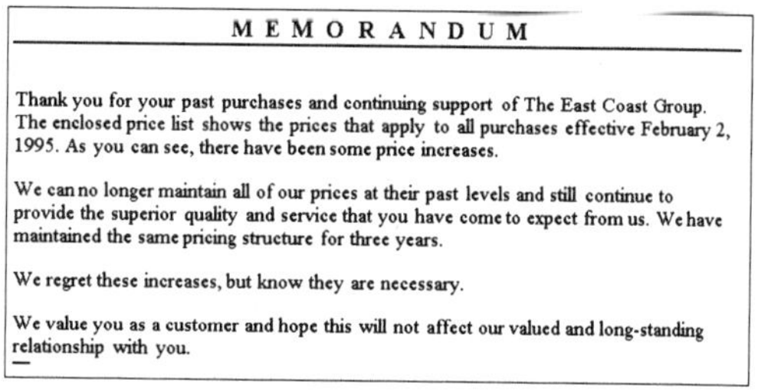

MEMORANDUM

Thank you for your past purchases and continuing support of The East Coast Group. The enclosed price list shows the prices that apply to all purchases effective February 2, 1995. As you can see, there have been some price increases.

We can no longer maintain all of our prices at their past levels and still continue to provide the superior quality and service that you have come to expect from us. We have maintained the same pricing structure for three years.

We regret these increases, but know they are necessary.

We value you as a customer and hope this will not affect our valued and long-standing relationship with you.

Figure 31. *Release the mouse button to drop the text.*

Selecting Objects

Passages of text, drawings, charts, scanned images, and other items you can select are called "objects." You can drag objects to reposition them on the page within an application, and you can usually drag them to other applications, too.

- In **Word**, select text to create an object that you can drag. **(Figure 32)**
  See Selecting Text, pages 23-25.
- In **Excel**, drag from one corner of a range of cells to the opposite corner to create a selected range. **(Figure 33)** The selected range, now enclosed in a box, is an object that you can drag. **(Figure 34)**
- In **PowerPoint**, each item on a page is an object. For example, a set of bulleted text items is an object that you can drag. **(Figure 35)**

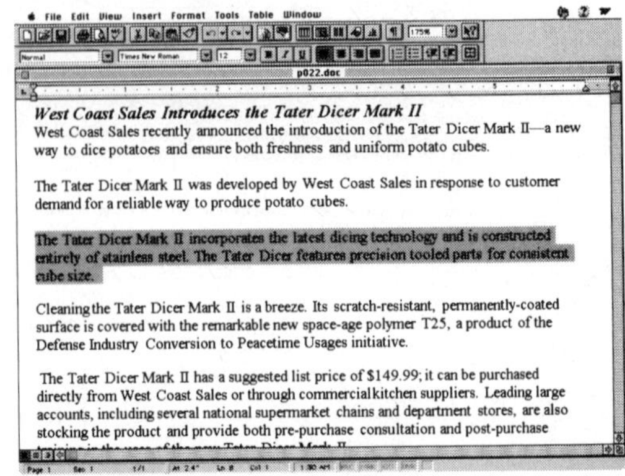

Figure 32. *Selected text is an object.*

You can insert data into the active, unhighlighted cell of a range by simply typing.

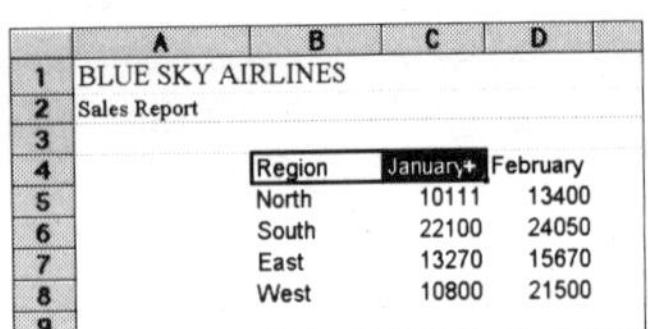

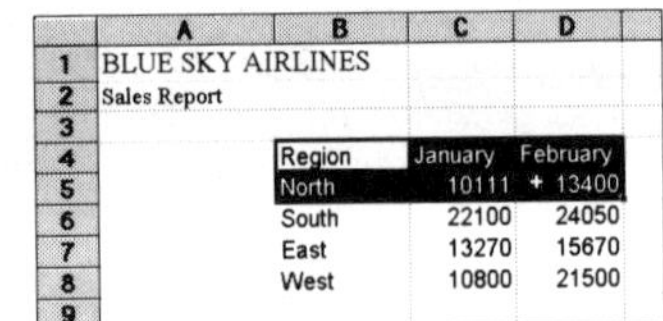

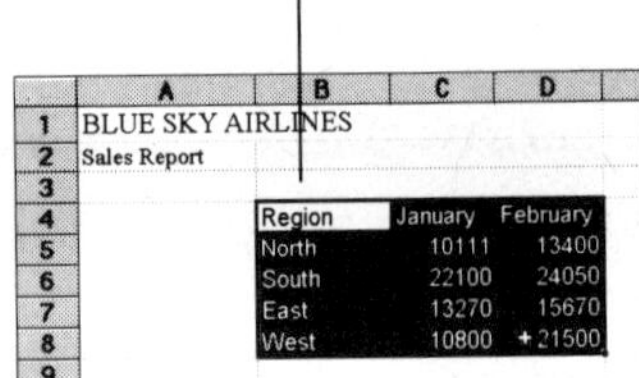

Figure 33. *Drag from the upper left corner cell to the lower right corner cell to select a range.*

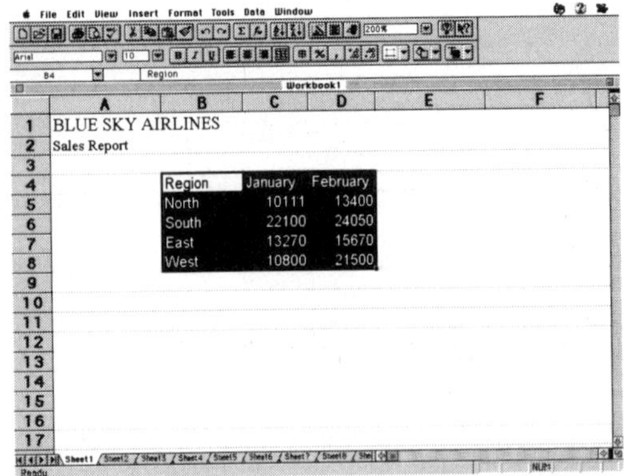

Figure 34. *A selected range of cells is highlighted and enclosed in a box.*

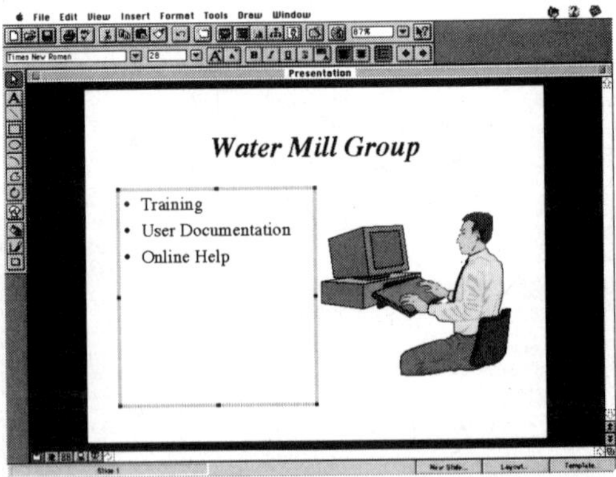

Figure 35. *Handles appear around selected objects in PowerPoint.*

A selected object is enclosed by handles.

Figure 36. *Selected object in PowerPoint.*

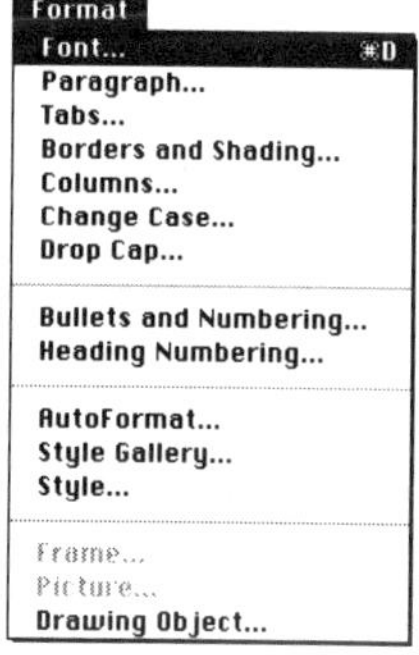

Figure 37. *The Word Format menu.*

Formatting Objects

You must always **first** select an object and **then** choose a formatting command, not the other way around.

1. Select the object to format. **(Figure 36)**
2. Choose a formatting option from the Format menu. **(Figure 37)**

   or

   Click the toolbar button for the formatting command.

   or

   Use the keyboard shortcut for the formatting command.

✔ Tips

- In **Excel** and **PowerPoint,** the first command on the Format menu always leads to a customized dialog box with special formatting options for the object you've selected. **(Figure 38)**
- The most popular formatting commands appear as buttons on the Formatting toolbar.

Table 2-2. ***Common Keyboard Shortcuts***

⌘+**b**	Bold
⌘+**i**	Italic
⌘+**u**	Underline

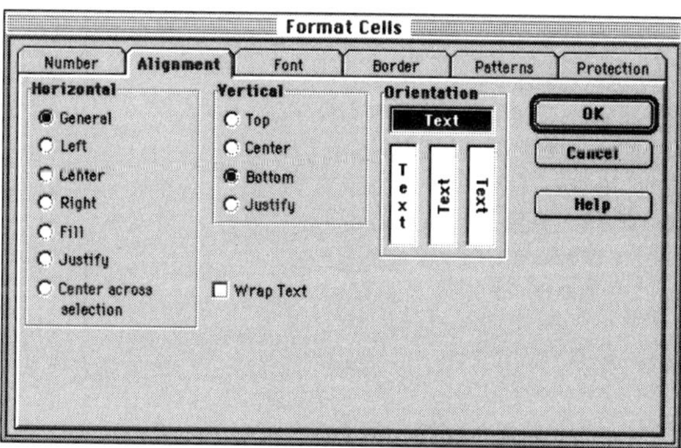

Figure 38. *The Excel Format Cells dialog box.*

Copying Formatting with the Format Painter

The Format Painter transfers formatting from one object to another.

1. Select an object that has the desired formatting. **(Figure 39)**
2. Click the Format Painter button in the Standard toolbar to pick up the object's formatting. **(Figure 40)**
3. Select the object to receive the formatting. If the object is a passage of text, drag across the text to format. **(Figures 41-42)**

✔ Tip

- To apply formatting to an entire sentence, press and hold the ⌘ key and then click any word in the sentence.

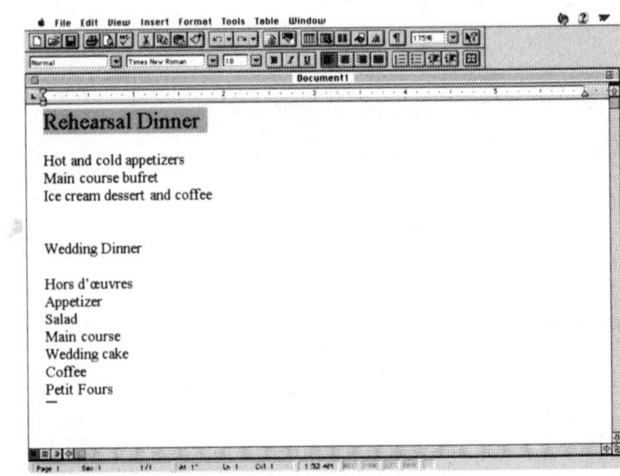

Figure 39. *Select the formatted object.*

The Format Painter button.

Figure 40. *The Format Painter button.*

Rehearsal Dinner

Hot and cold appetizers
Main course bufret
Ice cream dessert and coffee

Wedding Dinner

Hors d'œuvres
Appetizer
Salad
Main course
Wedding cake
Coffee
Petit Fours

Figure 41. *Drag across text with the Format Painter pointer.*

Rehearsal Dinner

Hot and cold appetizers
Main course bufret
Ice cream dessert and coffee

Wedding Dinner

Hors d'œuvres
Appetizer
Salad
Main course
Wedding cake
Coffee
Petit Fours

Figure 42. *The newly formatted object.*

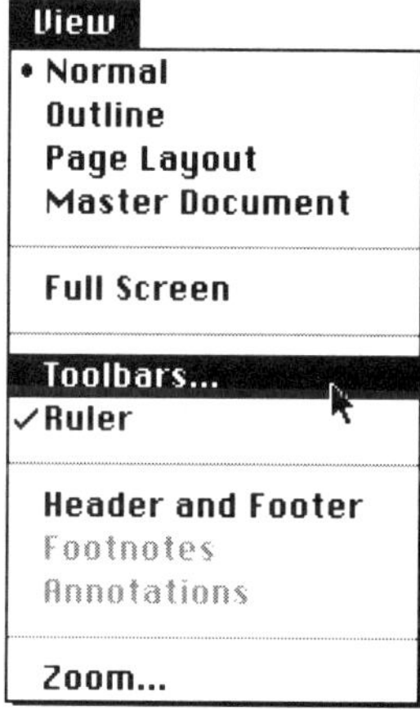

Figure 43. *The View menu.*

Selecting Toolbars

A default group of toolbars appears in each application, but you can select others to add to the screen to gain access to buttons for special tasks.

1. From the View menu, select Toolbars **(Figure 43),** and on the Toolbars dialog box click the checkboxes for the toolbars you want **(Figure 44),** and click OK.

   or

   Click any toolbar while holding down the ⌘ key and then choose the toolbar to add. **(Figure 45)**

✔ Tips

- To add new toolbar buttons to a toolbar, choose Toolbars from the View menu and then click Customize. On the Customize dialog box, choose a Category from the list and then drag the button you want from the dialog box to the toolbar. **(Figure 46)**
- To move a button within a toolbar or to a different toolbar, hold down the Option key and drag the button.

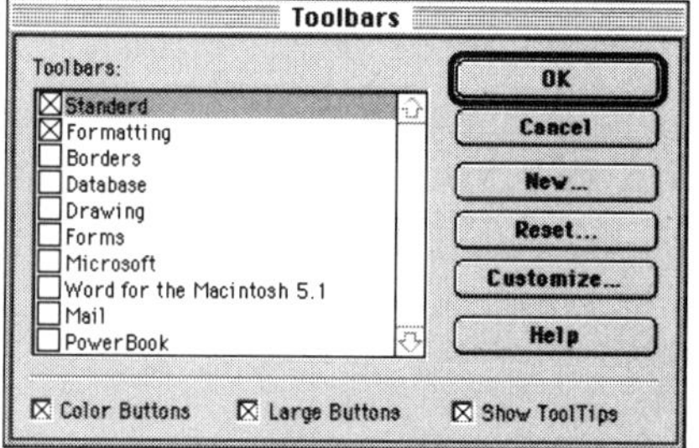

Figure 44. *Click the checkboxes for the toolbars you want and then click OK.*

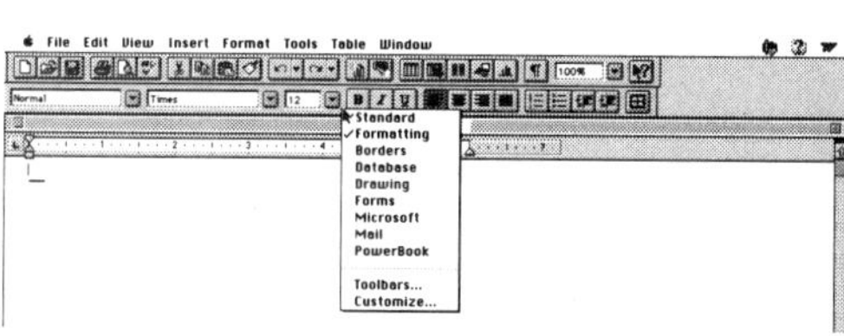

Figure 45. *Click a toolbar while holding down the ⌘ key to get the toolbar list.*

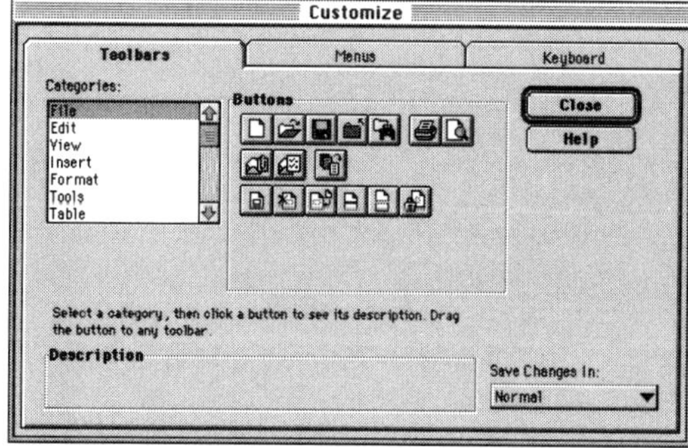

Figure 46. *The Customize dialog box.*

Getting a Shortcut Menu

A shortcut menu offers the commands you are most likely to need after you select an object. A shortcut menu shows only commands that are applicable to the selected object. **(Figures 47–49)**

1. In **Word**, select text.

   In **Excel**, select a range of cells.

   In **PowerPoint**, select any object.

2. Hold down the Control key and click the mouse button.

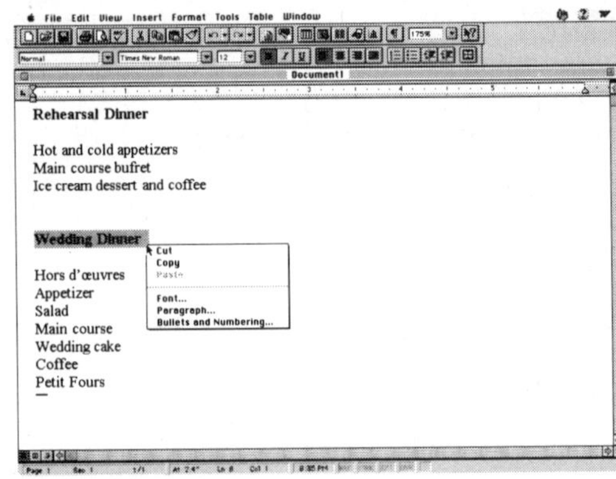

Figure 47. *Shortcut menu for selected text in Word.*

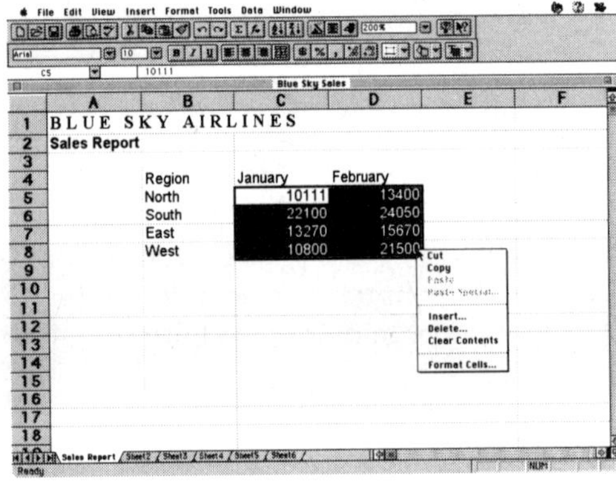

Figure 48. *Shortcut menu for a range of cells in Excel.*

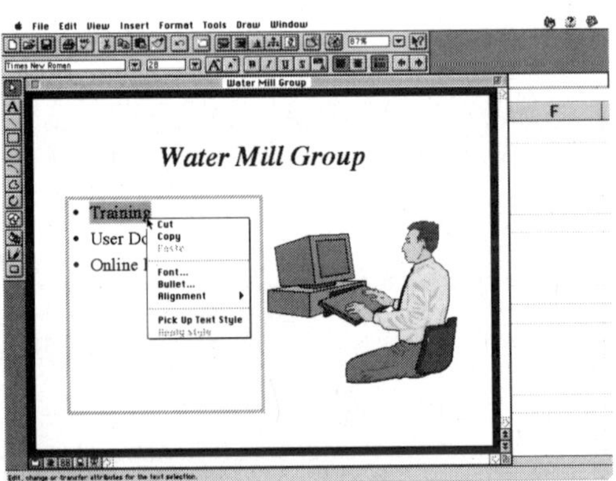

Figure 49. *Shortcut menu for a PowerPoint object.*

Zoom percentage.

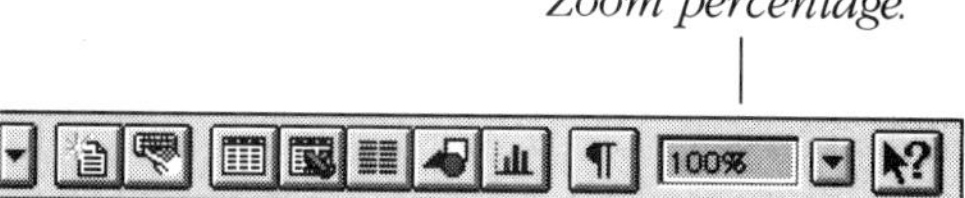

Figure 50. *Double-click the existing zoom percentage to select it and then enter a new percentage.*

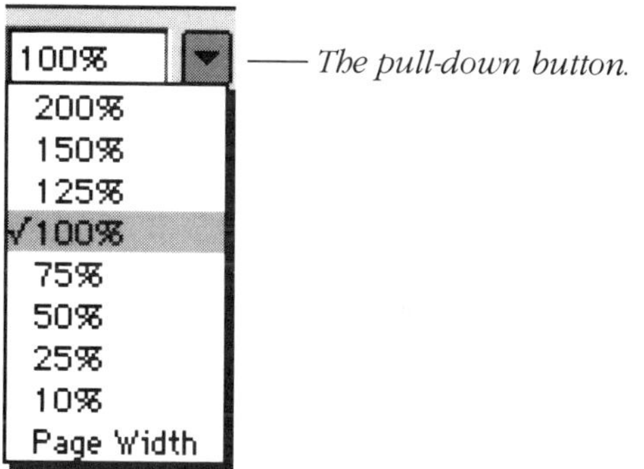

The pull-down button.

Figure 51. *The Zoom Control.*

Zooming In and Out

To magnify your work on the screen, choose one of the preset zoom percentages or enter your own. For example: 200% would make everything on the screen twice as large.

1. Double-click the current zoom percentage number, type a new zoom percentage, and press Enter. **(Figure 50)**

   or

   Click the pull-down button next to the Zoom Control and then choose a preset percentage from the list. **(Figure 51)**

   or

   From the View menu, choose Zoom and then choose a preset percentage or enter your own in the Zoom dialog box. **(Figure 52)**

✓ Tips

- In **Word**, Page Width zooms to a percentage that neatly fits the text across the screen.
- In **Excel**, Selection zooms to the percentage that neatly fits the selected range of cells to the screen.

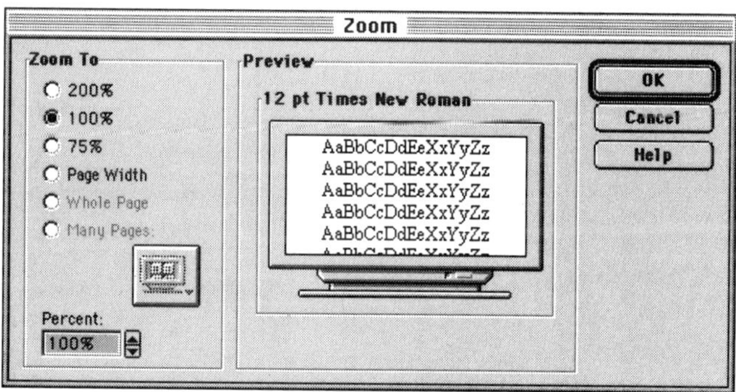

Figure 52. *The Zoom dialog box in Word.*

Setting up the Page Margins

The page margins give you white space at the top, bottom, left, and right sides of the page.

1. From the File menu, choose Document Layout. **(Figure 53)**
2. On the Document Layout dialog box, click the Margins tab. **(Figure 54)**
3. Double-click and then type over the margin settings. **(Figure 55)**

   or

   Click the arrow buttons next to each setting to incrementally increase or decrease it.

✔ Tips

- Click the Page Setup button in the Document Layout dialog box or choose Page Setup from the File menu to print landscape (sideways) rather than portrait, or to specify a paper size other than letter (8 1/2 x 11).
- The Page Setup choices are stored as part of the current document. The next new document you create will revert to the original, default page setup.
- In **Word**, you can click Default after changing the page setup to change the default for the following new documents.

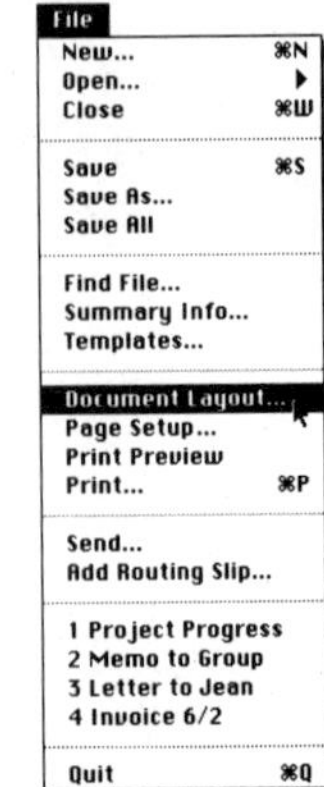

Figure 53. *The File menu.*

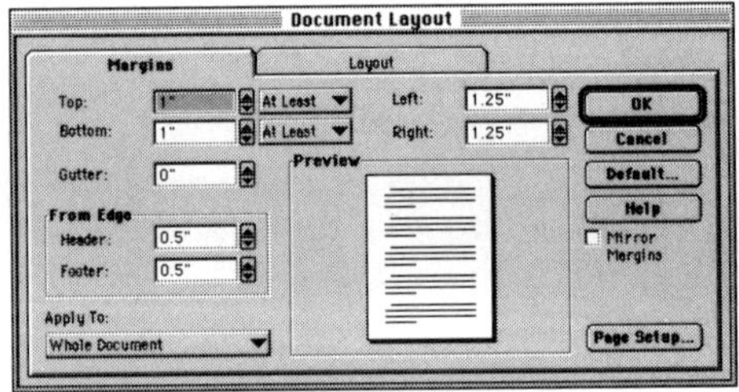

Figure 54. *The Document Layout dialog box.*

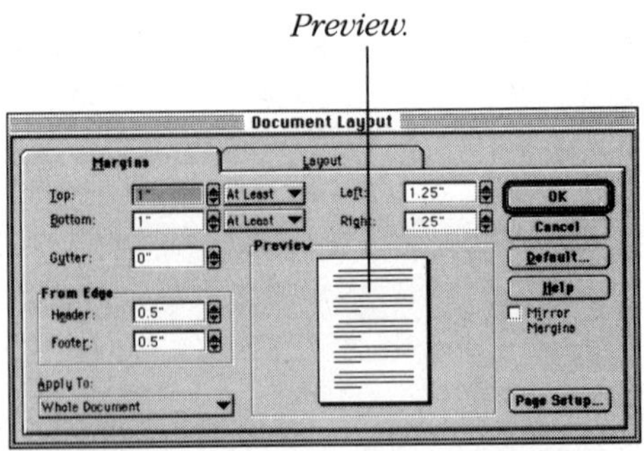

Figure 55. *The preview shows the current margin settings.*

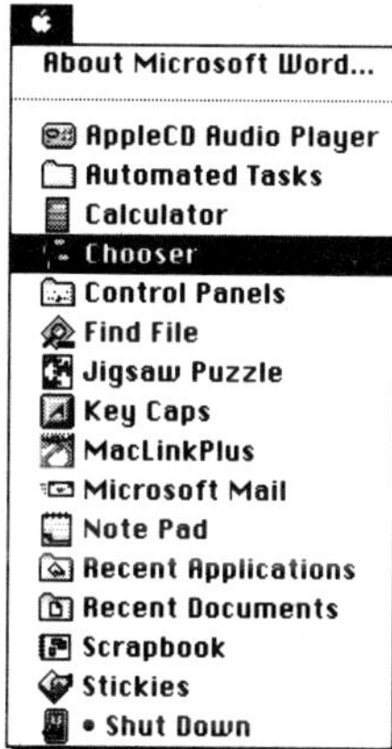

Figure 56. *The Apple menu.*

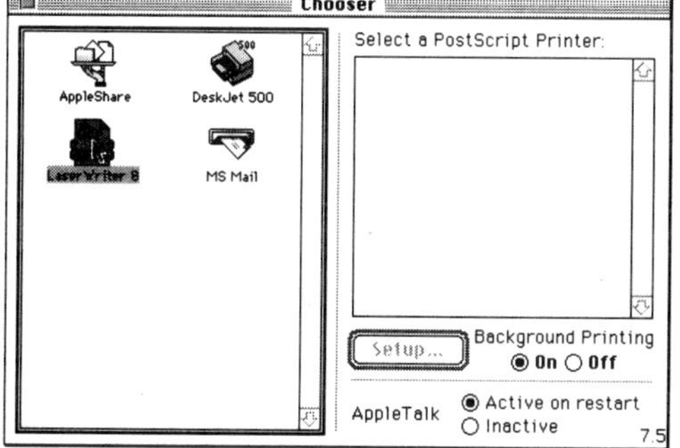

Figure 57. *The Chooser dialog box.*

Choosing a Printer

If you have more than one printer available, usually when you're on a network, you can choose a printer other than the default printer.

1. From the Apple menu, choose Chooser. **(Figure 56)**
2. On the Chooser dialog box, click the printer driver you want to use. **(Figure 57)**

✔ Tips

- The options that come up in the right half of the Chooser dialog box when you click a printer driver will vary depending upon your installation. Click the appropriate options for you and then click the window's close box.
- The good part about having only one printer is that you'll never need to choose a different printer with Chooser.

Printing

1. From the File menu, choose Print.

   or

   Press ⌘+P.
2. If necessary, choose different options on the Print dialog box.
3. Modify the number of copies, if you want.
4. Click All to print the entire document or enter starting and ending page numbers.

✔ Tip

- In **Word**, you can enter a range of pages and individual pages at the same time. Entering 1-3,5 would print pages 1 through 3 and also page 5. Entering 6,12 would print pages 6 and 12.

Choosing a Printer

Saving Your Work

1. From the File menu, choose Save. **(Figure 58)**
   or
   Click the Save button. **(Figure 59)**
   or
   Press ⌘+S.
2. On the Save dialog box, type a filename over the temporary document name in the Save Current Document as text box. **(Figure 60)**
3. Choose where you want the document to be stored and then click Save or press Enter.
4. If the Summary Info dialog box appears, enter as much information into the text boxes as you want and then click OK. Press Tab to move from text box to text box. Summary Info helps you find the file later. **(Figure 61)**

✔ Tip

- Each application has a way to set a default folder for your work. In the online help system, search for help on *defaults* and look for the sub-topic "Creating default directories or folders."

Figure 58. *The File menu.*

The Save button.

Figure 59. *The Save button.*

Enter a filename here.

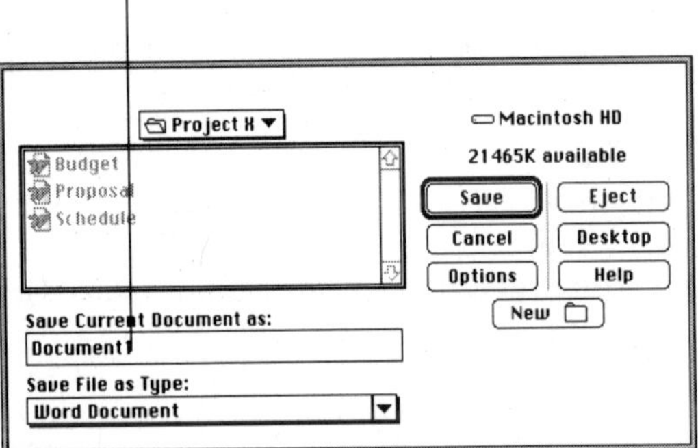

Figure 60. *The Save As dialog box.*

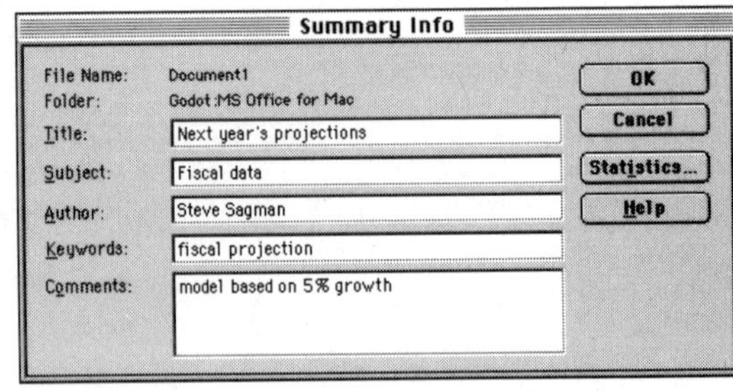

Figure 61. *The Summary Info dialog box.*

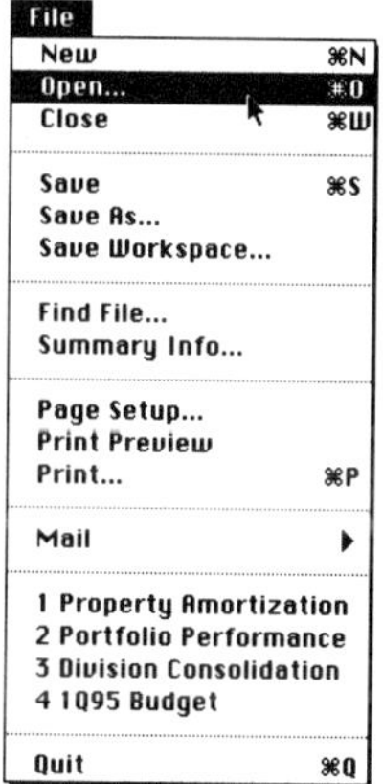

Figure 62. *The File menu.*

Reopening a Saved File

1. From the File menu, choose Open. **(Figure 62)**
   or
   Click the Open button. **(Figure 63)**
   or
   Press ⌘+O.
2. In the Open dialog box, double-click the filename to open. **(Figure 64)**
   or
   Click the filename and click OK.

✔ Tip

- You can use Find File on the File menu to search for files based on the Summary Info information you entered when you saved the file or the text contents of the file.

The Open button..

Figure 63. *The Open button.*

Special Note on Folders:

Folders are the way the Macintosh shows you the storage areas on your storage device. With the Macintosh system, you can add or delete folders and create folders within folders. The system also lets you manage (move, copy, rename, and delete) folders and the files you accumulate. You'll want to learn more about basic System 7 to understand folders and files.

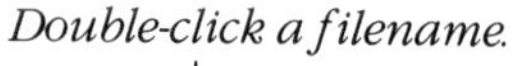

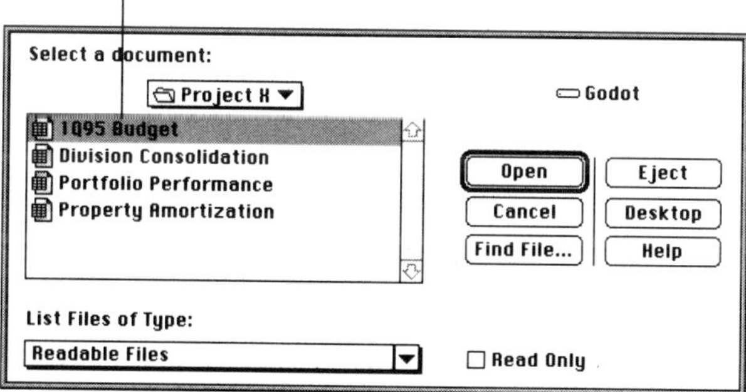

Figure 64. *Double-click a filename.*

Quitting an Office Application

From the File menu, choose Quit. **(Figure 65)**

or

Press ⌘+Q.

✔ Tip

- The Macintosh will not let you quit an application without offering the chance to save any open documents that have changed since you last saved them.

File
New... ⌘N
Open... ⌘O
Close ⌘W
Save ⌘S
Save As...
Save All
Find File...
Summary Info...
Templates...
Document Layout...
Page Setup...
Print Preview
Print... ⌘P
Send...
Add Routing Slip...
1 Project Progress
2 Memo to Group
3 Letter to Jean
4 Invoice 6/2
Quit ⌘Q

Figure 65. *The File menu.*

Word 6.0 Word Processing

Word 6.0 Word Processing

About Word

What is Word for Windows?
The Road to a Word Document
The Word Window
Key to the Word Window
Starting Word

Entering and Editing the Text

Starting a New Document
Entering the Text
About the Paragraph Marks
Text Editing
Finding Text
Replacing Text
Switching to Page Layout View
The Other Views

Font Formatting

About Font Formatting
Changing the Font and Font Size
Boldfacing, Italicizing, and Underlining
Expanding and Condensing Character Spacing
Changing the Case of Characters
Special Font Effects

Paragraph Formatting

About Paragraph Formatting
Selecting Paragraphs
Indenting Paragraphs with the Ruler
Changing the First Line Indent
Indenting with the Paragraph Dialog Box
Double Spacing Paragraphs
Centering and Justifying Paragraphs
Setting Tabs
Adding Bullets to Paragraphs
Numbering Paragraphs
Finding and Replacing Formatting

Automatic Text Formatting

About Styles
Choosing a Style from the Style List
Creating a Paragraph Style
Modifying a Paragraph Style
Creating a Character Style

Page Formatting

About Page Formatting
Changing the Page Size and Shape
Changing the Margins
Setting up Headers and Footers
Creating Multiple Sections
Paginating the Document
Numbering Pages
Setting up Multiple Columns
AutoFormatting a Document

Creating Tables

About Tables
Starting a Table
Using the Table Wizard
Entering Data in the Table
Deleting Columns or Rows
Inserting a Column or Row
Inserting Multiple Columns or Rows
Changing Column Width and Row Height
Turning on Borders and Shading
Converting Text to a Table

Special Word Techniques

Automatically Correcting Typos
Automatically Entering Text
Inserting Symbols from the Wingdings Font
Printing Envelopes
Envelope Printing Options
Saving a Document as a Template
Modifying an Existing Template
Using Automatic Saves
Creating Form Letters with Mail Merge
Changing the Appearance of the Word Window

About Word 3

What is Word?

Word 6, the word processing component of the Microsoft Office suite, creates letters, memos, invoices, proposals, reports, forms, and just about any other printed document that you might want.

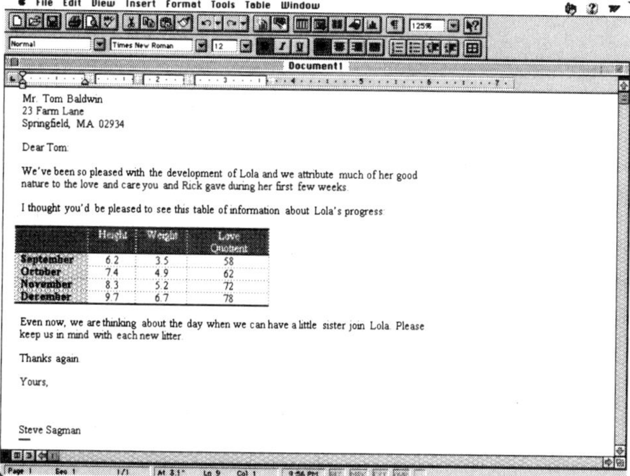

You can type text into Word and insert drawings or scanned photos from other applications, then format the text and graphics into sophisticated documents, complete with running headers and footers, footnotes, cross-references, page numbering, tables of contents, and indexes. On the other hand, you might need only to create a simple text memo with Word's easy-to-use features.

Word

Word's approach, as with other applications in the Office suite, is entirely visual. As you work in a document, you see all the text, graphics, and formatting exactly as they will appear when printed.

Word can easily work in concert with the other Office applications, too. It can display numbers from Excel or even a slide from PowerPoint.

The Road to a Word Document

The Bridgehampton Garden Club

Saturday, May 23, 1991

About the Bridgehampton Garden Club

Among the many activities offered by the Bridgehampton Garden Club is a monthly garden tour through the gardens of our members.

Each month, we will visit four gardens on a Saturday afternoon. During the tour, the gardener will present his or her concept for the garden, a brief history of the garden contained in the garden.

The monthly garden tour is a wonderful opportunity to expand your knowledge about gardens and gardening from your fellow gardeners.

Today's Event

Four superb English gardens.

24 Lily Pond Lane
117 Georgica St.
3 Heron Court
57 Hill Street

Entering and Editing the Text

Start a new document and type the text. Don't worry about formatting. You'll take care of that later with styles, or if you don't have styles, by manually formatting the characters and paragraphs. *Pages 47-54.*

Formatting the Characters

Select any words or paragraphs whose characters require a special look (a different font or font size, bold, italic, or underlined, or other special font effects) and "font format" them. If you've created styles that contain font formatting, you can apply the styles to save time. *Pages 55-60.*

Formatting the Paragraphs

Select any paragraphs which need a unique look and apply paragraph formats to them. Change their indents, line spacing, centering, and tab settings in this step. Also add bullets or numbers, if necessary. If you've created styles that contain preset combinations of paragraph formatting options, this is the time to use them. *Pages 61-74.*

Formatting the Pages

With the text in shape, you can make any overall adjustments to the page that are required. You can change the page size, page shape, and the margins; set up multiple columns of text, and repaginate the text to fit the pages. You can also set up the elements that will appear on all pages, such as headers, footers, and page numbers. *Pages 75-82.*

Adding Tables or Objects from Other Applications

Word's built-in table tools make creating and revising tables of text or numbers quick and easy. If the table you need is a range of numbers from Excel, you can simply drag the range from the Excel window into your document. The range appears with all the data and formatting you applied in Excel. You may want to augment the document with information from other Office applications, too, such as a slide from PowerPoint. *Pages 83-94.*

Proofing the Document

Word's AutoCorrect can catch many typing errors on the fly as you type, but you'll still want to check the document spelling to catch other possibly embarrassing typos. *Pages 95-106.*

Printing or Mailing the Document

Before you print, you can preview the document to find obvious formatting errors in advance. If you're ready for the "paperless office" you might want to attach the document to a Mail message instead, and send it to a recipient over your network.

Extras

Not in the everyday flow are these special features you'll learn about: printing envelopes, creating form letters, and using templates to create virtually automatic documents.

The Word 6 Window

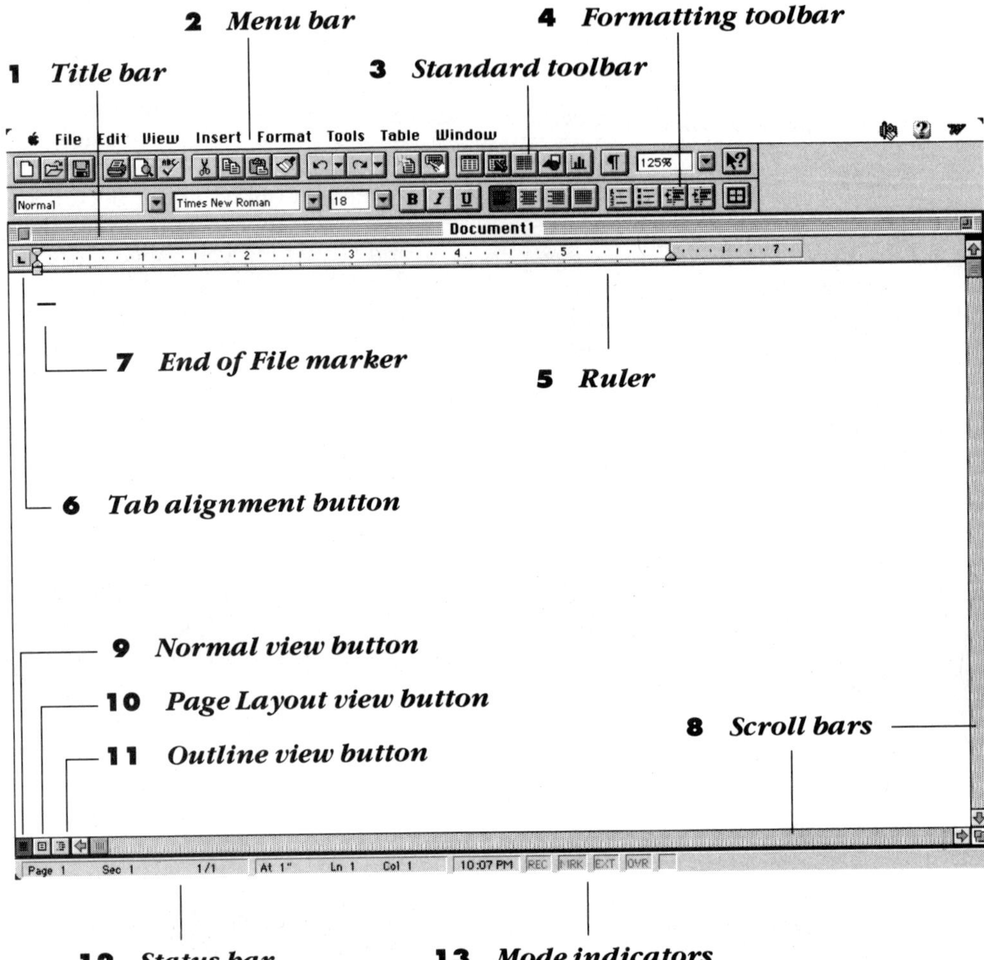

Key to the Word 6 Window

Word

1 ***Title bar***

Displays the document name. Drag the title bar to move the window.

2 ***Menu bar***

Click any name on the menu bar to pull down a menu.

3 ***Standard toolbar***

Toolbar with buttons for standard file management and text editing and proofing commands.

4 ***Formatting toolbar***

Toolbar with buttons for formatting characters and paragraphs.

5 ***Ruler***

Accurate horizontal ruler showing page width and position of tabs and indents.

6 ***Tab alignment button***

Click this button before setting a tab to select a tab type.

7 ***End of File marker***

Horizontal line showing the end of the current file. When you open a new document, the end of the file is at the top of the screen.

8 ***Scroll bars***

Use these scroll bars to move the view of the document up or down or to quickly jump to a spot in the document. The length of the vertical scroll bar represents the length of the entire document. The position of the scroll button represents the position of the insertion point in the document.

9 ***Normal view button***

Click this button to switch to a normal view of the document.

10 ***Page Layout view button***

Click this button to switch to Page Layout view, which shows page borders, accurate margins, headers and footers and other elements exactly as they'll appear when printed.

11 ***Outline view button***

Click this button to work with the document as an outline so you can develop the structure of a document.

12 ***Status bar***

Shows the current page number and position of the insertion point in the document.

13 ***Mode indicators***

Show special conditions that are in effect, such as a pressed Caps Lock key.

Starting Word

1. Double-click the Microsoft Word icon in its folder. **(Figure 1)**

   or

   Pull down the Microsoft Office Manager menu and choose Word. **(Figure 2)**

✓ Tip

- If Microsoft Word is already started, pull down the application menu and choose Microsoft Word from the list of running applications.

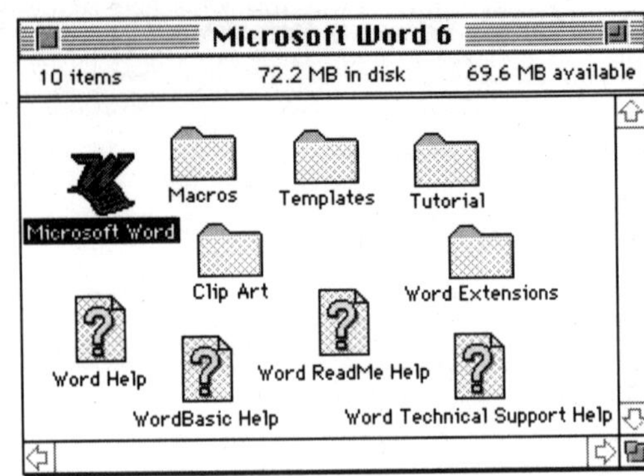

Figure 1. *The Microsoft Word icon in the Word folder.*

Select this menu item to start Word.

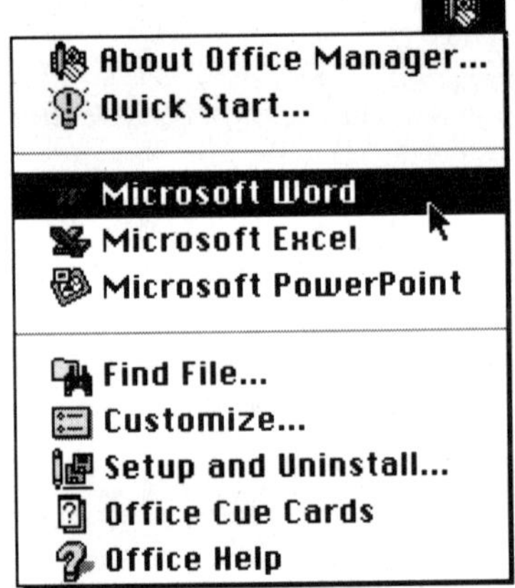

Figure 2. *The Microsoft Office Manager.*

Entering and Editing the Text 4

The New button.

Figure 1. *The New button.*

Figure 2. *The File menu.*

Figure 3. *The New dialog box.*

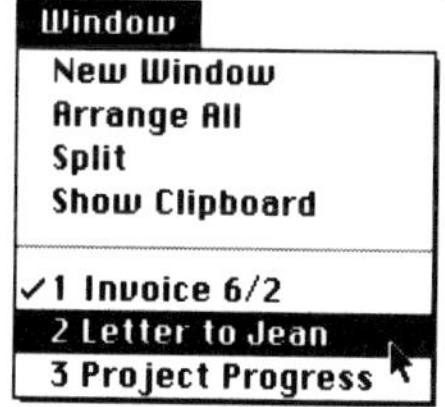

Figure 4. *The Window menu.*

Starting a New Document

When Word starts, `Document1` is open and ready for you to type text. Documents are numbered sequentially and several can be open simultaneously. To start `Document2` follow these steps:

1. Click the New button to open a new document. **(Figure 1)**

   or

   Press ⌘+N.

   or

   From the File menu, choose New **(Figure 2)** and then, in the New dialog box, click OK to use the default template named Normal. **(Figure 3)**
   To learn more about templates, see Saving a Document as a Template, page 101.

✔ Tips

- To switch from one open document to another, choose a document name from the list of open documents at the bottom of the Window menu. **(Figure 4)**
- A single document can be displayed within the Word window, or several documents can be arranged in their own windows within the Word window.

Word

Entering the Text

Typing in Word is just like typing with a typewriter except that you do **not** press Enter at the end of a line. When the insertion point reaches the right margin, it *wraps* automatically to the next line. Press Enter only to start a new paragraph. **(Figure 5)**

File Edit View Insert Format Tools Table Window
Document1
M E M O R A N D U M
DATE: January 14, 1995
TO: Eric Weinberger
FROM: John White
RE: ProjectX
Our initial survey of the market for pet care products indicates that an overwhelming

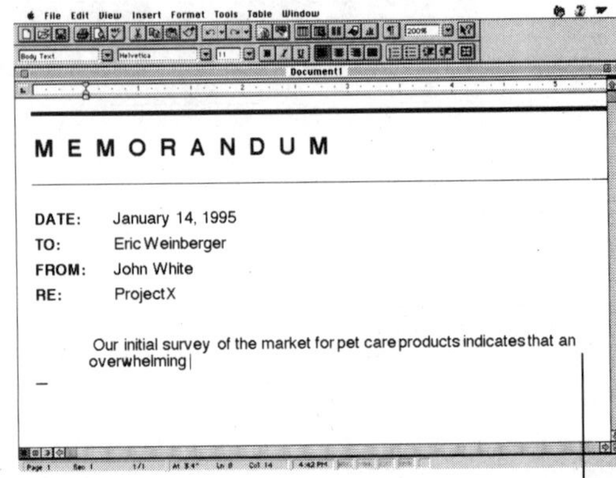

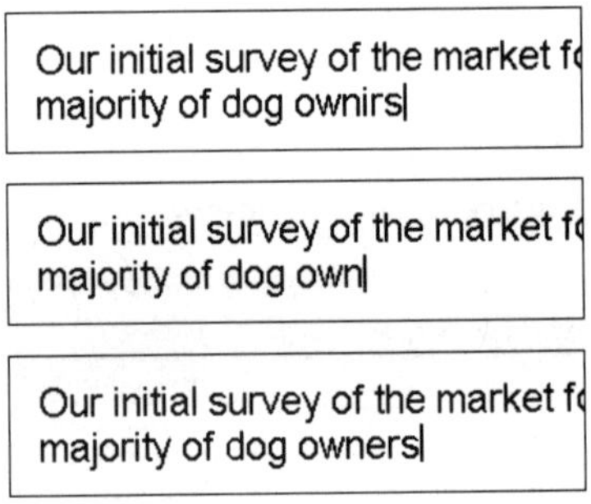

Figure 5. *Do not press Enter when you get here. Word will jump to the next line when no more text can fit on the current line.*

✔ Tips

- Press Delete to back up and delete mistakes to the left of the insertion point. **(Figure 6)**
- Press Clear or Del to delete characters to the right of the insertion point. **(Figure 7)**
- Word automatically corrects many common typos, such as forgetting to capitalize the first word in a sentence, or typing "teh" instead of "the." **(Figure 8)** *See Automatically Correcting Typos, page 95.*

Our initial survey of the market f
majority of dog ownirs
Our initial survey of the market f
majority of dog own
Our initial survey of the market f
majority of dog owners

Figure 6. *Press Delete to delete characters to the* ***left*** *of the insertion point.*

Our initial survey of the market f
majority of dog owners like
Our initial survey of the market f
majority of dog owners
Our initial survey of the market f
majority of dog owners prefer

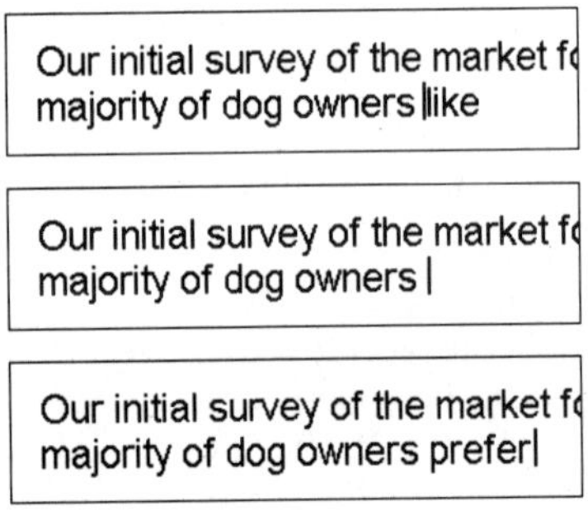

Figure 7. *Press Clear or Del to delete characters to the* ***right*** *of the insertion point.*

Our initial survey of the market for pe
majority of dog owners prefer teh
Our initial survey of the market for pe
majority of dog owners prefer the

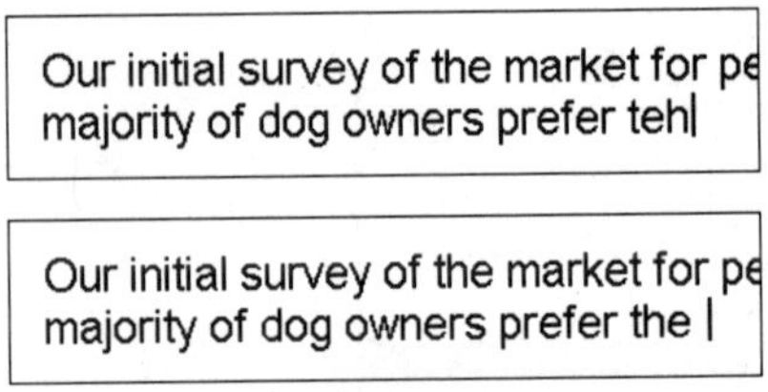

Figure 8. *Word automatically corrects typos when you finish a word.*

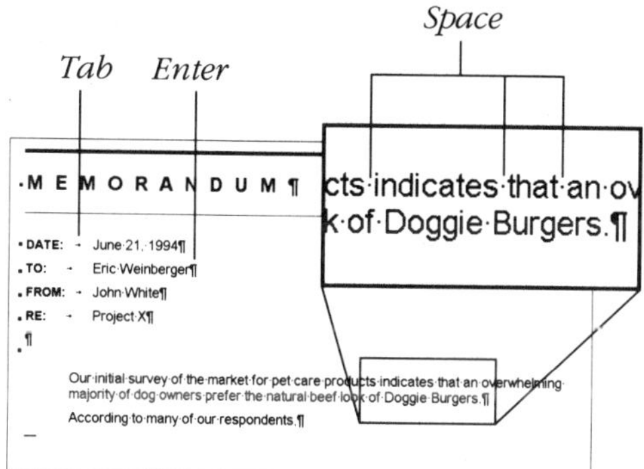

Figure 9. *Nonprinting characters.*

About the Paragraph Marks (Show/Hide ¶ button)

If nonprinting characters are turned on, you will see a ¶ at the end of each paragraph and a dot between words to help you understand the formatting in your document. **(Figure 9)**

1. Click the Show/Hide ¶ button to turn on nonprinting characters. **(Figure 10)**

✔ **Tip**

- If nonprinting characters are already on, click the Show/Hide ¶ button again to turn them off.

Table 4-1. *The Nonprinting Characters.*

¶	End of paragraph
Dot	Space
→	Tab
↵	New line, same paragraph

The Show/Hide ¶ button.

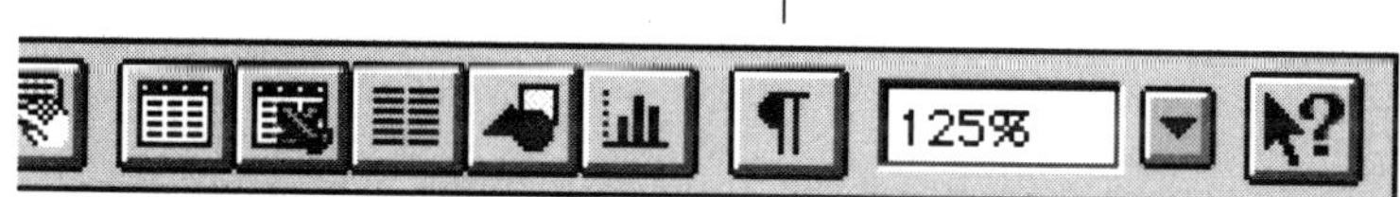

Figure 10. *The Show/Hide ¶ button.*

Text Editing

To insert new text, position the insertion point and then type new text at the insertion point. **(Figures 11-12)** *See Moving the Insertion Point, page 21.*

Press Delete to delete characters to the left of the insertion point or press Clear or del to delete characters to the right of the insertion point.

To move or copy text, use Drag and Drop. *See Dragging and Dropping Text, page 27.*

To replace existing text, select the text, and then type new text in its place. **(Figure 13)** *See Selecting Text with the Mouse, pages 23-24; Selecting Text with the Keyboard, page 25; and Deleting and Replacing Text, page 26.*

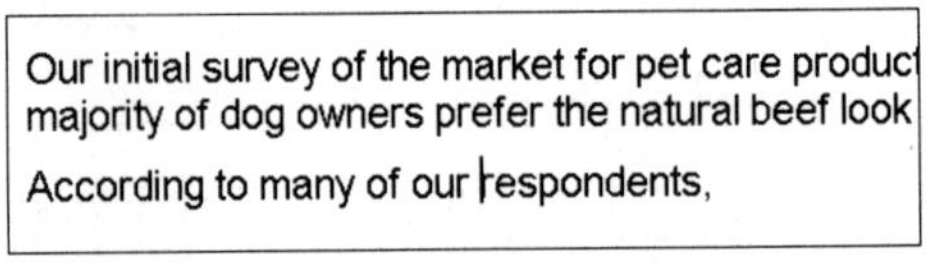

Our initial survey of the market for pet care produc
majority of dog owners prefer the natural beef look
According to many of our respondents,

Figure 11. *Place the insertion point at the location for the new text.*

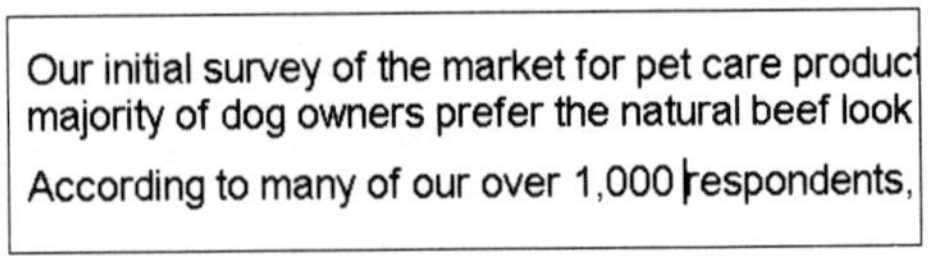

Our initial survey of the market for pet care produc
majority of dog owners prefer the natural beef look
According to many of our over 1,000 respondents,

Figure 12. *Anything you type is inserted at the insertion point.*

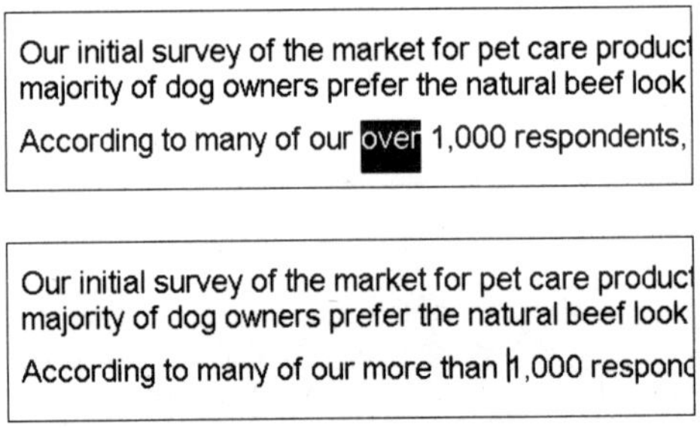

Our initial survey of the market for pet care produc
majority of dog owners prefer the natural beef look
According to many of our over 1,000 respondents,

Our initial survey of the market for pet care produc
majority of dog owners prefer the natural beef look
According to many of our more than 1,000 respond

Figure 13. *Anything you type while text is selected replaces the selected text.*

Word

Finding Text

1. From the Edit menu, choose Find. **(Figure 14)**

   or

   Press ⌘+F.
2. In the Find dialog box, type text in the Find What text box. **(Figure 15)**
3. Click Find Next.

✔ Tips

- Click the pull-down button next to the Find What text box to view a list of text items you've already searched for. Choose from the list to repeat an earlier search. **(Figure 16)**
- To search for special formatting, click the Format button and then select a format on the subsequent menu and dialog boxes. **(Figure 17)**
- To search for special characters, click the Special button and then select the special character to find.

Figure 14. *The Find command.*

Type the text to find here.

Figure 15. *The Find dialog box.*

Click here.

Figure 16. *Click here to choose an earlier text item to find again.*

Table 4-2. *Special Find Options*

Match Case	Finds words that contain the same combination of upper and lower case characters
Find Whole Words Only	Finds text when not part of a larger word. Ex: finds "art" but not "artistic."
Use Pattern Matching	Allows you to enter a code to specify a special character combination to find.
Sounds Like	Finds text that sounds like the Find What text.

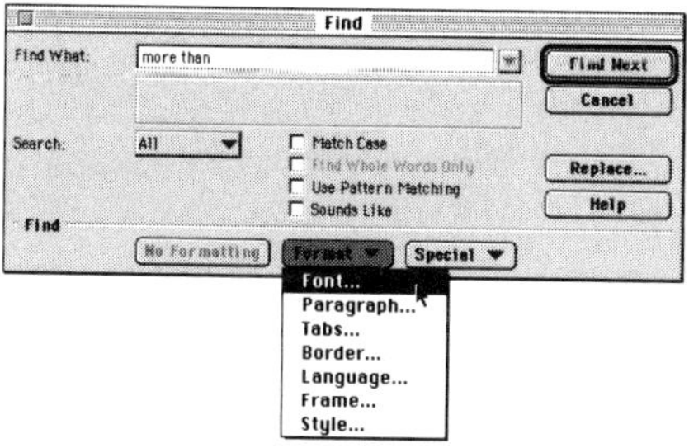

Figure 17. *Choose a format type here.*

Replacing Text

1. From the Edit menu, choose Replace. **(Figure 18)**

   or

   Press ⌘+H.
2. In the Replace dialog box, type the text to find in the Find What text box. **(Figure 19)**
3. In the Replace With text box, type the replacement text.
4. Click the Find Next button.
5. Click Replace to replace the text or click Find Next to skip to the next occurrence of the Find What text.

   or

   Click Replace All to replace all occurrences of the Find What text in the entire document.

✔ Tips

- The Search pull-down list gives you the choice to search Up from the insertion point, Down from the insertion point, or All (through the entire document). **(Figure 20)**
- You can replace formatting as easily as you can replace text.

Edit
Undo Typing ⌘Z
Repeat Typing ⌘Y
Cut ⌘X
Copy ⌘C
Paste ⌘V
Paste Special...
Clear Clear
Select All ⌘A
Find... ⌘F
Replace... ⌘H
Go To... ⌘G
AutoText...
Bookmark...
Links...
Object
Publishing

Figure 18. *The Edit menu.*

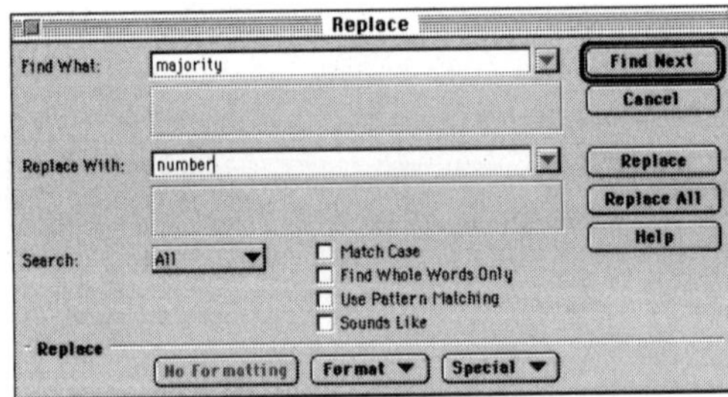

Figure 19. *The Replace dialog box.*

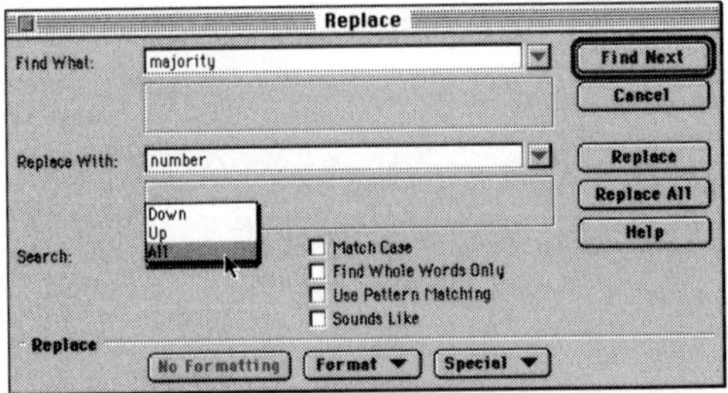

Figure 20. *The Search pull-down list.*

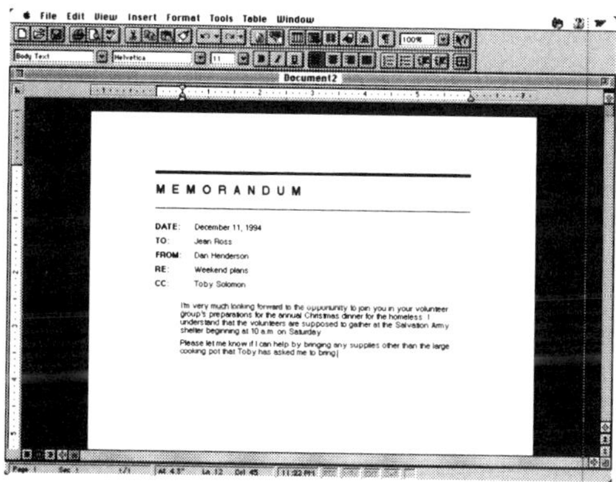

Figure 21. *Page Layout view*

The Page Layout View button.

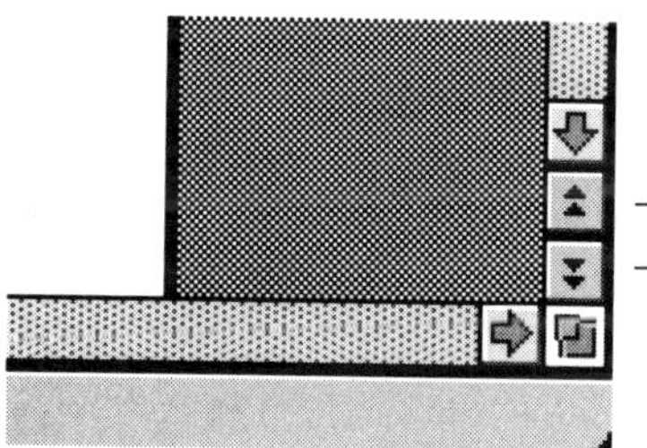

Figure 22. *The Page Layout View button.*

Switching to Page Layout view

Switch to Page Layout view **(Figure 21)** to see the document as it will look when printed, including the accurate page borders, page margins, headers and footers, multiple columns, and frames that contain images.

1. Click the Page Layout View button. **(Figure 22)**

   or

   From the View menu, choose Page Layout.

✔ Tips

- Page layout view is an actual working view of the document in which you can enter, edit, and format text.
- While in Page Layout view, turn from page to page by clicking the Next Page and Previous Page buttons. **(Figure 23)**
- While in Page Layout view, you can choose Whole Page from the Zoom Control list to see the entire page. **(Figure 24)** *See Zooming In and Out, page 33.*

Previous Page button.

Next Page button.

Figure 23. *The Next Page and Previous Page buttons.*

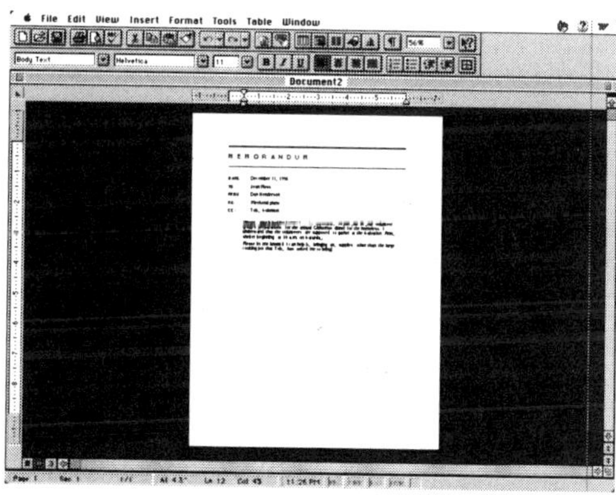

Figure 24. *Viewing the whole page in Page Layout view.*

The Other Views

In Outline view **(Figure 25)**, you can enter several levels of headings, type text underneath the headings, and rearrange both the headings and the text as you work out the structure of a document. To edit and rearrange the main headings, you can collapse any lower level headings underneath a heading at any level.

In Master Document view **(Figure 26)**, you form a compound document composed of individual documents. Any change made to one of the component documents shows up in the master document, and vice versa.

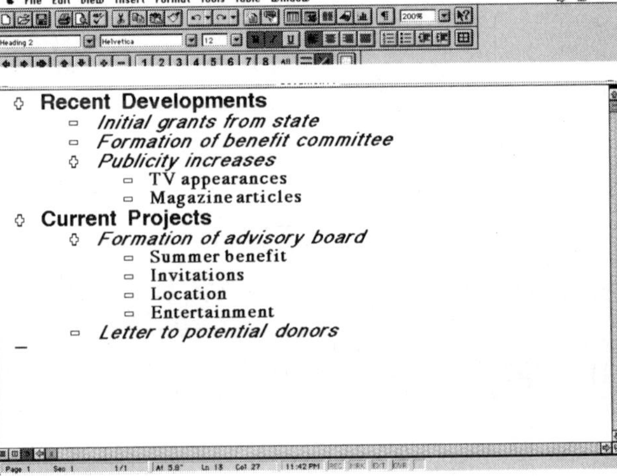

Figure 25. *Outline view.*

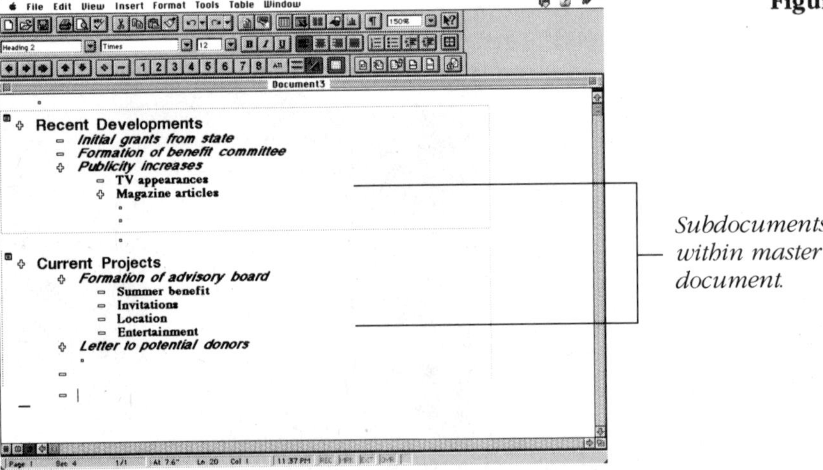

Figure 26. *Master Document view.*

Font Formatting 5

Word

About Font Formatting

The look of the characters you type (letters, numbers, and punctuation) is automatically set when you begin typing, but you can change it by choosing different *font formatting*. **(Figure 1)**

As with any change, you must select the text to format **first** (an individual character, a word or two, a paragraph, or the entire document) and **then** select font formatting with a menu selection, a click of a toolbar button, or a special keyboard shortcut. New text typed into the document assumes the character formatting of the text immediately to the left of the insertion point when typing begins.

For speedy document formatting, font formatting can be part of the information you record in a *Style*. Applying a style you've created to a paragraph automatically applies character formatting to the entire paragraph. *See About Styles, page 71.*

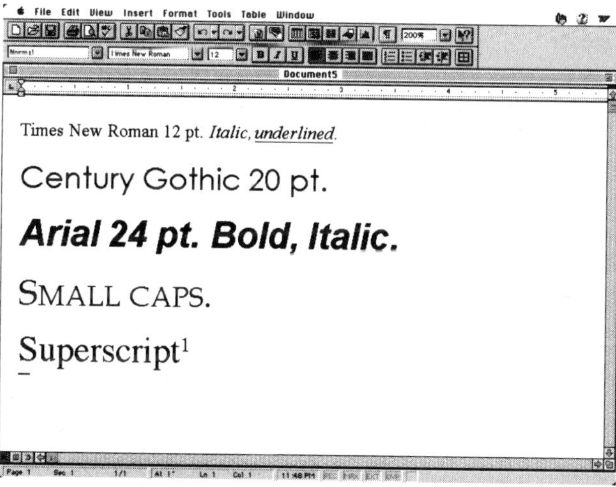

Figure 1. *Examples of different font formatting.*

Changing the Font and Font Size

1. Select the text to format. **(Figure 2)** *See Selecting Text, pages 23-25.*
2. Pull down the Font list on the Formatting toolbar and select a font name. **(Figure 3)**
3. Pull down the Font Size list and select a different size or double-click the current size and type a replacement. **(Figure 4)**

or

1. Select the text to format. **(Figure 2)**
2. From the Format menu, choose Font and then, on the Font dialog box, select a font on the scrollable list under Font and a Font Size on the scrollable list under Size. **(Figure 5)**

✔ Tips

- To use the keyboard to change the font of selected text, press ⌘+Shift+F, press the up or down arrow keys to select a font, and then press Enter.
- To return selected text to the standard font and size for the paragraph, select the text and press ⌘+Spacebar or ⌘+Shift+Z.
- To increase the font size of selected text, press ⌘+Shift+>.
- To decrease the font size of selected text, press ⌘+Shift+<.

Choose a font from this list.

Choose a font size from this list.

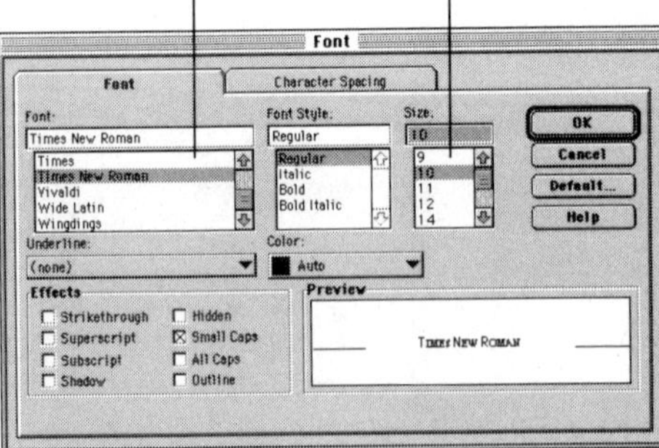

Figure 5. *The Font dialog box.*

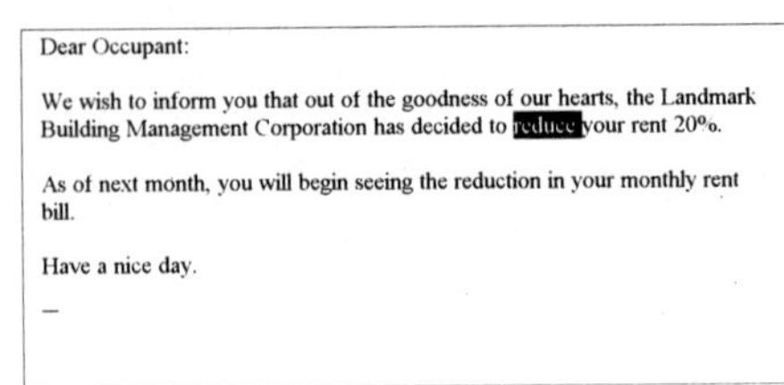

Dear Occupant:

We wish to inform you that out of the goodness of our hearts, the Landmark Building Management Corporation has decided to reduce your rent 20%.

As of next month, you will begin seeing the reduction in your monthly rent bill.

Have a nice day.

Figure 2. *Selected text.*

Click here to pull down the Font list.

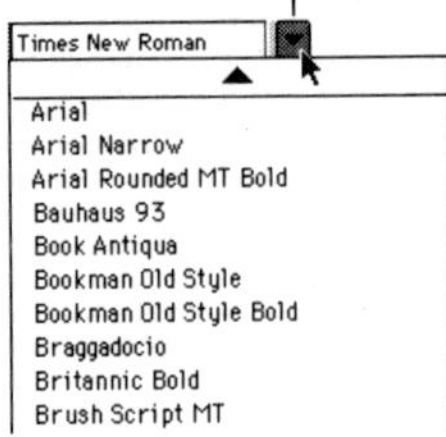

Figure 3. *The Font list.*

Click here to pull down the Font Size list.

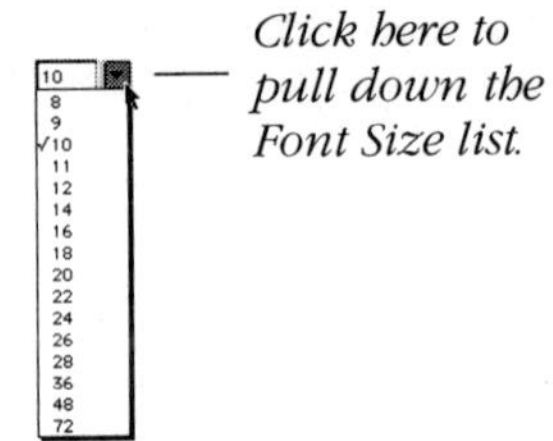

Figure 4. *The Font Size list.*

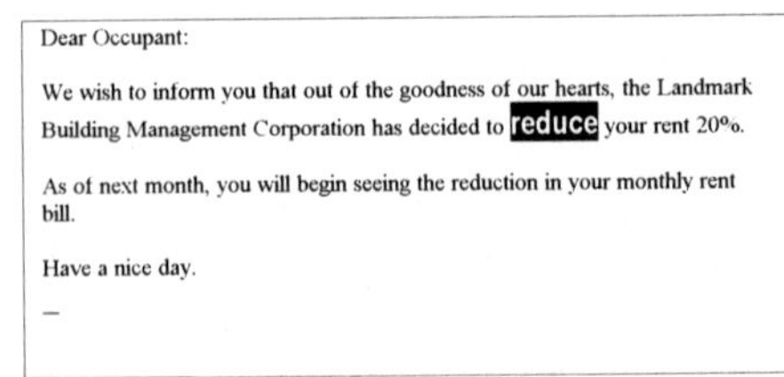

Dear Occupant:

We wish to inform you that out of the goodness of our hearts, the Landmark Building Management Corporation has decided to reduce your rent 20%.

As of next month, you will begin seeing the reduction in your monthly rent bill.

Have a nice day.

Figure 6. *Text with its new font and font size.*

As you know, your lease for office #200 in the East Coast Sales building will expire on December 31, 1994. Enclosed you will find a contract to extend your tenancy for an additional three years.

The contract includes a rental rate of $495.00 per month.

Figure 7. *Selected text.*

Figure 8. *The Bold, Italic, and Underline buttons.*

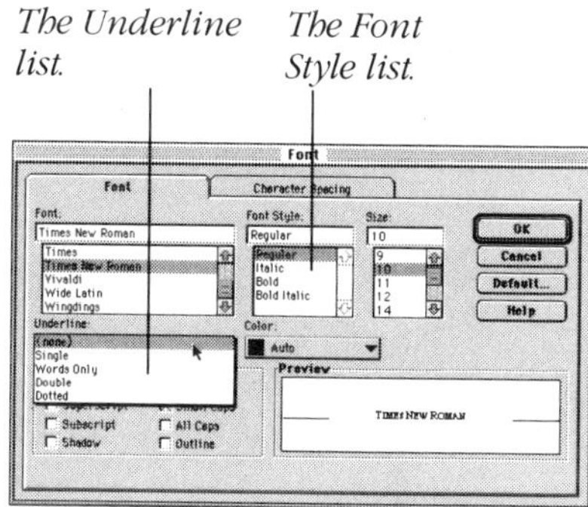

Figure 9. *The Font dialog box.*

As you know, your lease for office #200 in the East Coast Sales building will expire on **December 31, 1994**. Enclosed you will find a contract to extend your tenancy for an additional three years.

The contract includes a rental rate of $495.00 per month.

Figure 10. *Formatted text.*

Boldfacing, Italicizing and Underlining

1. Select the text to format. **(Figure 7)**
2. Click the Bold, Italic, or Underline buttons on the Formatting toolbar. **(Figure 8)**

   or

   From the Format menu, choose Font and then, in the Font dialog box, click an item on the list under Font Style. To change underlining, click the pull-down button next to the Underline text box and then select an underline option on the list. **(Figure 9)**

✔ Tip

- The Bold, Italic, and Underline buttons and keyboard shortcuts are toggles. Use them once to turn formatting on, again to turn formatting off.

Table 5-1. *Keyboard Shortcuts*

⌘+b	Bold
⌘+i	Italic
⌘+u	Underline

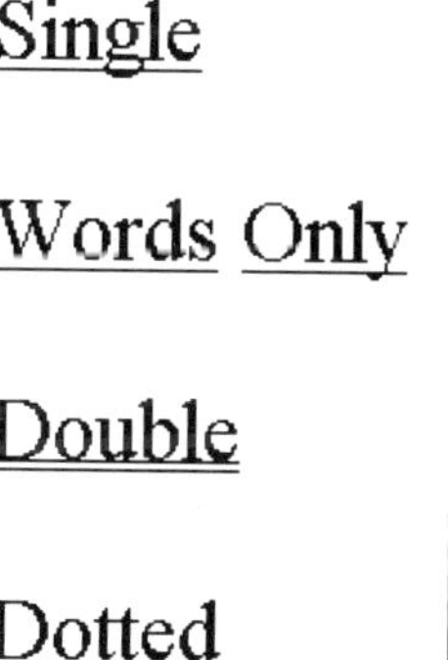

Figure 11. *Underline options.*

Expanding and Condensing Character Spacing

1. Select the text to format. **(Figure 12)**
2. From the Format menu, choose Font.
3. On the Character Spacing tab of the Font dialog box, click the up or down arrows next to the By text box to Expand or Condense the character spacing. **(Figure 13)**

✔ Tip

■ To quickly return expanded or condensed text to normal, select the text and then press ⌘+Spacebar or ⌘+Shift+Z.

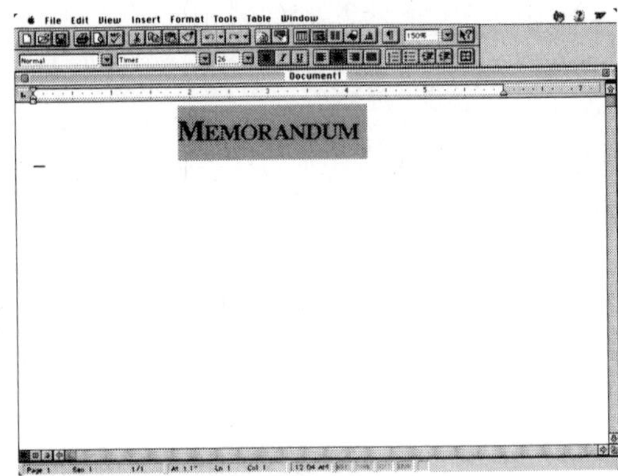

Figure 12. *Selected text.*

Click these arrows to expand or condense character spacing.

Font

Font | Character Spacing

Spacing: Expanded By: 6 pt

Position: Normal By:

☒ Kerning for Fonts: 14 Points and Above

Preview

MEMORANDUM

OK

Cancel

Default...

Help

This preview shows the current settings.

Figure 13. *The Character Spacing tab on the Font dialog box.*

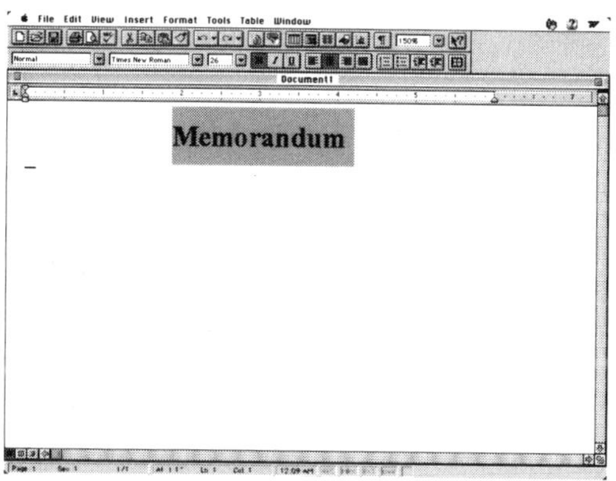

Figure 14. *Selected text.*

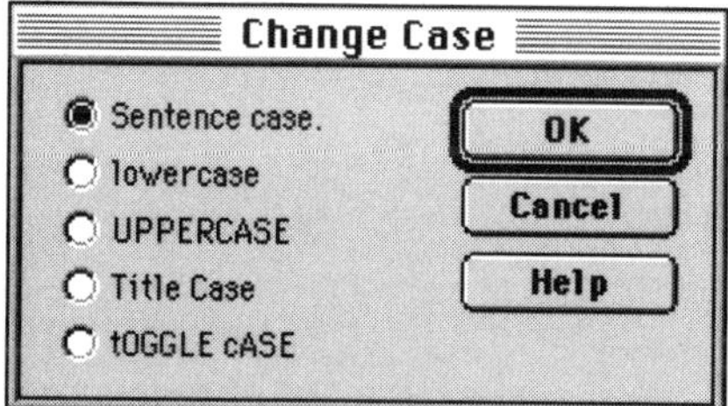

Figure 15. *The Change Case dialog box.*

Changing the Case of Characters

1. Select the text to format. **(Figure 14)**
2. Press Shift+F3 or ⌘+Option+C to toggle among Initial Caps, ALL CAPS, and all lower case.

   or

   From the Format menu, choose Change Case and select an option on the Change Case dialog box. **(Figure 15)**

   or

   From the Format menu, choose Font.
3. On the Font tab of the Font dialog box, click the Small Caps or All Caps checkboxes. Click either one again to clear it. **(Figure 16)**

Table 5-2. *Keyboard Shortcuts*

Shift+F3	Change the case of characters.
⌘+Shift+K	Small caps.
⌘+Shift+A	All caps.
⌘+Spacebar	Remove Small caps or All caps applied with keyboard shortcut.

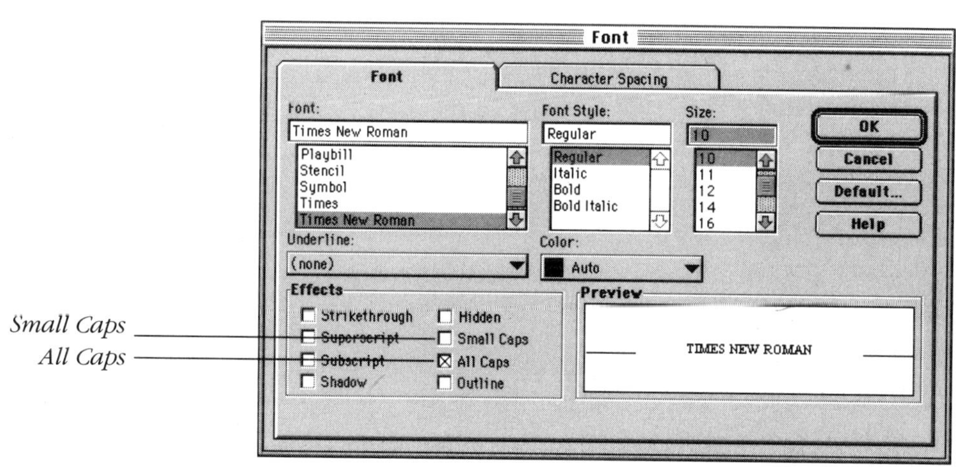

Figure 16. *The Font tab of the Font dialog box.*

Special Font Effects

On the Font tab of the Font dialog box, six checkboxes let you specify special effects for the selected text.

1. Select the text to format.
2. From the Format menu, choose Font.
3. On the Font tab of the Font dialog box, click as many effects as you'd like to apply to the selected text. **(Figure 17)**

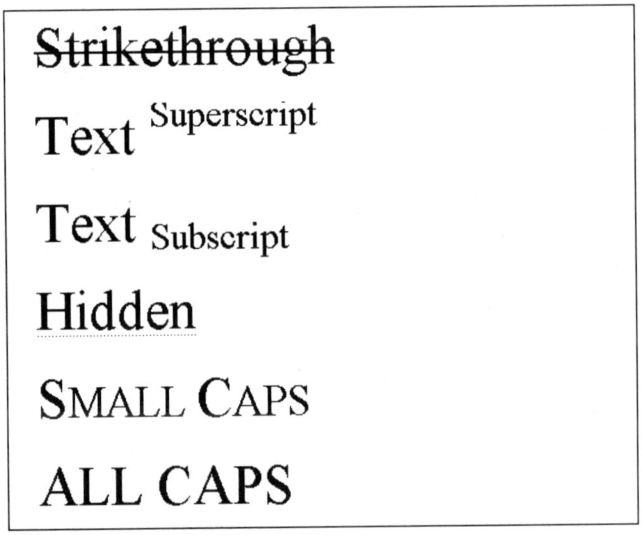

~~Strikethrough~~

Text ^{Superscript}

Text $_{\text{Subscript}}$

Hidden

SMALL CAPS

ALL CAPS

Figure 17. *The Font effects.*

Paragraph Formatting 6

About Paragraph Formatting

Paragraph formatting applies changes in appearance to entire paragraphs. The most popular paragraph formatting options include indenting, double spacing, centering, justifying, numbering, and adding bullets to paragraphs.

A paragraph is any amount of text that ends in a paragraph mark, from as little as a single word to multiple lines of text. **(Figure 1)**

M E M O R A N D U M ¶

DATE: November 24, 1994¶
TO: George Washington¶
FROM: Abraham Lincoln¶

I hope this letter finds you in good health and good spirits.¶

I am writing now to solicit your advice on several issues of great importance to the state and our good people. Among my concerns is the continuing difficulties I have had with gathering support for my plans.¶

Figure 1. *Paragraph marks.*

Tip

- Use the Format Painter to copy paragraph formatting from one paragraph to others. *See Copying Formatting with the Format Painter, page 30.*

Selecting Paragraphs

To select a paragraph for paragraph formatting, click anywhere in the paragraph. The paragraph containing the insertion point will be formatted. **(Figure 2)**

Insertion point *This paragraph will be formatted.*

I hope this letter finds you in good health and good spirits.¶

I am writing now to solicit your advice on several issues of great importance to the state and our good people. Among my concerns is the continuing difficulties I have had with gathering support for my plans.¶

Figure 2. *The paragraph containing the insertion point will be formatted.*

To select multiple paragraphs, drag from anywhere in the first paragraph to format to anywhere in the last paragraph to format. If the selection extends into a paragraph, the paragraph will be formatted. **(Figure 3)**

These two paragraphs will be formatted.

I hope this letter finds you in good health and good spirits.¶

I am writing now to solicit your advice on several issues of great importance to the state and our good people. Among my concerns is the continuing difficulties I have had with gathering support for my plans.¶

Figure 3. *Drag across multiple paragraphs to format.*

✔ Tips

- You do not have to select an entire paragraph to apply paragraph formatting.
- To select multiple paragraphs quickly, drag down through the left margin next to the paragraphs.

Indenting Paragraphs with the Ruler

1. Click in or select the paragraph or paragraphs to be formatted. **(Figure 4)**
2. Drag the left indent marker to set the left indent. **(Figures 5 and 7)**

   or

   Drag the rectangular button below the left indent marker to move the first line indent and the left indent markers simultaneously and maintain their relative positions. **(Figure 7)**
3. Drag the right indent marker to set the right indent. **(Figure 6)**

✔ Tips

- Click on a paragraph and then examine the indent markers on the ruler to check the indent settings for the paragraph.
- Click the Increase Indent button on the Formatting toolbar to increase the left indent one-half inch. **(Figure 8)**
- Click the Decrease Indent button to decrease the left indent one-half inch. **(Figure 8)**

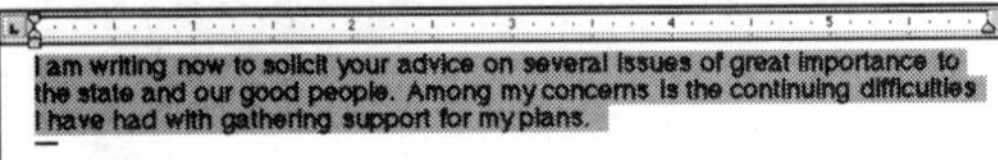

Figure 4. *Select a paragraph to format.*

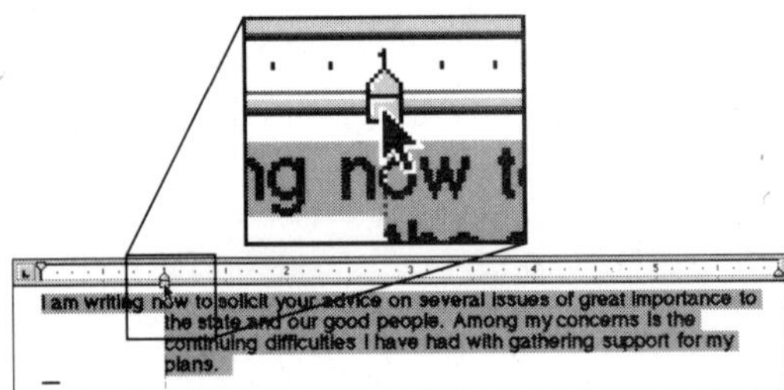

Figure 5. *The left indent marker.*

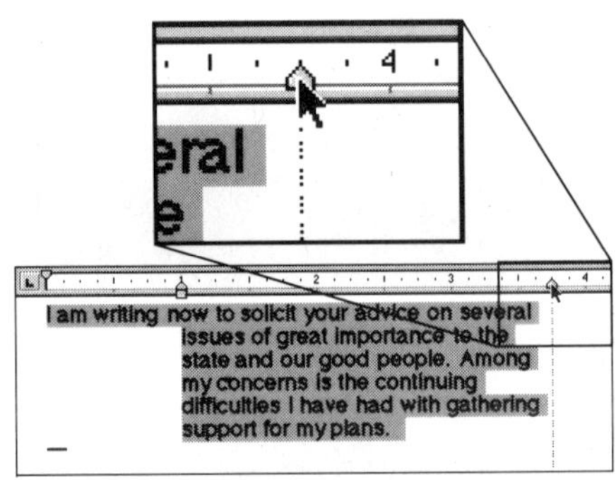

Figure 6. *The right indent marker.*

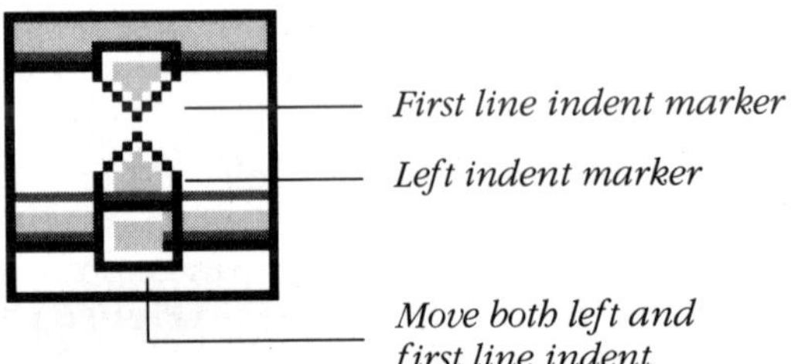

Figure 7. *The indent markers.*

Figure 8. *The Increase Indent and Decrease Indent buttons.*

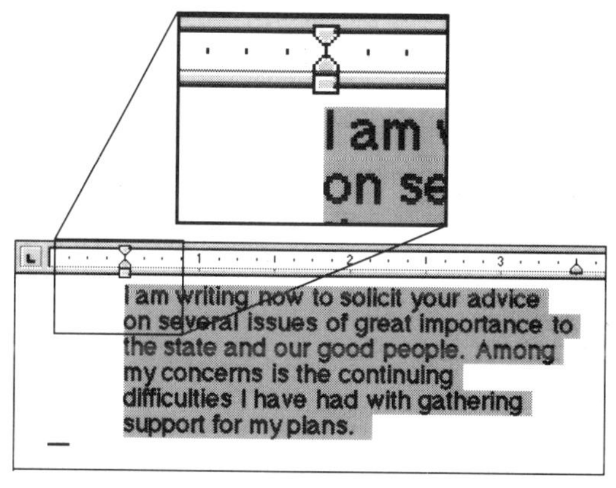

Figure 9. *Select a paragraph to format.*

Changing the First Line Indent

1. Select the paragraph or paragraphs to be formatted. **(Figure 9)**
2. Drag the first line indent marker to set the indent of the first line of a paragraph. **(Figure 10)**

✔ Tip

- Drag the first line indent to the left of the left indent marker to create a hanging indent. **(Figure 11)**

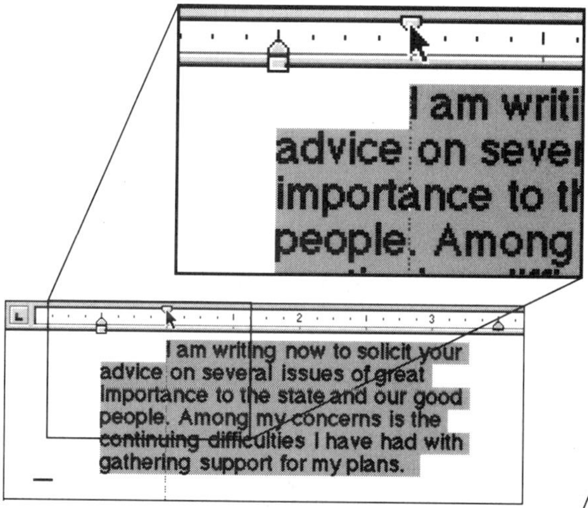

Figure 10. *Drag the first line indent marker to create a first line indent.*

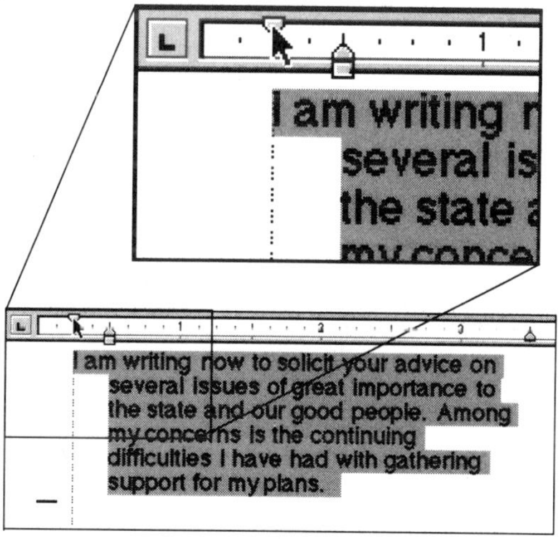

Figure 11. *A hanging indent.*

Indenting with the Paragraph Dialog Box

1. Select the paragraph or paragraphs to be formatted. **(Figure 12)**
2. From the Format menu, choose Paragraph. **(Figure 13)**
3. On the Indents and Spacing tab of the Paragraph dialog box, change the left or right indent settings by clicking the increment/decrement buttons **(Figure 14)** or by double-clicking the current setting and typing a replacement.
4. If you want a hanging or first line indent, pull down the list under Special and choose either First Line or Hanging. Then, set the amount of the indent in the By text box.
5. Click OK.

✔ **Tips**

- Using the Paragraph Dialog box gives you the precision to enter exact measurements.
- Indents are measured from the left and right margins.

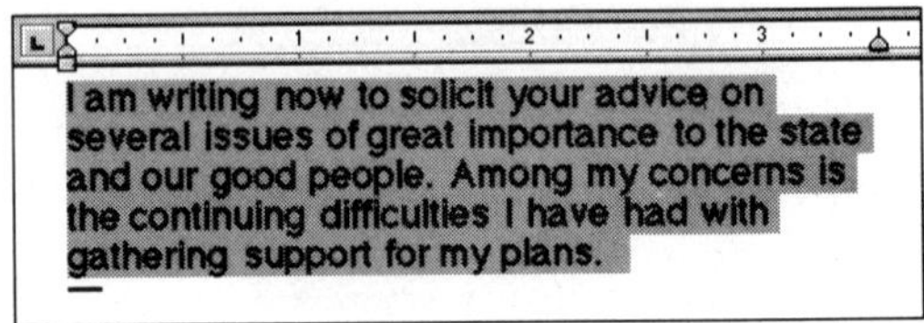

Figure 12. *Select a paragraph to format.*

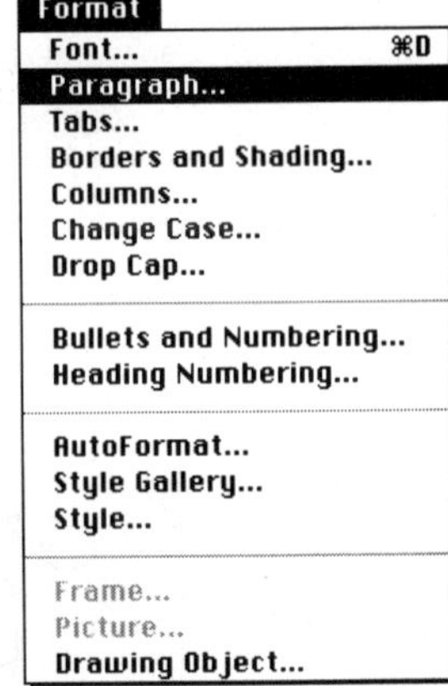

Figure 13. *The Format menu.*

The increment/decrement buttons.

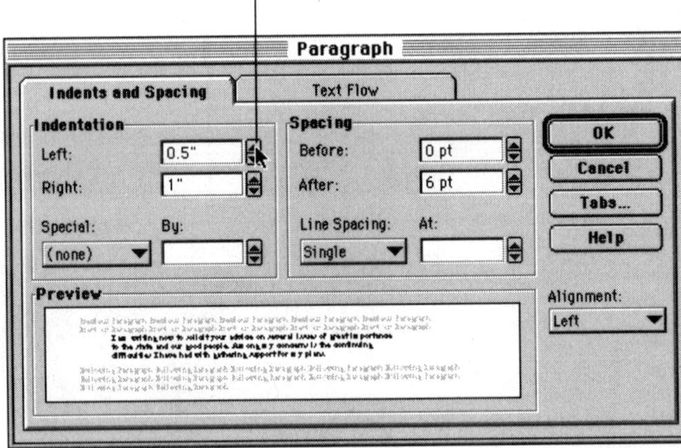

Figure 14. *The Paragraph dialog box.*

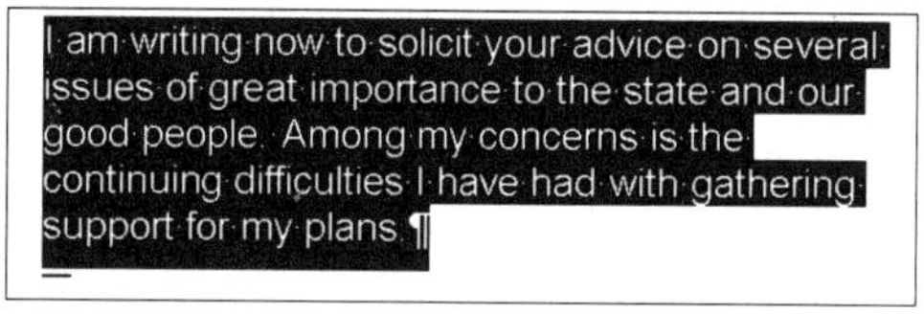

I am writing now to solicit your advice on several issues of great importance to the state and our good people. Among my concerns is the continuing difficulties I have had with gathering support for my plans.¶

Figure 15. *Select a paragraph to format.*

I am writing now to solicit your advice on several
issues of great importance to the state and our
good people. Among my concerns is the
continuing difficulties I have had with gathering
support for my plans.¶

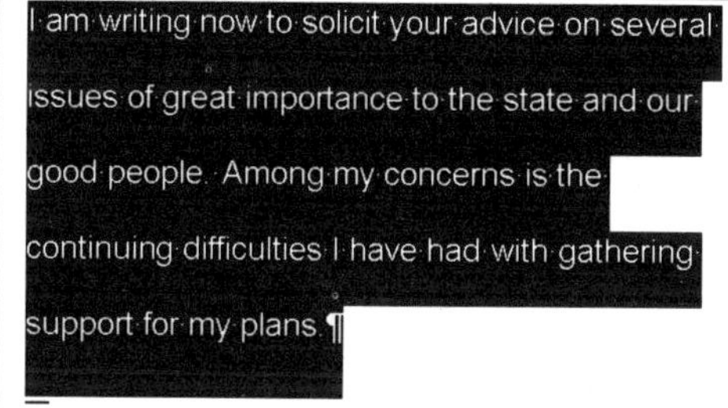

Figure 16. *Double-spaced paragraph.*

Double Spacing Paragraphs

1. Select the paragraph or paragraphs to be formatted. **(Figure 15)**
2. Press ⌘+2. **(Figure 16)**

   or

   From the Format menu, choose Paragraph and choose Double from the Line Spacing drop-down list. Then click OK. **(Figure 17)**

✔ Tips

- Press ⌘+1 to return a selected paragraph to single spacing.
- From the Line Spacing drop-down list on the Paragraph dialog box, you can also choose 1.5 lines, or set an exact line spacing by choosing Exactly and then selecting a measurement for At.

Choose an alternate line spacing here.

Paragraph
Indents and Spacing
Text Flow
Indentation
Left:
0"
Right:
2.5"
Special:
By:
(none)
Spacing
Before:
0 pt
After:
6 pt
Line Spacing:
At:
Single
1.5 Lines
Double
At Least
Exactly
Multiple
OK
Cancel
Tabs...
Help
Alignment:
Left
Preview

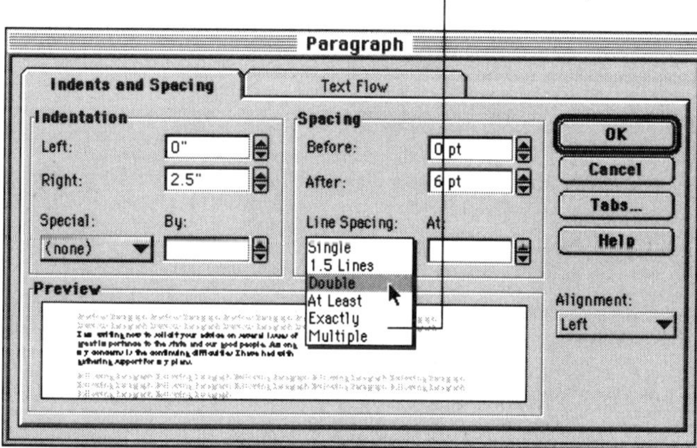

Figure 17. *The Line Spacing drop-down list.*

Centering and Justifying Paragraphs

Centered paragraphs are horizontally centered between the left and right margins. **(Figure 18)** The left and right sides of **justified** paragraphs are aligned with the left and right margins. **(Figure 19)**

1. Select the paragraph or paragraphs to be formatted.
2. Click the Center or Justify buttons on the Formatting toolbar. **(Figure 20)**

   or

   Press ⌘+E to center or ⌘+J to justify.

✔ Tips

- To return a paragraph to standard left alignment (aligned with the left margin and ragged right), click the Left button in the Formatting toolbar or press ⌘+L.
- You can also select Paragraph from the Format menu and then, on the Paragraph dialog box, choose an option from the Alignment drop-down list. **(Figure 21)**
- Paragraphs that are indented will not be centered properly so be sure to remove the indents first.
- To align paragraphs with the right margin, click the Align Right button or press ⌘+R.

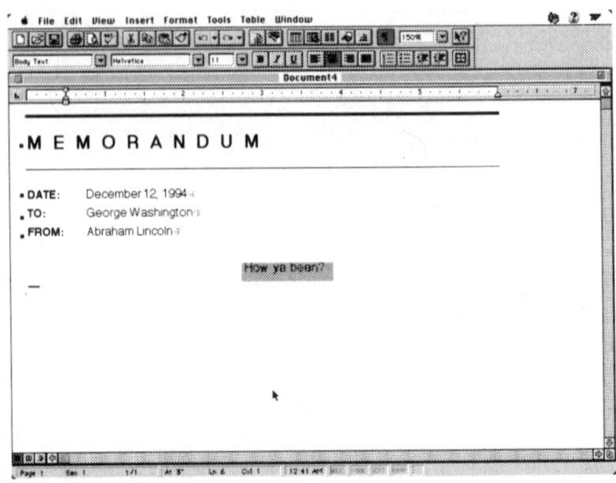

Figure 18. *Centered paragraph.*

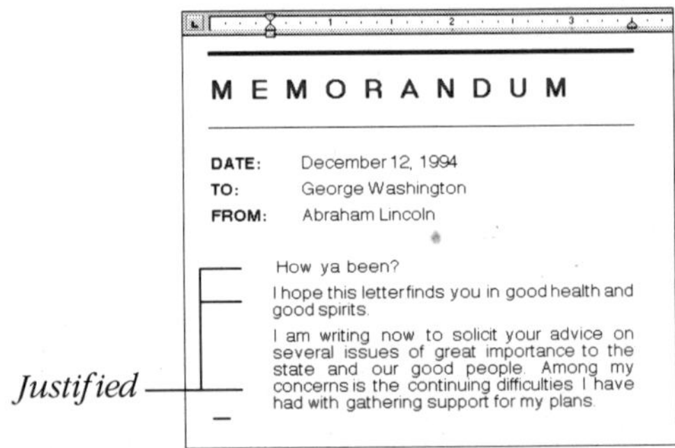

Figure 19. *Justified paragraph.*

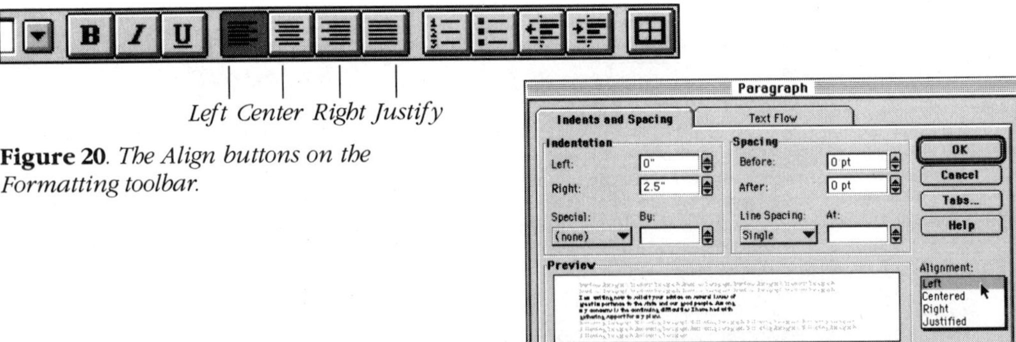

Figure 20. *The Align buttons on the Formatting toolbar.*

Figure 21. *The Alignment drop-down list.*

Bus Tours
New York Radio City Music Hall
Miami South Beach Art Deco District
Boston Harvard Square
Los Angeles Hollywood Bowl

Figure 22. *Selected paragraphs.*

Tab alignment button.

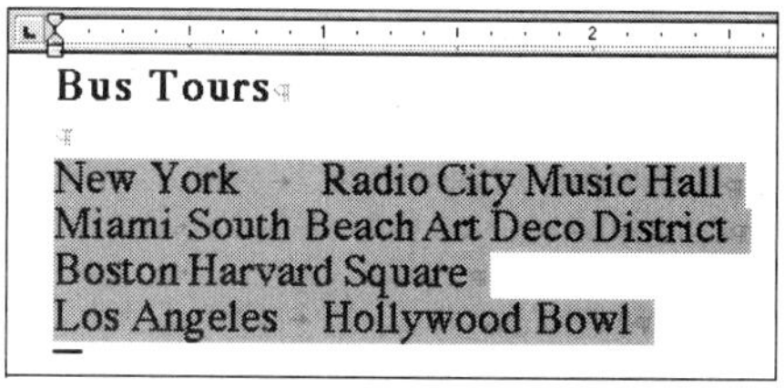

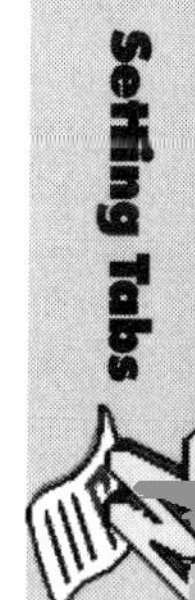

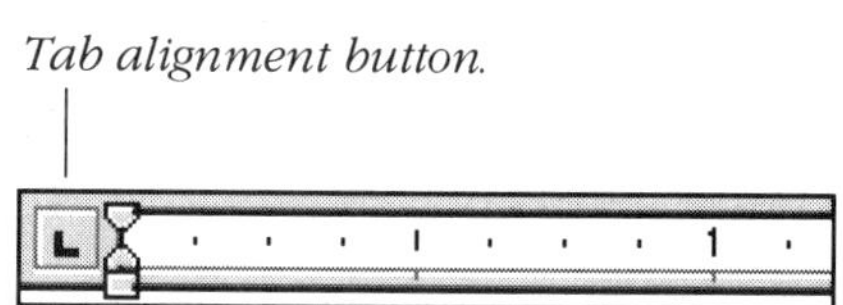

Figure 23. *The alignment marker.*

Click in the ruler to set a tab.

Bus Tours
New York Radio City Music Hall
Miami South Beach Art Deco District
Boston Harvard Square
Los Angeles Hollywood Bowl

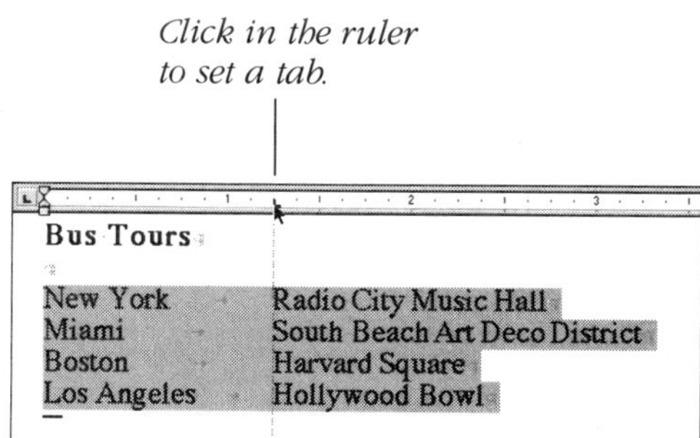

Figure 24. *Setting a tab.*

Setting Tabs

1. Select the paragraph or paragraphs to which you want to add tabs. **(Figure 22)**
2. Click the tab alignment button if you want to change the tab type. The default tab is left-aligned. **(Figure 23)**
3. Click in the ruler to set a tab of the type shown on the tab alignment button. **(Figure 24)**
4. Click again at a different spot in the ruler to set another tab of the same type.
   or
   Click the tab alignment button to select a different tab type before clicking in the ruler to set the tab.

✔ Tips

- To delete a tab, drag it up and off the ruler.
- To change tab settings, select the paragraphs to affect and then drag the tab markers left or right along the ruler.

Table 6-1. ***Tab Alignment Settings***

L	Left-aligned tab
⊥	Center-aligned tab
┘	Right-aligned tab
⊥.	Decimal-aligned tab

Adding Bullets to Paragraphs

1. Select the paragraph or paragraphs to be formatted. **(Figure 25)**
2. Click the Bullets button on the Formatting toolbar. **(Figure 26)**

   or, to select a bullet shape and other bullet options:

   From the Format menu, choose Bullets and Numbering.

   or

   Click while holding down the Control key and choose Bullets and Numbering from the shortcut menu.
3. On the Bulleted tab of the Bullets and Numbering dialog box, click one of the six large panes to select a bullet shape. **(Figure 27)**
4. Clear the Hanging Indent checkbox on the Bulleted tab only if you do not want the text to be aligned to the right of the bullet. **(Figure 27)**

✓ Tips

- To remove bullets, select the bulleted paragraphs and then click the Bullets button again.
- Bulleted paragraphs in a list have equal emphasis. To order the list, number the paragraphs instead. *See Numbering Paragraphs, page 69.*
- To set the bullet size, distance from text, and other options, click Modify on the Bulleted tab of the Bullets and Numbering dialog box.

Action Plan

Solicit proposals
Evaluate bids
Develop design
Hire contractor

Figure 25. *Select a paragraph to format.*

Figure 26. *The Formatting toolbar.*

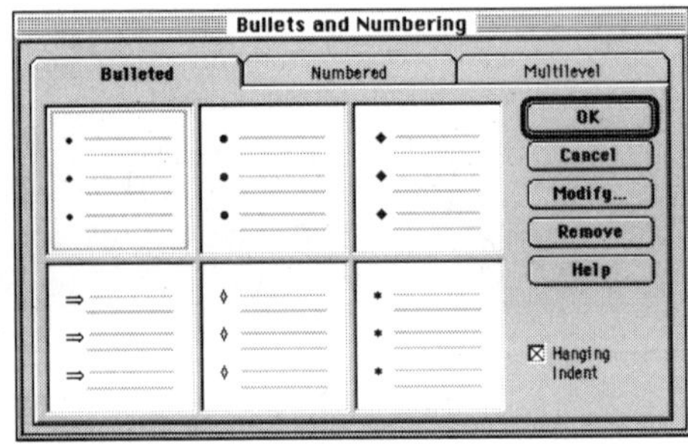

Figure 27. *The Bullets and Numbering dialog box.*

Action Plan

- Solicit proposals
- Evaluate bids
- Develop design
- Hire contractor

Figure 28. *The paragraphs with bullets.*

Action Plan

Solicit proposals
Evaluate bids
Develop design
Hire contractor

Figure 29. *Select a paragraph to format.*

The Numbering button.

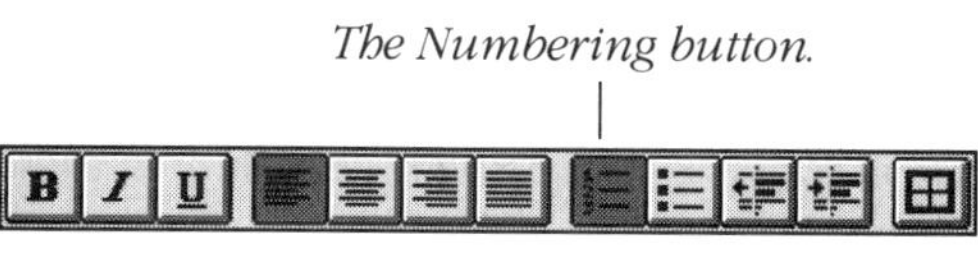

Figure 30. *The Formatting toolbar.*

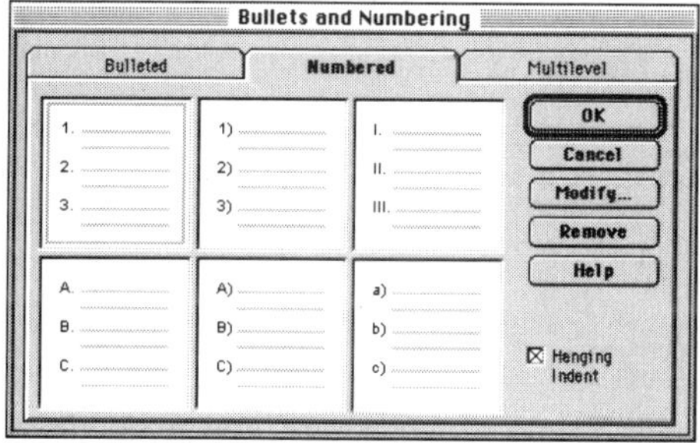

Figure 31. *The Bullets and Numbering dialog box.*

Action Plan

1. Solicit proposals
2. Evaluate bids
3. Develop design
4. Hire contractor

Figure 32. *The numbered list.*

Numbering Paragraphs

1. Select the paragraph or paragraphs to be formatted. **(Figure 29)**
2. Click the Numbering button on the Formatting toolbar. **(Figure 30)**

   or, to select a numbering style and other numbering options

   From the Format menu, choose Bullets and Numbering.

   or

   Click while holding down the Control key and choose Bullets and Numbering from the shortcut menu.
3. On the Numbered tab of the Bullets and Numbering dialog box, click one of the six large panes to select a numbering style. **(Figure 31)**
4. Clear the Hanging Indent checkbox only if you do not want the text to be aligned to the right of the numbers. **(Figure 32)**

✔ Tips

- To remove numbers, select the numbered paragraphs and then click the Numbering button again.
- To set the numbering style, distance from text, and other options, click Modify on the Numbered tab of the Bullets and Numbering dialog box.
- To stop numbering in a list of paragraphs or to skip over a paragraph in a list, select a paragraph in the list, click while holding down the Control key, and choose Skip Numbering or Stop Numbering.

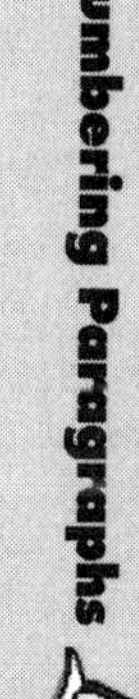

Word

Finding and Replacing Formatting

1. Press ⌘+F to Find or ⌘+H to replace text.

   or

   From the Edit menu, choose either Find or Replace. **(Figure 33)**
2. On the Find dialog box or the Replace dialog box, click the Format button to pull down a list of formats. **(Figure 34)**
3. Choose the formatting you want to find or replace. The formatting you choose will be described under the Find What text box. **(Figure 35)**
4. Click Find Next to find the formatting.

   or

   Click in the Replace With textbox, click the Format button, choose replacement formatting, and then click Find Next.

✔ Tips

- You can search for a style by clicking the Format button on the Find or Replace dialog box, selecting Style on the Format list, and then choosing a style. *To learn about styles, see Automatic Text Formatting, pages 71-74.*
- Type text into the Find What text box at Step 2 above to search for specific text with specific formatting.

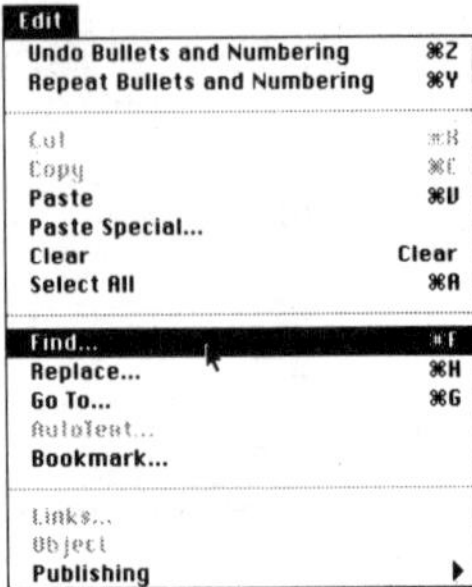

Figure 33. *The Edit menu.*

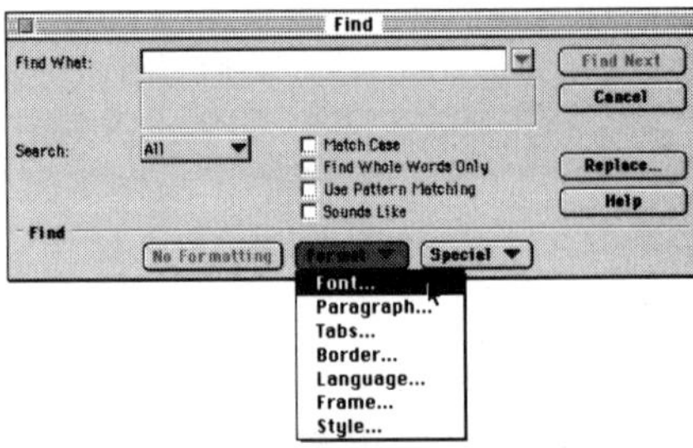

Figure 34. *The Format pull-down list.*

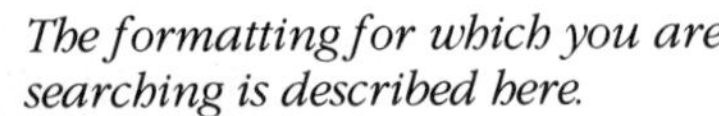

Figure 35. *The Find dialog box.*

Automatic Text Formatting

Before we complete the tour, I'd like to show you some superb English gardens:

24 Lily Pond Lane
117 Georgica St.
3 Heron Court
57 Hill Street

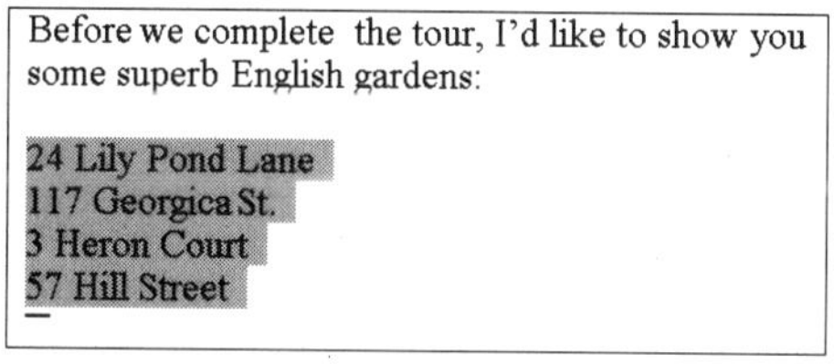

Figure 1. *Select the paragraphs to format.*

Click here to pull down the style list.

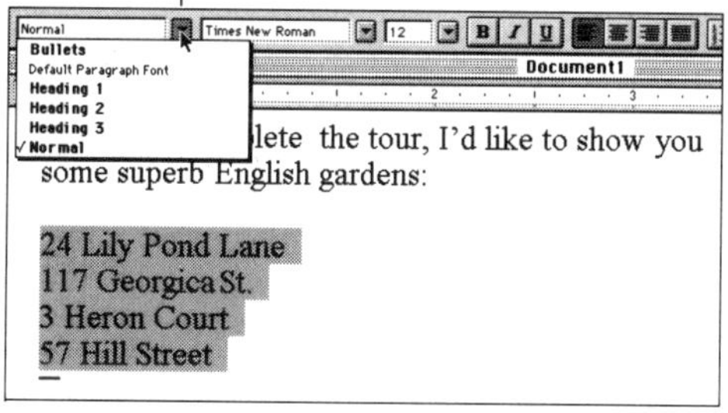

Normal | Times New Roman | 12 | B I U
Bullets
Default Paragraph Font
Heading 1
Heading 2
Heading 3
✓Normal
Document1
...lete the tour, I'd like to show you some superb English gardens:

24 Lily Pond Lane
117 Georgica St.
3 Heron Court
57 Hill Street

Figure 2. *The style list.*

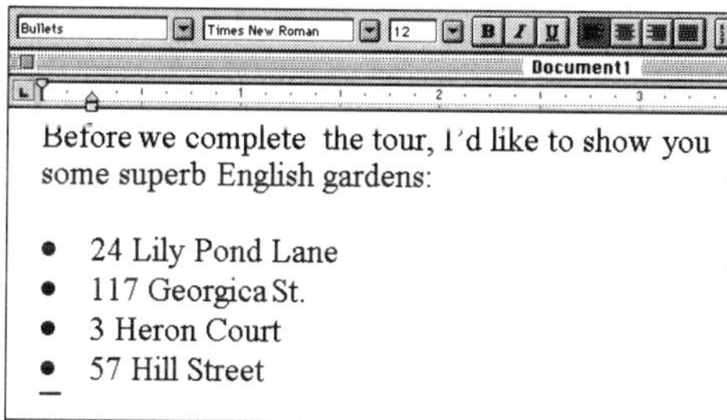

Figure 3. *Bullets style applied to selected paragraphs.*

About Styles

A *style*, which contains formatting choices, is useful for quickly and easily applying a preset combination of formatting to characters or paragraphs. A style you might create called Heading, for example, could contain all of the formatting for headings. To format a particular heading, you'd select the heading and then choose the style called Heading from the Style list.

Character styles, which can be applied to selected characters of text, contain font formatting. Paragraph styles, which are applied to entire paragraphs, hold both font and paragraph formatting.

By default, paragraphs get the Normal style and text gets the Default Paragraph Font style.

Choosing a Style from the Style List

1. Select the characters or paragraphs to format. **(Figure 1)**
2. On the Formatting toolbar, click the pull-down button next to the Style box to pull down the list of styles. **(Figure 2)**
3. Choose a style name from the style list.

✓ Tips

- Paragraph styles are bold on the style list. Character style names are not bold.
- You do not have to select an entire paragraph before you apply a style. Simply click anywhere in the paragraph.
- You can apply a style to several consecutive paragraphs by dragging from any point in the first paragraph to any point in the last paragraph and then selecting a paragraph style.

Creating a Paragraph Style

1. Apply font and paragraph formatting to a paragraph and then leave the paragraph selected. **(Figure 4)**
2. On the Formatting toolbar, double-click the current style name. **(Figure 5)**
3. Type the new style name in place of the old name and press Enter. **(Figure 6)**

✔ Tips

- You can also create a style by using the Style command on the Format menu. *See Creating a Character Style, page 74.*
- The styles you create are stored in the document. To use the styles in other documents, you must transfer them to a template.

The Bridgehampton Garden Club

Among the many activities offered by the Bridgehapton Garden Club is a monthly garden tour through the gardens of our members.

Each month, we will visit four gardens on a Saturday afternoon. During the tour, the gardener will present his or her concept for the garden, a brief history of the garden's development, and notable information about special flowers contained in the garden.

The monthly garden tour is a wonderful opportunity to expand your knowledge about gardens and gardening from your fellow gardeners.

Figure 4. *Format a sample paragraph.*

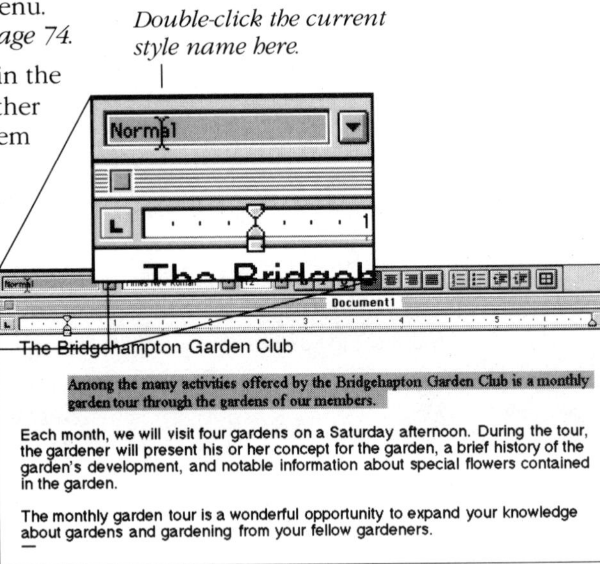

Figure 5. *Double-click the current style name.*

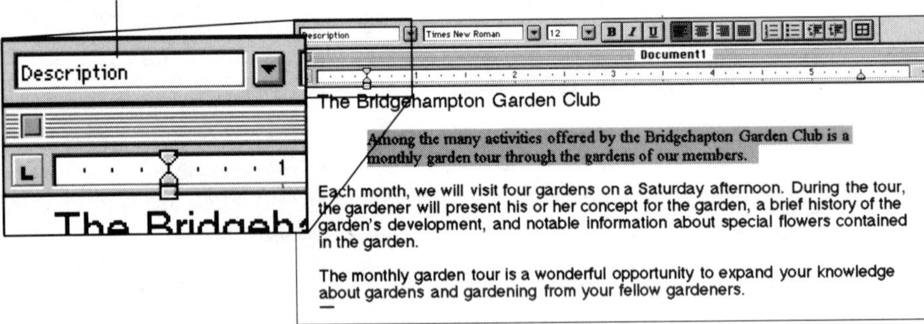

Figure 6. *Type the new style name.*

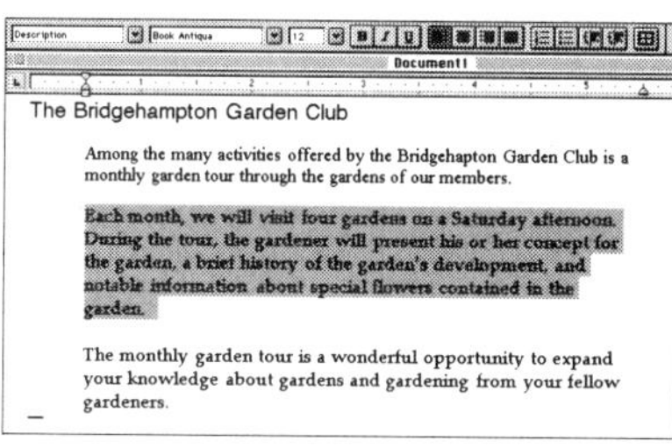

Figure 7. *Make font and paragraph formatting changes.*

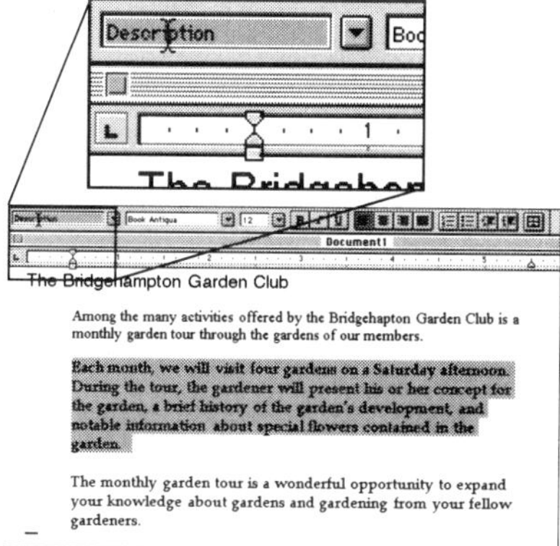

Figure 8. *Click the style name.*

Each month, we will visit four garden
During the tour, the gardener will pre
the garden, a brief history of the gard
notable information about special flov
garden.

The monthly garden tour is a wonder

Figure 9. *Click back on the modified text.*

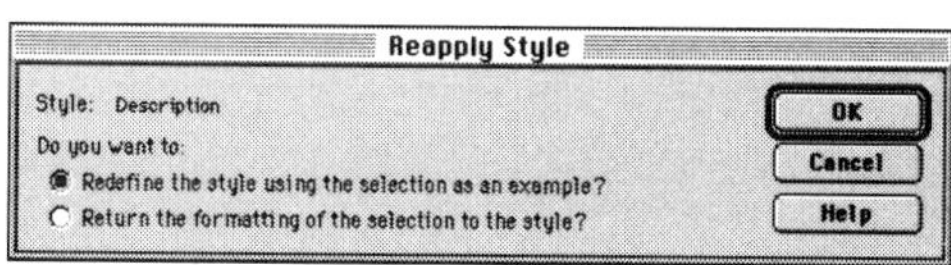

Figure 10. *The Reapply Style dialog box.*

Modifying a Paragraph Style

1. Make changes to the font or paragraph formatting of a paragraph that has been given the style that you want to modify. **(Figure 7)**
2. Click the current style name once. **(Figure 8)**
3. Click once anywhere in t he modified paragraph. **(Figure 9)**
4. On the Reapply Style dialog box, make sure "Redefine the style using the selection as an example?" is selected and click OK. **(Figure 10)** Every paragraph formatted by the modified style will be reformatted. **(Figure 11)**

✔ Tip

- When you redefine a paragraph style, all paragraphs that are formatted with the style will be redefined.

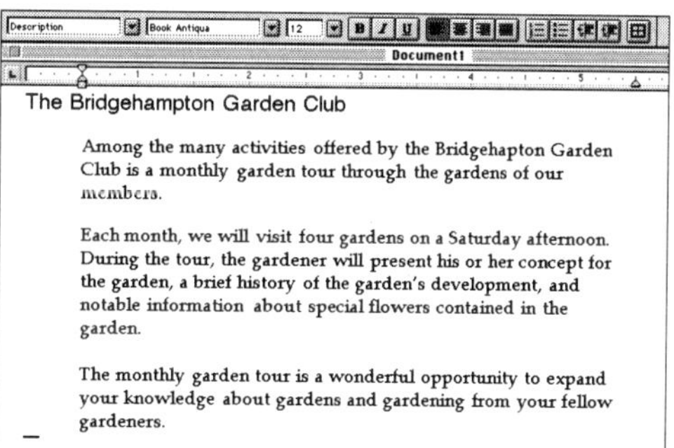

Figure 11. *All other paragraphs controlled by the modified style get the new formatting, too.*

Creating a Character Style

1. From the Format menu, select Style. **(Figure 12)**
2. On the Style dialog box, click New to create a new style. **(Figure 13)**
3. On the New Style dialog box, type a style name to replace the current, selected style name. **(Figure 14)**
4. Choose Character from the drop-down Style Type list.
5. Click the Format button and choose Font from the Format list. **(Figure 14)**
6. On the Font dialog box, select the formatting you'd like and then click OK. **(Figure 15)**
7. Click OK on the New Style dialog box.
8. Click Apply on the Style dialog box.

Figure 12. *The Format menu.*

Click here to create a new style.

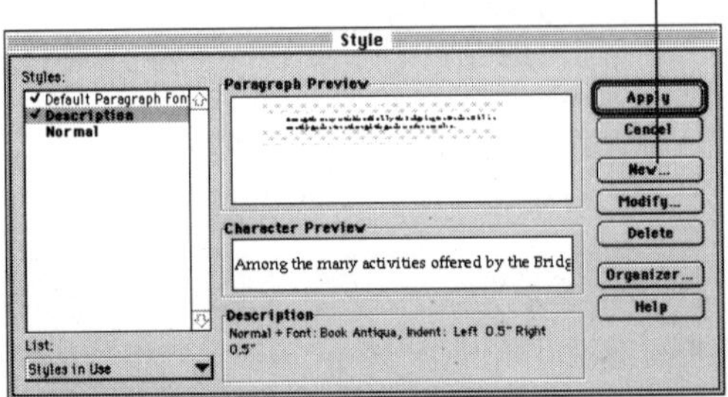

Figure 13. *The Style dialog box.*

Type a new style name here...

...then choose Character from the drop-down list.

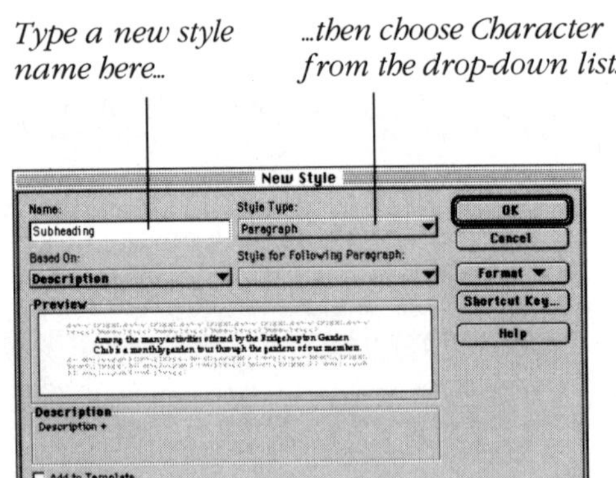

Figure 14. *The New Style dialog box.*

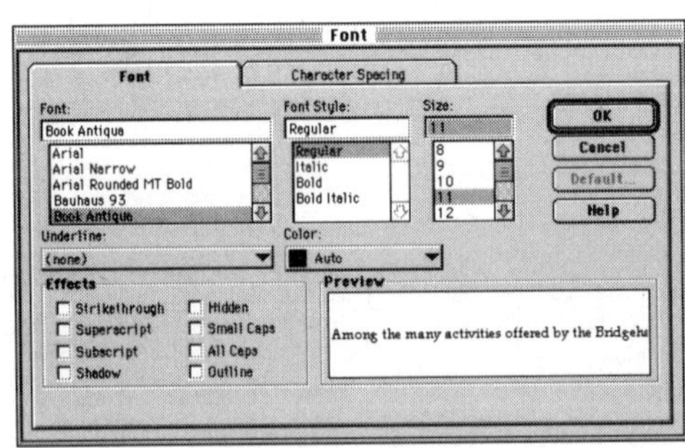

Figure 15. *The Font dialog box.*

Page Formatting 8

Figure 1. *The File menu.*

Click here to drop down the Paper list.

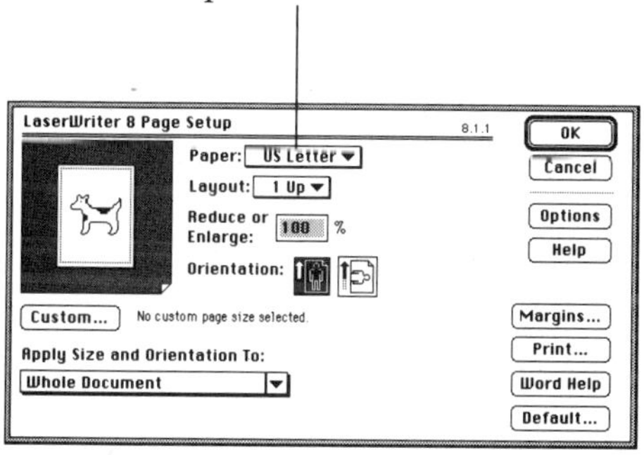

Figure 2. *The Paper drop-down list on the Page Setup dialog box.*

About Page Formatting

Page formatting can be the first step in creating a new document or the last. In page formatting, you set the size and shape of the page, the size of the margins, and certain printer information that should be recorded with the document, such as whether the paper will be manually fed or taken from the printer's paper tray. Word will adjust the text on the page to fit the new page size and margins.

If you always print portrait, 8 1/2 x 11 pages with standard margins, you won't need to worry about page formatting.

Word

Changing the Page Size and Shape

1. From the File menu, choose Page Setup. **(Figure 1)**
2. On the Page Setup dialog box, choose one of the standard paper sizes from the drop-down Paper list. **(Figure 2)**

   or

   Click the Custom button and enter a custom page size in the Width and Height text boxes.
3. Confirm that the Orientation setting you want for the page is selected: vertical or horizontal.

✔ **Tip**

- The selections you make for paper size and orientation are for the current document only. New documents revert to the default settings.

Changing the Margins

The margins are the blank space at the top, bottom, left, or right edges of the page. To provide extra space for hole punching, you might want to increase the left margin, for example. **(Figure 3)**

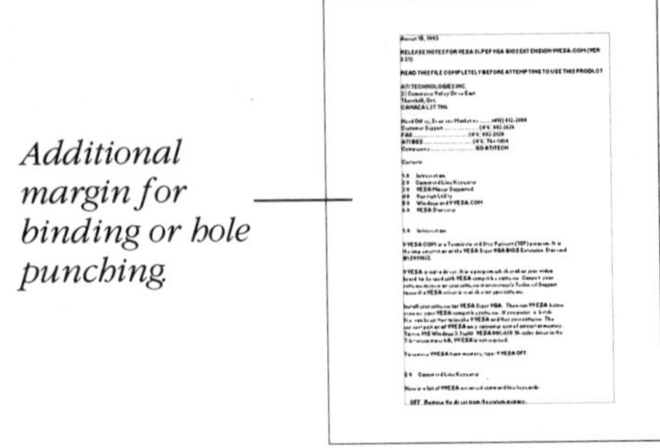

Figure 3. *Increase the left margin to provide space for hole punching.*

1. From the File menu, choose Page Setup. **(Figure 4)**
2. On the Margins tab of the Document Layout dialog box, alter the Top, Bottom, Left, or Right settings. **(Figure 5)**
3. Alter the gutter width if you want to change the space between multiple columns on the page. *See Setting up Multiple Columns, page 81.*

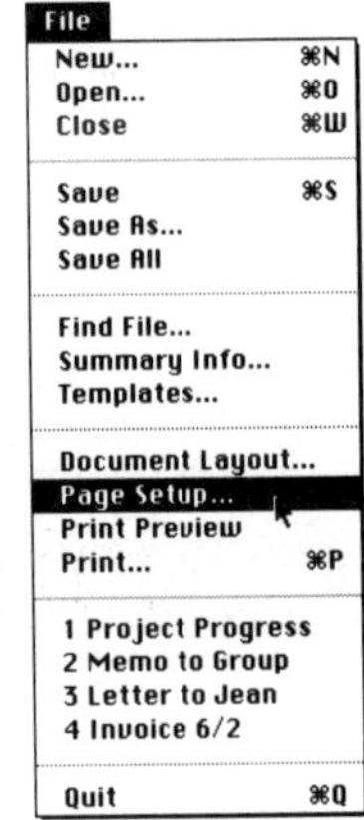

Figure 4. *The File menu.*

✔ Tip

- To print a book with text on both sides of the page, click the Mirror Margins checkbox on the Margins tab of the Page Setup dialog box. The Left margin of a right page becomes the Inside margin and the Right margin becomes the Outside margin. On left pages, it's vice versa. To leave space for binding on the left side of the right page and the right side of the left page, you'd increase the Inside margin, for example.

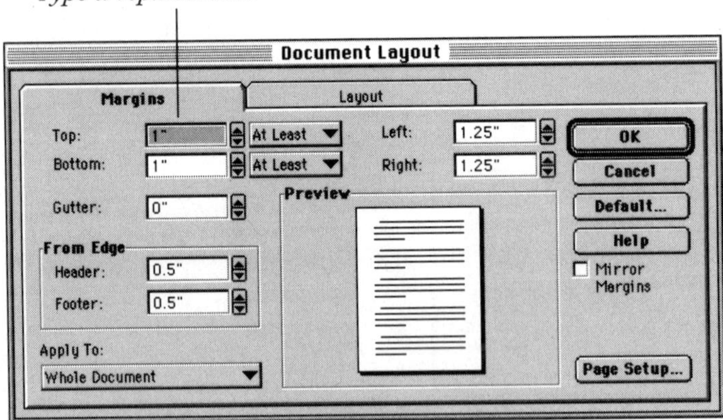

Figure 5. *The Margins tab of the Page Setup dialog box.*

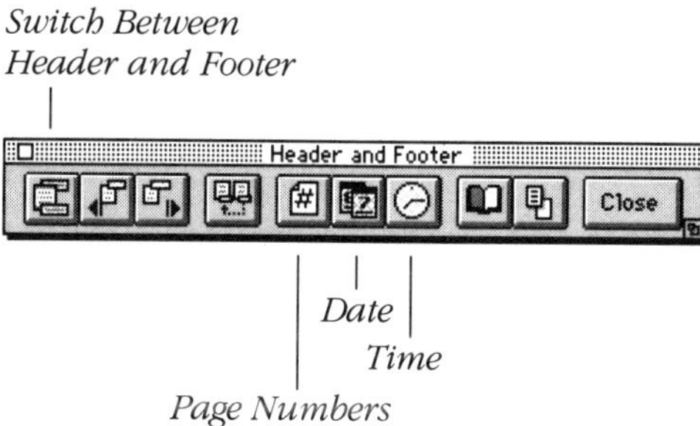

Figure 6. *The Header and Footer toolbar.*

Left side of the header.

Header
Proposal—The Water Mill Group

Figure 7. *Type text at the left side of the header or footer.*

Press Tab twice to move to the right side of the header.

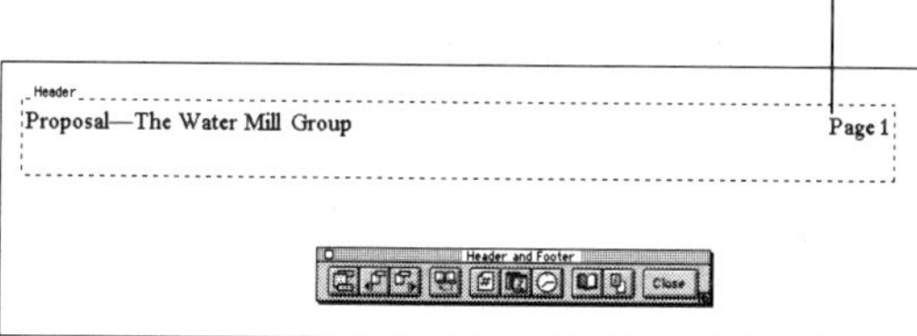

Figure 8. *Press Tab twice to skip to the right side of the header or footer.*

Setting up Headers and Footers

Headers are text that appears at the top of every page. Footers repeat at the bottom of every page.

1. From the View menu, choose Header and Footer. Word switches to Page Layout view, places the insertion point in the blank header space, and opens the Header and Footer toolbar. **(Figure 6)**
2. To edit the footer rather than the header, click the Switch Between Header and Footer button on the Header and Footer toolbar. **(Figure 6)**
3. Type text for the left side of the header or footer. **(Figure 7)**
4. Press Tab and type text for the center of the header or footer.

   or

   Press Tab again and type text for the right side of the header or footer. **(Figure 8)**
5. Click the Close button on the Header and Footer toolbar to finish editing the header or footer and return to the previous view.

✔ Tips

- You may want to change the Zoom setting to see the header or footer more clearly.
- Rather than type text, you can enter the page number, date, or time in the header or footer by clicking the appropriate buttons on the Header and Footer toolbar. **(Figure 6)**

Creating Multiple Sections

A document can contain multiple sections, each of which can have different page setup attributes: different margins, page numbering, and headers and footers. A new document contains only one section until you insert a section break. Then, you can page format the new section independently.

1. Place the insertion point at the location for the start of the new section. **(Figure 9)**
2. From the Insert menu, choose Break. **(Figure 10)**
3. On the Break dialog box **(Figure 11)**, choose one of the four Section Breaks options. Word inserts a double dotted line marked with End of Section. **(Figure 12)**

✔ Tip

■ Insert an Odd Page section break when you are printing left and right pages, you've started numbering on a right page (page 1), and you want each section to start on a new right page even if it means leaving a whole left page blank.

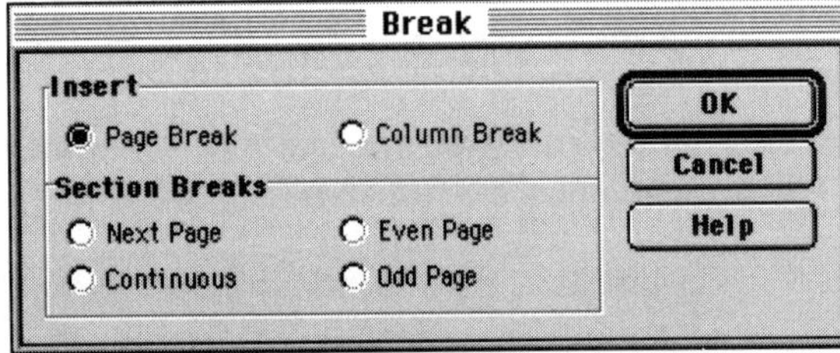

Figure 11. *The Break dialog box.*

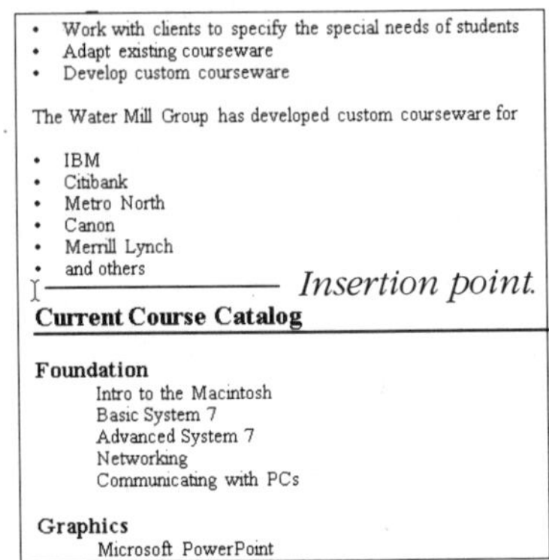

Figure 9. *Place the insertion point at the location for a section break.*

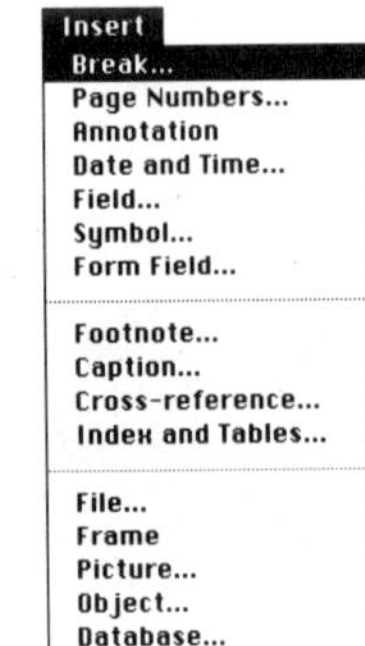

Figure 10. *The Insert menu.*

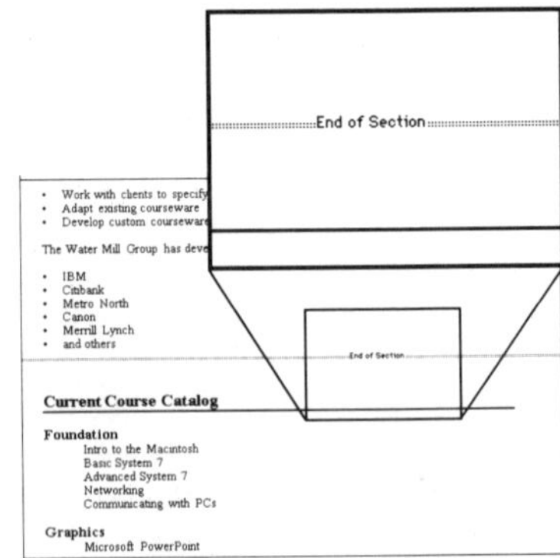

Figure 12. *A section break.*

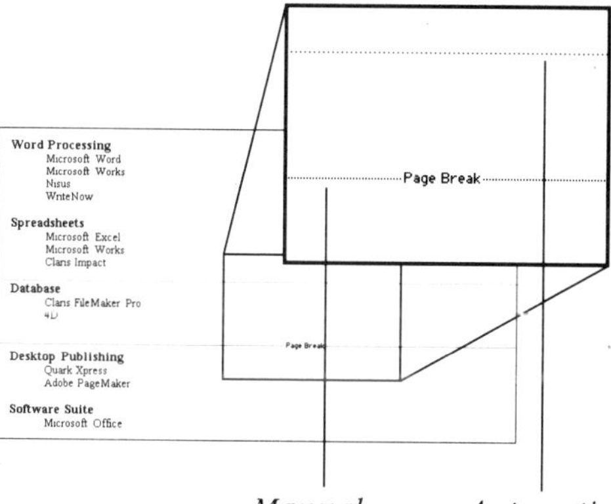

Figure 13. *Manual page break vs. Automatic page break.*

Table 8-1. ***Section Breaks***

Next Page	Starts a new section at the top of the next page.
Continuous	Starts a new section without moving the text after the section break to a new page. If the previous section has multiple columns, Word evens out the bottoms of the columns.
Even Page	If the section break falls on an odd page, Word starts the new section on the next page. Otherwise, Word leaves the next odd page blank and starts the new section on the next even page.
Odd Page	If the section break falls on an even page, Word starts the new section on the next page. Otherwise, Word leaves the next page blank and starts the new section on the next odd page.

Paginating the Document

As you work in Normal view, Word enters an automatic page break (a dotted line across the page) whenever you fill a page. Whenever you pause while typing, Word readjusts the automatic page breaks, if necessary.

To start a new page earlier than the automatic page break, enter a manual page break. **(Figure 13)**

1. Position the insertion point on the line that should be the first line of the new page.
2. Press ⌘+Enter.

   or

2. From the Insert menu, choose Break.
3. Make sure Page Break is selected and then click OK.

✔ Tips

- To delete a manual page break, select the page break and press the Delete key.
- You **cannot** delete an automatic page break or move it down. Your only option is to insert a manual page break above the automatic page break.
- Word's Widow/Orphan Control ensures that Word does not break the page and leave a single line of text at the top or bottom of a page.
- By switching to Page Layout view or a Print Preview, you can see how the text falls on pages with the current page breaks. In Page Layout view, you can enter manual page breaks.

Numbering Pages

As you create a document's header or footer, you can always enter page numbering. *See Setting up Headers and Footers, page 77.* Another approach is more direct and it gives you the option to choose a number format and a starting number.

1. From the Insert menu, choose Page Numbers. **(Figure 14)**
2. On the Page Numbers dialog box, choose Top of Page or Bottom of Page from the Position drop-down list. **(Figure 15)**
3. Choose an Alignment from the Alignment drop-down list. **(Figure 15)**
4. To show the page number on the first page, click the Show Number on First Page checkbox, otherwise the page numbers will first appear on page 2. **(Figure 15)**
5. Click the Format button and then, on the Page Number Format dialog box, choose a numbering style from the Number Format drop-down list. **(Figure 16)**

✔ **Tip**

■ While the Page Number Format dialog box is open, you can also enter a number in the Start At text box to start numbering at a number other than 1.

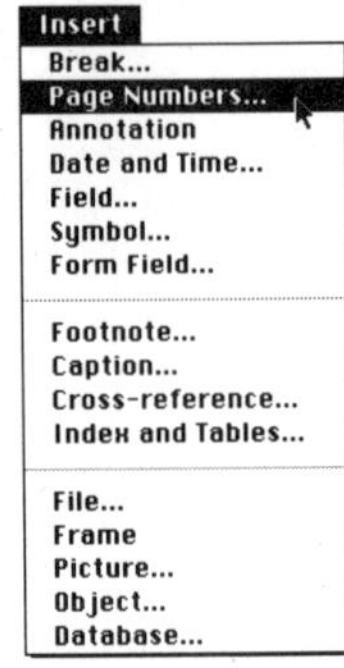

Figure 14. *The Insert menu.*

Position drop-down list box.

Alignment drop-down list box.

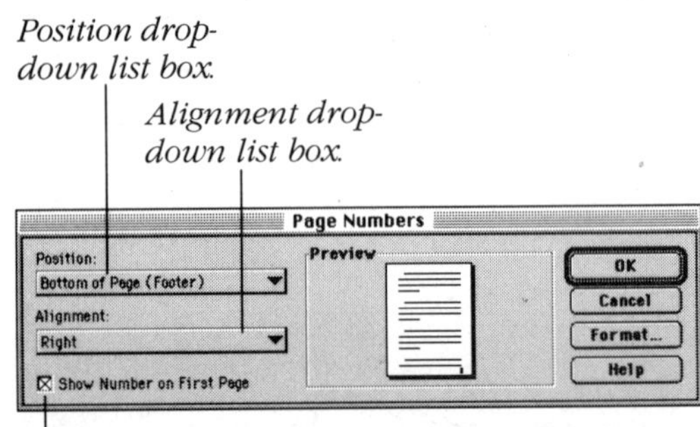

Click here to show a page number on the first page of a document.

Figure 15. *The Page Numbers dialog box.*

Choose a numbering style here.

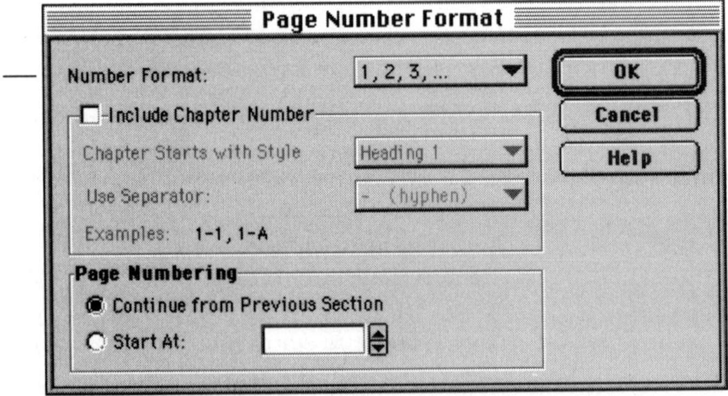

Figure 16. *The Page Number Format dialog box.*

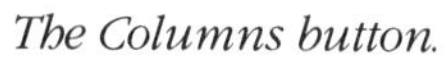
The Columns button.

Figure 17. *The Columns button.*

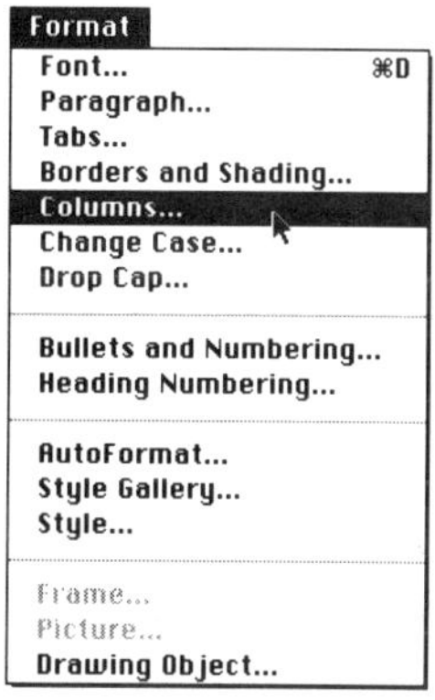

Figure 18. *The Format menu.*

Setting up Multiple Columns

1. Click the Columns button on the Standard toolbar and then drag across the number of columns you want. **(Figure 17)**

   or

1. From the Format menu, choose Columns. **(Figure 18)**
2. On the Columns dialog box, click one of the Presets or enter a number of columns in the Number of Columns text box. **(Figure 19)**
3. To obtain a vertical line between the columns, click the Line Between checkbox.

✔ Tips

- To vary the widths of columns, clear the Equal Column Width checkbox on the Columns dialog box and then use the Width and Spacing controls to modify the width and spacing for each column.
- The maximum number of columns on a page is 12.
- The gutter width on the Margins tab of the Page Setup dialog box determines the spacing between equal columns. *See Changing the Margins, page 76.*

Click one of these panels to choose a number of columns.

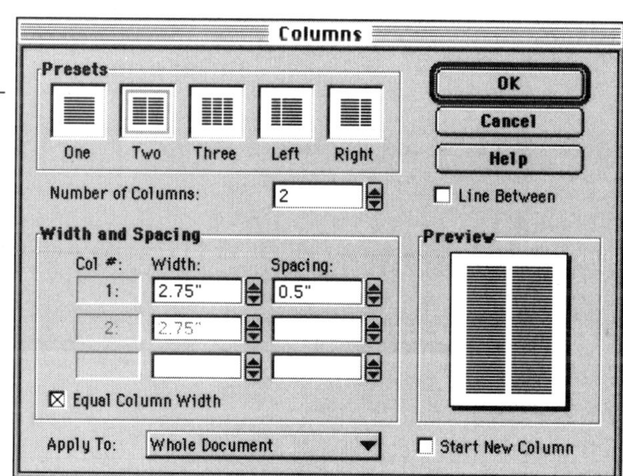

Figure 19. *The Columns dialog box.*

AutoFormatting a Document

AutoFormatting a document causes Word to analyze the document and apply styles to the text. AutoFormatting also removes extra paragraph marks, replaces indents created with spaces or tabs with paragraph indents, replaces asterisks or hyphens in bulleted lists with real bullets, and replaces (C), (R), and (TM) with copyright, registered trademark, and trademark symbols.

1. Click the AutoFormat button on the Standard toolbar. **(Figure 20)**

   or

1. From the Format menu, choose AutoFormat. **(Figure 21)**
2. On the AutoFormat dialog box, click OK. **(Figure 22)**

✔ Tip

■ To change the way AutoFormat analyzes the document and to specify which of the standard actions it will carry out, click Options on the AutoFormat dialog box.

The AutoFormat button.

Figure 20. *The AutoFormat button.*

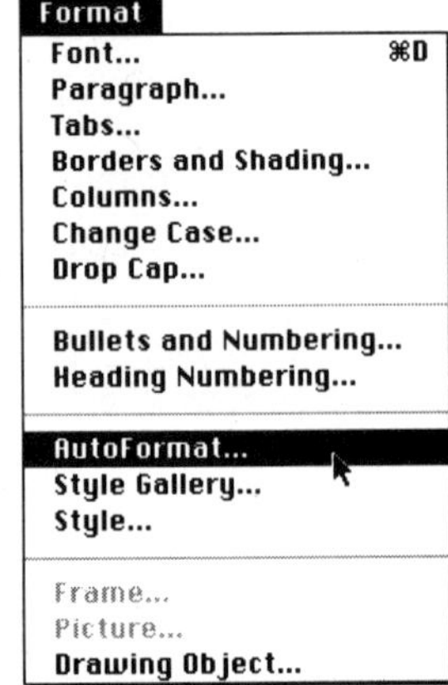

Figure 21. *The Format menu.*

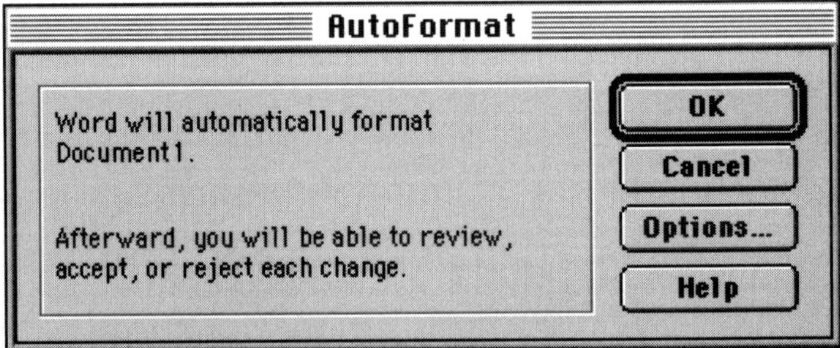

Figure 22. *The AutoFormat dialog box.*

Creating Tables 9

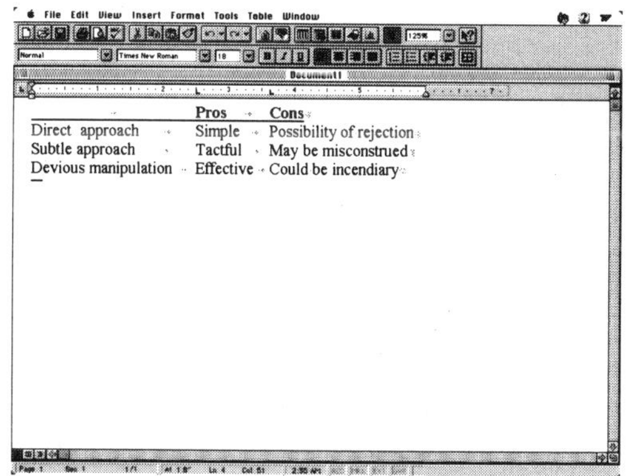

Figure 1. *Tabs used to align text in columns.*

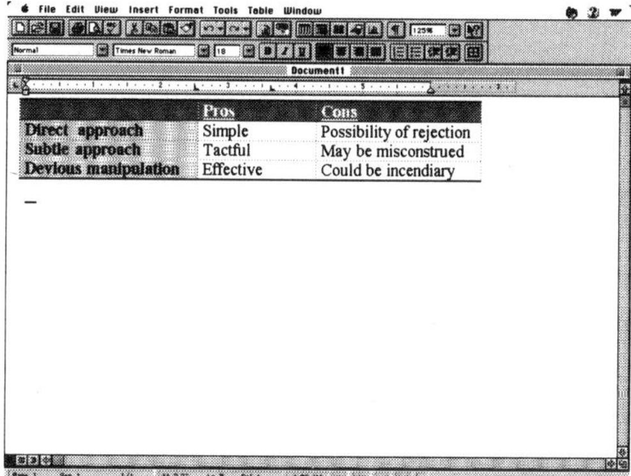

	Pros	Cons
Direct approach	Simple	Possibility of rejection
Subtle approach	Tactful	May be misconstrued
Devious manipulation	Effective	Could be incendiary

Figure 2. *A Word table.*

About Tables

Old fashioned word proccssors used tabs to align text and numbers in columns. **(Figure 1)** You can still use tabs in Word, but you're better off using Word's tables, which make it easy to both align data in columns and rows and to format the table so it looks professional. **(Figure 2)** Tables are so useful in Word that we're devoting an entire chapter to them.

You can create a table manually or use the Table Wizard, which guides you step by step through the table making and formatting process. **(Figure 3)**

Word

Figure 3. *Step 1 of the Table Wizard.*

Starting a Table

Word provides two ways to start a table. The first method gives you the option to use the Table Wizard, which helps set up more complex tables and provides automatic table formatting options. The second method gives you a quick and dirty table that requires manual formatting.

Method 1, for an automatically formatted table:

1. Position the insertion point at the location for the table.
2. From the Table menu, choose Insert Table. **(Figure 4)**
3. On the Insert Table dialog box, choose the number of columns and rows. **(Figure 5)**

Optional steps:

- Click the Wizard button to use the Table Wizard to create the table. *See Using the Table Wizard, page 86.*
- Click the AutoFormat button to choose a format for the table so you can see the formatting as you create the table. **(Figure 6)**

---

4. Click OK to create the table.

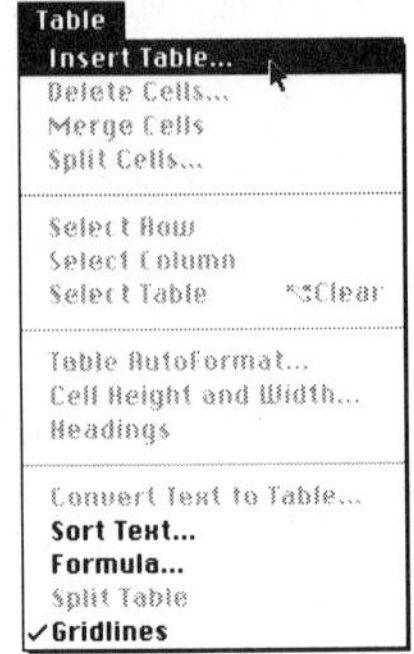

Figure 4. *The Table menu.*

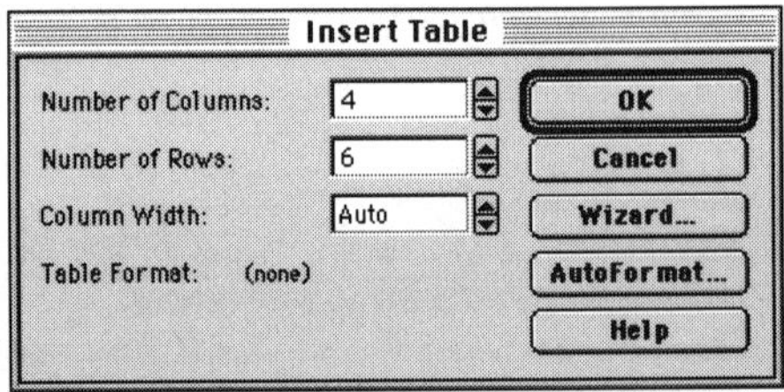

Figure 5. *The Insert Table dialog box.*

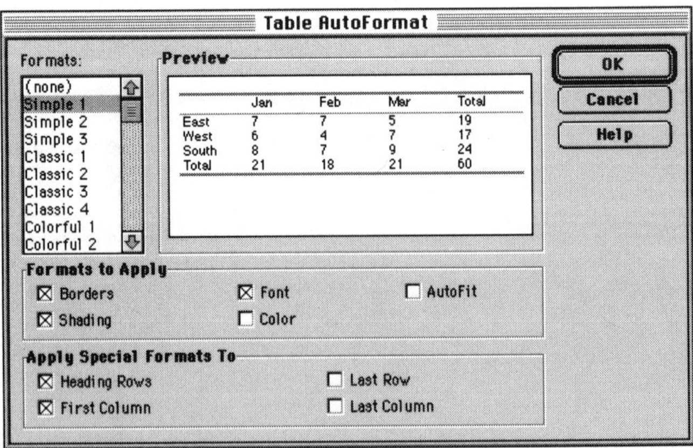

Figure 6. *The Table AutoFormat dialog box.*

The Insert Table button.

Figure 7. *The Insert Table button.*

Method 2, for a quick and dirty table:

1. Position the insertion point at the location for the table.
2. Click the Insert Table button on the Standard toolbar. **(Figure 7)**
3. Drag across the number of columns and down the number of rows you want. **(Figure 8)** An unformatted table appears. **(Figure 9)**

✔ **Tip**

- You can apply an AutoFormat to a table or change the AutoFormat applied at any time by clicking anywhere in the table and then choosing Table AutoFormat from the Table menu.

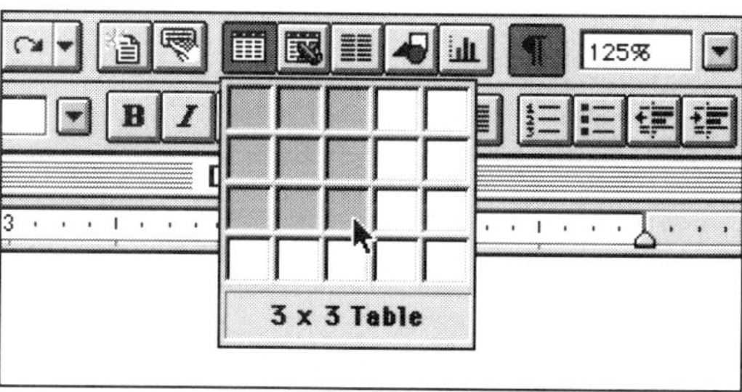

Figure 8. *Drag across the grid to specify the table dimensions.*

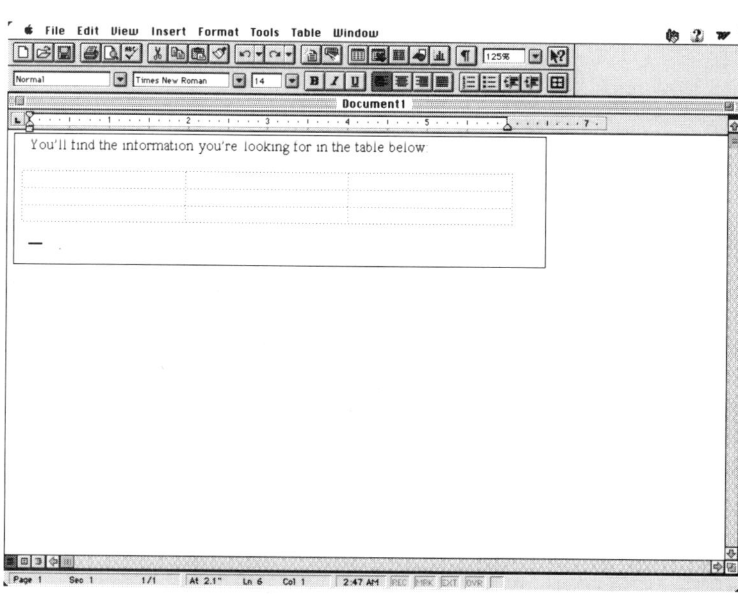

Figure 9. *The new table.*

Using the Table Wizard

1. On the Insert Table dialog box, click Wizard. **(Figure 9)**
2. Make selections on the following series of Table Wizard dialog boxes. **(Figures 10-16)** After you make a selection, click **Next** to go to the next step, **Back** to return to the previous step, or **Finish** to skip the rest of the steps and accept the defaults.
3. On the Table AutoFormat dialog box, click on Format names on the Formats list and examine the previews shown in the dialog box. Click OK when you find the format you want. **(Figure 17)**

✔ Tips

- When you insert a table within a document, be sure to select the same direction for the table (portrait vs. landscape) as the rest of the document, otherwise Word will create a separate section for the table on a new page.
- The checkboxes on the Table AutoFormat dialog box allow you to select which aspects of the formatting in the AutoFormat to apply to your table.

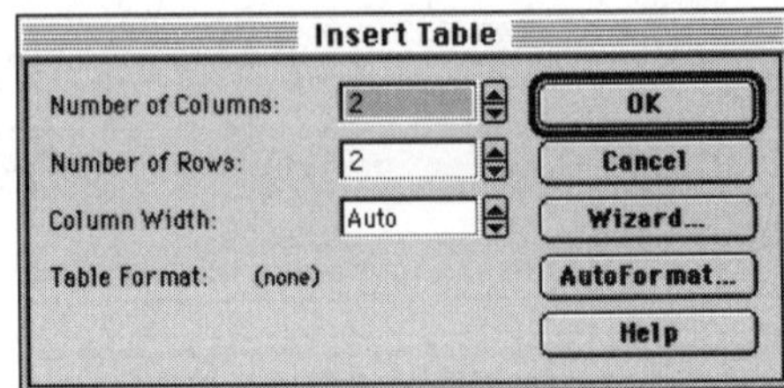

Figure 9. *The Insert Table dialog box.*

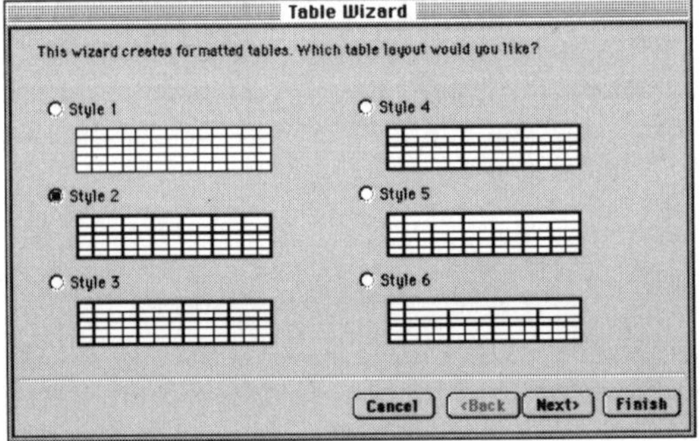

Figure 10. *Choose a table layout in the first step of the Table Wizard.*

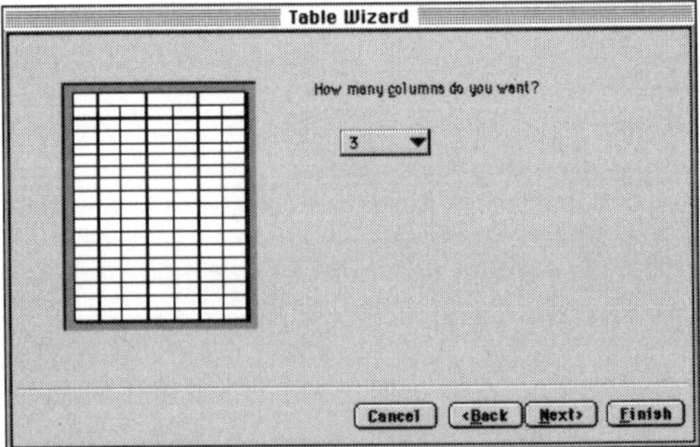

Figure 11. *Specify the number of columns in the second step of the Table Wizard.*

Word

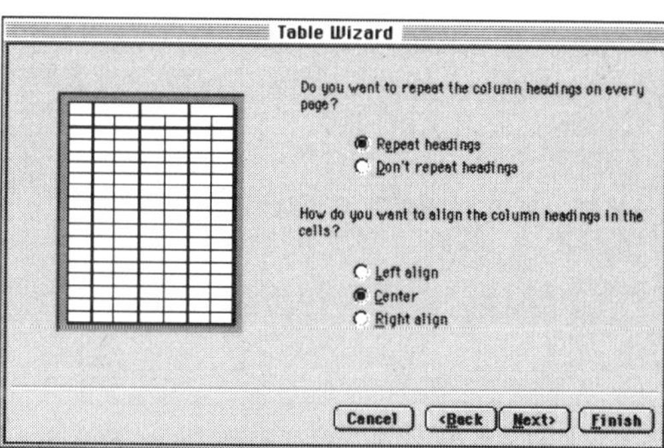

Figure 12. *Format the column headings in the third step of the Table Wizard.*

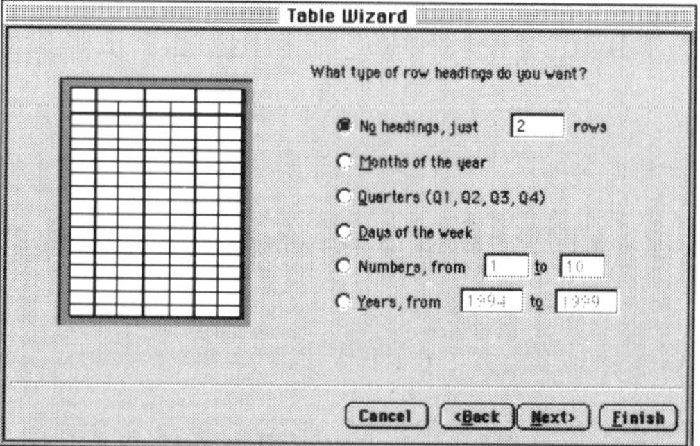

Figure 13. *Specify the row headings in the fourth step of the Table Wizard.*

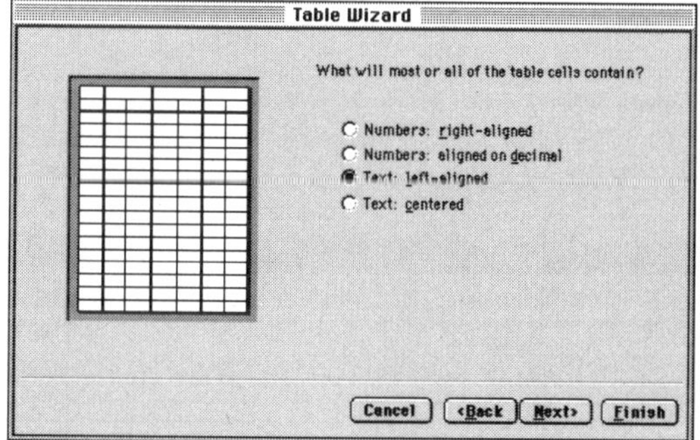

Figure 14. *Choose a default alignment for the cells in the fifth step of the Table Wizard.*

Figure 15. *Choose an orientation for the table in the sixth step of the Table Wizard.*

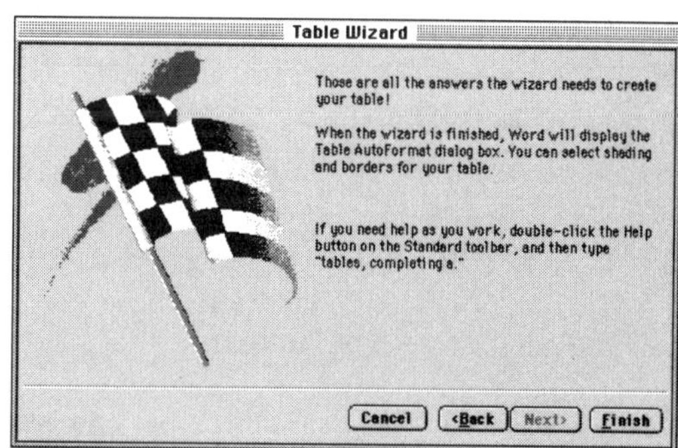

Figure 16. *The last step of the Table Wizard.*

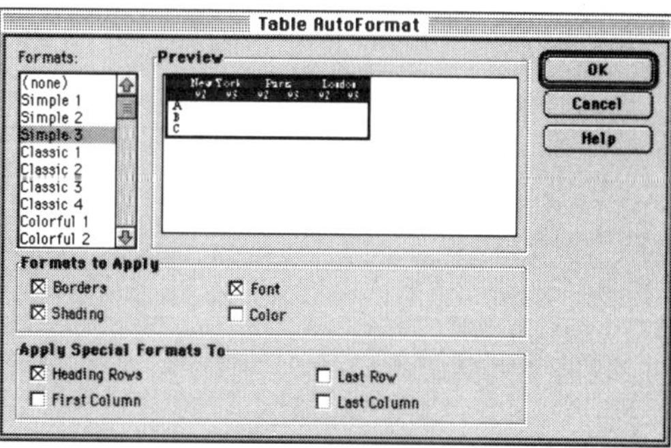

Figure 17. *The Table AutoFormat dialog box.*

Entering Data in the Table

1. Click in a cell and then type to insert data into the cell. As you type, the insertion point will wrap within the cell and the entire row will become taller to accommodate multiple lines of text, if necessary. **(Figure 15)**
2. Press Tab to move to the cell to the right. **(Figure 16)**
3. Type text into the next cell. **(Figure 17)**
4. Continue pressing Tab after you finish each cell. When you finish the last cell of the table, pressing Tab will create a new row.

✓ Tips

- When you reach the rightmost cell, pressing Tab moves the insertion point to the next line. **(Figure 18)**
- Press Shift+Tab to move back a cell.
- If there is already text in a cell, pressing Tab to move to the cell both moves to the cell and selects the text.

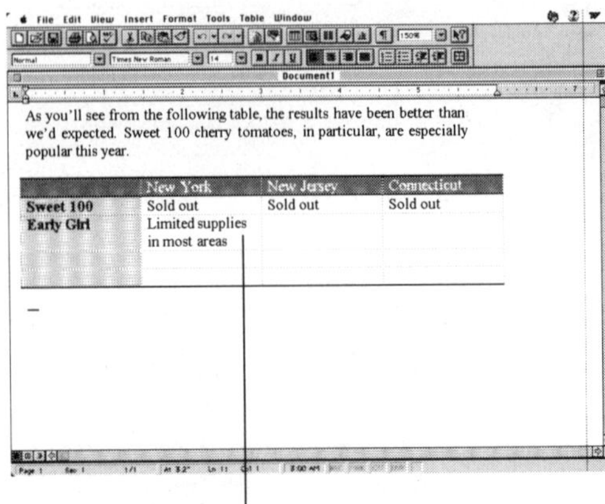

As you'll see from the following table, the results have been better than we'd expected. Sweet 100 cherry tomatoes, in particular, are especially popular this year.

	New York	New Jersey	Connecticut
Sweet 100	Sold out	Sold out	Sold out
Early Girl	Limited supplies in most areas		

Figure 15. *Rows grow in height to accommodate the largest entry.*

	New York	New Jersey	Connecticut
Sweet 100	Sold out	Sold out	Sold out
Early Girl	Limited supplies in most areas		

Figure 16. *Press Tab to move to the blank cell to the right.*

	New York	New Jersey	Connecticut
Sweet 100	Sold out	Sold out	Sold out
Early Girl	Limited supplies in most areas	In stock	

Figure 17. *Type into the cell.*

	New York	New Jersey	Connecticut
Sweet 100	Sold out	Sold out	Sold out
Early Girl	Limited supplies in most areas	In stock	In stock

Figure 18. *Press Tab at the rightmost cell to move to the next line.*

	New York	New Jersey	Connecticut
Sweet 100	Sold out	Sold out	Sold out
Early Girl	Limited supplies in most areas	In stock	In stock
Plum	Limited supplies	In stock	Limited supplies
Big Boy	In stock	In stock	Limited supplies

Figure 20. *Drag across a row...*

	New York	New Jersey	Connecticut
Sweet 100	Sold out	Sold out	Sold out
Early Girl	Limited supplies in most areas	In stock	In stock
Plum	Limited supplies	In stock	Limited supplies
Big Boy	In stock	In stock	Limited supplies

Figure 21. *...or drag down a column.*

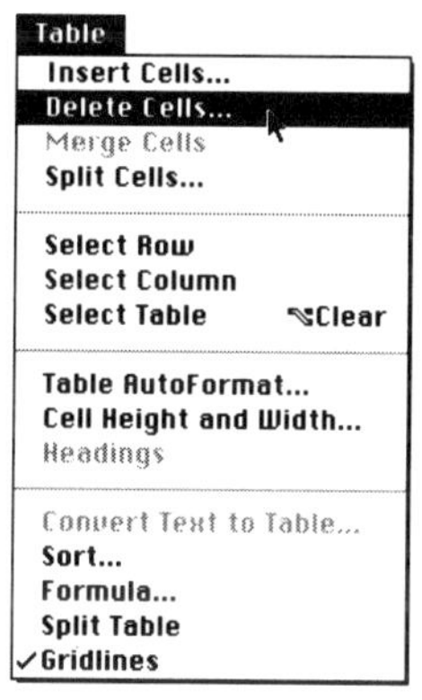

Figure 22. *The Table menu.*

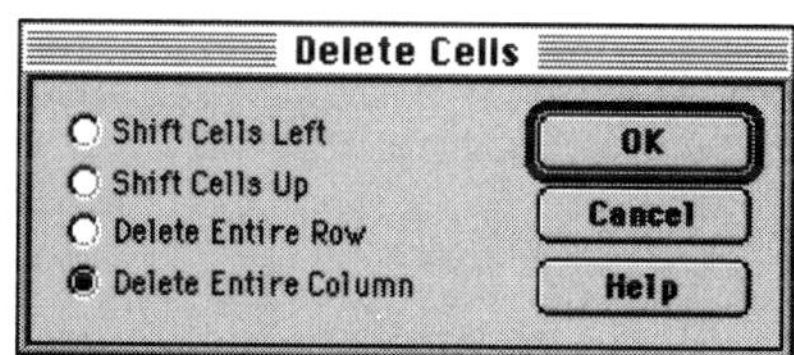

Figure 23. *The Delete Cells dialog box.*

Deleting Columns or Rows

1. Drag across any cells in the rows or the columns to delete. **(Figures 20–21)**
2. From the Table menu, choose Delete Cells. **(Figure 22)**
3. On the Delete Cells dialog box, choose Delete Entire Row or Delete Entire Column. **(Figure 23)**

✔ Tip

■ To delete an entire table, drag across all the columns and choose Delete Entire Column or drag down all the rows and choose Delete Entire Row.

Inserting a Column or Row

To insert a row:

1. Click in a cell at the location for the new, blank row. **(Figure 23)**
2. From the Table menu, choose Insert Rows. **(Figure 24)**

	New York	New Jersey	Connecticut
Sweet 100	Sold out	Sold out	Sold out
Early Girl	Limited supplies in most areas	In stock	In stock
Plum	Limited supplies	In stock	Limited supplies
Big Boy	In stock	In stock	Limited supplies

Figure 23. *Click at the destination of the new row.*

Table
Insert Rows
Delete Cells...
Merge Cells
Split Cells...
Select Row
Select Column
Select Table ⌥Clear
Table AutoFormat...
Cell Height and Width...
Headings
Convert Text to Table...
Sort...
Formula...
Split Table
✓Gridlines

Figure 24. *The Table menu.*

To insert a column:

1. Position the mouse pointer at the top of the column at the location for the new column. A large, down arrow appears. **(Figure 25)**
2. Click while the down arrow is visible to select the column. **(Figure 26)**
3. From the Table menu, choose Insert Columns. **(Figure 27)**

	New York	New Jersey	Connecticut
Sweet 100	Sold out	Sold out	Sold out
Early Girl	Limited supplies in most areas	In stock	In stock
Plum	Limited supplies	In stock	Limited supplies
Big Boy	In stock	In stock	Limited supplies

Figure 25. *Position the mouse pointer at the top of a column.*

	New York	New Jersey	Connecticut
Sweet 100	Sold out	Sold out	Sold out
Early Girl	Limited supplies in most areas	In stock	In stock
Plum	Limited supplies	In stock	Limited supplies
Big Boy	In stock	In stock	Limited supplies

Figure 26. *Click to select the entire column.*

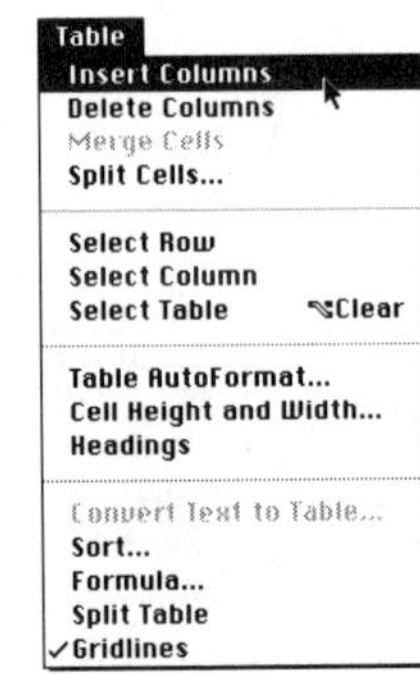

Figure 27. *The Table menu.*

	New York	New Jersey	Connecticut
Sweet 100	Sold out	Sold out	Sold out
Early Girl	Limited supplies in most areas	In stock	In stock
Plum	Limited supplies	In stock	Limited supplies
Big Boy	In stock	In stock	Limited supplies

Figure 28. *Drag across the number of columns to insert.*

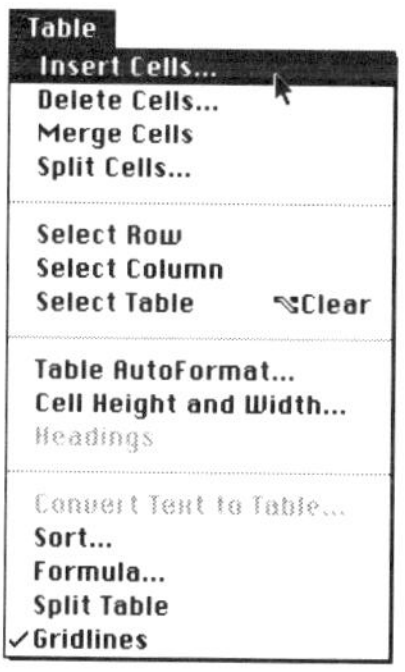

Figure 29. *The Table menu.*

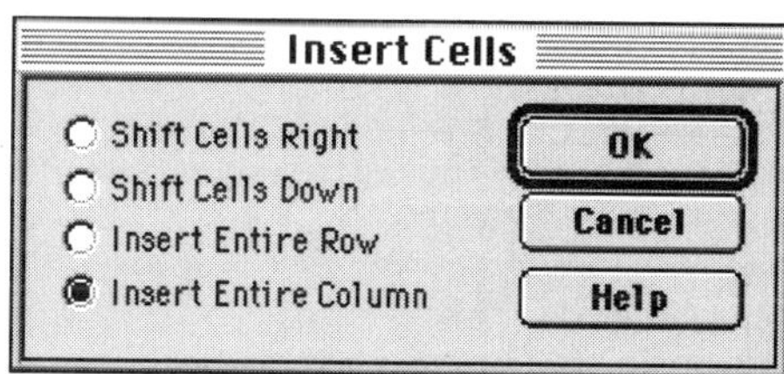

Figure 30. *The Insert Cells dialog box.*

Inserting Multiple Columns or Rows

1. Drag across the number of columns to insert or drag down the number of rows to insert. **(Figure 28)**
2. From the Table menu, choose Insert Cells. **(Figure 29)**
3. On the Insert Cells dialog box, choose either Insert Entire Row or Insert Entire Column. **(Figure 30)**

✔ **Tip**

- The new columns or rows will be inserted before the existing columns or rows.

Changing Column Width and Row Height

To change the column width by dragging:

1. Place the mouse pointer on the vertical border at the right edge of the column to widen.
2. Drag the border to the right. **(Figure 31)**

	New York	New Jersey	Connecticut
Sweet 100	Sold out	Sold out	Sold out
Early Girl	Limited supplies in most areas	In stock	In stock
Plum	Limited supplies	In stock	Limited supplies
Big Boy	In stock	In stock	Limited supplies

Figure 31. *Drag the right border of a column to widen the column.*

To change the height of a row:

1. Select any cells in the rows to heighten. **(Figure 32)**
2. From the Table menu, choose Cell Height and Width. **(Figure 33)**
3. On the Rows tab of the Cell Height and Width dialog box, modify the At setting. **(Figure 34)**

	New York	New Jersey	Connecticut
Sweet 100	Sold out	Sold out	Sold out
Early Girl	Limited supplies in most areas	In stock	In stock
Plum	Limited supplies	In stock	Limited supplies
Big Boy	In stock	In stock	Limited supplies

Figure 32. *Select cells.*

✔ Tips

- Select cells in columns and then use the controls on the Column tab of the Cell Height and Width dialog box to set exact column widths.
- On the Column tab, you can also add more space between columns.
- You can drag the right edge of the table to widen the last column.

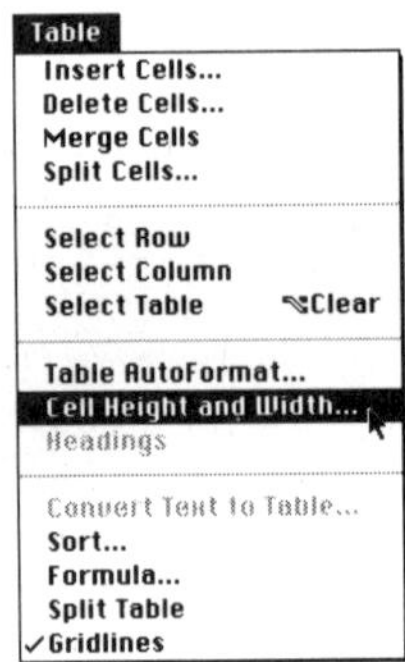

Figure 33. *The Table menu.*

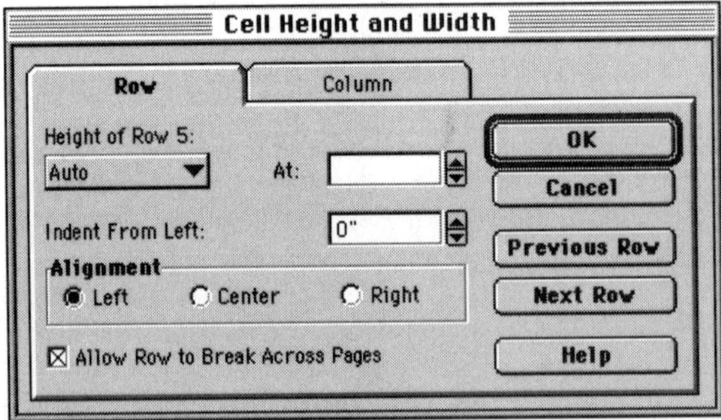

Figure 34. *The Cell Height and Width dialog box.*

First row is selected.

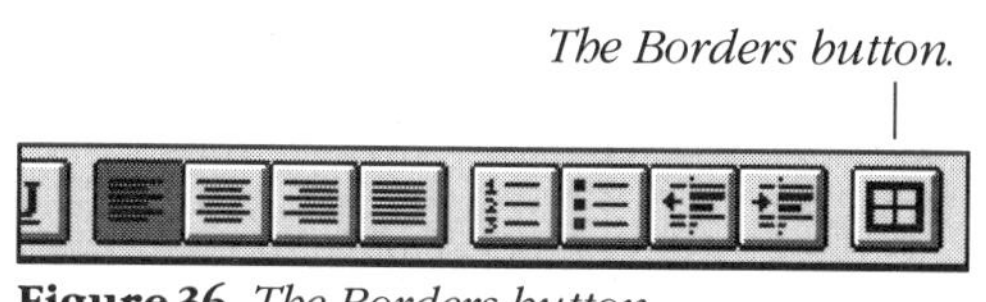

	New York	New Jersey	Connecticut
Sweet 100	Sold out	Sold out	Sold out
Early Girl	Limited supplies in most areas	In stock	In stock
Plum	Limited supplies	In stock	Limited supplies
Big Boy	In stock	In stock	Limited supplies

Figure 35. *Select cells first.*

The Borders button.

Figure 36. *The Borders button.*

Turning on Borders and Shading

Borders are lines surrounding the cells. Shading is a fill within the cells.

1. Select the cells for which you want to modify the borders or add shading. **(Figure 35)**
2. Click the Borders button on the Formatting toolbar. **(Figure 36)**
3. On the Borders toolbar, select a line style and thickness from the Line Style drop-down list. **(Figure 37)**
4. On the Borders toolbar, click the appropriate Border button to apply borders to the top, bottom, left, right, inside, or outside of the selected cells.
5. To apply a shading to the selected cells, select a shading from the Shading drop-down list.

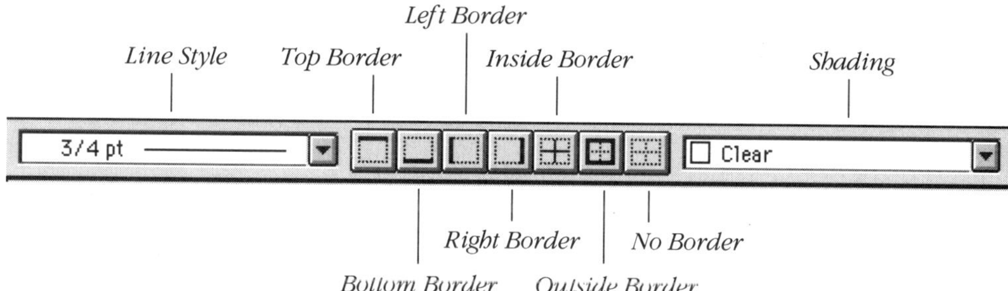

Figure 37. *The Borders toolbar.*

Different shadings in first row and first column.

	New York	New Jersey	Connecticut
Sweet 100	Sold out	Sold out	Sold out
Early Girl	Limited supplies in most areas	In stock	In stock
Plum	Limited supplies	In stock	Limited supplies
Big Boy	In stock	In stock	Limited supplies

Figure 38. *Shaded cells.*

Converting Text to a Table

When somebody else has created a table in a document with plain old tabs, you can easily convert the tab table to a standard Word table that can be more easily modified and formatted.

1. Select all the lines of the existing tab table. **(Figure 39)**
2. Click the Insert Table button on the Standard toolbar.

   or

   From the Table menu, choose Convert Text to Table. **(Figure 40)**
3. On the Convert Text to Table dialog box, click AutoFormat to select a format for the table if you want and then click OK. **(Figures 41-42)**

✓ Tip

- By using the Convert Text to Table command on the Table menu, you can convert a list of paragraphs to a table by choosing Paragraphs for Separate Text At.

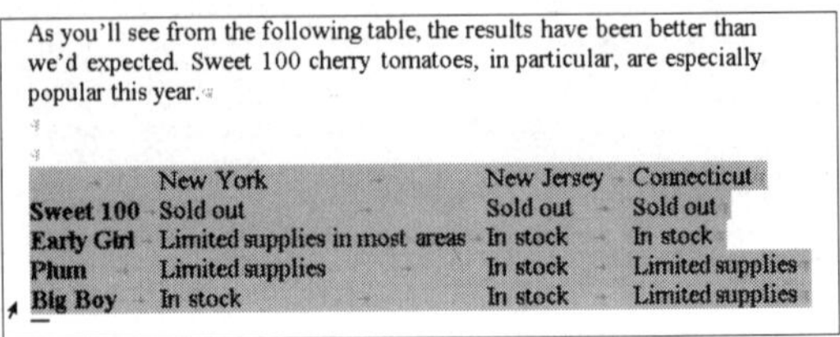

As you'll see from the following table, the results have been better than we'd expected. Sweet 100 cherry tomatoes, in particular, are especially popular this year.

	New York	New Jersey	Connecticut
Sweet 100	Sold out	Sold out	Sold out
Early Girl	Limited supplies in most areas	In stock	In stock
Plum	Limited supplies	In stock	Limited supplies
Big Boy	In stock	In stock	Limited supplies

Figure 39. *Select the existing table.*

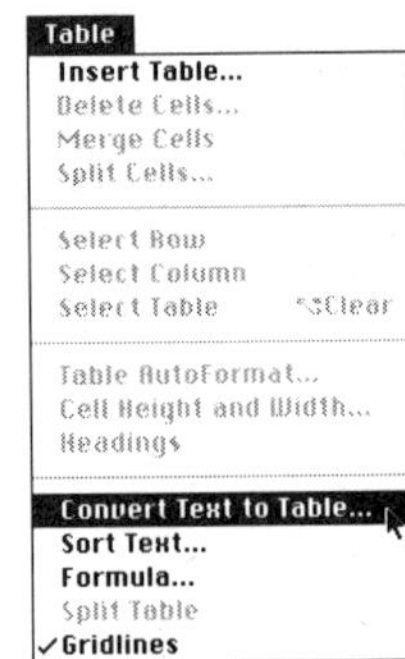

Figure 40. *The Table menu.*

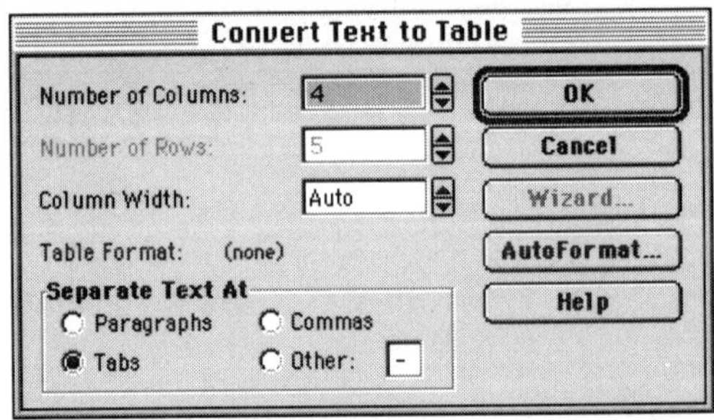

Figure 41. *The Convert Text to Table dialog box.*

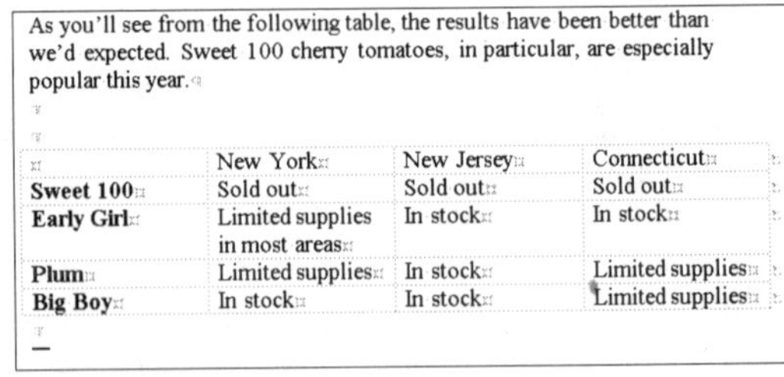

As you'll see from the following table, the results have been better than we'd expected. Sweet 100 cherry tomatoes, in particular, are especially popular this year.

	New York	New Jersey	Connecticut
Sweet 100	Sold out	Sold out	Sold out
Early Girl	Limited supplies in most areas	In stock	In stock
Plum	Limited supplies	In stock	Limited supplies
Big Boy	In stock	In stock	Limited supplies

Figure 42. *The unformatted table.*

Special Word Techniques

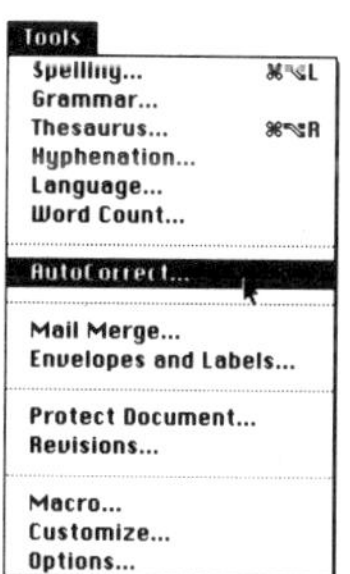

Figure 1. *The Tools menu.*

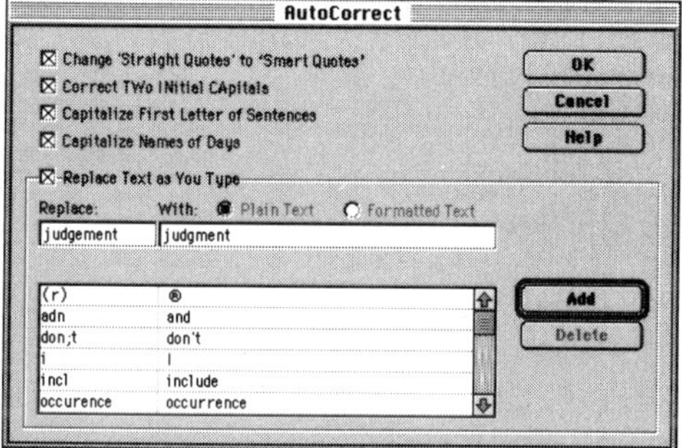

Figure 2. *The AutoCorrect dialog box.*

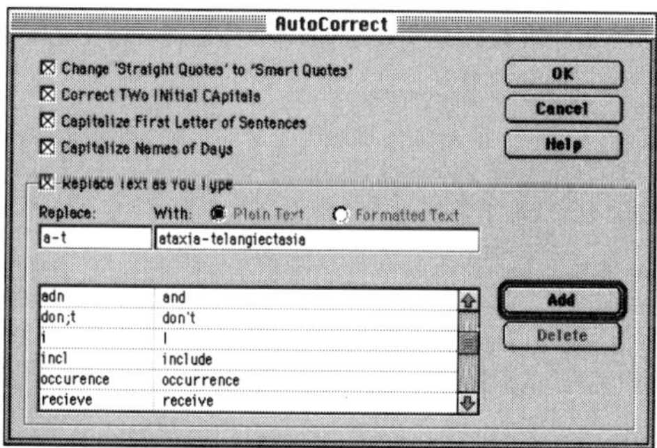

Figure 3. *You can use AutoCorrect to expand abbreviations.*

Automatically Correcting Typos

Word's AutoCorrect works quietly behind the scenes, automatically correcting many common typos as you type. It has its own short list of common typos and their corrections but you can add your own most frequent typos and the corresponding corrections to the list.

AutoCorrect also automatically capitalizes the first word in a sentence if you forget, removes instances of TWo capitals at the beginning of a word, and capitalizes the names of days for you.

To add typos and corrections to the AutoCorrect list:

1. From the Tools menu, choose AutoCorrect. **(Figure 1)**
2. Type the typo in the Replace text box.
3. Type the correction in the With text box. **(Figure 2)**
4. Click the Add button.

✔ Tips

- To insert text with a special font formatting, type the correction and format it in a document, then copy the correction and paste it into the With text box on the AutoCorrect dialog box. Be sure to click Formatted Text before you click Add.
- You can enter an abbreviation as the Replace term and the full technical, medical, or legal term as the With item and then have AutoCorrect enter long, complex terms for you whenever you type the abbreviation. **(Figure 3)**

Automatically Entering Text

AutoText saves you from repetitively typing text that you need frequently. With AutoText, you can insert any amount of text in a document, from a single word to multiple paragraphs. Assembling boilerplate documents from standard passages, such as putting together contracts by combining standard clauses, is an ideal task for AutoText.

To use AutoText, you type a passage of text once and then save it as an AutoText entry, giving it a name in the process, such as "closing." Then to recall an AutoText entry, you type the name and press F3. In previous versions of Word, AutoText was called the Glossary.

To create an AutoText entry:

1. Type the text to save and select it. **(Figure 4)**
2. Click the Edit AutoText button. **(Figure 5)**
   or
   Choose AutoText from the Edit menu.
3. In the Name text box, replace the suggested name that is highlighted with a name of your own. **(Figure 6)**
4. Click Add to add the text to the list of available AutoText entries.

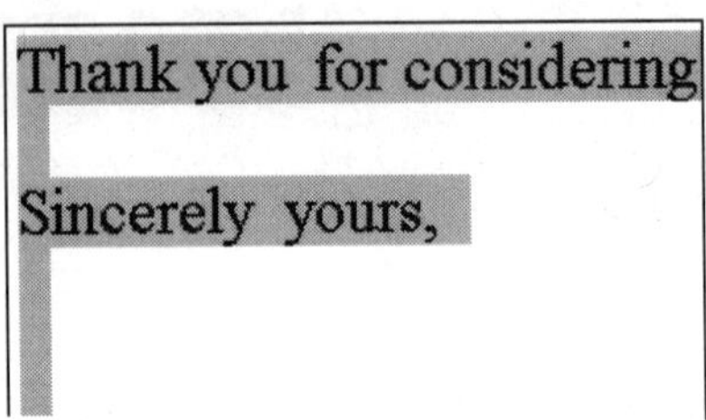

Figure 4. *Type and then select the AutoText entry.*

The Edit AutoText Button.

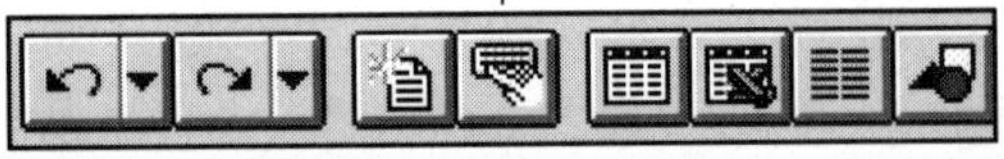

Figure 5. *The Edit AutoText button.*

Enter a name for the Autotext entry here.

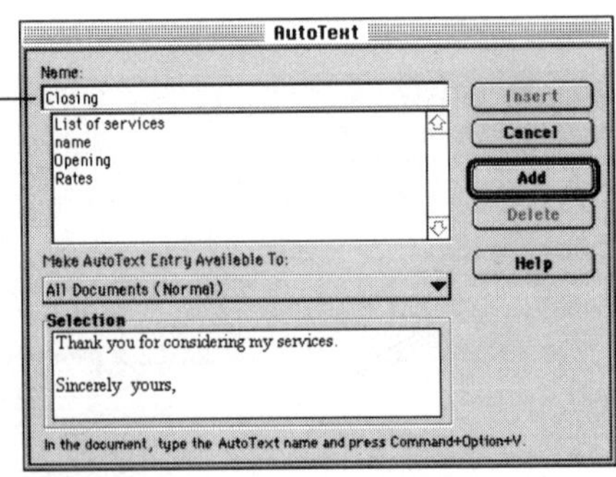

Figure 6. *The AutoText dialog box.*

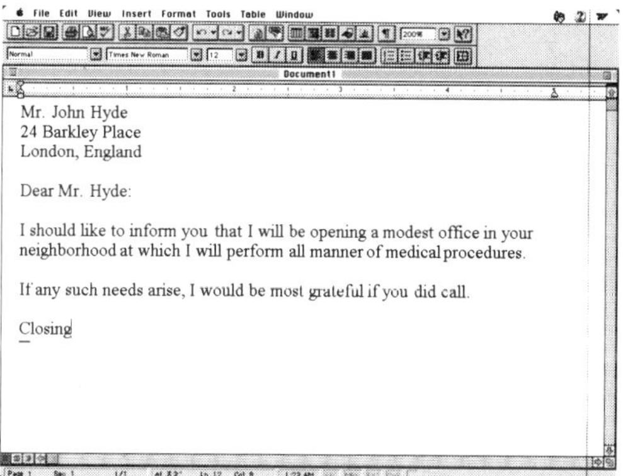

Figure 7. *Type the name of the AutoText entry.*

The Insert AutoText Button.

Figure 8. *The Insert AutoText button.*

To insert an AutoText entry:

1. Type the name of the AutoText entry. **(Figure 7)**
2. Click the Insert AutoText button. **(Figure 8)**

   or

   Press ⌘+Option+V.

   or

   From the Edit menu, choose AutoText. Select the name of the AutoText entry from the list, and click Insert.

✔ **Tips**

- You can include graphics in an AutoText entry to automatically insert a logo in a document.
- You can use AutoText to automatically enter long medical, legal, or technical terms.
- To save a formatted paragraph as an AutoText entry, select the paragraph mark at the end of the paragraph in Step 2. Otherwise, the text will be inserted as plain text.
- The Insert AutoText button becomes the Edit AutoText button when you select newly typed text.

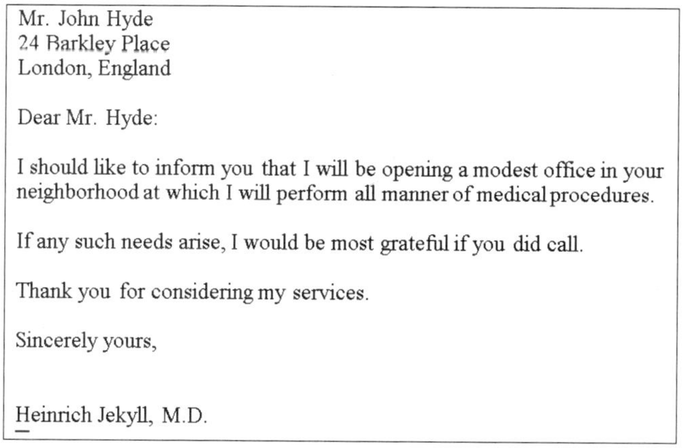

Mr. John Hyde
24 Barkley Place
London, England

Dear Mr. Hyde:

I should like to inform you that I will be opening a modest office in your neighborhood at which I will perform all manner of medical procedures.

If any such needs arise, I would be most grateful if you did call.

Thank you for considering my services.

Sincerely yours,

Heinrich Jekyll, M.D.

Figure 9. *The AutoText is inserted.*

Inserting Symbols from the Wingdings Font

The Wingdings font contains dozens of useful and fun pictures that you can embed in a document. Word provides an automatic way to insert symbols into a document.

1. Position the insertion point at the destination for the symbol. **(Figure 10)**
2. From the Insert menu, choose Symbol. **(Figure 11)**
3. On the Symbols tab of the Symbol dialog box, pull-down the list of Fonts and choose Wingdings. **(Figure 12)**
4. Click on any symbol to magnify it. **(Figure 13)**
5. Click the symbol you want and then click Insert.
6. Click Cancel to close the Symbol dialog box.

✔ Tips

- You can select symbols from other fonts, too.
- On the Special Characters tab of the Symbol dialog box, you'll find frequently used characters that you can select and insert in any document.

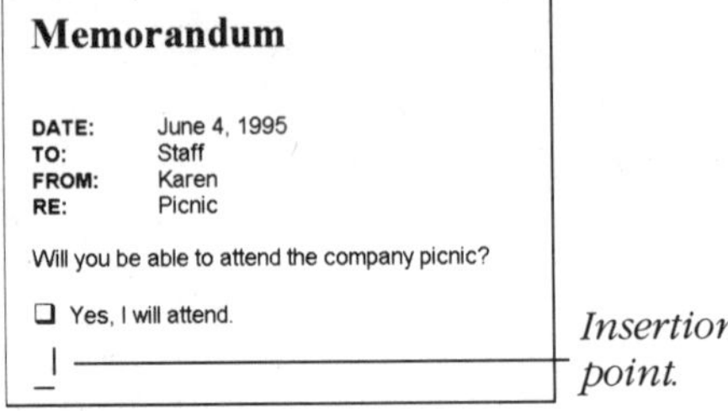

Memorandum

DATE: June 4, 1995
TO: Staff
FROM: Karen
RE: Picnic

Will you be able to attend the company picnic?

❑ Yes, I will attend.

Insertion point.

Figure 10. *Position the insertion point in the document.*

Figure 11. *The Insert menu.*

The list of fonts.

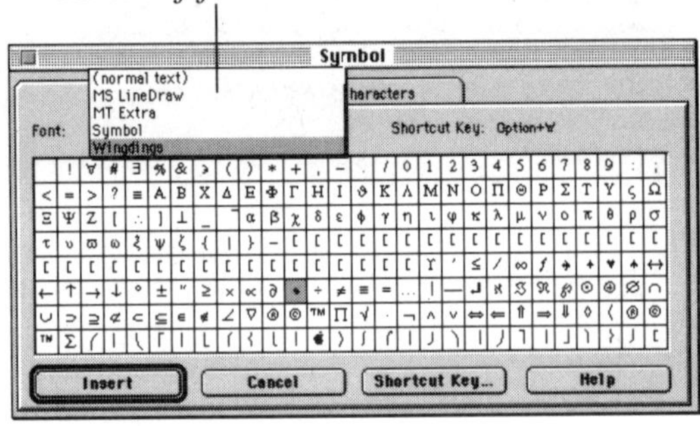

Figure 12. *The Font pull-down list.*

Click here to insert the symbol you've selected.

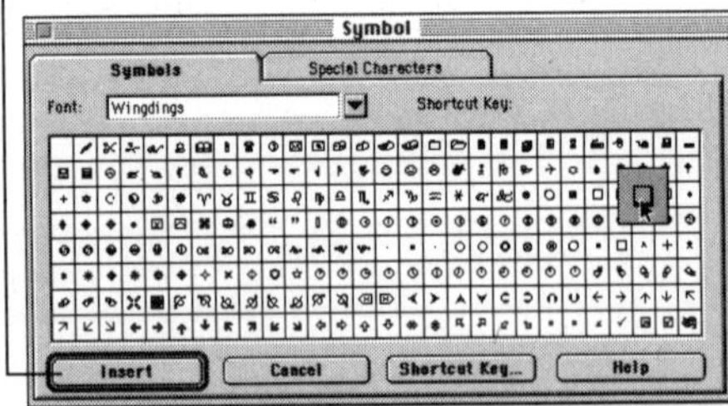

Figure 13. *Magnify a symbol by clicking on it.*

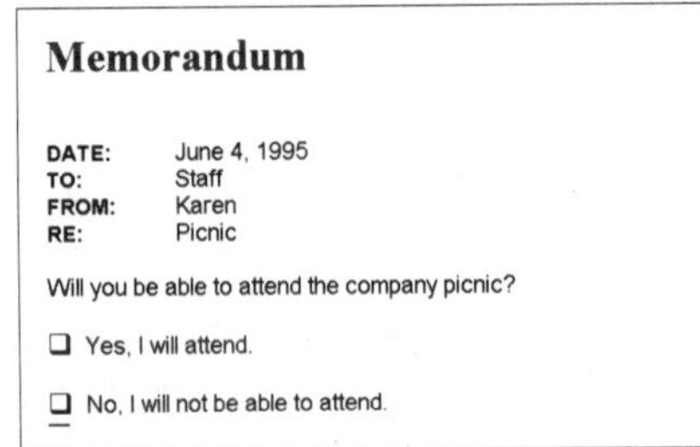

Memorandum

DATE: June 4, 1995
TO: Staff
FROM: Karen
RE: Picnic

Will you be able to attend the company picnic?

❑ Yes, I will attend.

❑ No, I will not be able to attend.

Figure 14. *The symbol inserted.*

Word

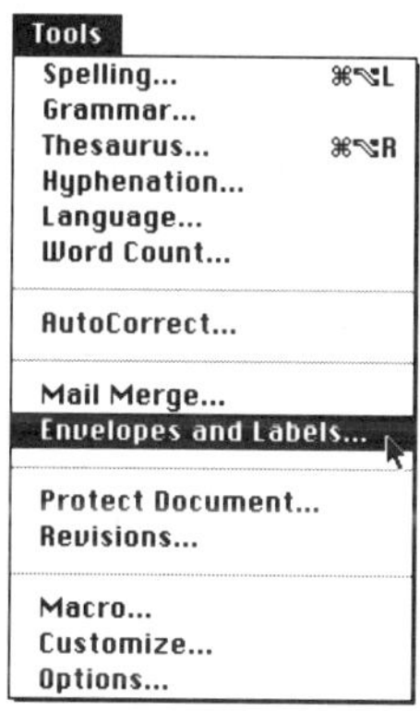

Figure 15. *The Tools menu.*

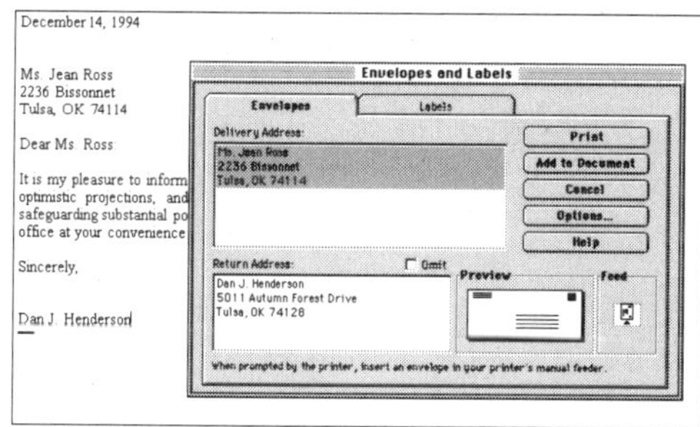

Figure 16. *Envelopes tab of the Envelopes and Labels dialog box.*

Printing Envelopes

Word can extract the mailing address from a letter and automatically format and print an envelope.

1. From the Tools menu, select Envelopes and Labels. **(Figure 15)**

   or, if the document contains more than one address, select the proper address before you select Envelopes and Labels.

2. If the address and return address are correct on the Envelopes tab of the Envelopes and Labels dialog box, click the Print button. **(Figure 16)**

   or

   Make any necessary modifications to the address and return address before clicking the Print button.

✔ Tips

- If your envelopes have a pre-printed return address, make sure the Omit checkbox is checked to omit the return address before clicking the Print button.
- To choose a different envelope size, or change the font and location of the addresses on the envelopes, click the Options button on the Envelopes and Labels dialog box to get to the Envelope Options dialog box. *See Envelope Printing Options, page 100.*

Envelope Printing Options

Before you print the envelopes, you can examine the Envelope Printing Options and change the way envelopes will print, if necessary.

1. On the Envelopes and Labels dialog box, click the Options button. **(Figure 17)**
2. On the Envelope Options tab of the Envelope Options dialog box, change the envelope size and font and location of the addresses. **(Figure 18)**
3. On the Printing Options tab of the Envelope Options dialog box choose the envelope feed direction that matches the way your printer works. **(Figure 19)**
4. If your printer has an envelope feeder, select the envelope tray from the Feed From drop-down list.

✔ Tips

- Word chooses the best options based on the current selected printer.
- The Delivery Point Bar Code option prints a machine-readable version of the zip code on the envelope.
- If you are printing Reply envelopes, you can also have word print a FIM code. FIMs are only necessary with Business Reply mail. Check with your post office for more information about FIMs.

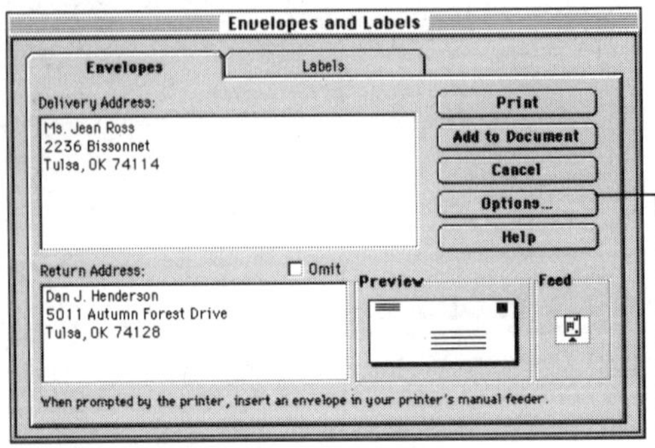

Figure 17. *The Options button on the Envelopes and Labels dialog box.*

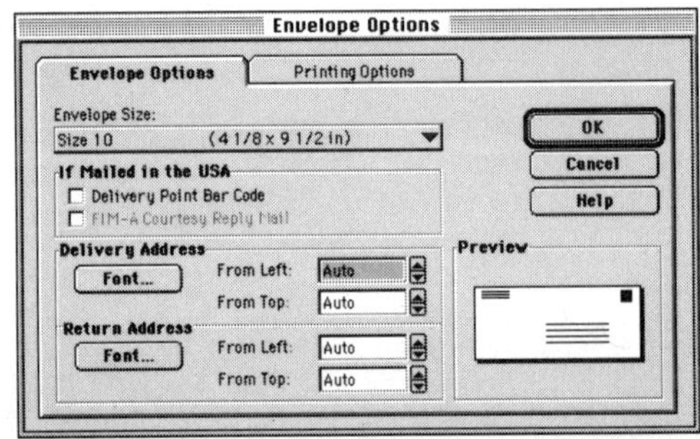

Figure 18. *The Envelope Options tab of the Envelope dialog box.*

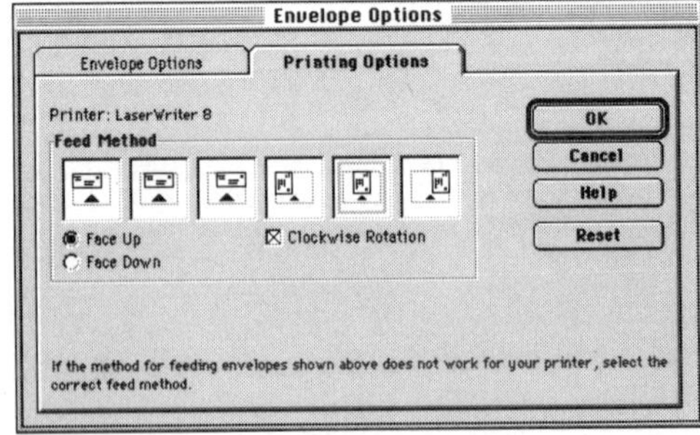

Figure 19. *The Printing Options tab of the Envelope Options dialog box.*

Figure 20. *The File menu.*

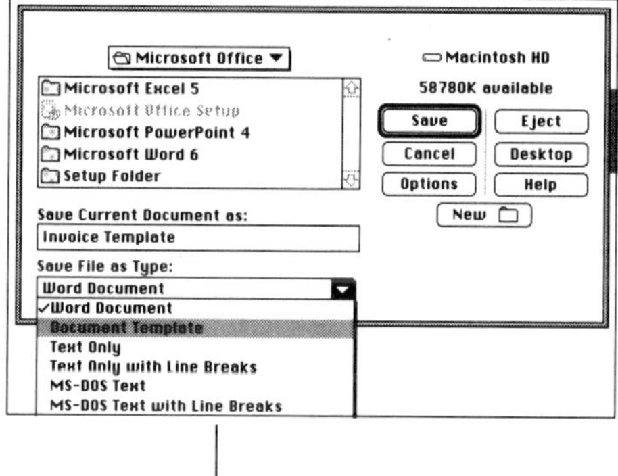

Choose Document Template here.

Figure 21. *Save As dialog box.*

Saving a Document as a Template

Templates contain entire document designs, possibly even including some of the text. When you start a new document with the New command on the File menu, you get the option to choose from among the many preformatted templates that come with Word. These include templates for popular business and professional documents. If none of the templates exactly suits your needs, you can modify them or save your own document designs as templates. Then, you can easily create other documents based on a design you like or need to use frequently.

1. Create a sample document and format it by creating and applying a set of styles. *See Creating a Paragraph Style, page 72 and Choosing a Style from the Style List, page 71.*
2. Delete any text that you do not want saved as part of the template. To save only the styles and page formatting, delete all the text, for example.
3. From the File menu, choose Save As. **(Figure 20)**
4. From the Save File as Type pull-down list, choose Document Template. **(Figure 21)**
5. Type a name for the template in the File Name text box.
6. Click OK.

✓ Tips

- Document Templates are automatically stored with all the other templates.
- AutoText entries, macros, and custom toolbars are saved in the template, so you may want to create AutoText entries and modify the toolbars before saving the document as a template. *See Automatically Entering Text, page 96, and Selecting Toolbars, page 31.*

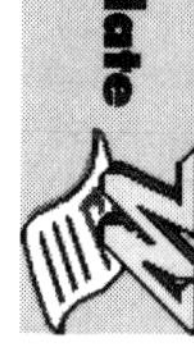

Modifying an Existing Template

1. From the File menu, choose Open. **(Figure 22)**

   or

   Press ⌘+O.
2. On the Open dialog box, choose Document Templates from the List Files of Type drop-down list. **(Figure 23)**
3. Double-click a template name on the list to open the template.
4. Make editing and formatting changes to the template.
5. From the File menu, choose Save. **(Figure 24)**

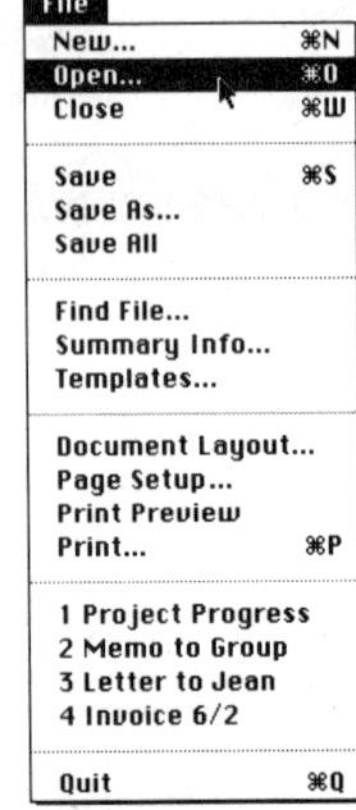

Figure 22. *The File menu.*

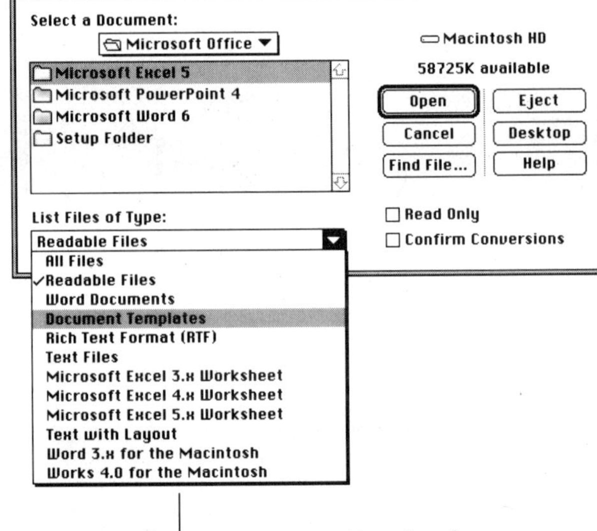

Figure 23. *Choose a Document Template here.*

Figure 24. *The File menu.*

Figure 25. *The Tools menu.*

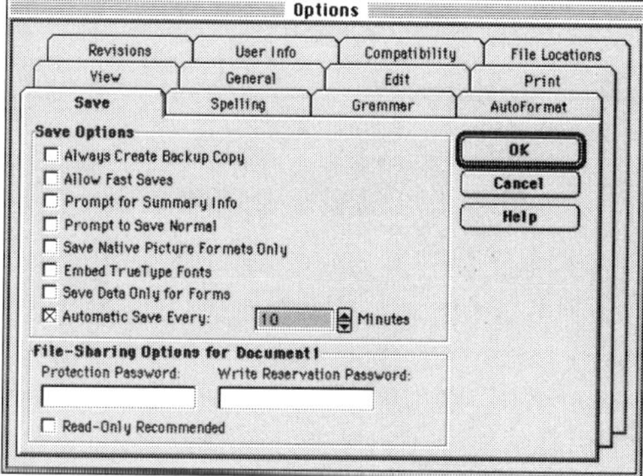

Figure 26. *The Options dialog box.*

Using Automatic Saves

You can have Word automatically save your document at preset intervals. You'll want to turn this feature on as it gives you protection in case of a power loss or other calamity, and the saving process occurs very quickly and will not disturb your work.

1. From the Tools menu, select Options. **(Figure 25)**
2. Click the Save tab of the Options dialog box. **(Figure 26)**
3. Make sure Automatic Save Every __ Minutes is turned on.
4. Change the number of minutes if you wish.
5. Click OK.

✓ Tips

- Even though Word can automatically save your work, you must still save your work in a file as usual when you finish a document. Word's automatic saving simply creates a special file on disk so Word can restore the file if your typing session is interrupted before you perform a normal save.
- If the power fails or disaster strikes while you're working, Word will display a list of automatically saved documents when you next start the program. Simply select from the list the document you were working on when you were so rudely interrupted.

Creating Form Letters with Mail Merge

Word provides built-in, guided help for performing the three major steps in creating mail merged letters, labels, or envelopes: **1.** Creating the merge letter; **2.** Creating or opening the data source; and **3.** Printing the mail merge.

Word will have you create a merge document, prepare or open a data source, and then return to the merge document where you will create the merge

1. From the Tools menu, select Mail Merge. **(Figure 27)**
2. On the Mail Merge Helper, click each option and then follow the onscreen instructions. Before Word helps you create the actual merge letter, it helps you create or open the data source for the database. Then, it returns to the merge document and displays the Mail Merge toolbar. **(Figure 28)**
3. Type the text of the merge document, clicking the Insert Merge Field button whenever you want to include information from the data source.
4. When the merge document is complete, click the Check for Errors button and then click the Merge to Printer button or the Merge to New Document button to create a document you can print later.

✔ Tips

- Click the Mail Merge button on the Mail Merge toolbar to choose a destination for the merge and to select data for the merge.

Figure 27. *The Tools menu.*

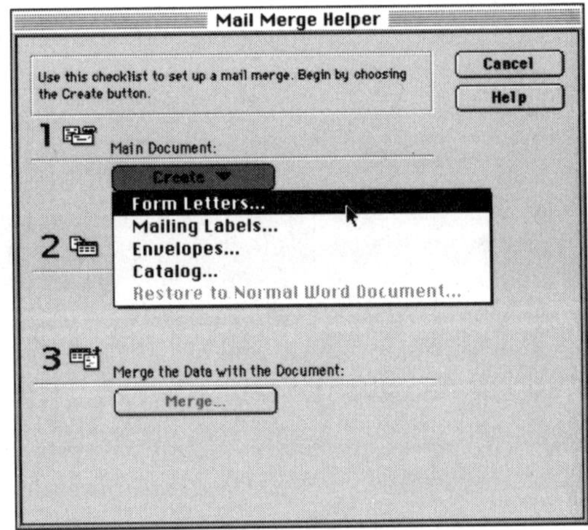

Figure 28. *The Mail Merge Helper.*

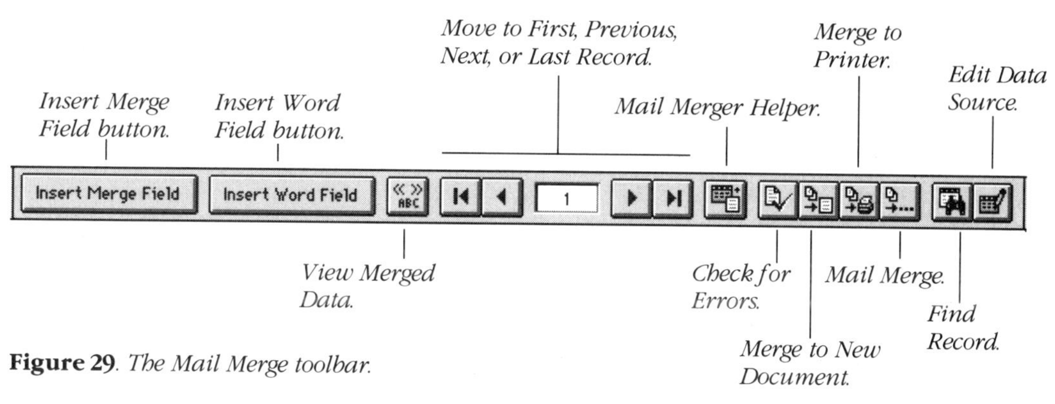

Figure 29. *The Mail Merge toolbar.*

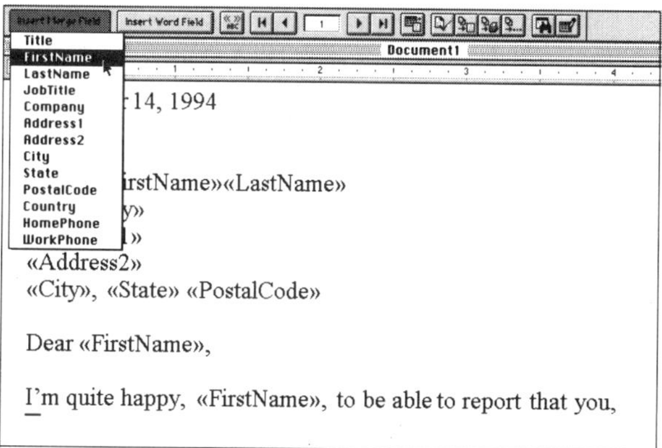

Figure 30. *Choose field names from the Insert Merge Field list as you type the mail merge letter.*

Data Form

Title:	Ms.
FirstName:	Patricia
LastName:	Paul
JobTitle:	
Company:	Honorable Mensans
Address1:	7855 E. Marshall Place
Address2:	
City:	Rockville
State:	MD

OK
Add New
Delete
Restore
Find...
View Source
Help

Record: 1

Figure 31. *You can use the Data Form provided by the Mail Merge helper to enter the data.*

Changing the Appearance of the Word Window

You can choose whether to display the status bar, the scroll bars, and the toolbars, or whether to keep a minimalist view devoted to the text. You can also decide which of the nonprinting characters to display. *See About the Paragraph Marks, page 49.*

1. From the Tools menu, choose Options. **(Figure 29)**
2. On the View tab of the Options dialog box, use the checkboxes in the Window and Nonprinting Characters areas to decide which elements to display. **(Figure 30)**
3. On the View tab you can also turn on Wrap to Window to keep all the text in view even when you reduce the size of the Word window or increase the Zoom factor. When Wrap to Window is on, the arrangement of words onscreen may not match the arrangement on the printed page.

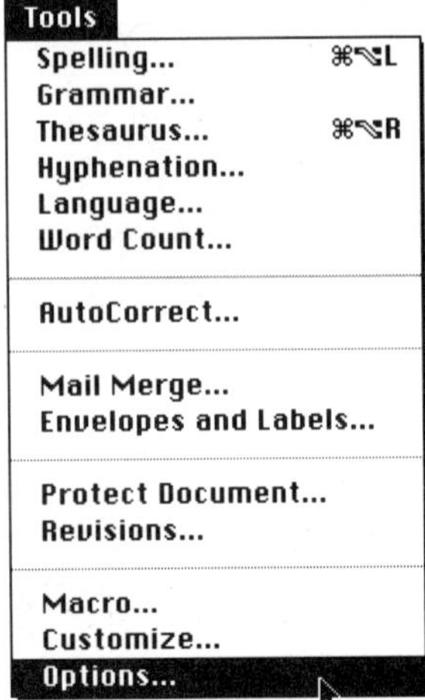

Figure 32. *The Tools menu.*

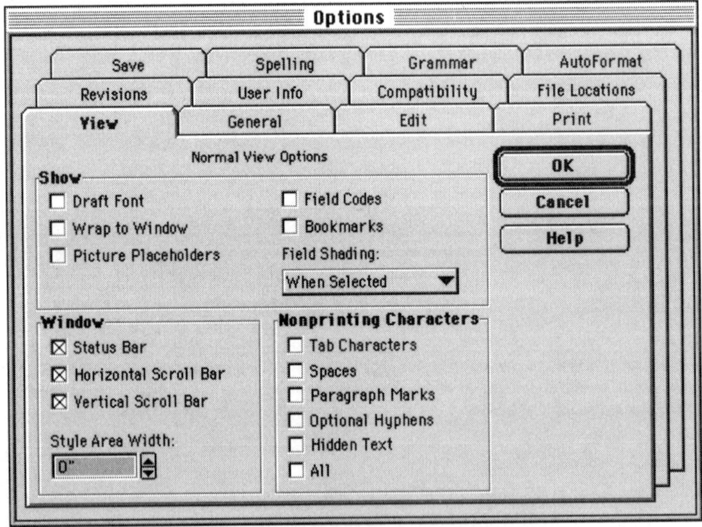

Figure 33. *The View tab of the Options dialog box.*

Excel 5.0 Number Crunching

Excel 5.0 Number Crunching

About Excel

What is Excel?
The Road to an Excel Sheet
The Excel 5 Window
Key to the Excel 5 Window
Starting Excel

Entering Headings and Data

Planning the Worksheet
Moving Within a Sheet
Typing Data into a Cell
Editing Cells
Filling an Entry Range
AutoFilling a Range

Entering the Calculations

Entering Simple Calculations
Building a Simple Formula
Summing Columns or Rows
Totaling a Column with the Sum Function
Copying Formulas to Adjacent Cells
Another Example of a Function: Averaging Numbers
Calculating Numbers in Non-Adjacent Cells
Using Functions
Some Useful Functions

Changing the Sheet's Structure

Widening Columns and Rows
Inserting and Deleting Rows and Columns
Inserting and Deleting Cells
Moving and Copying Data
Freezing the Headings
Splitting a Sheet

Formatting the Sheet

Choosing an AutoFormat
Text Formatting
Centering a Title Above a Range
Number Formatting
Adding Borders to a Range
Adding Shading to a Range
Selecting Styles
Creating Styles

Working with Multiple Sheets

About Using Multiple Sheets
Changing to Another Sheet
Naming Sheets
Referring to Data from Other Sheets in Formulas
Consolidating to a Sheet

Special Excel Techniques

Inserting Notes in Cells
Naming Ranges
Auditing a Worksheet
Creating a Chart with the Chart Wizard
Modifying a Chart

Excel Database Techniques

About Excel's Database Capabilities
Setting up the Database
Creating a Form
Sorting the Database
Extracting Data
Totaling Numeric Data in a Database

About Excel

What is Excel?

Excel, the spreadsheet of the Microsoft Office suite, tracks, calculates and analyzes numbers, and creates charts to depict them visually.

After typing numbers into a grid of cells on an Excel sheet, you enter formulas into adjacent cells that total, subtract, multiply, or divide the numbers. You can also enter functions (special Excel formulas) that perform dozens of complex calculations on the numbers, from simple averaging to sophisticated financial calculations such as Net Present Value. Excel can even calculate highly involved statistics, such as the inverse of the one-tailed probability of the chi-squared distribution.

Ad Budget			
	Magazine	TV	Radio
Jan	$ 16,000	$ 78,000	$ 8,200
Feb	16,000	78,000	8,200
Mar	17,500	82,500	11,000
Apr	17,500	82,500	11,000
May	14,000	64,000	6,700
Jun	15,000	64,000	7,200
Total	$ 96,000	$ 449,000	$ 52,300

Excel also offers simple database capabilities. You can accumulate records of information that are both textual and numeric, and sort, search for, and extract data from a database.

To view numbers graphically, you can have Excel create a chart. Excel uses the same charting program as PowerPoint, so its charts are professional and presentable.

The Road to an Excel Sheet

The Bridgehampton Garden Club

Sheet1

Fund Raising Events	Spring	Summer	Fall
Garden Tour	240	310	120
Bulb Planting	350	-	510
Cuttings Club	100	465	275
Plant Auction	580	-	430
Flower Festival	335	250	145
	S 1,605	S 1,025	S 1,480

Fill Cells with Row and Column Headings and Data

Into the worksheet grid of cells, enter the row and column headings and the numbers that go underneath. Use AutoFill, if you can, to enter sequences like month names. *Pages 115-120.*

Enter the Calculations

Into cells that are adjacent to the data, enter the formulas that will calculate the results you need. Summing a column is the most familiar formula, but Excel provides dozens of special "functions" that can perform sophisticated calculations on your data. *Pages 121-130.*

Changing the Sheet Structure

With the numbers and calculations in place, you can structure the sheet to make it easy to interpret. You might widen a column, lock the headings so they remain on the screen at all times, or split the sheet into panes you can use to view or edit different areas of a sheet simultaneously. *Pages 131-136.*

Formatting the Sheet

AutoFormatting a sheet can enhance the sheet's appearance and make it more presentable or easier to understand. Excel's dozens of AutoFormat designs make designing the sheet a simple menu pick. Then, to refine the sheet, you can further format sheet elements. You can format the text or numbers, add borders and shading to cells, or use styles to apply formatting automatically. *Pages 137-144.*

Annotating and Auditing the Sheet

Add notes to cells to attach text messages or even voice annotations. Name the sheets in a workbook to make them easier to understand. And, before you stake your reputation on the accuracy of the sheet, use Excel's built-in auditing tools to check the formulas. *Pages 149-151.*

Printing or Mailing the Sheet

Excel's print preview gives you a bird's eye view of your work before you commit it to paper. To send a sheet to a colleague, you can attach it to a Microsoft Mail note.

Extras

Excel also includes sophisticated charting and database capabilities so you can graphically represent numeric data or collect and store large quantities of information. *Pages 152-160.*

The Excel 5 Window

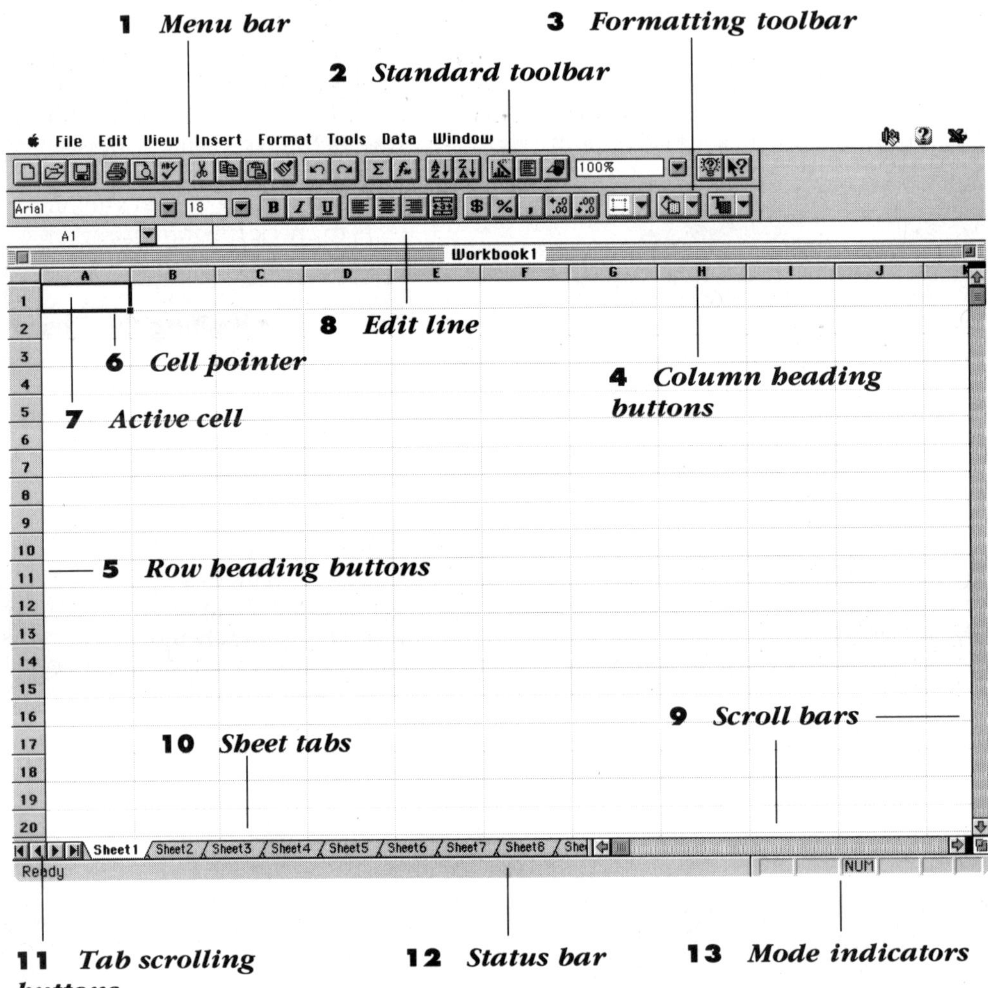

Key to the Excel 5 Window

1 *Menu bar*

Click any name on the menu bar to pull down a menu.

2 *Standard toolbar*

Toolbar with buttons for standard file management and text editing and proofing commands.

3 *Formatting toolbar*

Toolbar with buttons for formatting cells and the contents of cells.

4 *Column heading buttons*

Column labels. Click a column heading button to select a column. Drag across column heading buttons to select multiple columns.

5 *Row heading buttons*

Row labels. Click a row heading button to select a row. Drag across row heading buttons to select multiple rows.

6 *Cell pointer*

The cell pointer surrounds the currently selected cell. To move the cell pointer, click a different cell or press the arrow keys.

7 *Active cell*

The cell into which data is placed when you start to type. When you select a range, the active cell is the only cell that remains unhighlighted.

8 *Edit line*

Displays the contents of the selected cell. You can edit the contents here or within the cell.

9 *Scroll bars*

Use these scroll bars to move the view of the document up or down or to quickly jump to a spot in the document. The length of the vertical scroll bar represents the length of the entire document. The position of the scroll button represents the position of the insertion point in the document.

10 *Sheet tabs*

Click these tabs to switch from sheet to sheet. Double-click a tab to rename a sheet.

11 *Tab scrolling buttons*

Use these buttons to scroll forward or back a sheet or to jump to the first or last sheet.

12 *Status bar*

Provides information about the current sheet or the current operation.

13 *Mode indicators*

Show special conditions that are in effect, such as a pressed Caps Lock key.

Starting Excel

1. Double-click the Microsoft Excel icon in its folder. **(Figure 1)**

   or

   Pull down the Microsoft Office Manager menu and choose Microsoft Excel. **(Figure 2)**

✔ Tip

- If Microsoft Excel is already started, pull down the application menu and choose Microsoft Excel from the list of running applications. You can also press ⌘+Tab repeatedly until Microsoft Excel appears.

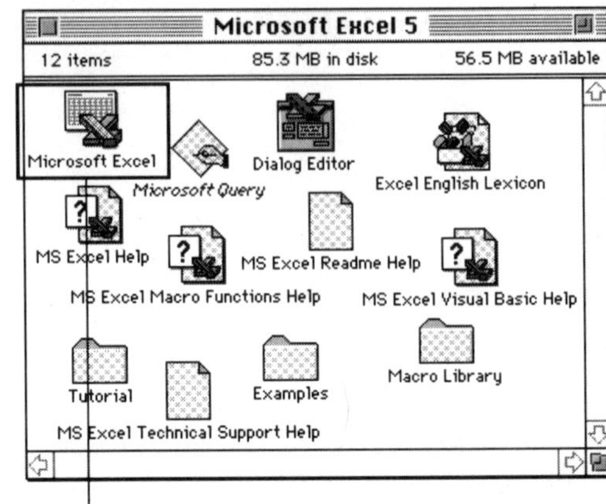

Figure 1. *The Microsoft Excel icon in its folder.*

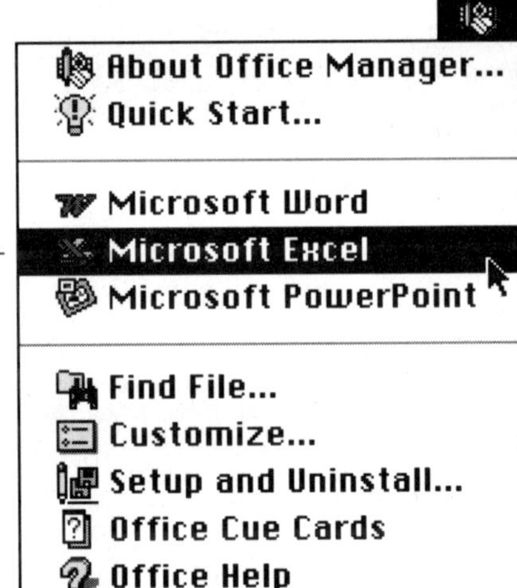

Select this item to start Excel.

Figure 2. *The Microsoft Office Manager.*

Entering Headings and Data

Planning the Worksheet

Most worksheets conform to a standard design, with rows and columns of data, headings at the tops of columns and left ends of rows, and calculations at the bottoms of columns and/or the right ends of rows. **(Figure 1)**

Because everyone is familiar with this basic structure, your worksheet will be universally understood.

Excel is a blank slate, though, onto which you can write any worksheet design. The 256 columns and 16,384 rows should give you ample space to be creative.

Ad Budget

	Magazine	TV	Radio
Jan	$ 16,000	$ 78,000	$ 8,200
Feb	$ 16,000	$ 78,000	$ 8,200
Mar	$ 17,500	$ 82,500	$ 11,000
Apr	$ 17,500	$ 82,500	$ 11,000
May	$ 14,000	$ 64,000	$ 6,700
Jun	$ 15,000	$ 64,000	$ 7,200
Total	$ 96,000	$ 449,000	$ 52,300

Figure 1. *The most common worksheet structure.*

Moving Within a Sheet

To enter data into a cell, you must move to the cell first.

1. Click in the cell. **(Figure 2)**

   or

   Press the arrow keys to move the cell pointer to the cell.

   or

   Click the current cell address on the edit line and type the new cell address to jump to. **(Figure 3)**

✔ Tips

- The cell surrounded by the cell pointer is called the *active cell.*
- You can use the scroll bars to scroll through the document without changing the active cell.

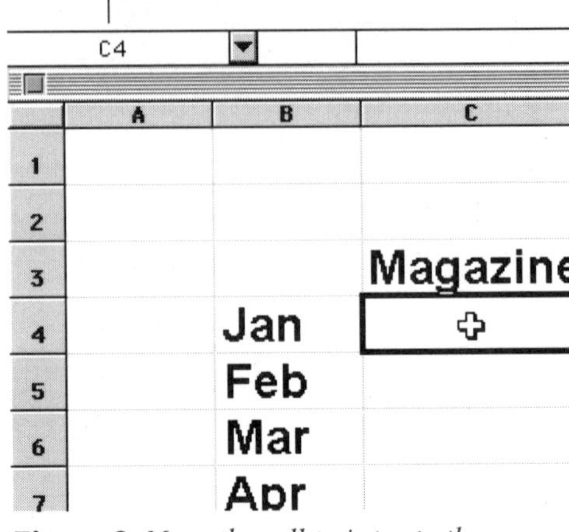

Figure 2. *Move the cell pointer to the cell into which you want to enter data and then click.*

Table 12-1. ***Keyboard Shortcuts for Moving Within a Worksheet***

Key	Action
Arrow key	Move to the adjacent cell up, down, left, or right.
⌘+Up arrow or ⌘+Down arrow	Move up or down one screenful.
⌘+Left arrow or ⌘+Right arrow	Move left or right one screenful.
Tab	Move right one screenful.
Shift+Tab	Move left one screenful.
⌘+Home	Move to cell A1.
Home	Move to first cell of the row.
⌘+End	Move to last cell of last row that contains data.

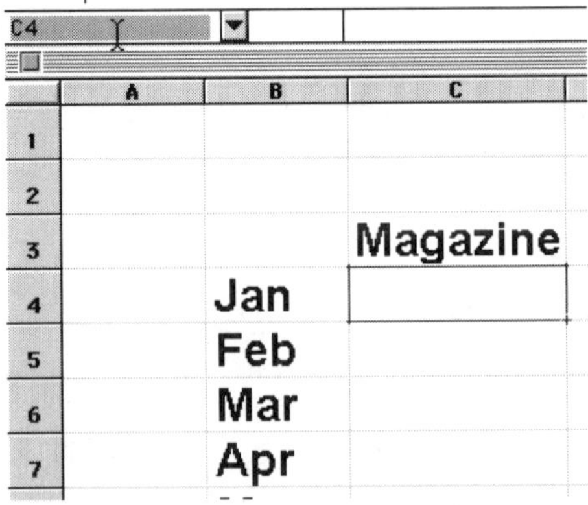

Figure 3. *Editing the current cell address.*

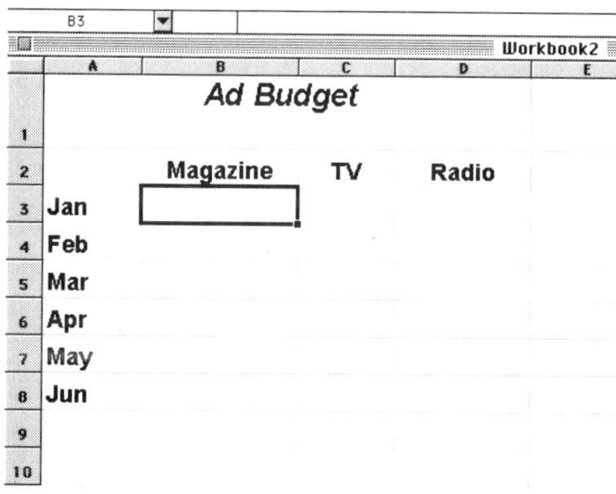

Figure 4. *Select the cell.*

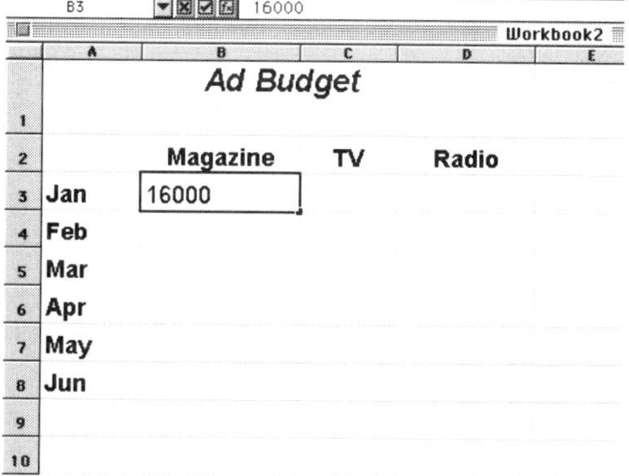

Figure 5. *Type the entry.*

Text is left-aligned.

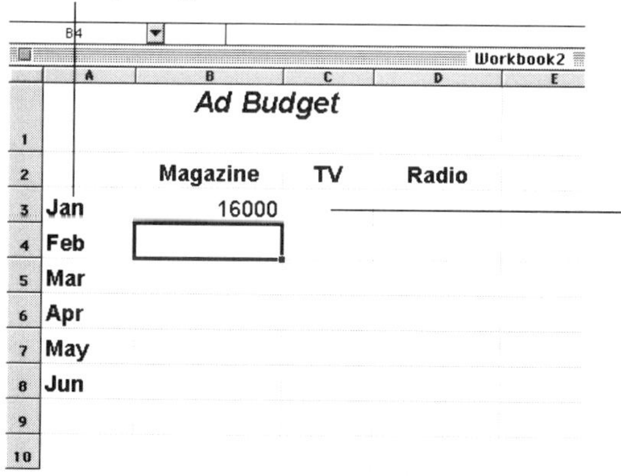

Numbers are right-aligned.

Figure 6. *Move to the next cell.*

Typing Data into a Cell

1. Select the cell. **(Figure 4)** *See Moving Within a Sheet, page 116.*
2. Type text, a number, or a formula. **(Figure 5)**
3. Move to the next cell. The data is entered in the previous cell automatically. **(Figure 6)**

✔ Tips

- You don't have to press Enter after you type the contents of a cell. You can simply press an arrow key to move to the next cell.
- Text is automatically left-aligned in cells. Numbers are right-aligned. **(Figure 6)**
- If you need a series of consecutive dates or numbers for column or row headings (month names, for example), use AutoFill to enter them automatically. *See AutoFilling a Range, page 120.*

Editing Cells

The easiest way to change the text or number in a cell is to click the cell and then type right over the contents. But if you have a formula in the cell, you may want to edit the formula instead, so you don't have to retype the whole entry.

1. Click on the cell and then type over the contents. **(Figure 7)**

   or

1. Double-click the cell to place an insertion point in the contents.
2. Edit the contents as though you were editing text in **Word**. *See Text Editing, page 50.*
3. Press Enter to enter the revision into the cell. **(Figure 8)**

✔ Tips

- When you click a cell, the cell contents appears on the edit line also. **(Figure 9)** You can click on the edit line and edit the cell contents there.
- To abandon any revisions you've made, press Esc to leave the original contents of a cell intact before you press Enter to exit the cell.

B3 | 10000 — Workbo

	A	B	C	D
1		Ad Budget		
2		Magazine	TV	Radio
3	Jan	10000	78000	11500
4	Feb	16000	78000	11500
5	Mar	21500	82500	9000
6	Apr	21500	82500	9000
7	May	14000	64000	6500
8	Jun	14000	64000	6500
9				
10				

Figure 7. *Select a cell and then type to replace the cell's contents.*

H13 — Workbo

	A	B	C	D
1		Ad Budget		
2		Magazine	TV	Radio
3	Jan	18000	78000	11500
4	Feb	16000	78000	11500
5	Mar	21500	82500	9000
6	Apr	21500	82500	9000
7	May	14000	64000	6500
8	Jun	14000	64000	6500
9				
10				

Figure 8. *The revised entry.*

The contents of the cell you select appears here.

B2 | Magazine — Workbook1

	A	B	C	D
1		Ad Budget		
2		Magazine	TV	Radio
3	Jan	18000	78000	11500
4	Feb	16000	78000	11500
5	Mar	21500	82500	9000
6	Apr	21500	82500	9000
7	May	14000	64000	6500
8	Jun	14000	64000	6500
9				
10				

Figure 9. *The contents of the currently selected cell appears on the edit line.*

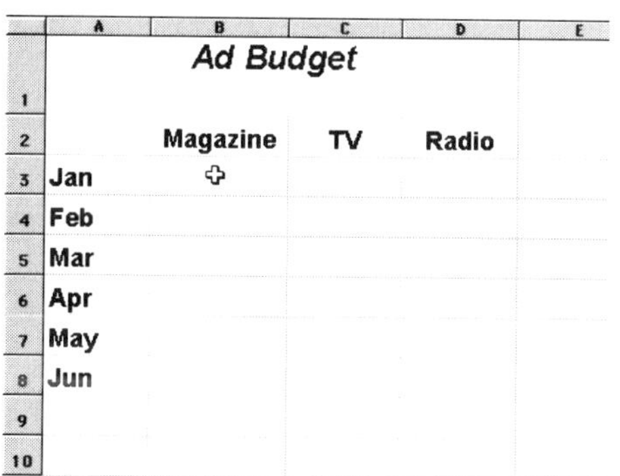

Figure 10. *Place the mouse pointer at the first cell for the range.*

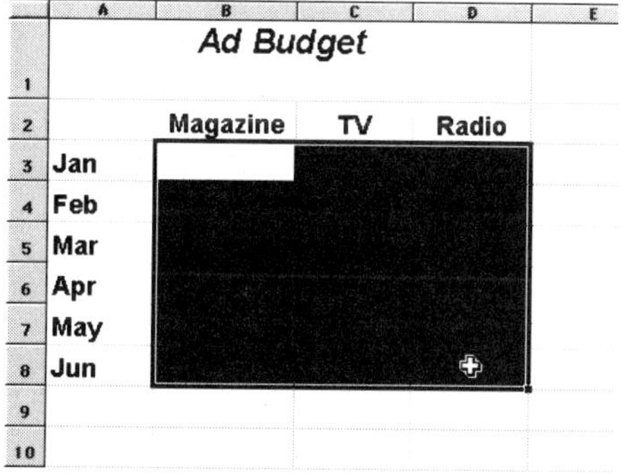

Figure 11. *Drag to the last cell.*

Filling an Entry Range

To quickly enter data into a rectangular range of cells, create an entry range.

1. Place the mouse pointer on the upper left corner cell of the range. **(Figure 10)**
2. Click and drag to the lower right corner cell of the range. **(Figure 11)** The active cell is the cell at the upper left corner of the entry range.
3. Type data into each cell and then press Enter. The cell pointer moves down each column from cell to cell automatically. When it reaches the bottom of a column, it jumps to the top of the next column within the entry range. **(Figures 12-13)**

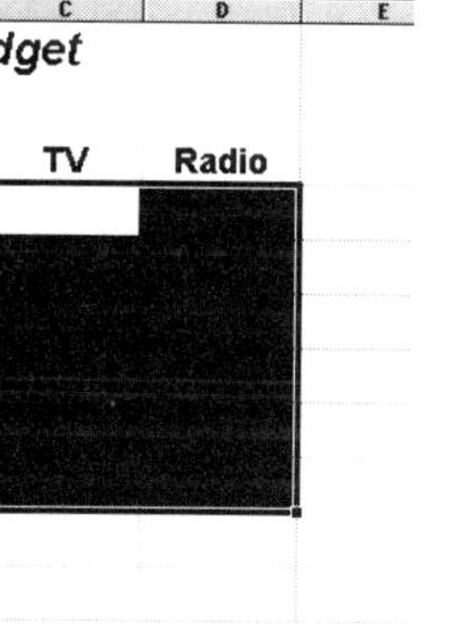

Figure 12. *Press Enter at the bottom of a column to continue at the top of the next column.*

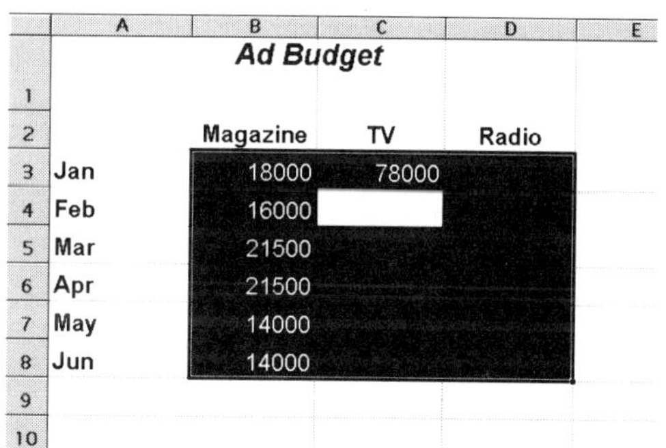

Figure 13. *Press Enter after typing a value into a cell to move to the cell below.*

AutoFilling a Range

When a range of cells should be filled with consecutive numbers, numbers that follow a specific pattern, dates, or dates that follow a specific pattern, such as every Monday, use AutoFill as a quick and convenient method of automatically entering the sequence.

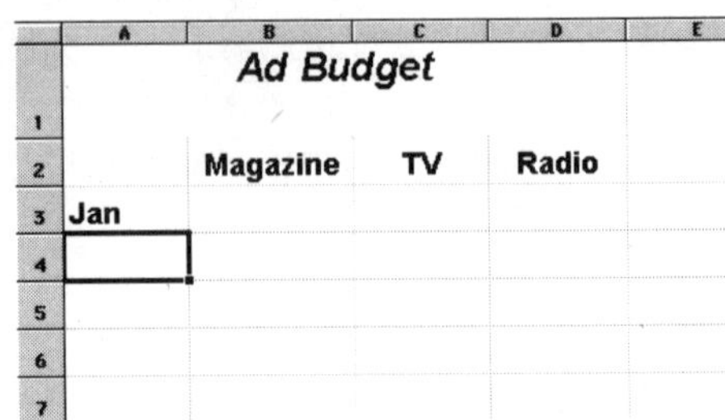

Figure 14. *Enter the first number or date.*

1. Into the first cell of the sequence, type the first number or date. **(Figure 14)**
2. Into an adjacent cell, type the next number or date. **(Figure 15)**
3. Select the two cells. **(Figure 16)**
4. Carefully place the mouse pointer on the Fill handle at the lower right corner of the border surrounding the two cells.
5. Drag the Fill handle to extend the sequence. **(Figure 17)**
6. Release the mouse button when the sequence is complete. **(Figure 18)**

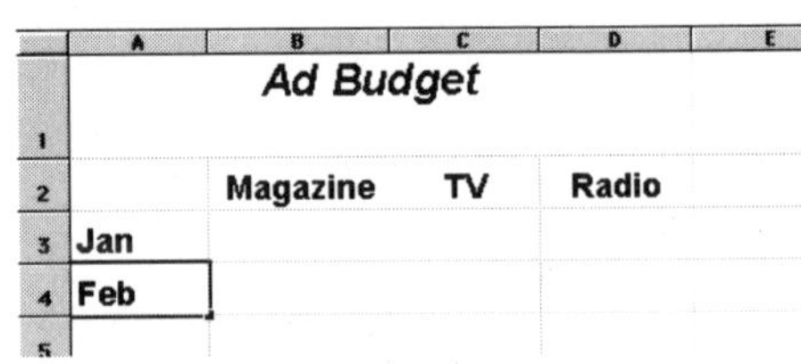

Figure 15. *Type the next number or date in an adjacent cell.*

✔ Tip

- As you drag to extend the sequence, the current value appears at the left end of the edit line.

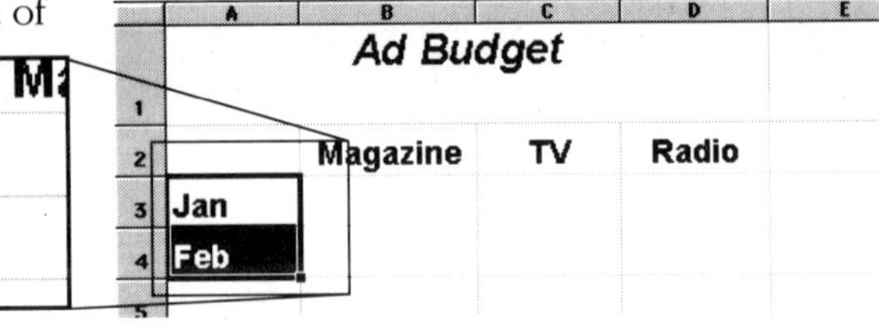

The Fill handle.

Figure 16. *Select the two cells.*

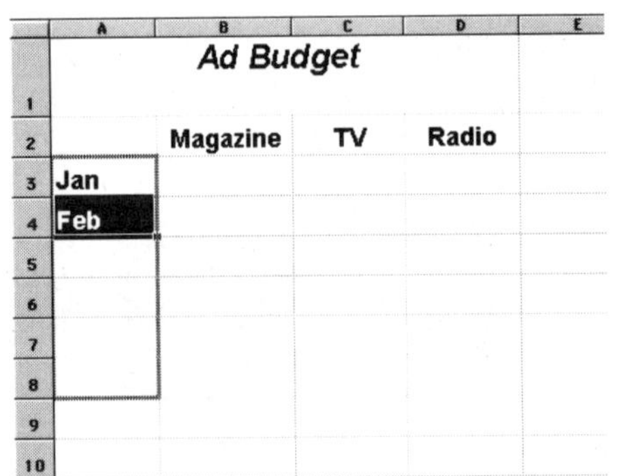

Figure 17. *Drag the Fill handle to extend the pattern established in the first two cells.*

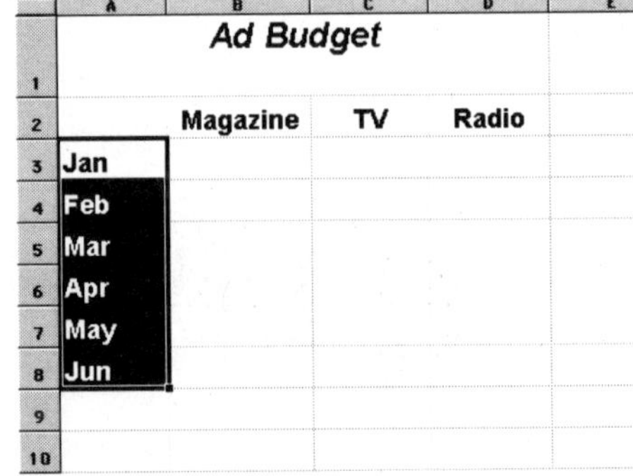

Figure 18. *Release the mouse button to complete the sequence.*

Entering the Calculations 13

Entering Simple Calculations

A calculation can be simple (a sum of a column of numbers) or complex (a financial, statistical, or scientific computation) but it is always entered as a *formula* that begins with an equal sign (=).

To sum two numbers in a cell, you could type =23+43, for example. To sum the contents of two cells, you would include their cell addresses in the formula, such as =B3+B4. The cell into which you type the formula displays the result of the calculation. **(Figure 1)**

If any numbers change in the cells that supply values to the formula, the result of the calculation changes immediately. This immediate recalculation lets you perform what-if analyses; you can see the change in the bottom line immediately when you change any of the contributing numbers.

	A	B	C	D
1	Simple calculation	Sum a column	Mortgage Payment	
2				
3		23	Interest/month	0.71%
4		43	# of payments	360
5		54	Mortgage amt.	167,000
6	101	120	Monthly payment	($1,286.45)
7				

=26+75   =SUM(B3:B5)   =PMT(D3,D4,D5)

Figure 1. *Some typical calculations.*

Building a Simple Formula

1. Click the destination cell for the formula. **(Figure 2)**
2. Type an equal sign (press the equal sign key.) **(Figure 3)**
3. Click in the first cell whose address you want in the formula. **(Figure 4)**
4. Type an operator. *See Table 13-1. Table of Operators, this page.* **(Figure 5)**
5. Click the next cell whose address should appear in the formula. **(Figure 6)**
6. Type another operator to continue the formula if you want.

   or

   Press Enter to enter the formula into the cell and display the result of the calculation.

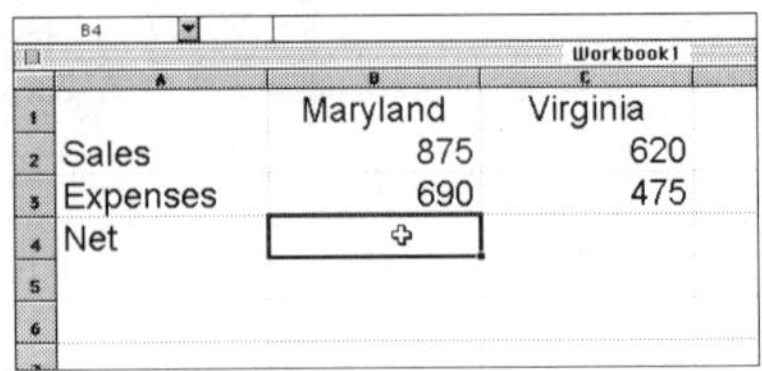

Figure 2. *Click at the destination for the formula.*

Figure 3. *The formula builds both in the cell and on the edit line.*

Click here to add B2 to the formula.

Figure 4. *Click on a cell.*

Figure 5. *Type an operator.*

Figure 6. *The address of each cell you click adds to the formula.*

✔ Tips

- If adjacent cells require a similar formula, you can copy the formula from cell to cell. *See Copying Formulas to Adjacent Cells, page 125.*
- You can enter a combination of typed numbers and cell addresses in formulas, such as =C2*2.5 (the contents of cell C2 multiplied by 2.5).

Table 13-1. *Table of Operators*

+	Plus
–	Minus
*	Multiply (asterisk)
/	Divide

	A	B	C	D
1		Jimmy	Pete	
2	Mon	17.50	12.00	
3	Tue	14.25	13.50	
4	Wed	16.50	12.75	
5	Thu	16.00	14.00	
6	Fri	18.00	14.50	
7				
8				
9				
10				

Figure 7. *Click at the destination for the sum.*

The AutoSum button.

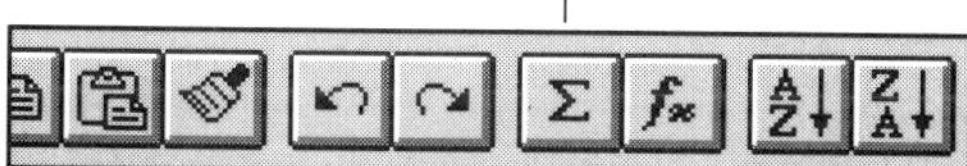

Figure 8. *The AutoSum button. Excel creates the formula for you.*

Summing Columns or Rows

Excel includes special help for summing a column or row.

1. Click in the empty cell below the last entry in the column or to the right of the last entry in the row. **(Figure 7)**
2. Click the AutoSum button. **(Figure 8)**
3. Press Enter to enter the formula that has automatically appeared in the cell. **(Figure 9)**

✔ Tips

- Excel looks for a range of numbers it can sum that is above the cell you've selected for the total. If it does not find a range of numbers or if it finds text, it looks to the left for a range of numbers.
- To quickly enter sums below a number of adjacent columns, select the empty cells at the bottoms of all the columns before clicking the AutoSum button. Excel will insert a sum in each selected cell. **(Figure 10)**

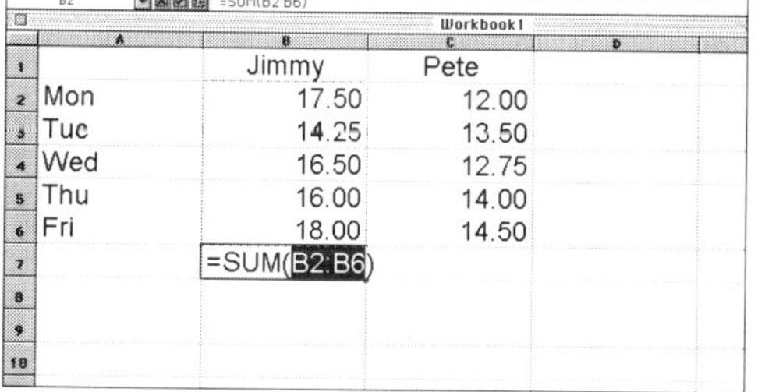

	A	B	C	D
1		Jimmy	Pete	
2	Mon	17.50	12.00	
3	Tue	14.25	13.50	
4	Wed	16.50	12.75	
5	Thu	16.00	14.00	
6	Fri	18.00	14.50	
7		=SUM(B2:B6)		
8				
9				
10				

Figure 9. *Excel has created the formula for you.*

	A	B	C	D
1		Jimmy	Pete	Tommy
2	Mon	17.50	12.00	9.00
3	Tue	14.25	13.50	9.80
4	Wed	16.50	12.75	11.00
5	Thu	16.00	14.00	12.80
6	Fri	18.00	14.50	15.00
7				
8				
9				
10				

Figure 10. *You can select the cells below any number of adjacent columns before clicking the AutoSum button.*

Totaling a Column with the Sum Function

1. Click in the destination cell for the formula. **(Figure 11)**
2. Enter an equal sign to start the formula. **(Figure 12)**
3. Type the word SUM. **(Figure 13)**
4. Enter a left parenthesis (Shift-9). **(Figure 14)**
5. Drag down the column of numbers to sum. **(Figure 15)**
6. Press Enter. **(Figure 16)**

✔ Tips

- You don't need to close the parentheses before pressing Enter. Excel will do it for you.
- The word SUM is an example of an Excel *function*. Excel contains hundreds of functions for common and uncommon math, statistical, financial, date, time, and other calculations. *See Using Functions, page 128.*

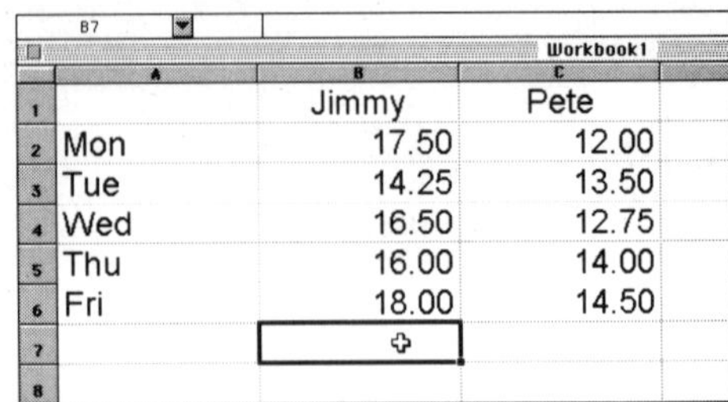

	A	B	C
1		Jimmy	Pete
2	Mon	17.50	12.00
3	Tue	14.25	13.50
4	Wed	16.50	12.75
5	Thu	16.00	14.00
6	Fri	18.00	14.50
7			
8			

Figure 11. *Click at the destination for the formula.*

	A	B	C
1		Jimmy	Pete
2	Mon	17.50	12.00
3	Tue	14.25	13.50
4	Wed	16.50	12.75
5	Thu	16.00	14.00
6	Fri	18.00	14.50
7		=	
8			

Figure 12. *Start a formula with an equals sign.*

=sum

Figure 13. *Type "sum."*

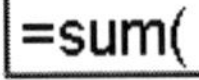

=sum(

Figure 14. *Type a left parenthesis.*

	A	B	C
1		Jimmy	Pete
2	Mon	17.50	12.00
3	Tue	14.25	13.50
4	Wed	16.50	12.75
5	Thu	16.00	14.00
6	Fri	18.00	14.50
7		=sum(B2:B6	
8			

Figure 15. *Drag across the range of numbers to sum. In this case, from B2 to B6.*

	A	B	C
1		Jimmy	Pete
2	Mon	17.50	12.00
3	Tue	14.25	13.50
4	Wed	16.50	12.75
5	Thu	16.00	14.00
6	Fri	18.00	14.50
7		82.25	
8			

Figure 16. *The sum.*

Copying Formulas to Adjacent Cells

Rather than retype the formula in adjacent cells, copy it across. Excel will adjust the formula in the direction of the copy.

1. Click on the cell containing the formula. **(Figure 17)**
2. Drag the Fill handle at the lower right corner of the cell across the adjacent cells to which you want to copy the formula. **(Figures 18-19)**

✔ Tip

- When the mouse pointer is positioned properly on the Fill handle, the pointer becomes a small plus sign. Otherwise, the mouse pointer is a large, heavy plus sign.

B7 =SUM(B2:B6)

Workbook1

	A	B	C	D
1		Jimmy	Pete	Tommy
2	Mon	17.50	12.00	9.00
3	Tue	14.25	13.50	9.80
4	Wed	16.50	12.75	11.00
5	Thu	16.00	14.00	12.80
6	Fri	18.00	14.50	15.00
7		82.25		
8				

The Fill handle.

Figure 17. *Click on the cell with the formula.*

=SUM(B2:B6)

Workbook1

	A	B	C	D
1		Jimmy	Pete	Tommy
2	Mon	17.50	12.00	9.00
3	Tue	14.25	13.50	9.80
4	Wed	16.50	12.75	11.00
5	Thu	16.00	14.00	12.80
6	Fri	18.00	14.50	15.00
7		82.25		
8				

Figure 18. *Drag the Fill handle across adjacent cells.*

Excel adjusts the formula as it copies the formula across to column D so the formula in column D refers to other cells in Column D.

D7 =SUM(D2:D6)

Workbook1

	A	B	C	D
1		Jimmy	Pete	Tommy
2	Mon	17.50	12.00	9.00
3	Tue	14.25	13.50	9.80
4	Wed	16.50	12.75	11.00
5	Thu	16.00	14.00	12.80
6	Fri	18.00	14.50	15.00
7		82.25	66.75	57.60
8				

Figure 19. *The formula copied to adjacent cells.*

Another Example of a Function: Averaging Numbers

1. Click in the destination cell for the formula that will calculate the average. **(Figure 20)**
2. Enter an equal sign.
3. Type the word AVERAGE. **(Figure 21)**
4. Enter a left parenthesis. (Shift-9)
5. Drag across the cells to average. **(Figure 22)**
6. Press Enter. **(Figure 23)**

E2 — Workbook1

	Jimmy	Pete	Tommy	Average
Mon	17.50	12.00	9.00	
Tue	14.25	13.50	9.80	
Wed	16.50	12.75	11.00	
Thu	16.00	14.00	12.80	
Fri	18.00	14.50	15.00	
	82.25	66.75	57.60	

Figure 20. *Click at the destination for the formula.*

E2 =average(— Workbook1

	Jimmy	Pete	Tommy	Average
Mon	17.50	12.00	9.00	=average(
Tue	14.25	13.50	9.80	
Wed	16.50	12.75	11.00	
Thu	16.00	14.00	12.80	
Fri	18.00	14.50	15.00	
	82.25	66.75	57.60	

Figure 21. *Type the formula.*

B2 =average(B2:D2 — Workbook1

	Jimmy	Pete	Tommy	Average
Mon	17.50	12.00	9.00	=average(B2:D2
Tue	14.25	13.50	9.80	
Wed	16.50	12.75	11.00	
Thu	16.00	14.00	12.80	
Fri	18.00	14.50	15.00	
	82.25	66.75	57.60	

Figure 22. *Drag across the cells to average.*

E3 — Workbook1

	Jimmy	Pete	Tommy	Average
Mon	17.50	12.00	9.00	12.83
Tue	14.25	13.50	9.80	
Wed	16.50	12.75	11.00	
Thu	16.00	14.00	12.80	
Fri	18.00	14.50	15.00	
	82.25	66.75	57.60	

Figure 23. *The cell displays the result of the formula.*

D9

Workbook1

	A	B	C	D	
1		Jimmy	Pete	Tommy	Ave
2	Mon	17.50	12.00	9.00	
3	Tue	14.25	13.50	9.80	
4	Wed	16.50	12.75	11.00	
5	Thu	16.00	14.00	12.80	
6	Fri	18.00	14.50	15.00	
7		82.25	66.75	57.60	
8					
9	Total of Jimmy and Tommy				
10					

Figure 24. *Click at the destination for the formula.*

D9 =sum(

Workbook1

	A	B	C	D	
1		Jimmy	Pete	Tommy	Ave
2	Mon	17.50	12.00	9.00	
3	Tue	14.25	13.50	9.80	
4	Wed	16.50	12.75	11.00	
5	Thu	16.00	14.00	12.80	
6	Fri	18.00	14.50	15.00	
7		82.25	66.75	57.60	
8					
9	Total of Jimmy and Tommy			=sum(	
10					

Figure 25. *Enter the function.*

Calculating Numbers in Non-Adjacent Cells

1. Click on the destination cell for the formula. **(Figure 24)**
2. Start the formula as usual with an equal sign.
3. Enter a function followed by the left parenthesis. **(Figure 25)**
4. Click on the first cell to include. **(Figure 26)**
5. Type a comma.
6. Click on the next cell to include. **(Figure 27)**
7. Repeat Steps 5-6 until you have included as many cells as necessary.
8. Press Enter to enter the formula.

✔ Tip

- A formula can contain a combination of discrete cells and ranges, such as =SUM(B2,B4,B9:B11). This formula will add the contents of B2, B4, and B9 through B11.

Non-adjacent Cells

Excel

Click on this cell and type a comma...

B7 =sum(B7

Workbook1

	A	B	C	D	
1		Jimmy	Pete	Tommy	Ave
2	Mon	17.50	12.00	9.00	
3	Tue	14.25	13.50	9.80	
4	Wed	16.50	12.75	11.00	
5	Thu	16.00	14.00	12.80	
6	Fri	18.00	14.50	15.00	
7		82.25	66.75	57.60	
8					
9	Total of Jimmy and Tommy			=sum(B7	
10					

Figure 26. *Click on a cell to include.*

...then click on this cell.

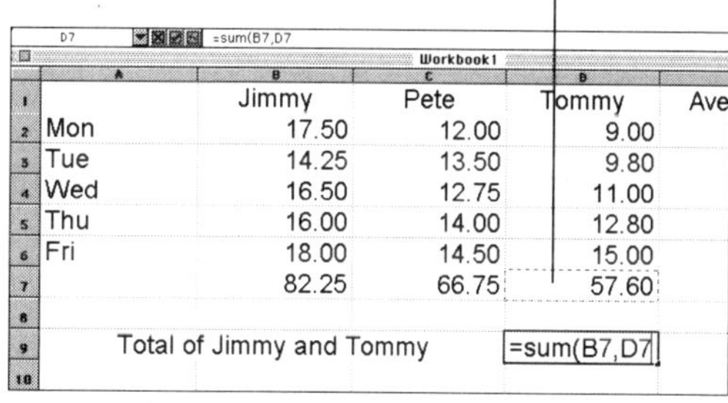

D7 =sum(B7,D7

Workbook1

	A	B	C	D	
1		Jimmy	Pete	Tommy	Ave
2	Mon	17.50	12.00	9.00	
3	Tue	14.25	13.50	9.80	
4	Wed	16.50	12.75	11.00	
5	Thu	16.00	14.00	12.80	
6	Fri	18.00	14.50	15.00	
7		82.25	66.75	57.60	
8					
9	Total of Jimmy and Tommy			=sum(B7,D7	
10					

Figure 27. *Type a comma and then click on the next cell to include.*

Using Functions

SUM and AVERAGE are only two of the dozens of functions that are included in Excel. To find others, click the Function Wizard button on the edit line **(Figure 28)** as you are building the formula. The Function Wizard takes you through the steps of building a formula. **(Figures 29-34)**

Function Wizard button.

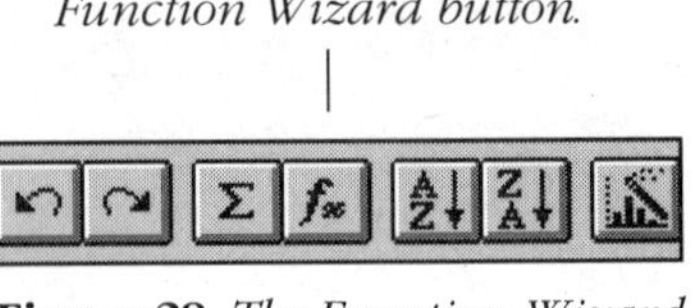

Figure 28. *The Function Wizard button.*

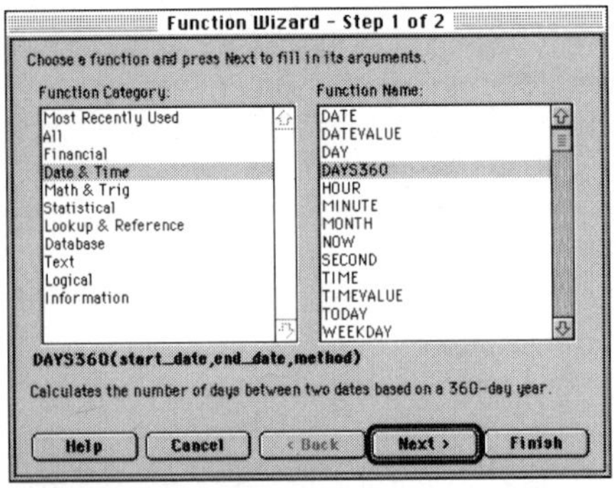

Figure 29. *Selecting the function that calculates the number of days between two dates.*

Function Wizard button.

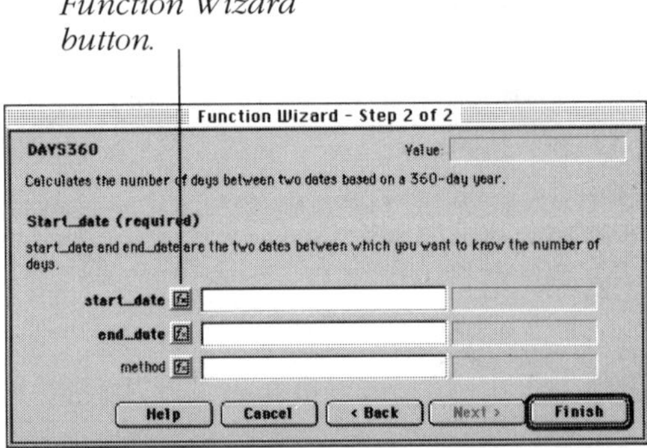

Figure 30. *Step 2 asks you to enter the numbers of the start and end dates. To use the DATE function to calculate the date numbers, you can click the Function Wizard button next to the entry.*

"Nested" indicates that you are running the Function Wizard from within a function you are building.

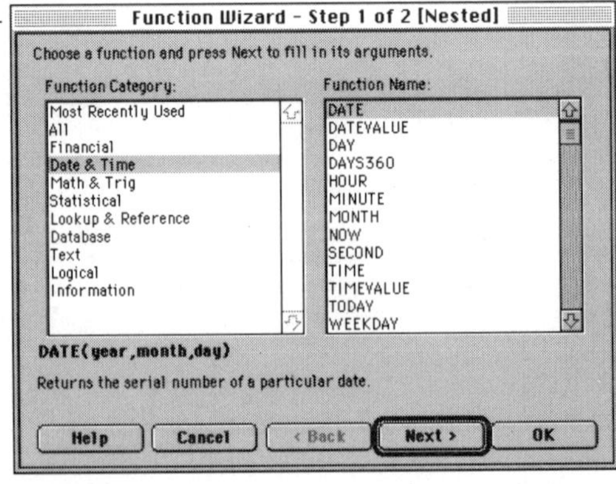

Figure 31. *Select the DATE function on Step 1 of the Function Wizard.*

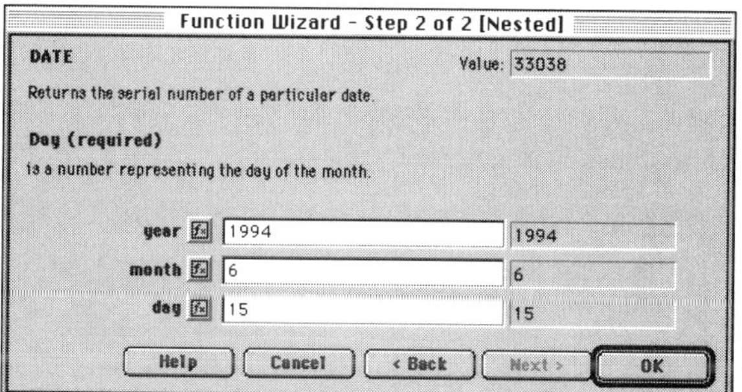

The date number.

Figure 32. *Enter the year, month, and day to obtain the date number and click OK.*

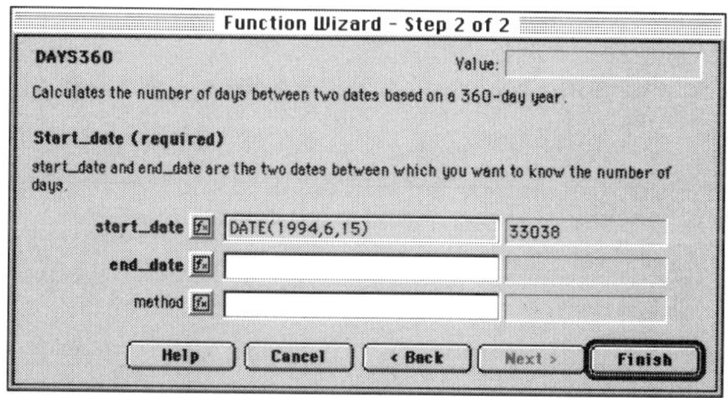

Figure 33. *The DATE function is entered into the start_date text box automatically.*

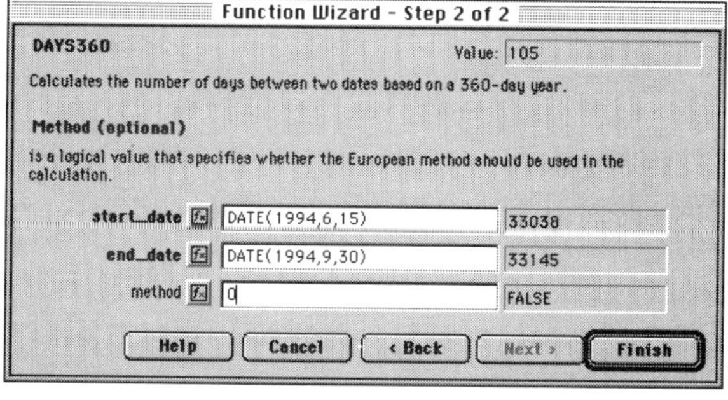

Figure 34. *Complete the end_date entry and then click Finish to end the Wizard.*

Figure 35. *The completed function.*

Some Useful Functions

DATE(year, month, day)	Provides the serial number of a particular date.
DAYS360(start_date, end_date, method)	Calculates the number of days between two dates based on a 360-day year.
TODAY( )	Provides the serial number of today's date.
NOW( )	Provides the serial number of the current date and time.
DDB(cost, salvage, life, period, factor)	Provides the depreciation of an asset for a spcified period using the double-declining balance method or some other method you specify.
FV(rate, nper, pmt, pv, type)	Calculates the future value of an investment.
IRR(values, guess)	Provides the internal rate of return for a series of cash flows.
NPV(rate, value1, value2, ...)	Calculates the net present value of an investment based on a series of periodic cash flows and a discount rate
PMT(rate, nper, pv, fv, type)	Calculates the periodic payment for an annuity or loan.
PV(rate, nper, pmt, fv, type)	Calculates the present value of an investment
ROUND(number, num_digits)	Rounds a number to a specified number of digits.
SUM(number1, number2, ...)	Calculates the sum of all the numbers in the list of arguments.*
AVERAGE(number1, number2, ...)	Calculates the average (arithmetic mean) of the arguments.*
MAX(number1, number2, ...)	Calculates the maximum value in a list of arguments.*
MEDIAN(number1, number2, ...)	Calculates the median of the given numbers.*
MIN(number1, number2, ...)	Calculates the smallest number in the list of arguments.*
STDEV(number1, number2, ...)	Estimates standard deviation based on a sample. The standard deviation is a measure of how widely values are dispersed from the average value (the mean).*
VAR(number1, number2, ...)	Estimates variance based on a sample.*
VALUE(text)	Converts text to a number.

*(number1, number 2, ...) can also be specified as a range (C25:C47).

Changing the Sheet's Structure

	A	B	C	
1		Q1 94	Q2 94	Q
2	Income			
3	Beans	12400	13200	
4	T-Shirts	2600	2800	
5	Baked Goods	8800	9000	
6	Coffeemakers	1900	2100	
7	Gelato	5600	6700	

Figure 1. *The mouse pointer changes to a double arrow.*

	A	B	C	
1		Q1 94	Q2 94	Q3
2	Income			
3	Beans	12400	13200	
4	T-Shirts	2600	2800	
5	Baked Goods	8800	9000	
6	Coffeemakers	1900	2100	
7	Gelato	5600	6700	

Figure 2. *Drag right or left to widen or narrow the column below.*

	A	B	C
1		Q1 94	Q2 94
2	Income		
3	Beans	12400	1320
4	T-Shirts	2600	280
5	Baked Goods	8800	900
6	Coffeemakers	1900	210
7	Gelato	5600	670

Figure 3. *The newly widened column.*

	A	B
1		Q1 94
2	Income	
3	Beans	12
4	T-Shirts	2
5	Baked Goods	8

Figure 4. *The mouse pointer changes to a double arrow.*

Widening Columns and Rows

To change the width of a column:

1. Place the mouse pointer on the right edge of the gray column heading button for the column to widen. **(Figure 1)**
2. When the mouse pointer changes to a double arrow, drag right or left. **(Figures 2–3)**

To change the height of a row:

1. Place the mouse pointer on the bottom edge of the gray row heading button for the row to heighten. **(Figure 4)**
2. When the mouse pointer changes to a double arrow, drag up or down.

✔ Tips

- To change the width of multiple columns or rows, select the columns or rows by dragging across their column heading or row heading buttons. Then drag the edge of any column heading or row heading button that is selected. All the selected columns or rows will change uniformly.
- You can also select Column or Row on the Format menu and then choose Width or Height on the submenu to get to the Column Width or Row Height dialog boxes. On these dialog boxes, you can choose an exact setting.

Inserting and Deleting Rows and Columns

1. Click in any cell of the row or column where you'd like the new blank row or column. The remaining rows or columns will be pushed down or to the right. **(Figure 5)**
2. From the Insert menu choose Rows or Columns. **(Figures 6–7)**

✔ Tips

- To insert multiple columns, drag across the column heading buttons (labeled A, B, C, and so on) to highlight the locations of the new columns instead of Step 1 above. **(Figure 8)** To insert multiple rows, drag across row heading buttons, instead.
- You can also click a column or row heading button to select the destination for a new column or row or the column or row to be deleted. Next, while holding down the Control key, click the mouse button and choose Insert or Delete from the shortcut menu.

	A	B	C	D	
1		Q1 94	Q2 94	Q3 94	Q4
2	Income				
3	Beans	12400	13200	15000	
4	T-Shirts	2600	2800	3100	
5	Baked Goods	8800	9000	10100	
6	Coffeemakers	1900	2100	2400	
7	Gelato	5600	6700	11200	
8					
9	Expenses				
10	Personnel	6200	6500	6900	
11	Overhead	4100	4100	4300	
12	Taxes	1900	1900	1900	
13	Services	950	990	1100	
14					

Figure 5. *Click in a cell in the column where you'd like a new column inserted.*

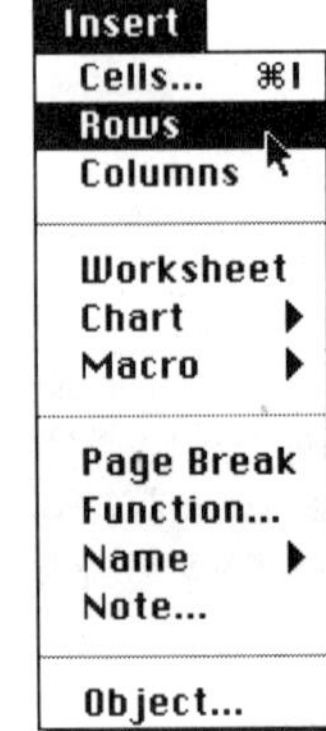

Figure 6. *The Insert menu.*

	A	B	C	D	
1		Q1 94	Q2 94	Q3 94	Q4
2	Income				
3	Beans	12400	13200	15000	
4	T-Shirts	2600	2800	3100	
5	Baked Goods	8800	9000	10100	
6	Coffeemakers	1900	2100	2400	
7	Gelato	5600	6700	11200	
8					
9					
10	Expenses				
11	Personnel	6200	6500	6900	
12	Overhead	4100	4100	4300	
13	Taxes	1900	1900	1900	
14	Services	950	990	1100	

Figure 7. *New blank row.*

	A	B	C	
1		Q1 94	Q2 94	Q3
2	Income			
3	Beans	12400	13200	
4	T-Shirts	2600	2800	
5	Baked Goods	8800	9000	
6	Coffeemakers	1900	2100	
7	Gelato	5600	6700	
8				

Figure 8. *Drag across two row heading buttons to specify two rows for insertion.*

	A	B	C	D	E
1		Q1 94	Q2 94	Q3 94	Q4 94
2	Income				
3	Beans	12400	13200	15000	16900
4	T-Shirts	2600	2800	3100	4700
5	Baked Goods	8800	9000	10100	11500
6	Coffeemakers	1900	2100	2400	2600
7	Gelato	5600	6700	11200	9400
8	Grinders	2200	2400	2800	
9					

Figure 9. *Click a cell.*

Inserting and Deleting Cells

When you tell Excel to insert or delete a cell within a range of data, Excel needs to know how to move the data that's in adjacent cells. You specify your choice on the Insert or Delete dialog box.

1. Click at the destination for the new, blank cell. **(Figure 9)**

   or

   Click on the cell you want to delete.
2. To insert a cell, choose Cells from the Insert menu **(Figure 10)** or click the mouse button while pressing Control and choose Insert from the shortcut menu.

   or

   To delete a cell, choose Delete from the Edit menu **(Figure 11)** or click the mouse button while pressing Control and choose Delete from the shortcut menu.
3. On the Insert dialog box, select either Shift Cells Right or Shift Cells Down. **(Figure 12)**

   or

   On the Delete dialog box, select either Shift Cells Left or Shift Cells Up. **(Figure 13)**

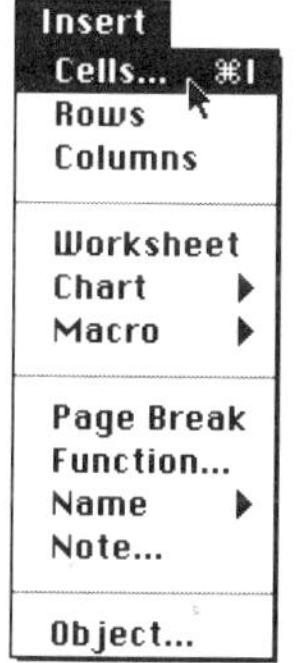

Figure 10. *The Insert menu.*

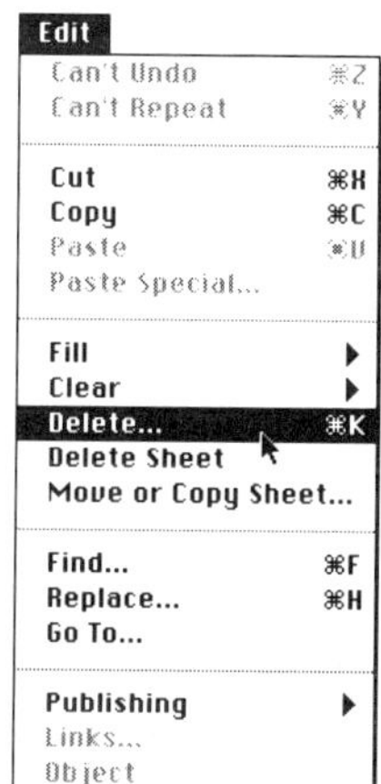

Figure 11. *The Edit menu.*

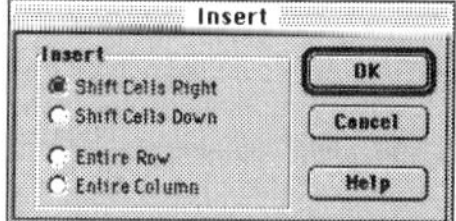

Figure 12. *The Insert dialog box.*

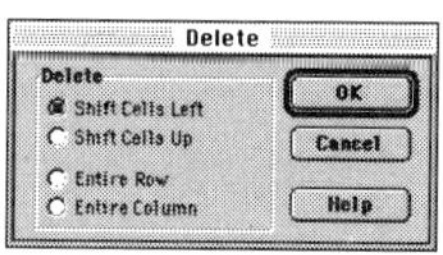

Figure 13. *The Delete dialog box.*

	A	B	C	D	E
1		Q1 94	Q2 94	Q3 94	Q4 94
2	Income				
3	Beans	12400	13200	15000	16900
4	T-Shirts	2600	2800	3100	4700
5	Baked Goods	8800	9000	10100	11500
6	Coffeemakers	1900	2100	2400	2600
7	Gelato	5600	6700	11200	9400
8	Grinders		2200	2400	2800

Cells shifted to the right.

Figure 14. *Inserted cell.*

Moving and Copying Data

Excel's drag and drop makes moving and copying data especially easy.

1. Select the range of cells to move or copy. **(Figure 15)**
2. Place the mouse pointer on the border of the range so the pointer becomes an arrow. **(Figure 16)**
3. To move the cells, drag the border of the range to move the range to a new location. **(Figure 17)**

   or

   To copy the cells, press and hold Option while dragging the border of the range. A small plus appears next to the mouse pointer to indicate that you are copying rather than moving. **(Figure 18)**
4. Release the mouse button to drop the range at the new location. **(Figure 19)**

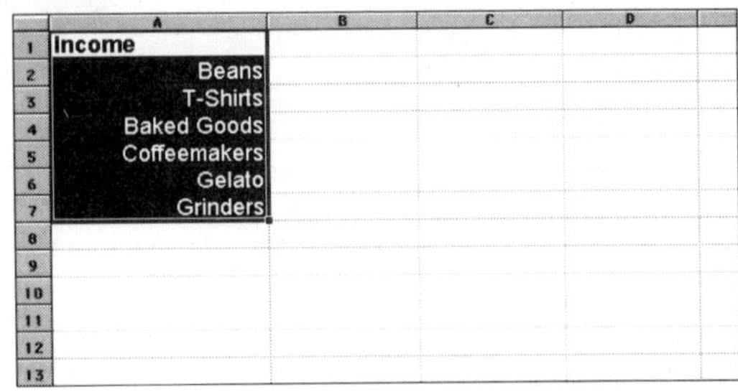

Figure 15. *Select a range of cells.*

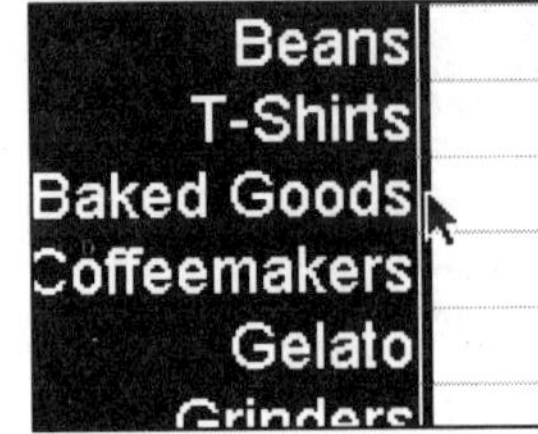

Figure 16. *The mouse pointer on the range border.*

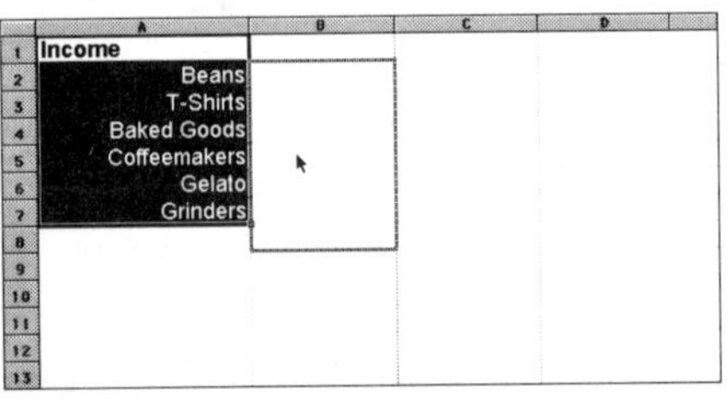

Figure 17. *Drag the border of the range to move the range.*

Figure 18. *The small plus sign next to the mouse pointer shows that a copy is in progress.*

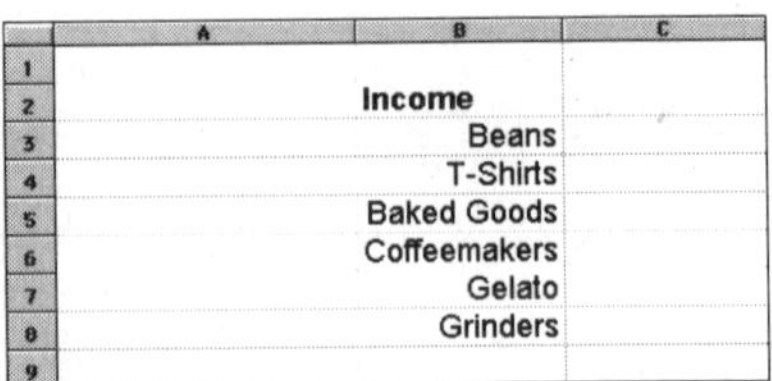

Figure 19. *The range moved to its new location.*

Moving/Copying Data

Microsoft Excel

	A	B	C	D	E
1		Q1 94	Q2 94	Q3 94	Q4 94
2	Income				
3	Beans	12400	13200	15000	16900
4	T-Shirts	2600	2800	3100	4700
5	Baked Goods	8800	9000	10100	11500
6	Coffeemakers	1900	2100	2400	2600
7	Gelato	5600	6700	11200	9400
8	Grinders	2100	2200	2400	2800
9					
10	Expenses				
11	Personnel	6200	6500	6900	7200
12	Supplies	4100	4100	4300	4500
13	Utilities	820	840	840	880
14	Packaging	1100	1200	1400	1500
15	L&P	2000	0	1200	0
16	Accounting	620	740	750	1000
17	Taxes	1900	1900	1900	1900
18	Other Services	950	990	1100	1150
19					
20	Net	15710	19730	25810	29770
21	Cumulative	15710	35440	61250	91020
22					

Figure 20. *Click at the upper left corner of the data range.*

Freezing the Headings

To keep the column and row headings from scrolling off the screen while you scroll through a large worksheet, you can *freeze* the headings.

1. Click on the cell at the upper left corner of the region that contains the data. **(Figure 20)**
2. From the Window menu, choose Freeze Panes. **(Figures 21-22)**

✓ Tips

- Pressing ⌘+Home now moves the cell pointer to the upper left corner of the data range.
- To unfreeze the panes, choose Unfreeze Panes from the Window menu.

Figure 21. *The Window menu.*

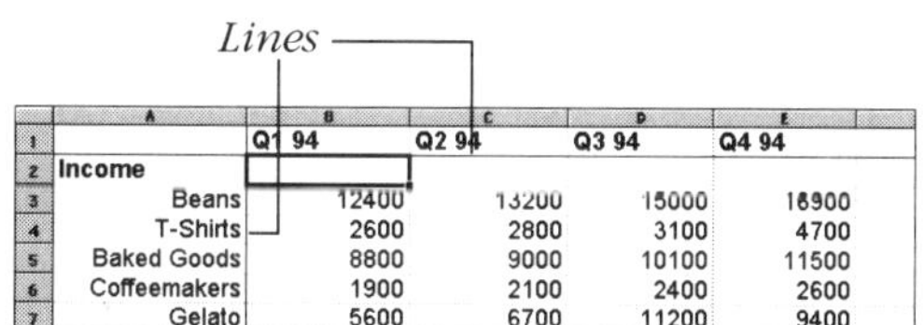

	A	B	C	D	E
1		Q1 94	Q2 94	Q3 94	Q4 94
2	Income				
3	Beans	12400	13200	15000	16900
4	T-Shirts	2600	2800	3100	4700
5	Baked Goods	8800	9000	10100	11500
6	Coffeemakers	1900	2100	2400	2600
7	Gelato	5600	6700	11200	9400

Figure 22. *Lines appear to indicate which areas of the sheet are frozen.*

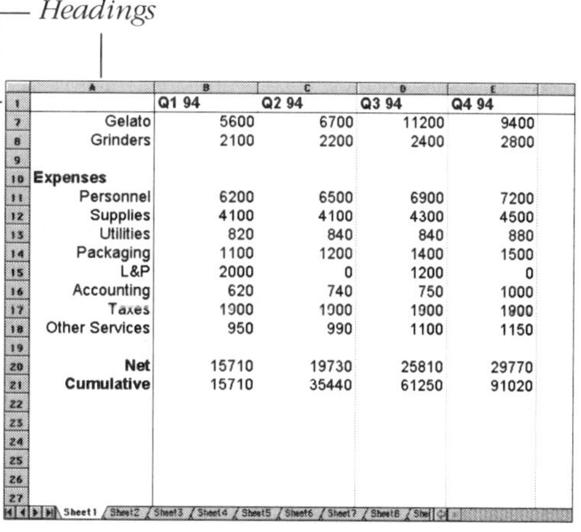

	A	B	C	D	E
1		Q1 94	Q2 94	Q3 94	Q4 94
7	Gelato	5600	6700	11200	9400
8	Grinders	2100	2200	2400	2800
9					
10	Expenses				
11	Personnel	6200	6500	6900	7200
12	Supplies	4100	4100	4300	4500
13	Utilities	820	840	840	880
14	Packaging	1100	1200	1400	1500
15	L&P	2000	0	1200	0
16	Accounting	620	740	750	1000
17	Taxes	1900	1900	1900	1900
18	Other Services	950	990	1100	1150
19					
20	Net	15710	19730	25810	29770
21	Cumulative	15710	35440	61250	91020
22					
23					
24					
25					
26					
27					

Figure 23. *The headings stay frozen when you scroll through the data..*

Splitting a Sheet

Splitting a sheet lets you display and scroll through four different regions of the sheet independently.

1. Click in the cell that you want to become the upper left corner of the bottom right pane. **(Figure 24)**
2. From the Window menu, choose Split. **(Figure 25)**

✔ Tips

- To remove the split, choose Remove Split from the Window menu.
- You can drag the thick split lines to change the relative sizes of the panes. **(Figure 26)**

	A	B	C	D	E
1		Q1 94	Q2 94	Q3 94	Q4 94
2	Income				
3	Beans	12400	13200	15000	16900
4	T-Shirts	2600	2800	3100	4700
5	Baked Goods	8800	9000	10100	11500
6	Coffeemakers	1900	2100	2400	2600
7	Gelato	5600	6700	11200	9400
8	Grinders	2100	2200	2400	2800
9					
10	Expenses				
11	Personnel	6200	6500	6900	7200
12	Supplies	4100	4100	4300	4500
13	Utilities	820	840	840	880
14	Packaging	1100	1200	1400	1500
15	L&P	2000	0	1200	0
16	Accounting	620	740	750	1000
17	Taxes	1900	1900	1900	1900
18	Other Services	950	990	1100	1150
19					
20	Net	15710	19730	25810	29770

Figure 24. *Click on a cell.*

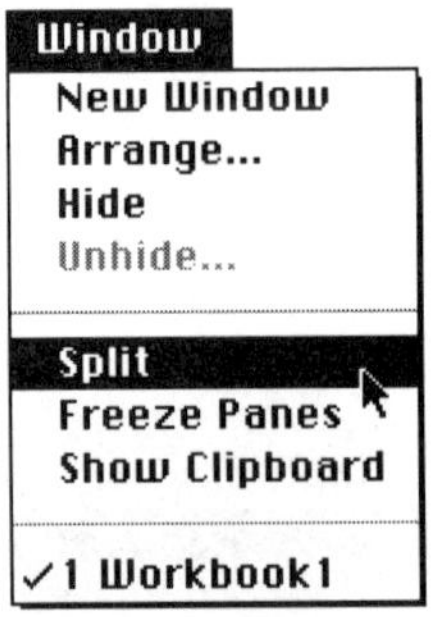

Window
New Window
Arrange...
Hide
Unhide...
Split
Freeze Panes
Show Clipboard
✓1 Workbook1

Figure 25. *The Window menu.*

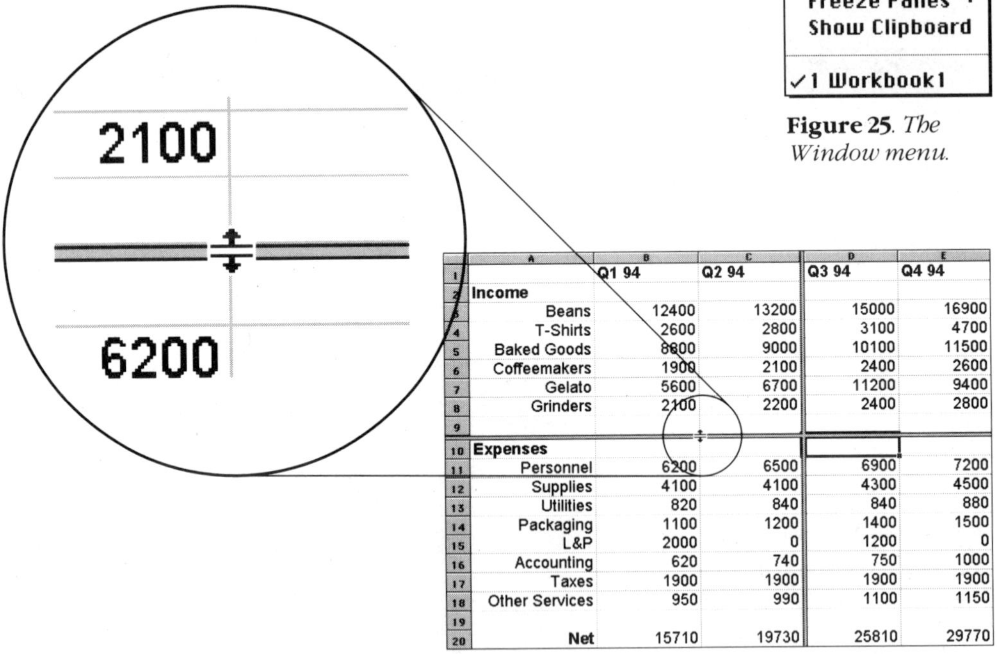

	A	B	C	D	E
1		Q1 94	Q2 94	Q3 94	Q4 94
2	Income				
3	Beans	12400	13200	15000	16900
4	T-Shirts	2600	2800	3100	4700
5	Baked Goods	8800	9000	10100	11500
6	Coffeemakers	1900	2100	2400	2600
7	Gelato	5600	6700	11200	9400
8	Grinders	2100	2200	2400	2800
9					
10	Expenses				
11	Personnel	6200	6500	6900	7200
12	Supplies	4100	4100	4300	4500
13	Utilities	820	840	840	880
14	Packaging	1100	1200	1400	1500
15	L&P	2000	0	1200	0
16	Accounting	620	740	750	1000
17	Taxes	1900	1900	1900	1900
18	Other Services	950	990	1100	1150
19					
20	Net	15710	19730	25810	29770

2100

6200

Figure 26. *Click and drag here to change the sizes of the panes.*

Formatting the Sheet

	A	B	C	D
1	Book Sales			
2				
3		Hardcover	Paperback	Total
4	Jan	160	535	695
5	Feb	158	570	728
6	Mar	173	595	768
7	Apr	156	547	703
8	May	190	580	770
9	Jun	210	595	805
10	1st Half	1,047	3,422	4,469
11	Jul	225	620	845
12	Aug	230	816	1,046
13	Sep	189	585	774
14	Oct	202	612	814
15	Nov	212	690	902
16	Dec	525	1,139	1,664
17	2nd Half	1,583	4,462	6,045
18	Total	2,630	7,884	10,514
19				

Figure 1. *Click on a cell in the range to format.*

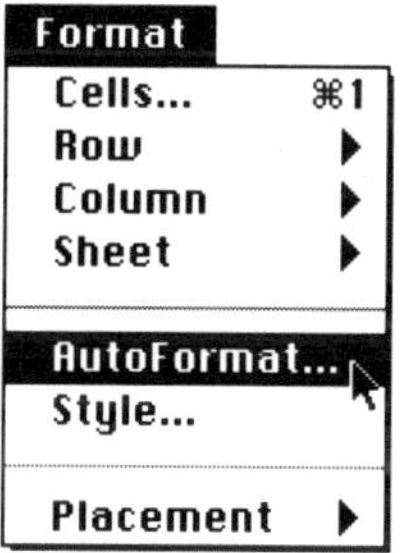

Figure 2. *The Format menu.*

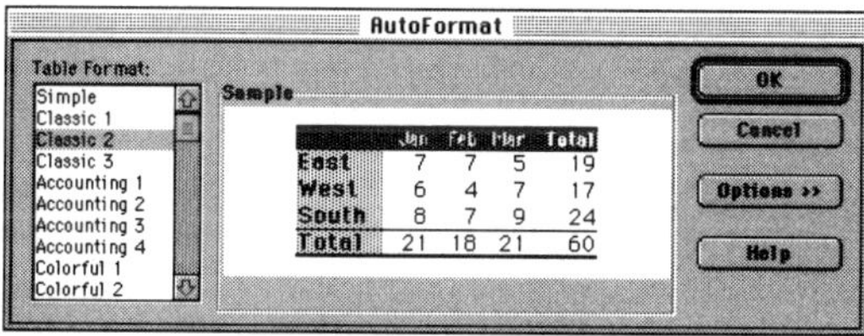

Figure 3. *The AutoFormat dialog box.*

Choosing an AutoFormat

The fastest and easiest way to make a sheet presentable is to give it an AutoFormat. An AutoFormat contains a complete look for a range of data by changing the font, text alignment, number formatting, borders, patterns, colors, column widths, and row heights. Excel provides a selection of AutoFormats, each with a different look.

1. Click any cell in the range to format. **(Figure 1)**
   or
   Select the range to format.
2. From the Format menu, choose AutoFormat. **(Figure 2)**
3. On the AutoFormat dialog box, select an AutoFormat from the list and then click OK. **(Figures 3–4)**

✔ Tips

- To remove an AutoFormat immediately after applying it, use Undo.
- To remove an AutoFormat later, select the range, follow Steps 2 and 3 above, and then choose None from the list of AutoFormats.

	A	B	C	D	E
1	Book Sales				
2					
3		Hardcover	Paperback	Total	
4	Jan	160	535	695	
5	Feb	158	570	728	
6	Mar	173	595	768	
7	Apr	156	547	703	
8	May	190	580	770	
9	Jun	210	595	805	
10	1st Half	1,047	3,422	4,469	
11	Jul	225	620	845	
12	Aug	230	816	1,046	
13	Sep	189	585	774	
14	Oct	202	612	814	
15	Nov	212	690	902	
16	Dec	525	1,139	1,664	
17	2nd Half	1,583	4,462	6,045	
18	Total	2,630	7,884	10,514	
19					

Figure 4. *The AutoFormatted range.*

Text Formatting

1. Select the cell or cells that contain the text to format. **(Figure 5)**
2. Choose formatting options by clicking the text formatting buttons on the Formatting toolbar. **(Figure 6)**

or

1. Select the cell or cells that contain the text to format.
2. From the Format menu, choose Cells or click while pressing Control and choose Format Cells from the shortcut menu.
3. On the Format Cells dialog box, change options on the Alignment and Font tabs. **(Figures 7-8)**

	A	B	C
1	Book Sales		
2			
3		Hardcover	Paperba
4	Jan	160	5
5	Feb	158	5
6	Mar	173	5

Figure 5. *Select the cells with the text to format.*

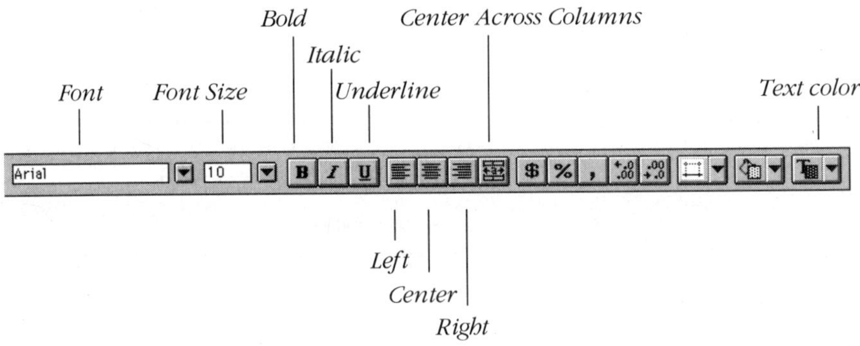

Figure 6. *The text formatting buttons on the Formatting toolbar.*

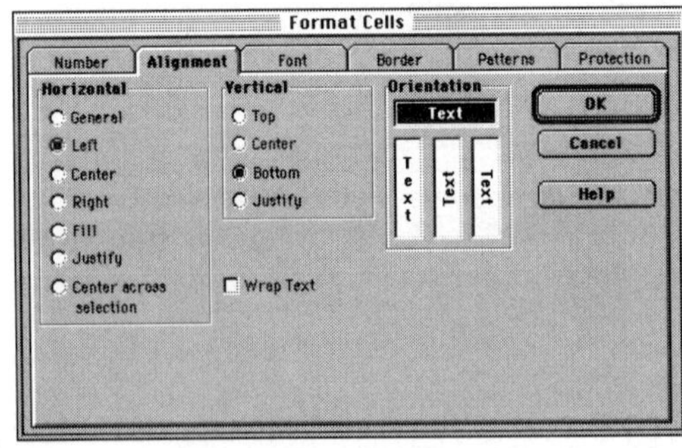

Figures 7. *The Alignment tab.*

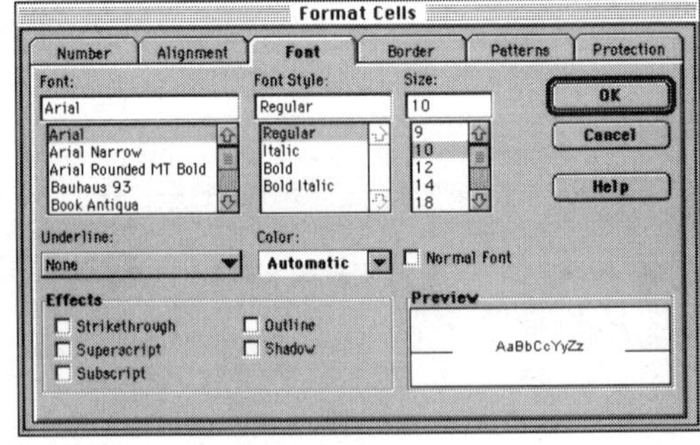

Figure 8. *The Font tab.*

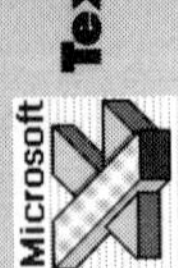

	A	B	C	D
1	Book Sales			
2				
3		Hardcover	Paperback	Total
4	Jan	160	535	695
5	Feb	158	570	728
6	Mar	173	595	768
7	Apr	156	547	703
8	May	190	580	770

Figure 9. *Enter the title in the leftmost cell above the range.*

Centering a Title Above a Range

1. Type the title into the leftmost cell above the range. **(Figure 9)**
2. Select the cells above the range. **(Figure 10)**
3. Click the Center Across Columns button. **(Figure 11)**

   or

   From the Format menu, choose Cells. Then choose Center Across Selection on the Alignment tab of the Format Cells dialog box. **(Figure 12)**

✔ Tip

- Click the Center Across Columns button again to return the text to left aligned.

	A	B	C	D
1	Book Sales			
2				
3		Hardcover	Paperback	Total
4	Jan	160	535	695
5	Feb	158	570	728
6	Mar	173	595	768
7	Apr	156	547	703
8	May	190	580	770

Figure 10. *Select the cells above the range.*

Center Across Columns button.

Figure 11. *The Center Across Columns button.*

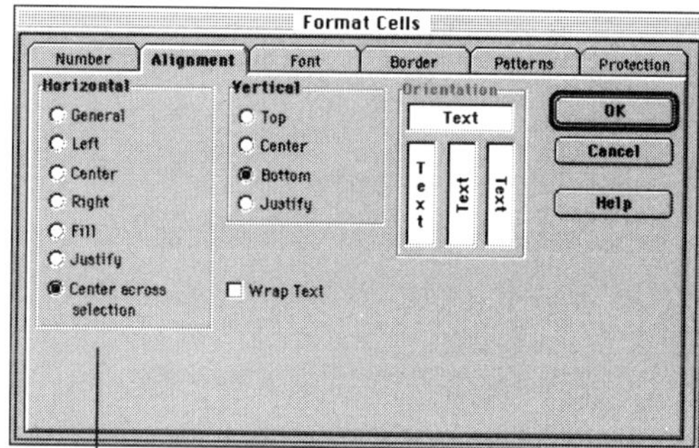

Figure 12. *Click here to center the text across the selected cells.*

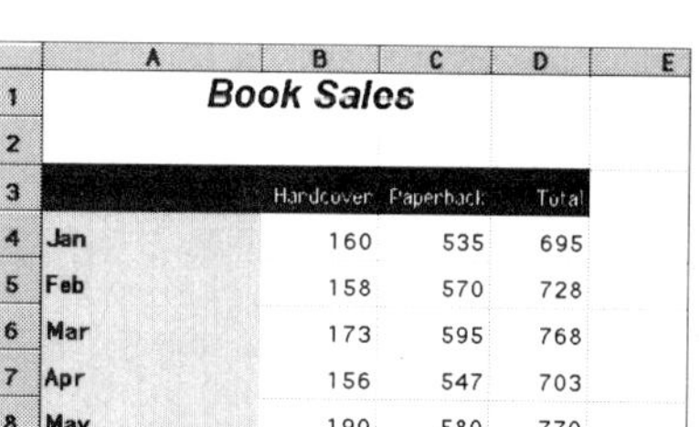

	A	B	C	D	E
1		Book Sales			
2					
3		Hardcover	Paperback	Total	
4	Jan	160	535	695	
5	Feb	158	570	728	
6	Mar	173	595	768	
7	Apr	156	547	703	
8	May	190	580	770	

Figure 13. *The centered title.*

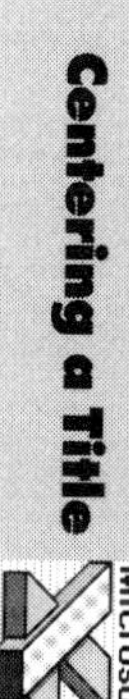

Excel

Number Formatting

1. Select the numbers to format. **(Figure 14)**
2. Click the appropriate number formatting button on the Formatting toolbar. **(Figure 15)**

   or

   From the Format menu, choose Cells and then, on the Number tab of the Format Cells dialog box, choose a Category and Formatting Code. **(Figure 16)**

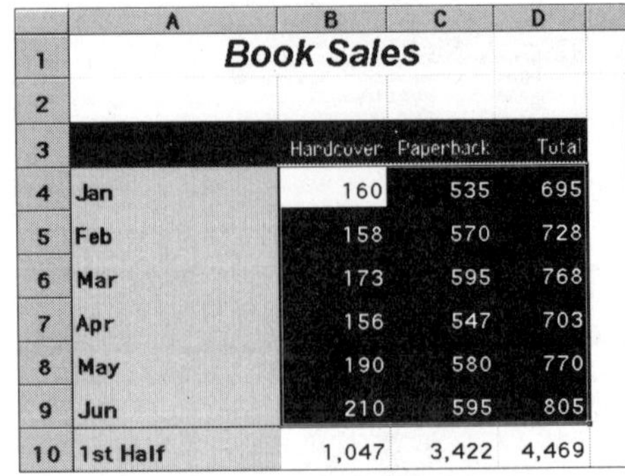

	A	B	C	D
1	Book Sales			
2				
3		Hardcover	Paperback	Total
4	Jan	160	535	695
5	Feb	158	570	728
6	Mar	173	595	768
7	Apr	156	547	703
8	May	190	580	770
9	Jun	210	595	805
10	1st Half	1,047	3,422	4,469

Figure 14. *Select the numbers to format.*

✔ Tips

- Until you choose a special number format, numbers are formatted with the General number format (right aligned, up to 11 decimal places).
- If you enter numbers preceded by a dollar sign, Excel automatically applies Currency formatting. If you enter numbers followed by a percent sign, Excel automatically applies Percentage formatting.
- Number formatting can be saved as a style. *See Creating Styles, page 144.*

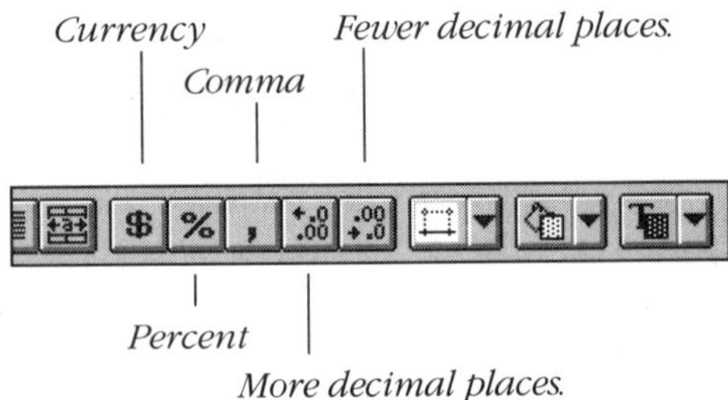

Figure 15. *The number formatting buttons on the Formatting toolbar.*

Number Formatting

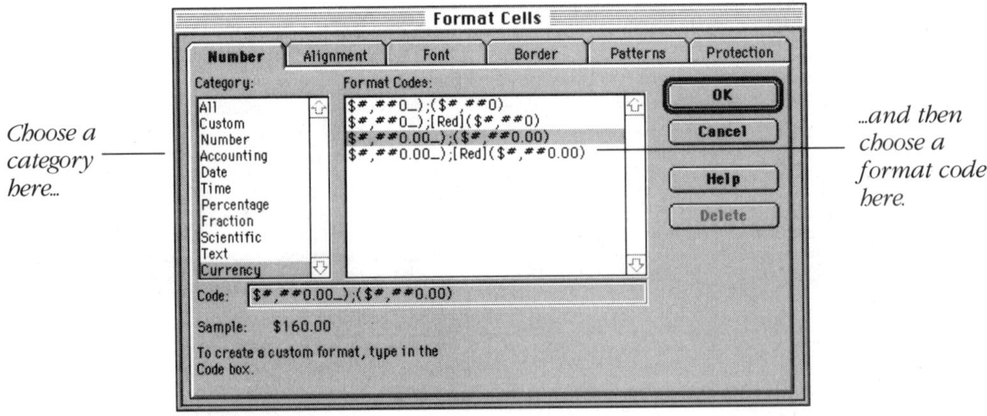

Figure 16. *The Number tab of the Format Cells dialog box.*

	A	B	C	D
1		Book Sales		
2				
3		Hardcover	Paperback	Total
4	Jan	160	535	695
5	Feb	158	570	728
6	Mar	173	595	768
7	Apr	156	547	703
8	May	190	580	770

Figure 17. *Select the range first.*

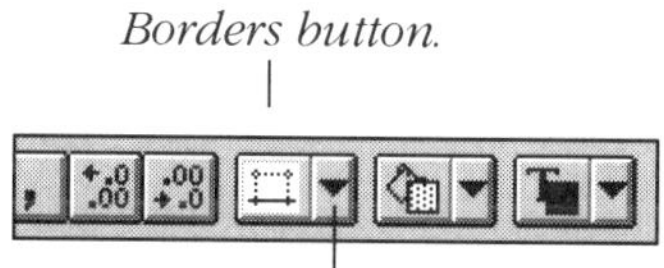

Figure 18. *Click here to see the available borders.*

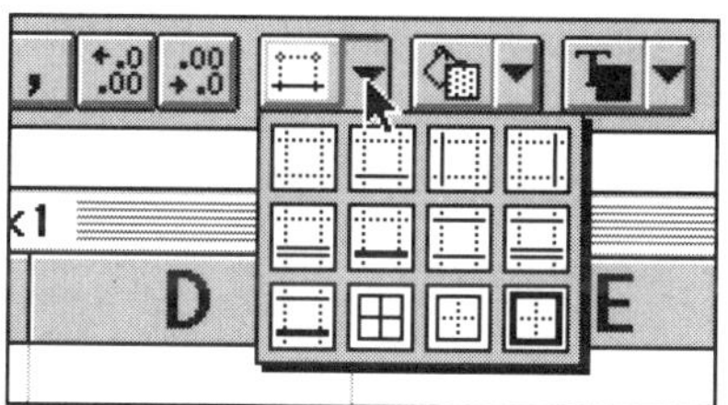

Figure 19. *Select one of these panes to choose the border it displays.*

	A	B	C	D
1		Book Sales		
2				
3		Hardcover	Paperback	Total
4	Jan	160	535	695
5	Feb	158	570	728
6	Mar	173	595	768
7	Apr	156	547	703
8	May	190	580	770

Figure 20. *A border added to the range.*

Adding Borders to a Range

A border is a line at the edge of a cell. You can use borders to divide the information on the sheet into logical regions. Borders both appear on the screen and print out when you print the sheet.

1. Select the range to which you'd like to apply a border. **(Figure 17)**
2. Click the pull down button next to the Borders button to see the full range of borders. **(Figure 18)**
3. Select the pane on the display of borders that matches the border you want for the range. **(Figures 19-20)**

or

1. Select the range to which you'd like to apply a border.
2. From the Format menu, choose Cells or click while pressing Control and choose Format Cells from the shortcut menu.
3. On the Border tab of the Format Cells dialog box, choose a border, a border style, and a color. **(Figure 21)**

✔ Tips

- To choose the most recently used border, you can click the Borders button.
- To remove the borders around a range, select the range, pull down the display of borders and choose the pane at the upper left corner.

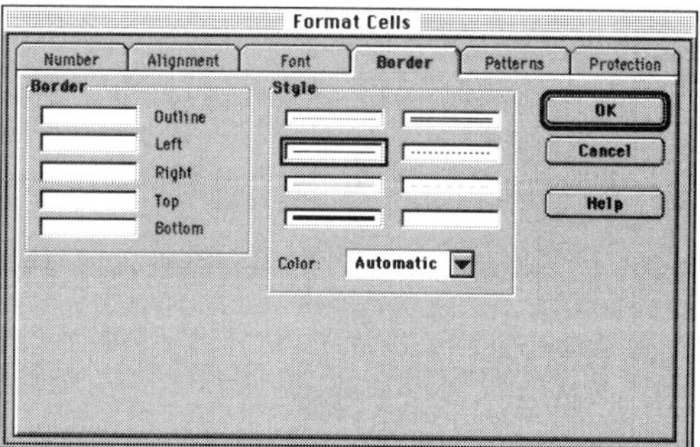

Figure 21. *The Border tab of the Format Cells dialog box.*

Adding Shading to a Range

1. Select the range to which you'd like to add shading. **(Figure 22)**
2. From the Format menu, choose Cells, or click while pressing Control and choose Format Cells from the shortcut menu.
3. On the Patterns tab of the Format Cells dialog box, choose a color if you want the shading to be other than gray. Otherwise, pull down the list of patterns and choose one of the shades of gray at the top of the display of patterns. **(Figures 23–24)**

✔ **Tip**

- Shading is often applied automatically to parts of a range when you select an AutoFormat.

	A	B	C	D
1	Book Sales			
2				
3		Hardcover	Paperback	Total
4	Jan	160	535	695
5	Feb	158	570	728
6	Mar	173	595	768
7	Apr	156	547	703
8	May	190	580	770
9	Jun	210	595	805
10	1st Half	1,047	3,422	4,469
11	Jul	225	620	845
12	Aug	230	816	1,046
13	Sep	189	585	774
14	Oct	202	612	814
15	Nov	212	690	902
16	Dec	525	1,139	1,664
17	2nd Half	1,583	4,462	6,045
18	Total	2,630	7,884	10,514
19				

Figure 22. *Select the range to shade.*

Shades of gray

Figure 23. *Choose one of these patterns to shade the selected cells.*

	A	B	C	D
1	Book Sales			
2				
3		Hardcover	Paperback	Total
4	Jan	160	535	695
5	Feb	158	570	728
6	Mar	173	595	768
7	Apr	156	547	703
8	May	190	580	770
9	Jun	210	595	805
10	1st Half	1,047	3,422	4,469
11	Jul	225	620	845

Figure 24. *The shaded cells.*

	A	B	C	D
1	Book Sales			
2				
3		Hardcover	Paperback	Total
4	Jan	160	535	695
5	Feb	158	570	728
6	Mar	173	595	768
7	Apr	156	547	703
8	May	190	580	770
9	Jun	210	595	805
10	1st Half	1,047	3,432	4,469
11	Jul	225	620	845
12	Aug	230	816	1,046
13	Sep	189	585	774
14	Oct	202	612	814
15	Nov	212	690	902
16	Dec	525	1,139	1,664
17	2nd Half	1,583	4,462	6,045
18	*Total*	2,630	7,884	10,514
19				

Figure 25. *Select the cells to format.*

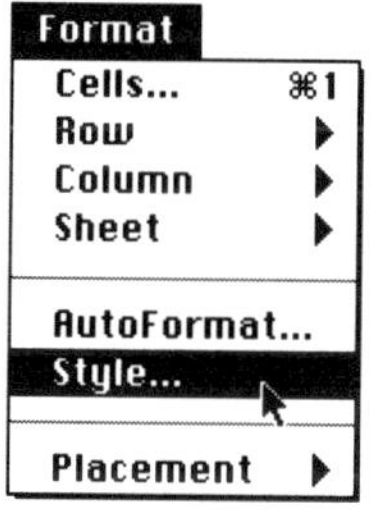

Figure 26. *The Format menu.*

Selecting Styles

A style is a preset combination of formatting. You can choose one of the existing styles or create your own.

1. Select the cells to format. **(Figure 25)**
2. From the Format menu, choose Style. **(Figure 26)**
   or
   Press ⌘+Shift+L.
3. On the Style dialog box, choose a style from the drop-down Style Name list. **(Figure 27)**
4. Make sure the checkboxes on the Style dialog box are checked for the formatting aspects that you'd like the style to apply.

✔ Tips

- Styles on the style list that are followed with a (0) are formatted to zero decimal places.
- Cells are given the Normal style unless you specify a different style.
- To change the default cell formatting, modify the Normal style. *See Creating Styles, page 144.*

Choose a style here.

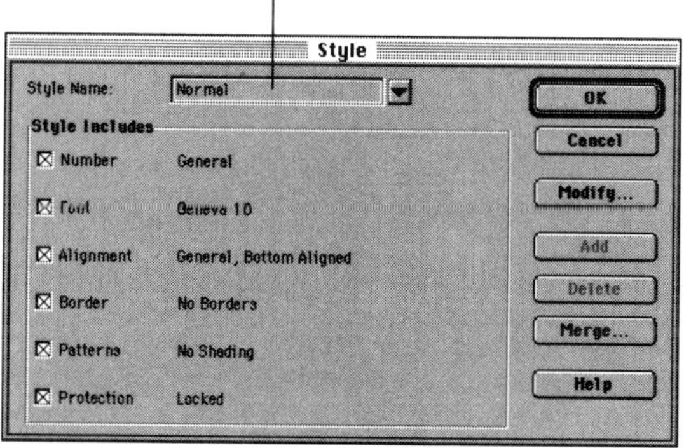

Figure 27. *The Style dialog box.*

Creating Styles

1. Format a cell with all the formatting you want. **(Figure 28)** *See Text Formatting, page 138, and Number Formatting, page 140.*
2. From the Format menu, choose Style. **(Figure 29)**

   or

   Press ⌘+Shift+L.
3. Type a new style name into the Style text box. **(Figure 30)**
4. Click OK.

✔ Tip

- By clicking the Merge button on the Style dialog box, you can copy the styles from another open workbook.

12	Aug	230	816	1,046
13	Sep	189	585	774
14	Oct	202	612	814
15	Nov	212	690	902
16	Dec	525	1,139	1,664
17	2nd Half	1,583	4,462	6,045
18	Total	$ 2,630	7,884	10,514
19				

Figure 28. *Format a sample cell.*

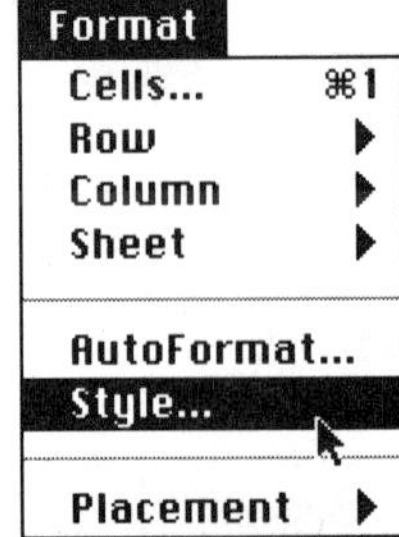

Figure 29. *The Format menu.*

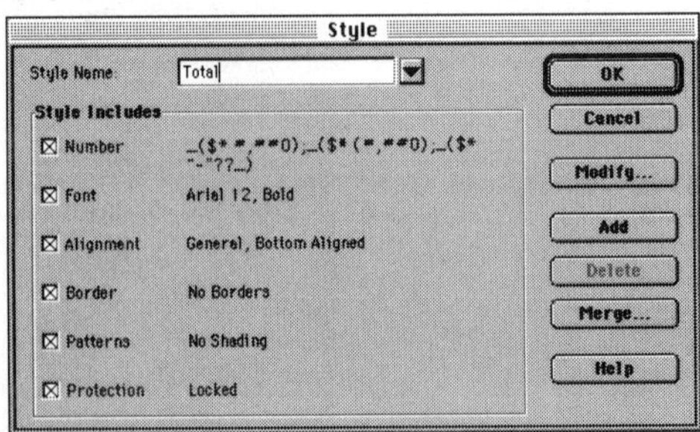

Figure 30. *Type a new style name into the Style text box.*

Working with Multiple Sheets

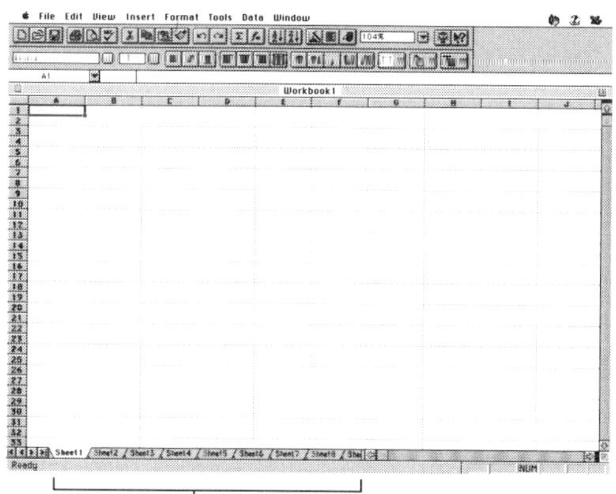

Figure 1. *The Worksheet tabs.*

Figure 2. *To bring a worksheet to the front, click its tab.*

About Using Multiple Sheets

Each Excel workbook contains 16 worksheets. You may use only the first worksheet for all your data and calculations. But you also might want to organize your information by placing certain data on each worksheet and then consolidating the results on a grand total worksheet.

The worksheet tabs that are visible below the current sheet let you switch easily from sheet to sheet. **(Figure 1)**

Changing to Another Sheet

1. Click the tab of the sheet to display. **(Figure 2)**

✔ Tips

- If the tab is not visible, use the Tab scrolling buttons to scroll through the tabs. **(Figure 3)**
- You can rearrange the order of sheets by dragging their tabs to the left or right.

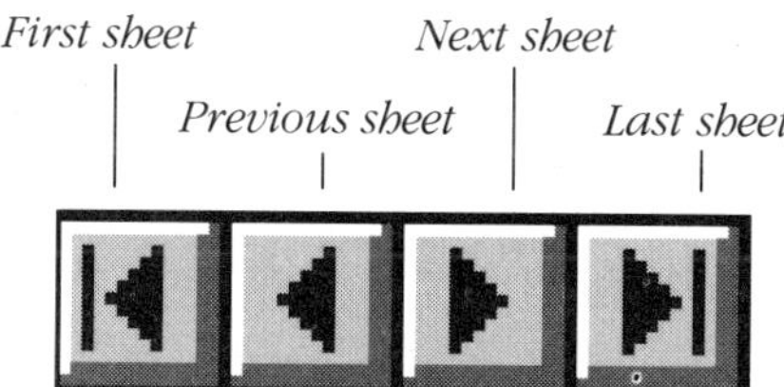

Figure 3. *The Tab scrolling buttons.*

Naming Sheets

Naming the sheets you use replaces the default names (Sheet1, Sheet2, and so on) with useful, informative names (Marketing, Manufacturing, Personnel, for example).

1. Double-click the tab of the sheet to rename. **(Figure 4)**
2. On the Rename Sheet dialog box, type the new name over the current name in the Name text box. **(Figure 5)**
3. Click OK. **(Figure 6)**

✔ **Tips**

- You can also choose Sheet Rename from the Format menu to get to the Rename Sheet dialog box.
- Sheet names can be up to 31 characters long and can include spaces.

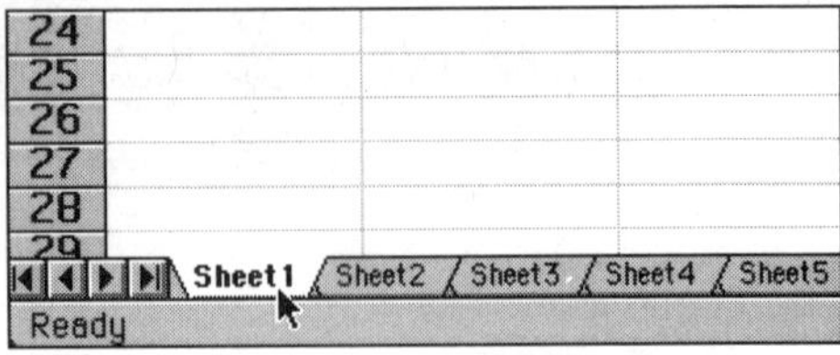

Figure 4. *Double-click a tab to rename the sheet.*

Figure 5. *The Rename Sheet dialog box.*

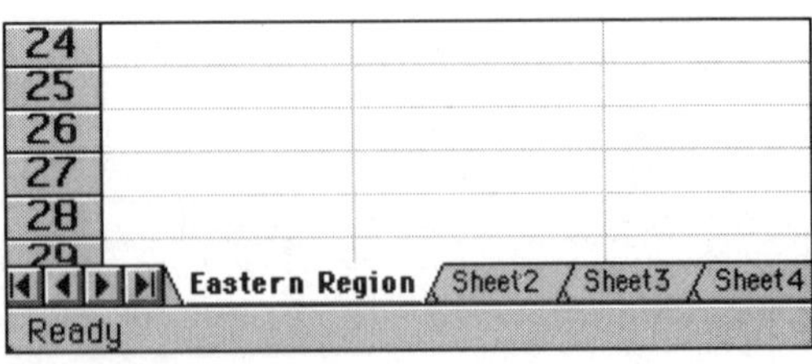

Figure 6. *The new name appears on the tab.*

Referring to Data from Other Sheets in Formulas

While building a formula, you can include data from another sheet.

1. Click in the destination cell for the formula. **(Figure 7)**
2. Start the formula as usual by entering an equals sign.
3. Refer to cells on other sheets by switching to the sheets and then selecting the cell or cells. **(Figure 8)**
4. Press Enter when you finish building the formula. You will be returned to the sheet where you started the formula. **(Figure 9)**

✔ Tip

- If you've named ranges in other sheets, you can enter the range names in the formula without worrying about which sheet the data is on. Excel will find the range on any sheet in the workbook.

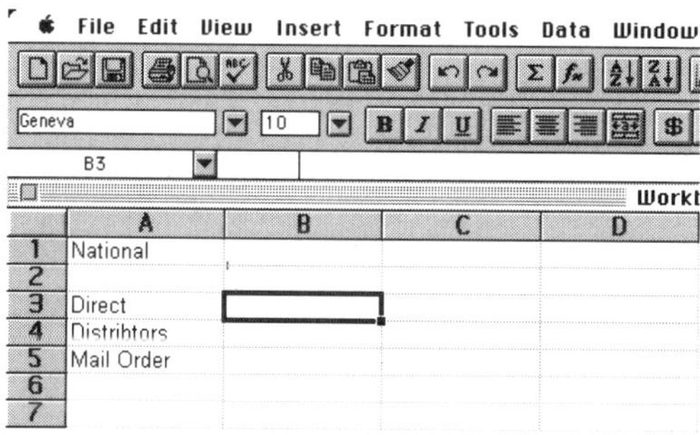

Figure 7. *Start the formula.*

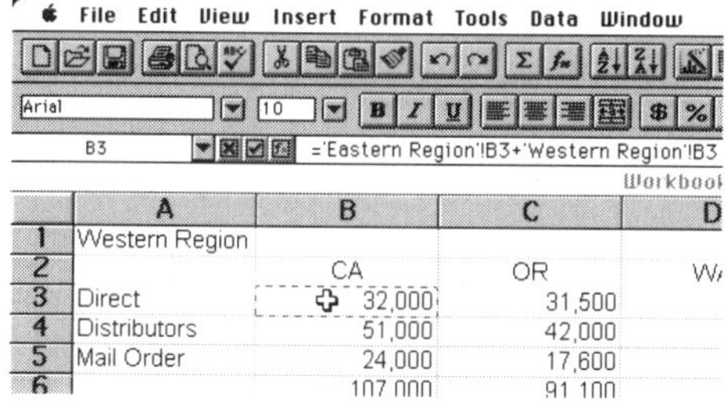

Figure 8. *Switch to another sheet and select the cells to include in the formula.*

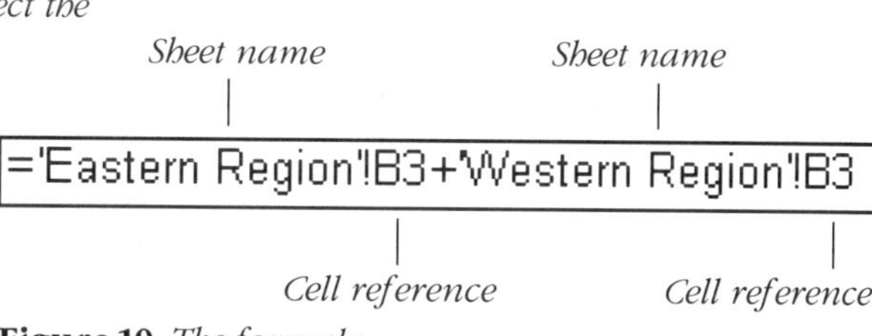

Figure 10. *The formula.*

Figure 9. *Press Enter to complete the formula.*

Referring to Sheets

Excel

Consolidating to a Sheet

When successive sheets of a workbook contain the exact same arrangement of data, you can sum ranges that extend "down" from sheet to sheet data rather than across a single sheet. This is called 3-D referencing. **(Figure 11)**

1. On the consolidation sheet, click in the destination cell for the formula. **(Figure 12)**
2. Start the formula by entering an equal sign followed by the function or operator, such as SUM, and the left parenthesis. **(Figure 13)**
3. Select the range on the first sheet in the range of sheets. **(Figure 14)**
4. Press and hold the Shift key on the keyboard.
5. Click the tab of the last sheet in the range. **(Figure 15)**
6. Press Enter. **(Figure 16)**

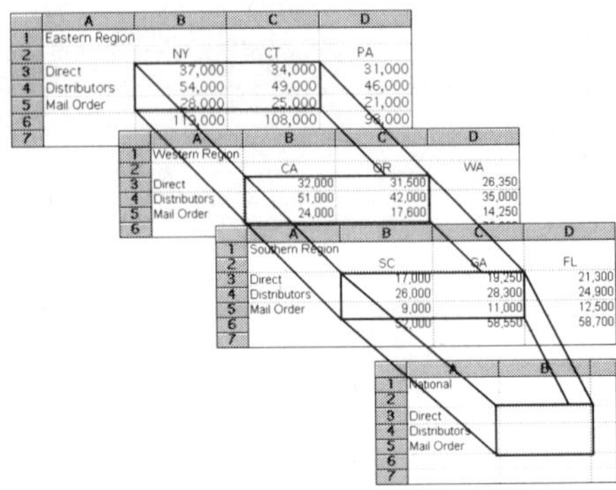

Figure 11. *3-D referencing*

	A	B
1	National	
2		
3	Direct	
4	Distributors	
5	Mail Order	
6		

Figure 12. *Click at the destination for the formula. (B3, in this case)*

	A	B
1	National	
2		
3	Direct	=sum(
4	Distributors	
5	Mail Order	
6		

Figure 13. *Start the formula as usual.*

B3 =sum('Eastern Region'!B3:D3

Workbook1

	A	B	C	D
1	Eastern Region			
2		NY	CT	PA
3	Direct	37,000	34,000	31,000
4	Distributors	54,000	49,000	46,000
5	Mail Order	28,000	25,000	21,000
6		119,000	108,000	98,000
7				

Figure 14. *Select the range on the first sheet.*

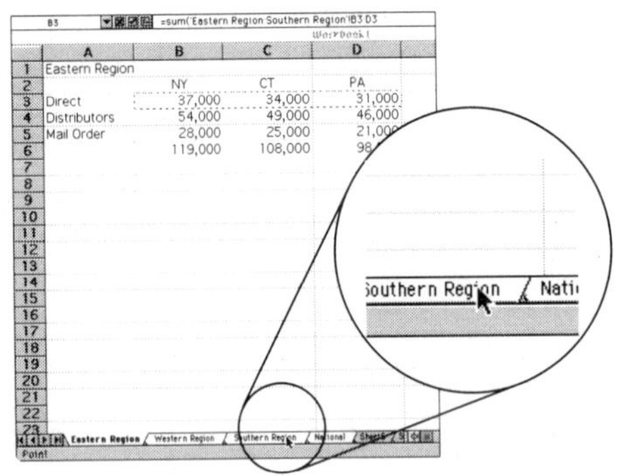

Figure 15. *While holding the Shift key, click the tab on the last range.*

The reference in the formula contains both a range of sheets and a range of cells.

B3 =SUM('Eastern Region:Southern Region'!B3:D3)

Workbook1

	A	B	C	D
1	National			
2				
3	Direct	249,400		
4	Distributors			
5	Mail Order			
6				

Figure 16. *The formula.*

Special Excel Techniques

Inserting Notes in Cells

A note is an annotation that you attach to a cell to provide information about the cell's contents. Notes can be text or sound.

1. Select the cell to which you want to attach a note. **(Figure 1)**
2. From the Insert menu, choose Note. **(Figure 2)**
3. On the Cell Note dialog box, type the text for the note into the Text Note box. **(Figure 3)**
4. Click OK.

✔ Tips

- A note is indicated by a note marker at the upper right corner of the cell (a small red dot). **(Figure 4)**
- To remove a note, double-click the cell containing the note, select the note on the Cell Note dialog box, and then click the Delete button on the dialog box.

Fundraiser Projected Revenue	Week 1	Week 2	Week 3	Week 4
Personal invitations	$ 2,600.00	$ 3,120.00	$ 2,470.00	$ 2,130.00
Mailing lists	650.00	1,300.00	1,560.00	1,040.00
Radio sales	1,105.00	1,235.00	780.00	260.00
Association list	2,340.00	4,030.00	1,820.00	1,235.00
Donations	390.00	650.00	520.00	325.00
	$ 7,085.00	$ 10,335.00	$ 7,150.00	$ 4,990.00

Figure 1. *Select a cell.*

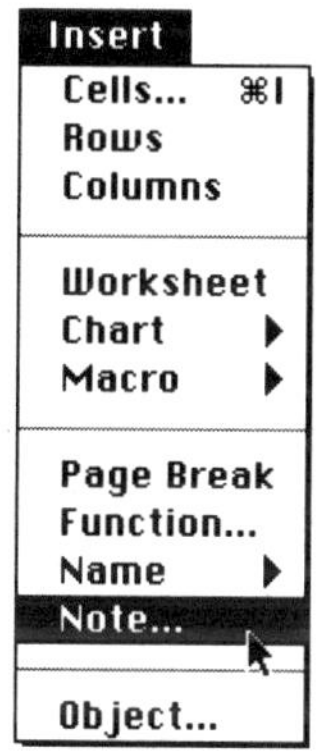

Figure 2. *The Insert menu.*

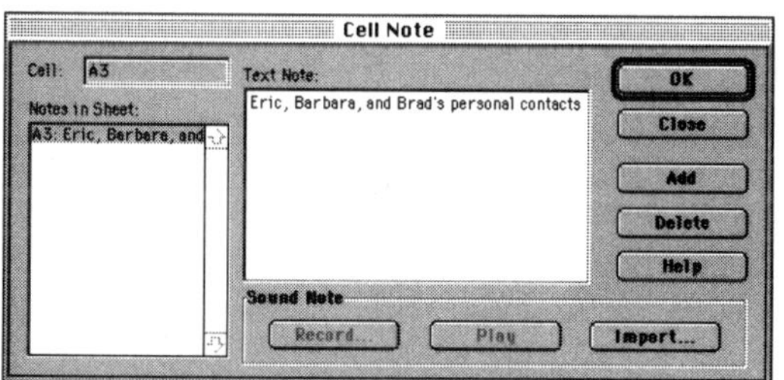

Figure 3. *The Cell Note dialog box.*

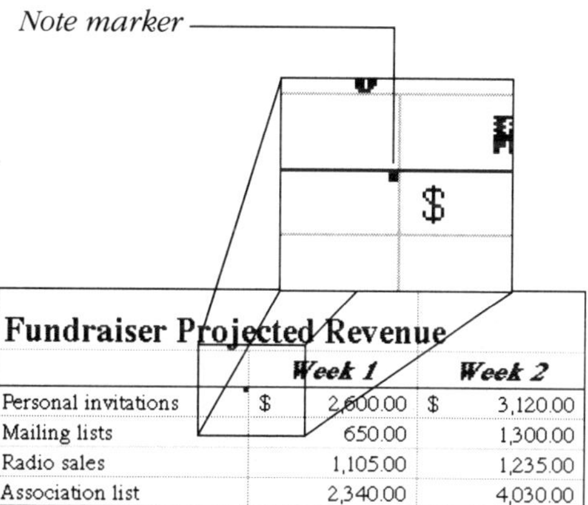

Figure 4. *Note marker.*

Naming Ranges

When you give a range a name, you can use the name in formulas rather than the range address. **(Figure 5)** Range names make it easier to refer to data and easier to understand formulas.

1. Select the range that you want to name. **(Figure 6)**
2. From the Insert menu, choose Name. **(Figure 7)**
3. On the Name submenu, choose Define.
4. Enter the name into the Define Name dialog box. **(Figure 8)**
5. Click OK.

✔ Tip

- You can give a name to an individual cell or a range of cells.

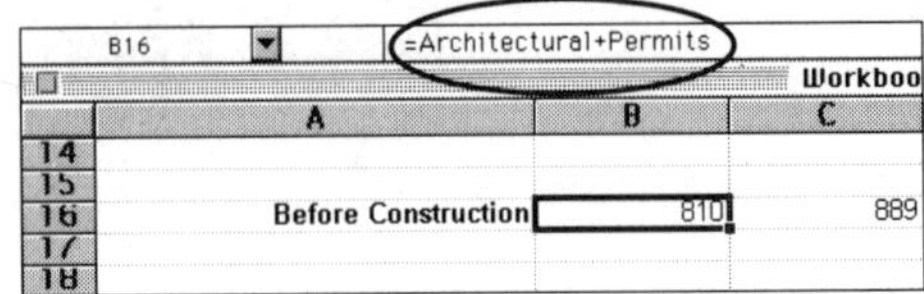

Figure 5. *Using range names in a formula.*

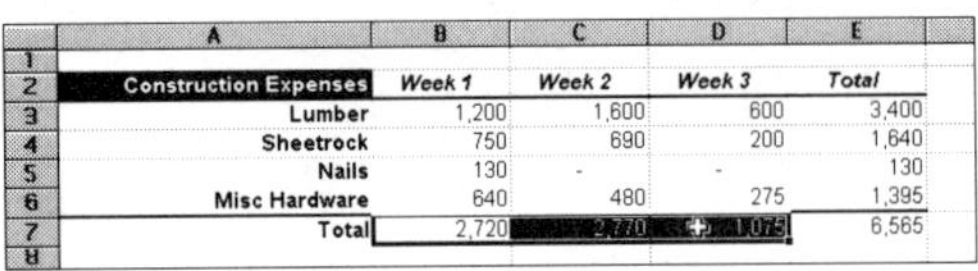

Figure 6. *Select the range to name.*

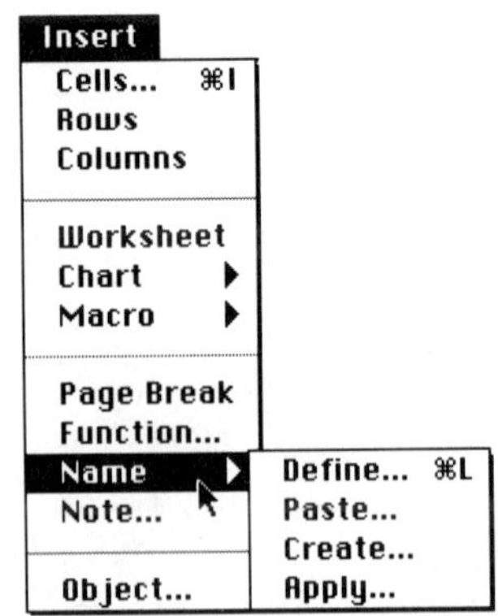

Figure 7. *The Insert menu.*

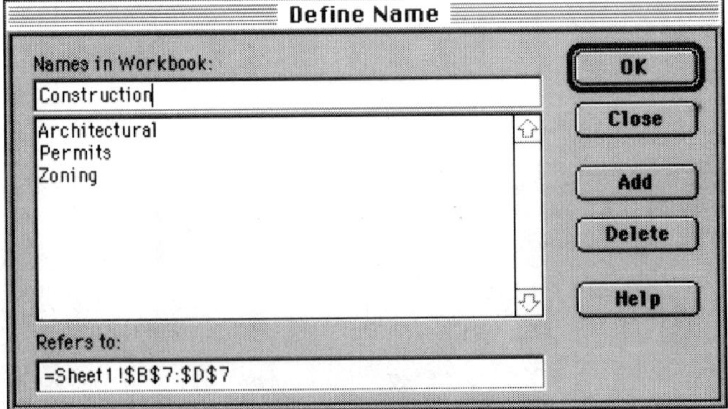

Figure 8. *The Define Name dialog box.*

	A	B	C	D	E
2	Construction Expenses	Week 1	Week 2	Week 3	Total
3	Lumber	1,200	1,600	600	3,400
4	Sheetrock	750	690	200	1,640
5	Nails	130	-	-	130
6	Misc Hardware	640	480	275	1,395
7	Total	2,720	2,770	1,075	6,565
8					

Figure 9. *Select the formula or formulas to trace.*

Auditing a Worksheet

To avoid bogus results from incorrect formulas, you can have Excel show you which cells have supplied data for a formula.

1. Select the cell or cells that contain the formulas. **(Figure 9)**
2. From the Tools menu, choose Auditing. **(Figure 10)**
3. On the Auditing submenu, choose Trace Precedents.
4. Choose Trace Precedents again to see an additional level of precedents, if it exists.

✓ Tips

- To clear the arrows, choose Remove All Arrows from the Auditing submenu.
- The Auditing toolbar contains Trace Precedents and Remove All Arrows buttons. **(Figure 12)** *See Selecting Toolbars, page 31.*

	A	B	C	D	E
2	Construction Expenses	Week 1	Week 2	Week 3	Total
3	Lumber	1,200	1,600	600	3,400
4	Sheetrock	750	690	200	1,640
5	Nails	130	-	-	130
6	Misc Hardware	640	400	275	1,395
7	Total	2,720	2,770	1,075	6,565
8					

Figure 11. *Arrows show the links between a formula and the cells that have supplied data to it.*

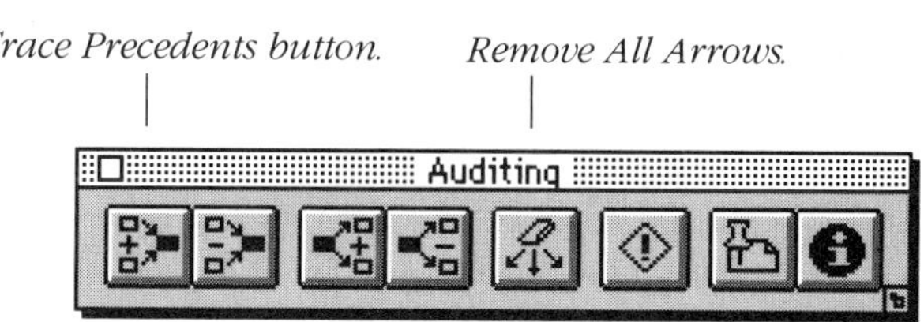

Figure 12. *The Auditing toolbar.*

Creating a Chart with the Chart Wizard

1. Select the data to chart. **(Figure 13)**
2. Click the ChartWizard button in the Standard toolbar. **(Figure 14)**
3. Drag out a box that marks the location for the chart on a clear area of the worksheet. **(Figure 15)**
4. Follow the instructions and make selections on the series of steps in the Chart Wizard dialog boxes that follow. **(Figures 16-20)**

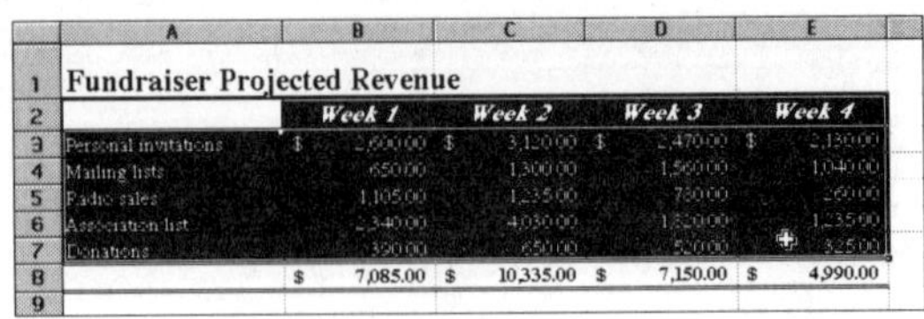

	A	B	C	D	E
1	Fundraiser Projected Revenue				
2		Week 1	Week 2	Week 3	Week 4
3	Personal invitations	$ 2,600.00	$ 3,120.00	$ 2,470.00	$ 2,130.00
4	Mailing lists	650.00	1,300.00	1,560.00	1,040.00
5	Radio sales	1,105.00	1,235.00	780.00	260.00
6	Association list	2,340.00	4,030.00	1,820.00	1,235.00
7	Donations	390.00	650.00	520.00	325.00
8		$ 7,085.00	$ 10,335.00	$ 7,150.00	$ 4,990.00
9					

Figure 13. *Select the data to chart.*

The ChartWizard button.

Figure 14. *The ChartWizard button.*

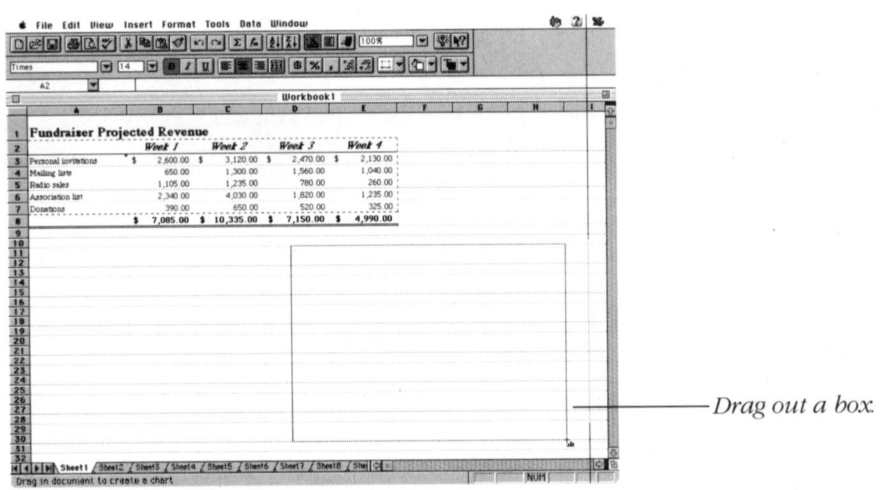

Figure 15. *Drag out a box.*

Figures 16. *Confirm the range to chart in ChartWizard Step 1.*

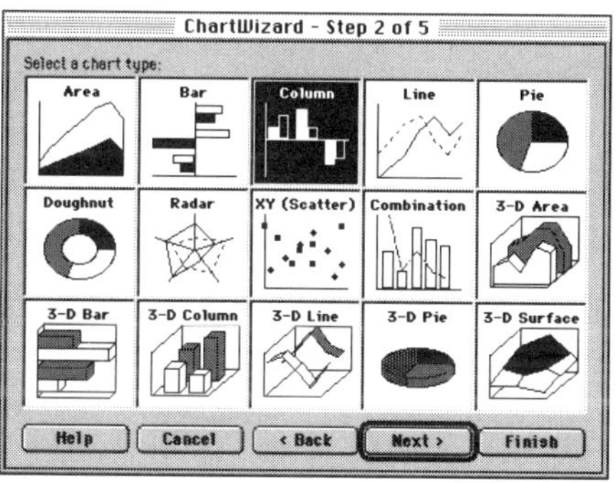

Figure 17. *Select a chart type in ChartWizard Step 2.*

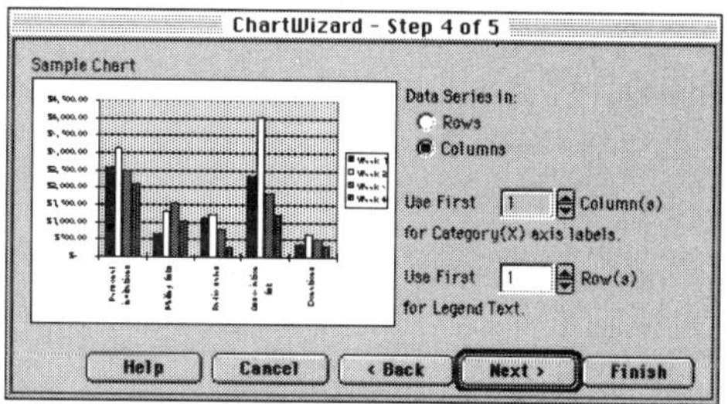

Figure 19. *Confirm the structure of the chart in ChartWizard Step 4.*

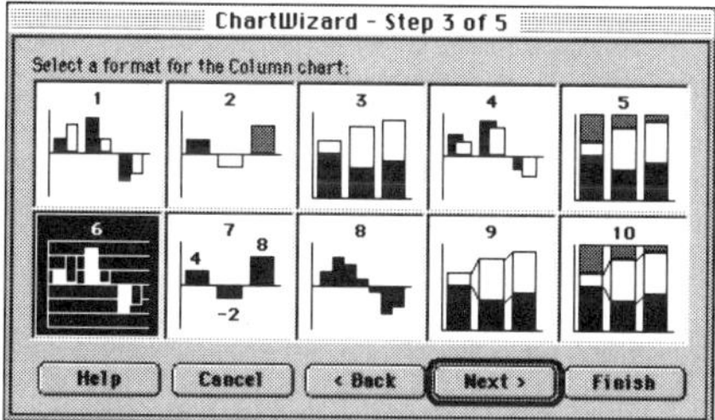

Figure 18. *Select a chart format in ChartWizard Step 3.*

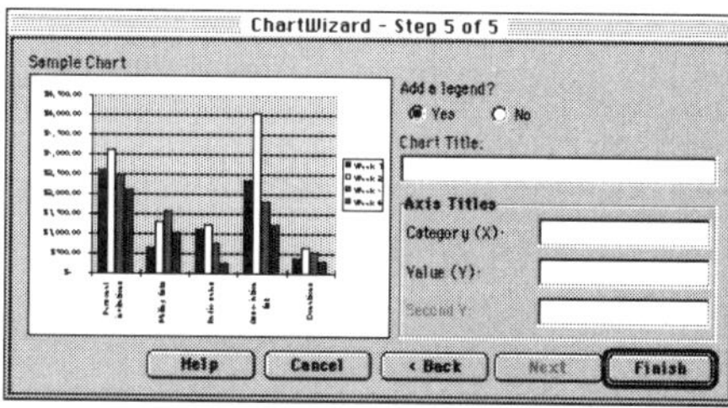

Figure 20. *Title the chart in ChartWizard Step 5, then click Finish.*

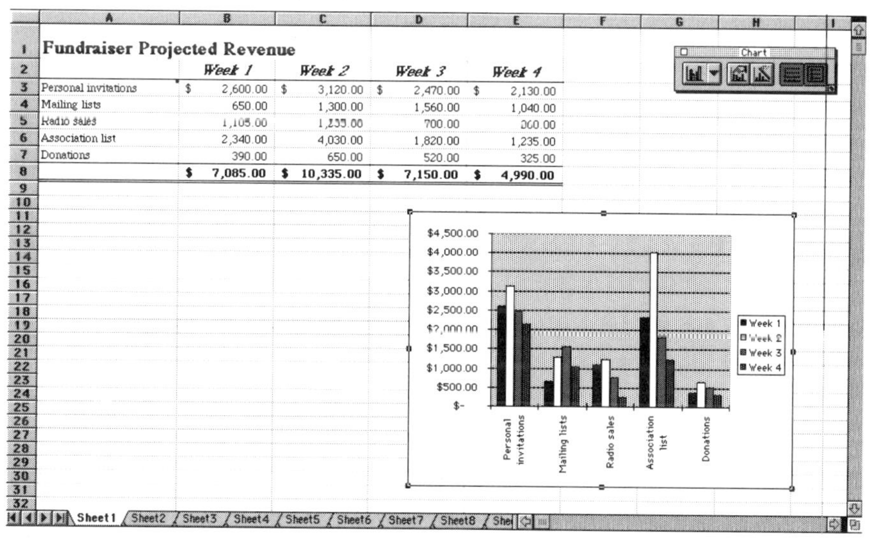

Figure 21. *Completed chart.*

Modifying a Chart

1. Double-click a chart to activate it. **(Figure 22)**
2. Use commands on the Insert and Format menus to change the design of the chart. **(Figure 23)**
3. Click outside the border surrounding the chart to finish modifying the chart.

✓ Tips

- While a chart is active, you can click any part of the chart once to select it and then double-click to obtain a dialog box that contains options for the selected part. **(Figure 24)**
- Drag the chart to move it on the sheet or drag the handles of its window to resize the chart.

Note: *You'll find far more detail about modifying charts on pages 189-196, which cover creating graphs in PowerPoint. Charting is identical in Excel 5 and PowerPoint 4.*

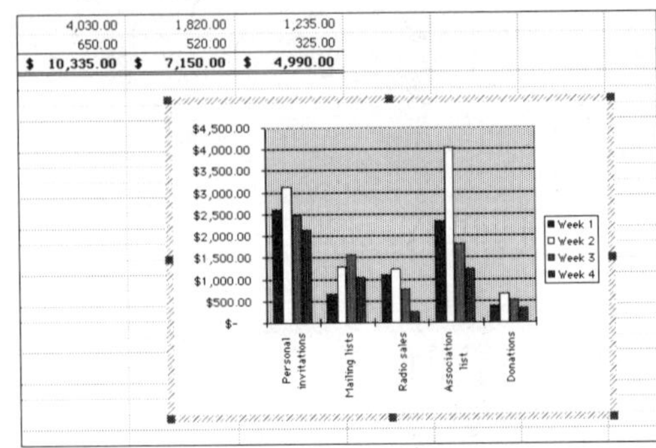

Figure 22. *A thick gray border appears around a chart when you double-click it.*

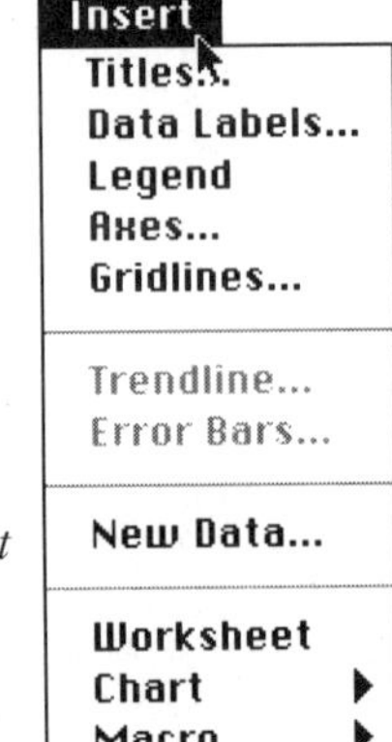

Figure 23. *While a chart is activated, the Insert menu displays chart commands and options.*

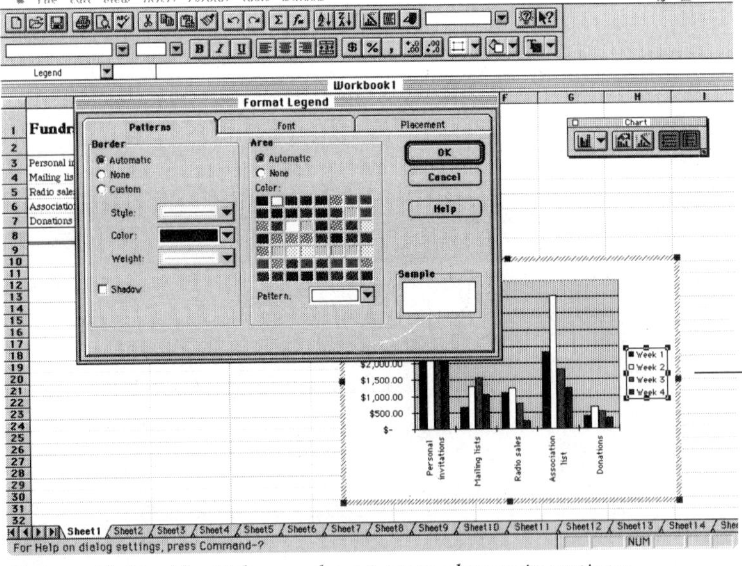

Figure 24. *Double-click any chart part to change its options.*

Excel Database Techniques 18

	A	B	C	D	E
1	Fname	Lname	Employee no.	Total vacation days	Vacation days used
2	Eric	Weinberger	2394	15	5
3	Audrey	Marr	2089	20	12
4	David	Lawrence	3132	20	14
5	Thomas	Speeches	3082	50	28
6	Robert	Westover	2965	20	12
7	Cohen	Susan	2075	10	5
8	Cohen	Aaron	2104	10	5
9					

Figure 1. *Each* **record** *of information occupies a row. Each column is a* **field**.

About Excel's Database Capabilities

Unless you work with extremely large databases (thousands and thousands of sets of data) or need a complex database structure, Excel can provide all the database power you'll need.

In Excel, you enter data in rows. Each row is a *record* (one complete set of information). Each column in the row, called a *field*, contains one particular type of information in the record. **(Figure 1)**

Rather than enter information directly into the cells of a sheet, you can also create a fill-in-the-blanks data *form* to make it easier to enter, edit, delete and search through information. **(Figure 2)**

After you enter the data, you can search through it, sort it, and pull out only the information that matches particular criteria.

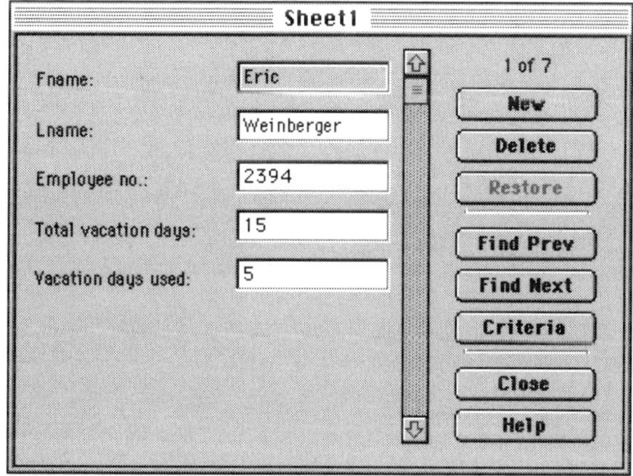

Figure 2. *A data form.*

Setting up the Database

1. Enter the field names at the tops of a group of adjacent columns. **(Figure 3)**
2. Enter the data into rows below the field names. **(Figure 4)**

✔ **Tips**

- Press Tab when you complete a cell to move to the next cell to the right.
- Press Enter when you complete a cell to move to the next cell below.

	A	B	C	D	E
1	Fname	Lname	Employee no.	Total vacation days	Vacation days used
2					
3					
4					
5					

Figure 3. *The field names.*

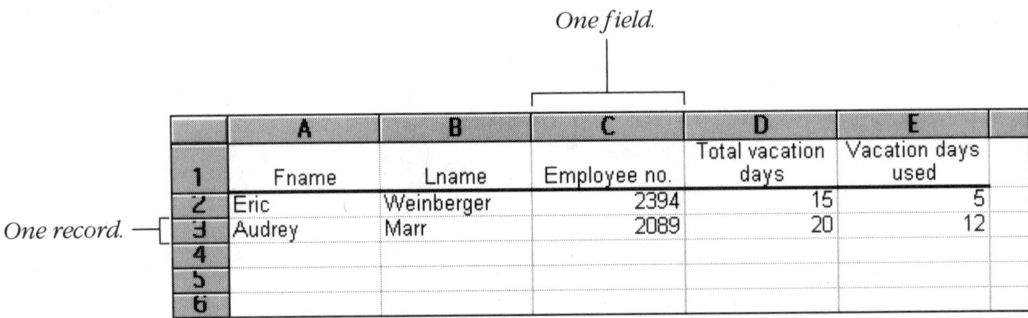

	A	B	C	D	E
1	Fname	Lname	Employee no.	Total vacation days	Vacation days used
2	Eric	Weinberger	2394	15	5
3	Audrey	Marr	2089	20	12
4					
5					
6					

Figure 4. *Data entered below the field names.*

Creating a Form

1. Click any cell that contains data. **(Figure 5)**
2. From the Data menu, choose Form. **(Figures 6-7)**

✔ **Tips**

- To put away the form, click Close.
- Press Tab to move from field to field on a form.
- Press Shift+Tab to return to the previous field on a form.

	A	B	C	D	E
1	Fname	Lname	Employee no.	Total vacation days	Vacation days used
2	Eric	Weinberger	2394	15	5
3	Audrey	Marr	2089	20	12
4	David	Lawrence	3132	20	14
5	Thomas	Speeches	3082	50	28
6	Robert	Westover	2965	20	12
7					

Figure 5. *Click a cell in the database.*

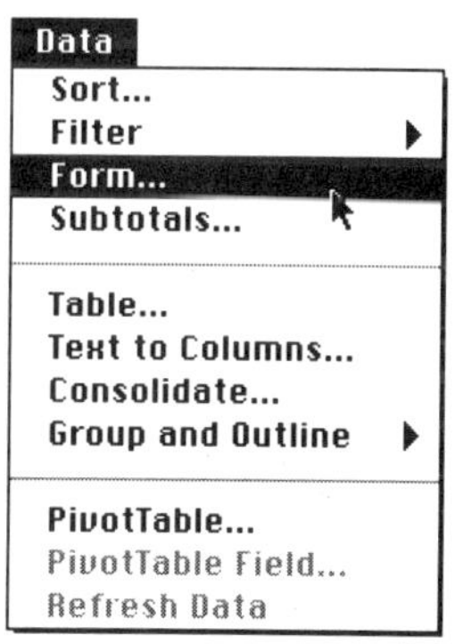

Figure 6. *The Data menu.*

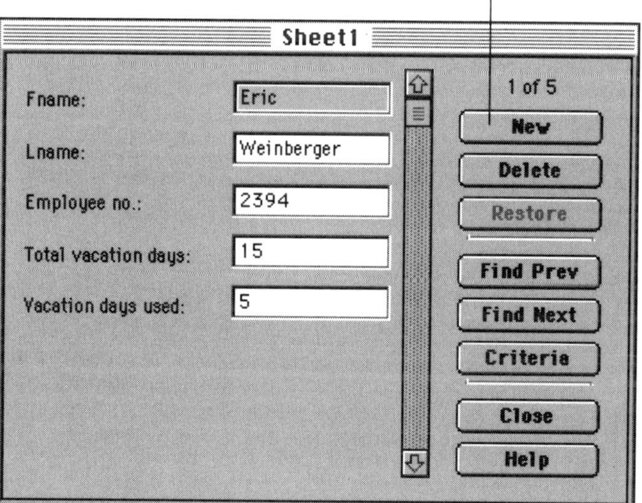

Figure 7. *The data form.*

Creating a Form

Excel

Sorting the Database

1. Click any cell in the database. **(Figure 8)**
2. From the Data menu, choose Sort. **(Figure 9)**
3. On the Sort dialog box, choose a field name from the Sort By drop-down list. **(Figure 10)**
4. To perform secondary and tertiary sorts on the data, choose additional fields from the two Then By drop-down lists also on the Sort dialog box.
5. To sort from smallest to largest or earliest to latest, choose Ascending. To sort from largest to smallest or latest to earliest, choose Descending.
6. Click OK. **(Figure 11)**

	A	B	C	D	E
1	Fname	Lname	Employee no.	Total vacation days	Vacation days used
2	Eric	Weinberger	2394	15	5
3	Audrey	Marr	2089	20	12
4	David	Lawrence	3132	20	14
5	Thomas	Speeches	3082	50	28
6	Robert	Westover	2965	20	12
7					

Figure 8. *Click a cell in the database.*

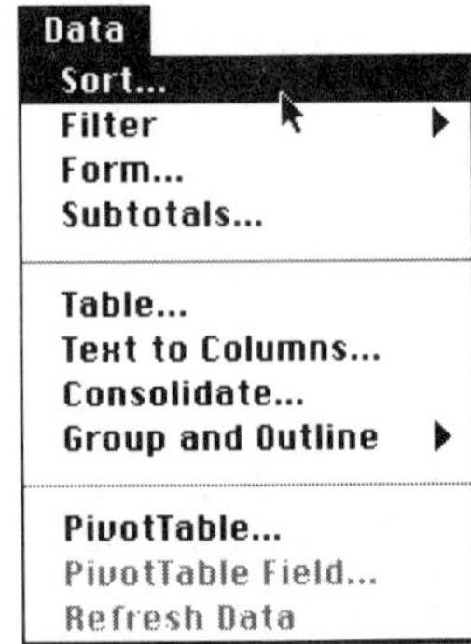

Figure 9. *The Data menu.*

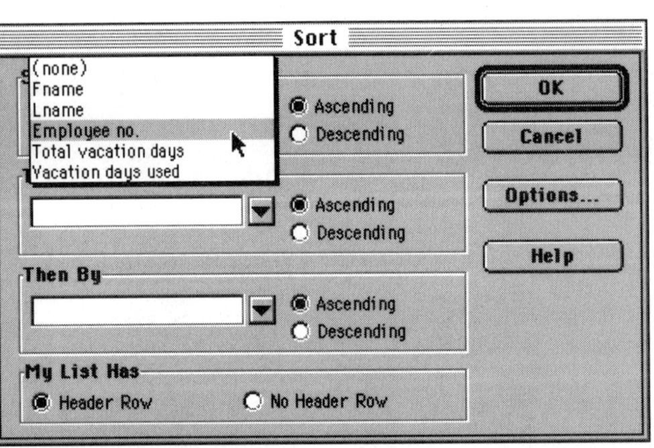

Figure 10. *The Sort dialog box.*

	A	B	C	D	E
1	Fname	Lname	Employee no.	Total vacation days	Vacation days used
2	Audrey	Marr	2089	20	12
3	Eric	Weinberger	2394	15	5
4	Robert	Westover	2965	20	12
5	Thomas	Speeches	3082	50	28
6	David	Lawrence	3132	20	14
7					

Figure 11. *The sorted data.*

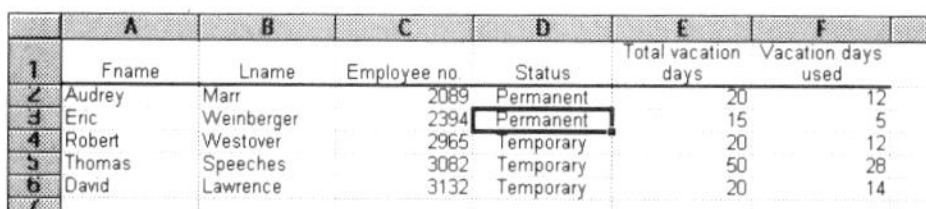

	A	B	C	D	E	F
1	Fname	Lname	Employee no	Status	Total vacation days	Vacation days used
2	Audrey	Marr	2089	Permanent	20	12
3	Eric	Weinberger	2394	Permanent	15	5
4	Robert	Westover	2965	Temporary	20	12
5	Thomas	Speeches	3082	Temporary	50	28
6	David	Lawrence	3132	Temporary	20	14
7						

Figure 12. *Click on any cell in the database.*

Extracting Data

1. Click any cell in the database. **(Figure 12)**
2. From the Data menu, choose Filter.
3. On the Filter submenu, choose AutoFilter.
4. Click any of the pull-down buttons next to the field names to see a list of the entries in that field. **(Figure 13)**
5. Choose an entry on the list to view only those records that match the entry. **(Figure 14)**

✔ Tips

- Click a cell outside the database and then choose AutoFilter from the Filter submenu again to display the entire database.
- When the data is filtered, the row headings of the extracted data are blue.
- The field upon which the data is filtered shows a blue drop-down button.

	A	B	C	D	E	F
1	Fname	Lname	Employee n		Total vacation days	Vacation days used
2	Audrey	Marr	2089		20	12
3	Eric	Weinberger	2394		15	5
4	Robert	Westover	2965		20	12
5	Thomas	Speeches	3082		50	28
6	David	Lawrence	3132	Temporary	20	14
7						

(All)
(Custom...)
Permanent
Temporary
(Blanks)
(NonBlanks)

Figure 13. *Select an entry from one of the pull-down lists.*

	A	B	C	D	E	F
1	Fname	Lname	Employee n	Status	Total vacation days	Vacation days used
2	Audrey	Marr	2089	Permanent	20	12
3	Eric	Weinberger	2394	Permanent	15	5
7						

Figure 14. *Only records that match the selected entry appear.*

Totaling Numeric Data in a Database

1. Select any cell in the database.
2. From the Data menu, choose Subtotals. **(Figure 15)**
3. On the Subtotal dialog box, select a field from the At Each Change in drop-down list. A subtotal will appear each time this field changes value. A grand total appears at the bottom of the list. **(Figures 16)**

✔ **Tip**

- Use the controls to the left of the database to show only the subtotals. **(Figure 17)**

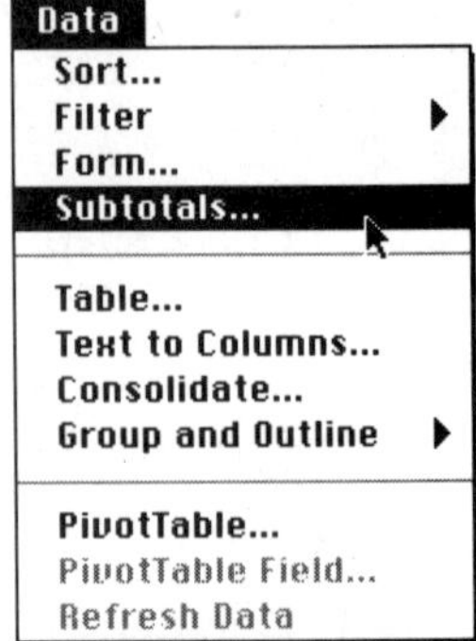

Figure 15. *The Data menu.*

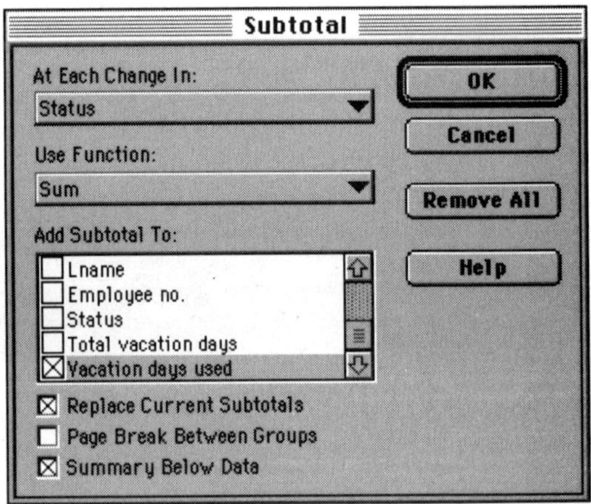

Figure 16. *The Subtotals dialog box.*

Click the minus buttons to hide detail and show only the totals.

	A	B	C	D	E	F
1	Fname	Lname	Employee no.	Status	Total vacation days	Vacation days used
2	Audrey	Marr	2089	Permanent	20	12
3	Eric	Weinberger	2394	Permanent	15	5
4				**Permanent Total**		17
5	Robert	Westover	2965	Temporary	20	12
6	Thomas	Speeches	3082	Temporary	50	28
7	David	Lawrence	3132	Temporary	20	14
8				**Temporary Total**		54
9				**Grand Total**		71
10						

Figure 17. *Use these controls to show only the totals.*

PowerPoint 4.0 Presenting

PowerPoint 4.0 Presenting

About PowerPoint

What is PowerPoint?
The Road to a PowerPoint Presentation
The PowerPoint Window
Key to the PowerPoint Window
Starting PowerPoint

Starting a Presentation

About Starting a Presentation
Using the AutoContent Wizard
Using the Pick a Look Wizard
Changing Views
Adding Slides

Outlining the Presentation

About Outlining
Switching to Outline View
Entering the Text
Replacing Existing Text
Reorganizing the Slides
Showing Only the Slide Titles
Inserting Slides
Deleting Slides

Creating Text Slides

Starting a Text Slide
Filling in Text Placeholders
Selecting Text Blocks
Moving and Resizing Text Blocks
Formatting Text
Rearranging Text in a Block

Creating Graph Slides

About Graphing
Starting a Chart
Replacing the Sample Data on the Data Sheet
Changing the Chart Type
Choosing an AutoFormat
Displaying a Legend and Grid Lines
Adding Chart Titles
Adding Data Labels
By Rows vs. By Columns

Formatting Charts

About Chart Formatting
Formatting a Chart Element
Formatting a Group
Cutting a Pie Chart Slice
Creating High-Low-Close Charts
Switching Between 3-D and 2-D Chart Types
Changing the View of 3D Graphs

Organization Charts and Tables

Starting an Org Chart
Entering Org Members
Adding Subordinates
Adding an Assistant
Formatting the Boxes, Text, and Lines
Finishing the Chart and Leaving Microsoft Organization Chart
Starting a Table
Entering the Data and Formatting the Table

Using the Slide Sorter

About the Slide Sorter
Switching to Slide Sorter View
Reordering Slides
Changing the Overall Design in Slide Sorter View
Duplicating and Deleting Slides

Customizing a Presentation

Selecting a New Design
Adding a Logo to the Background
Changing the Background Color and Shading
Changing the Text Fonts
Changing the Color Scheme
Saving a Custom Design

Drawing on Slides

Drawing Shapes
Grouping and Ungrouping Shapes
Aligning and Rotating Shapes
Overlapping Shapes

Creating Slide Shows

Adding Transition Effects
Adding Build Effects
Displaying the Show
Using the PowerPoint Viewer

About PowerPoint

What is PowerPoint?

PowerPoint is the presentation graphics component of the Microsoft Office suite. It creates charts and graphs, slides, handouts, overheads, and any other presentation materials you might use during a stand-up, dog and pony show. PowerPoint even creates slide shows, which are electronic presentations that you can run on your computer screen or on a projection in front of an audience.

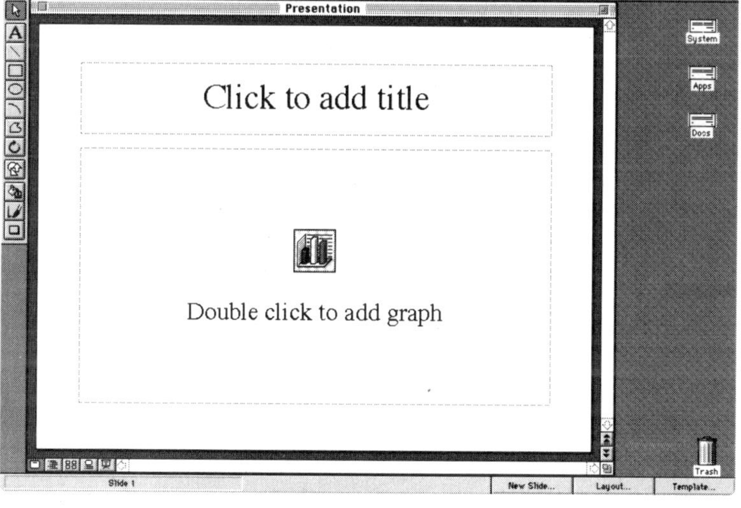

PowerPoint comes with dozens of professionally designed templates that take care of the look of a presentation so you can focus on the message. It even comes with a selection of sample presentation outlines from which you can choose to get a start on the presentation content.

Bulleted text slides, graphs, tables, organization charts, clip art, and drawing tools are all elements of PowerPoint's powerful arsenal.

The Road to a PowerPoint Presentation

Starting the Presentation

PowerPoint offers not one, but several different ways to start a presentaton, including using the Pick a Look Wizard to choose a design first, or the AutoContent Wizard to choose a presentation outline first. *Pages 169-176.*

Creating the Text Slides

You may prefer to develop the text in Outline view, where you can see all the text in one place. Or, you can generate slides one at a time, typing text directly into the special text placeholders on the slides as you go. Creating slides with PowerPoint is no more difficult than filling in the blanks. If you've outlined the presentation in Word, you can even transfer the outline to a new PowerPoint presentation automatically. *Pages 177-188.*

Creating Graphs and Tables

If the information you need to get across is numeric, you might want to consider a graph slide. PowerPoint also makes organization charts and tables to depict other sorts of information visually. *Pages 189-210.*

Customizing the Presentation

In Slide Sorter view, you get a bird's eye view of the entire presentation. You can rearrange slides, change the overall design, and delete extraneous slides. In Slide view, you can add a logo to or change the color or design of the background, change the font and color schemes, or change the template, which governs the overall look of the presentation. *Pages 211-214.*

Adding Special Graphics

PowerPoint's sophisticated drawing tools and commands make it easy to embellish slides with special graphics. You can even import a scanned photograph or a graphic from another application. *Pages 221-224.*

Creating a Slide Show

The big payoff comes when you're ready to present the presentation. You can generate 35mm slides and handouts just as you'd expect, but you can also create an onscreen, electronic presentation complete with TV-like special effects and transitions, and sound and music. Then, you can even send the slide show, along with the special PowerPoint Viewer module, to another computer user who is not fortunate enough to have PowerPoint. *Pages 225-228.*

The PowerPoint 4 Window

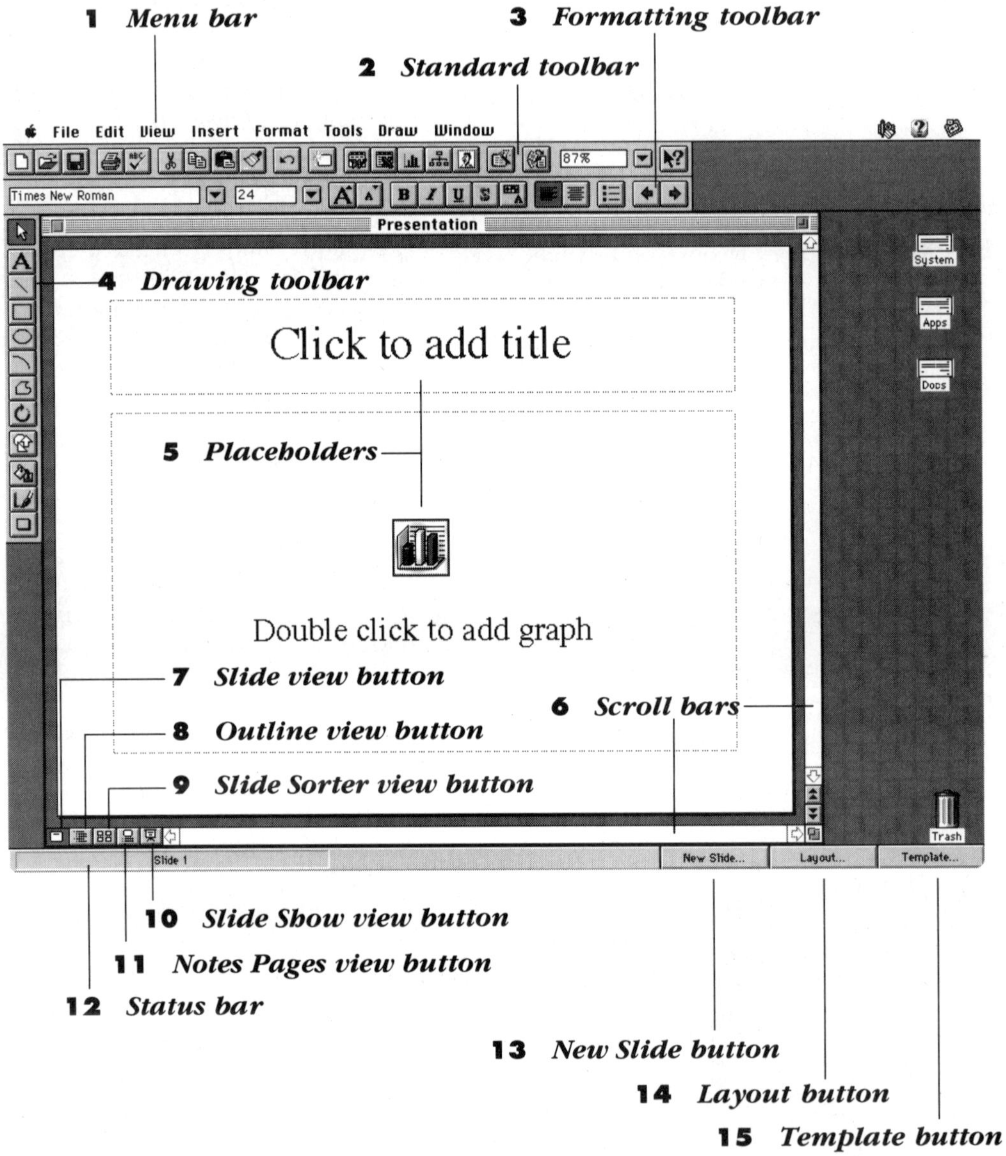

1 *Menu bar*

3 *Formatting toolbar*

2 *Standard toolbar*

File Edit View Insert Format Tools Draw Window

Times New Roman 24 87%

Presentation

System

Apps

Docs

4 *Drawing toolbar*

Click to add title

5 *Placeholders*

Double click to add graph

7 *Slide view button*

6 *Scroll bars*

8 *Outline view button*

9 *Slide Sorter view button*

Trash

Slide 1 New Slide... Layout... Template...

10 *Slide Show view button*

11 *Notes Pages view button*

12 *Status bar*

13 *New Slide button*

14 *Layout button*

15 *Template button*

Key to the PowerPoint 4 Window

1 ***Menu bar***

Click any name on the menu bar to pull down a menu.

2 ***Standard toolbar***

Toolbar with buttons for file management, editing, and proofing commands.

3 ***Formatting toolbar***

Toolbar with buttons for formatting text.

4 ***Drawing toolbar***

Toolbar with buttons for adding graphic objects to slides.

5 ***Placeholders***

Double-click these placeholders to add elements to slides.

6 ***Scroll bars***

Use these scroll bars to move the view of the document up or down or to quickly jump to a spot in the document. The length of the vertical scroll bar represents the length of the entire document. The position of the scroll button represents the position of the insertion point in the document.

7 ***Slide view button***

Click this button to switch to Slide view which shows a single slide.

8 ***Outline view button***

Click this button to switch to Outline view, which shows the text of the presentation in outline form.

9 ***Slide Sorter view button***

Click this button to switch to Slide Sorter view, which shows miniatures of slides arranged in a grid.

10 ***Slide Show view button***

Click this button to view the slides of the presentation in sequence, as a slide show.

11 ***Notes Pages view button***

Click this button to view a slides and notes you've typed about the slide for the presenter.

12 ***Status bar***

Shows the current slide number.

13 ***New Slide button***

Click this button to start a new slide.

14 ***Layout button***

Click this button to summon the dialog box that shows sample layouts for the slide.

15 ***Template button***

Click this button to choose a different template to redesign the appearance of the presentation.

Starting PowerPoint

1. Double-click the Microsoft PowerPoint icon in its folder. **(Figure 1)**
   or
   Choose Microsoft PowerPoint from the Microsoft Office Manager menu. **(Figure 2)**

✔ Tip

■ If PowerPoint is already started, choose Microsoft PowerPoint from the list of running applications on the application menu. You can also press ⌘+Tab repeatedly until Microsoft PowerPoint appears.

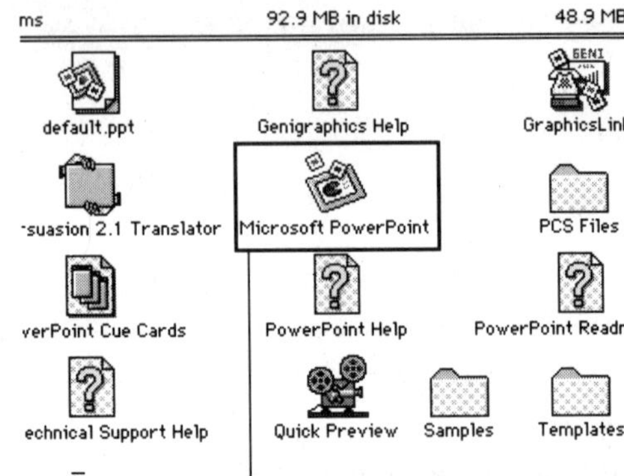

Figure 1. *The Microsoft PowerPoint icon in its folder.*

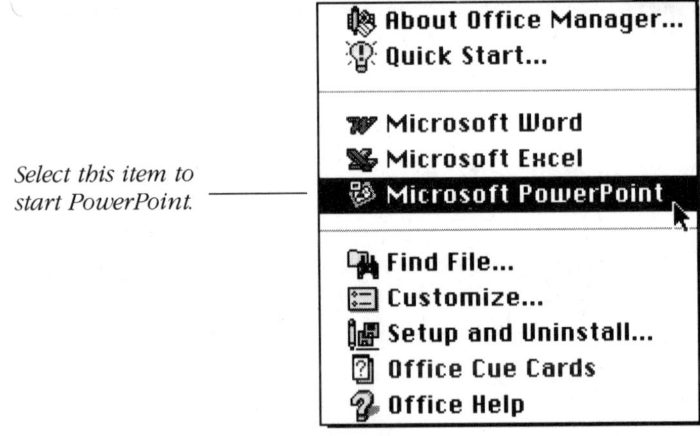

Figure 2. *The Microsoft Office Manager.*

Starting a Presentation

About Starting a Presentation

Whenever you start a new presentation, PowerPoint offers several choices on the PowerPoint dialog box. To concentrate on content first, choose one of the suggested presentation outlines offered by the AutoContent Wizard. To concentrate on appearance first, use the Pick a Look Wizard.

The New button.

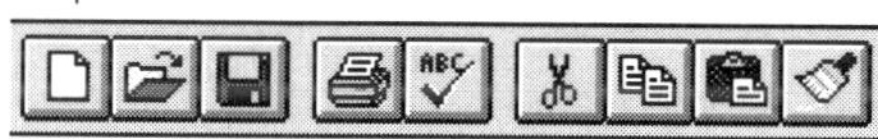

Figure 1. *The New button.*

1. Click the New button on the Standard toolbar. **(Figure 1)**

or

Press ⌘+N.

or

From the File menu, choose New. **(Figure 2)**

File
New... ⌘N
Open... ⌘O
Close ⌘W
Save ⌘S
Save As...
Find File...
Summary Info.
Slide Setup...
Page Setup...
Print... ⌘P
Quit ⌘Q

Figure 2. *The File menu.*

2. On the PowerPoint dialog box, double-click AutoContent Wizard or Pick a Look Wizard. **(Figure 3)**

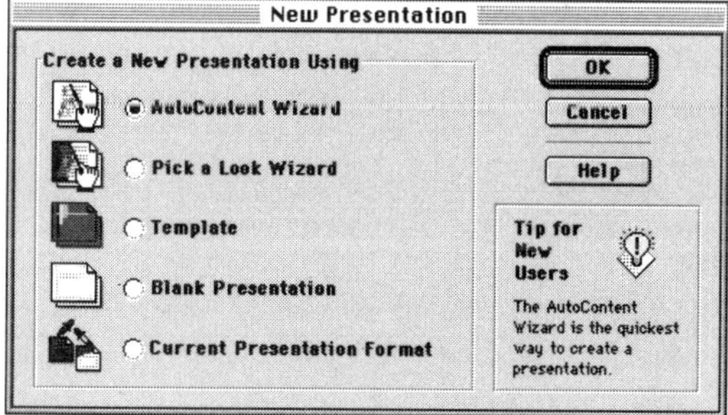

Figure 3. *The PowerPoint dialog box.*

✔ Tips

- If you've already created a presentation during the current PowerPoint session, the PowerPoint dialog box is named the New Presentation dialog box, instead.
- To choose a presentation look by filename, double-click Template on the PowerPoint dialog box.
- To start with a blank presentation and then add formatting later, double-click Blank Presentation on the PowerPoint dialog box.

Using the AutoContent Wizard

The AutoContent Wizard offers a choice of sample presentation outlines, then drops you off in Outline view, where you can replace the sample outline text provided by the Wizard with your own.

1. Click Next on the Step 1 screen of the AutoContent Wizard. **(Figure 4)**
2. In Step 2, enter a presentation title and other information for the opening slide and then click Next. **(Figure 5)**
3. In Step 3, select an outline by name and click Next. **(Figure 6)**
4. In Step 4, click the Finish button. **(Figures 7-8)**

✔ Tips

- To return to a previous step, click Back on any Wizard dialog box.
- To skip the following steps and accept their default choices, click Finish.
- Each outline generates a presentation with a preset look. You can change the look by choosing a different template. *See Selecting a New Design, page 215.*
- The Cue Cards window may open on top of the outline to offer onscreen help. You can close the Cue Cards window just as you can any other window.

Figure 4. *Step 1 of the AutoContent Wizard.*

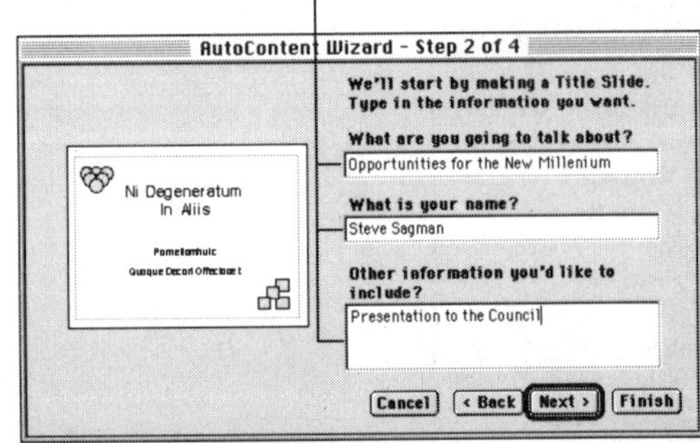

Figure 5. *Step 2 of the AutoContent Wizard.*

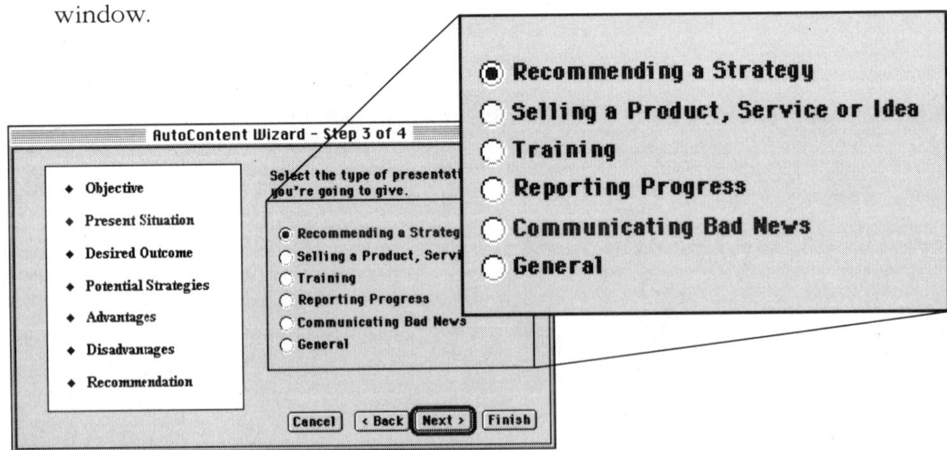

Figure 6. *Step 3 of the AutoContent Wizard.*

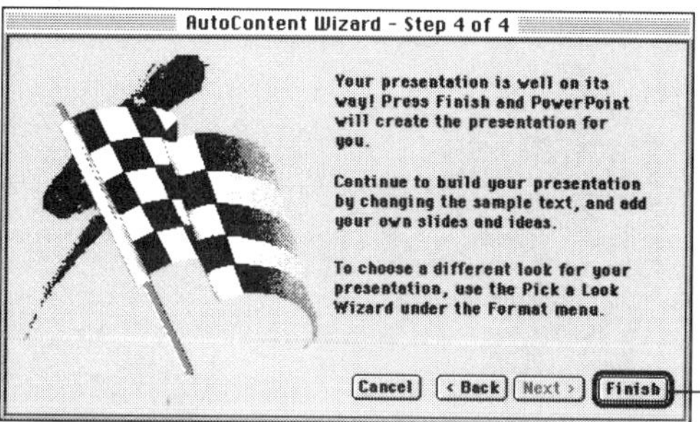

Figure 7. *Step 4 of the AutoContent Wizard.*

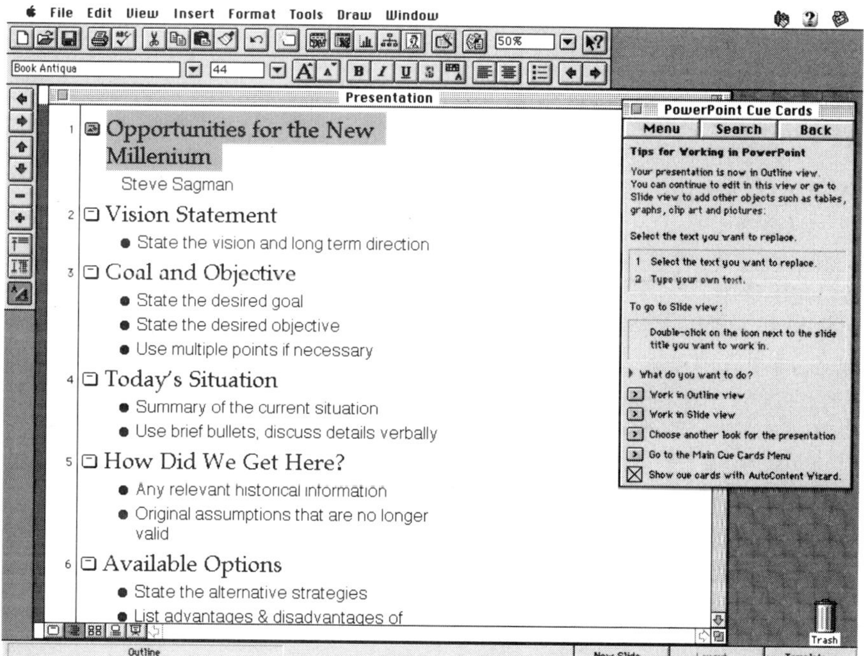

Figure 8. *The sample outline provided by the "Recommending a Strategy" option.*

Using the Pick a Look Wizard

The Pick a Look Wizard guides you in selecting a template that will govern the appearance of a presentation and in choosing a format for the presentation output.

1. In Step 1 of the Wizard, click Next. **(Figure 9)**
2. In Step 2, choose an output format for the presentation by clicking one of the four radio buttons, and click Next. **(Figure 10)**
3. In Step 3, choose one of the four templates shown, or click More to choose from the full list of templates, and then click Next. **(Figure 11)**
4. In Step 4, choose the output formats you'll use and click Next. **(Figure 12)**
5. In the next several steps, enter the special text that will appear on each output option selected in Step 4, and then click Next. **(Figure 13)**
6. When you reach the final step, click Finish. **(Figure 14)**

✓ Tips

- The Pick a Look Wizard drops you off in Slide View, where you can begin adding slides. **(Figure 15)**
- You can change the look of the presentation at any time by choosing a different template. *See Selecting a New Design, page 215.*

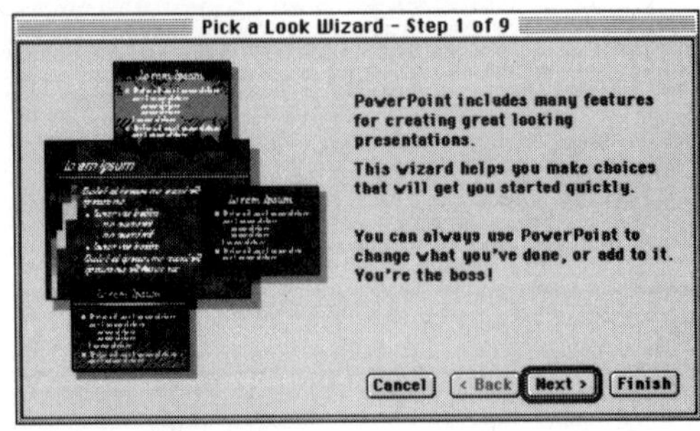

Figure 9. *Step 1 of the Pick a Look Wizard.*

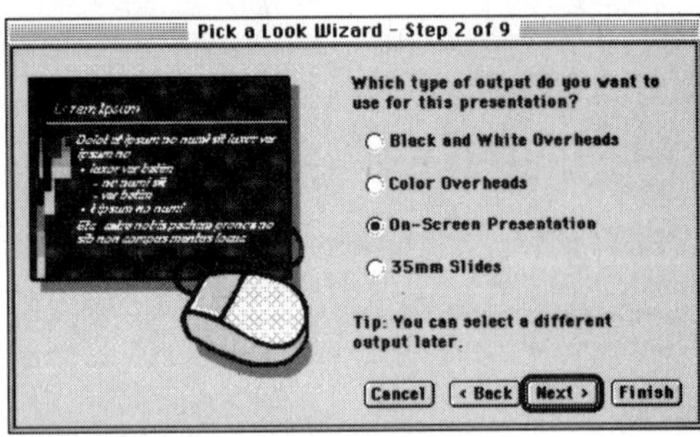

Figure 10. *Step 2 of the Pick a Look Wizard.*

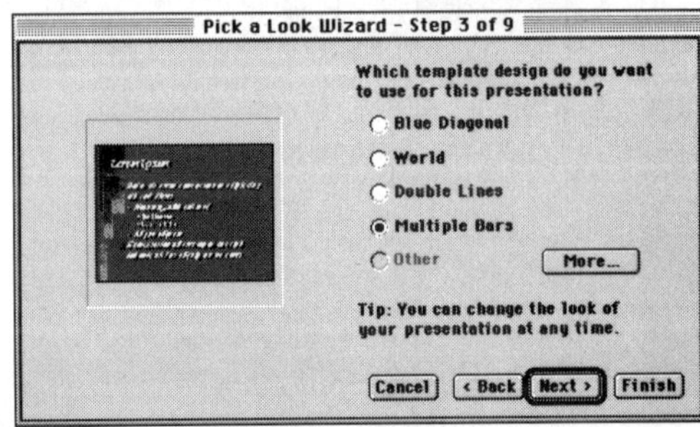

Figure 11. *Step 3 of the Pick a Look Wizard.*

Pick a Look Wizard

Power-Point

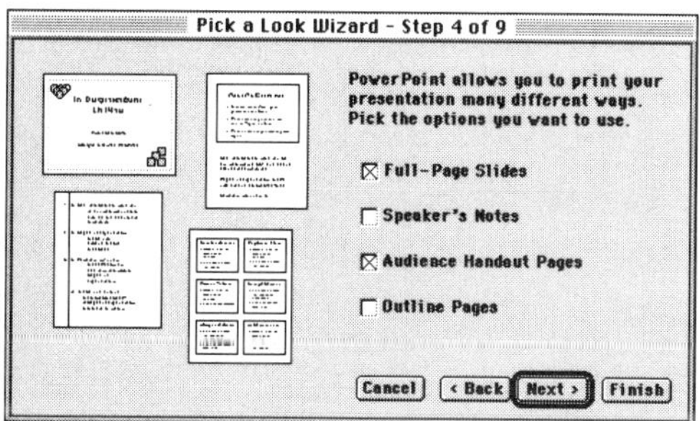

Figure 12. *Step 4 of the Pick a Look Wizard.*

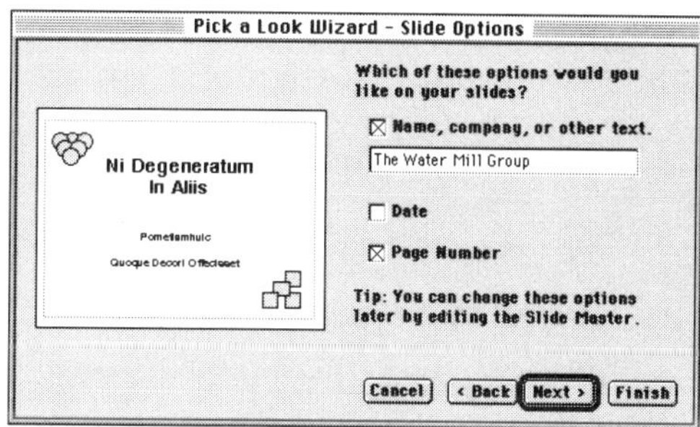

Figure 13. *Step 5 of the Pick a Look Wizard.*

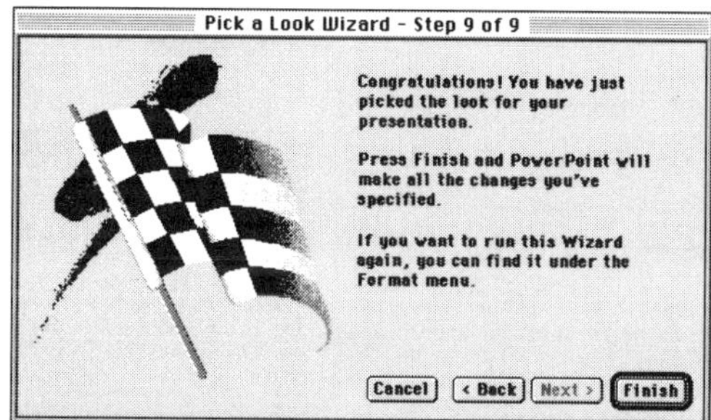

Figure 14. *The final step of the Pick a Look Wizard.*

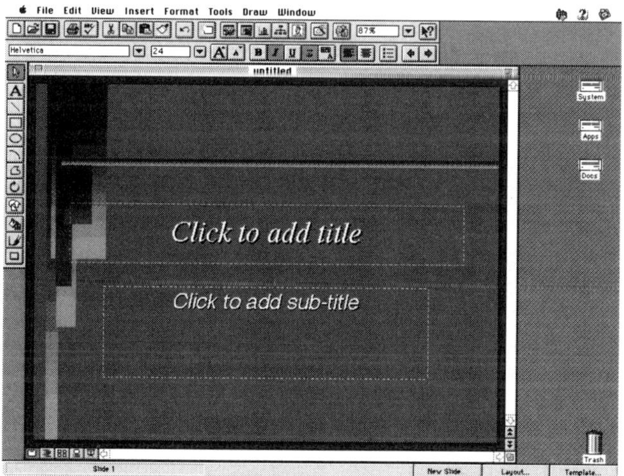

Figure 15. *The PowerPoint window after the completion of the Pick a Look Wizard.*

Changing Views

Slide View displays one slide at a time so you can enter text and graphics. **(Figure 16)**

Outline view displays only the text of the presentation in outline form so you can work easily with the content. **(Figure 17)**

Slide Sorter View displays miniatures of multiple slides so you can reorganize the slides and change the overall look of the presentation. Here you can also add and edit the transition effects for the slide show. **(Figure 18)**

Notes Pages View lets you enter and edit speaker's notes for the presenter. **(Figure 19)**

Slide Show View displays the presentation one slide after another in sequence as an automatic slide show (electronic presentation).

1. Click the appropriate button at the lower left corner of the presentation window. **(Figure 19-20)**

   or

   From the View menu, choose the view you want. **(Figure 21)**

✔ Tips

- Each view shows a different aspect of the same presentation.
- You can switch from one view to another at any time.

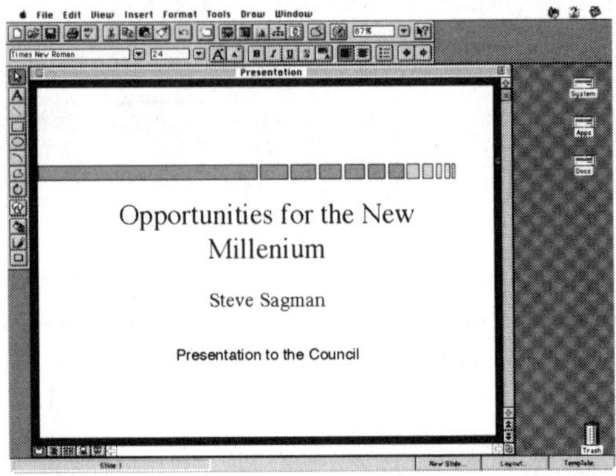

Figure 16. *Slide view.*

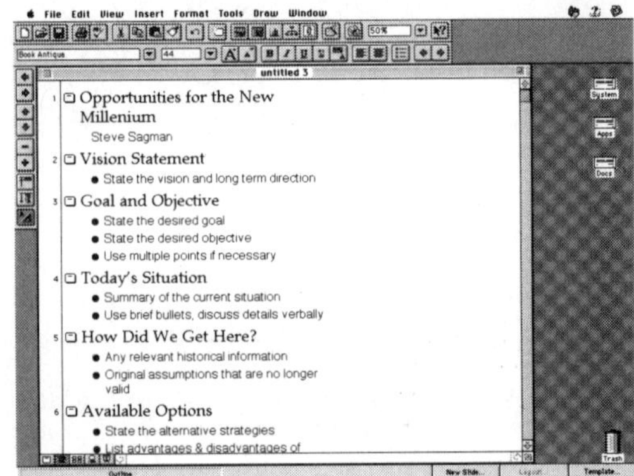

Figure 17. *Outline view.*

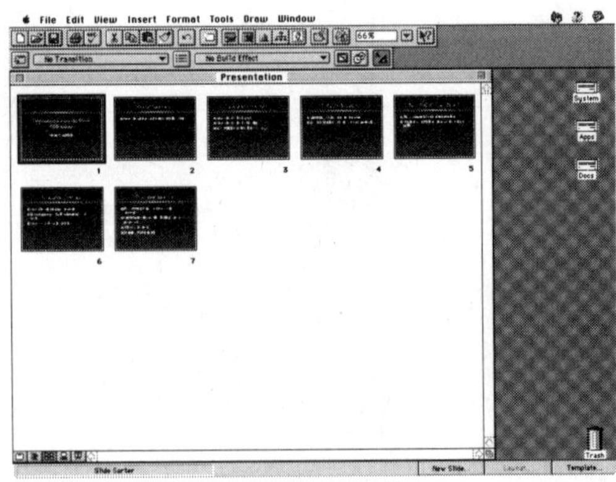

Figure 18. *Slide Sorter view.*

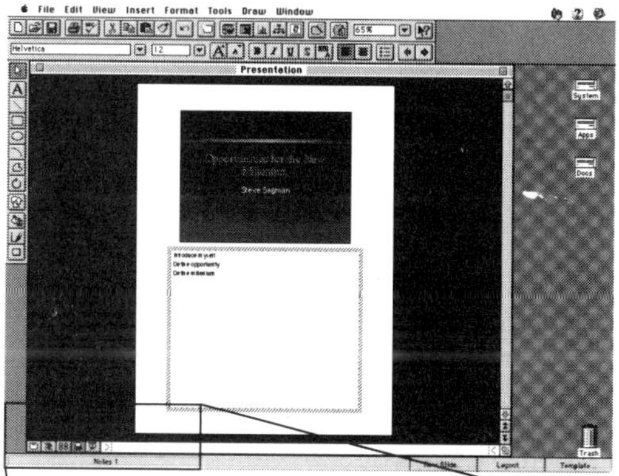

Figure 19. *Notes Pages view.*

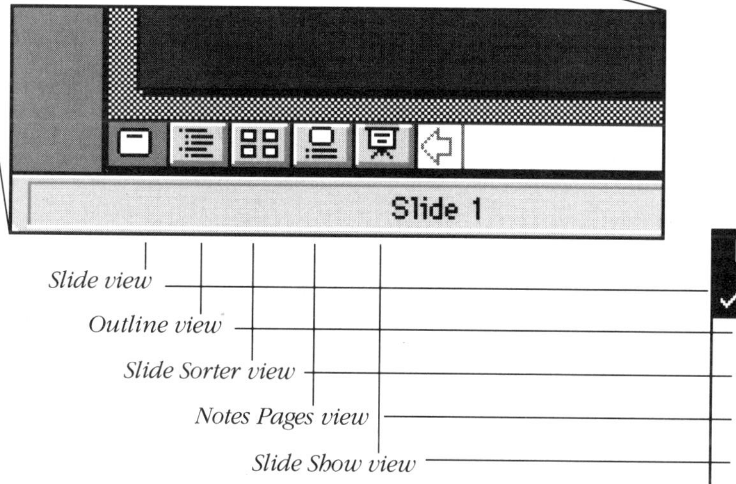

Slide 1

Slide view

Outline view

Slide Sorter view

Notes Pages view

Slide Show view

Figure 20. *The View buttons.*

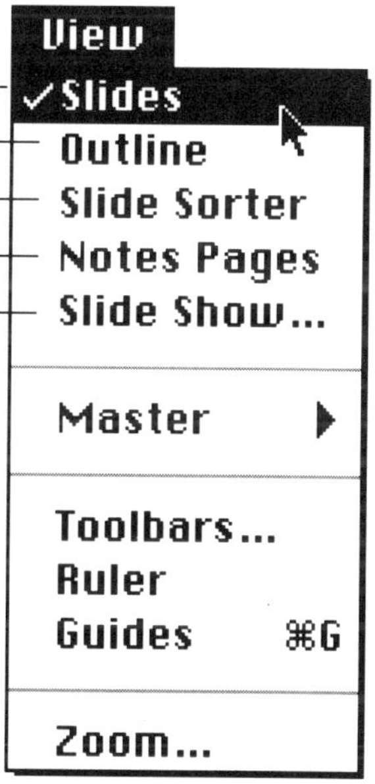

View
✓Slides
Outline
Slide Sorter
Notes Pages
Slide Show...
Master ▶
Toolbars...
Ruler
Guides ⌘G
Zoom...

Figure 21. *The View menu.*

Adding Slides

1. Click the New Slide button. **(Figure 22)**

   or

   Press ⌘+M.

2. On the New Slide dialog box, double-click a slide layout. **(Figure 23)**

✔ Tips

- If Show New Slide Dialog is turned off on the Options dialog box, a Bulleted List slide will appear each time you click the New Slide button.
- If you choose the wrong slide layout, click the Layout button and then choose the correct layout on the Slide Layout dialog box.

Figure 22. *The New Slide button.*

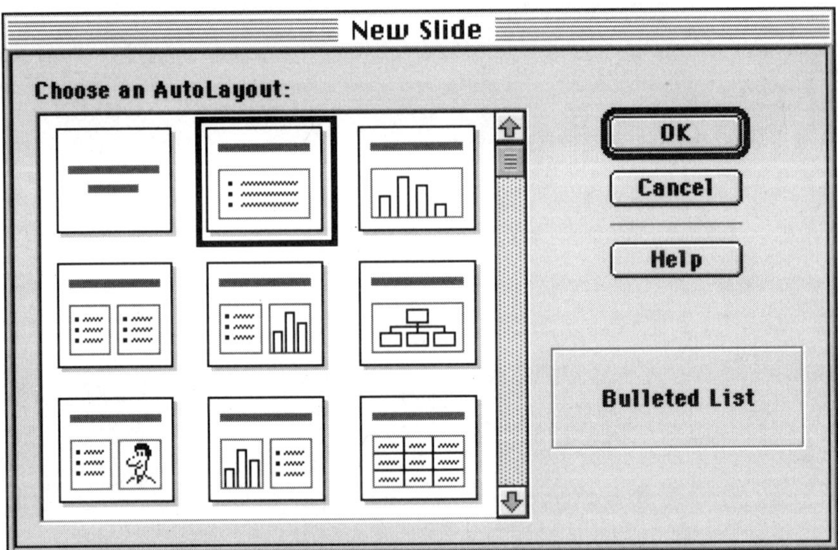

Figure 23. *The New Slide dialog box.*

Outlining the Presentation 21

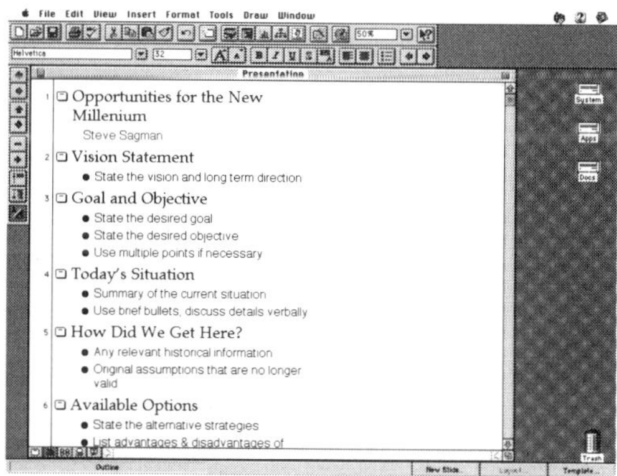
Figure 1. *Outline view.*

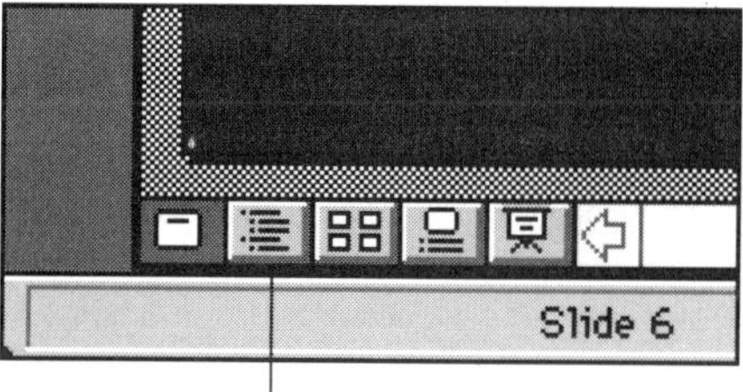

Figure 2. *The Outline view button.*

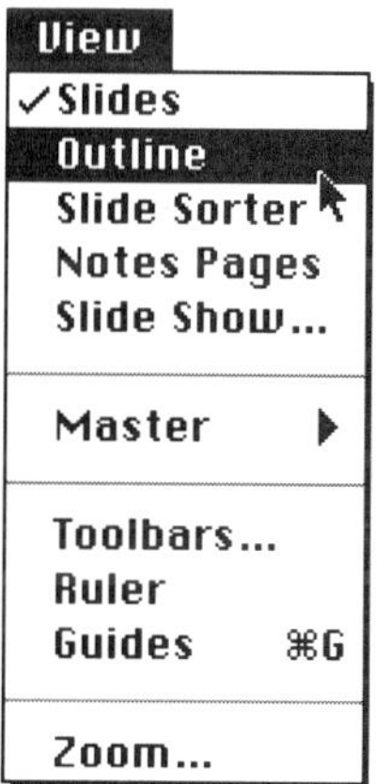

Figure 3. *The View menu.*

About Outlining

Outline view shows only the presentation text in outline form so you can focus exclusively on the content. **(Figure 1)** In Outline view, you see the text of the presentation on one screen so you can rearrange the flow, add or delete topics, and refine the wording of slides.

The AutoContent Wizard drops you off in Outline view automatically so you can modify the sample presentation outline it provides. You can also start in Outline view and enter the text of a presentation before switching to Slide view to add charts and graphs, tables, drawings, and other elements to individual slides. Even if you've already created a full presentation in Slide view, you can still switch to Outline view temporarily to focus on the text.

Switching to Outline View

1. Click the Outline view button. **(Figure 2)**

   or

2. From the View menu, choose Outline. **(Figure 3)**

Entering the Text

1. Type the title for a slide next to the slide icon and press Enter. **(Figure 4)**
2. Type the title of the next slide and press Enter. **(Figure 5)**

   or

   Press Tab, type the first bulleted text line for the current slide, and press Enter. **(Figure 6)**
3. Type any more bulleted text items, pressing Enter after each.

   or

   Press Shift+Tab to start a new slide. **(Figure 7)**
4. Continue as above to create new slides or add bulleted text points to the current slide.

✔ Tip

- To create a slide for a graph, organization chart, table, or drawing, simple type a slide title without entering bulleted text items underneath.

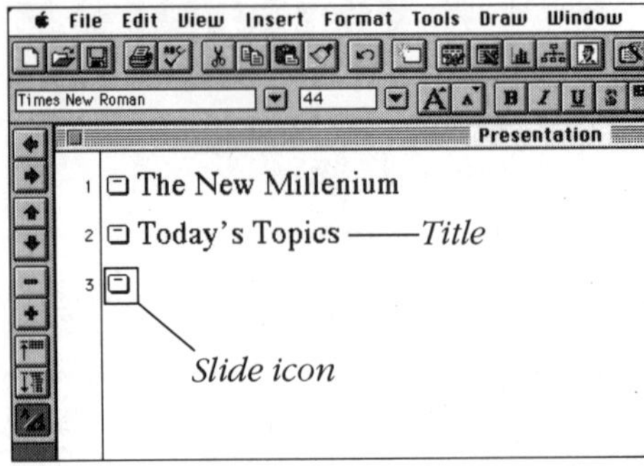

Figure 4. *Type the slide title.*

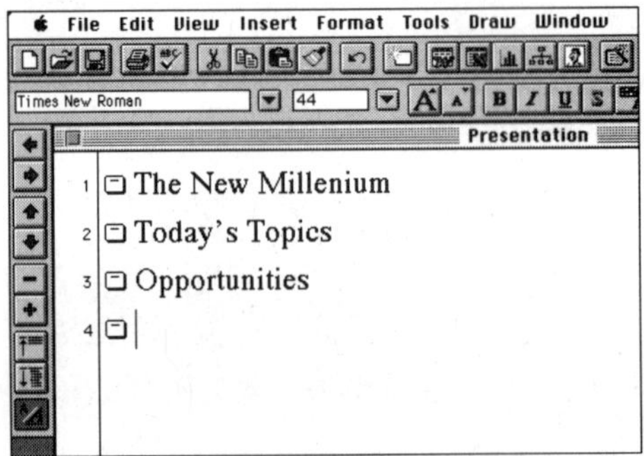

Figure 5. *Press Enter to begin a new slide.*

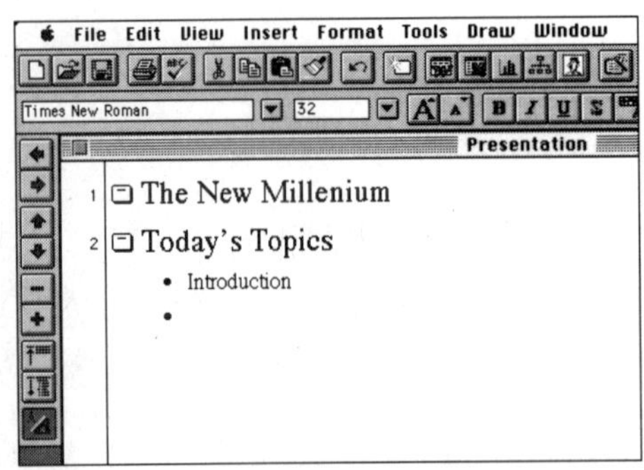

Figure 6. *Press Tab to begin typing bulleted items.*

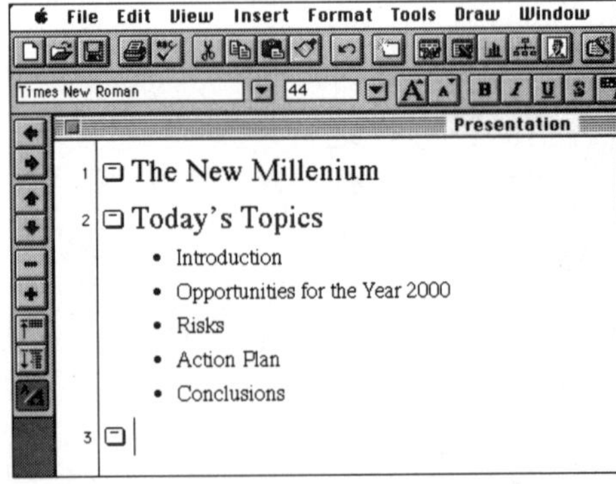

Figure 7. *Press Shift+Tab to type the next slide's title.*

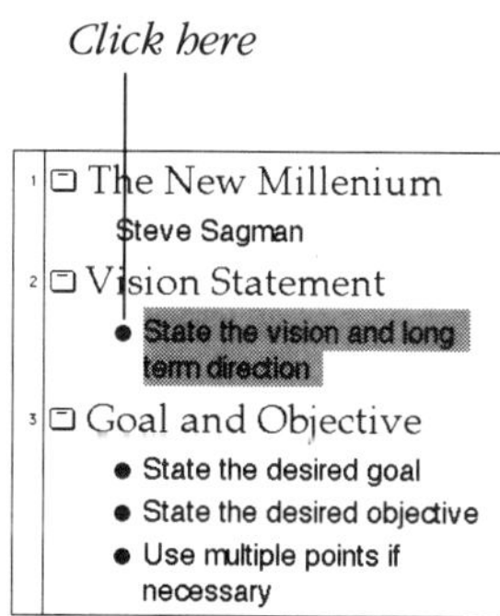

Figure 8. *Click a bullet.*

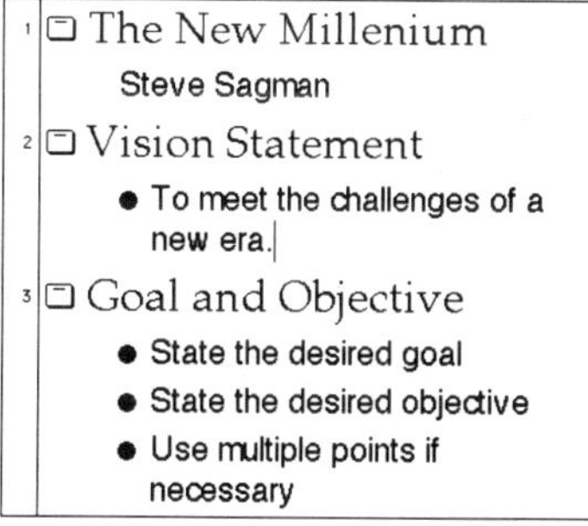

Figure 9. *Type a replacement.*

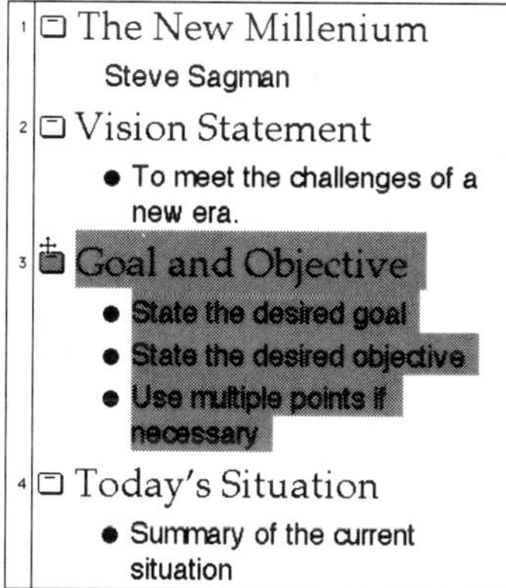

Figure 10. *Click a slide icon to select all the text on the slide.*

Replacing Existing Text

If you use the AutoContent Wizard to obtain one of the sample outlines, you must replace the sample text with your own.

1. Click a bullet to select a bulleted text line. **(Figure 8)**

   or

   Triple-click anywhere on a bulleted text line.
2. Type replacement text. **(Figure 9)**

✔ **Tip**

- Click a slide icon to select all the text on a slide. Then type replacement text, slide title and all. **(Figure 10)**

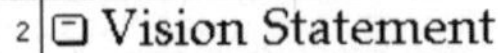

Reorganizing the Slides

1. Click a slide icon. **(Figure 11)**
2. Drag the icon up or down in the outline. **(Figure 12)**

   or

   Click the Move Up or Move Down buttons on the Outlining toolbar. **(Figure 13)**
3. Release the mouse button to drop the slide at its new position. **(Figure 14)**

✔ Tip

■ You can click the bullet at the beginning of a text item and then click the Move Up or Move Down buttons to move an individual line on a single slide.

2 Vision Statement
- To meet the challenges of a new era.

3 Goal and Objective
- State the desired goal
- State the desired objective
- Use multiple points if necessary

4 Today's Situation
- Summary of the current situation
- Use brief bullets, discuss details verbally

5 How Did We Get Here?
- Any relevant historical information

Figure 11. *Click a slide icon.*

The double-arrow mouse pointer and line show the proposed destination.

2 Vision Statement
- To meet the challenges of a new era.

3 Goal and Objective
- State the desired goal
- State the desired objective
- Use multiple points if necessary

4 Today's Situation
- Summary of the current situation
- Use brief bullets, discuss details verbally

5 How Did We Get Here?
- Any relevant historical information

Figure 12. *A horizontal line indicates the new position for the slide.*

Move Up button.

Move Down button.

Figure 13. *The Move Up and Move Down buttons.*

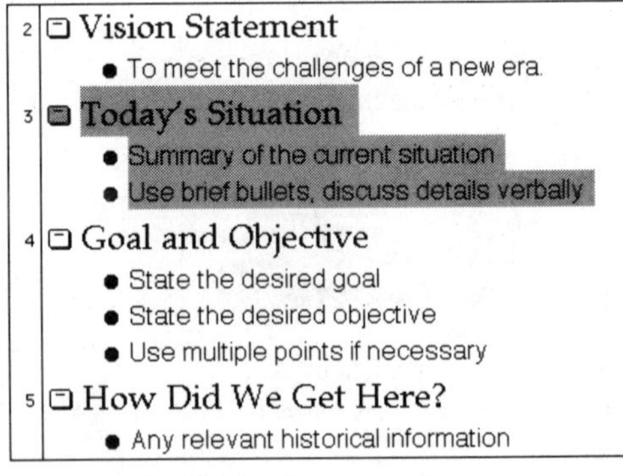

Figure 14. *Release the mouse button to drop the slide text.*

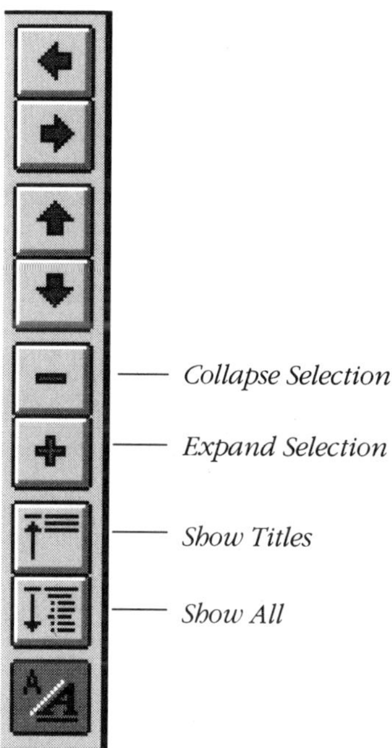

Figure 15. *The Outlining toolbar.*

Showing Only the Slide Titles

Show only the slide titles to temporarily disregard the detail in an outline.

1. Click the Show Titles button on the Outlining toolbar. **(Figure 15)**

✔ Tips

- To once again reveal the text on the slides, click the Show All button on the Outlining toolbar. **(Figure 15)**
- To hide or reveal text on a single slide, click the slide icon and then click the Collapse Selection button on the Outlining toolbar. **(Figure 17)** To see the text again, click the Expand Selection button.

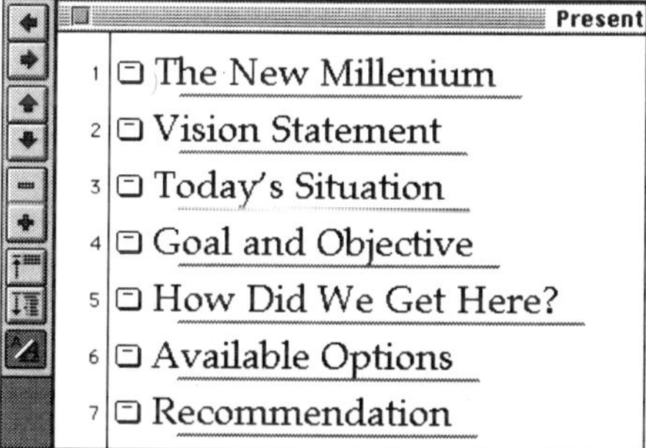

Figure 16. *Lines under the slide titles indicate that text is collapsed underneath.*

3 Today's Situation
- Summary of the current situation
- Use brief bullets, discuss details verbally

4 Goal and Objective
- State the desired goal
- State the desired objective
- Use multiple points if necessary

5 How Did We Get Here?
- Any relevant historical information

3 Today's Situation
- Summary of the current situation
- Use brief bullets, discuss details verbally

4 Goal and Objective

5 How Did We Get Here?
- Any relevant historical information
- Original assumptions that are no longer valid

6 Available Options

Figure 17. *Before and After: Collapsing the Goal and Objective text.*

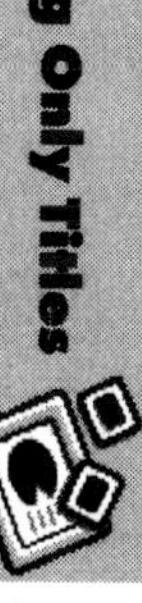

Inserting Slides

1. Click at the end of the last line of a slide. **(Figure 18)**
2. Click the New Slide button. **(Figure 19)**

- To meet the challenges of a new era.
3 Today's Situation
- Summary of the current situation
- Use brief bullets, discuss details verbally
4 Goal and Objective
- State the desired goal
- State the desired objective
- Use multiple points if necessary
5 How Did We Get Here?
- Any relevant historical information

Figure 18. *Click at the end of a slide.*

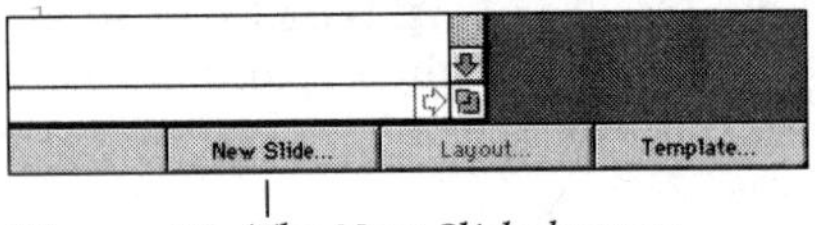

New Slide... Layout... Template...

Figure 19. *The New Slide button.*

- To meet the challenges of a new era.
3 Today's Situation
- Summary of the current situation
- Use brief bullets, discuss details verbally
4
5 Goal and Objective
- State the desired goal
- State the desired objective
- Use multiple points if necessary
6 How Did We Get Here?

Figure 20. *The new, blank slide appears.*

Deleting Slides

1. Click a slide icon to select an entire slide. **(Figure 21)**
2. Press the Delete key on the keyboard. **(Figure 22)**

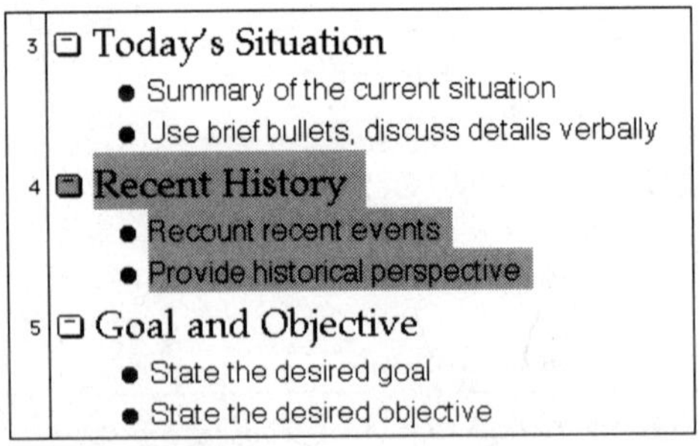

3 Today's Situation
- Summary of the current situation
- Use brief bullets, discuss details verbally
4 Recent History
- Recount recent events
- Provide historical perspective
5 Goal and Objective
- State the desired goal
- State the desired objective

Figure 21. *Click a slide icon and press Delete.*

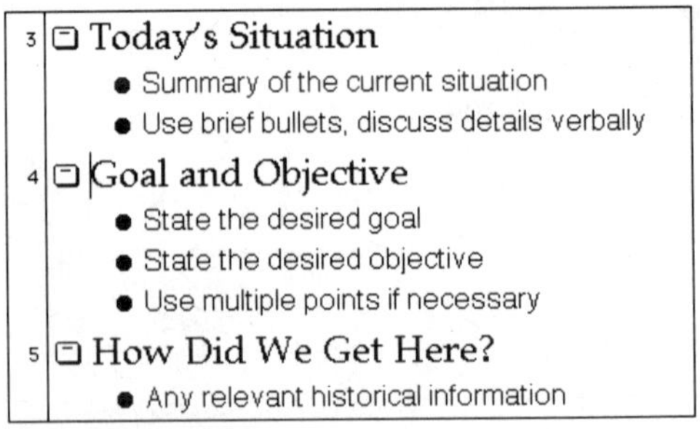

3 Today's Situation
- Summary of the current situation
- Use brief bullets, discuss details verbally
4 Goal and Objective
- State the desired goal
- State the desired objective
- Use multiple points if necessary
5 How Did We Get Here?
- Any relevant historical information

Figure 22. *The slide is deleted.*

Creating Text Slides 22

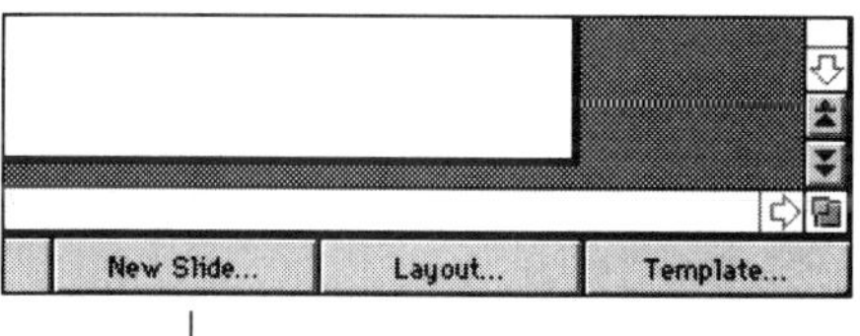

Figure 1. *The New Slide button.*

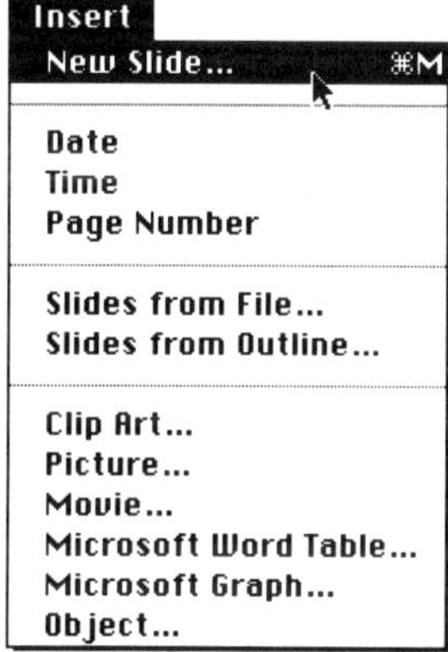

Figure 2. *The Insert menu.*

Starting a Text Slide

If you don't usc Outlinc vicw to enter the text of slides, you can create text slides in Slide view.

1. In Slide view, click the New Slide button. **(Figure 1)**

   or

   From the Insert menu, choose New Slide. **(Figure 2)**

   or

   Press ⌘+M.

2. On the New Slide dialog box, choose the second layout, Bulleted List, and then click OK. **(Figures 3-4)**

Bulleted List layout.

New Slide

Choose an AutoLayout:

OK

Cancel

Help

Bulleted List

Figure 3. *The New Slide dialog box.*

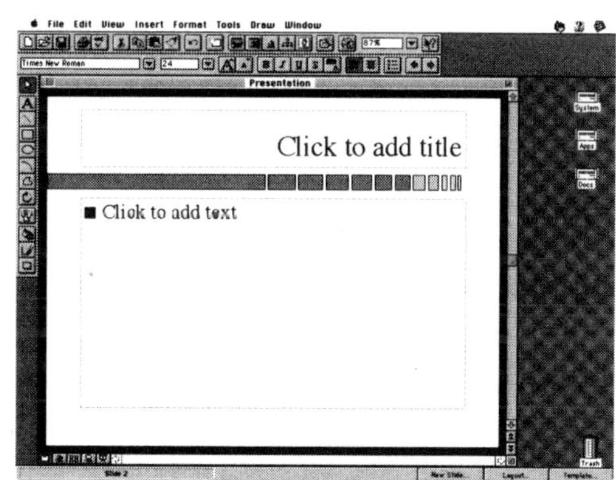

Figure 4. *The Bulleted List layout.*

Filling in Text Placeholders

1. Click a "Click to add title" or "Click to add text" placeholder. **(Figure 5)**
2. Type text. **(Figure 6)**
3. Click the next placeholder and type the next text. **(Figure 7)**

✔ Tips

- When you finish typing text into a placeholder, press ⌘+Enter to jump to the next placeholder.
- When you finish the text in the last placeholder on the page, you can press ⌘+Enter to add a new bulleted list slide.

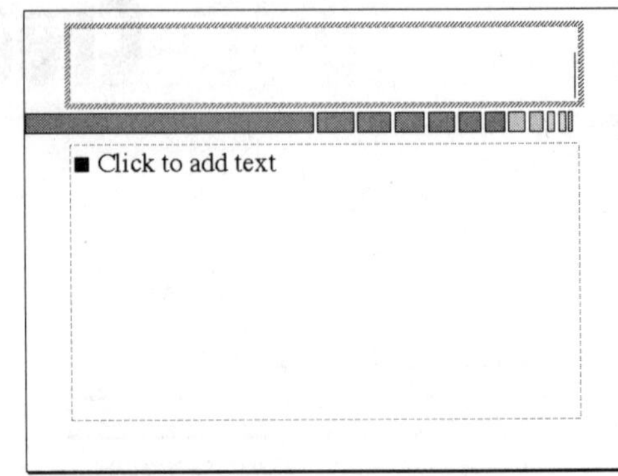

Figure 5. *Click the "Click to add title" placeholder.*

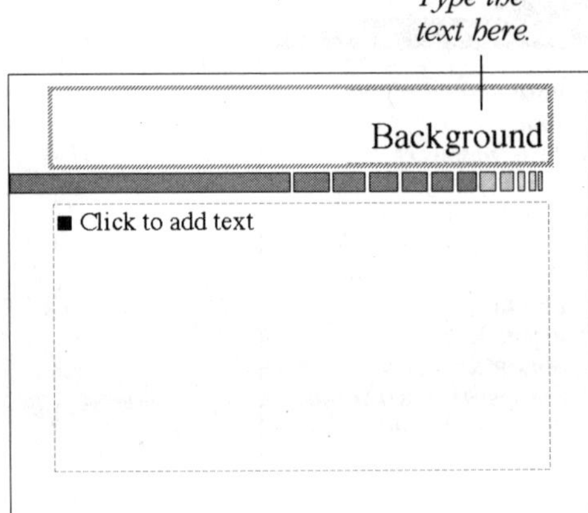

Figure 6. *Type text.*

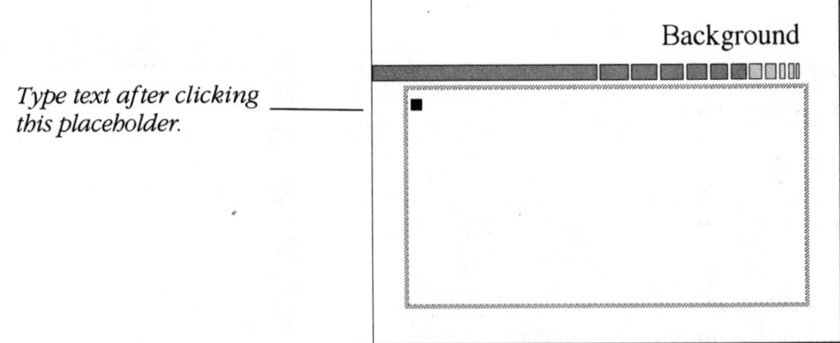

Figure 7. *Click the next text placeholder.*

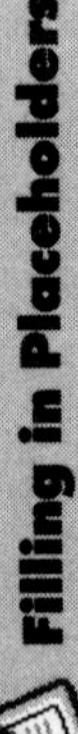

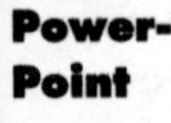

Selecting Text Blocks

Selecting characters, words, or paragraphs within a text block is just like selecting them in a **Word** document. *See Selecting Text, page 23-25.*

To move or format an entire text block, though, PowerPoint makes it easy to select the entire text block.

1. Click anywhere on a text block. **(Figure 8)**
2. Click on the border surrounding the text block. Handles appear. **(Figures 9-10)**

✔ Tips

- Click within a selected text block to select text within the block.
- To select a bulleted item in a text block, click the bullet.

Background

■ Pine Preservation Group meets in May.

■ Town Council meeting scheduled for July.

■ Meeting postponed until August.

Figure 8. *Click on the text block.*

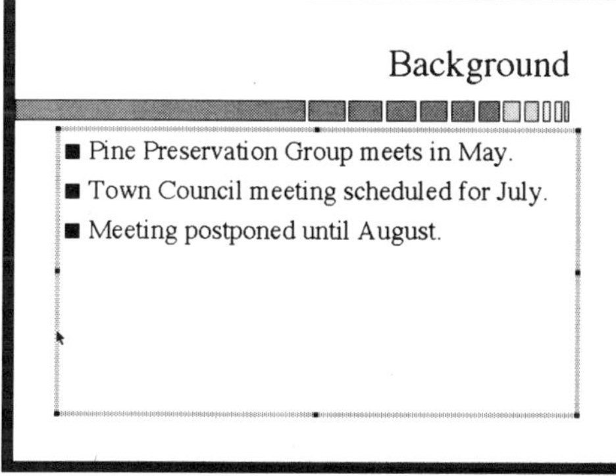

Figure 9. *Click on a border.*

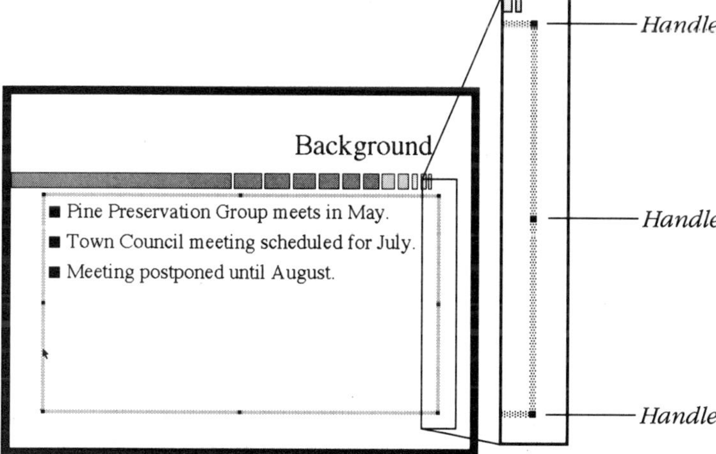

Figure 10. *Handles appear.*

Moving and Resizing Text Blocks

1. To move a selected text block, place the pointer on the border surrounding a selected text block. **(Figure 11)** *See Selecting Text Blocks, page 185.*

   or

   To resize a text block, place the pointer on a handle. **(Figure 12)**
2. Hold down the mouse button and drag the mouse. **(Figure 13)**

✔ Tips

- The text inside a text block re-wraps to fit within the new size of the block.
- Hold down the ⌘ key as you resize a text block to resize the block about its center.

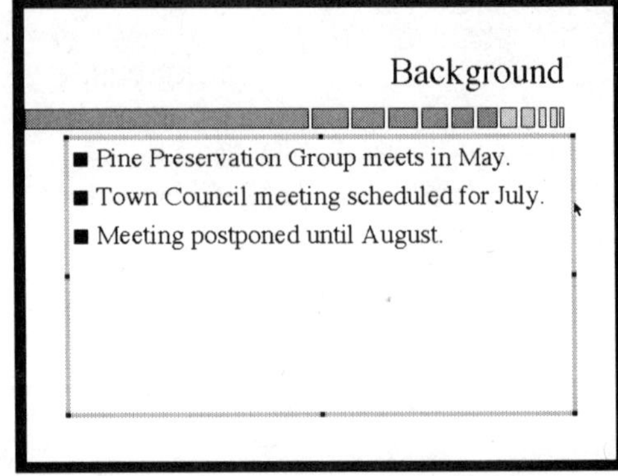

Figure 11. *Place the pointer on the border.*

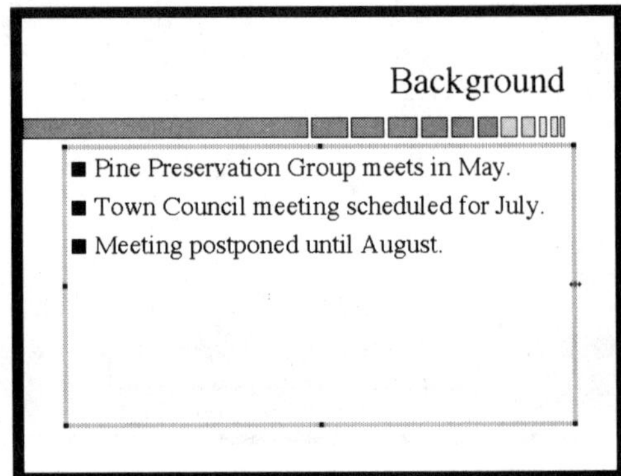

Figure 12. *Place the pointer on a handle.*

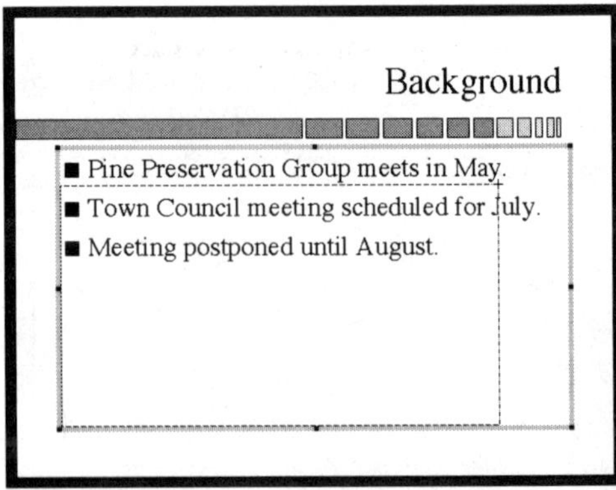

Figure 13. *Drag the handle to resize a text block.*

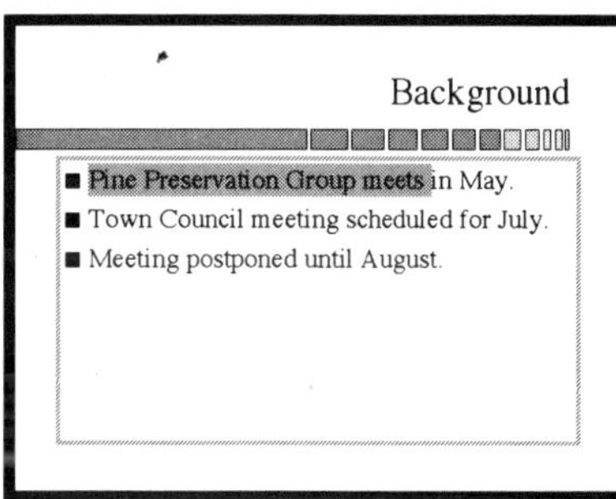

Figure 14. *Select text to format.*

Figure 15. *The Formatting toolbar.*

Figure 16. *The Format menu.*

Formatting Text

1. Select the text within a text block to format. **(Figure 14)**

   or

   Select the text block to format.

2. Click a text formatting button on the Formatting toolbar. **(Figure 15)** *See Font Formatting, pages 55-60.*

   or

   From the Format menu, choose Font, Bullet, Alignment, Line Spacing, or Change Case and make selections on the next dialog box to appear. **(Figure 16)**

   or

   Press and hold the Control key and click the mouse button. Then choose Font or Bullet from the shortcut menu, and make selections on the Font or Bullet dialog box. **(Figures 17-18)**

✔ Tips

- Any text formatting changes you make are preserved when you choose a different template to change the overall design of the presentation.
- To quickly add periods to the ends of all bulleted lines in a text block, select the block and choose Periods from the Format menu. Then select Add Periods or Remove Periods from the Periods dialog box.

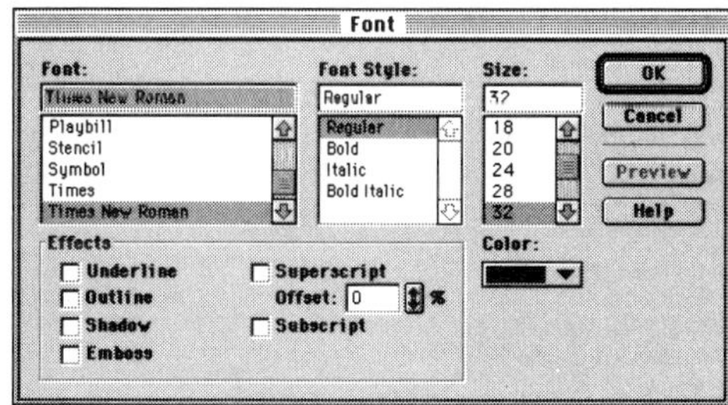

Figure 17. *The Font dialog box.*

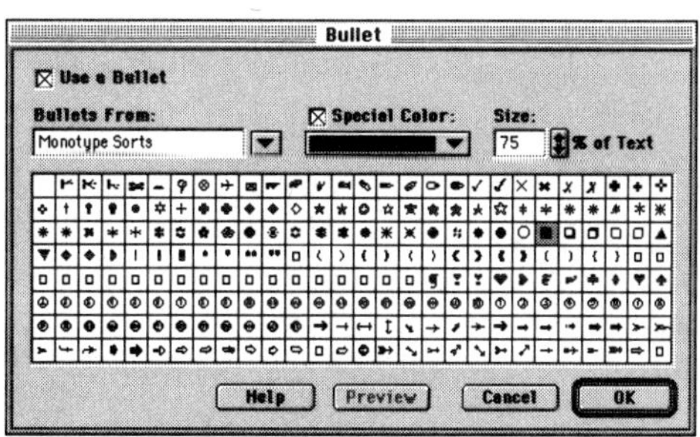

Figure 18. *The Bullet dialog box.*

Rearranging Text in a Block

1. Drag the bullet at the beginning of a text item up, down, left, or right to change the position of the text item within the block. **(Figures 19-20)**

   or

   Click on a bulleted text item and press Option+Shift+Arrow key to move the text item up, down, left, or right.

✔ Tips

- When you move a text item to the right, it appears to be indented under the previous text item. **(Figure 21)**
- When you move a text item to the left or right, you move the text item to a different level. Each level may have a different default text format and bullet style.

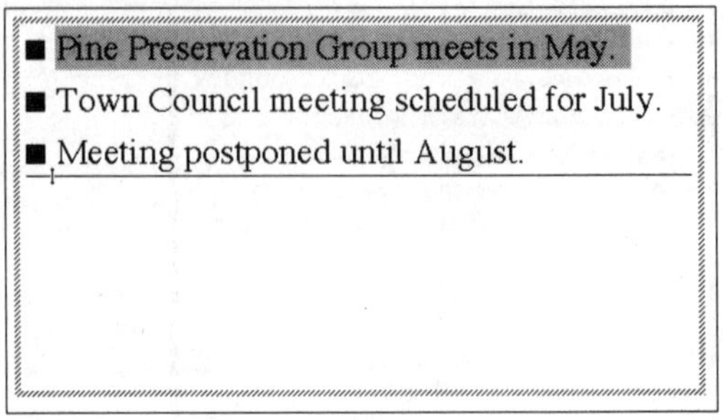

■ Pine Preservation Group meets in May.
■ Town Council meeting scheduled for July.
■ Meeting postponed until August.

Figure 19. *Drag the bullet at the beginning of a text item.*

■ Town Council meeting scheduled for July.
■ Meeting postponed until August.
■ Pine Preservation Group meets in May.

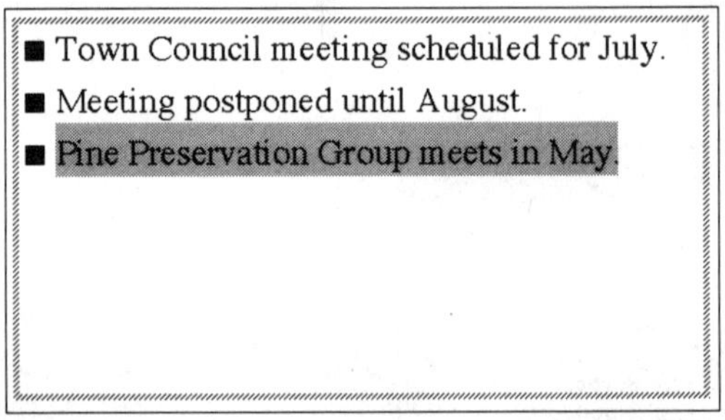

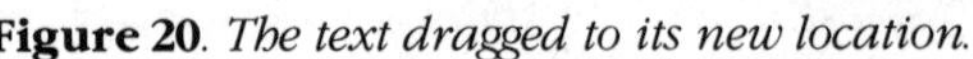

Figure 20. *The text dragged to its new location.*

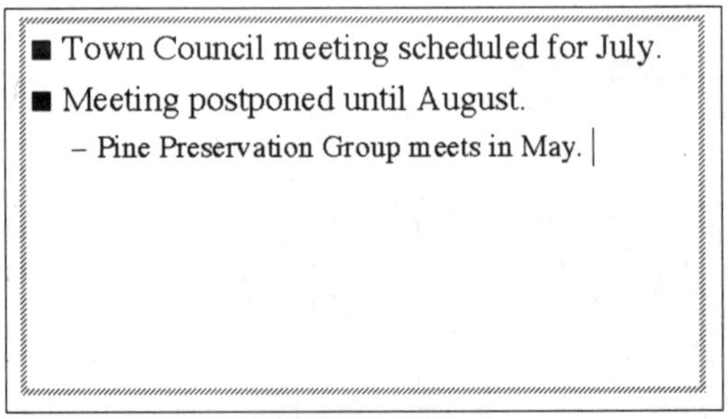

■ Town Council meeting scheduled for July.
■ Meeting postponed until August.
– Pine Preservation Group meets in May.

Figure 21. *Text moved to the right one level appears indented.*

Creating Graph Slides

Choose one of these three layouts.

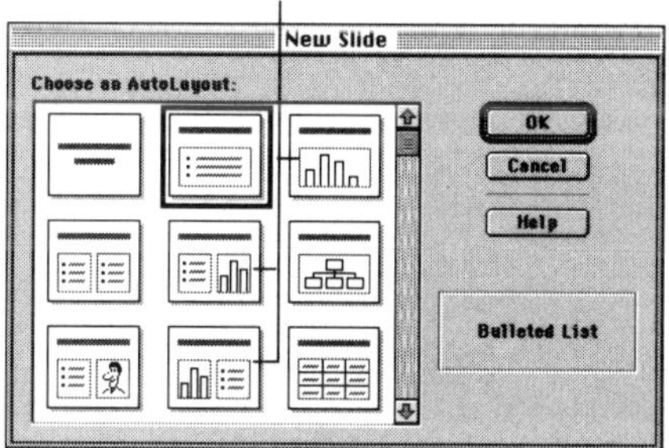

Figure 1. *The New Slide dialog box.*

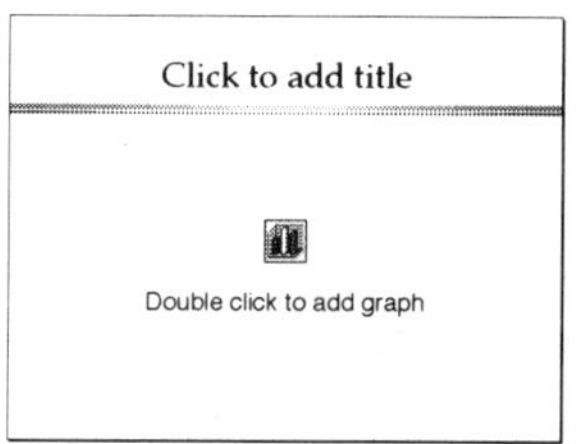

Figure 2. *Double click a graph placeholder.*

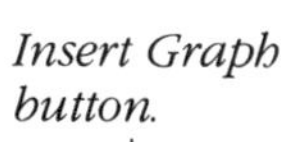

Insert Graph button.

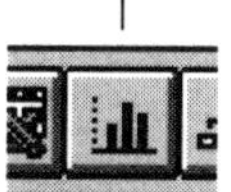

Figure 3. *The Insert Graph button.*

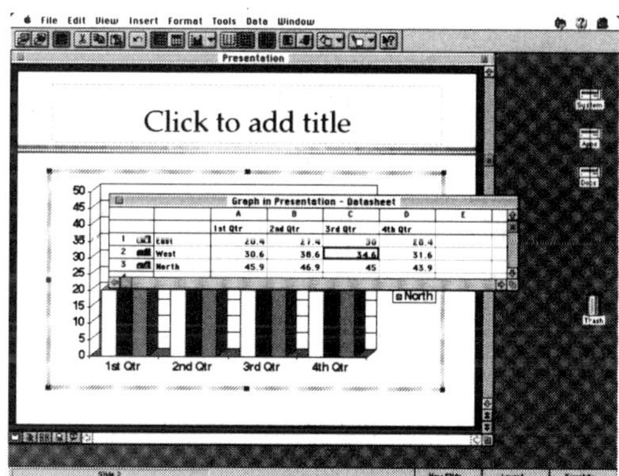

Figure 4. *A sample graph and datasheet appear within a border on the current slide.*

About Graphing

When chosen wisely, a graph can make even complex numeric information visual and therefore easy to interpret and communicate.

To create or edit a graph, PowerPoint uses Graph 5, the same graphing module used by Excel. Graph 5 creates a *chart*, and while doing so commandeers the PowerPoint window, replacing PowerPoint's menus and toolbars with its own. When you click outside the border of the completed chart, the PowerPoint menus and toolbars reappear.

Starting a Chart

1. Click the New Slide button.
2. On the New Slide dialog box, choose one of the three layouts that includes a graph placeholder (Graph, Text & Graph, Graph & Text.) **(Figure 1)**
3. Double-click the "Double click to add graph" placeholder. **(Figure 2)**

   or

1. Turn to the slide to which you'd like to add a graph.
2. Click the Insert Graph button on the Standard toolbar. **(Figure 3)**

   or

   From the Insert menu, choose Microsoft Graph.

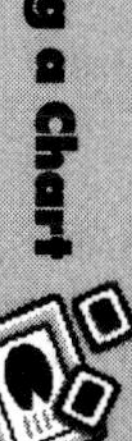

Replacing the Sample Data on the Data Sheet

1. Click any cell in the Excel-like grid and type over its contents. **(Figure 5)**

   or

   Select all the cells that contain data and begin typing new data in columns. Press Enter after typing each new heading or number. When the cell pointer reaches the bottom of a column, it jumps to the top of the next column automatically. **(Figure 6)**

2. Click the View Datasheet button in the Graph toolbar to close the datasheet and view the graph. **(Figure 7)**

   or

   Click any part of the graph that is visible.

✔ Tip

■ To exclude a row or column of data from the graph, double-click the row or column heading button. **(Figure 8)**

Graph in Presentation - Datasheet

		A	B	C	D	E
		1st Qtr	2nd Qtr	3rd Qtr	4th Qtr	
1	East	20.4	27.4	30	20.4	
2	West	30.6	38.6	34.6	31.6	
3	North	45.9	46.9	45	43.9	

Figure 5. *The data sheet.*

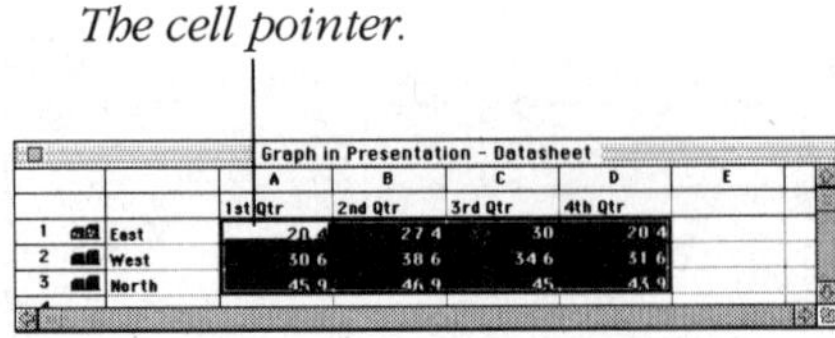

Figure 6. *Select the cells that contain data to replace.*

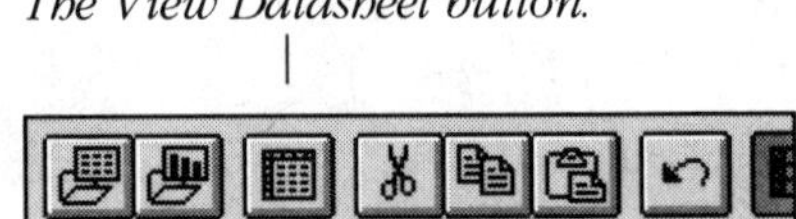

Figure 7. *The View Datasheet button.*

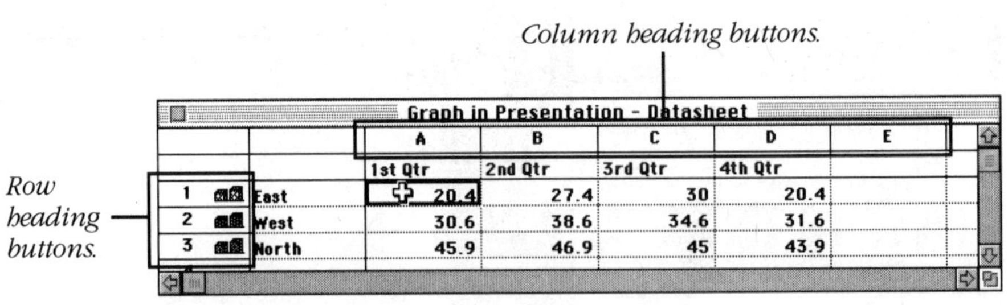

Figure 8. *The row and column heading buttons.*

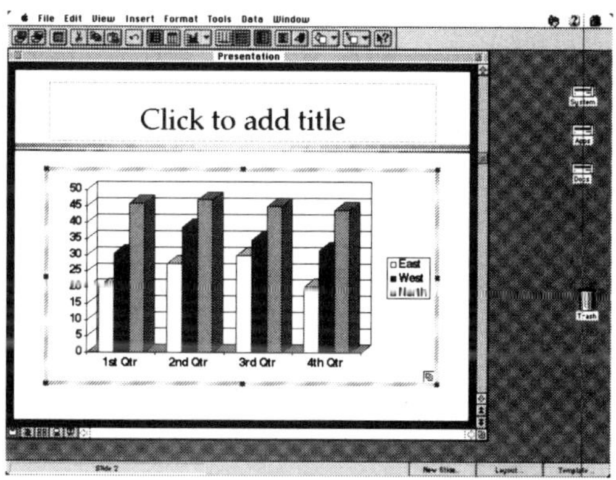

Figure 9. *Double-click the chart to format.*

The Chart Type button.

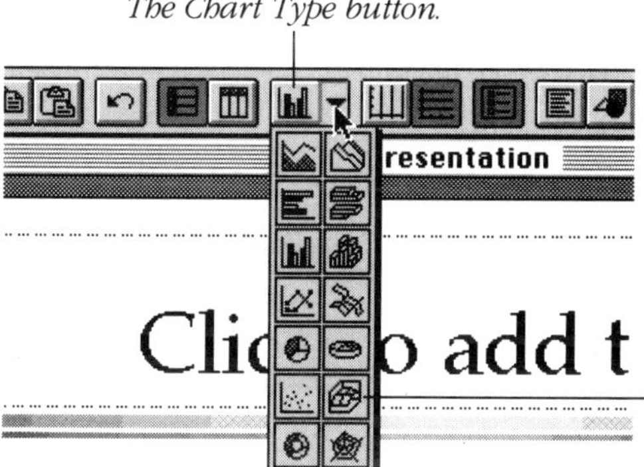

Chart type pane.

Figure 10. *The Chart Type button.*

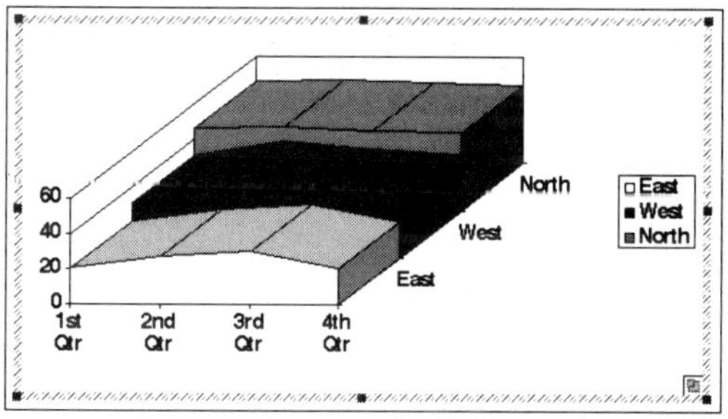

Figure 11. *The modified chart.*

Changing the Chart Type

The most basic commands to format a new chart are available as buttons on the Graph toolbar.

1. Double-click the chart if necessary to make it active (surrounded by a thick border). **(Figure 9)**
2. Click the pull-down button next to the the Chart Type button on the Graph toolbar. **(Figure 10)**
3. Select a chart type pane to change the chart type of the chart.

✔ Tips

- Choosing an AutoFormat for the chart gives you many more chart type options. *See Choosing an AutoFormat, on the next page.*
- You can create a Chart Type toolbar by positioning the pointer on the pull-down Chart Type button, holding down the mouse button, and then dragging to another point on the screen.

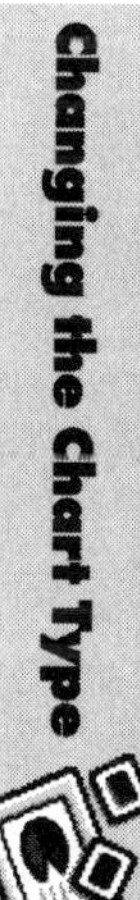

Choosing an AutoFormat

Choosing an AutoFormat for a chart is a shortcut for formatting the chart. An AutoFormat specifies a chart type and sets many chart formatting options automatically.

1. Double-click the chart if necessary to make it active. **(Figure 12)**
2. From the Format menu, choose AutoFormat. **(Figure 13)**
3. Select a chart type from the Galleries list. **(Figure 14)**
4. Double-click on one of the numbered panes which display charts with various option settings. **(Figure 14)**

✔ Tips

- Click User-Defined on the AutoFormat dialog box to choose one of the special chart formats you've created and added to the selection.
- To add a chart format, format a chart manually and select the chart. Then, on the AutoFormat dialog box, choose User-Defined and click the Add button.

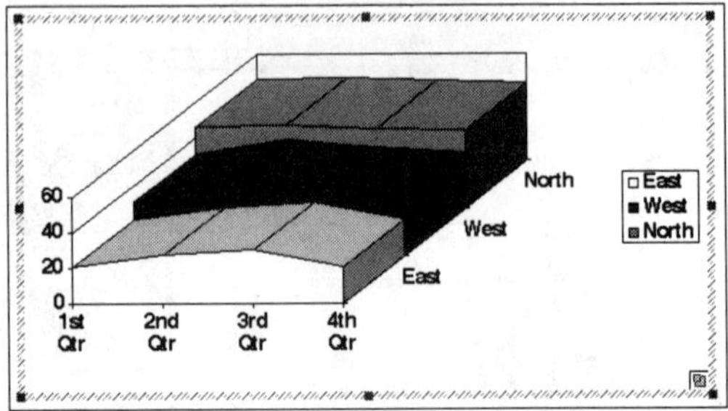

Figure 12. *Double-click the chart to format.*

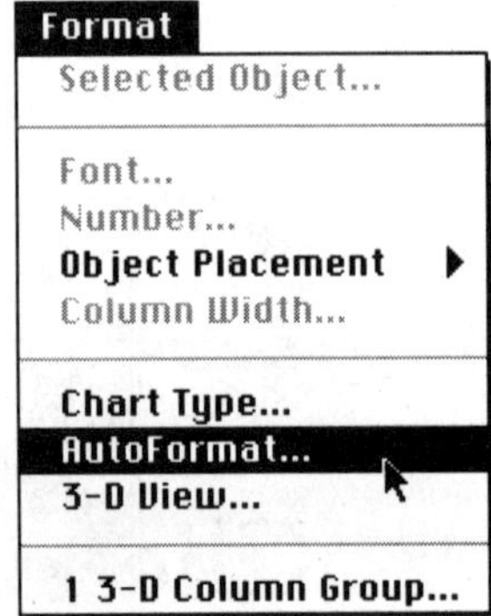

Figure 13. *The Format menu.*

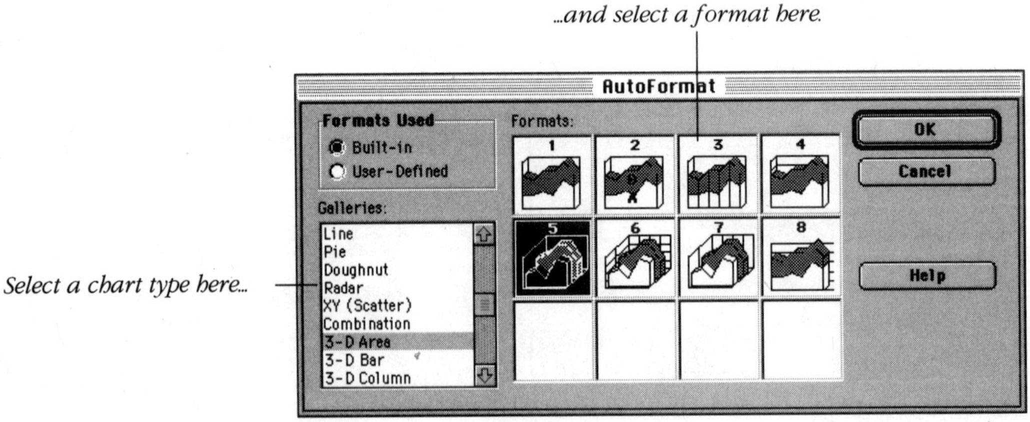

...and select a format here.

Select a chart type here...

Figure 14. *The AutoFormat dialog box.*

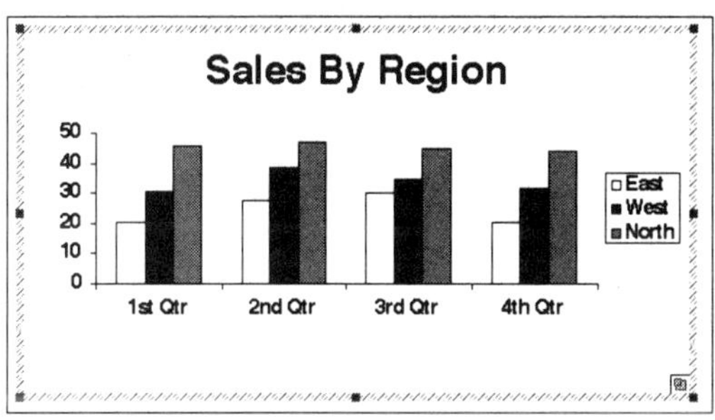

Figure 15. *Double-click the chart to format.*

Displaying a Legend and Grid Lines

1. Double-click the chart to make it active, if necessary. **(Figure 15)**
2. To turn the legend on or off, click the Legend button on the Graph toolbar. **(Figure 16)**

   or

   To turn the grid lines on or off, click the Vertical Gridlines and/or Horizontal Gridlines buttons on the Graph toolbar. **(Figure 16)**

✔ Tips

- You can also add a legend or gridlines by selecting Legend or Gridlines from the Insert menu.
- When you add gridlines from the Insert menu, you can choose Major Gridlines or Minor Gridlines for each axis. **(Figure 17)**

Vertical Gridlines button.

Legend button.

Horizontal Gridlines button.

Figure 16. *The Graph toolbar.*

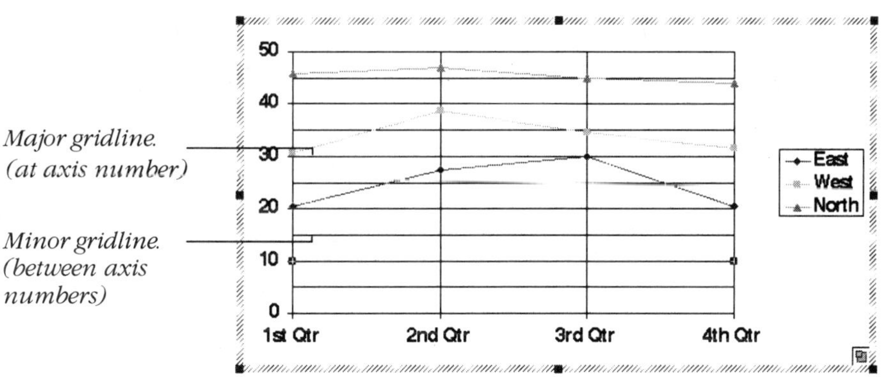

Figure 17. *Major vs. Minor Gridlines.*

Adding Chart Titles

1. Double-click the chart to make it active, if necessary.
2. From the Insert menu, choose Titles. **(Figure 18)**
3. On the Titles dialog box, click the checkboxes for the titles you'd like to add. **(Figure 19)**
4. On the chart, click a title placeholder and then type the new title. **(Figures 20-21)**

✔ **Tips**

- To remove a title, choose Titles from the Insert menu again and then, on the Titles dialog box, clear the checkbox for the title to remove.

Figure 18. *The Insert menu.*

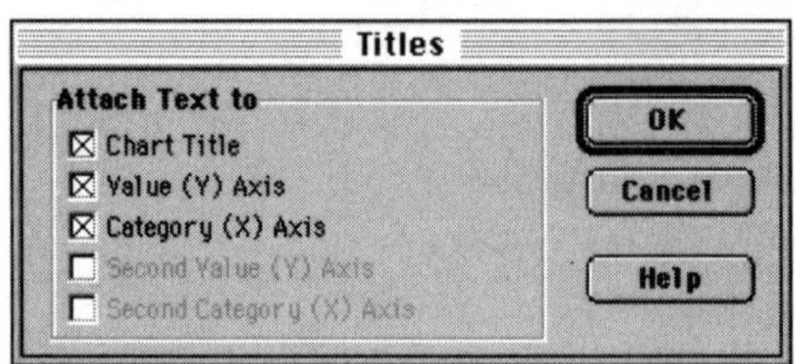

Figure 19. *The Titles dialog box.*

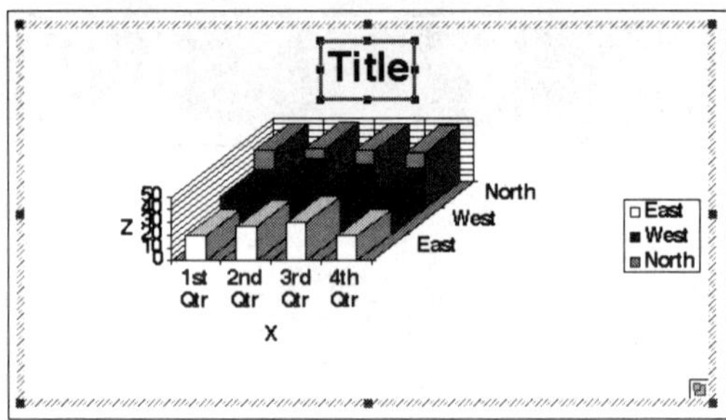

Figure 20. *Click a title placeholder...*

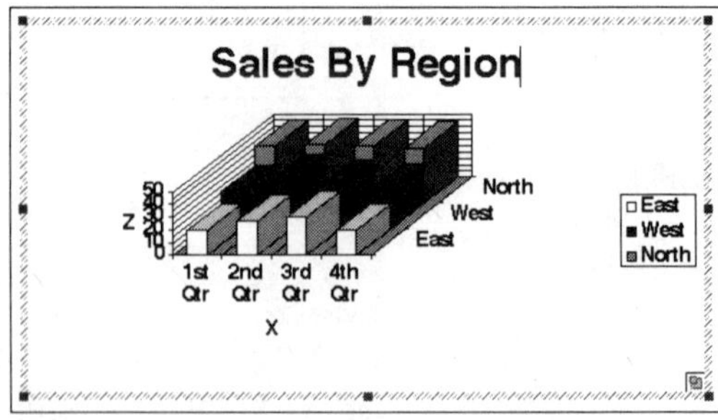

Figure 21. *...and then type the new title.*

Insert
Insert Cells... ⌘I
Titles...
Data Labels...
Legend
Axes...
Gridlines...
Trendline...
Error Bars...

Figure 22. *The Insert menu.*

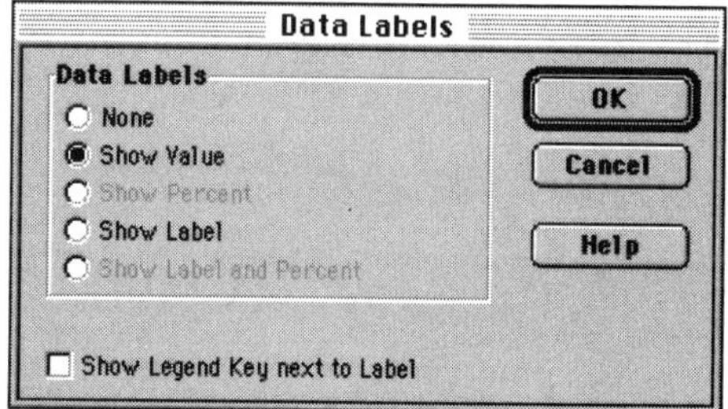

Figure 23. *The Data Labels dialog box.*

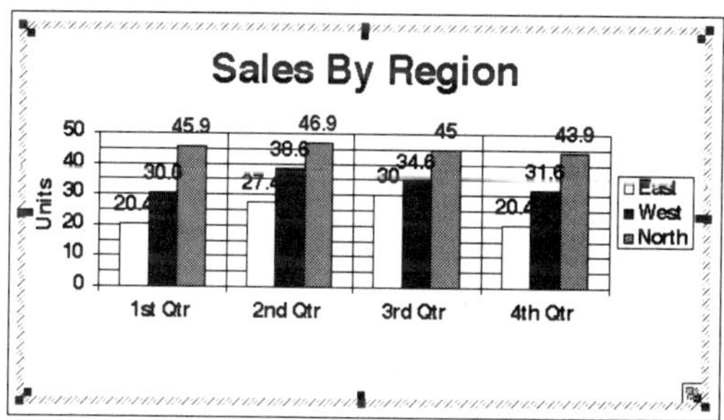

Figure 24. *Data Labels on all series.*

Adding Data Labels

To turn on data labels for every series in the chart:

1. Double-click the chart if necessary to make it active.
2. From the Insert menu, choose Data Labcls. **(Figure 22)**
3. On the Data Labels dialog box, choose one of the options other than None and click OK. **(Figures 23-24)**

To turn on data labels for a single series:

1. Click one set of bars, one line, one pie slice, or similar chart element. **(Figure 25)**
2. Follow Steps 2 and 3 above.

✔ **Tips**

- To remove data labels, choose None on the Data Labels dialog box.
- To format data labels, double-click the series to which they are attached and then make changes on the Data Labels tab of the Format Data Series dialog box.

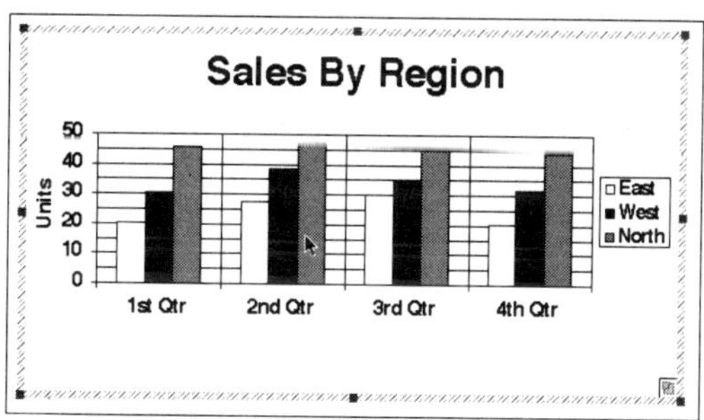

Figure 25. *Select one series before turning on data labels.*

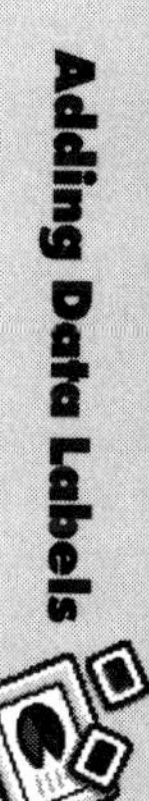

By Rows vs. By Columns

The sets of data that you need to chart are arranged either in rows or in columns on the data sheet. **(Figures 26-28)** To inform Graph how your data is arranged, click the By Rows or By Columns button.

1. Double-click the chart if necessary to make it active.
2. Click the By Columns or By Rows button. **(Figure 29)**

   or

   From the Data menu, choose Series in Rows or Series in Columns. **(Figure 30)**

✔ Tip

- Choosing an alternate view of the data (By Rows rather than By Columns, or vice versa) is legitimate only when both the columns and rows of the datasheet hold related series of data.

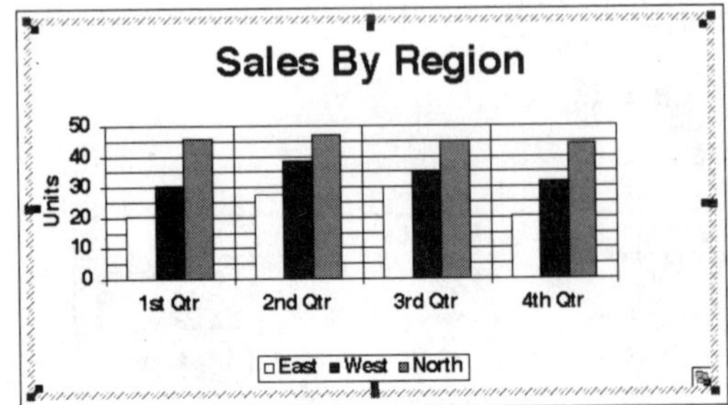

Graph in Presentation - Datasheet

		A	B	C	D	E
		1st Qtr	2nd Qtr	3rd Qtr	4th Qtr	
1	East	20.4	27.4	30	20.4	
2	West	30.6	38.6	34.6	31.6	
3	North	45.9	46.9	45	43.9	

Figure 26. *The datasheet.*

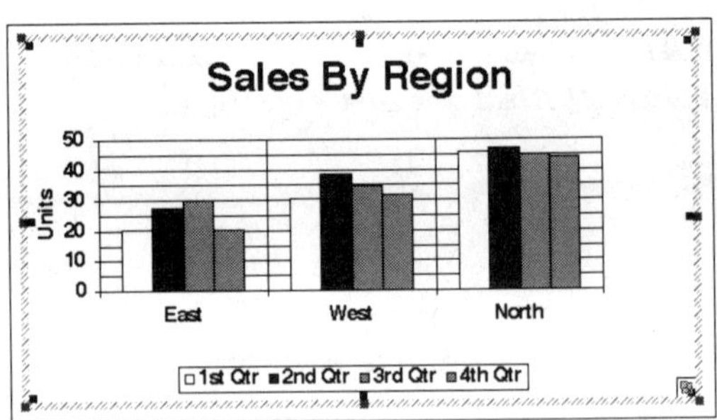

Figure 27. *Data charted by rows.*

Sales By Region

Units

50 40 30 20 10 0

East West North

1st Qtr 2nd Qtr 3rd Qtr 4th Qtr

Figure 28. *Same data charted by columns.*

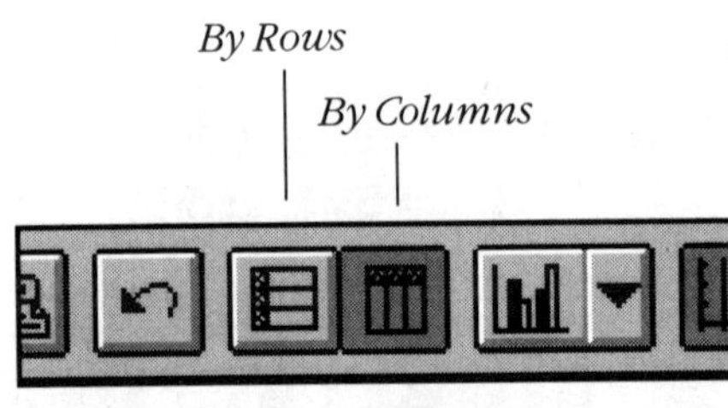

Figure 29. *The By Columns and By Rows buttons.*

Figure 30. *The Data menu.*

Formatting Charts

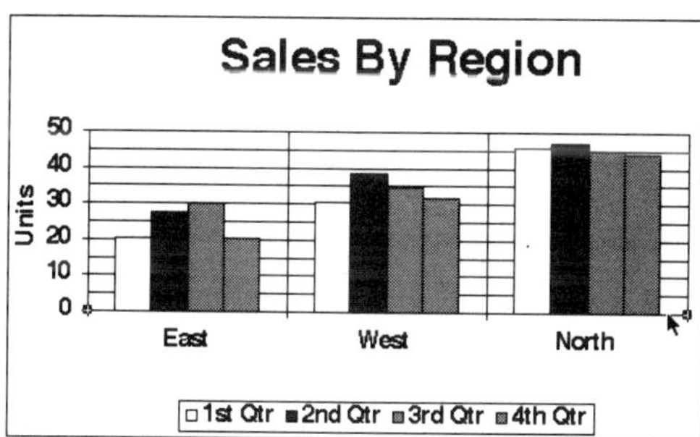

Figure 1. *Double-click an axis to format the axis.*

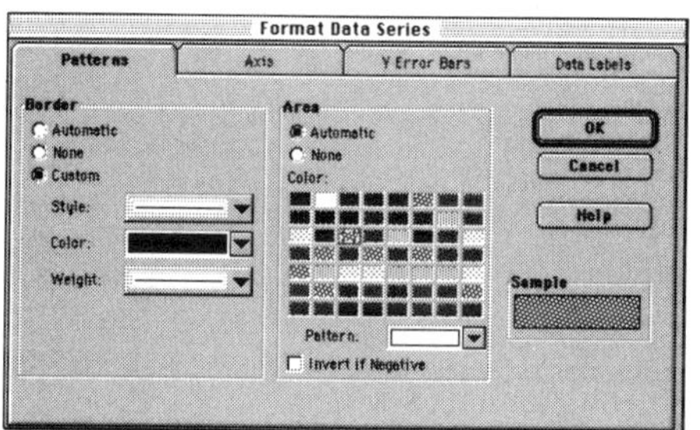

Figure 2. *The Format Data Series dialog box has four tabs of settings.*

About Chart Formatting

The easiest way to change the overall appearance of a chart is to choose a different AutoFormat. *See Choosing an AutoFormat, page 192.* You can also format the appearance of an individual element of the chart (one set of bars, one line, an axis, etc.) or change the style of the series in the chart by formatting a *series group*.

Formatting a Chart Element

1. Double-click the chart if necessary to make it active.
2. Double-click the chart element to format. **(Figure 1)**
3. On the Format dialog box, choose formatting settings on the appropriate tab or tabs. **(Figure 2)**

✔ Tips

- You can also select a chart element choose the first command on the Format menu, which reads "Selected *Chart Element*."
- After you format one chart element, you can double-click a different chart element to format.

Formatting a Group

1. Double-click the chart to make it active, if necessary.
2. At the bottom of the Format menu, choose the Format Group command. **(Figure 3)**
3. On the Subtype tab of the Format Group dialog box, click the pane that displays the subtype you want. **(Figure 4)**

   or

   Change the settings on the other tabs in the Format Group dialog box.
4. Click OK.

✓ Tip

- The sample on the Format Group dialog box previews the effect of any setting change.

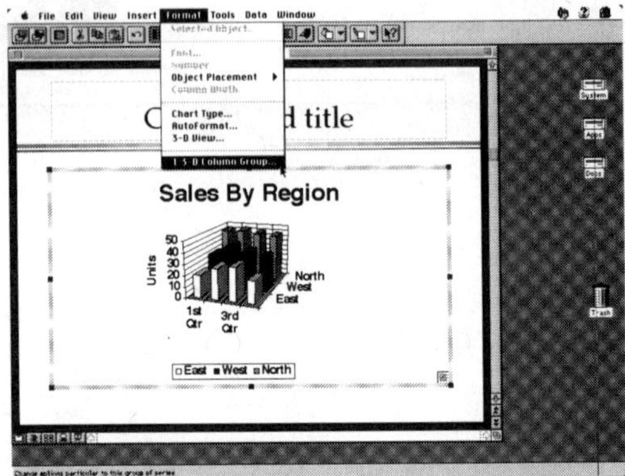

Figure 3. *The Format 3-D Column Group command.*

Figure 4. *The Subtype tab for a 3-D Column chart.*

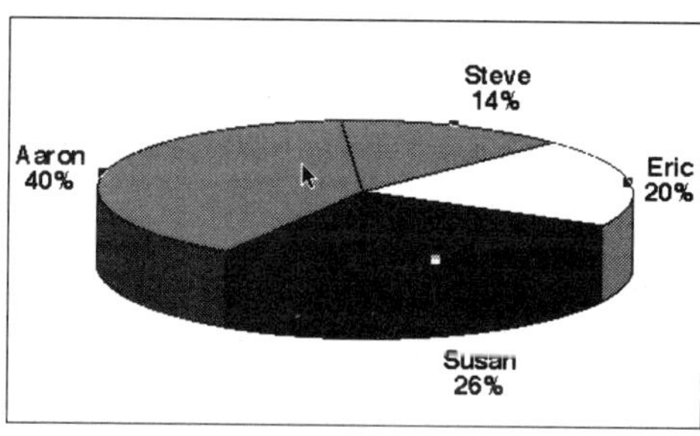

Figure 5. *Click the pie.*

Cutting a Pie Chart Slice

1. Double-click the chart to make it active, if necessary.
2. Click the pie once to select the entire pie. **(Figure 5)**
3. Click the slice to cut. **(Figure 6)**
4. Drag the slice away from the pie. **(Figures 7-8)**

✓ Tip

- To rejoin the slice with the pie, drag the slice back toward the center of the pie.

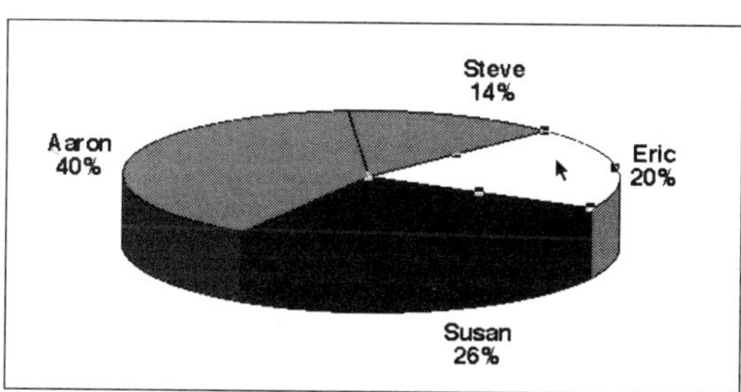

Figure 6. *Click the slice to cut.*

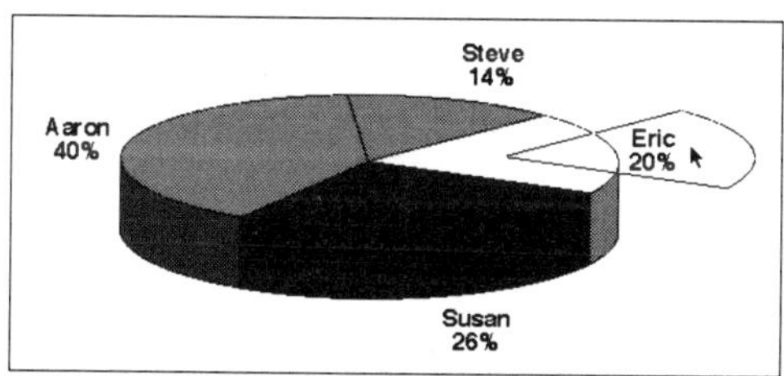

Figure 7. *Drag the slice away from the pie.*

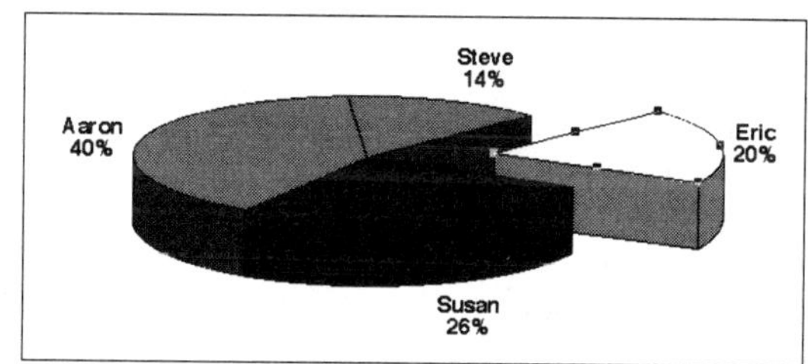

Figure 8. *The cut slice.*

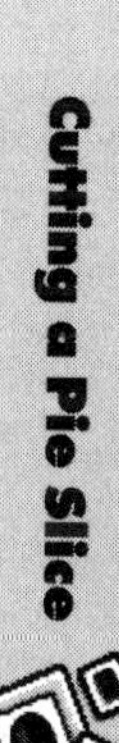

Creating High-Low-Close Charts

1. Double-click the chart to make it active, if necessary.
2. On the datasheet, make sure the data is ordered either High-Low-Close or Open-High-Low-Close. **(Figure 9)**
3. Choose the 2-D Line chart type. **(Figure 10)**
4. From the Format menu, choose Line Group. **(Figure 11)**
5. On the Options tab of the Format Line Group dialog box, turn on Up-Down Bars and High-Low Lines. **(Figure 12)**
6. If you want, double-click each line and then, on the Format Data Series dialog box, set Line to None on the Patterns tab.

Graph in Presentation - Datasheet

		A	B	C	D	E
		Mon	Tue	Wed	Thu	Fri
1	Open	11.00	12.00	13.00	17.00	17.00
2	High	14.00	14.00	16.00	19.00	22.00
3	Low	10.38	11.00	13.50	15.00	18.00
4	Close	12.00	13.00	16.00	18.00	21.38
5						
6						

Figure 9. *The datasheet for a High-Low-Close chart.*

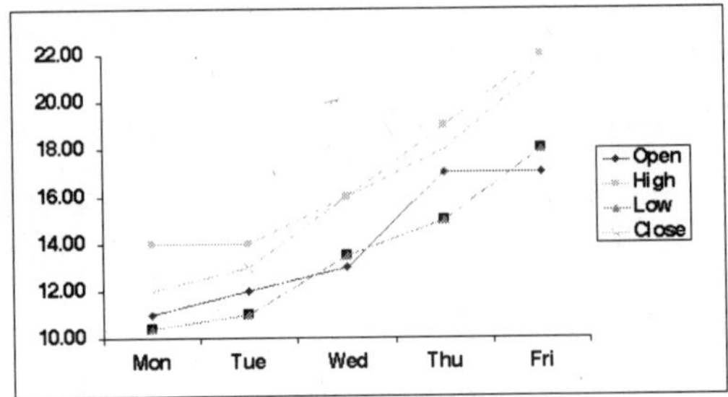

Figure 10. *The 2-D Line chart type.*

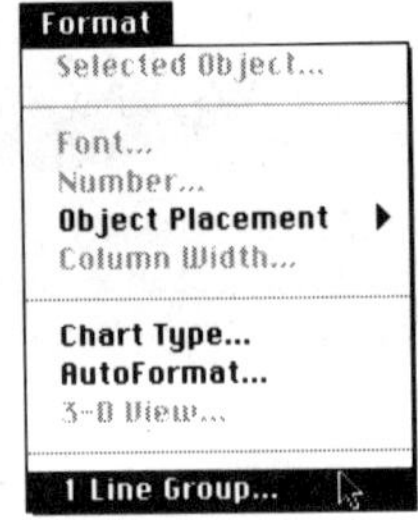

Figure 11. *The Format menu.*

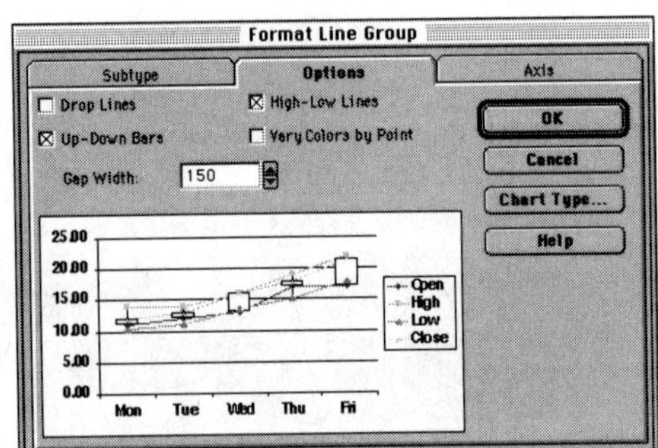

Figure 12. *The Options tab of the Format Line Group dialog box.*

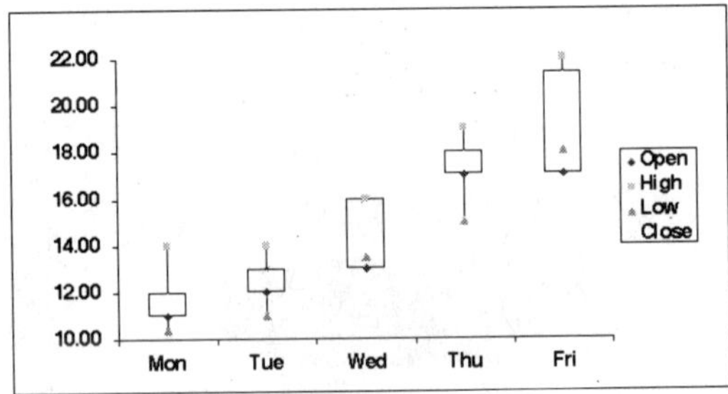

Figure 13. *The High-Low-Close chart.*

High-Low-Close Charts

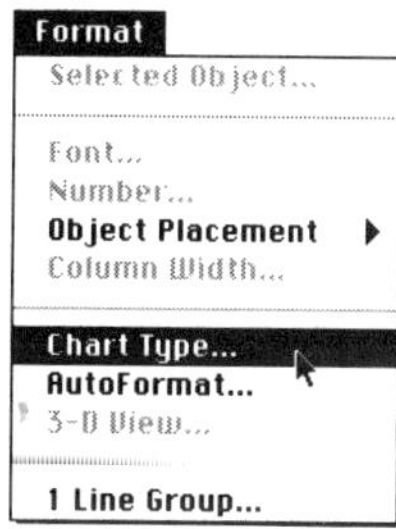

Figure 14. *The Format menu.*

Switching Between 3-D and 2-D Chart Types

1. Double-click the chart to make it active, if necessary.
2. From the Format menu, choose Chart Type. **(Figure 14)**
3. On the Chart Type dialog box, click the appropriate Chart Dimension setting, either 2-D or 3-D. **(Figure 15)**
4. Click OK. **(Figure 16)**

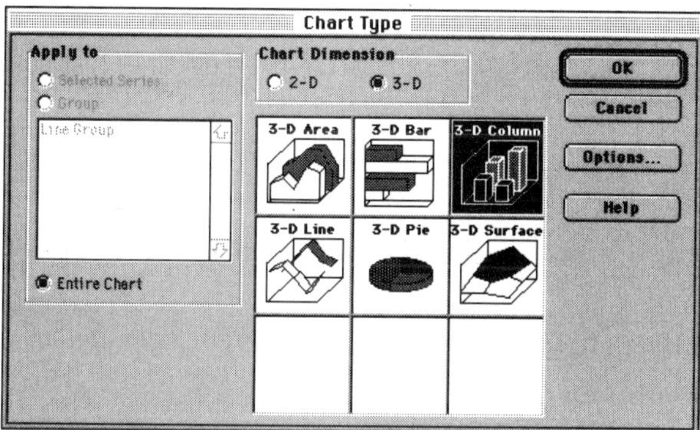

Figure 15. *The Chart Type dialog box.*

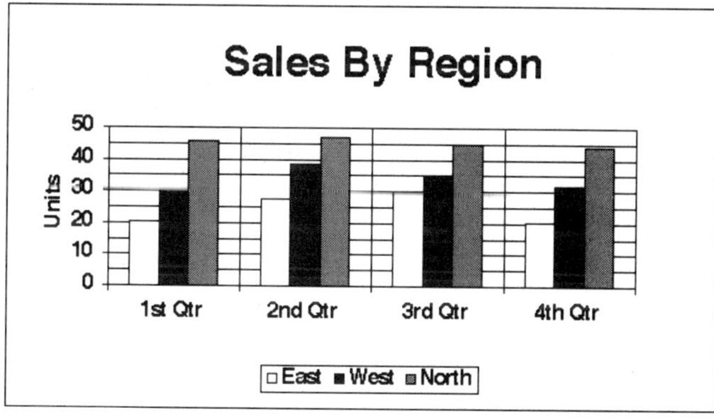

Figure 16. *The 2-D Chart.*

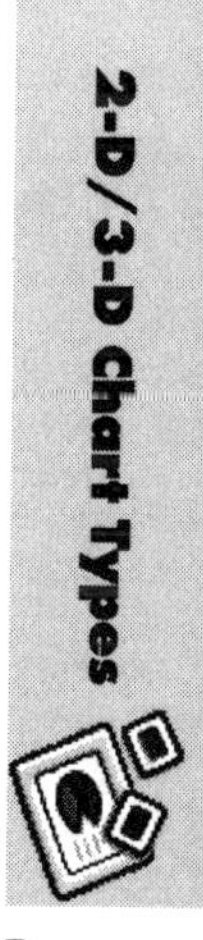

Changing the View of 3-D Charts

1. Double-click the chart to make it active, if necessary.
2. From the Format or shortcut menus, choose 3-D View. **(Figure 17)**
3. Click the large buttons on the 3-D View dialog box to rotate the 3-D wireframe model shown on the dialog box. **(Figure 18)**
4. To add perspective, clear the Right Angle Axes checkbox and then click the Perspective buttons to increase or decrease the perspective. **(Figure 19)**
5. Click Apply to apply the 3-D view of the model to your chart.

✔ Tips

- To change the proportions of the chart, clear the Auto Scaling checkbox and change the Height of Base percentage.
- You may prefer to change the 3-D view of a graph by dragging a corner handle of the graph. Release the corner handle when the wireframe representation of the graph is positioned to your liking. **(Figure 20)**

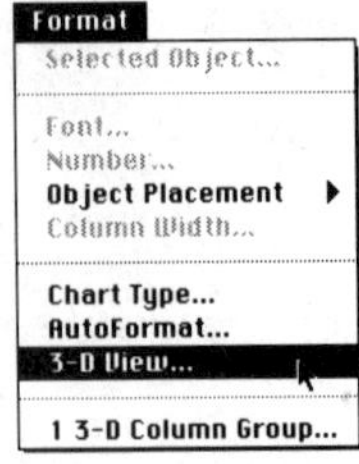

Figure 17. *The Format menu.*

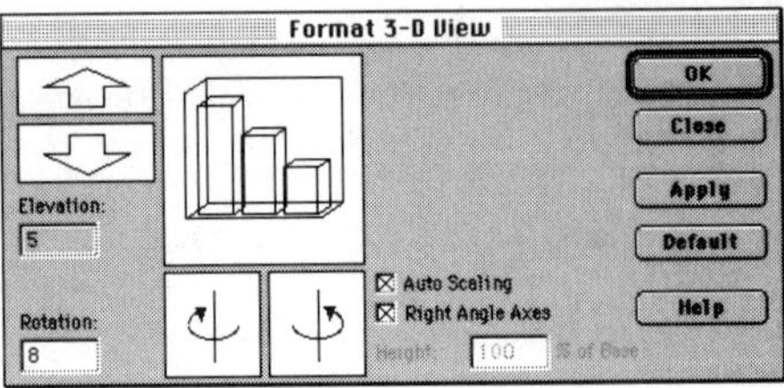

Figure 18. *The Format 3-D View dialog box.*

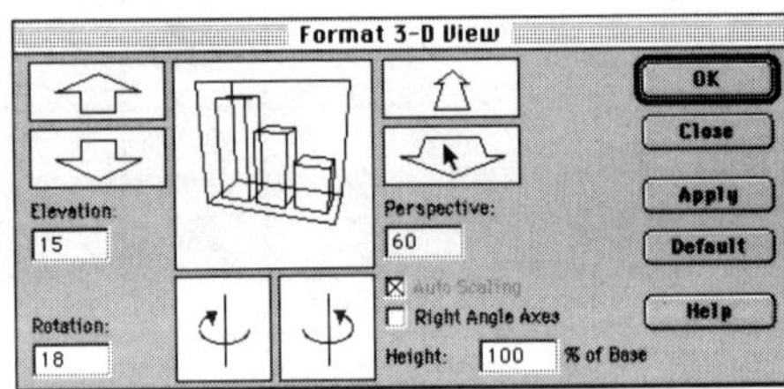

Figure 19. *Adding Perspective.*

Drag a corner handle.

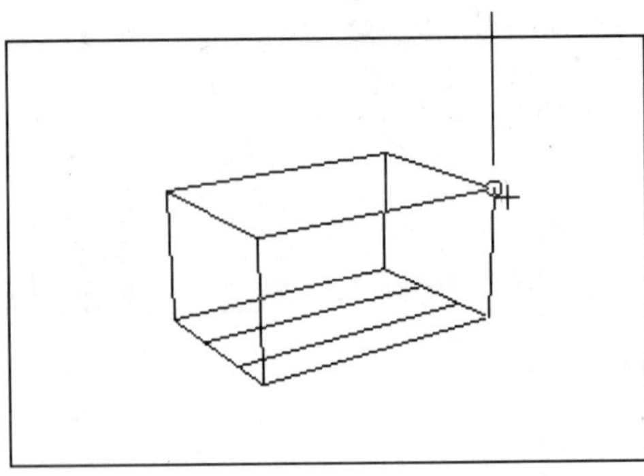

Figure 20. *Dragging a corner handle to rotate a wireframe of a 3-D graph.*

Organization Charts and Tables 25

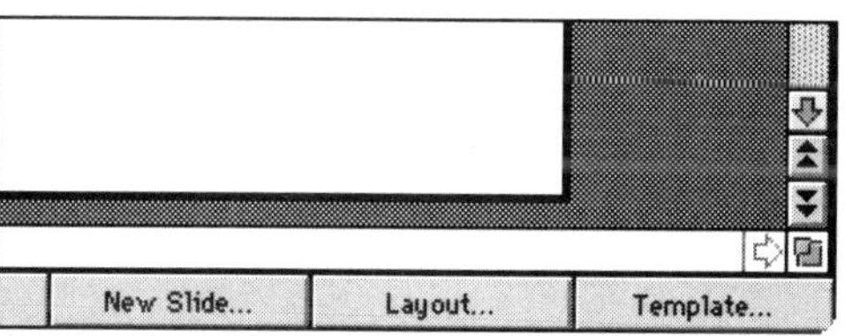

Figure 1. *The New Slide button.*

Double-click the Org Chart layout.

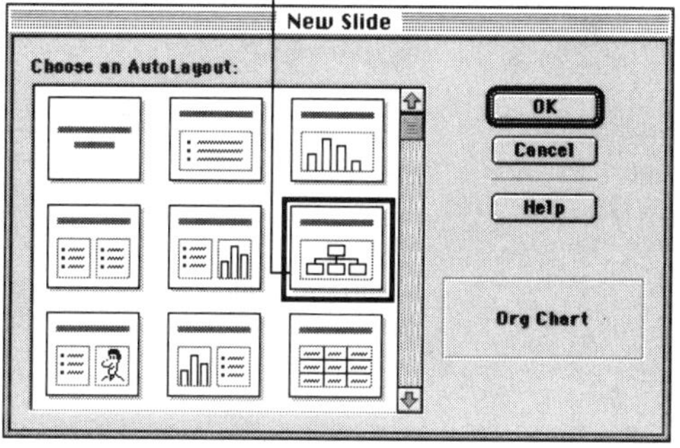

Figure 2. *The New Slide dialog box.*

Insert Org Chart button.

Figure 3. *The Insert Org Chart button.*

Starting an Org Chart

1. Click the New Slide button to start a new slide. **(Figure 1)**
2. On the New Slide dialog box, double-click the Org Chart layout. **(Figure 2)**
3. On the new slide, double-click the "Double click to add org chart" placeholder.

or, to add an org chart to an existing slide

1. Turn to the slide to which you want to add an org chart.
2. Click the Insert Org Chart button on the Standard toolbar. **(Figure 3)**

✔ Tip

- Org charts are created by a module called Microsoft Organization Chart, which appears in a separate window. **(Figure 4)** When you finish the org chart, the chart will be placed on the current slide.

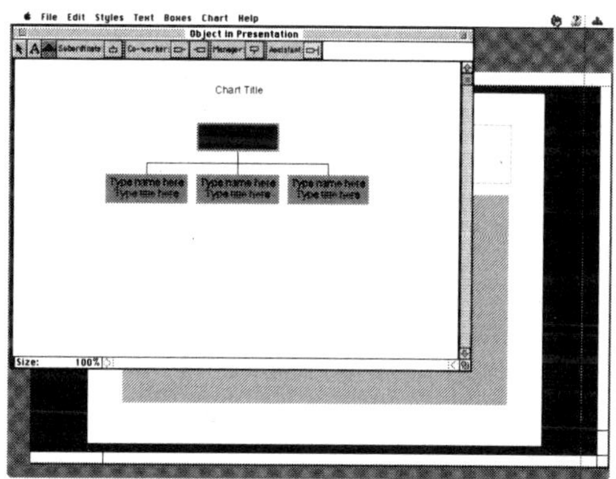

Figure 4. *The Microsoft Organization Chart window.*

Entering Org Members

1. Into the box at the top of the hierarchy, type the head of the hierarchy's name. **(Figure 5)**
2. Press Tab to highlight the next line within the same box and type the organization member's title. **(Figure 6)**

   or

   Click in a different box and enter a name. **(Figure 7)**

   or

   Press ⌘+Down arrow to move to the box below and enter a name.
3. If you want to enter additional information in the same box, press Tab to highlight each successive line and then type over the prompt text.

✔ Tip

■ To edit the information in a box, click the box, pause briefly, and then click again to place an insertion point in the box. If you double-click without pausing between the clicks, the program thinks that you intend to select the box and others at the same level.

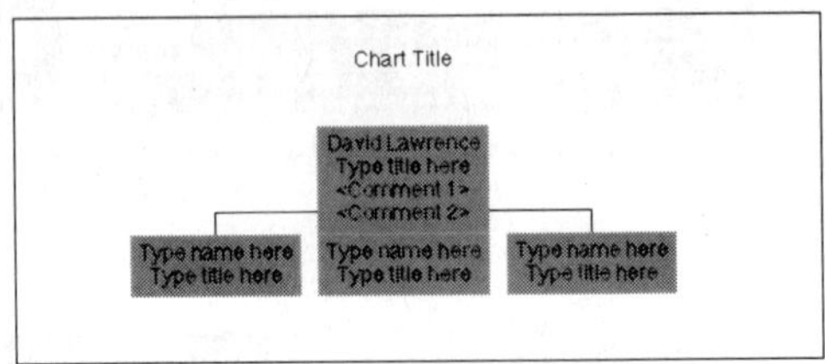

Figure 5. *Type the name of the head of the hierarchy.*

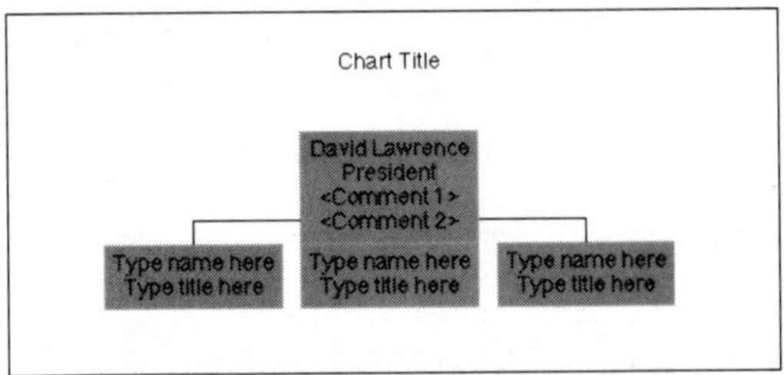

Figure 6. *Press Tab to move to the next line.*

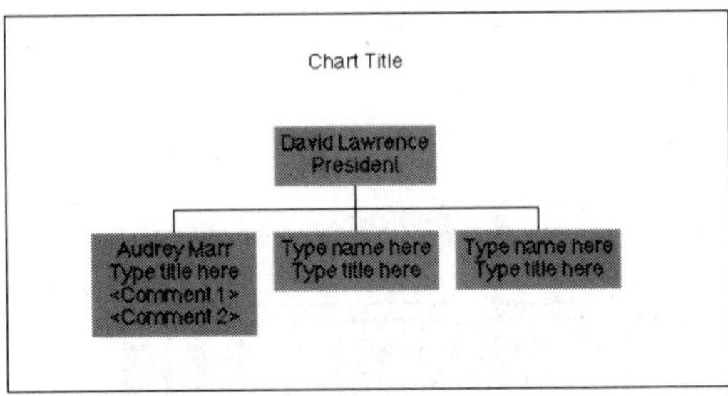

Figure 7. *Click in a different box to fill.*

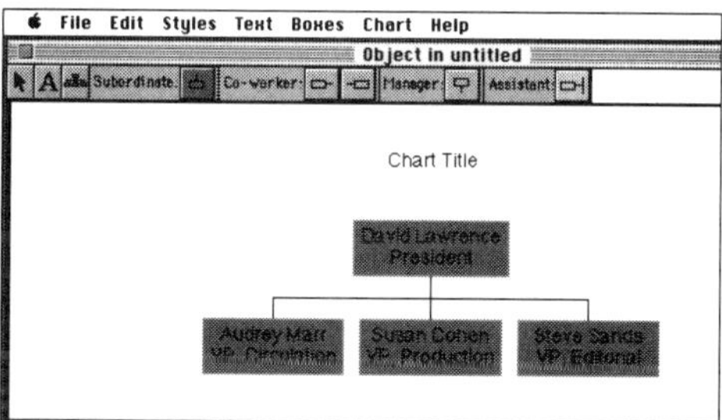

Figure 8. *Click the subordinate button.*

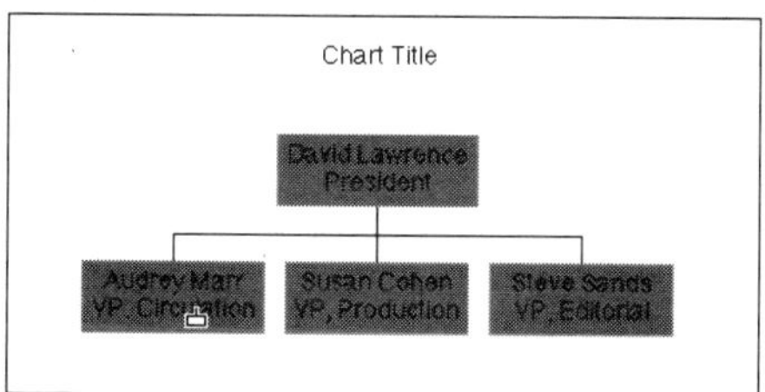

Figure 9. *Place the mouse pointer on a box.*

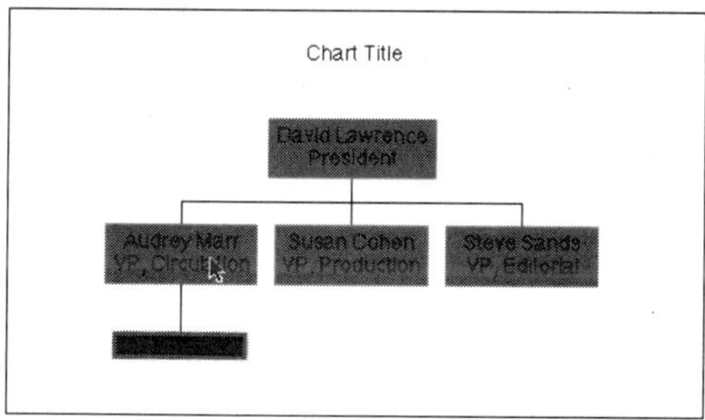

Figure 10. *Click to add a subordinate.*

Adding Subordinates

The initial structure contains only four organization members, a manager and three subordinates. To build a more complete structure, you will need to add more subordinates.

1. Click the Subordinate button. **(Figure 8)**
2. Place the mouse pointer on a box that requires a subordinate. **(Figure 9)**
3. Click to add a subordinate. **(Figure 10)**

✔ Tips

- To add multiple subordinates, click the Subordinate button several times (once for each subordinate to add) and **then** click an organization member.
- To add a coworker beside a box, click one of the Co-worker buttons and then click a box. **(Figures 11-12)**
- To **move** a subordinate to another organization member, drag the subordinate on top of the other member's box and then release the mouse button.

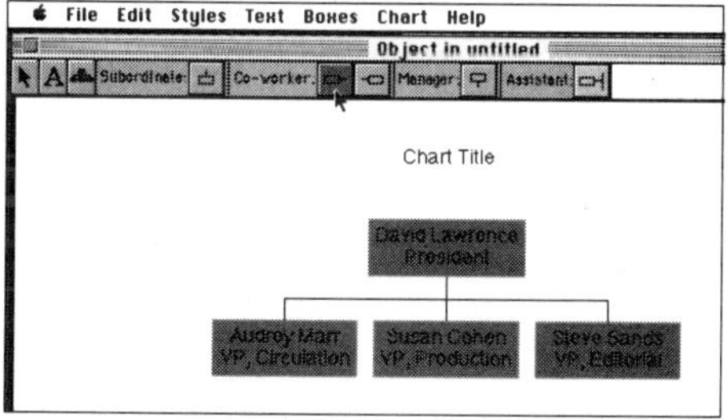

Figures 11. *The Co-worker buttons.*

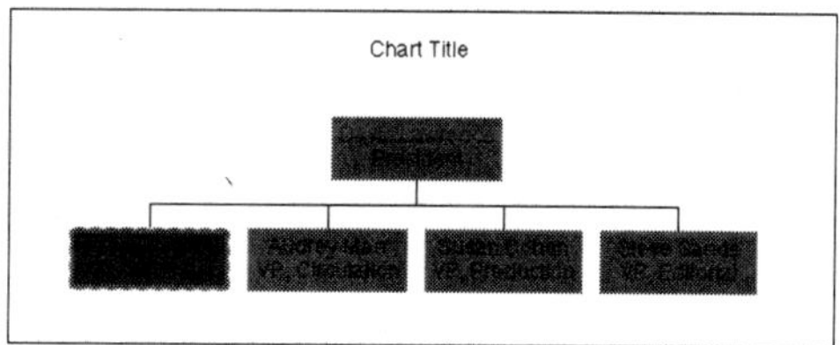

Figure 12. *A Co-worker added to a box.*

Adding an Assistant

1. Click the Assistant button. **(Figure 13)**
2. Click the box for the member who is to receive an assistant. **(Figures 14–15)**

✔ **Tips**

- You can add several assistants to a single organization member.
- To delete an assistant, click the box and then press the Delete key.

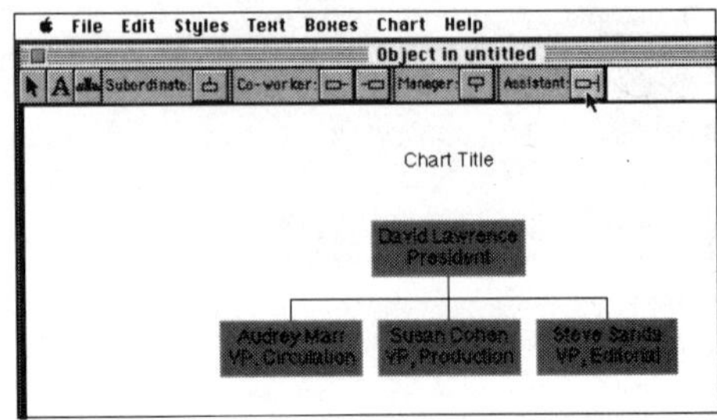

Figure 13. *The Assistant button.*

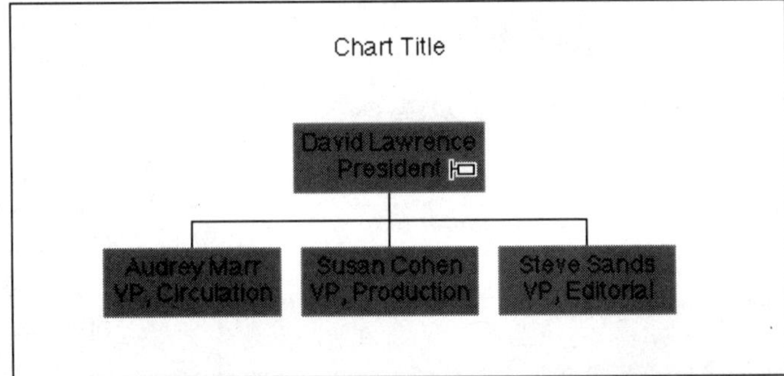

Figure 14. *Position the mouse pointer on the box for the member who is to receive the assistant.*

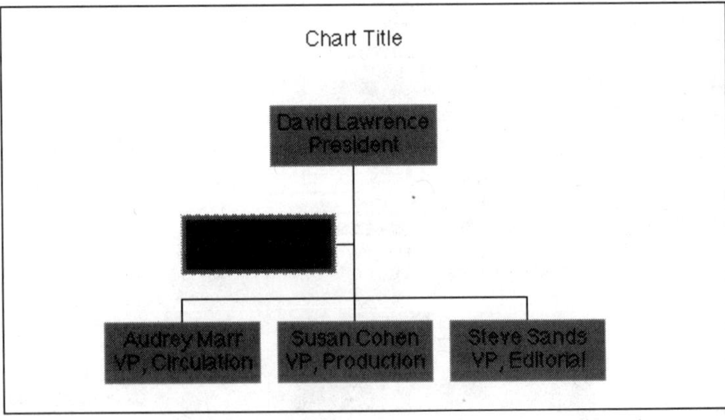

Figure 15. *Click the box to add the assistant.*

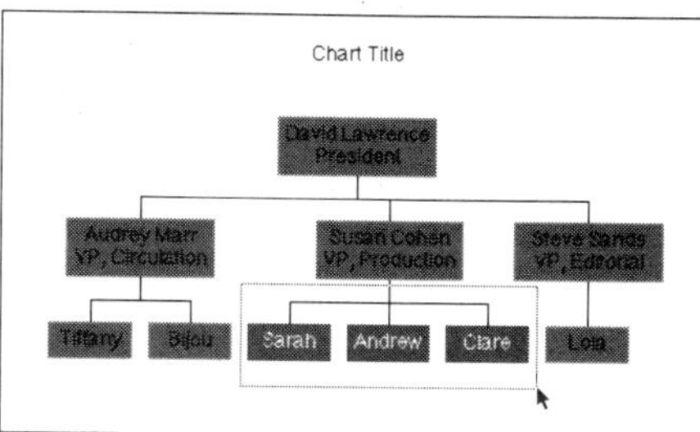

Figure 16. *Dragging a selection box.*

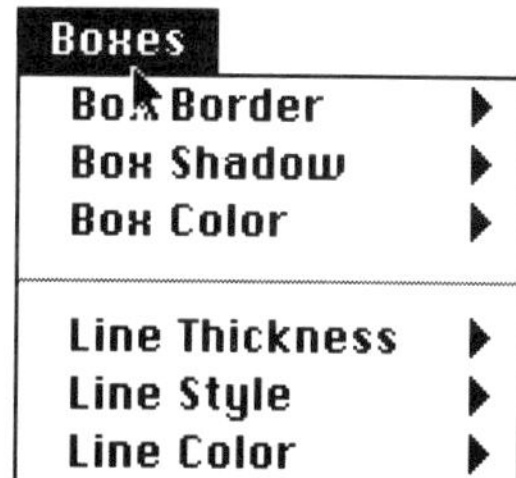

Figures 17. *The Boxes menu.*

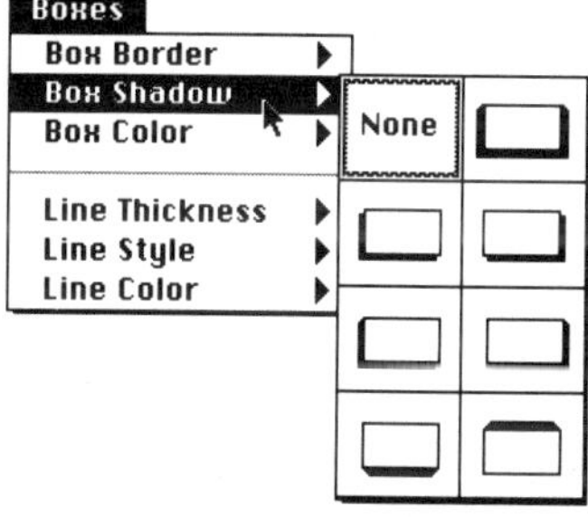

Figure 18. *Choose an option from the submenu.*

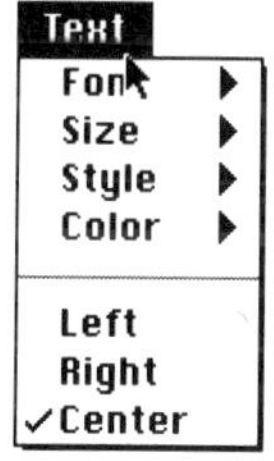

Figure 19. *The Text menu.*

Formatting the Boxes, Text, and Lines

1. Click a box or line.

   or

   Drag a selection box that encloses multiple boxes or lines to format. **(Figure 16)**

2. To format a box, choose one of the Box options on the Boxes menu and choose a setting from the submenu that appears. **(Figures 17–18)**

   or, to format the text

   Choose an option on the Text menu and then choose a setting for the option. **(Figure 19)**

   or, to format the connecting lines

   Choose one of the Line options on the Boxes menu. **(Figure 17)**

✔ Tips

- To select multiple boxes, you can also hold down the Shift key while clicking each box.
- Double-click a box to select all boxes at the same level.
- The shadow color of boxes is set by the Line color.

Finishing the Chart and Leaving Microsoft Organization Chart

1. Complete the chart. **(Figure 21)**
2. From the File menu, choose the Update Presentation command. **(Figure 22)**
3. From the File menu, choose Quit and return to Presentation. **(Figure 23)**
4. Drag the chart or drag the chart's handles to move or resize the chart on the PowerPoint slide as necessary. **(Figure 24)**

✔ **Tip**

- Anytime you want to edit an existing chart, double-click the chart.

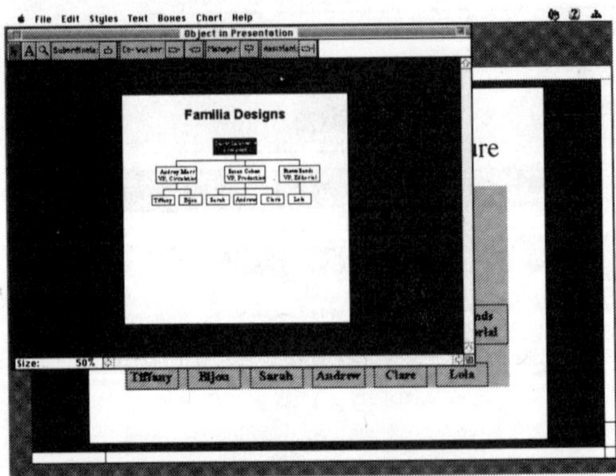

Figure 21. *The completed org chart.*

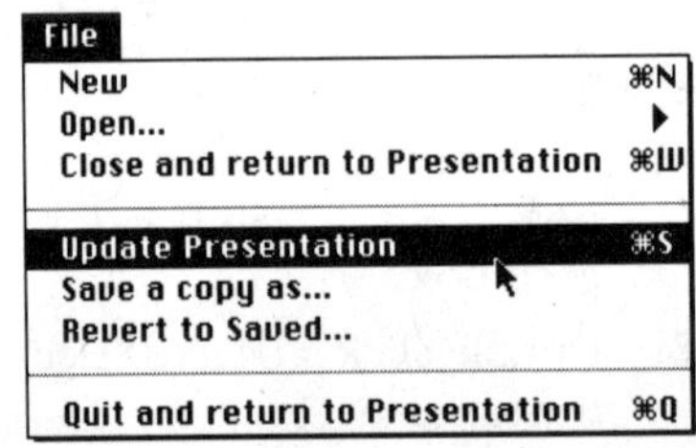

Figure 22. *The File menu.*

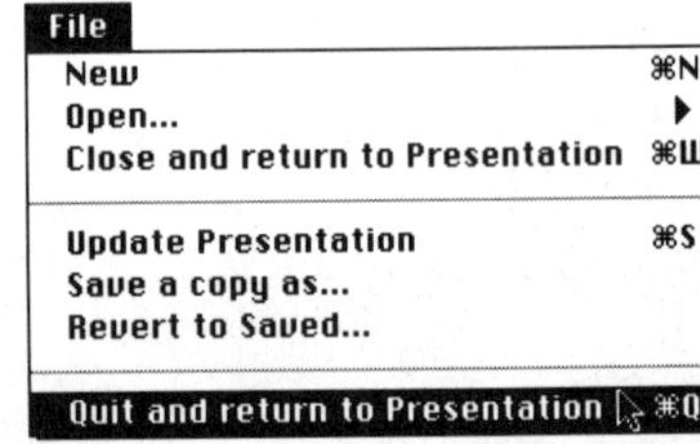

Figure 23. *The File menu.*

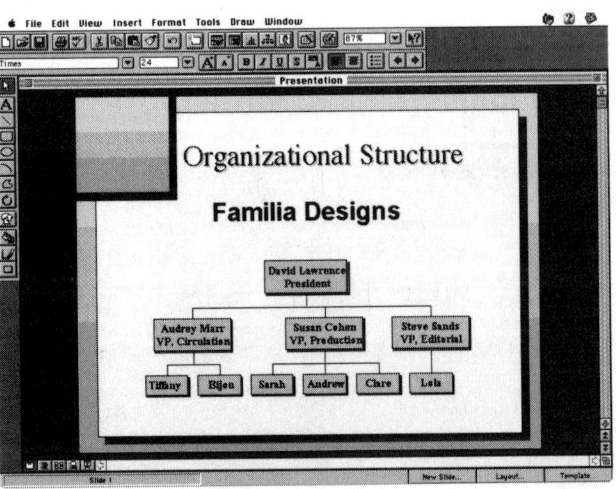

Figure 24. *The organization chart on the PowerPoint slide.*

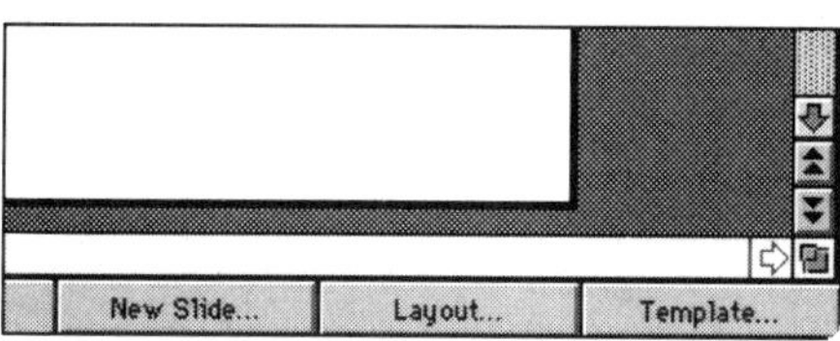

Figure 25. *The New Slide button.*

Double-click the Table layout.

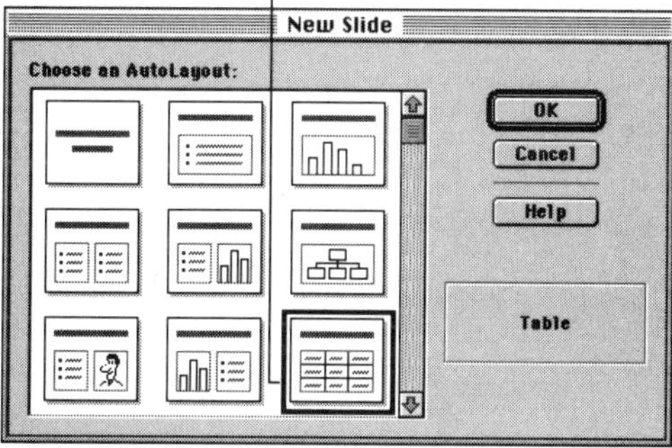

Figure 26. *The New Slide dialog box.*

Starting a Table

1. Click the New Slide button to start a new slide. **(Figure 25)**
2. On the New Slide dialog box, double-click the Table layout. **(Figure 26)**
3. Double click the "Double click to add table" placeholder on the new slide.
4. On the Insert Word Table dialog box, set the number of columns and number of rows. Then click OK. **(Figure 27)**

or, to add a table to an existing slide:

1. Turn to the slide to which you want to add a table.
2. Click the Insert Microsoft Word Table button in the Standard toolbar and drag across the number of rows and columns you want in the new table. **(Figure 28)**

   or

   Choose Microsoft Word Table from the Insert menu.

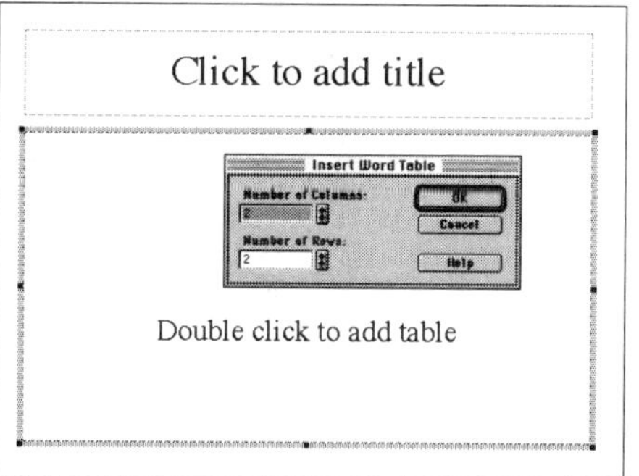

Figure 27. *The Insert Word Table dialog box.*

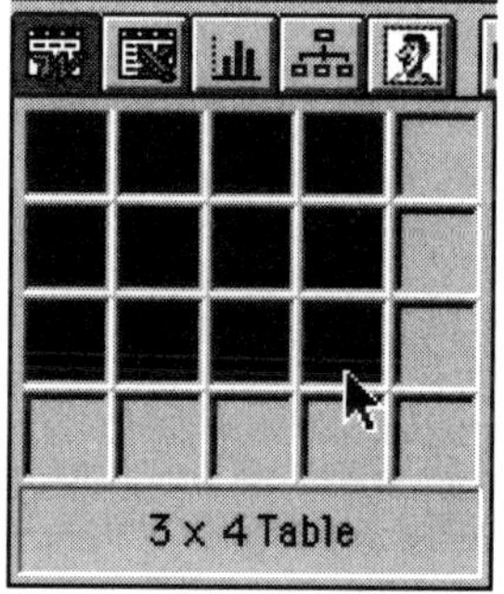

Figure 28. *Drag across the number of rows and columns you want.*

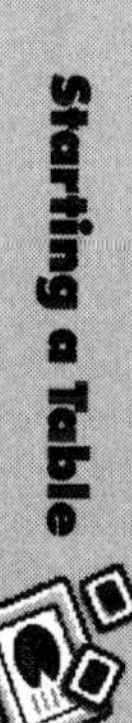

Entering the Data and Formatting the Table

PowerPoint uses the **Microsoft Word** table module to create and format tables. Therefore, creating a table in PowerPoint is just like creating a table in **Word**. In fact, if you double-click the "Double click to add table" placeholder in **PowerPoint**, the Insert *Word* Table dialog box appears to request the number of columns and rows you want in the table. **(Figure 29)**

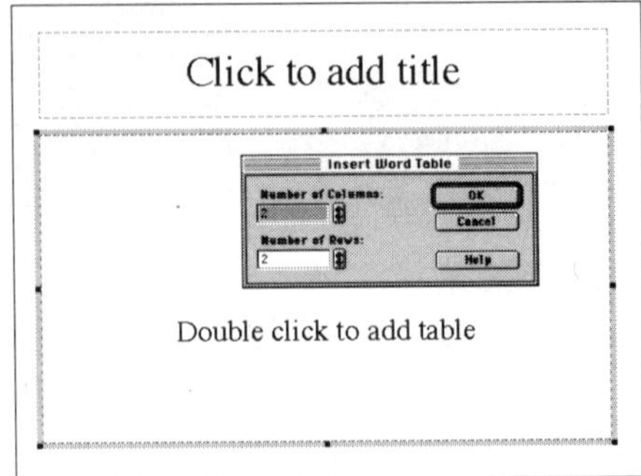

Figure 29. *The Insert Word Table dialog box.*

While you are creating or editing the table, **Microsoft Word's** menus and toolbars occupy the **PowerPoint** window and the table is surrounded by a heavy gray frame. **(Figure 30)**

When you finish the table, click outside the frame and **PowerPoint's** menus and toolbars regain the screen.

To edit an existing table, double-click the table. The familiar gray frame will reappear around the table and **Word's** menus and toolbars reemerge.

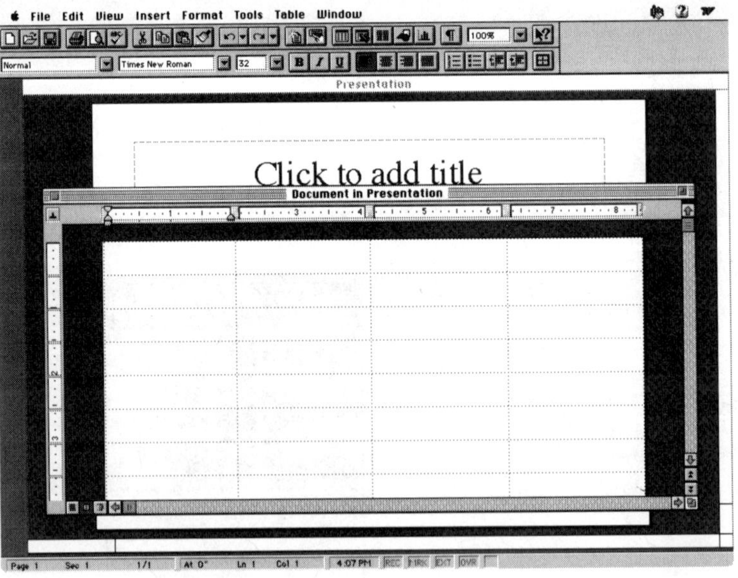

Figure 30. *Editing a table.*

Using the Slide Sorter 26

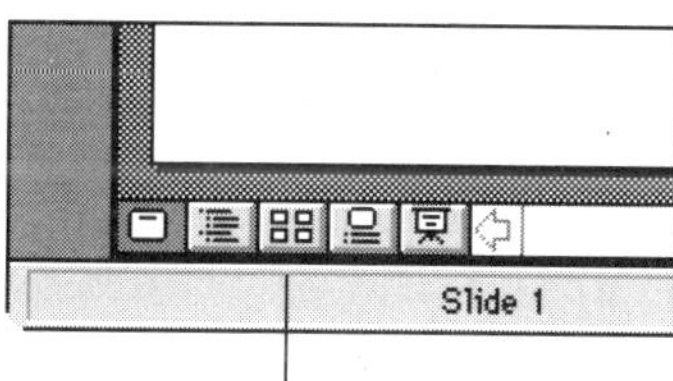

Figure 1. *The Slide Sorter View button.*

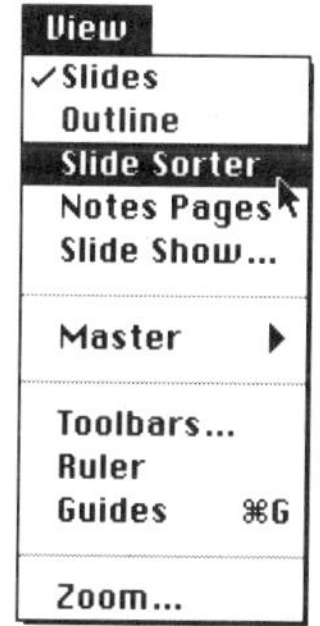

Figure 2. *The View menu.*

About the Slide Sorter

Slide Sorter view is just another of PowerPoint's views of a presentation. It displays rows of slides in miniature the way you place 35mm slides in rows on a light table to get an overview of the presentation. In Slide Sorter view, you can rearrange slides, delete or duplicate slides, and change the template to change the overall look of the presentation.

Switching to Slide Sorter View

1. Click the Slide Sorter View button. **(Figure 1)**

   or

   From the View menu, choose Slide Sorter. **(Figure 2)**

✔ Tip

- To switch to a view of a single slide, double-click the slide or click the slide and then click the Slide View button.

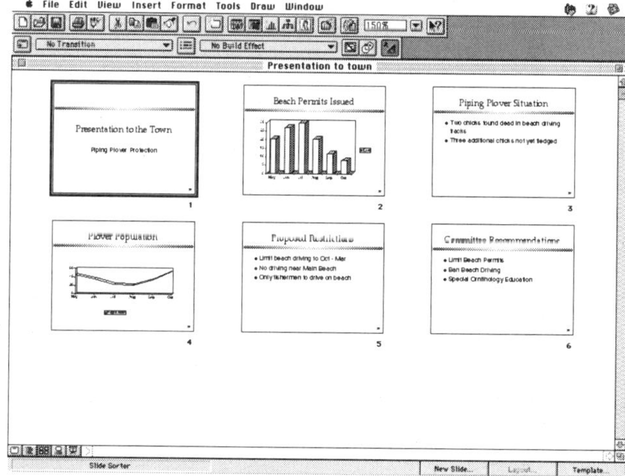

Figure 3. *Slide Sorter view.*

Reordering Slides

1. Place the mouse pointer on the slide to reposition in the presentation. **(Figure 4)**
2. Hold down the mouse button and drag the slide to a new position. A vertical line appears to indicate where the slide will drop when you release the mouse button. **(Figure 5)**
3. Release the mouse button to drop the slide. **(Figure 6)**

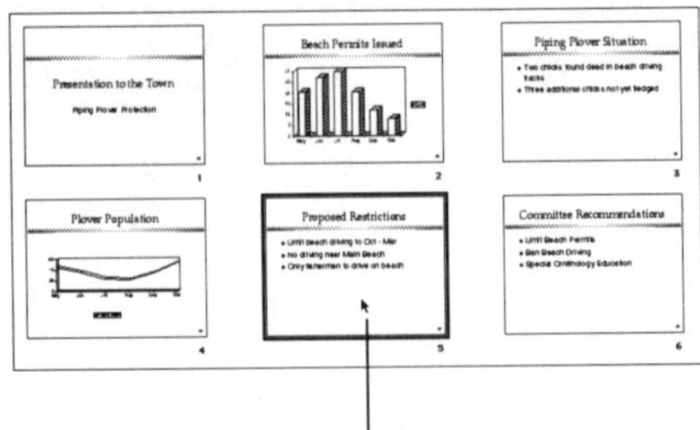

Figure 4. *Place the mouse pointer on a slide.*

✔ Tips

- You can select several slides to move by drawing a selection box around the group of slides then dragging the group to the new position. **(Figure 7)**
- To gather slides from different parts of a presentation, hold down the Shift key as you click each slide. Then drag any one slide to a new point in the presentation. All the selected slides will appear in sequence and in the same relative order at the new position.

The slide will drop here if you release the mouse button.

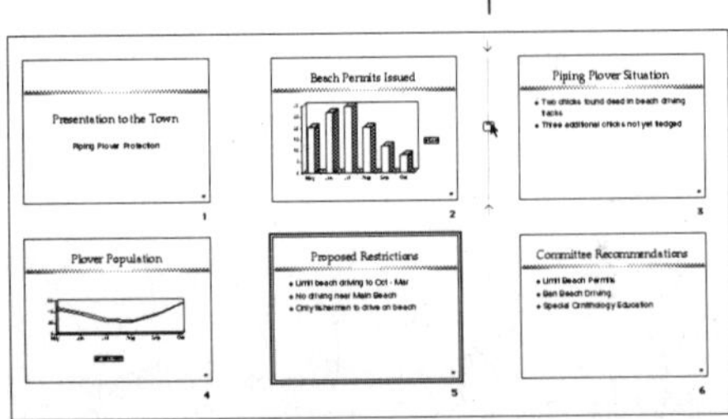

Figure 5. *A line indicates the position at which the slide will drop.*

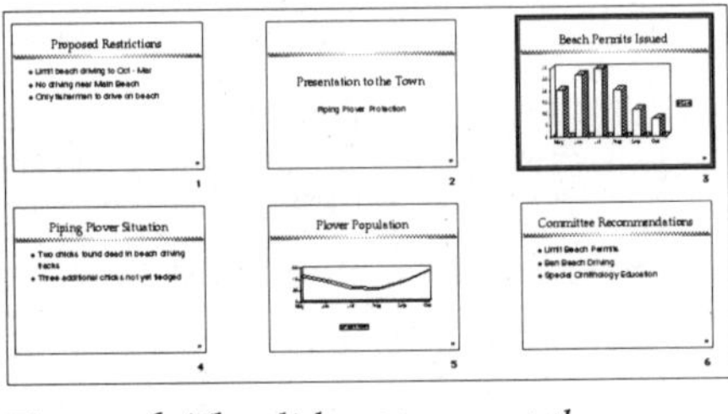

Figure 6. *The slide appears at the new position.*

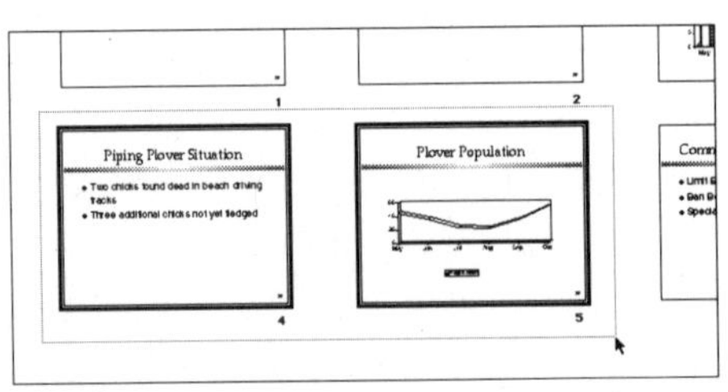

Figure 7. *Drag a selection box around several slides to select the slides.*

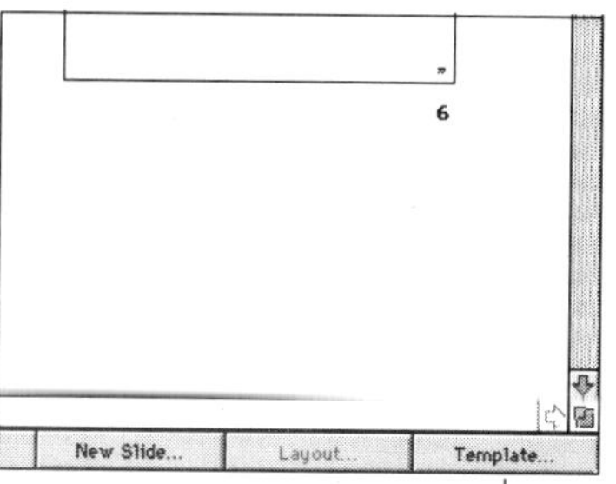

The Template button.

Figure 8. *The Template button.*

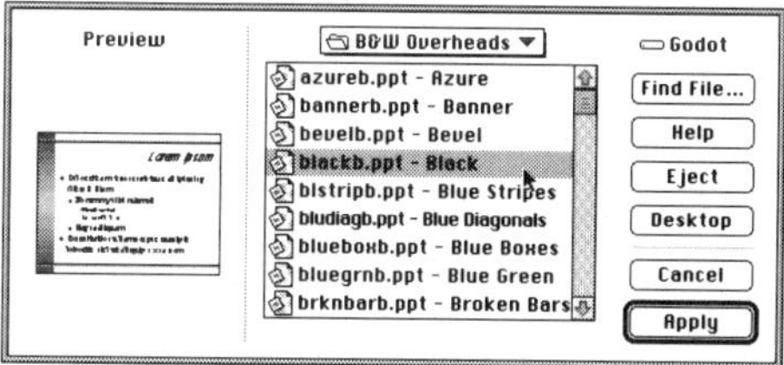

Figure 9. *The Presentation Template dialog box.*

Changing the Overall Design in Slide Sorter View

1. Click the Template button. **(Figure 8)**

   or

   From the Format menu, choose Presentation Template.

2. On the Presentation Template dialog box, select a template from the list of templates at the left. **(Figure 9)**

   or

   Double-click the template directory icon (yellow folder) in the Directories box and then double-click a different category of templates before selecting a template from the list at the left. *For more on templates, see Selecting a New Design, page 215.*

✔ Tip

- To change the appearance of one segment of the presentation, you can select certain slides in the Slide Sorter, choose Slide Background from the Format menu, and choose a different background color or design.

Table 26-1. ***Template Categories***

B&W Overheads	Black and white templates.
Color Overheads	Color printer templates (lighter colors, suitable for printing).
On Screen & 35mm Slides	Slide show templates (vivid colors suitable for display on the screen and 35mm slides).

Duplicating and Deleting Slides

1. Select the slide or slides to delete or duplicate. **(Figure 10)**
2. Press ⌘+D to duplicate the slide. **(Figure 11)**

   or

   Press Delete to delete the slide. **(Figure 12)**

✔ Tips

- To delete a slide, you can also choose Delete Slide from the Edit menu.
- To duplicate a slide, you can also choose Duplicate from the Edit menu.

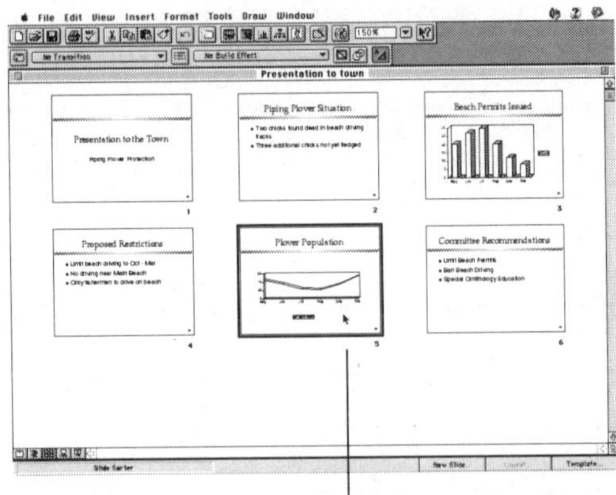

Figure 10. *Select the slide to duplicate or delete.*

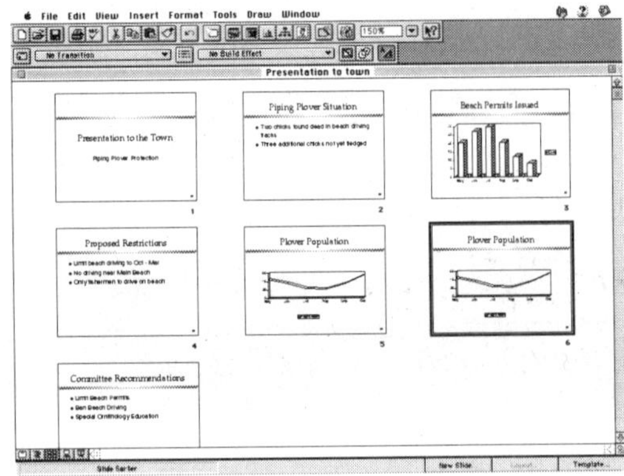

Figure 11. *The slide is duplicated.*

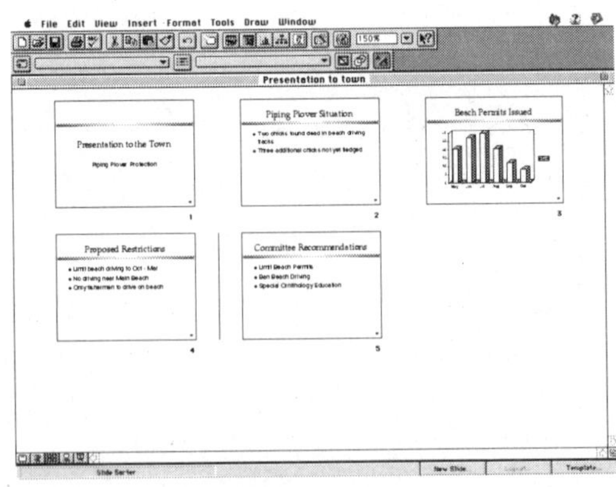

Figure 12. *The slide is deleted.*

Customizing a Presentation

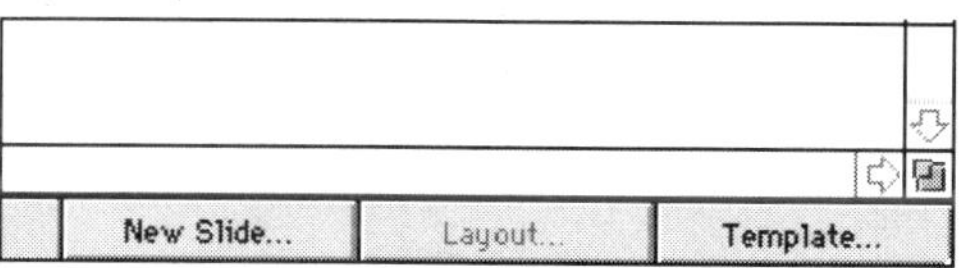

Figure 1. *The Template button.*

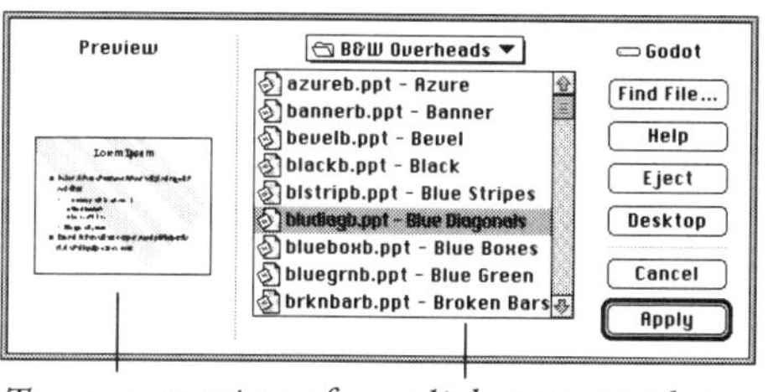

Figure 2. *The Presentation Template dialog box.*

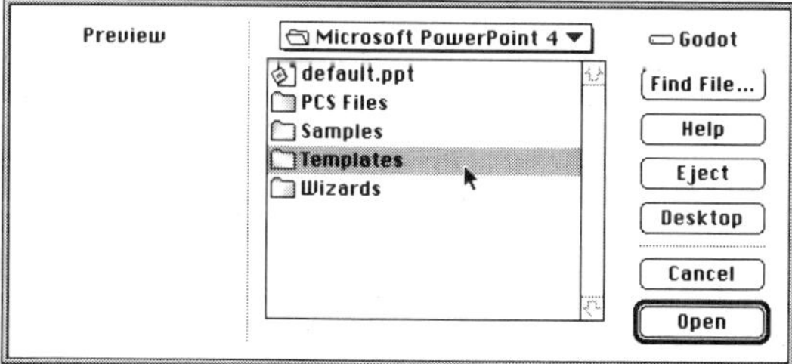

Figure 3. *Double-click the template folder to see the template sub-folders inside.*

Selecting a New Design

Changing a presentation's *template* can give a presentation an entirely new look, perhaps for a different audience. If you'll be printing black & white handouts on a laser printer, you might want to apply a black & white template to a color presentation.

A template contains a color scheme (a combination of colors used for text and other foreground presentation elements) and a slide master design (a background color, a selection of text fonts and formatting, and a background graphic design).

1. In any view, click the Template button. **(Figure 1)**
   or
   From the Format menu, choose Presentation Template.
2. On the Presentation Template dialog box, select a template from the list of templates. **(Figure 2)**
   or
   Select a different folder under the Templates folder and then choose a template name from the list of templates. **(Figure 3)**

Adding a Logo to the Background

Your company's or client's logo can give a stock presentation that important made-to-order look.

1. From the View menu, choose Master and then choose Slide Master from the submenu. **(Figure 4)**

   or

   Hold down the Shift key as you click the Slide View button.
2. With PowerPoint's drawing tools on the Drawing toolbar, modify the existing background graphic objects or add new objects. **(Figure 5)** *See Drawing Shapes, page 221.*

   or, to insert a logo stored in a graphic file:

   From the Insert menu, choose Picture and then select a graphic file on the Insert Picture dialog box.
3. Click one of the View buttons to leave Slide Master view and see the effect of the changes you've made. **(Figure 6)**

✓ Tips

- You can copy and paste a graphic image from another program onto the slide master, or copy and paste graphics from the slide master of another presentation onto the slide master of the current presentation.
- Any graphics that are already on the slide master as part of the template background must be ungrouped before you can modify them. *See Grouping and Ungrouping Shapes, page 222.*
- Click the Drawing toolbar with the right mouse button and then click Drawing+ on the list of toolbars to add a special toolbar with advanced drawing commands.

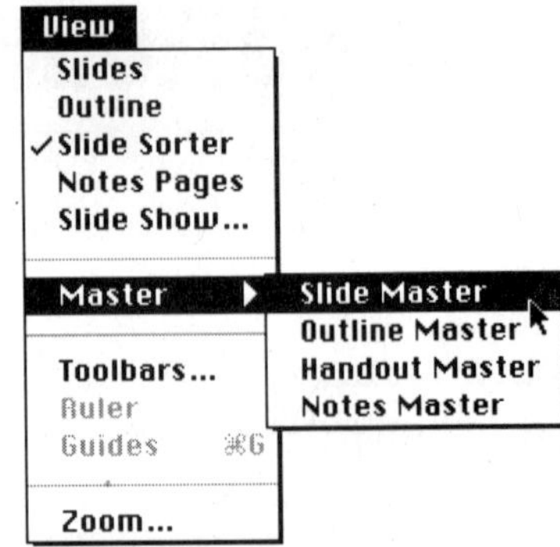

Figure 4. *The View menu.*

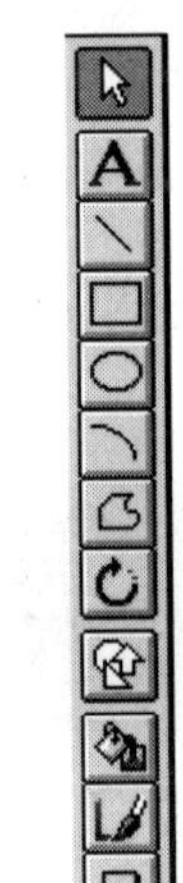

Figure 5. *The Drawing toolbar.*

The logo.

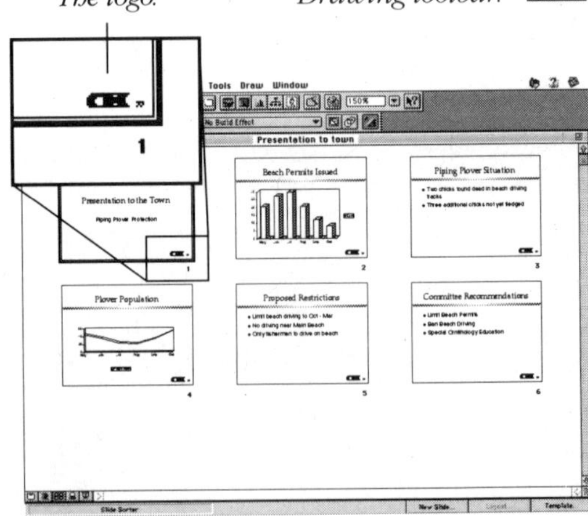

Figure 6. *An inserted logo on every slide in Slide View.*

Adding a Logo

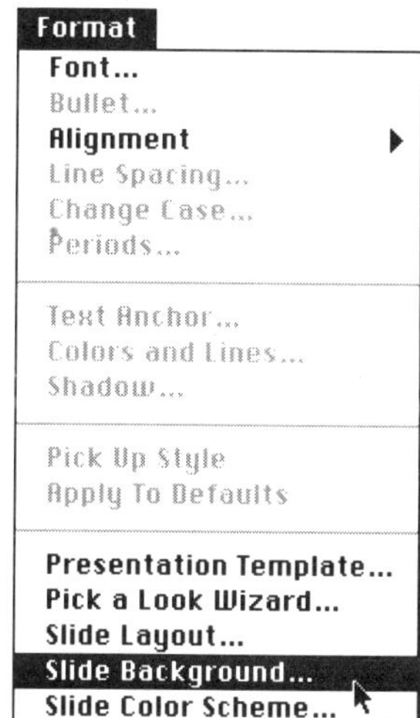

Figure 7. *The Format menu.*

Changing the Background Color and Shading

1. In Slide view or Slide Master view, choose Slide Background from the Format menu. **(Figure 7)**
2. On the Slide Background dialog box, choose a Shade Style and a Variant. **(Figure 8)**
3. To modify the background color, click Change Color on the Slide Background dialog box and use the Dark to Light scroll bar to change the darkness of the shading, if necessary.
4. Click Apply to All to apply the changes to all the slides. **(Figure 9)**

   or

   Click Apply to change the background of the current slide only.

✔ Tip

■ To see the new background shading while the Slide Background dialog box is still open, click the Preview button and then move the dialog box to the side.

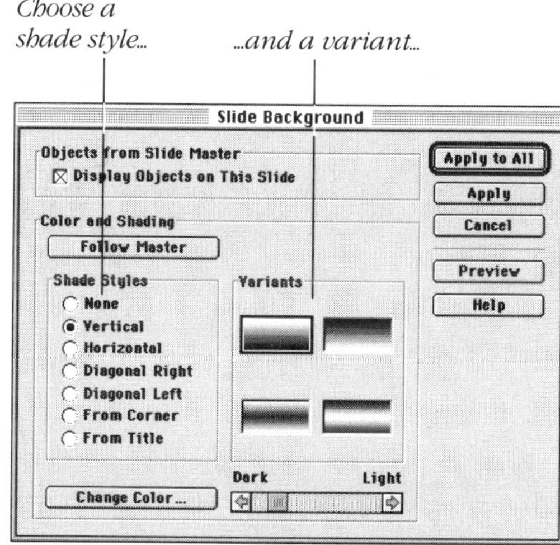

Figure 8. *The Slide Background dialog box.*

Figure 9. *The new shading on a slide.*

Changing the Text Fonts

1. From the View menu, choose Master and then choose Slide Master from the submenu. **(Figure 10)**

   or

   Hold down the Shift key as you click the Slide View button.

2. Select the text in the Title Area or the text in the Object Area on the Slide Master and then change the text formatting as you would text on any slide. **(Figure 11)** *See Formatting the Text, page 187.*

   or, to format the text at a particular bullet level on bullet slides

   Select the text in the Object area at the bullet level to format and then make formatting changes. **(Figure 12)**

3. Click any View button to switch to another view. **(Figure 13)**

✔ Tips

- To change the bullet style at a bullet level, select the text at that level, choose Bullet from the Format menu and then choose a different bullet style, size, and color on the Bullet dialog box.
- The color of the text is determined by the color scheme, but changing the color of text on the slide master overrides the color scheme.

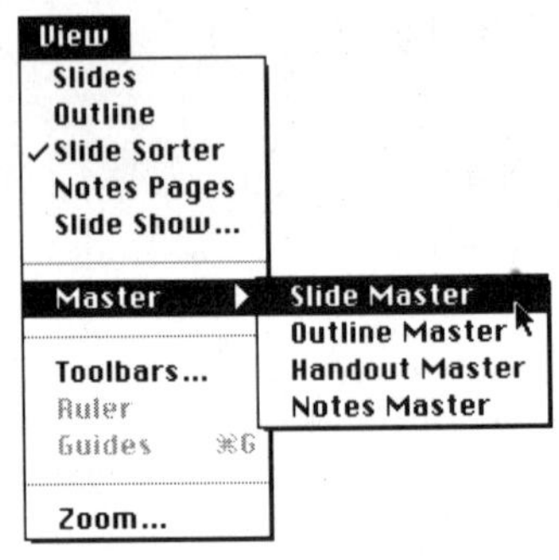

Figure 10. *The View menu.*

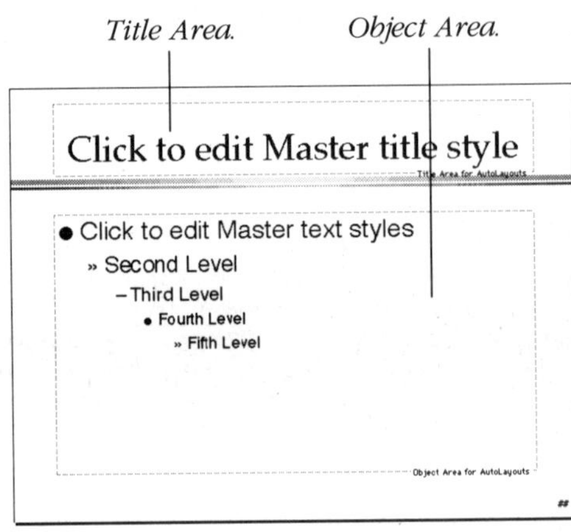

Figure 11. *The Slide Master.*

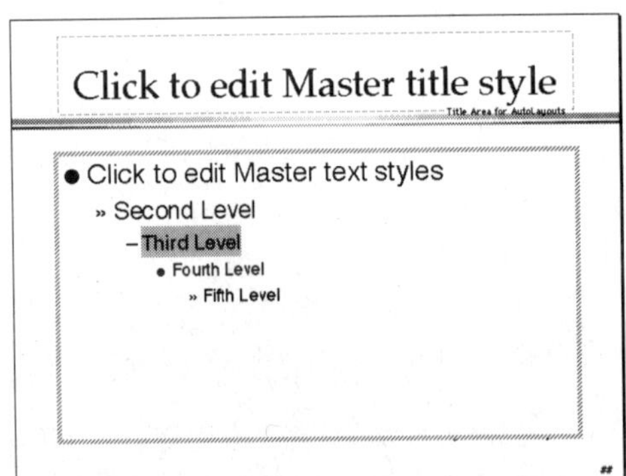

Figure 12. *Select the text at a particular bullet level to change text formatting at that level throughout the presentation.*

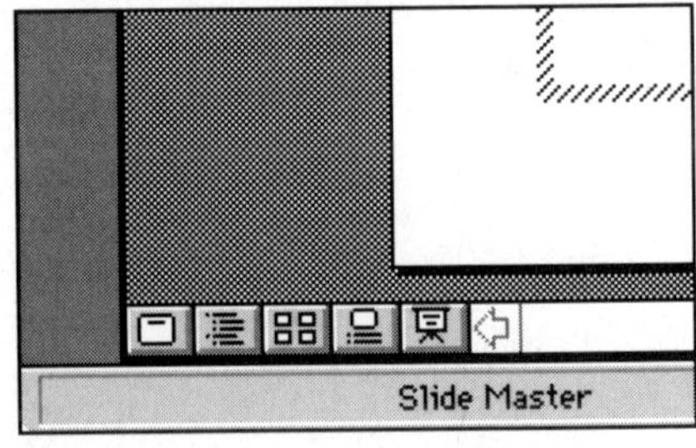

Figure 13. *Click any View button.*

Figure 14. *The Format menu.*

Click here to choose a different scheme.

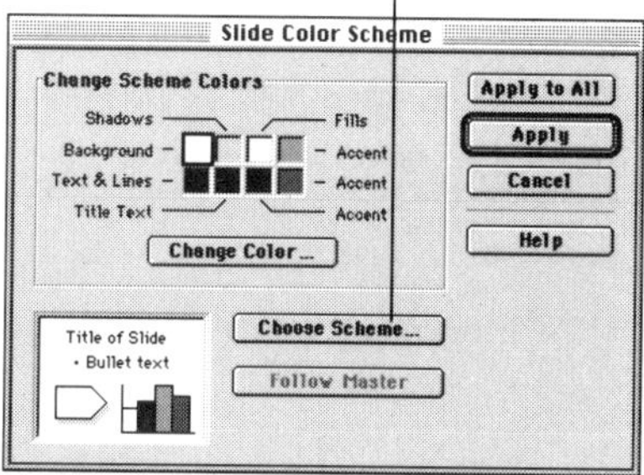

Figure 15. *The Color Scheme dialog box.*

Click a color here... ...then here... ...then click a pane.

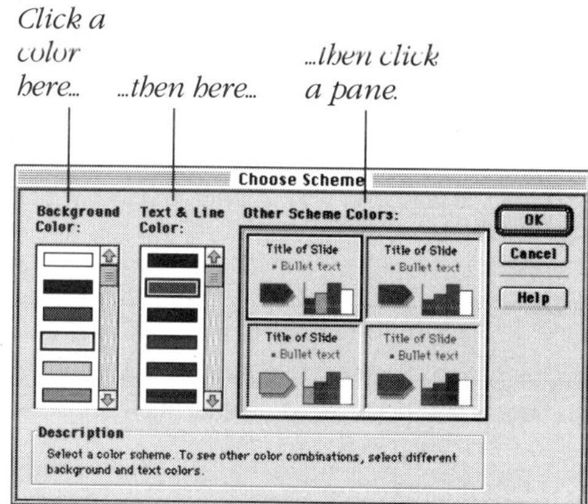

Figure 16. *Choose a Background color and then a Text & Line color.*

Changing the Color Scheme

The eight colors of the *color scheme* are the colors used by all the elements on slides unless you change the color of a specific element. The color scheme is stored in a template, so when you switch templates, you end up switching color schemes, too.

You can select predefined color schemes or create your own.

1. From the Format menu, choose Slide Color Scheme. **(Figure 14)**
2. On the Color Scheme dialog box, click the Choose Scheme button. **(Figure 15)**
3. On the Choose Scheme dialog box, click a Background color, then click one of the coordinating Text & Line colors that appears. **(Figure 16)**
4. Click one of the large panes that displays other scheme colors and click OK.
5. On the Slide Color Scheme dialog box, click Apply to All.

✔ Tips

- To change a color in the color scheme, double-click the color or click the color and click the Change Color button. Then choose a color on the Color dialog box that appears. **(Figure 17)**
- To return to the original color scheme in the template, click the Follow Master button on the Slide Color Scheme dialog box.

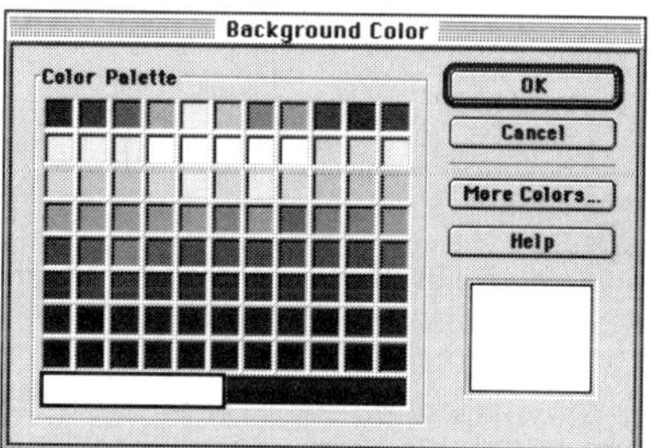

Figure 17. *The Background Color dialog box.*

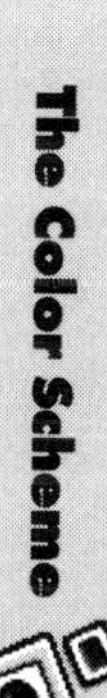

Saving a Custom Design

Simply by saving a specially formatted presentation, you've created a design you can apply to other presentations later. Simply open the presentation, start a new presentation, and choose Current Presentation Format on the New Presentation dialog box.

You can also open a template, make any or all of the changes detailed in this chapter, and then save the custom template for use with future presentations.

1. Click the Open button on the Standard toolbar. **(Figure 18)**
2. On the Open dialog box, select one of the three folders under the template folder. **(Figure 19)**
3. Double-click the template to edit.
4. Make formatting changes to the color scheme and slide master.
5. From the File menu, choose Save As. **(Figure 20)**
6. Save the template with a new name. **(Figure 21)**

✔ **Tip**

- You do not need to specify that you want to save a design as a template. Simply save the presentation. You'll use it as a template later.

Figure 18. *The Open button.*

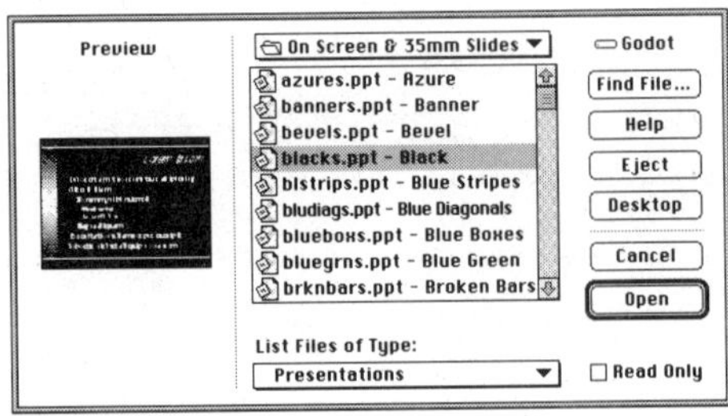

Figure 19. *The Open dialog box.*

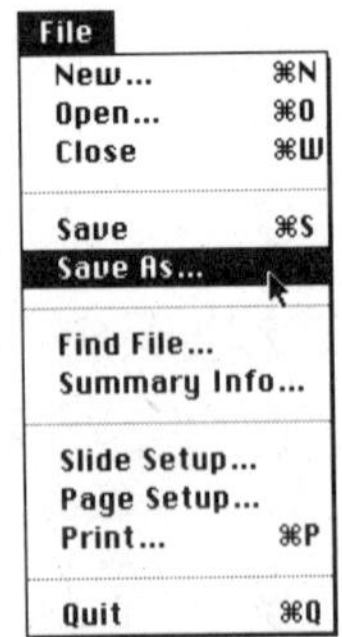

Figure 20. *The File menu.*

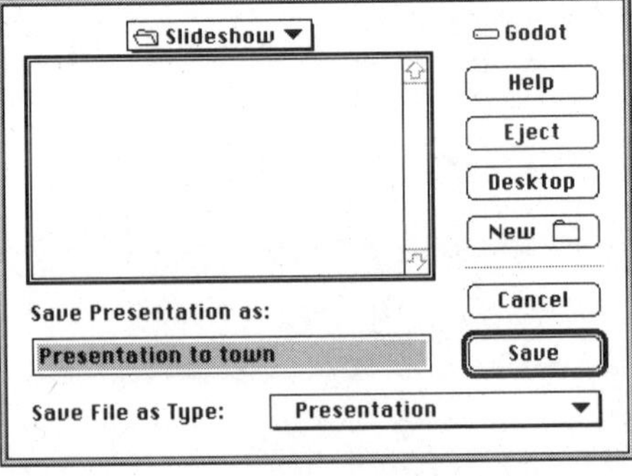

Figure 21. *The Save As dialog box.*

Drawing on Slides 28

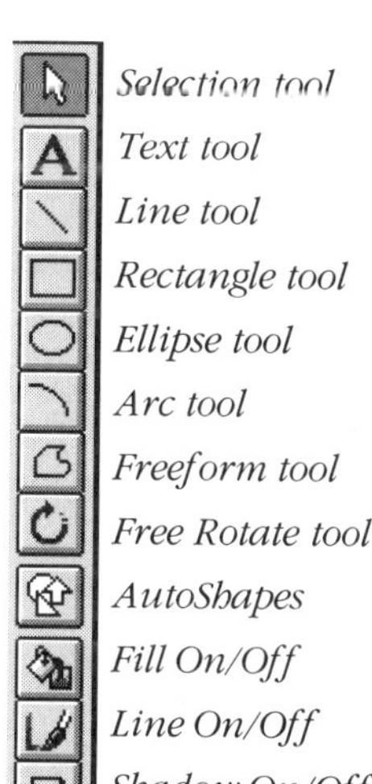

Figure 1. *The Drawing toolbar.*

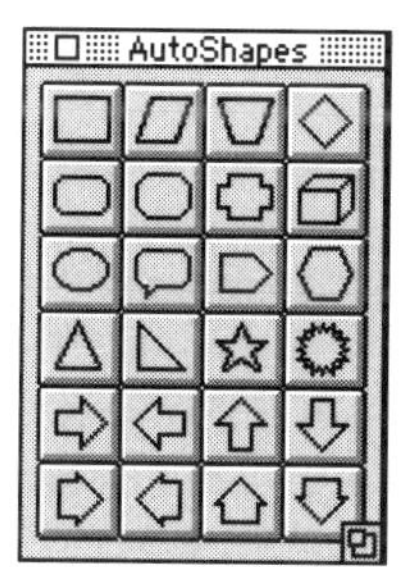

Figure 2. *The AutoShapes toolbar.*

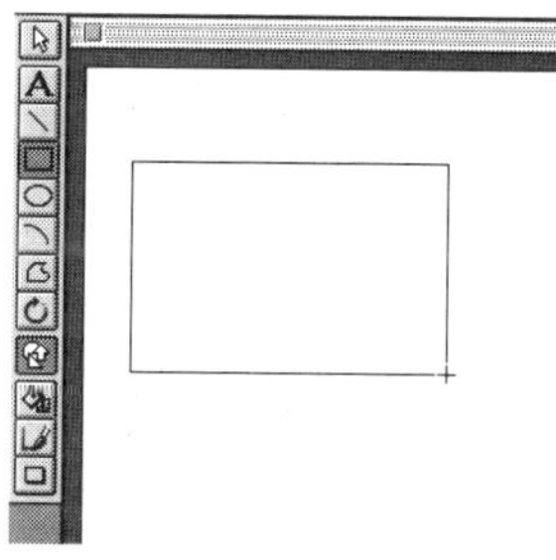

Figure 3. *Drag to create the shape.*

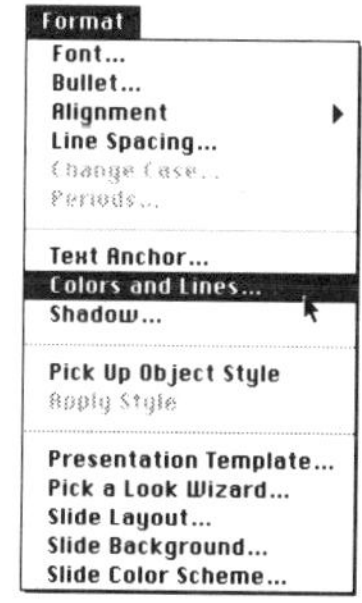

Figure 4. *The Format menu.*

Drawing Shapes

1. In Slide view, click one of the drawing tools on the Drawing or AutoShapes toolbars. **(Figures 1-2)**
2. Drag with the mouse pointer to create the shape. **(Figure 3)**
3. Click the shape and choose Colors and Lines from the Format menu. **(Figure 4)**
4. On the Colors and Lines dialog box, choose a fill color, line color, and line style. **(Figure 5)**

✔ Tips

- Click the AutoShapes button to summon the AutoShapes toolbar. Then select any AutoShape and drag across the slide to create the shape. Click the AutoShapes button again to put away the AutoShapes toolbar. **(Figure 2)**
- To add or remove the fill color, the surrounding line, or a shadow, click the Fill On/Off, Line On/Off, or Shadow On/Off buttons.
- To add text to the center of any shape, click the shape and then begin typing.

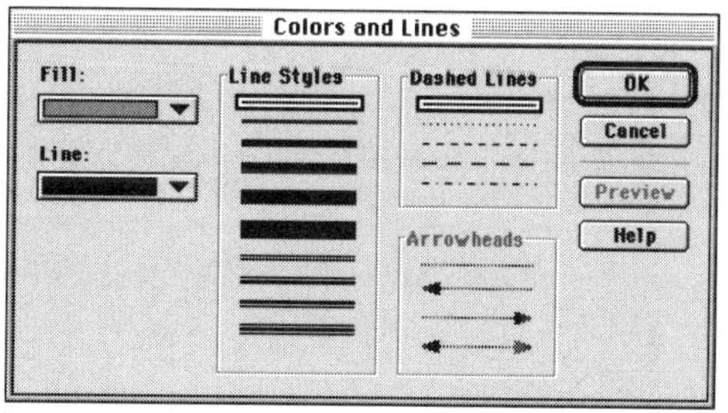

Figure 5. *The Colors and Lines dialog box.*

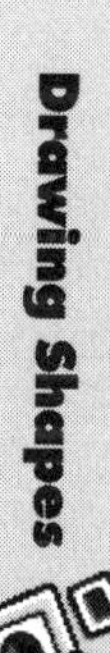

Grouping and Ungrouping Shapes

By grouping several objects, you can treat them as a single object. Simply select and then move, copy, or format the group.

1. Hold down the Shift key as you click each object for the group. **(Figure 6)**

   or

   With the Selection Tool, draw a selection box that entirely encloses only the objects to group. **(Figure 7)**
2. From the Draw or shortcut menus, choose Group. A single set of handles surrounds the objects in the group. **(Figures 8-9)**

✓ Tips

- To ungroup objects, select the group and then choose Ungroup from the Draw or shortcut menus.
- The Regroup command reestablishes the last group that was ungrouped.

Figures 6. *Hold down Shift as you click objects one after another.*

Figure 7. *Draw a selection box around objects to group with the Selection Tool.*

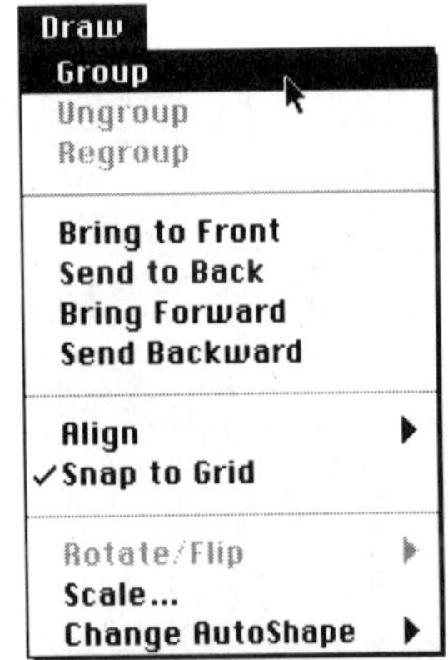

Figures 8. *The Draw menu.*

Figure 9. *Handles surround the group.*

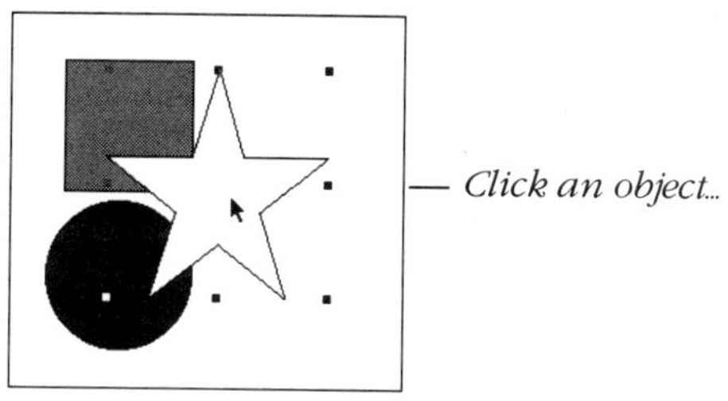

Figure 10. *Select an object to rotate.*

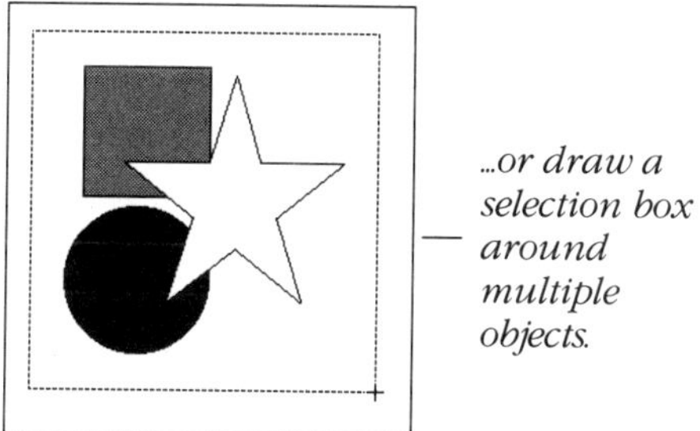

Figure 11. *Select the objects to align.*

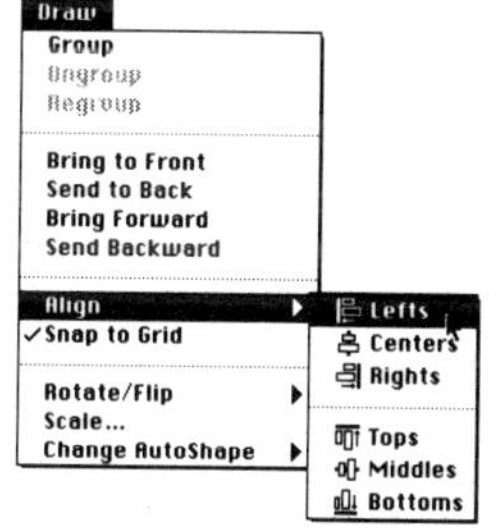

Figure 12. *The Align submenu.*

Aligning and Rotating Shapes

1. Select the object to rotate or the objects to align. **(Figures 10-11)**
2. From the Draw menu, choose Align and then choose an option on the submenu. **(Figure 12)**

   or

   From the Draw menu, choose Rotate/Flip and choose an option on the submenu. **(Figure 13)**

✔ Tips

- Objects align with the object that extends farthest from the center of all the objects.
- If you choose Free Rotate, place the pointer on a corner handle and drag around the center of the object to the desired angle. **(Figure 14)**

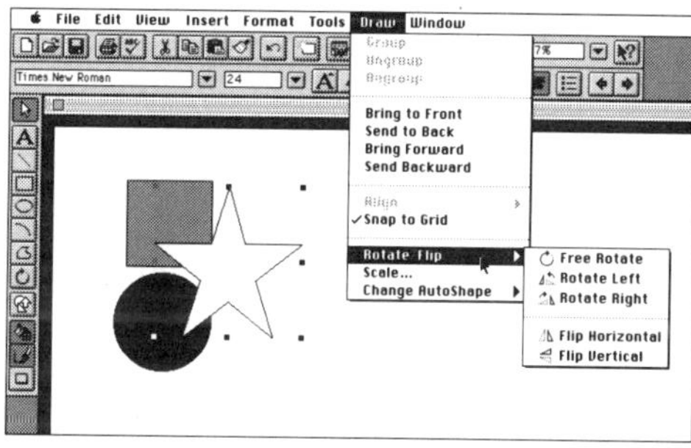

Figure 13. *The Rotate/Flip submenu.*

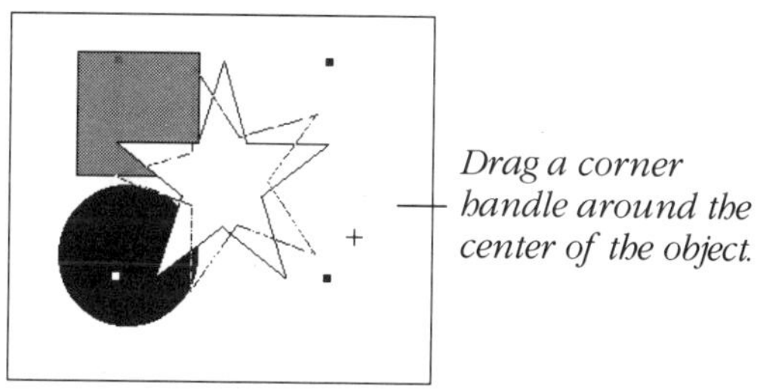

Figure 14. *Free Rotating an object.*

Overlapping Shapes

1. Select an object to move above or below other overlapping objects. **(Figure 15)**
2. From the Draw menu, choose Send to Back, Send to Front, Bring Forward (one level) or Send Backward (one level). **(Figures 16-17)**

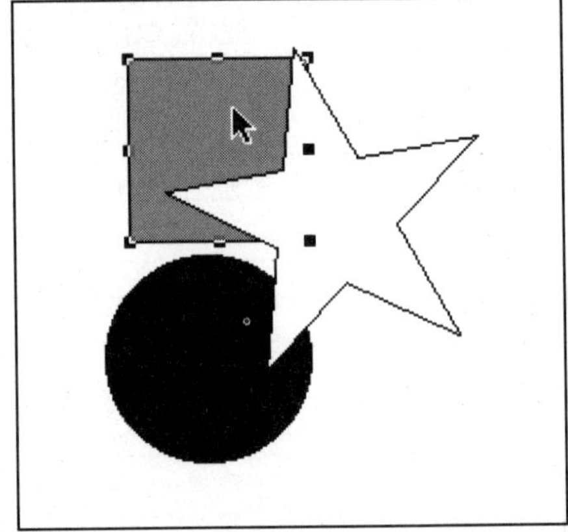

Figure 15. *Select an object to shift in the overlapping pile.*

Table 28-1. *Overlap Options*

Send to Back	Moves an object to the bottom of an overlapping pile.
Bring to Front	Moves an object to the top of an overlapping pile.
Bring Forward	Moves an object one layer closer in the pile.
Send Backward	Moves an object one layer farther down in the pile.

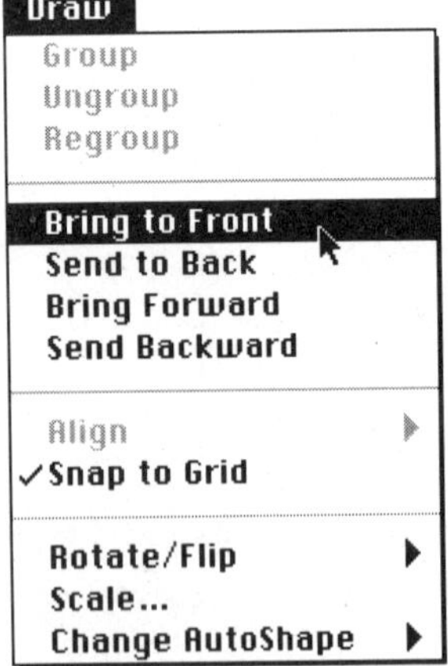

Figure 16. *The Draw menu.*

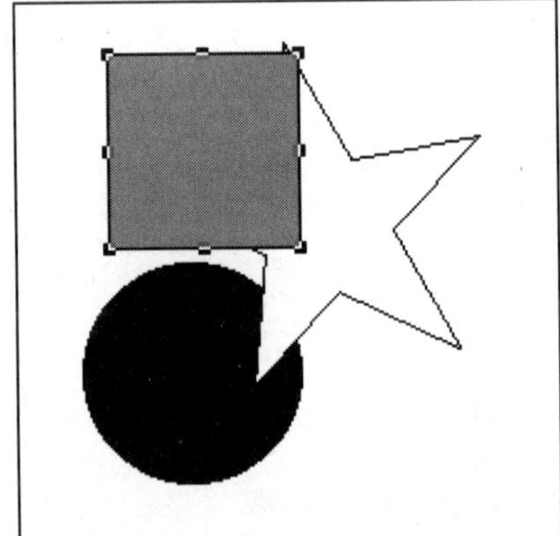

Figure 17. *The object after it is brought to the front.*

Creating Slide Shows 29

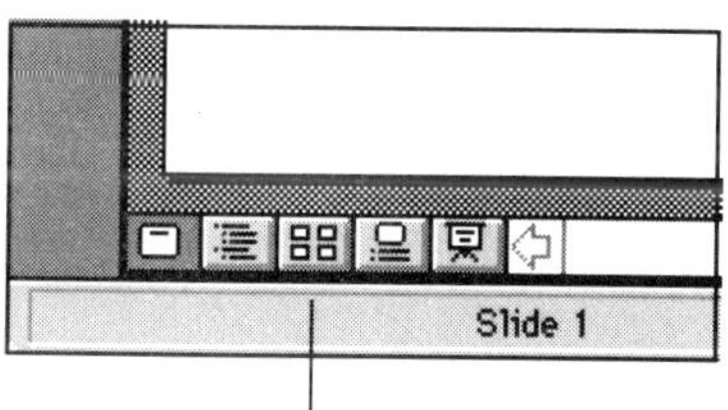

Figure 1. *Slide Sorter View button.*

Transition button. *Transition Effects box.*

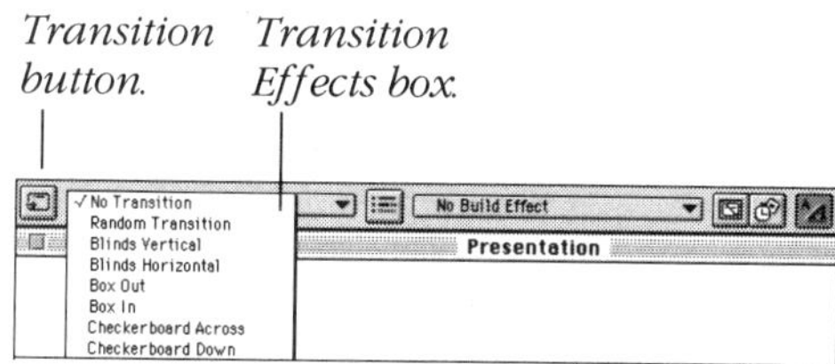

Figure 2. *The Slide Sorter toolbar.*

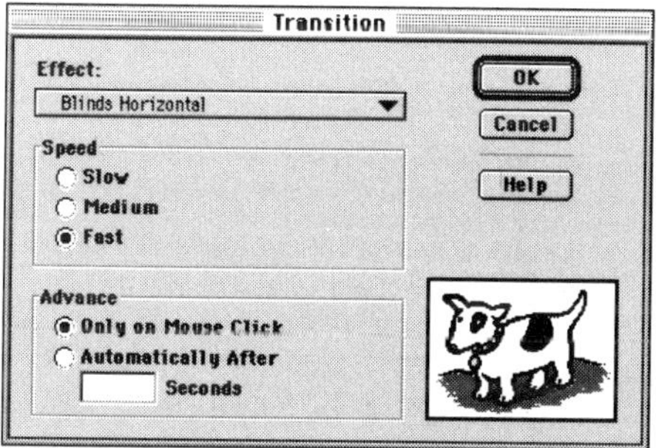

Figure 3. *The Transition dialog box.*

Adding Transition Effects

Transition effects are the dissolves, splits, wipes, and other TV-like effects that a slide show can use to bring each new slide into view.

1. Click the Slide Sorter View button to switch to the Slide Sorter. **(Figure 1)**
2. Click the slide for which you want to change the transition effect.
3. Click the pull-down button next to the Transition Effects box on the Slide Sorter toolbar and select a transition effect from the list. **(Figure 2)**

   or

   Click the Transition button and choose a transition Effect, Speed, and Advance option on the Transition dialog box. **(Figure 3)**

✔ Tips

- To apply the same transition effect to multiple slides, hold down the Shift key and click the slides and then choose a transition effect.
- To preview the transition effect in Slide Sorter view, click the transition icon that appears below each slide that has a transition effect. **(Figure 4)**

The transition icon.

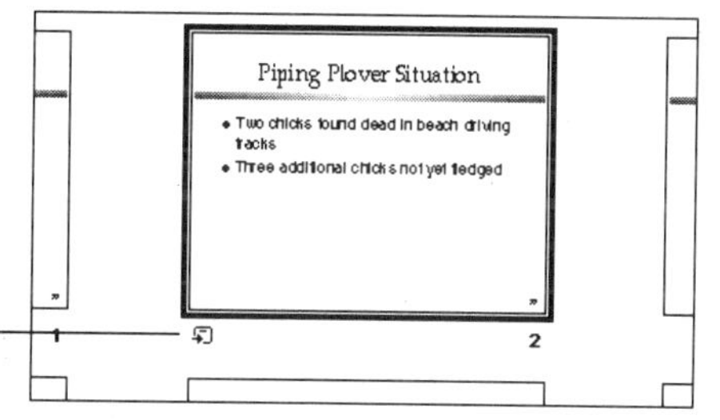

Figure 4. *The transition icon.*

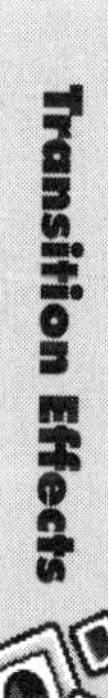

Adding Build Effects

A build effect brings each bullet on a bullet slide into view with a special effect.

1. In Slide Sorter view, click the bullet slide that requires a build effect. **(Figure 5)**
2. Click the pull down button next to the Build Effects box on the Slide Sorter toolbar and select a build effect from the list. **(Figure 6)**

   or

   Click the Build button and, on the Build dialog box, choose whether to dim previous bullets, select the color of dimmed bullets, and choose a build effect. **(Figure 7)**

✔ Tips

- To apply the same build effect to multiple slides, hold down the Shift key and click the slides and then choose a build effect.
- A slide with a build effect shows a build icon at the lower left corner. Unlike the transition icon, you cannot click the build icon to preview the build. **(Figure 8)**

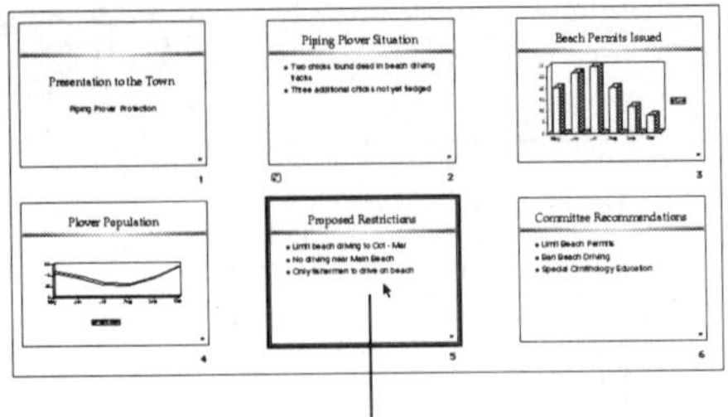

Figure 5. *Select the bullet slide.*

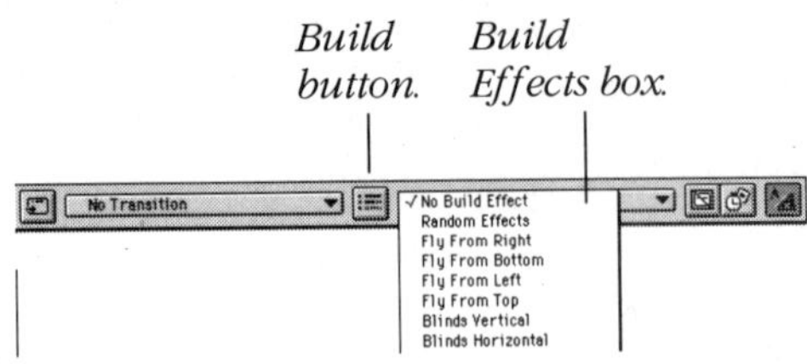

Figure 6. *The Slide Sorter toolbar.*

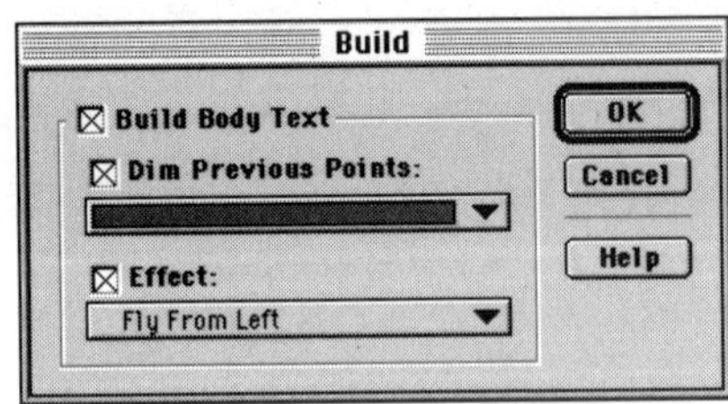

Figure 7. *The Build dialog box.*

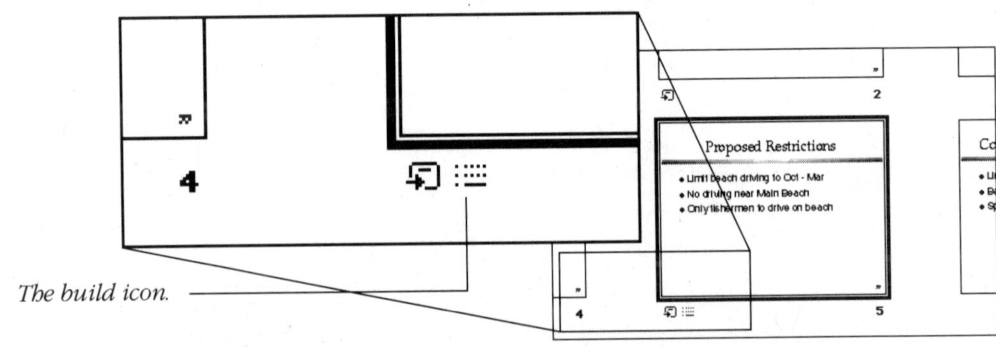

Figure 8. *The build icon.*

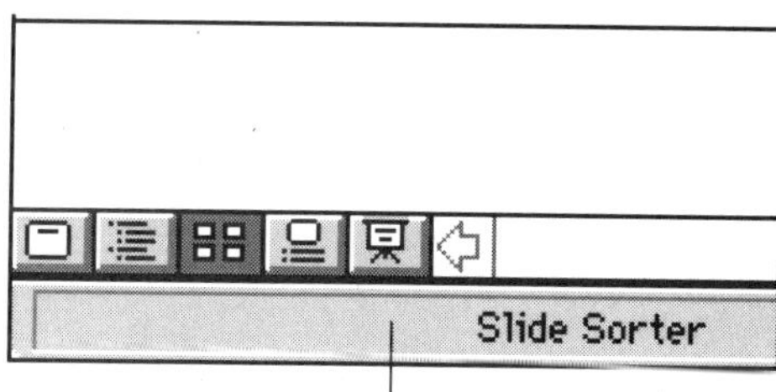

Slide Show view button.

Figure 9. *The Slide Show view button.*

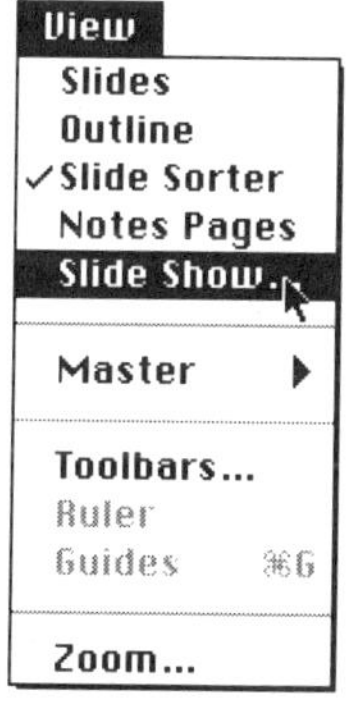

Figure 10. *The View menu.*

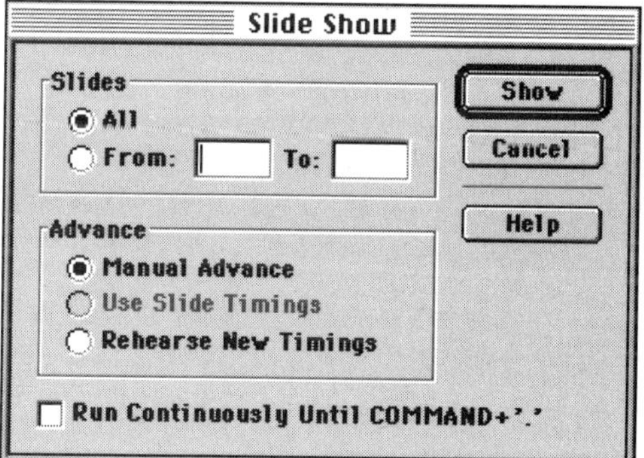

Figure 11. *The Slide Show dialog box.*

Displaying the Show

1. In Slide Sorter view, click on the first slide to view in the show and then click the Slide Show view button. **(Figure 9)**

   or

   From the View menu, choose Slide Show. **(Figure 10)**
2. On the Slide Show dialog box, choose All and click Show or enter From and To slide numbers and click Show to display only a segment of the show. **(Figure 11)**

✓ Tips

- Choose Rehearse New Timings on the Slide Show dialog box or click the Rehearse Timings button on the Slide Sorter toolbar to practice the show and record the overall length of the show and the duration of each slide as you advance the show manually. To use the slide timings you recorded during rehearsal, choose Use Slide Timings on the Slide Show dialog box.

Table 29-1. ***Slide Show Keystrokes and Mouse Clicks.***

Advance to the next slide	Mouse button, Spacebar, Right arrow, Down arrow, PgDn, or N.
Back up to previous slide	Backspace, Left arrow, Up arrow, PgUp, or P
Go to slide number	Slide number+Enter
Pause/Resume automatic show	S or + on the numeric keypad
Switch to temporary black screen	B or period. B or period again to resume.

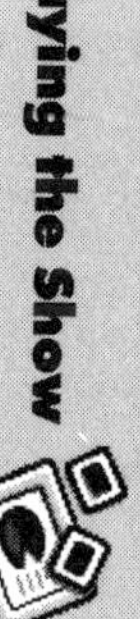

Using the PowerPoint Viewer

The PowerPoint Viewer can display a slide show without the rest of the PowerPoint program installed. You can send the slide show file and PowerPoint Viewer to another user without PowerPoint so they can view your presentation.

1. Create the show, add the transition and build effects, and rehearse the show to set the slide timings.
2. Make sure Use Slide Timings is set on the Slide Show dialog box.
3. Save the presentation in a file.
4. Start the PowerPoint viewer by double-clicking the PowerPoint Viewer icon in the PowerPoint folder. **(Figure 12)**
5. In the Microsoft PowerPoint Viewer, select the presentation and click Show.

✔ Tips

- Click Run Continuously Until 'Esc' to run the presentation unattended.
- Click Use Automatic Timings to use the automatic timings you recorded during rehearsal.
- To send a slide show and the PowerPoint Viewer to someone else, copy PowerPoint Viewer and your slide show to a diskette.

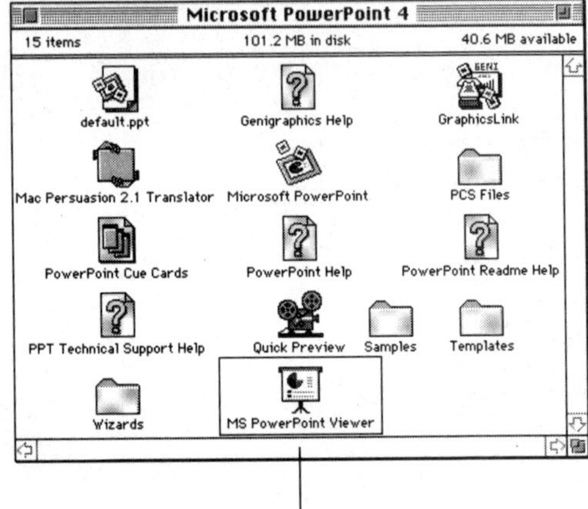

Figure 12. *The PowerPoint Viewer icon.*

Mail 3.1 Communicating

Mail 3.2 Communicating

About Mail

What is Mail?
The Microsoft Mail Window
Key to the Microsoft Mail Window
Starting Microsoft Mail
Quitting Microsoft Mail

Reading Messages

Selecting a Message to Read
Sorting Your Mail
Replying to a Message
Forwarding a Message
Printing a Message
Deleting a Message

Sending Messages

Starting and Addressing a Message
Entering the Text and Sending the Message
Selecting Message Options
Enclosing a File with a Message
Setting the Address Book to Open Automatically
Creating a Personal Address Book
Using the Personal Address Book
Creating a Personal Group
Sending a Document from Within an Office Application

Managing Your Mail

Filing a Message in a Folder
Creating Folders
Deleting Folders
Changing Your Password
Setting Mail Preferences

About Mail 30

What is Mail?

Microsoft Mail is a communications program that lets everyone on a network send messages back and forth. If you are not connected to a local area network (LAN), you cannot use Mail.

Publication Contracts

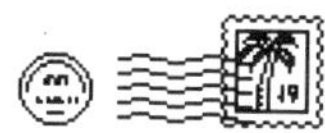

Your Message: Publication Contracts
Was Read By: LolaW
On: Sun, Jan 29, 1995 3:20 PM

Mail lets users compose text messages and attach files created by the Office applications. It also lets users read incoming messages and file messages in folders according to any organization scheme.

Mail includes special capabilities that let you sort messages and print them to maintain a record of your electronic correspondence.

The Microsoft Mail system at your organization may have the capability to connect to individuals at other organizations or electronic mail addresses if the proper gateway software is installed. You should check with the individual who administers your system to see whether this capability is available.

The Microsoft Mail Window

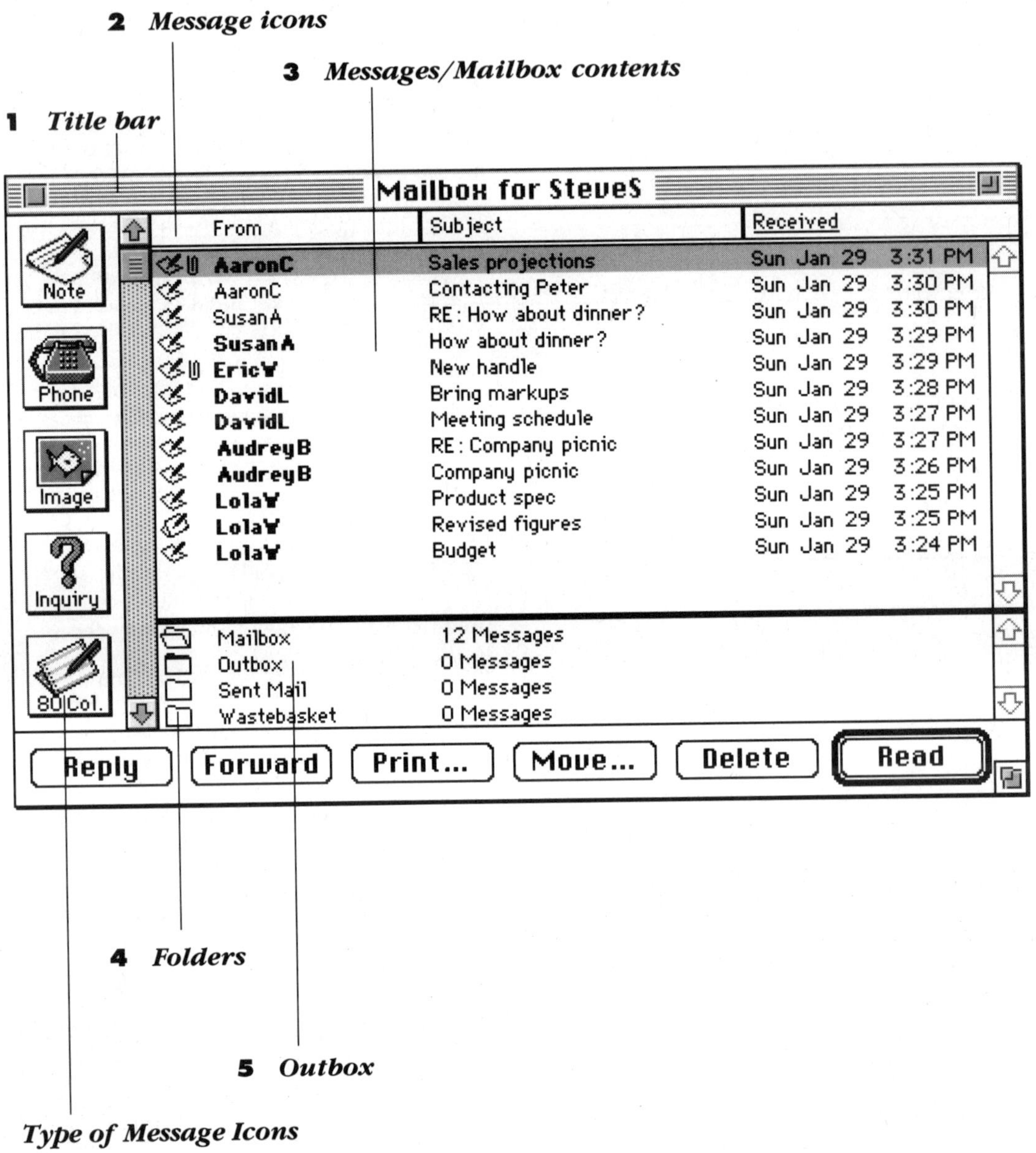

2 ***Message icons***

3 ***Messages/Mailbox contents***

1 ***Title bar***

Mailbox for SteveS

Note

Phone

Image

Inquiry

80 Col.

From	Subject	Received	
AaronC	Sales projections	Sun Jan 29	3:31 PM
AaronC	Contacting Peter	Sun Jan 29	3:30 PM
SusanA	RE: How about dinner?	Sun Jan 29	3:30 PM
SusanA	How about dinner?	Sun Jan 29	3:29 PM
EricV	New handle	Sun Jan 29	3:29 PM
DavidL	Bring markups	Sun Jan 29	3:28 PM
DavidL	Meeting schedule	Sun Jan 29	3:27 PM
AudreyB	RE: Company picnic	Sun Jan 29	3:27 PM
AudreyB	Company picnic	Sun Jan 29	3:26 PM
LolaV	Product spec	Sun Jan 29	3:25 PM
LolaV	Revised figures	Sun Jan 29	3:25 PM
LolaV	Budget	Sun Jan 29	3:24 PM

Mailbox	12 Messages
Outbox	0 Messages
Sent Mail	0 Messages
Wastebasket	0 Messages

Reply | Forward | Print... | Move... | Delete | Read

4 ***Folders***

5 ***Outbox***

Type of Message Icons

Key to the Microsoft Mail Window

1 *Title bar*

Displays the window name. Drag the title bar to move the window.

2 *Message icons*

These icons indicate the status of the messages they accompany:

 80-characters-per-line note.

 Regular note.

 Note with an enclosure.

 Urgent message.

 Sound.

 Image.

 Phone message.

3 *Mailbox Messages*

The Mailbox is a rcpository of messages that have been sent to you. The message headers are sorted according to the underlined field in the window (From, Subject, or Received). To sort on a different field, move the cursor to the field name and click once when the cursor becomes a down arrow. If you sort by Subject, any prefixes (such as RE: and FW:) are ignored.

4 *Folders*

Some folders already exist when you start using Mail. You can add more folders to store messages in any logical arrangement you'd like.

5 *Outbox*

Temporarily stores outgoing messages that the system has been instructed to send, but that have not yet been sent. The Outbox holds outgoing mail when you work offline, perhaps on a portable computer. When you reconnect to the network, the messages are sent from the Outbox.

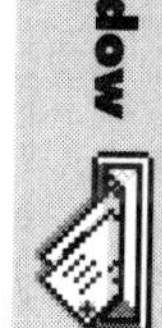

Starting Microsoft Mail

1. Pull down the Apple menu and select Microsoft Mail. **(Figure 1)**

   or

   Pull down the Microsoft Office Manager menu and select Microsoft Mail.
2. On the Mail Sign In dialog box, enter your password and click OK or press Enter. **(Figure 2)**

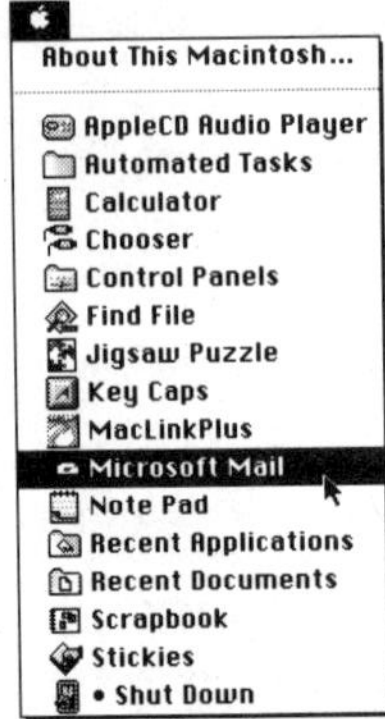

Figure 1. *The Apple menu.*

✔ Tip

- You can sign in to Mail automatically when you start your computer by clicking the MS Mail icon on the Chooser, selecting your mail server, clicking Setup, and then selecting Sign In To Mail Automatically. Then, click OK and close the Chooser. If the AppleTalk Zones box appears during this procedure, select your mail server's zone.

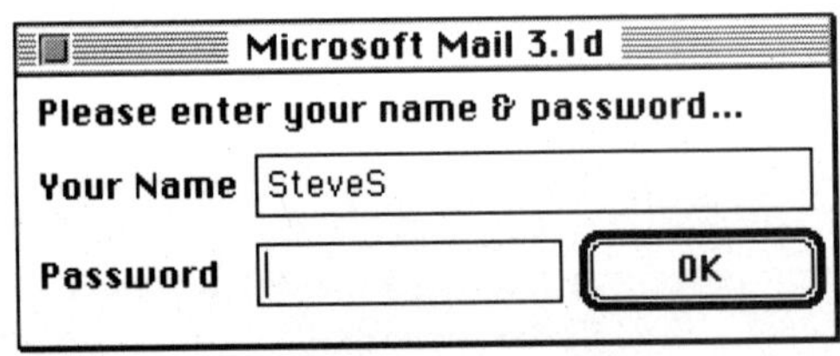

Figure 2. *The Mail Sign In dialog box.*

Starting/Quitting Mail

Mail

Quitting Microsoft Mail

1. From the Mail menu, choose Close & Sign Out. **(Figure 3)**

   or, to quit mail but remain signed in so you can be notified of incoming mail while using other applications

   From the File menu, choose Close Mailbox.

Figure 3. *The Mail menu.*

Reading Messages

Figure 1. *The Mailbox.*

Figure 2. *Double-click a message.*

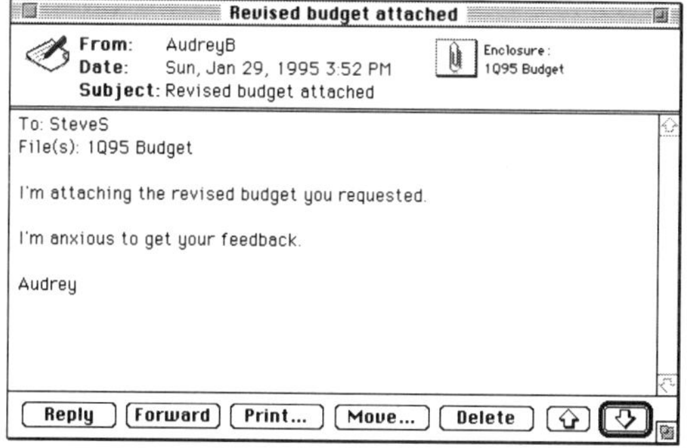

Figure 3. *Reading a message.*

Selecting a Message to Read

The Mailbox shows a list of messages that have been sent to you. Messages that you have not yet read show the name of the sender in bold. **(Figure 1)**

1. Double-click a message header to open the message. **(Figures 2-3)**

   or

   Use the arrow keys to move the highlight to the message and then press Enter.

2. Click the down arrow button to read the next message if you'd like.

✔ Tips

- You can sort the Mailbox. *See Sorting Your Mail, page 236.*
- If the message contains an Enclosure, click the Enclosure icon (paper clip). In the Enclosures dialog box, select the enclosure(s) to save and click Save or Save All.

Sorting Your Mail

You can sort the messages in your Mailbox according to the sender (From), the subject, or the date and time received. An underlined column heading indicates the sort method. **(Figure 4)**

1. Place the mouse pointer on the column heading by which you want the messages to be sorted. **(Figure 5)**
2. When the pointer changes to a down arrow, click once. **(Figure 6)**

✔ Tip

- When you sort the messages by Received, the most recent messages are shown first.
- When you sort by subject, the message type prefixes (RE: for regarding, and FW: for forwarded) are ignored.

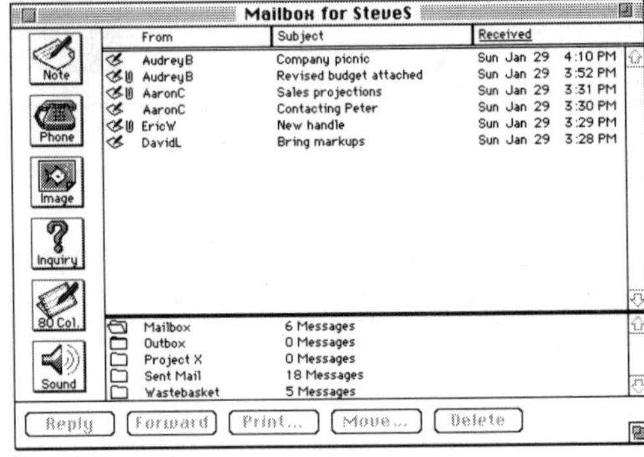

Figure 4. *Mailbox messages sorted according to the date and time received.*

Click here to sort the messages by "From".

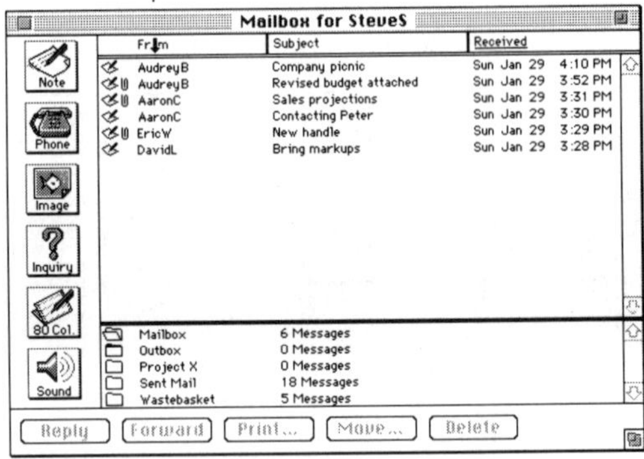

Figure 5. *The pointer positioned on the From column heading.*

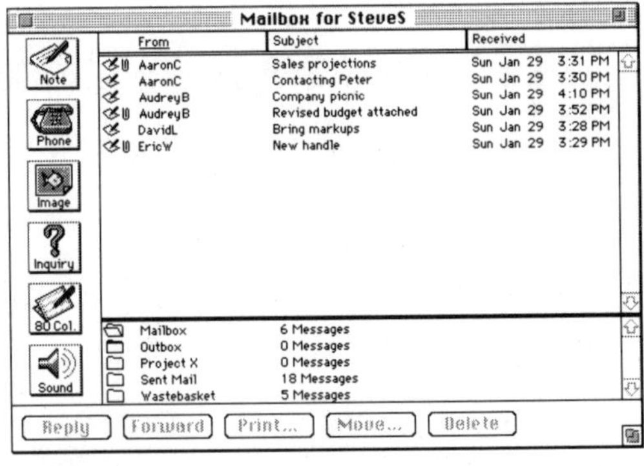

Figure 6. *Messages sorted according to "From."*

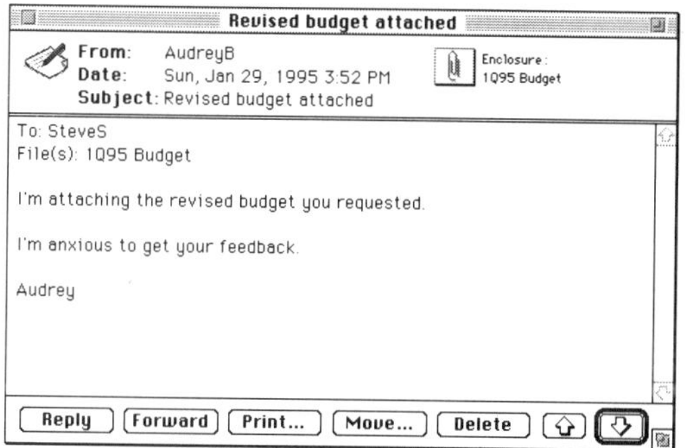

Figure 7. *Open the message.*

Reply button.

Figure 8. *The Reply button.*

Replying to a Message

1. Open the message to which you want to reply. **(Figure 7)**
   or
   Select the message on the Mailbox list.
2. Click the Reply button to reply to the sender. **(Figure 8)**
   or
   If there is more than one name on the To: or Cc: list, hold down the Option key to change the Reply button to Reply All. When you click Reply All, your reply will be sent to everyone on the To: and Cc: lists.
3. Enter the reply text at the current location of the insertion point (above the line). The original message appears below the line. **(Figure 9)**
4. Click Send.
   or
   Click the Enclosure or Options buttons before clicking Send to customize the message. *See Selecting Message Options, page 243; and Enclosing a File with a Message, page 244.*

✔ Tip

- To remove the contents of the original message to which you're replying, delete the original message text before you send the reply.

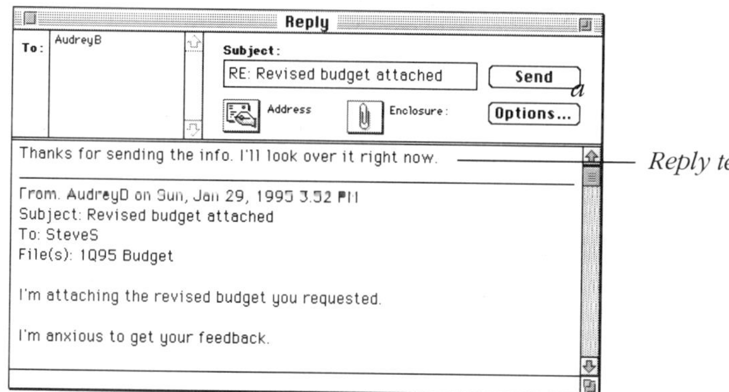

Figure 9. *Enter the reply text above the dashed line.*

Forwarding a Message

1. While reading a message, click the Forward button. **(Figure 10)**
2. On the Send Note form that appears, enter an address, optional Cc, and subject after the FW: in the Subject text box. (The FW indicates to the recipient that the message has been forwarded.) **(Figure 11)**
3. Enter any explanatory text to the forwarded message above the line.
4. Click the Send button.

✔ Tip

- When you forward a message, you can change the Options or enclose files as if you'd created the message. *See Selecting Message Options, page 243; and Enclosing a File with a Message, page 244.*

Forward button.

Figure 10. *The Forward button.*

The FW indicates that the message is being forwarded.

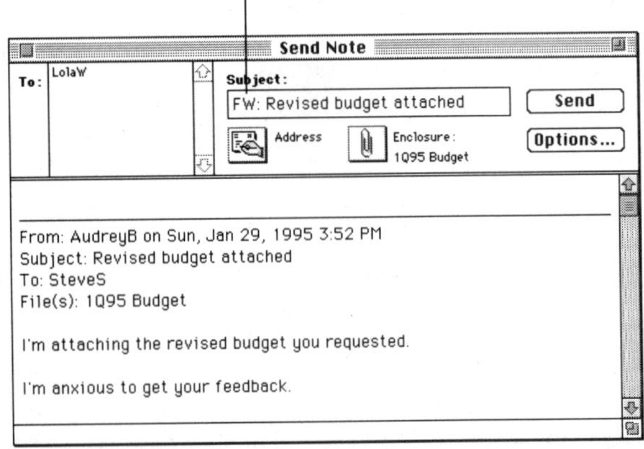

Figure 11. *The Send Note form.*

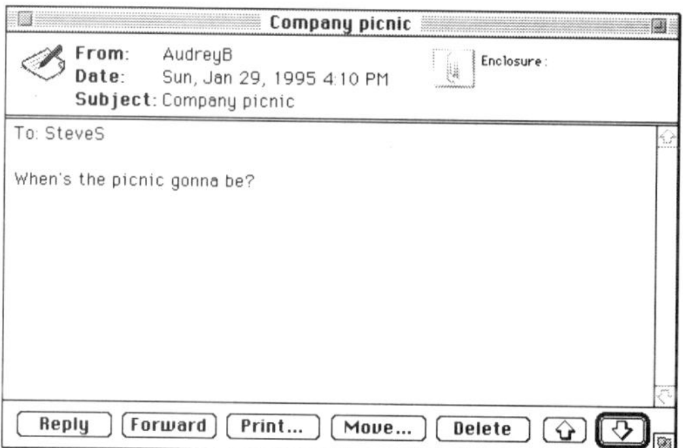

Figure 12. *Open a message.*

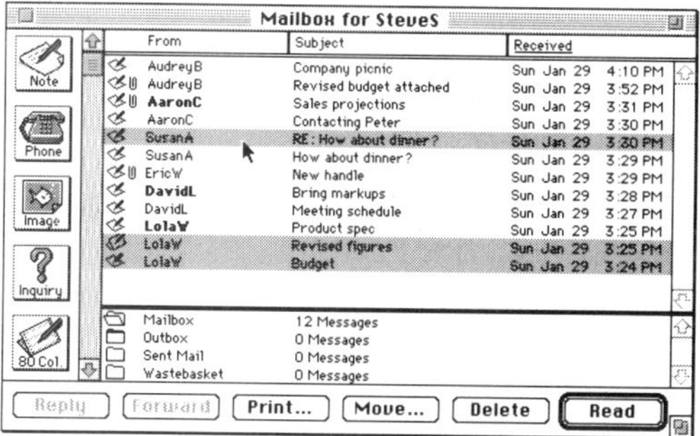

Figure 13. *Selecting multiple messages.*

Printing a Message

1. Open a message. **(Figure 12)**

   or

   In the Mailbox window, hold down Shift and click each message to include in the printout. **(Figure 13)**
2. Click Print.
3. On the Print dialog box, choose print options and then click Print.

✔ Tip

- Enclosures are not printed. You must print an enclosure from an application that can read that type of file.

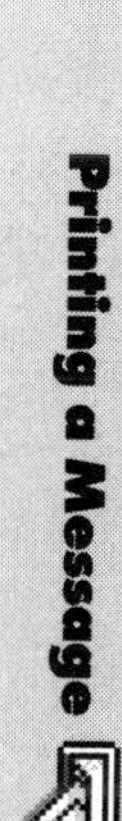

Mail

Deleting a Message

1. Open a message.

   or

   Select one or more messages on the Mailbox list. **(Figure 14)**

2. Click the Delete button. **(Figure 15)**

   or

   Press ⌘+D.

   or

   Press the Delete key on the keyboard.

✔ Tip

- Messages that you delete are moved to the Wastebasket folder. To retrieve deleted messages, open the Wastebasket folder and drag the messages back to the Mailbox.

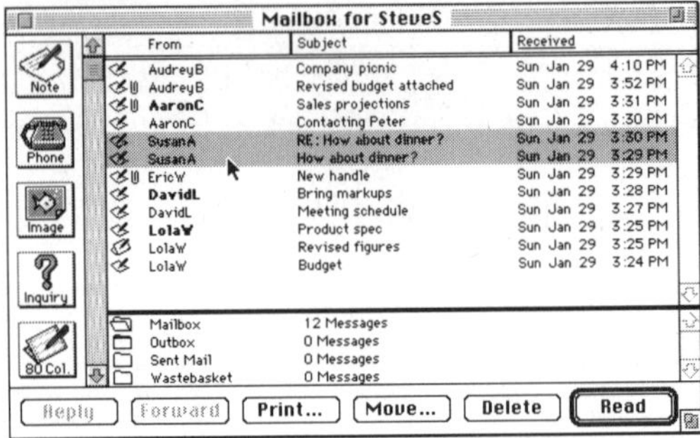

Figure 14. *Select one or more messages on the Inbox list.*

Figure 15. *The Delete button.*

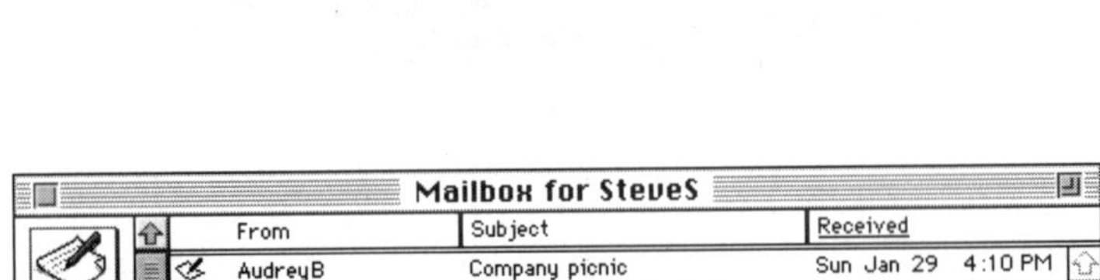

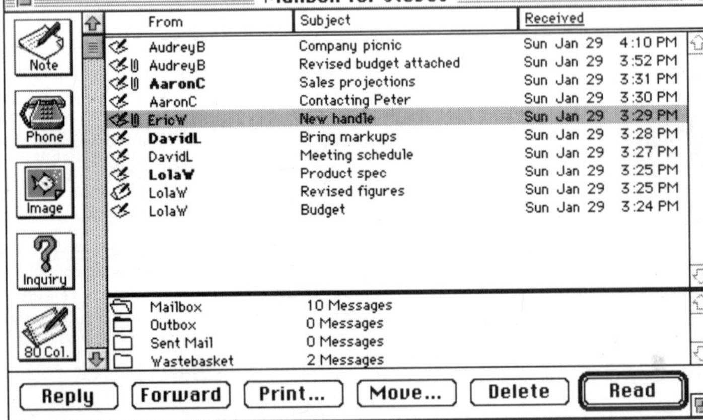

Figure 16. *The messages are deleted.*

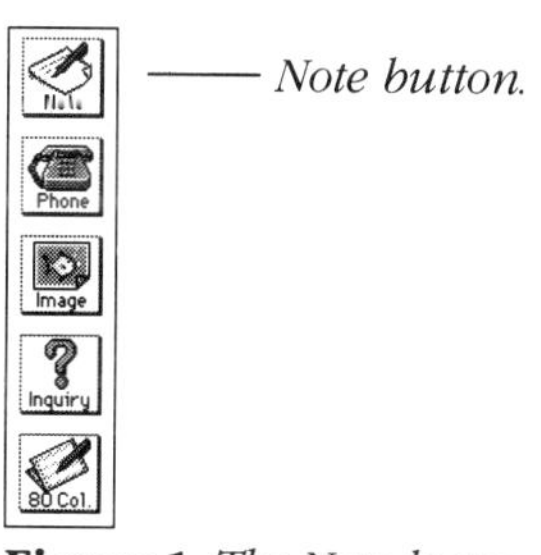

Figure 1. *The Note button.*

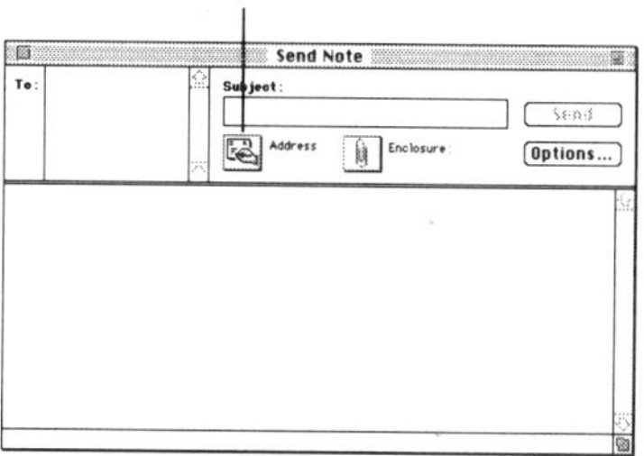

Figure 2. *The Address button.*

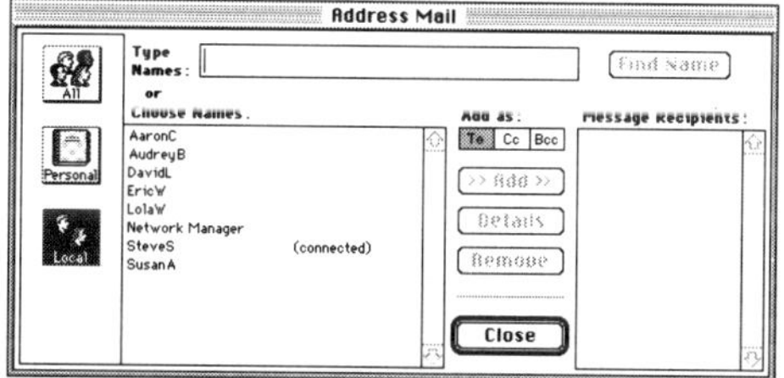

Figure 3. *The Address dialog box.*

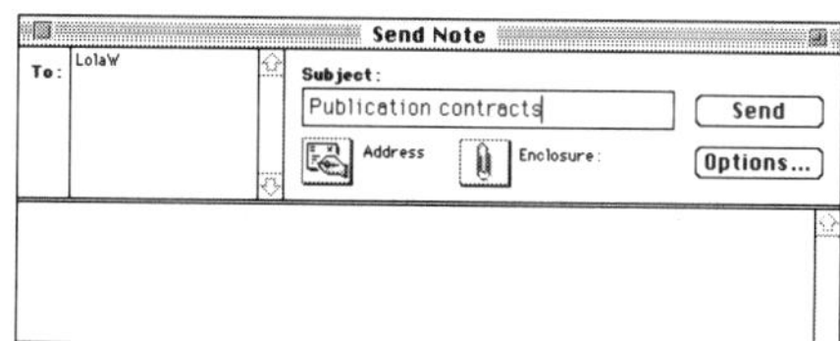

Figure 4. *Enter a subject.*

Starting and Addressing a Message

1. Click the Note button. **(Figure 1)**
2. On the new Send Note form, click the Address button to select addresses from the Address book. **(Figure 2)** You may also set preferences to have the address book come up automatically when you create a new Mail document.
3. On the Address dialog box, double-click the name of each recipient for the message. **(Figure 3)**

   or

   Select names from the list, click the To, Cc, or Bcc button, and click Add.
4. On the Address dialog box, click Close.
5. Enter a message subject in the Subject text box. **(Figure 4)** *Don't skip this step. A subject is helpful when the recipient views his or her Mailbox.*

✔ Tips

- To view details about a name on the address list, click the name and click the Details button.
- To remove a name from the Message Recipients list on the Address dialog box, select the name and press the Delete key.
- If you know a recipient's address, you can also type the address into the To text box on the Send Note form without using the Address book.
- Click the All button to see the addresses of all users on all Mail servers on your network. Click the Personal button to see only the addresses in your Personal Address book. Click the Local button to see only the addresses on your local Mail server, even if there are other servers on the network.

Entering the Text and Sending the Message

1. On the Send Note form, click the message text area.

   or

   After typing the subject, press the Tab key to move the insertion point to the message text area.
2. Type the text of the message. **(Figure 5)**
3. Click the Send button. **(Figure 6)**

   or

   Press ⌘+S.

✔ Tips

- Messages you send are transferred to the Outbox temporarily until they are actually sent by the system to the recipient.
- Messages that are successfully sent are transferred to the Sent mail folder where you can review them. **(Figure 7)**

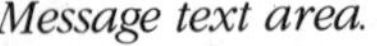

Message text area.

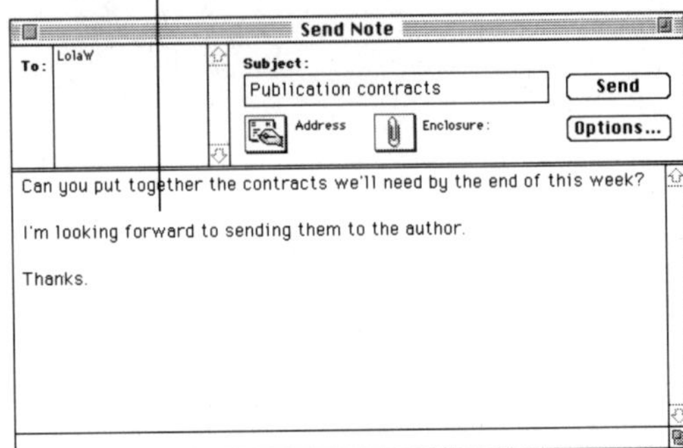

Figure 5. *Type the message text in the message text area.*

Click here to send the message.

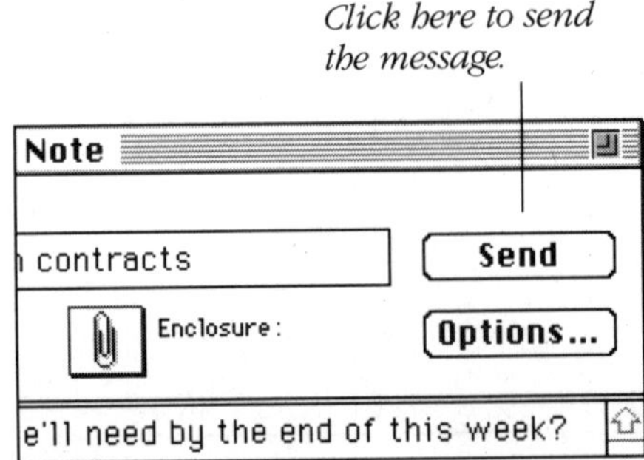

Figure 6. *The Send button.*

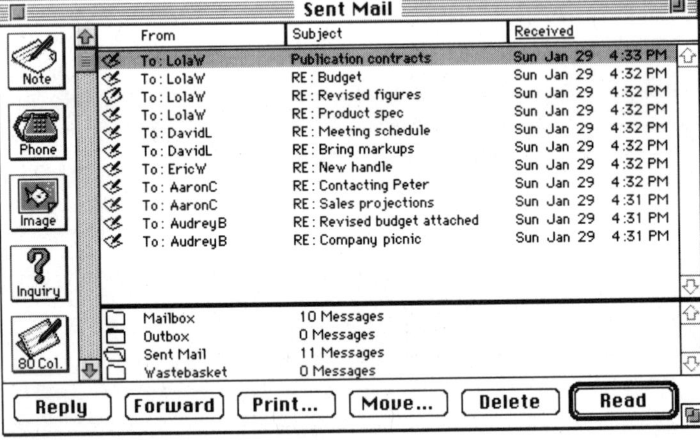

Figure 7. *The Sent Mail folder.*

Options button.

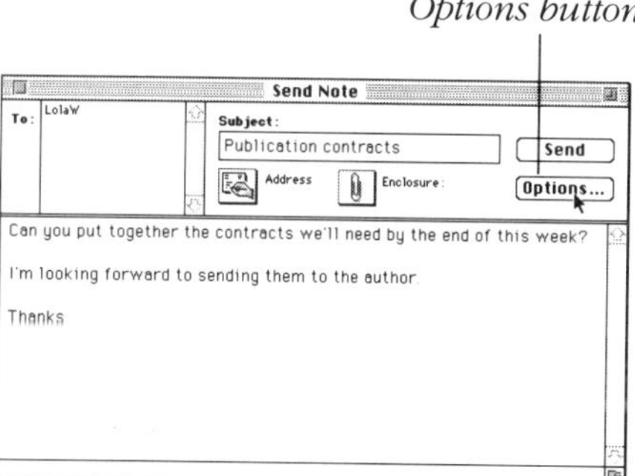

Figure 8. *The Options button.*

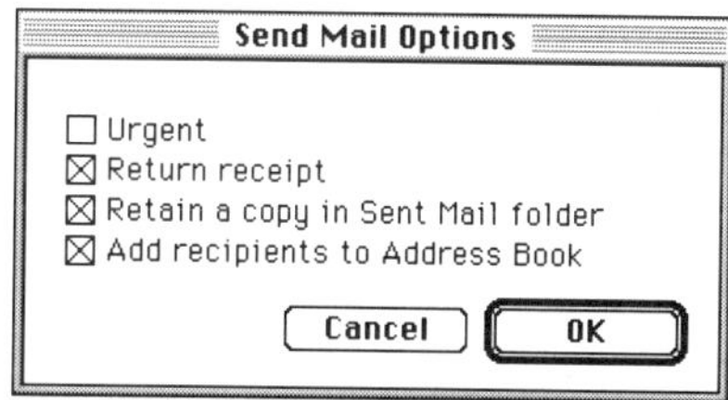

Figure 9. *The Options dialog box.*

Figure 10. *A return receipt.*

Selecting Message Options

1. While composing a message, click the Options button. **(Figure 8)**
2. On the Send Mail Options dialog box, click Return Receipt to be notified when the recipient opens the message. **(Figures 9–10)**
3. Clear the Retain a copy in Sent Mail folder checkbox if you do not want messages that have been sent to be transferred to the Sent mail folder.
4. Click the Urgent checkbox if you want to place an exclamation point next to the message header in the recipient's Mailbox. **(Figure 11)**
5. Click OK.

Urgent message.

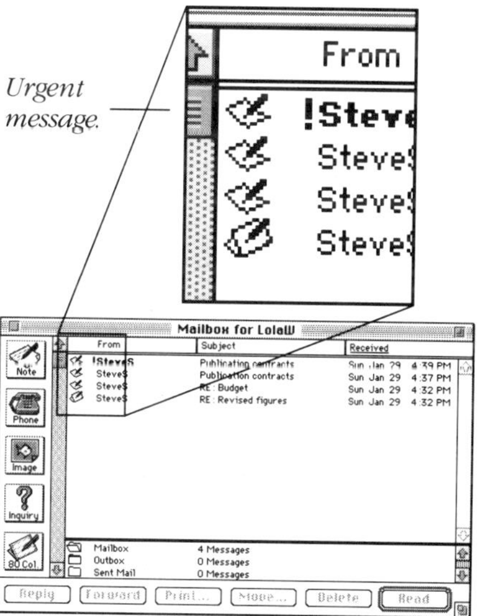

Figure 11. *The recipient's Inbox.*

Enclosing a File with a Message

1. While composing a message, click the Enclosure button. **(Figure 12)**
2. On the Enclosure dialog box, select a file and click add. **(Figure 13)**
3. To enclose another file, repeat Step 2.

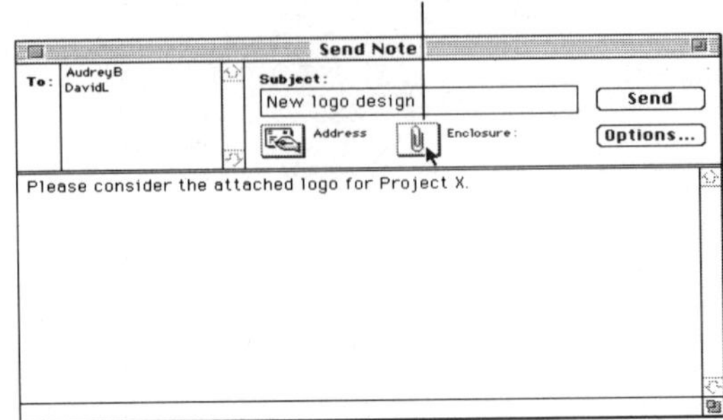

Figure 12. *The Enclosure button.*

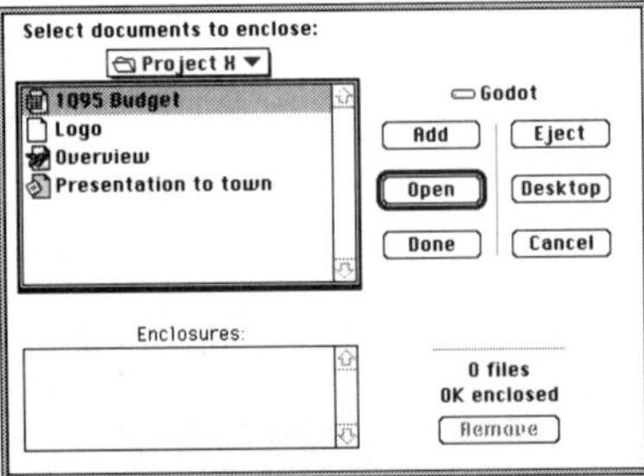
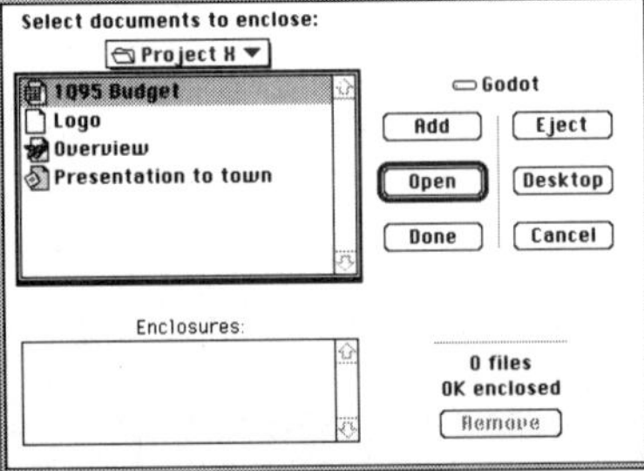

Figure 13. *The Select documents to enclose dialog box.*

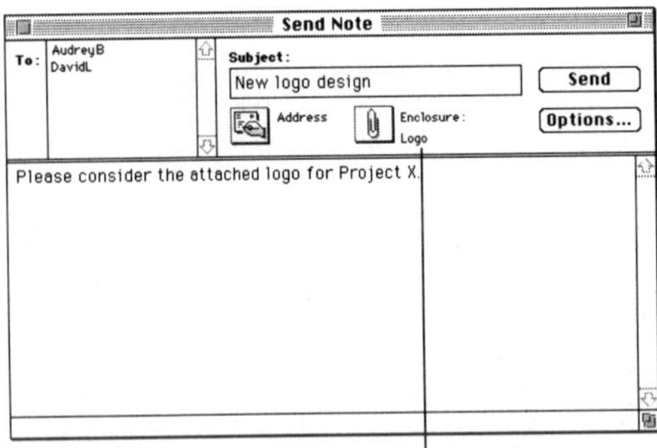

Figure 14. *An enclosed document ("Logo").*

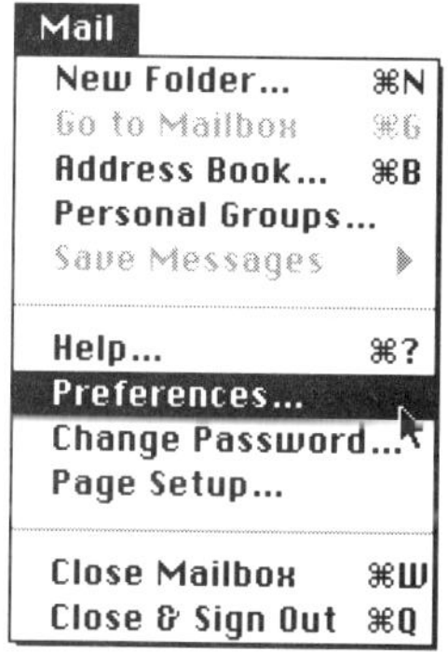

Figure 15. *The Mail menu.*

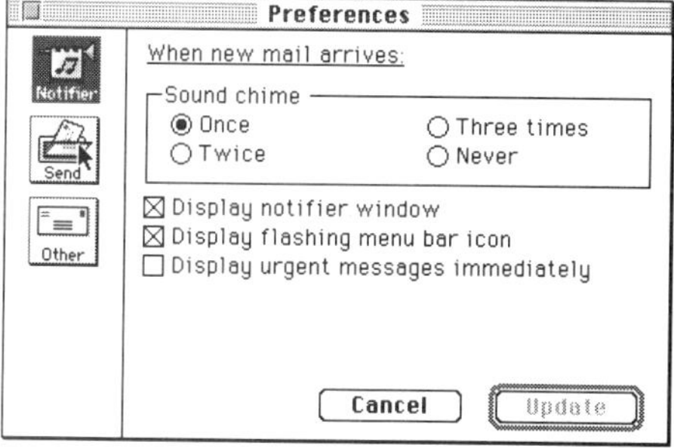

Figure 16. *The Notifier preferences.*

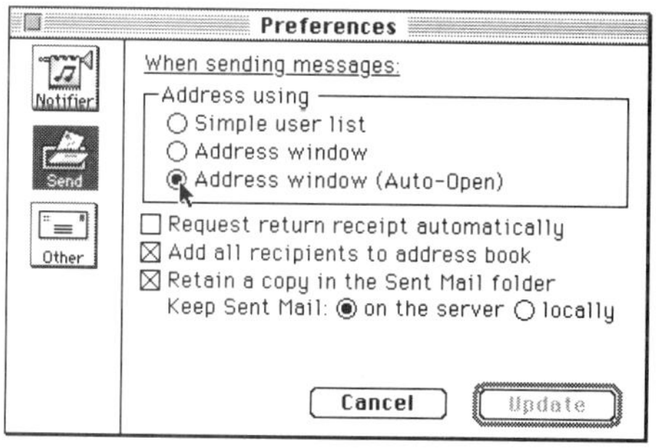

Figure 17. *The Send preferences.*

Setting the Address Book to Open Automatically

You may set your mail preferences so that whenever you compose a new message, the system automatically opens the Address Book for your convenience.

1. From the Mail menu, choose Preferences. **(Figure 15)**
2. On the display of Notifier preferences, click the Send button. **(Figure 16)**
3. On the Send Preferences dialog box, click the Address window (Auto-Open) button. **(Figure 17)**

✔ Tip

- You may set other preferences (besides Notifier and Send preferences) by clicking the Other button. **(Figure 18)**

Mail

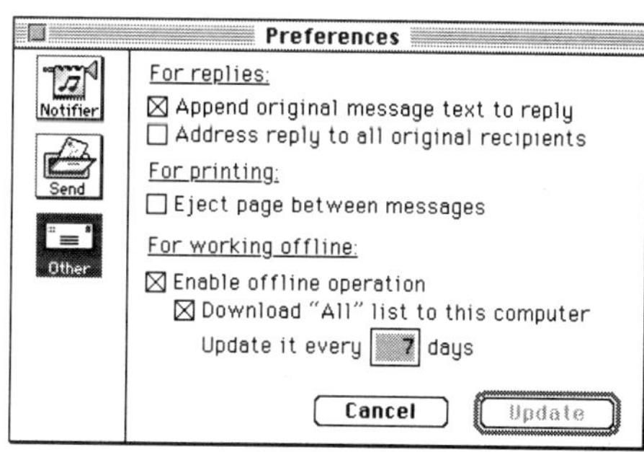

Figure 18. *The Other preferences.*

Creating a Personal Address Book

1. From the Mail menu, choose Address Book. **(Figure 19)**
2. On the Address Book dialog box, select as many names as you'd like to add to your personal address book. **(Figure 20)**
3. Click the Add button. **(Figure 20)**
4. Click Save.

✔ Tip

- To remove a name from the Personal Address Book, click the name on the Personal Address Book and click Remove. **(Figure 21)**

Figure 19. *The Mail menu.*

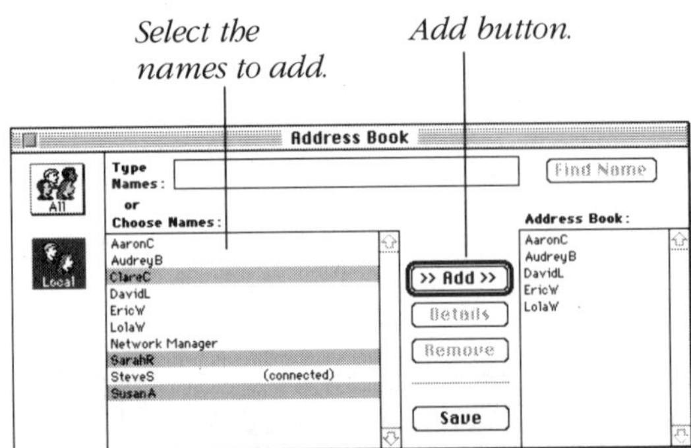

Figure 20. *The Address Book dialog box.*

Using the Personal Address Book

1. While composing a message, click the Address button.
2. On the Address dialog box, click the Personal Address Book button. **(Figure 22)**
3. Use the Personal Address Book as you would the Local Address book.

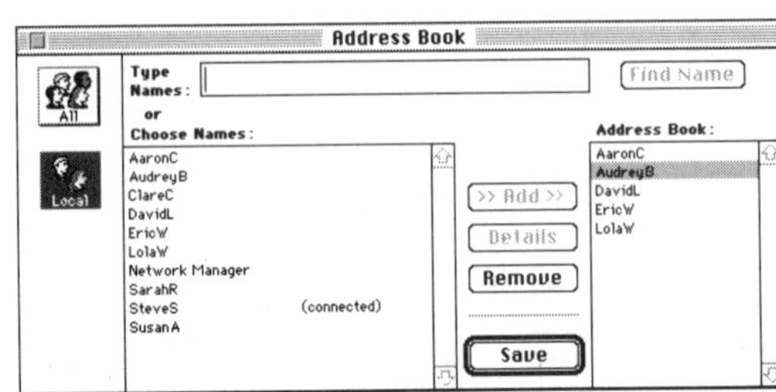

Figure 21. *The Personal Address Book.*

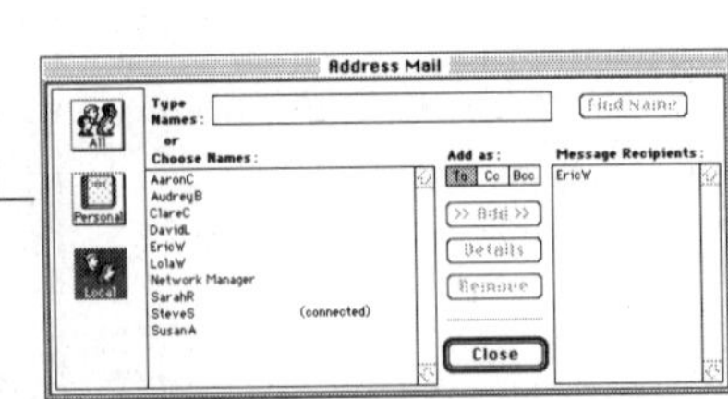

Figure 22. *The Address dialog box.*

Figure 23. *The Mail menu.*

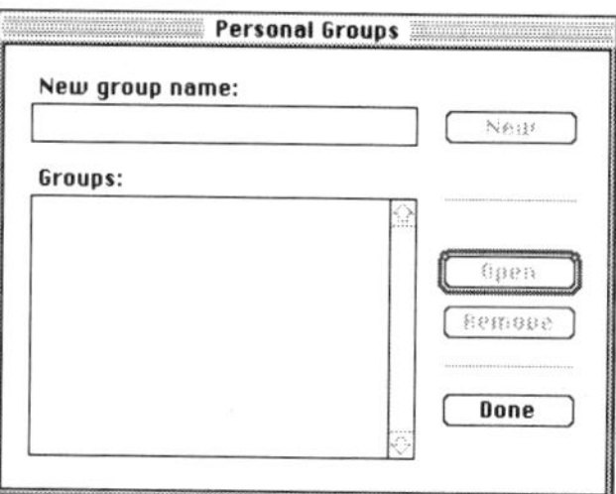

Figure 24. *The Personal Groups dialog box.*

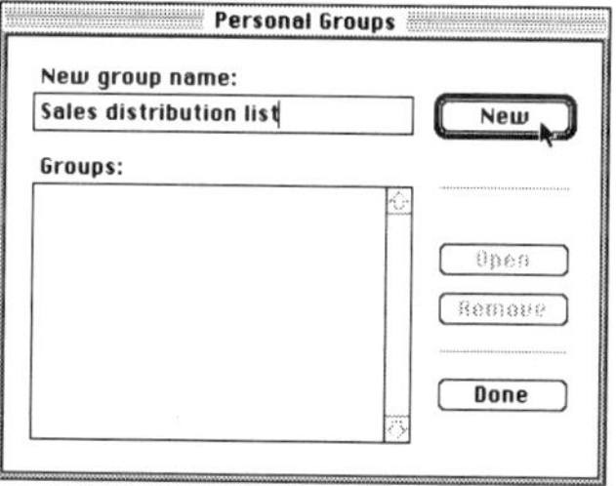

Figure 25. *Enter a name and click New.*

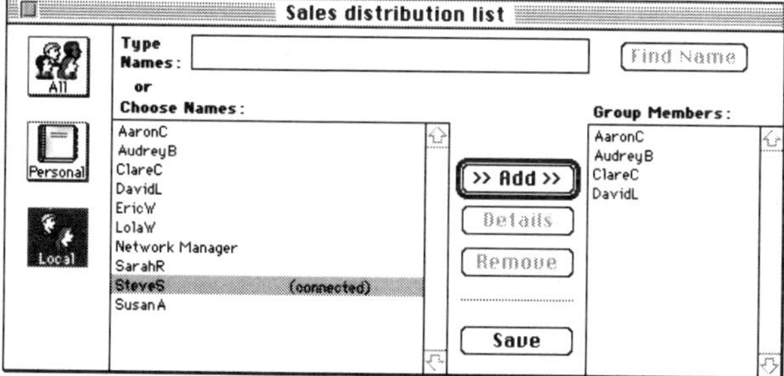

Figure 26. *The distribution list dialog box.*

Creating a Personal Group

A personal group is like a distribution list. By entering the personal group name as the recipient of a message, you can automatically send the message to everyone in the group.

1. From the Mail menu, choose Personal Groups. **(Figure 23)**
2. On the Personal Groups dialog box, enter a name for the group and click New. **(Figures 24-25)**
4. On the next dialog box, choose names from the Choose Names list and click Add. **(Figure 26)**
5. Click Save. **(Figure 26)**

Mail

Sending a Document from Within an Office Application

1. From the File menu of the application, select Send. **(Figure 27)**
2. On the Send Note form, enter an address, subject, and any additional text you want in the message body. **(Figure 28)**
3. Click Send to send the document as a Mail message.

✔ Tip

- Choose Add Routing Slip from the application's File menu to automatically send the document to others for their edits or annotations. **(Figure 29)**

Figure 27. *The File menu of Word.*

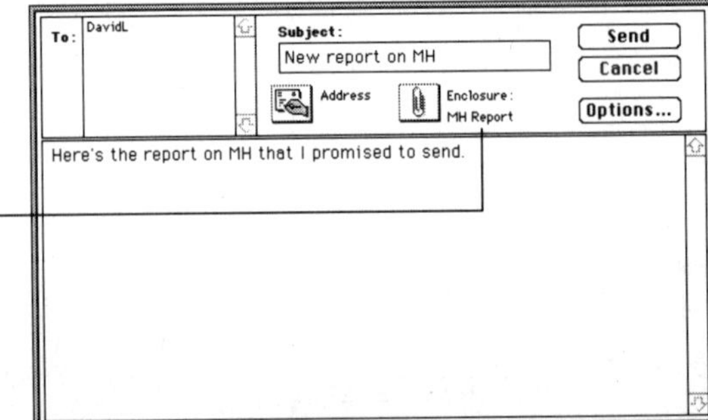

The document you are sending is shown as an enclosure.

Figure 28. *The Send Note form.*

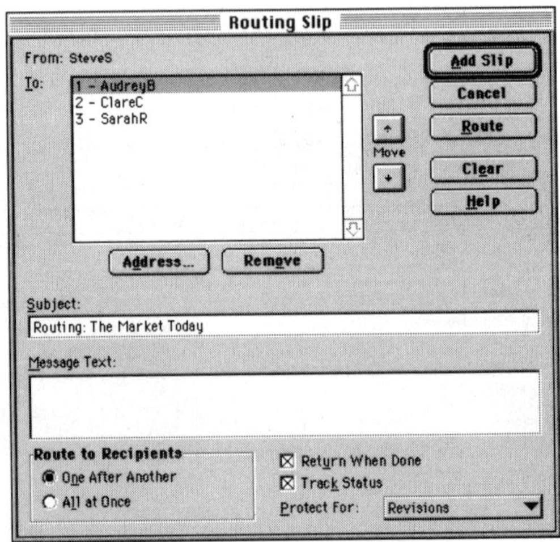

Figure 29. *The Routing Slip dialog box.*

Managing Your Mail

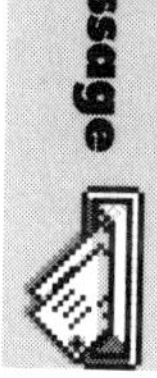

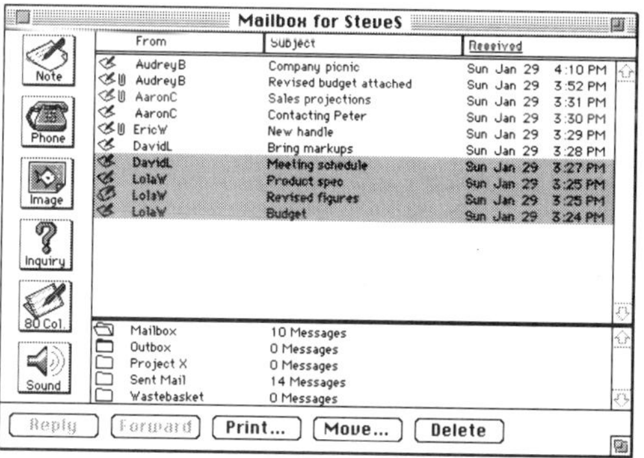

Figure 1. *The Mailbox.*

Filing a Message in a Folder

You can add folders to the list of private folders that you see in the Mailbox window and then easily move messages to any folder you create. Folders allow you to organize messages by sender, project, department, or any other plan.

1. On the Mailbox, select one or more messages. **(Figure 1)**
2. Drag the selected message or messages to the folder on the list of Private Folders. **(Figure 2)**

   or

   Click the Move button and then select a folder on the Move Message dialog box. **(Figure 3)**

✔ Tips

- The currently open folder shows an open folder icon. **(Figure 4)**
- To view the contents of a folder, double-click the folder name.

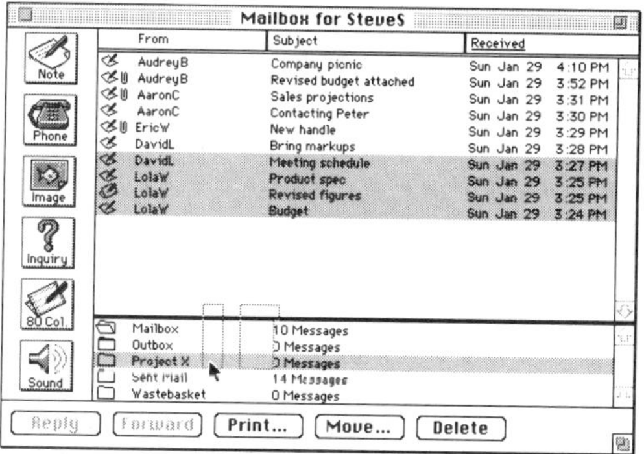

Figure 2. *Drag a message to a folder.*

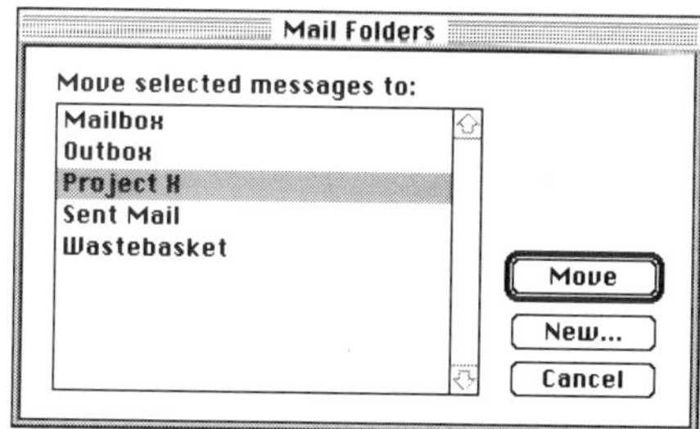

Figure 3. *The Move Message dialog box.*

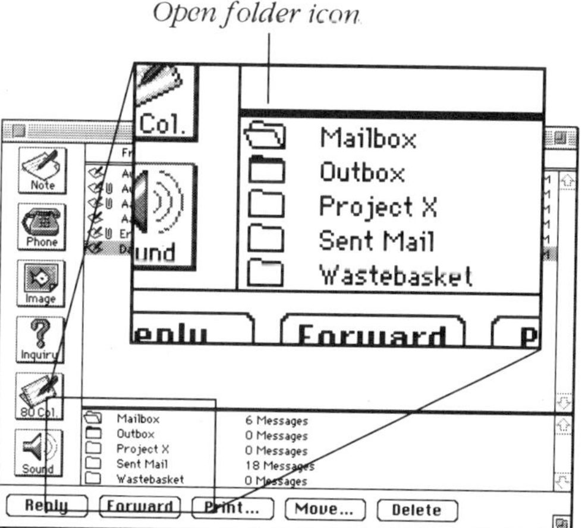

Figure 4. *Folder list.*

Creating Folders

New folders can be on your local Mac or on the Mail server if you are connected to a network.

1. From the Mail menu, choose New Folder. **(Figure 5)**
2. In the New Folder dialog box, enter a name for the folder and then click the button corresponding to where you would like the folder stored, on the mail server or on your own computer. **(Figure 6)**

✔ Tips

- Each folder can have its own Sort order for the messages inside.

Figure 5. *The File menu.*

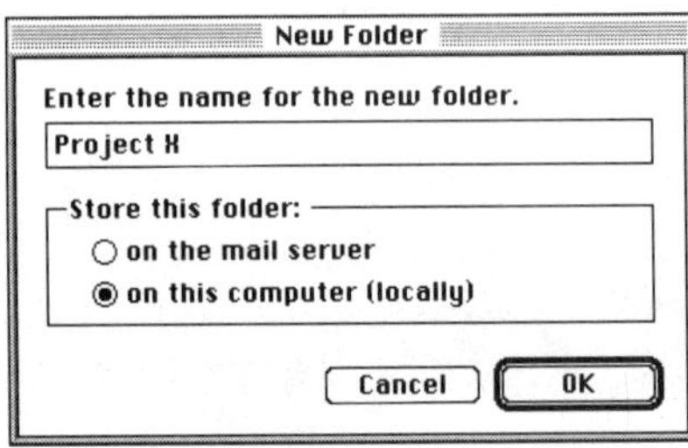

Figure 6. *The New Folder dialog box.*

Deleting Folders

1. Click a folder on the Private Folders list.
2. Click the Delete button or press the Delete key on the keyboard. **(Figure 7)**

✔ Tip

- When you delete a folder, you also delete all messages and subfolders it contains.

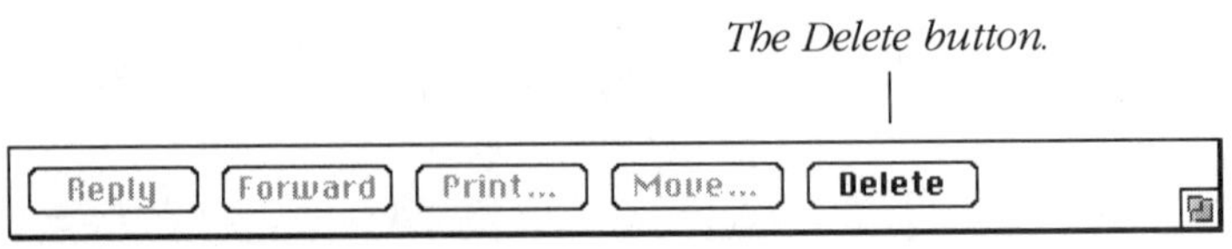

Figure 7. *The Delete button.*

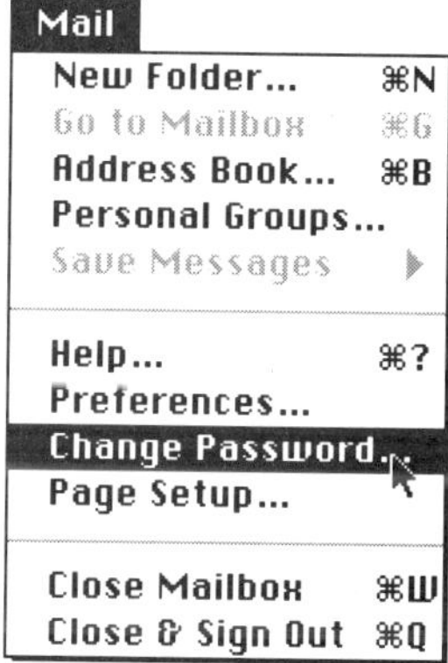

Figure 8. *The Mail menu.*

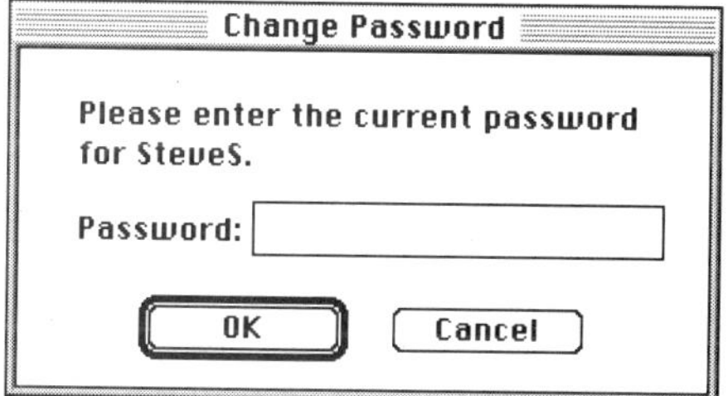

Figure 9. *The Change Password dialog box.*

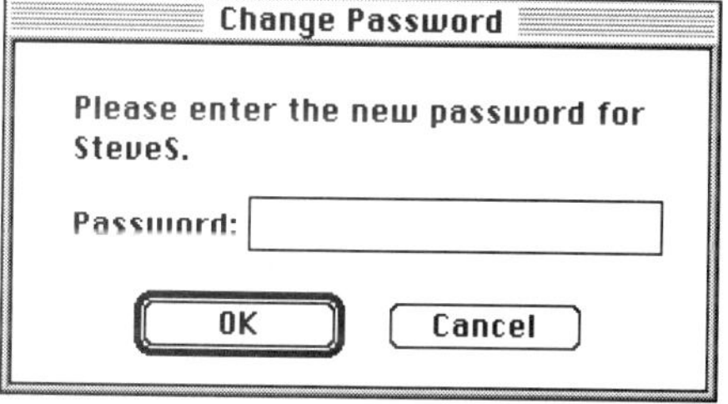

Figure 10. *Enter the new password.*

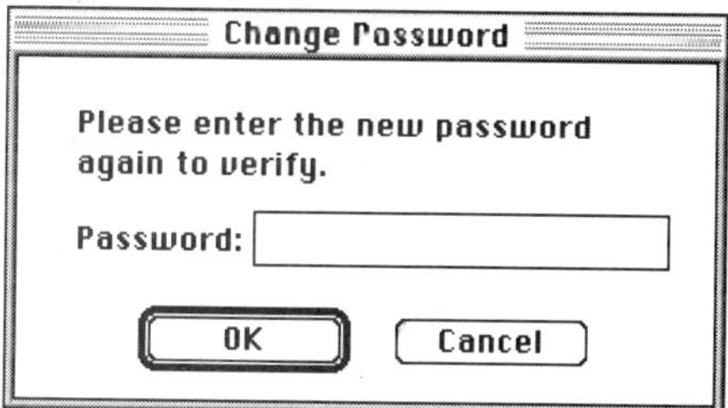

Figure 11 . *Verify the new password.*

Changing Your Password

1. From the Mail menu, choose Change Password. **(Figure 8)**
2. In the Change Password dialog box, enter your existing password into the Password text box and click OK. **(Figure 9)** For security, the characters you type are shown as bullets.
3. Into the New Password text box, enter the new password. **(Figure 10)**
4. Enter the new password again to confirm it. **(Figure 11)**

Setting Mail Preferences

1. From the Mail menu, choose Preferences. **(Figure 12)**
2. On the Preferences dialog box, click the Notifier, Send, or Other button, change the appropriate preferences, and then click Update or press Enter. **(Figures 13–15)**

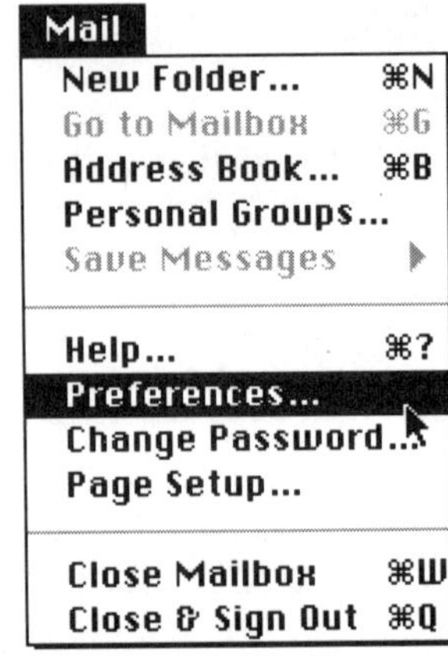

Figure 12. *The Mail menu.*

Figure 13. *The Notifier preferences.*

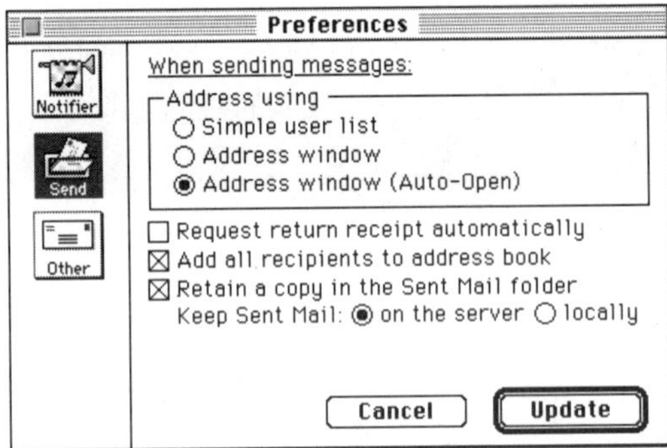

Figure 14. *The Send preferences.*

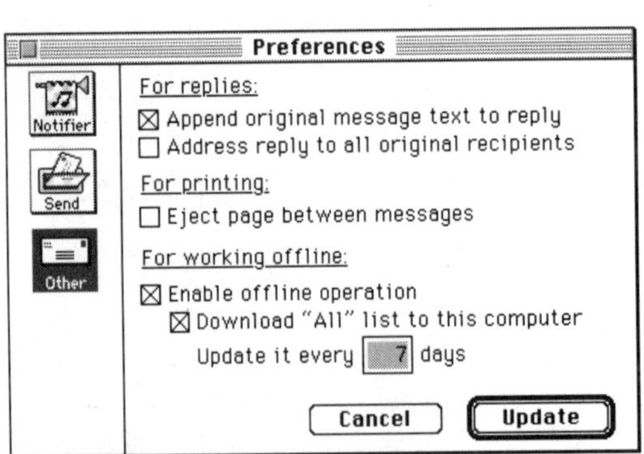

Figure 15. *The Other preferences.*

Combining the Office Applications

Combining the Office Applications

Basic Techniques

Combining Applications

Basic Techniques

About Sharing Information Among the Office Applications

Alone, each Office application is impressive enough, but combined, they form a powerful system that can pass information among the applications.

To add some numbers to a memo, you can copy a table of numeric data from **Excel** to a **Word** document. To ensure that future changes to the **Excel** numbers will flow through to the document in **Word**, you can even create a link between the original numbers in **Excel** and the copies in **Word**. Then, whenever the **Excel** numbers are updated, the copies in **Word** will be updated, too. **(Figure 1)**

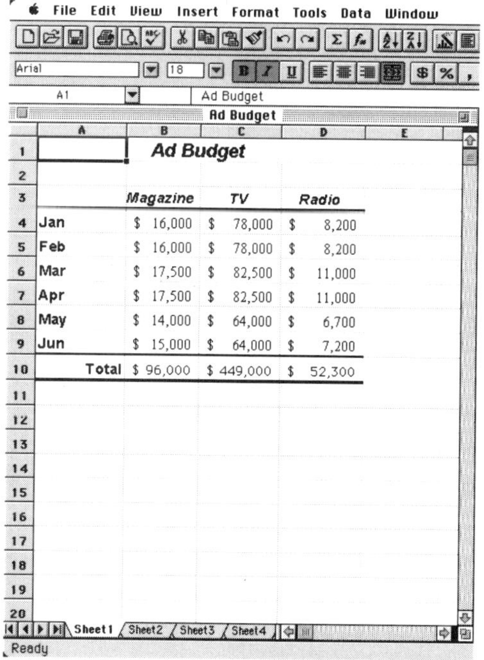

	Magazine	TV	Radio
Jan	$ 16,000	$ 78,000	$ 8,200
Feb	$ 16,000	$ 78,000	$ 8,200
Mar	$ 17,500	$ 82,500	$ 11,000
Apr	$ 17,500	$ 82,500	$ 11,000
May	$ 14,000	$ 64,000	$ 6,700
Jun	$ 15,000	$ 64,000	$ 7,200
Total	$ 96,000	$ 449,000	$ 52,300

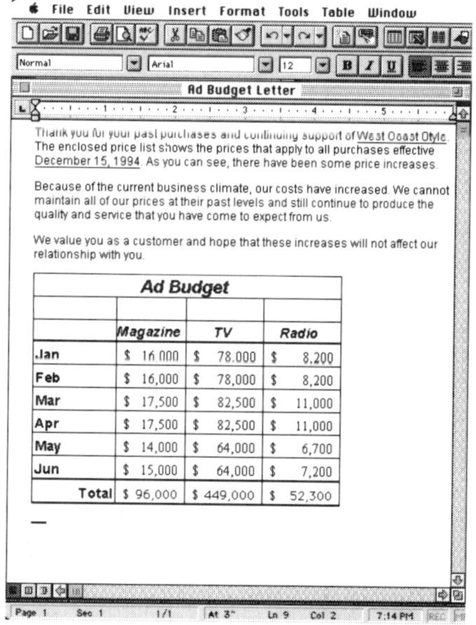

	Magazine	TV	Radio
Jan	$ 16,000	$ 78,000	$ 8,200
Feb	$ 16,000	$ 78,000	$ 8,200
Mar	$ 17,500	$ 82,500	$ 11,000
Apr	$ 17,500	$ 82,500	$ 11,000
May	$ 14,000	$ 64,000	$ 6,700
Jun	$ 15,000	$ 64,000	$ 7,200
Total	$ 96,000	$ 449,000	$ 52,300

Figure 1. *A table copied from Excel to Word.*

About Dragging and Dropping Among the Applications

The easiest way to move something from one application to another is with *Drag and Drop*. Dragging and dropping *between* applications works just like dragging and dropping *within* an application. You select an item to drag, called an *object*, and then drag it between two application windows that are arranged so that you can see them both. You can select a range of numbers or a chart in **Excel**, for instance, and drag it to a **Word** document. **(Figures 2-3)**

Table 41-1. ***Drag and Droppable Objects***

Word	• Selected text. • A table
Excel	• A cell • Selected range of numbers • A chart • Drawn graphics
PowerPoint	• A slide from Slide Sorter view

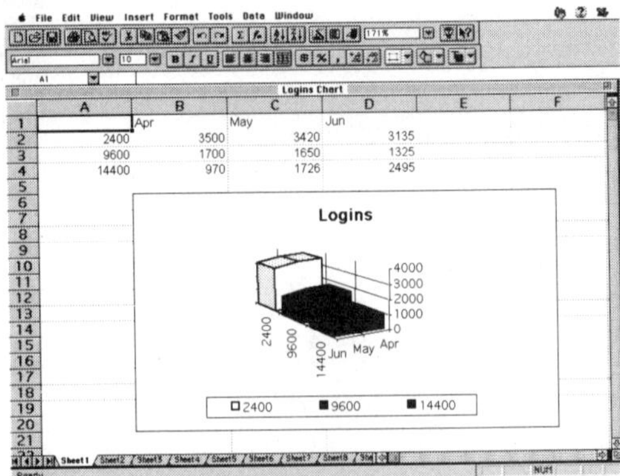

Figure 2. *An Excel chart.*

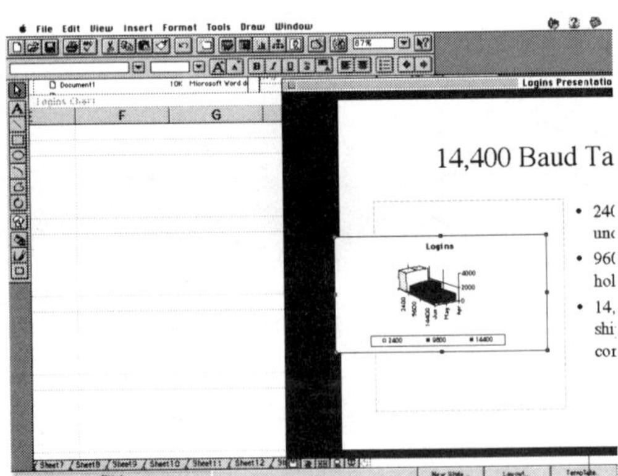

Figure 3. *The Excel chart dragged to a PowerPoint slide.*

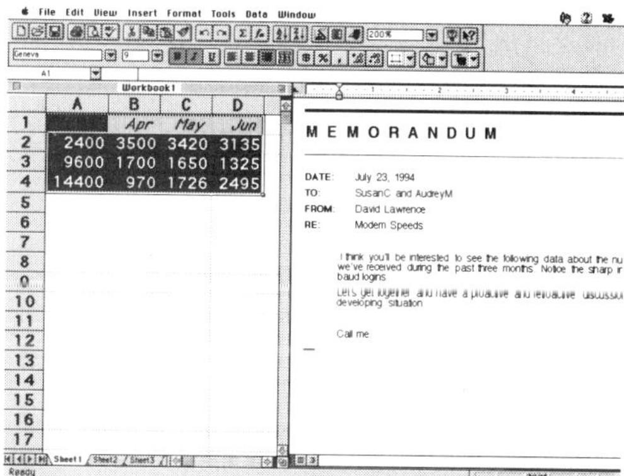

Figure 4. *Excel and Word windows.*

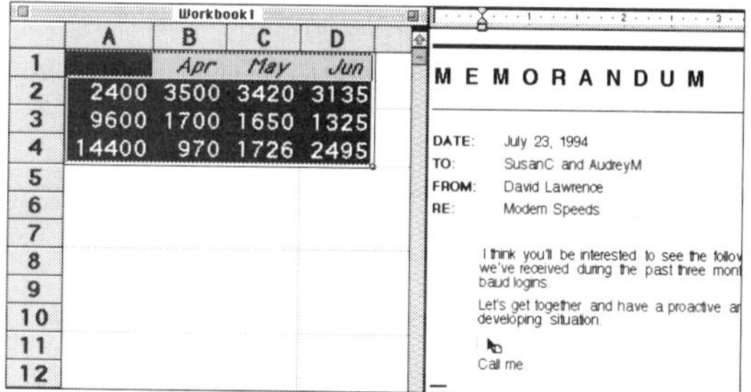

Figure 5. *A selected range in Excel.*

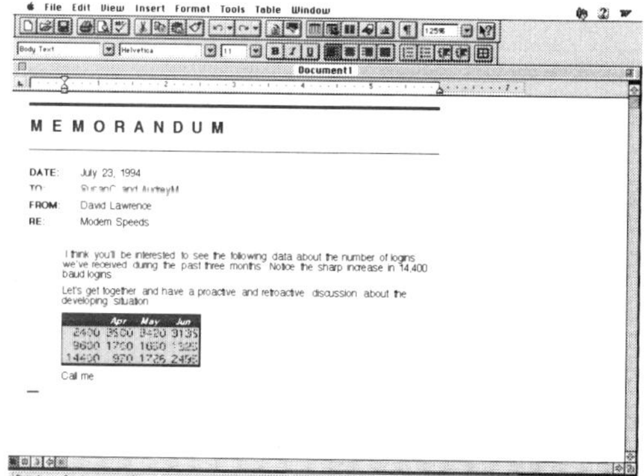

Figure 6. *Dragging the Excel range to Word.*

Figure 7. *The range as it appears in Word.*

Drag and Drop: Moving an Object

1. Arrange the two application windows so you can see both the object and its destination. **(Figure 4)**
2. Select the object. **(Figure 5)**
3. Drag the border of the object to the other window. **(Figure 6)**
4. Release the mouse button to drop the object at its destination. **(Figure 7)**

✔ Tips

- To arrange the windows so that you can see more than one at once, drag the title bar of the windows and/or drag the resize boxes of the windows.
- To **copy** rather than **move** an object with Drag and Drop, hold down the Option key as you drag the object. **(Figure 8)**
- When you drag and drop an object, it becomes embedded in the destination application. Any changes to the original are not reflected in the copy unless you establish a link using Copy and Paste Link. *See Linking Objects with Copy and Paste Link, page 261.*

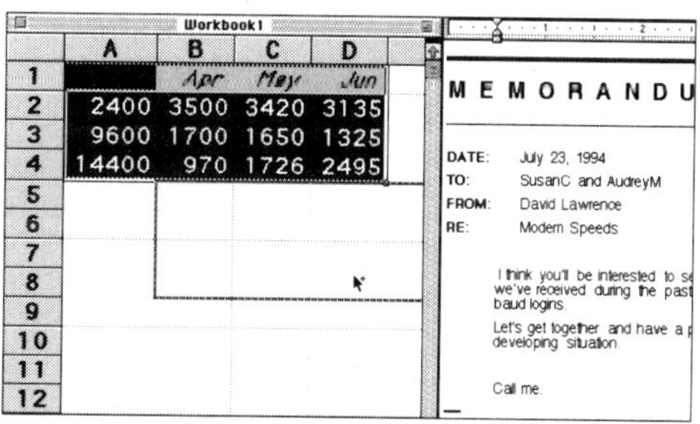

Figure 8. *Copying an object with Drag and Drop.*

Editing an Object After Dragging and Dropping

Even though you've dragged an object to another application, you can still edit the dragged object using the tools of the original application in which it was created. If the original application is **Word**, **Excel**, or **PowerPoint**, you may even be able to edit the object *in place*.

During in-place editing, the menus, toolbars, and other controls of the originating application temporarily appear within the application window in which you have been working.

1. Double-click an object that has been dragged from another application. **(Figures 9-10)**

   or

   Click the object with the Control key held down and then choose the Edit command on the shortcut menu. **(Figure 11)**

✓ Tip

- If you select an object, you'll see whether you can edit the object in its original application. The status line at the bottom of the application will advise you to double-click if you can edit the object. **(Figure 9)**

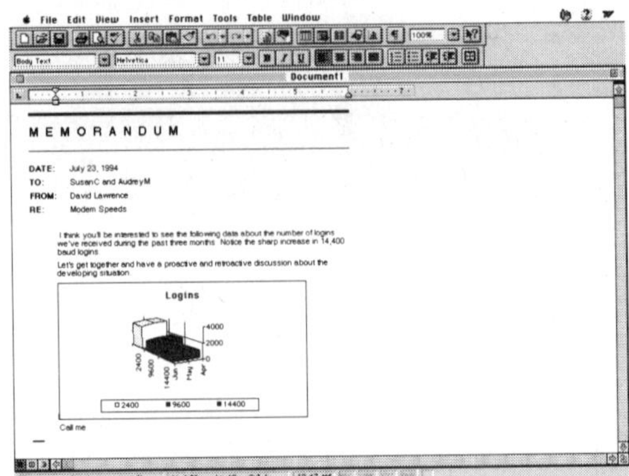

Figure 9. *Double-click an Excel chart in Word to edit the slide with Excel's tools.*

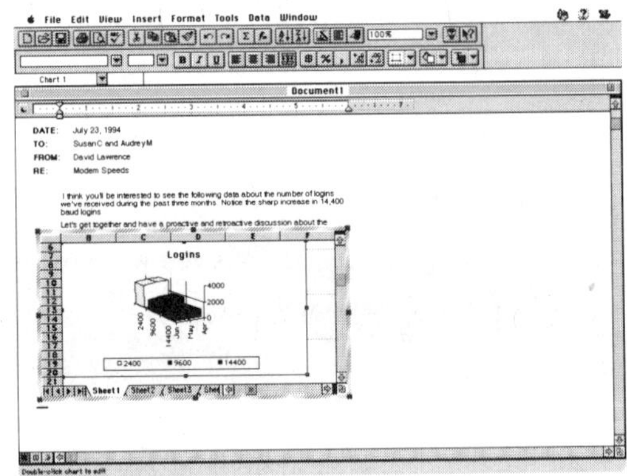

Figure 10. *The chart appears for editing along with the tools of its originating application.*

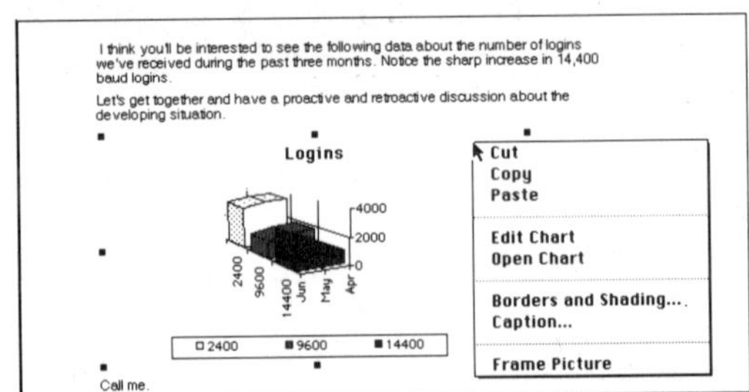

Figure 11. *The shortcut menu for an Excel chart that has been dragged to Word.*

	A	B	C
1		Orange	Riverside
2	2400	65	43
3	9600	52	45
4	14400	26	79
5			
6			

Figure 12. *Selecting an Excel range.*

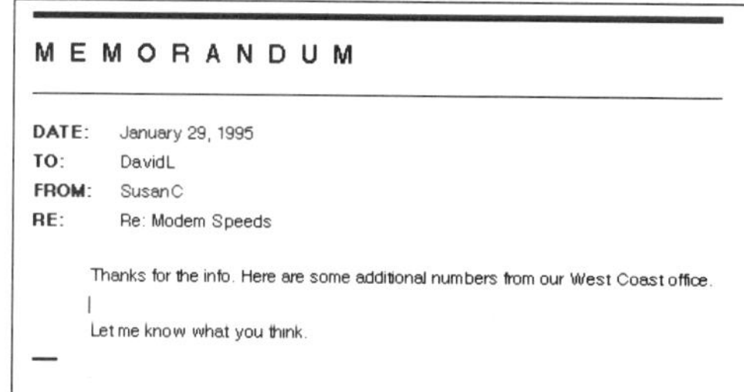
MEMORANDUM

DATE: January 29, 1995
TO: DavidL
FROM: SusanC
RE: Re: Modem Speeds

Thanks for the info. Here are some additional numbers from our West Coast office.

Let me know what you think.

Figure 13. *Click at the destination for the Excel object.*

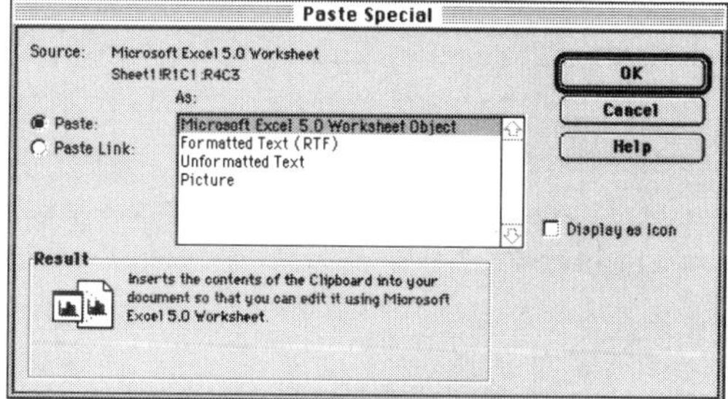

Figure 14. *The Paste Special dialog box.*

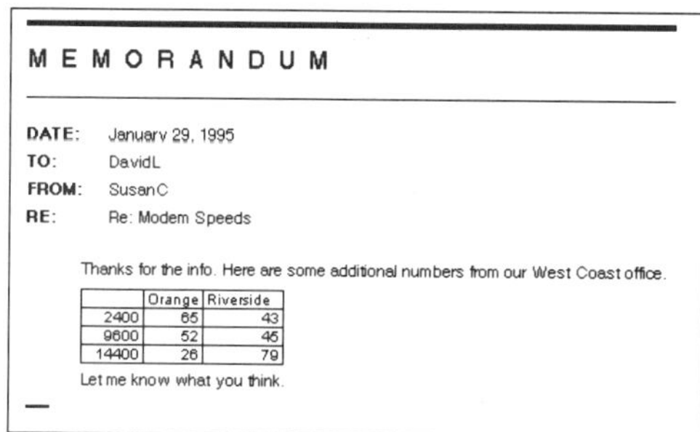
MEMORANDUM

DATE: January 29, 1995
TO: DavidL
FROM: SusanC
RE: Re: Modem Speeds

Thanks for the info. Here are some additional numbers from our West Coast office.

	Orange	Riverside
2400	65	43
9600	52	45
14400	26	79

Let me know what you think.

Figure 15. *The Excel range appears in the Word document.*

Embedding an Object with Copy and Paste Special

To transfer an existing object to another application, you can *embed* the object. Embedded objects are not linked to their original application. Instead, all the data for the object is transferred to the destination application. As a result, you can move the destination file to another computer, and the object, which has become an integral part of the destination file, is moved, too. Objects that are dragged and dropped become embedded.

1. Select the object in its originating application. **(Figure 12)**
2. From the Edit menu, choose Copy.
3. Switch to the other application and click at the destination for the object. **(Figure 13)**
4. From the Edit menu of the destination application, choose Paste Special.
5. On the Paste Special dialog box, double-click the item that is referred to as an "object" on the list. **(Figure 14)**

✔ Tips

- To edit an embedded object, double-click the object. Either the originating application will open in a separate window or the controls of the originating application will take over the current window. After you edit the object in a separate window, select Update from the File menu, and then Exit and Return from the File menu. If the controls of the originating application take over the current window, click outside the frame that contains the object when you finish.
- Any changes to the original object are not reflected in copies that are embedded in other applications.
- If you move a file with an embedded object to another computer, you must have installed the application that created the object in order to edit it.

Creating an Embedded Object

Rather than embed in a document an object that you've already created in a different application, you can create the object in the alternate application as you work in your main application. This gives you access to the tools of other Office applications at any time.

1. From the Insert menu of your main application, choose Object. **(Figure 16)**
2. On the Object dialog box, double-click the appropriate object type. **(Figure 17)**
3. In the other application, create the object.
4. From the File menu of the other application, select Quit. **(Figure 18)**
5. On the dialog box that asks if you want to save changes, click Yes. **(Figure 19)**

✔ Tips

- To edit an embedded object, double-click the object.
- If the second application allows in-place editing (the menus and toolbars of the other application appear in the current window) click outside the frame of the new object you are creating rather than follow Steps 4 and 5.

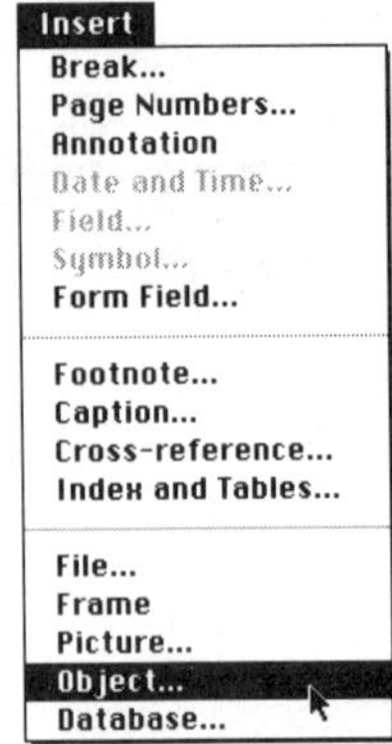

Figure 16. *The Word Insert menu.*

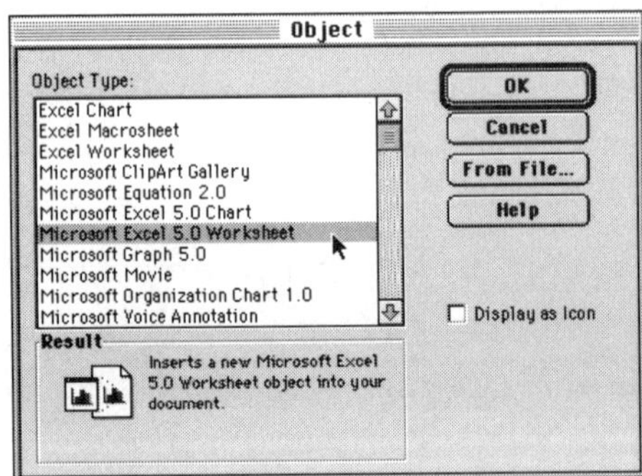

Figure 17. *The Object dialog box.*

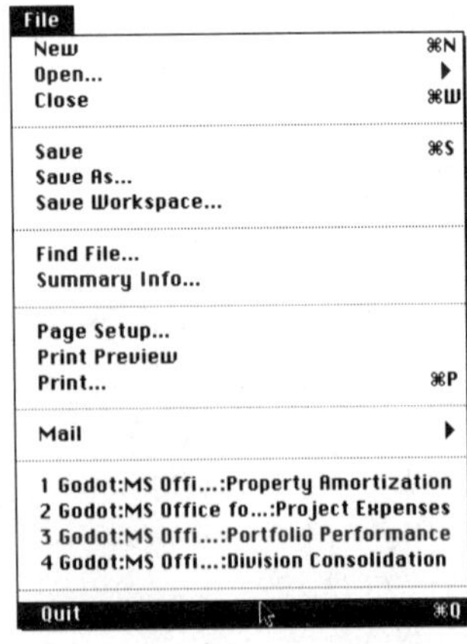

Figure 18. *The File menu.*

Figure 19. *The "Save changes?" dialog box.*

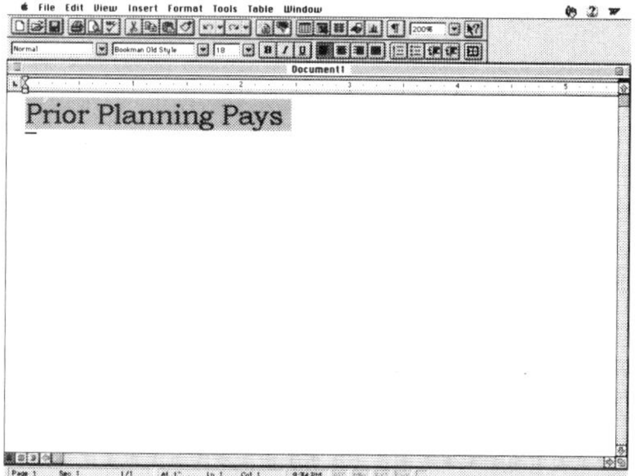

Figure 20. *Select text in Word.*

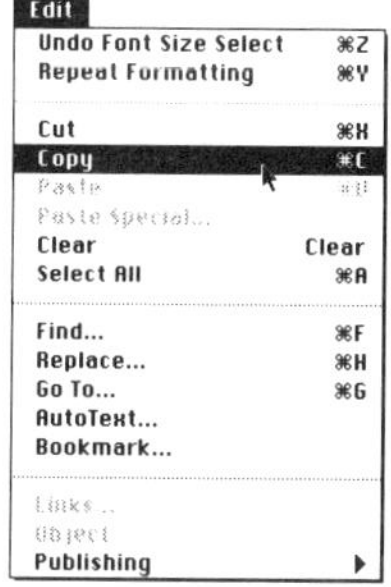

Figure 21. *The Edit menu of the first application.*

Figure 22. *The Edit menu of the second application.*

Click Paste Link

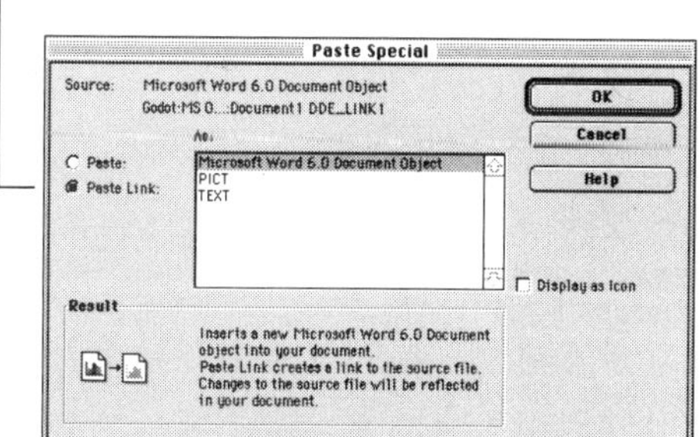

Figure 23. *The Paste Special dialog box.*

Linking Objects with Copy and Paste Link

When you *link* rather than embed an object, the object remains in its originating application. A copy, which is linked to the original, is displayed in the second application. Any changes to the original show up in the linked copy.

When an object will need frequent updating, link it to be sure that the changes to the original will flow to all other applications that display a linked copy.

1. Save the file in which you've created the object.
2. Select the object to link. **(Figure 20)**
3. From the Edit menu, choose Copy. **(Figure 21)**
4. Switch to the other application.
5. From the Edit menu of the other application, choose Paste Special. **(Figure 22)**
6. On the Paste Special dialog box, click Paste Link and then double-click the description of the object to link. **(Figures 23-24)**

✔ Tips

- Double-click the pasted copy to edit the original object.
- Each link automatically updates every time you open a document containing links.

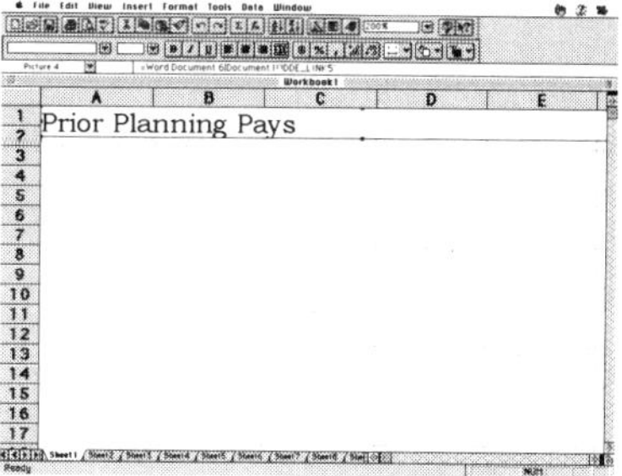

Figure 24. *The linked copy in Excel.*

Updating a Link

Links created with Copy and Paste Link update whenever you reopen a file in which they're found. You can manually update a link at any time, though.

1. From the Edit menu, choose Links. **(Figure 25)**
2. On the Links dialog box, select the link on the list of links. **(Figure 26)**
3. On the Links dialog box, click Update Now.
4. Click OK or Close to put away the Links dialog box.

✔ **Tip**

- To set the link so that it updates only when you choose Update Now, choose Manual as the Update option on the Links dialog box.

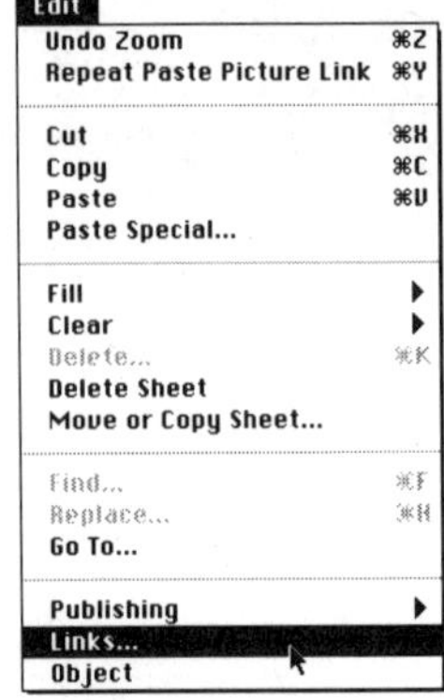

Figure 25. *The Edit menu.*

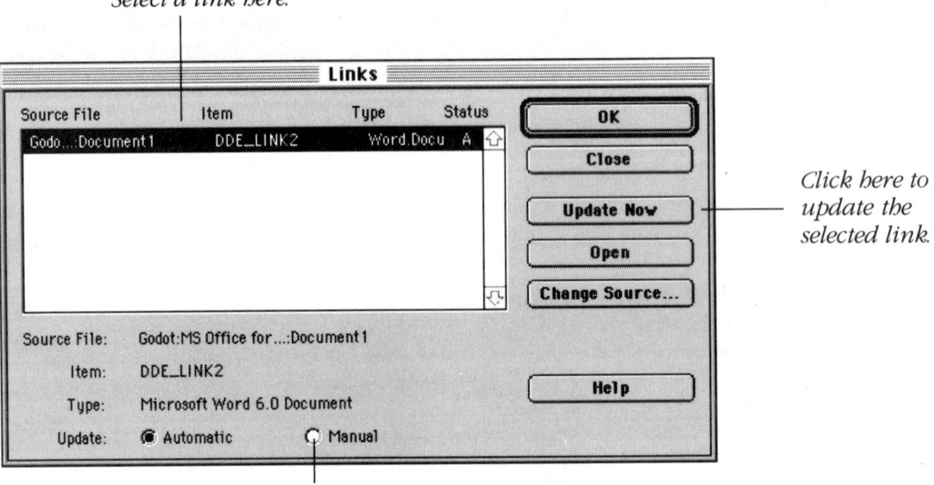

Figure 26. *The Links dialog box.*

Combining Applications

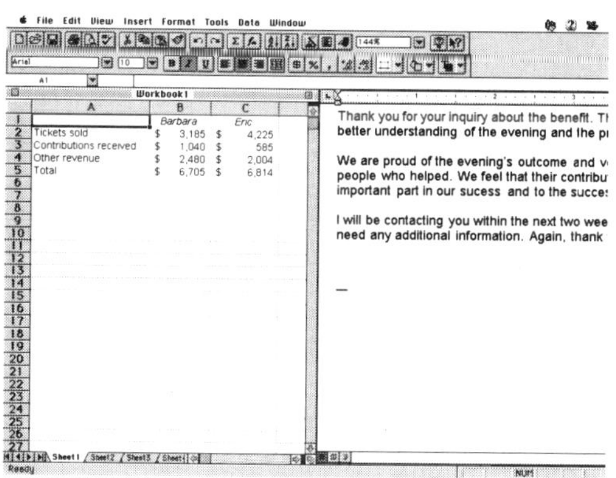

Figure 1. *Word and Excel windows arranged side-by-side.*

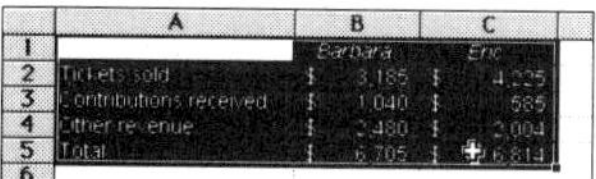

	A	B	C
1		Barbara	Eric
2	Tickets sold	$ 3,185	$ 4,225
3	Contributions received	$ 1,040	$ 585
4	Other revenue	$ 2,480	$ 2,004
5	Total	$ 6,705	$ 6,814
6			

Figure 2. *Select the range to copy.*

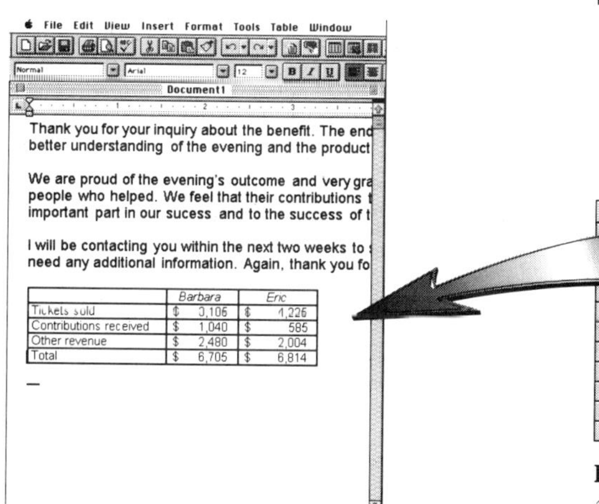

Figure 4. *Release the mouse button to drop the Excel range in the document.*

Excel to Word: Copying Ranges of Numbers

1. Arrange the **Word** and **Excel** documents so you can see them both. **(Figure 1)**
2. Select the range of numbers in **Excel**. **(Figure 2)**
3. Press and hold the Option key.
4. Place the mouse pointer on the border of the range and drag the range to the **Word** window. **(Figure 3)**
5. Release the mouse button when the insertion point is properly positioned in the **Word** document. **(Figure 4)**

✔ Tips

- The **Excel** range becomes embedded in the **Word** document, not linked. Changes to the numbers in **Excel** do not flow through to the **Word** document.
- To modify the numbers in **Word** using the **Excel** menus and toolbars, double-click the range in **Word**. Click in the document outside the range to return the **Word** menus and toolbars to the window.

	A	B	C
1		Barbara	Eric
2	Tickets sold	$ 3,185	$ 4,225
3	Contributions received	$ 1,040	$ 585
4	Other revenue	$ 2,480	$ 2,004
5	Total	$ 6,705	$ 6,814
6			
7			
8			
9			
10			
11			

Figure 3. *Drag the range from the Excel window to the Word window.*

Excel to Word: Linking Numbers

1. Select the range of numbers in **Excel**. **(Figure 5)**
2. From the Edit menu, choose Copy.
3. Switch to **Word**.
4. Position the insertion point at the destination for the copy of the range. **(Figure 6)**
5. From the Edit menu, choose Paste Special.
6. On the Paste Special dialog box, choose Paste Link. **(Figure 7)**
7. On the Paste Special dialog box, double-click Microsoft Excel 5.0 Worksheet Object.

✔ Tips

- Because you pasted a link, any changes to the range in **Excel** will be reflected in the **Word** document. If the **Word** document is not open, the changes will appear the next time you open the document.
- To update the link, choose Links from the Edit menu and then click Update Now on the Links dialog box, or click the range while holding down the Control key and choose Update Link from the shortcut menu.
- If you move the document to another computer, you must also move the **Excel** file to the other computer.
- To edit the range in **Excel**, double-click the range in **Word.**

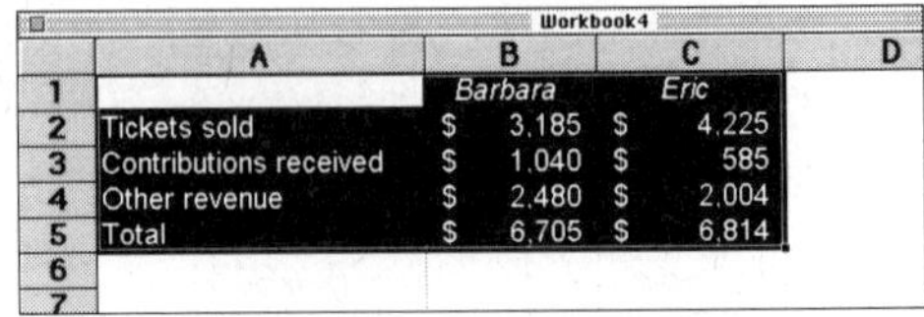

Workbook4

	A	B	C	D
1		Barbara	Eric	
2	Tickets sold	$ 3,185	$ 4,225	
3	Contributions received	$ 1,040	$ 585	
4	Other revenue	$ 2,480	$ 2,004	
5	Total	$ 6,705	$ 6,814	
6				
7				

Figure 5. *Select the range to link.*

Thank you for your inquiry about the benefit. The en
better understanding of the evening and the produc

We are proud of the evening's outcome and very gr
people who helped. We feel that their contributions
important part in our sucess and to the success of

I will be contacting you within the next two weeks to
need any additional information. Again, thank you f

Figure 6. *Click at the destination for the Excel range.*

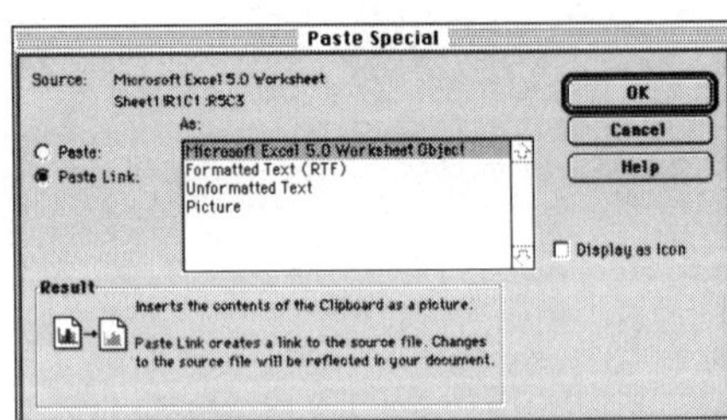

Figure 7. *The Paste Special dialog box.*

Thank you for your inquiry about the benefit. The en
better understanding of the evening and the produc

We are proud of the evening's outcome and very gr
people who helped. We feel that their contributions
important part in our sucess and to the success of

I will be contacting you within the next two weeks to
need any additional information. Again, thank you f

	Barbara	Eric
Tickets sold	$ 3,185	$ 4,225
Contributions received	$ 1,040	$ 585
Other revenue	$ 2,480	$ 2,004
Total	$ 6,705	$ 6,814

Figure 8. *The Excel range copied to a Word document.*

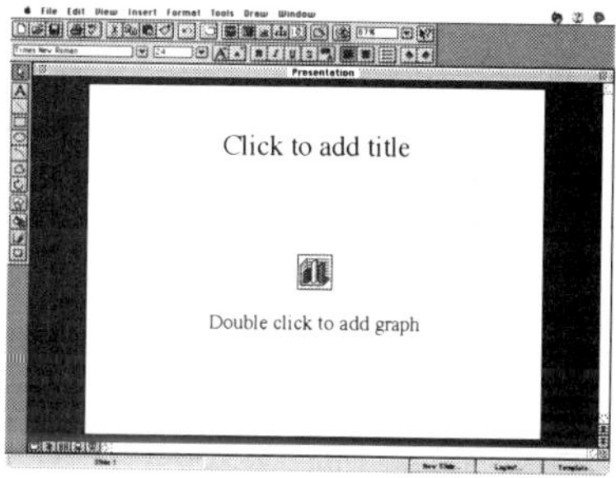

Figure 9. *The PowerPoint Graph slide.*

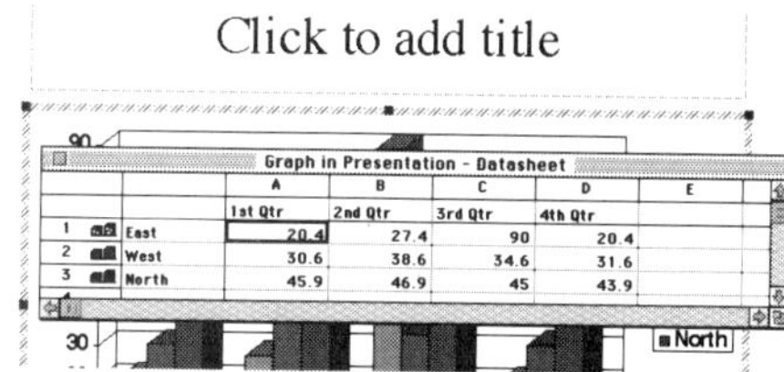

Figure 10. *The datasheet.*

Figure 11. *The Graph Edit menu.*

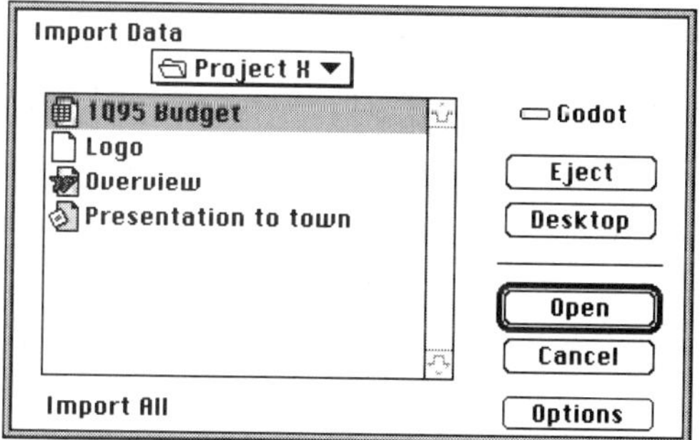

Figure 12. *The Import Data dialog box.*

Excel to PowerPoint: Graphing Numbers

1. In **PowerPoint**, create a slide for a graph. **(Figure 9)**
2. Double-click the "Double click to add graph" placeholder.
3. Click the cell on the datasheet at the upper left corner of the range of cells into which you want to import data from **Excel**. **(Figure 10)**
4. From Graph's Edit menu, choose Import Data. **(Figure 11)**
5. On the Import Data dialog box, select Entire File or click the Options button and select Range, depending on whether you want to import all the data in the **Excel** file or just a range. If you select Range, enter the range address or range name in the Range text box. **(Figure 12)**
6. On the Import Data dialog box, double-click the filename of the worksheet you want. The imported data appears on the worksheet. **(Figure 12)**

✔ Tips

- The data must be on the first worksheet of an **Excel** workbook. Otherwise, you must change the order of the worksheets.
- You can consolidate data from several worksheets in a single **PowerPoint** graph by importing data from different ranges.
- The procedure above imports the data but does not establish a link. *See Excel to PowerPoint: Linking Excel Data to a PowerPoint Graph, page 266.*

Excel to PowerPoint: Linking Excel Data to a PowerPoint Chart

1. In **PowerPoint**, start a Graph slide and double-click the "Double click to add graph" placeholder so the datasheet is open. **(Figure 13)**
2. Switch to **Excel** and then select the range to link. **(Figure 14)**
3. From the **Excel** Edit menu, choose Copy.
4. Switch to **PowerPoint** and click the datasheet cell at the upper left corner of the destination for the data.
5. From Graph's Edit menu, choose Paste Link. **(Figure 15)**
6. On the ChartWizard dialog box, make selections to identify whether the data series are in rows or columns, and whether the first row and column contain labels or data. **(Figure 16)**
7. Click OK.

✔ Tips

- Any changes to the numbers in **Excel** will be reflected in the **PowerPoint** graph.
- To update the link, choose Links from the Edit menu and then click Update Now on the Links dialog box, or click the range while holding down the Control key and choose Update Link from the shortcut menu.
- Be sure not to include totals in the data imported. If you **do** include a total row, double-click the row header button for the total row on the datasheet so the row won't be graphed.

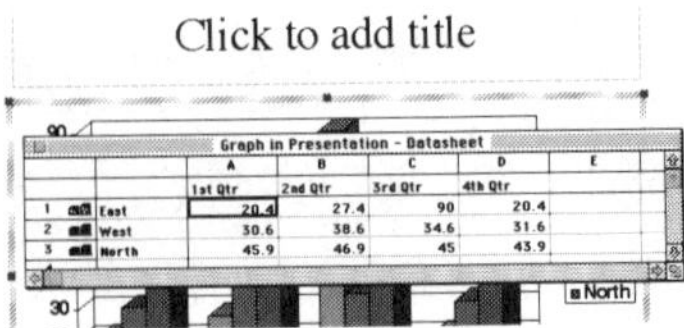

Figure 13. *Open a datasheet for a new graph.*

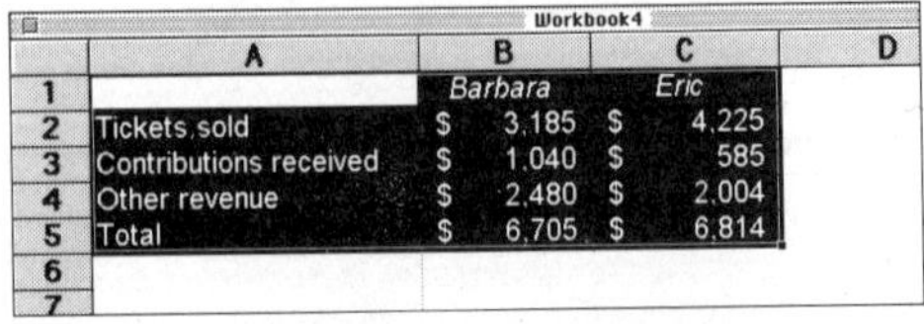

Workbook4

	A	B		C		D
1		Barbara		Eric		
2	Tickets sold	$	3,185	$	4,225	
3	Contributions received	$	1,040	$	585	
4	Other revenue	$	2,480	$	2,004	
5	Total	$	6,705	$	6,814	
6						
7						

Figure 14. *Select the range to link.*

Figure 15. *Graph's Edit menu.*

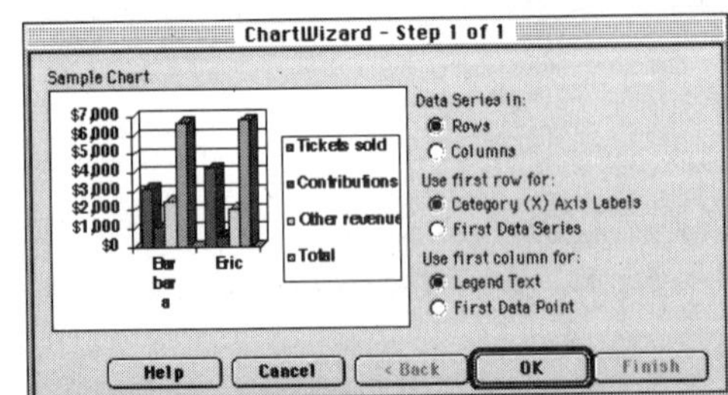

Figure 16. *The ChartWizard dialog box.*

Graph in Presentation - Datasheet

		A	B	C	D
		Barbara	Eric		
1	Tickets sold	$3,185	$4,225		
2	Contribution	$1,040	$585		
3	Other revenu	$2,480	$2,004		
4	Total	$6,705	$6,814		
5					

Figure 17. *The data appears in the datasheet.*

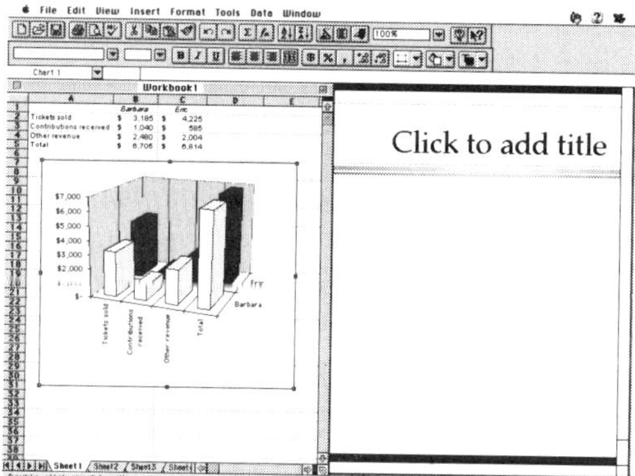

Figure 18. *The Excel and PowerPoint windows arranged.*

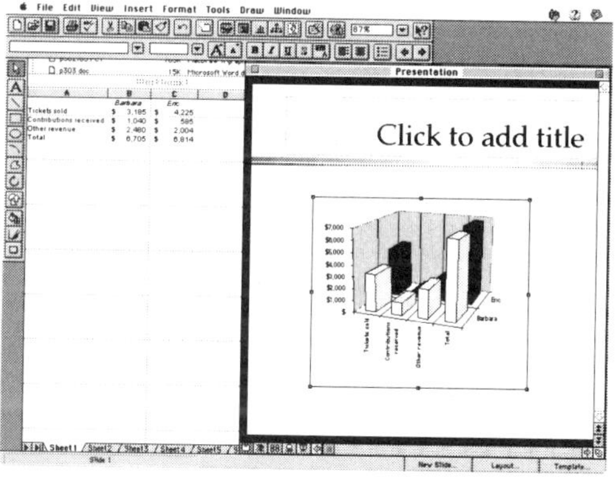

Figure 19. *Drag the chart to a PowerPoint slide.*

Excel to PowerPoint: Excel Chart to a Presentation

1. Arrange the **Excel** and **PowerPoint** windows so that you can see them both. **(Figure 18)**
2. Select the chart in **Excel**.
3. Drag the chart to a **PowerPoint** slide. **(Figure 19)**

✔ Tips

- Press the Option key while you drag if you want to **copy** rather than **move** the chart.
- You can also Copy and Paste the chart.
- To edit the chart in **PowerPoint** with **Excel's** menus and toolbars, double-click the chart. **(Figure 20)**

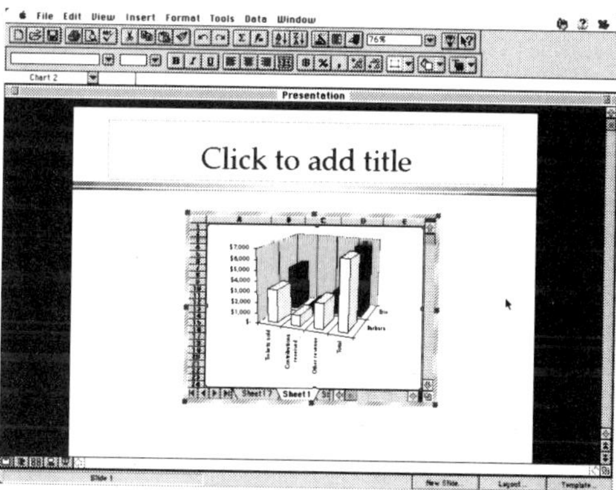

Figure 20. *Editing the chart in PowerPoint with Excel's controls.*

Excel to Word: Publish and Subscribe

Office for Macintosh provides an alternative to Copy and Paste Link, called Publish and Subscribe. When you publish a segment of a document, it is saved as an Edition file, to which other documents can subscribe. Changes made later in the published document are reflected in the documents that have subscribed to that edition.

1. Select a range of cells in Excel.
2. From the Edit menu, choose Publishing.
3. From the submenu that pops out, choose Create Publisher. **(Figure 21)**
4. Choose a name and location for the edition file and click Publish. **(Figure 22)**
5. In the Word document, click where you want the Excel edition inserted.
6. From the Edit menu, choose Publishing.
7. From the submenu that pops out, choose Subscribe To. **(Figure 23)**
8. Locate the edition you want to subscribe to and click Subscribe. **(Figure 24)**. The information is inserted in your Word document.

✔ Tips

- Excel cell ranges are subscribed into Word documents as Word tables.
- To edit all subscribed copies of a published edition, edit the data in the original document that published the edition. Do not attempt to edit the edition file.

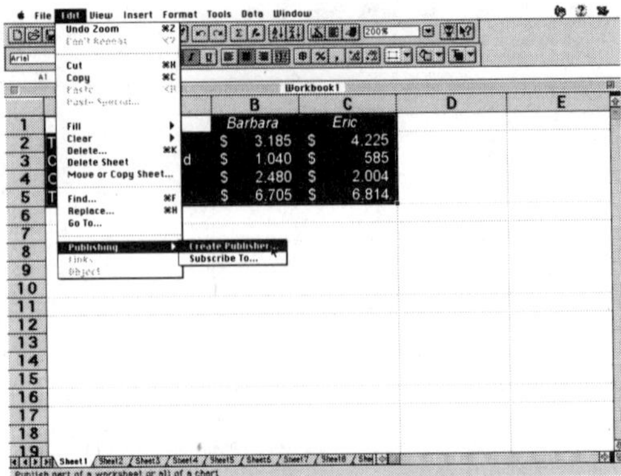

Figure 21. *Choose Create Publisher from the Publishing submenu.*

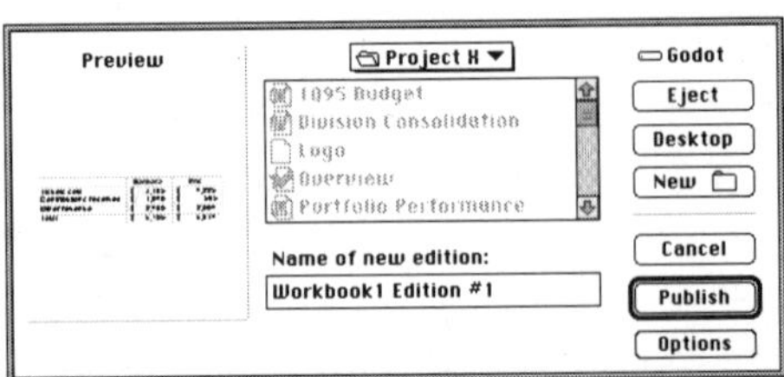

Figure 22. *Choose a name and location for the edition file and click Publish.*

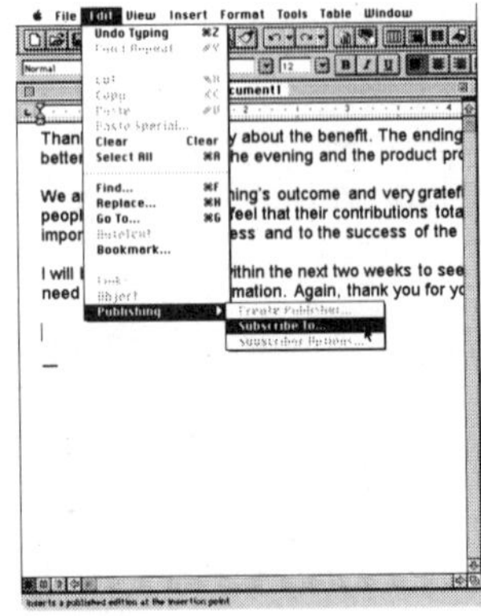

Figure 23. *Choose Subscribe To from the Publishing submenu.*

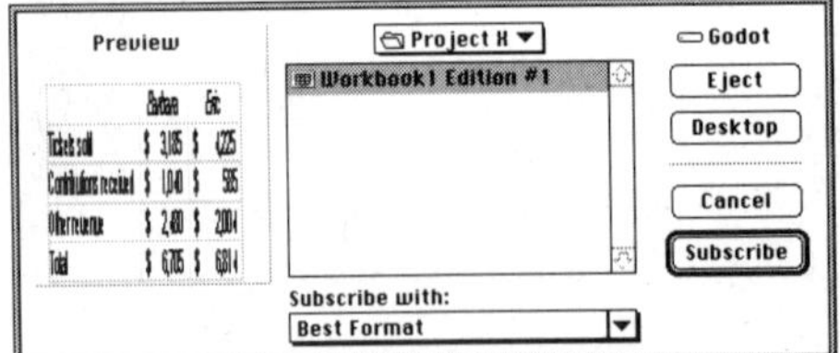

Figure 24. *Locate the edition and click Subscribe.*

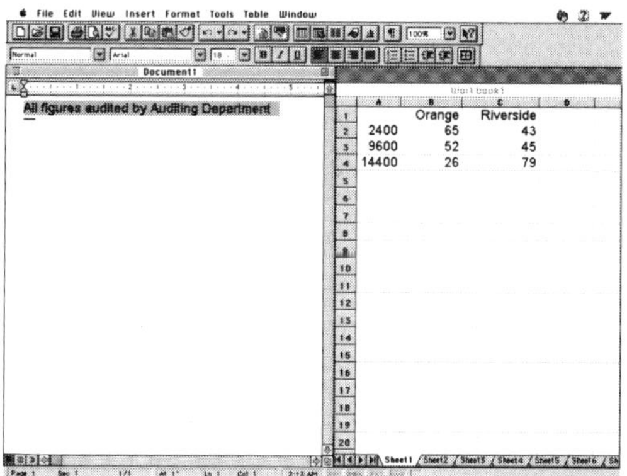

Figure 25. *Select text to copy.*

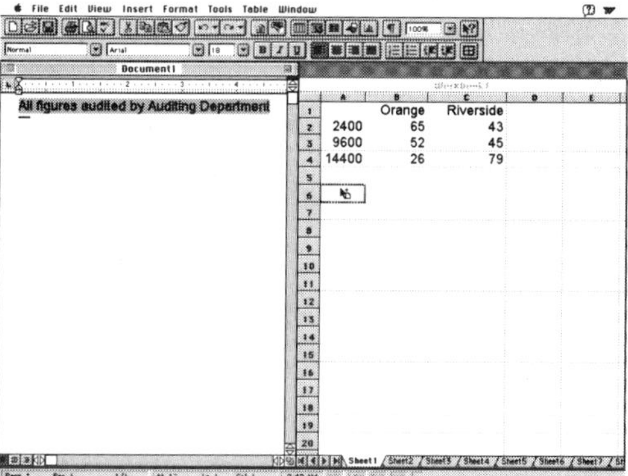

Figure 26. *Drag the text to the Excel or PowerPoint window.*

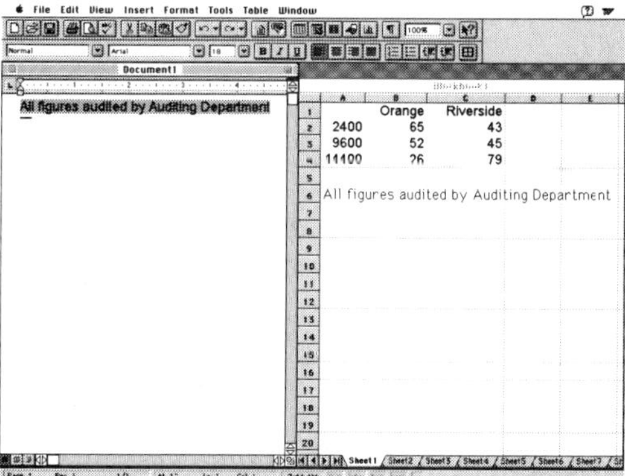

Figure 27. *The text on an Excel worksheet.*

Word to Excel or PowerPoint: Copying Text

1. Arrange the **Word** window side by side with the **Excel** or **PowerPoint** window.
2. In **Word**, select the text to copy. **(Figure 25)**
3. Place the mouse pointer on the text.
4. Hold down the Option key.
5. Drag the text to a destination cell in **Excel** or to a slide in **PowerPoint**. **(Figures 26-27)**

✓ Tips

- In **PowerPoint**, the text appears as a picture of the text as it was formatted in **Word** so you should format it in **Word** first.
- In **Excel**, the text goes into a cell as though you'd typed it into the cell.
- To edit or format the text after you copy it to **PowerPoint**, double-click the text. Then edit or format the text with **Word's** menus and toolbars. Click outside the text block to return to **PowerPoint's** menus and toolbars.

Word to PowerPoint: Using a Word Outline File

1. Create a presentation outline in **Word** and save it in a file. Each level 1 item will be the title of a new slide. **(Figure 28)**
2. In the Finder, drag and drop the **Word** outline file on top of the **PowerPoint** icon. **(Figure 29)**

✓ Tips

- Generating the outline in **Word** allows you to use such **Word** tools as the thesaurus.

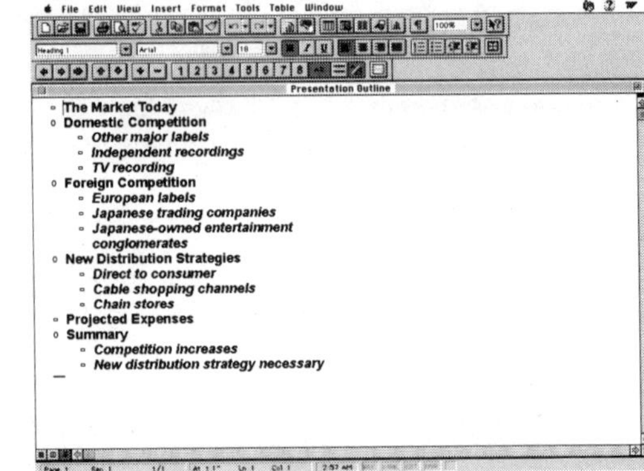

Figure 28. *The presentation outline in Word.*

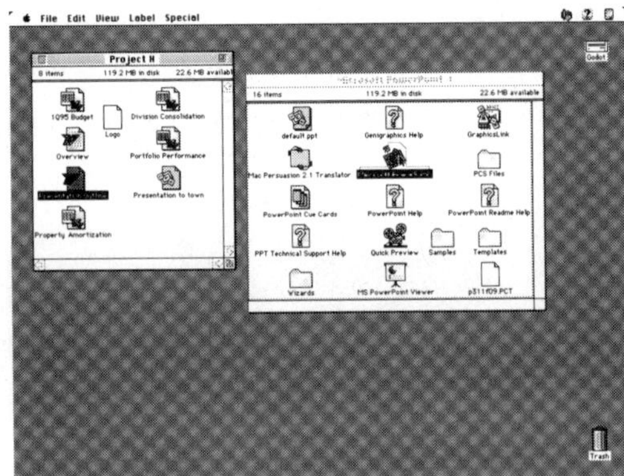

Figure 29. *Drag and drop the outline file to the PowerPoint window.*

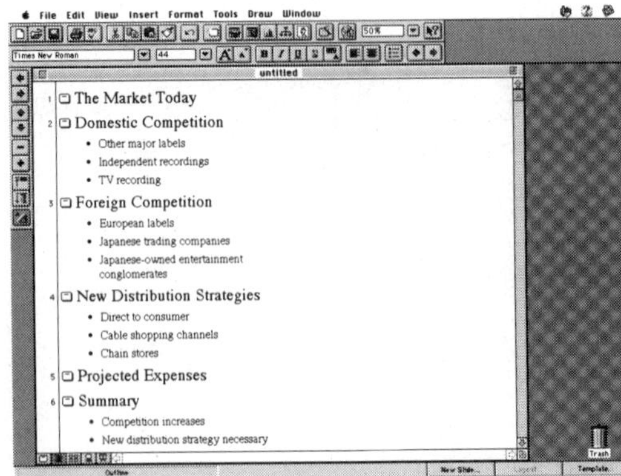

Figure 30. *A new presentation opens in PowerPoint based on the Word outline.*

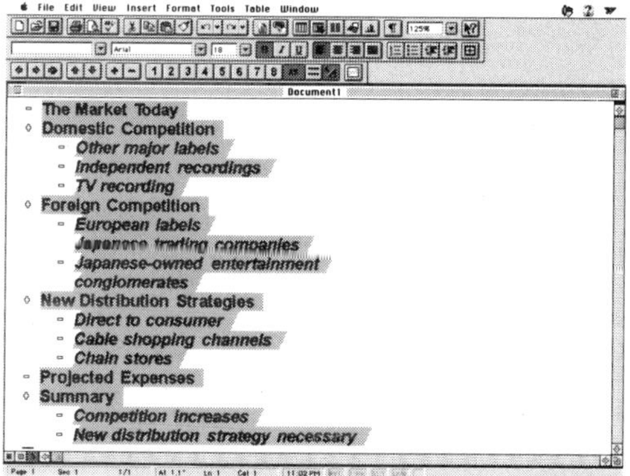

Figure 31. *A selected Word outline.*

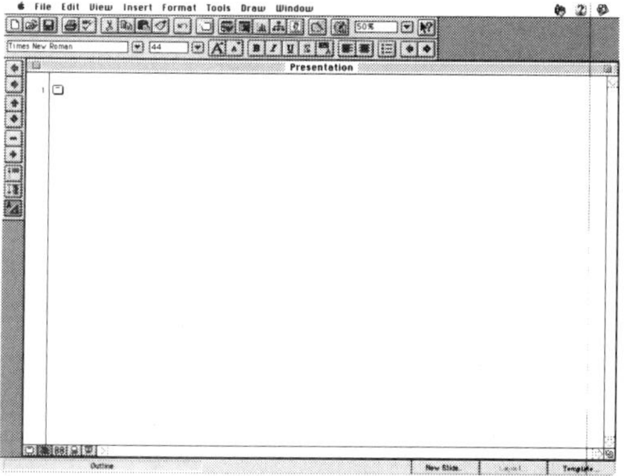

Figure 32. *PowerPoint's Outline view.*

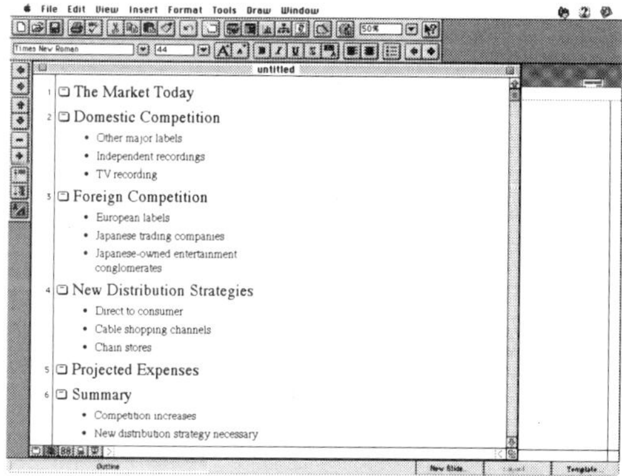

Figure 34. *The outline in PowerPoint.*

Word to PowerPoint: Copying a Word Outline to PowerPoint

1. Create and select an outline in a **Word** document. **(Figure 31)**
2. From the Edit menu, choose Copy.
3. Switch to **PowerPoint's** Outline view. **(Figure 32)**
4. Click at the destination for the **Word** outline.
5. From the Edit menu, choose Paste.

✔ Tip

- You can also use **Word's** Present It button **(Figure 33)** to copy an outline to **PowerPoint**, but first you must install the Present It button if it is not already available.

  To install the button, copy the Present It macro from the Macros folder to the current document using the Organizer dialog box. Then in the Customize dialog box, click the Toolbars tab and drag the Present It macro to any toolbar.

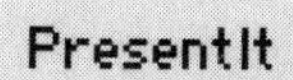

Figure 33. *The Present It Button.*

PowerPoint to Word: Copying a Presentation Outline to Word

1. Make sure both the **Word** and **PowerPoint** applications are running.
2. Switch to Outline view in **PowerPoint**. **(Figure 35)**
3. Click the Report It button on the Standard toolbar. **(Figure 36)**
4. In **Word**, save the temporary file that is created using a permanent file name. **(Figure 37)**

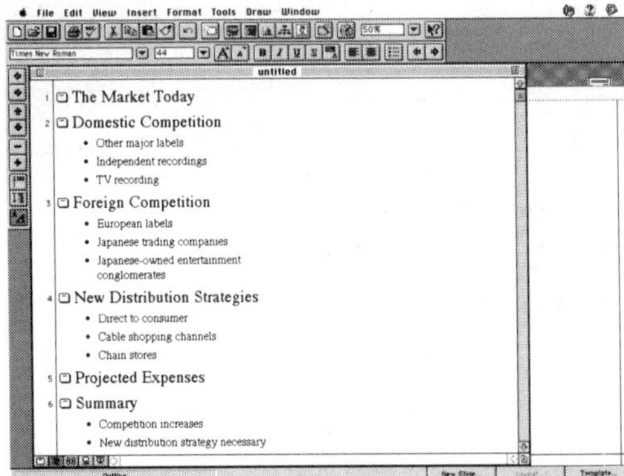

Figure 35. *Outline view.*

Figure 36. *The Report It button.*

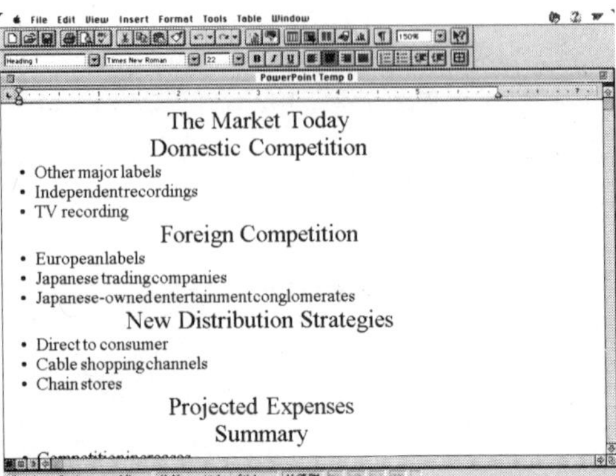

Figure 37. *The outline as it appears in a temporary Word file.*

Index

D

U

V

W

Z

Understanding of Plant and Crop Physiology

Understanding of Plant and Crop Physiology

C.S. Chandoliya
Vaibhav Suri

CYBER TECH PUBLICATIONS
4264/3, Ansari Road, Daryaganj, New Delhi-110002 (India)
Ph.: 011-23244078, 011-43559448 Fax: 011-23280028
E-Mail: cyberpublicationsdelhi@yahoo.com
Website: www.cybertechpublications.com

UNDERSTANDING OF PLANT AND CROP PHYSIOLOGY

C.S. Chandoliya, Vaibhav Suri

First Edition 2011

Published by :

G.S. Rawat for Cyber Tech Publications
4264/3, Ansari Road, Daryaganj, New Delhi-110002 (India)
Ph.: 011-23244078, 011-43559448 Fax: 011-23280028
E-Mail: cyberpublicationsdelhi@yahoo.com
Website: www.cybertechpublications.com

Contents

Preface

The growing demand for food and increasing scarcity of fertile land and other resources (water, energy, etc.) present multiple challenges to plant and crop scientists to meet the demands of future generations while protecting the environment and conserve biological diversity. Novel directions in linking basic plant sciences to crop and systems research are needed to meet the growing demand for food in a sustainable way.

Crop performance can be changed by modifying genetic traits of the plant through plant breeding or changing the crop environment through agronomic management practices. To achieve that, systems analysis and modelling play an important role by integrating and evaluating new findings at the gene and plant level at higher scales of aggregation. Robust crop-physiological modelling can become an essential tool to use insights from functional genomics in explaining crop behaviour. Current crop models can predict crop performance over a range of environmental conditions. Recently QTL information has been incorporated into crop models, and this has proved the potential of narrowing genotype-phenotype gaps and of applying QTL-based models for the analysis of genotype-by environment interactions. To make further progress, model structure must be upgraded to allow for more physiological feedback features.

Model input parameters should be designed to be potentially grounded in gene-level understanding. Integration of crop modelling into genetic and genomic researches can enhance the future position of crop physiology in 'plant breeding by design'. Role of crop physiology in predicting gene-to phenotype relationships. New tools derived from advances in molecular biology, genomics and plant physiology have yet not been widely adopted in plant breeding and integrated crop management because of inability to connect information at the gene level to the phenotype, crop and agro-ecosystem level.

— *Author*

1

Introduction

BIOTECHNOLOGY

The term biotechnology represents a fusion or an alliance between biology and technology. Biotechnology is as old as human civilization and is an integral part of human life. There are records that wine and beer were prepared in as early as 600 B.C. bread and curd in 4000 B.C. The term biotechnology was introduced in 1917 by Hungarian engineer, Karl Ereky.

It concerns with the exploitation of biological agents or their components for generating useful products / services. The area covered under biotechnology is very vast and the techniques involved are highly divergent.

Definition of Biotechnology

- Biotechnology consists of 'the controlled use of biological agents, such as, micro-organisms or cellular components, for beneficial use".
- Biotechnology is "the integrated use of biochemistry, microbiology and engineering sciences in order to achieve technological application of the capabilities of micro organisms, cultured tissues / cells and parts thereof".

  European Federation of Biotechnology (1981)
- Biotechnology comprises the "controlled and deliberate application of simple biological agents – living or dead, cells or cell components – in technically useful operations,

either of productive manufacture or as service operation". — J.D. Bu'lock (1987)

- The application of biological organisms, systems or process constitutes biotechnology. — British Biotechnologist
- Biotechnology is "the use of living organisms in system or processes for the manufacture of useful products, it may involve algae, bacteria, fungi, yeast, cells of higher plants and animals or sub systems of any of these or isolated components from living matter". — Gibbs and Greenhalgh (1983)
- Biotechnology is the application of scientific and engineering principles to the processing of materials by biological agents to provide goods and services". — Organization of Economic Co-operation and Development (1981)
- Biotechnology is the application of biochemistry, biology, microbiology and chemical engineering to industrial process and products and on environment. —International Union of Pure and Applied Chemistry (1981)

Importance of Biotechnology

Biotechnology has rapidly emerged as an area of activity having a worked realized as well as potential impact on virtually all domains of human welfare ranging from food processing, protecting the environment, to human health. It how plays a very important role in employment, production and productivity, trade, economics and economy, human health and the quality of human life throughout the world. The importance of biotechnology to human welfare as for the protection of human health, production of monoclonal antibodies, DNA & RNA probes (for disease diagnosis), artificial vaccines (for inoculation), rare and highly valuable drugs, such as human interferon, insulin etc. (for disease treatment) and the technology for gene therapy (for treatment of genetic diseases) are some of the notable achievements.

Micro-organisms are being employed since several decades for the large scale production of a variety of biochemical's ranging from alcohol to antibiotics in processing of foods and feeds. Enzymes, isolated mainly from microorganisms and immobilized in suitable polymers (called matrices) are preferred over the whole organisms for a variety of reasons; they are becoming increasing popular in many commercial ventures.

Several biological agents, such as, viruses, fungi, amoebae etc. are being exploited for the control of plant diseases and insect pests. Bacteria are being utilized for detoxification of industrial effluent (wastes), for treatment of sewage and for biogas production.

Invitro fertilization and embryo transfer techniques have permitted childless couples, suffering from one or the there kind of sterility, to have their own babies (test tube babies).

Genetic engineering is being employed to develop transgenic animals / plants resistant to certain diseases.

In agriculture, rapid and economic clonal multiplication of fruit and forest trees, production of virus free stocks of clonal crops through genetic engineering have opened up exciting possibilities in crop production, protection and improvement.

PLANT BIOTECHNOLOGY

Plant Biotechnology in the implication of biotechnological tools for improving the genotype, phynotypic tool for improving the genotype, phenotype, performance, multiplication rate of plant or exploiting cell constituent, generating useful products.

Plant biotechnology may be defined as generations of useful products or services from plant cells, tissue & organs. Such cells, tissues and organs are either continuously maintained *invitro* or they pass through a variable.

In vitro phase to enable generation from them of complete plantlets which is ultimately transferred to field therefore plant tissue culture technique form an integral part of plant biotech activities.

Objectives : The various objectives achievable / achieved by plant biotechnology may be summarized as under :

1. Rapid clonal multiplication (adventitious shoots / bulb/ protocorm or SE regeneration, axillary bud proliferation).
2. Germplasm conservation of vegetatively reproducing plants or those producing recalcitrant seeds (cryo-preservation, slow – growth cultures, DNA clones).
3. Production / recovery of difficult to produce hybrids (embryo rescue, *invitro* pollination).
4. Virus elimination (thermo-cryo or chemo - therapy coupled with ç meristem culture).
5. Rapid development of homozygous lines by producing haploids (anther culture, ovary culture, interspecific hybridization).
6. Useful biochemical production (large scale cell culture).
7. Genetic modification of plants (somaclonal variation, somatic hybridization, cybridization and genetic engineering).
8. Creation of genome maps and use of molecular markers to assist conventional breeding efforts.
9. Haploid production.

TECHNIQUES IN PLANT BIOTECHNOLOGY

Plant biotechnology comprises two major techniques

1. Plant Genetic Engineering
2. Plant Tissue Culture

Plant Genetic Engineering

Genetic engineering is an umbrella term, which can cover a wide range of way of changing the genetic material the DNA code – in living organisms. This code contains all the information, stored in a long chain chemical molecule which determines the nature of the organisms. The technique not only allows more precise changes, but also it greatly increases the efficiency of generating genetically engineered plants to use as food, fuel or to absorb carbon and cleaning the environment. Genetically engineering plants is a time intensive process. Methods currently used to deliver genetic changes are imprecise, so its often necess any to generate thousands of plants to find one that happens to have the desired alteration.

Concept : Genetic engineering is the alteration of genetic material by direct intervention in genetic processes with the purpose of producing new substances or improving functions of existing organisms. It is a very young, exciting, and controversial branch of the biological sciences. On the one hand, it offers the possibility of cures for diseases and countless material improvements to daily life. The Human Genome Project, a vast international effort to categorize all the genes in the human species, symbolizes hopes for the benefits of genetic engineering. On the other hand, genetic engineering frightens many with its potential for misuse; either in Nazi-style schemes for population control or through simple bungling that might produce a biological holocaust caused by a man-made virus. Symbolic of the alarming possibilities if the furor inspired by a single concept on the cutting edge of genetic engineering : cloning.

Principles : Just as DNA is at the core of studies in genetics, recombinant DNA (rDNA) that is, DNA that has been genetically altered through a process known as *gene splicing* – is the focal point of genetic engineering. In gene splicing, a DNA strand is cut in half lengthwise and joined with strand from another organism or perhaps even another species. Use of gene splicing makes possible two other highly significant techniques. Gene transfer, or incorporation of new DNA into an organism's cells, usually is carried out with the help of a microorganism that serves as a vector, or carrier. Gene therapy is the introduction of normal or genetically altered genes to cells, generally to replace defective genes involved in genetic disorders.

DNA also can be cut into shorter fragments through the use of restriction enzymes. (An enzyme is a type of protein that speeds up chemical reactions). The ends of these fragments have an affinity for complementary ends on other DNA fragments and will seek those out in the target DNA. By looking at the size of the fragment created by a restriction enzyme, investigators can determine whether the gene has the proper genetic code. This technique has been used to analyze genetic structures in fetal cells and to diagnose certain blood disorders, such as sickle cell anemia.

The ability to isolate and clone genes, coupled with the development of reliable techniques for introducing genes into plants has opened a new route to genetic improvement of plants that can circumvent the limitations of conventional breeding methods.

Once a useful gene is isolated, it can be transferred to many different crops without a lengthy breeding program.

Such useful traits as resistance to herbicides and disease have been identified and gene transfer herbicide resistant and disease resistant has produced plants.

A model genetic engineering of a plant comprised of the following general steps:-

1. Selection of a plant gene, whose introduction in other plants would be of positive agricultural value,
2. Identification and isolation of such genes.
3. Transfer of isolated genes to the plant cell and
4. Regeneration of complete plants from transferred cells or tissues.

Successful attempts at introducing disease, herbicide and pesticide resistance in plants following the aforesaid steps have already been reported from several laboratories.

Some of the goals of plant genetic engineers include production of plants that are

a. Resistant to herbicide, insect, fungal and viral pathogens,
b. Improved protein quality and amino acid composition,
c. Improved photosynthetic efficiency, and
d. Improved post harvest handling.

Plant Tissue Culture

Plant tissue culture broadly refers to the *invitro* cultivation of plants, seeds and various parts of the plants (organs, embryos, tissues, single cells protoplasts). The cultivation process is invariably carried out in a nutrient culture medium under aseptic conditions.

It has advanced the knowledge of fundamental botany, especially in the field of agriculture, horticulture, plant breeding, forestry, somatic cell hybridization, phytopathology and industrial production of plant metabolites etc.

The term tissue culture is actually a misnomer borrowed from the field of animal tissue culture. It is a misnomer because plant micropropagation is concerned with the whole plantlet and not just isolated tissues, though the explant may be a particular tissue. The terms plantlet culture or micropropagation, therefore are more accurate. However, whether we call it cloning, tissue culture, micropropagation or growing *in vitro.*

Plant cells have certain advantages over animal cells in culture system unlike 'animal cells'; highly mature and differentiated plant cells retain the ability of totipotency i.e. the ability of change in meristematic state and differentiate into a whole plant.

Definition : Culturing of living plant material (explant axillary bud, apical meristem, leaf and root tip) under aseptic condition on an artificial media is called tissue culture.

Some Salient Features of Tissue Culture are :

1. The culture of the cells / tissues is carried out in a sterile medium under controlled conditions.
2. Clones generated through tissue culture are identical in terms of size, development stage and rate of metabolic activities.
3. The rate of tissue multiplication is rapid within a small area.
4. The clones are capable of performing the transformative activity c involves biotransformation to produce primary and secondary metabolites in the tissue culture medium.

Principle of PTC : The principles of tissue culture are all around us in nature, in the field and in the greenhouse.

The technique has developed around the concept that a cell is totipotent that is has the capacity and ability to develop into whole organism. The principles involve in plant tissue culture are very simple & primarily an attempt, whereby an explant can be to some extent freed from inter-organ, inter-tissue and inter-cellular interactions and subjected to direct experimental control.

Cell culture is the cultivation of cells on a solid gel medium, the latter commonly known as cell suspension culture. Callus culture is the multiplication of callus (a mass of disorganized, mostly undifferentiated or undeveloped cells) usually on a solid medium. The apical meristem is the new, undifferentiated tissue of the microscopic tip of a shoot. It is often virus free even in diseased plants because these meristematic cells are not yet joined to the plant's vascular system and perhaps they grow faster than the viruses. Thus, if the few virus free cells that make up the microscopic dome of apical meristem are removed from the plant and placed in a culture, they can grow and produce healthy, disease free plants.

Importance of Plant Tissue Culture :

1. Plant tissue culture enables to develop better strains at a high multiplication rate.
2. It is clean and rapid way for genetic engineers to grow material for identifying and manipulating genes.
3. It provides reliable and economic method for maintenance of pathogen free plantlets in such a state to allow rapid clonal propogation.
4. Plant tissue culture can be initiated with a small explant if limited tissue is available.
5. Micropropagation can be carried out throughout year independent of seasons.
6. The variety of technique that collectively comprise plant tissue culture have permitted investigation at many levels, molecular, cellular, organismal and have been applied to

a range of disciplines biochemistry, genetics, physiology, anatomy and cell biology.

7. Plant tissue culture is preferable in case of recalcitrant and endangered species and in following situations :
   a. Seeds nongerminable or shows long dormancy period.
   b. Species highly heterozygous.
   c. Species does not produce seeds.

Pathways in Tissue Culture Technique:

Morphogenesis : Organs such as shoots leaves and flowers can frequently be induced to form adventitiously on cultured plant tissues. The creation of new form and organization where previously it was lacking is termed morphogenesis or organogenesis.

OR

Formation of morphological organs under *in vitro* condition is known as morphogenesis or organogenesis.

Hicks (1980) described the two methods of morphogenesis as direct and indirect organogenesis respectively.

Direct Organogenesis : When relatively large pieces of intact plants are transferred to nutrient media, new shoots, roots, somatic embryos and even flower initials are often formed without the prior growth of callus tissue, small explant show organogenesis only rarely, although some exceptions have been reported. The part of the original plant from which the explant is taken is important in influencing its morphogenetic potential.

Indirect Organogenesis: In this pathway media and plant growth regulator which favour rapid cell proliferation and formation of callus from an explant, are not usually conducive to the initiation of the morphogenetic meristems which give rise to roots or shoots. However, organogenesis is medium, but may be prevented if it is subcultured onto a fresh medium. In other cases unorganized callus initiated on one medium needs to be transferred to another of a different position with different combinations of growth regulators (a regeneration medium) for shoot initiation to occur. Organs are formed in callus tissues from single cells or several cells which divide to give rise to groups of small meristematic cells filled with densely staining cytoplasm and containing large nuclei. These specialized cells or cell groups are termed 'meristemoids' by some research workers .

Growth Profile of The Plant Culture and Its Measurement

a. Cell culture

b. Callus culture

Growth profile for cell culture : The various stages of the growth exhibited by the plant cell culture are to a great extent similar to those of the microorganisms. The various stages of growth are displayed in figure & can be enumerated as.

1. Lag Phase : In this phase, the cell regains the ability of division & the tissue shows show growth.
2. Exponential Phase : This stage involves rapid cell division the duration of this stage varies according to the cell and its nutrient regime . In majority of the cases it is a short one & lasts for only 3-4 generations.
3. Linear Phase : The growth in this phase follows a linear pattern with respect to time.
4. Progressive deceleration Phase : In this stage the rate of cell division declines ç the aging of the culture.
5. Stationary Phase : During this phase the rate of production of cells is equal to the rate of their death.
6. Senescent phase : During this phase the cells are dying.

Growth profile for callus culture: The growth profile for the callus to a great extent is similar to that of cells suspension culture. The various stages of growth are :

1. Lag Phase : Following inoculation of an explant, there is a lag time before the cells undergo cell division. Then a few cells start to divide and the tissue resumes its growth, albeit a slower one.

2. Exponential Phase : This stage involves vigorous growth owning to the rapid cell division. During this phase, the tissues consume nutrients from the medium leading to their depletion.
3. Decline Phase : The depletion of elements from the medium leads to starvation of some cells. This leads to a decline in the growth of callus tissues.
4. Stationary Phase : From this stage onwards no growth is evident. For further growth and development subculture is an imperative.

Basic Stages of Plant Tissue Culture : There are five basic stages of plant tissue culture mentioned below

A. Stage 0 : Preparative

B. State I : Establishment

C. State II : Multiplication

D. Stage III : Production

E. Stage IV : Hardening

A. Stage 0 : Preperative : Selection of healthy and disease free explants.

B. Stage I : Establishment : Success at this stage firstly requires that explant should be safely transferred to the culture environment and secondly that there should be an appropriate reaction (eg. growth of a shoot tip or formation of callus on a stem piece).

C. Stage II : Multiplication : Stage II is to being about multiplicaton of organs and structure that are able to give rise to new intact plants.

D. Stage III : Production : At stage III steps are taken to grow individual plantlets that can carry out photosynthesis and survive without an artificially supply of carbohydrate.

Stage III is often conveniently divided into :

Stage IIIa : The elongation of buds formed during stage II to uniform shoots for stage III.

Stage III b : Roofing of stage IIIa shoots *invitro* or extra vitrum.

E. Stage IV : Hardening : This stage involves the establishment of plantlets in soil. This is done by transferring the plantlets of stage III from the laboratory to the environment of greenhouse. For some plant species, stage III is skipped, and unrooted stage II shoots are planted in pots or in suitable compost mixture.

Types of Plant Tissue Culture : On the basis of explants, the plant tissue culture technique can be of following types :

1. Organ culture
   (a) Meristem and shoot tip culture
   (b) Leaf disc culture
   (c) Root tip culture
   (d) Bud culture
   (e) Storage organ culture
2. Cell culture
3. Callus culture
4. Embryo culture
5. Somatic embryogenesis
6. Anther and pollen culture
7. Ovary culture
8. Protoplast culture

Organ culture : The. term 'organ – culture' includes the isolation from whole plants of such definite structures as leaf primordial, immature flowers and traits etc. and their growth *in-vitro*. For the purposes of plant propagation, the most important kinds of organ culture are given below:

a. Meristem and shoot tip culture : Culture of the extreme tip of the shoot (the shoot meristem) is used as a technique to free plant from virus infections. Very small stem apices (0.2 – 1.0 mm in length), consisting of just the apical meristem and one or two leaf primordia, must be transferred to culture. This is usually described as 'meristem culture'.

Culture of slightly larger stem apices (sometimes 5 or 10 mm in length) is used as a very successfully method of propagation plants. Most workers use the term 'shoot tip culture' for this technique.

Both types of culture ultimately give rise to small shoots. With appropriate treatments, the original shoots can either be rooted to produce small plants or 'plantlets' or axillary bud can be induced to grow to form a cluster of shoots. Tissue cultured plantlets can then be removed from aseptic conditions, hardened off and grown normally.

b. Leaf disc culture : Leaf disc culture can be established by keeping leaf tips (apical portion) in suitable MS medium. After certain period of time; growth of shoot and root takes place.

c. Root tip culture : Root cultures can be established from root tips taken from primary or lateral roots of many plants. Suitable explants are small sections of aseptic roots bearing a primary or lateral root meristem. These explants may be obtained, for example, from surface sterilized seeds germinated in aseptic conditions. If the small root meristems continue normal growth on a suitable medium, they produce a root system consisting only of primary and lateral roots. No organized shoot buds will be formed. Isolated root cultures do not feature in current micropropagation techniques although shoots can be regenerated from root segments of some species. It has however, been suggested that root cultures could afford are means of germplasm storage.

d. Bud culture : The plant buds possess quiescent or active meristems depending on the physiological state of the plant. Two types of bud cultures are used : – single node culture and axillary bud culture.

Single node culture : This is a natural method for vegetative propagation of plants both in *in-vitro* and *in-vitro* conditions. The bud found in the axil of leaf is comparable to the stem tip, for its ability in micorpropagation. A bud along with a piece of stem is isolated and cultured to develop into a plantlet. Closed buds are used to reduce the chances of infections. In single node culture, no cytokinine is added.

Axillary bud culture : In this method, a shoot tip along with axillary bud is isolated. The cultures are carried out with high cytokinine concentration. As a result of this, apical dominance stop and axillary buds develop.

e. Storage organ culture : Many ornamental and crop species that naturally produce bulbs can be induced to form small bulbs in culture. They arise on cultured tissues either at the base of a previously form vegetative shoot or as a directly initiated storage organ with no extended vegetative leaves. Buds giving rise to bulbils may arise adventitiously on pieces of leaf on inflorescence stalks or on ovaries, but particularly on detached pieces of bulb scale.

Many small dormant tubers of the crops can be obtained from virus free shoots and have the great advantage that they can be readily removed from culture flasks, stored without aseptic precautions and than distributed to growers fro the production of plants.

Cell culture **:** The culture of isolated individual cells, obtained from an explant tissue or callus is regarded as cell culture. These cultures are carried out in dispension medium and are referred to as cell suspension cultures.

Callus culture **:** Callus is a coherent but unorganized and amorphous tissue, formed by the vigorous division of plant cells. In culture, callus is initiated by placing small pieces of the whole plant (explants) into a growth supporting medium under sterile conditions. With the stimulus of endogenous growth substances or growth regulating chemicals added to the medium.

Embryo culture **:** Seed embryos are often used advantageously as explants in plant tissue culture. In embryo culture, however, embryos are individually isolated and 'germinated' *in-vitro* to provide one plant per explant.

Types of embryo culture : (a) Mature embryo culture , (b) Immature embryo culture

(a) Mature embryo culture : Mature embryos are isolated from ripe seeds & cultured *in vitro*.

(b) Immature embryo culture : Immature embryos are isolated from unripe or hybrid seeds which fail to germinate and cultured *in vitro*.

Somatic embryogenesis : A somatic embryo in as embryo derived from a somatic cell, other than zygote and obtained usually on culture of the somatic cells *in vitro*.

Anther and Pollen culture : Haploids plants may be obtained from pollen grains by placing anthers or isolated pollen grains on a suitable culture medium, this constitutes anther and pollen culture, respectively.

Flower buds of the appropriate developmental stage are collected, surface sterilized and their anthers are excised and placed horizontally on culture medium. Alternatively, pollen grains may be separated from anthers and cultured on a suitable medium.

Ovary culture : Culture of unfertilized ovaries to obtain haploid plants from egg cell or other haploid cells of the embryo sac is called ovary culture and the process is termed as gynogenesis. Ovaries / ovules are generally cultured in light, but at least in some species dark incubation favours gynogenesis and minimizes somatic callusing.

Protoplast culture : Protoplasts have been isolated from virtually all plant parts, but leafy mesophyll is the most preferred tissue. The protoplasts cultured in a suitable medium. The media are supplemented with a suitable osmoticum and almost always, with an auxin and a cytokinine.

After 7-10 days of culture, protoplasts regenerate cell wall, and the osmolarity of medium is gradually reduced to that of normal medium. The macroscopic colonies are transferred into normal tissue culture media. In 1971 an entire plant was first regenerated from a callus originating from an isolated protoplast.

The formation of embryoids directly from cultured protoplasts has also been observed.

Applications of Plant Tissue Cultures :Plant tissue cultures are associated with a wide range of application the most important being the production of pharmaceutical, medicinal and other industrially important compounds. In addition, tissue cultures are useful for several other purposes listed below :

1. To study the respiration and metabolism of plants.
2. For the evaluation of organ functions in plants.
3. To study the various plant diseases and work out methods for their elimination.
4. Single cell clones are useful for genetic, morphological and pathological studies.
5. Embryonic cell suspensions can be used for large scale clonal propagation.
6. Somatic embryos from cell suspensions can be stored for long term in germplasm banks.
7. In the production of variant clones with new characteristics, a phenomenon referred to as somaclonal variations.
8. Production of haploids (with a single set of chromosomes) for improving crops.
9. Mutant cells can be selected from cultures and used for crop improvement.
10. Immature embryos can be cultured *in vitro* to produce hybrids, a process referred to as embryo rescue.

Terms Used In Plant Tissue Culture

A selected list of the most commonly used terms in tissue culture are briefly explained.

Explant or Donor plant : An excised piece of differentiated tissue or organ is regarded as an explant. The explain may be taken from any part of the plant body eg. leaf, stem, root.

Callus: The organized and undifferentiated mass of plant cells is referred to as callus i.e. a mass of parenchymatous cells.

Clone : The entire vegetatively produced descendants from a single original seedling.

Dedifferentiation : The phenomenon of mature cells reverting to meristematic state to produce callus is differentiation.

Redifferentiation : The ability of the callus cells to differentiate into a plant organ or a whole plant is regarded as redifferentiation.

Totipotency : The ability of an individual cell to develop into a whole plant is referred to as cellular totipotency. The inherent characteristic features of plant cells namely dedifferentiation and redifferentiation are responsible for the phenomenon of totipotency.

Laboratory requirements : A standard tissue culture laboratory should provide facilities for :

a. Washing and storage of glassware, plastic wares and other lab wares.

b. Preparation, sterilization and storage of nutrient media.

c. Aseptic manipulation of plant material.

d. Maintenance of cultures under controlled conditions of temperature, light and if possible, humidity.

e. Observation of cultures.

f. Acclimatization of *in-vitro* developed plants.

Apparatus required for Plant Tissue Culture :

I. Culture vessels and other wares

  a. Conical flasks

  b. Volumetric flasks

  c. Measuring cylinders

  d. Graduated pipettes, test tubes, bottles , beakers, funnel, plastic baskets, test tube and bottle caps, test-tube stands and filter paper.

  e. Scalpal, blade, forceps, scissors, cotton, muslin cloths, chemicals, burner, spatula etc.

II. Other large instruments

a. Double distilled water unit.

b. Electric hot air oven – for labwares drying.

c. Electronic balance – for weighing chemicals.

d. pH meter – for pH adjustment of media and other solutions.

e. Microwave – for melting agar

g. Shaker – for maintenance of suspension culture.

h. Autolcave (vertical and horizontal) - For steam sterilization of media and apparatus.

i. Laminar air flow cabinet - For constant flow of purified air for aseptic manipulation (Pore size – 45 um).

j. Air conditioner - For maintenance of temperature of culture room.

Sterilization Techniques involved in Plant Tissue Culture are

All the materials, e.g., vessels, instruments, medium, plant material, etc., used in culture work most be freed from microbes. This is achieved by one of the following approaches (i) dry heat, (ii) flame sterilization, (iii) autoclaving, (iv) filter sterilization, (v) wiping with 70% ethanol, and (vi) surface sterilization.

Dry Heat : Glassware and Teflon plastic ware (empty vessels), and instruments may be sterilized by dry heat in an oven at 160-180°C for 3 hr. But most workers prefer to autoclave glassware and plastic ware etc. and flame sterilize instruments like forceps, etc. More recently, glass bead sterilizers (300°C) are being employed for the sterilization of forceps, scalpels, etc. these devices use dry heat.

Flame Sterilization: Instruments like forceps, scalpals, needles, etc. are ordinarily flame sterilized by dipping them in 95% alcohol followed by flaming. These instruments are repeatedly sterilized during the operation to avoid contamination. It is customary to flame the mouths of culture vessels prior to inoculation / subculture.

Autoclaving : Culture vessels, etc. (both empty and containing media) are genrally sterilized by heating in an autoclave or a pressure cooker to 121°C at 15 p.s.i. (pounds per square inch, 1.06 kg/cm^2) for 30 to 40 minutes.

Filter Sterilization : Some growth regulators, e.g., GA3, zeatin, ABA (abscisic acid), urea, certain vitamins, and enzymes are heat labile. Such compounds are filter sterilized by passing their solution through a membrane filter of 0.45 u or lower pore size. The membrane filter is held in a suitable assembly, the assembly together with the filter is sterilized by autoclaving before use. Filter a suitable assembly; the assembly together with the filter is sterilized by autoclaving before use. Filter sterilized heat labile compounds are added to autoclaved and cooled media, in case of agar medium, they are added when the medium has cooled to about 40°C and is still liquefied.

Wiping with 70% ethanol :The surfaces that can not be sterilized by other techniques, e.g., platform of the laminar flow cabinet, hands of the operator, etc. are sterilized by wiping them thoroughly with 70% ethyl alcohol and the alcohol is allowed to dry.

Surface sterilization : All materials to be used for culture are treated with an appropriate sterilizing agent to inactivate the microbes present on their surface, this is called surface sterilization. Surface sterilization protocol will depend mainly on the source and the type of tissue of the explant, which will determine the contamination load and tolerance to the sterilizing agent. An explant is the excised piece of tissue or organ used for culture.

The sterilizing agents used for surface disinfection are calcium hypochlorite (9-10%), H_2O_2 (10-12%) and antibiotics (4-50 mg/l). Of these, calcium or sodium hypochlorite (very good results) and $HgCl_2$ (satisfactory results) are the most commonly used. The duration of treatment varies from 15-30 min. Since these agents are also toxic to plant tissues, the duration and the concentration used should be such as to cause minimum tissue death, and the rinsing after treatment should remove them as completely as possible.

Plant Tissue Culture Media

Culture media are largely responsible for the *in-vitro* growth and morphogenesis of plant tissues. The success of the plant tissue culture depends on the choice of the nutrient medium. In fact, the cells can be grown in culture media.

Basically, the plant tissue culture media should contain the same nutrients as required by the whole plant. It may be noted that plants in nature can synthesize their own food material. However, plants growing *in vitro* are mainly heterotrophic i.e. they cannot synthesize their own food.

Composition of media

The composition of the culture media is primarily dependent on two parameters.

1. The particular species of the plant.
2. The type of material used for culture i.e. cells, tissues, organs, protoplasts.

Thus, the composition of a medium is formulated considering the specific requirements of a given culture system. The media used may be solid (solid medium) or liquid (liquid medium) in nature. The selection of solid or liquid medium is dependent on the better response of a culture.

Major types of media :- The composition of the most commonly used tissue culture media is briefly described below.

- White's medium : This is one of the earliest plant tissue culture media developed for root culture.
- MS medium : Murashige and Skoog (MS) originally formulated a medium to induce organogenesis, and regeneration of plants in cultured tissues. These days, MS medium is widely used for many types of culture systems.

- B5 medium : Developed by Gamborg, B5 medium was originally designed for cell suspension and callus cultures. At present with certain modifications, this medium is used for protoplast culture.
- N6 medium : Chu formulated this medium and it is used for cereal anther culture, besides other tissue cultures.
- Nitsch's medium : This medium was developed by Nitsch and Nitsch and frequently used for anther cultures.

Among the media referred above, MS medium is most frequently used in plant tissue culture work due to its success with several plant species and culture systems.

Synthetic and natural media : When a medium is composed of chemically defined components, it is referred to as a synthetic medium. On the other hand, if a medium contains chemically undefined compounds (e.g., vegetable extract, fruit juice, plant, extract), it is regarded as a natural medium.

Expression of concentration in media : The concentrations of inorganic and organic constituents in culture media are usually expressed as mass values (mg/l or ppm or mg l^{-1}).

However, as per the recommendations of the international Association of Plant Physiology, the concentrations of macronutrients should be expressed as mmol/l^{-1} and micronutrients as mmol/l.

Constituents of media

Many elements are needed for nutrition and their physiological functions. Thus, these elements have to be supplied in the culture medium to support adequate growth of cultures *in vitro*.

The culture media usually contain the following constituents:

1. Inorganic nutrients
2. Carbon and energy sources
3. Organic supplements
4. Growth regulators

5. Solidifying agents
6. pH of medium

Inorganic nutrients

The inorganic nutrients consist of macronutrients (concentration > 0.5 mmol/l$^-$) and micronutrients (concentratioin <0.5 mmol/l$^-$). A wide range of mineral salts (elements) supply the macro and micronutrients. The inorganic salts in water undergo dissociation and ionization. Consequently, one type of ion may be contributed by more than one salt for instance, in MS medium, K+ ions are contributed by KNO_3 and KH_2PO_4 while NO_3 – ions come from KNO_3 and NH_4NO_3.

Macronutrient elements: The six elements namely nitrogen, phosphorus, potassium, calcium, magnesium and sulfur are the essential macronutrients for tissue culture. The ideal concentration of nitrogen, and potassium is around 25 mmol l^{-1} while for calcium, phosphorus, sulfur and magnesium, it is in the range of 1-3 mmol l^{-1} for the supply of nitrogen in the medium, nitrates and ammonium salts are together used.

Micronutrients : Although their requirement is in minute quantities, micronutrients are essential for plant cells and tissues. These include iron, manganese, zinc, boron, copper and molybdenum. Among the microelements, iron requirement is very critical. Chelated forms of iron and copper are commonly used in culture media.

Carbon and energy sources

Plant cells and tissues in the culture medium are heterotrophic and therefore, are dependent on the external carbon for energy. Among the energy sources, sucrose is the most preferred. During the course of sterilization (by autoclaving) of the medium, sucrose gets hydrolyzed to glucose and fructose. The plant cells in culture first utilize glucose and then fructose. In fact, glucose or fructose can be directly used in the culture media. It may be noted that for energy supply, glucose is as efficient as sucrose while fructose is less efficient.

Table : A selected list of elements and their functions in plants

Element:	Function(s)
Nitrogen:	Essential component of proteins, nucleic acids and some coenzymes. (Required in most abundant quantity)
Calcium:	Synthesis of cell wall, membrane function, cell signaling
Magnesium:	Component of chlorophyll, cofactor for some enzymes.
Potassium:	Major inorganic cation, regulates osmotic potential.
Phosphorus:	Component of nucleic acids and various intermediates in respiration and photosynthesis, involved in energy transfer.
Sulfur:	Component of certain amino acids (methionine, cysteine and cystine, and some cofactors).
Manganese:	Cofactor for certain enzymes.
Iron:	Component of cytochromes, involved in electron transfer.
Chlorine:	Participates in photosynthesis.
Copper:	Involved in electron transfer reactions, cofactor for some enzymes.
Cobalt :	Component of vitamin B_{12}.
Molybdenum:	Component of certain enzymes (e.g., nitrate reductase), cofactor for some enzymes.
Zinc:	Required for chlorophyll biosynthesis, cofactor for certain enzymes.

It is a common observation that cultures grow better on a medium with autoclaved sucrose than on a medium with filter-sterilized sucrose. This clearly indicates that the hydrolyzed products of sucrose (particularly glucose) are efficient sources of energy. Direct use of fructose in the medium subjected to autoclaving, is found to be detrimental to the growth of plant cells.

Besides sucrose and glucose, other carbohydrates such as lactose, maltose, galactose, raffinose, trehalose and cellobiose have been used in culture media but with a very limited success.

Organic Supplements

The organic supplements include vitamins, amino acids, organic acids, organic extracts, activated charcoal and antibiotics.

Vitamins : Plant cells and tissues in culture (like the natural plants) are capable of synthesizing vitamins but in suboptimal quantities, inadequate to support growth. Therefore, the medium should be supplemented with vitamins to achieve good growth of cells. The vitamins added to the media include thiamine, riboflavin, niacin, pyridoxine, folic acid, pantothenic acid, biotin, ascorbic acid, myoinositol, para-amino benzoic acid and vitamin E.

Amino acids : Although the cultured plant cells can synthesize amino acids to a certain extent, media supplemented with amino acids stimulate cell growth and help in establishment of cells lines. Further, organic nitrogen (in the form of amino acids such as L-glutamine, L-asparagine, L-arginine, L-cysteine) is more readily taken up than inorganic nitrogen by the plant cells.

Organic acids : Addition of Krebs cycle intermediates such as citrate, malate, succinate or fumarate allow the growth of plant cells. Pyruvate also enhances the growth of cultured cells

Organic extracts : It has been a practice to supplement culture media with organic extracts such as yeast, casein hydrolysate coconut milk, orange juice, tomato juice and potato extract.

It is however, preferable to avoid the use of natural extracts due to high variations in the quality and quantity of growth promoting factors in them. In recent years, natural extracts have been replaced by specific organic compounds e.g., replacement of yeast extract by L-asparagine, replacement of fruit extracts by L-glutamine.

Activated charcoal : Supplementation of the medium with activated charcoal stimulates the growth and differentiation of certain plant cells (carrot, tomato, orchids). Some toxic inhibitory compounds (e.g. phenols) produced by cultured plants are removed (by adsorption) by activated charcoal, and this facilitates efficient cell growth in cultures.

Addition of activated charcoal to certain cultures (tobacco, soybean) is found to be inhibitory, probably due to adsorption of growth stimulants such as phytohormones.

Antibiotics : It is sometimes necessary to add antibiotics to the medium to prevent the growth of microorganisms. For this purpose, low concentration of streptomycin or kanamycin are used. As far as possible, addition of antibiotics to the medium is avoided as they have an inhibitory influence on the cell growth.

Plant Growth Regulators

The naturally occurring compounds within plant tissue (endogenously) and have a regulatory rather than a nutritional role in growth and development are called as growth hormones. These compounds are generally active at very low concentrations. Synthetic chemicals with similar physiological activities to plant growth hormones or compounds having an ability to modify plant growth by some means are termed as plant growth regulators.

Ratio of auxins and cytokinins : The relative concentrations of the growth factors namely auxins and cytokinins are crucial for the morphogenesis of culture systems. When the ratio of auxins to cytokinins to high, embryogenesis, callus initiation and root initiation occur. On the other hand, for axillary and shoot proliferation, the ratio of auxins to cytokinins is low. For all practical purposes, it is considered that the formation and maintenance of callus cultures require both auxin and cytokinin, while auxin in needed for root culture and cytokinin for shoot culture. The actual concentration of the growth regulators in culture media are variable depending on the type of tissue explant and the plant species.

Abscisic acid (ABA) : The callus growth of cultures may be stimulated or inhibited by ABA. This largely depends on the nature of the plant species. Abscisic acid is an important growth regulation for induction of embryogenesis.

Solidifying agents

For the preparation of semisolid or solid tissue culture media, solidifying or gelling agents are required. In fact, solidifying agents extend support to tissues growing in the static conditions.

Agar : Agar, a polysaccharide obtained from seaweeds, is most commonly used as a gelling agent for the following reasons

1. It does not react with media constituents.
2. It is not digested by plant exzymes and is stable at culture temperature.

Agar at a concentration of 0.5 to 1% in the medium can form a gel.

Gelatin : It is used at a high concentration (10%) with a limited success. This is mainly because gelatin melts at low temperature (25°C) and consequently the gelling property is lost.

Other gelling agents : Biogel (polyacrylamide pellets), phytagel, gelrite and purified agarose are other solidifying agents, although less frequently used. It is in fact advantageious to use synthetic gelling compounds, since they can form gels at a relatively low concentration (1.0 to 2.5 g l^{-1}).

pH of medium

The optimal pH for most tissue cultures in the range of 5.0 – 6.0. The pH generally falls by 0.3 – 0.5 units after autoclaving. Before sterilization, pH can be adjusted to the required optimal level while preparing the medium. It is usually not necessary to use buffers for the pH maintenance of culture media. At a pH higher than 7.0 and lower than 4.5, the plant cells stop growing in cultures. If the pH falls during the plant tissue culture, then fresh medium should be prepared. In general, pH above 6.0 gives the medium hard appearance, while pH below 5.0 does not allow gelling of the medium.

CHEMOTAXONOMY

The use of biochemistry in taxonomic studies is called chemotaxonomy. Living organisms produce many types of natural products in varying amounts, and quite often the biosynthetic pathways responsible for these compounds also differ from one taxonomic group to another. The distribution of these compounds and their biosynthetic pathways correspond will with existing taxonomic arrangements based on more traditional criteria such as morphology. In some cases, chemical data have contradicted existing hypotheses, which necessitates a reexamination of the problem or, more positively, chemical data have provided decisive information in situations where other forms of data are insufficiently discriminatory.

Modern chemotaxonomists often divide natural products into two classes (1) micromolecules, that is, those compounds with a molecular weight of 1000 or less, such as alkaloids, terpenoids, amino acids, fatty acids, flavonoid pigments and other phenolic compounds, mustard oils, and simple carbohydrates, and (2) macromolecules, that is, those compounds (often polymers) with a molecular weight over 1000, including complex polysaccharides, proteins, and the basis of life itself, deoxyribonucleic acid (DNA).

A crude extract of a plant can be separated into its individual components, especially in the case of micromolecules, by using one or more techniques of chromatography, including paper, thin-layer, gas, or high-pressure liquid chromatography. The resulting chromatogram provides a visual display or "fingerprint" characteristics of a plant species for the particular class of compounds under study.

The individual, separated spots can be further purified and then subjected to one or more types of spectroscopy, such as ultraviolet, infrared, or nuclear magnetic resonance or mass spectroscopy (or both), which may provide information about the structure of the compound. Thus, for taxonomic purposes both visual patterns and structural knowledge of the compounds can be compared from species to species.

CHROMATOGRAPHY

The term chromatography (chroma^G = a colour, graphein^G = to write) was originally applied by a Russian chemist, Mechael Semonovich Twsett (LT. 1872-1919), in 1906 to a procedure where a mixture of different colored pigments (chlorophylls and xanthophylls) is separated from each other. He used a column of CaCO3 to separate the various components of petroleum either chlorophyll extract into green and yellow zones of pigments. He termed such a preparation as chromatogram and the procedure as chromatography. Chromatography may be defined as the technique of separation of substances according to their partition coefficients below (i.e., their relative solubilities in) two immiscible phases. In this method, the separation of the components of a mixture is a function of their different affinities for a fixed or stationary phase (such as a solid or a liquid) and their differential solubility in a moving or mobile phase (such as a liquid or a gas, Separation starts to occur when one component is held more firmly by the stationary phase than the other which tends to move on faster in the mobile phase.

PRINCIPLE - The various chromatographic techniques fall principally under 2 categories: adsorption chromatography and partition chromatography. In adsorption chromatography, the stationary phase is a finely divided adsorbent such as alumina or silica gel and the mobile phase can be a gas or more commonly a liquid. Partition chromatography involves partition between two liquids rather than adsorption by a solid from a liquid. Here the stationary phase a liquid, which is held on an inert porous supporting liquid.

Types of Chromatography : Some major chromatographic techniques are discussed below :

1. Paper Chromatography
2. Thin layer Chromatography
3. Column Chromatography : a. Affinity Chromatography

   b. Ion - exchange Chromatography

   c. Size exclusion Chromatography
4. Gas Chromatography
5. Liquid Chromatography

Paper Chromatography

Paper chromatography is an analytical chemistry technique for separating and identifying mixtures that are or can be colored, especially pigments.Two Russian workers, Izmailov and Schraiber (1938) discovered this important techniques. This method is especially useful for the detection and separation of amino acids. Here the filter paper strips are used to support a stationary water phase while a mobile organic phase moves down the suspended paper strip in a cylinder. Separation is based on a liquid partition of the components. Thus, this is essentially a form of partition chromatography between two liquid phases through adsorption to the paper may also take place.

In this method, a drop of solution containing a mixture of amino acids (or other compounds) to be separated is applied at a marked point, about 3 cm from one end of a strip of filter paper. Whatman No. 1 paper is most frequently used for this purpose.

The filter paper is then dried and 'equilibrated' by putting it into an air-tight cylindrical jar which contains an aqueous solution of a solvent. The most widely applicable solvent mixture is n-butanol acetic acid: water (4:1:5), which is abbreviated as BAW. The end of the filter paper nearest the applied drop is inserted into the solvent mixture at the bottom of the jar, taking care that the marked point of application remains will above the level of the solvent in the jar. The paper is suspended in such a manner so that it hangs freely without touching the sides of the container. Thus, the solvent will ascend into the paper and different components of a mixture are separated.

Thin Layer Chromatography

Thin layer chromatography is adsorption chromatography performed on open layers of adsorbent materials supported in glass plates. This technique combines many of the advantages of paper such a preparation as chromatogram and the procedure as chromatography.

Thin layer Chromatography chromatography with those of column chromatography. Here a thin uniform film of adsorbent (like silica gel or alumina powder) containing a binding medium (like calcium sulfate) is spread onto a glass plate. The thin layer is allowed to dry at room temperature and is then activated by bearing in an oven between 100°C to 250°C. The activated plate is then placed flat and samples spotted with micropipettes carefully on the surface of the thin layer. After the solvent has evaporated, the plates are placed vertically in glass tank containing a suitable rising through the thin layer. The glass plate is a variety of reagents.

Column Chromatography

Column chromatography is a separation technique in which the stationary bed is within a tube. The particles of the solid stationary phase or the support coated with a liquid stationary phase may fill the whole inside volume of the tube (packed column) or e concentrated on or along the inside tube wall leaving an open, unrestricted path for the mobile phase in the middle part of the tube (open tubular column). Differences in rates of movement through the medium are calculated to different retention times of the sample.

Types of column chromatography:

a. Affinity chromatography

b. Ion exchange chromatography

c. Size exclusion chromatography

a. Affinity chromatography is based on selective non-covalent interaction between an analyte and specific molecules. It is very specific, but not very robust. It is often used in biochemistry in the purification of proteins bound to tags. These fusion proteins are labeled with compounds such as His-tags, biotin or antigens, which bind to the stationary phase specifically. After purification, some of these tags are usually removed and the pure protein is obtained.

b. Ion exchange chromatography uses ion exchange mechanism to separate analytes. It is usually performed in columns but can also be useful in planar mode. Ion exchange chromatography uses a charged stationary phase to separate charged compounds including amino acids, peptides, and proteins. In conventional groups which interact with oppositely charged groups of the compound to be retained. Ion exchange chromatography is commonly used to purify proteins.

c. Size exlusion chromatography (SEC) is also known as gel permeation chromatography (GPc) or gel filtration chromatography and separates molecules according to their size (or more accurately according to their hydrodynamic diameter or hydrodynamic volume). Smaller molecules are able to enter the pores of the media and, therefore, take longer to elute, whereas larger molecules are excluded from the pores and elute faster. It is generally a low-resolution chromatography technique and thus it is often reserved for the final, "polishing" step of purification. It is also useful for determining the tertiary structure and quaternary structure of purified proteins, especially since it can be carried out under native solution conditions.

Gas Chromatography (OR GC)

Gas chromatography is a dynamic method of separation and detection of volatile organic compounds and several inorganic permanent gases in a mixture. GC as an instrumental technique was first introduced in the 1950s and has evolved into a primary tool used in many laboratories. Significant technological advance in the area of electronics, computerization and column technology have yielded lower and lower detectable limits and more accurate identification of substances through improved resolution and qualitative analysis techniques. GC is very versatile technique that can be used in most industry area, environmental, pharmaceutical, petroleum, chemical manufacturing, clinical, forensic, food science and many more. Several leading manufactures of gas chromatographs provide fairly extensive resources for training, method development and operational support services.

Liquid Chromatography

Liquid chromatography (LC) is a separation technique in which the mobile phase is a liquid. Liquid chromatography can be carried out either in a column or a plane. Present day liquid chromatography that generally utilizes very small packing particles and a relatively high pressure is referred to as high performance liquid chromatography (HPLC).

In the HPLC technique, the sample is forced through a column that is packed with irregularly or spherically shaped particles of a porous monolithic layer (stationary phase) by a liquid (mobile phase) at high pressure. HPLC is historically divided into two different sub-classes based on the polarity of the mobile and stationary phases. Technique mobile phase, silica as the stationary phase) is called normal phase liquid chromatography (NPLC) and the opposite (e.g. water-methanol mixture as the mobile phase and C18 = octadecylsilyl as the stationary phase) is called reversed phase liquid chromatography (RPLC). Ironically the "normal phase" has fewer applications and RPLC is therefore used considerably more.

HIGH PERFORMANCE LIQUID CHROMATOGRAPHY

HPLC was developed in the late 1960s & 1970s. Today it is a widely accepted separation technique for both sample analysis and purification in a variety of areas including the pharmaceutical, biotechnological, environmental, polymer and food industries. HPLC is enjoying a steady increase in no. of both instrumental sales and publications that describe new and innovative applications. Some recent growth areas include miniaturization of HPLC analysis of nucleic acids intact proteins and protein digests, analysis of CBH and chiral analysis.

Basic Principle

The basic principle of reverse phase HPLC separation is the hydrophobic interaction between the own polar hydrocarbonaceous matrix of the column material and the hydrophobic groups of the analyte. Two different mechanisms, adsorption and partition are responsible for retention of solutes in the stationary phase.

In the adsorption model, a solute is adsorbed on the hydrophobic surface of the solid support the remains adsorbed until the attractive forces are weakened by a sufficiently high concentration of the organic modifier in the mobile phase. At this critical concentration, the adsorbed solute molecules are replaced by the molecules of the organic modifier and eluted from the column e little further interaction e the stationary phase. The process can be regarded as endothermic and entropically driven.

In the partition model the solid surface is considered a hydrophobic bulk phase and equilibrium is achieved when a solute partitions between this solid phase and the mobile phase. With the downward flow of the mobile phase, the solute moves in and out of the stationary phase. Solutes e higher equilibrium constants are retained longer in the column. The equilibrium can be shifted toward the liquid phase by increasing the concentration of the organic modifier.

Working

Chromatography is a technique in which solutes are resolved by differential rates of elution as they pass through a chromatographic column. Their separation is governed by their distribution bet the mobile and the stationary phases. The successful use of liquid chromatography for a given problem requires the right combination of a variety of operating conditions such as the type of column packing and mobile phase, column length and diameter, mobile phase flow rate, column temperature sand sample size. HPLC instrumentation is made up of eight basic components :-

1. Mobile phase reservoir
2. Solvent delivery system
3. Sample introduction device
4. Column
5. Detector
6. Waste reservoir
7. Connective tubing
8. Computer

Required Sample Properties:-

State : Sample must be in liquid form for injection into the instrument, solid samples must be dissolved in a solvent compatible with the mobile and stationary phases.

Amount: 1-100 ml injected (generally 5-10 ml); mass amounts injected vary depending on the sensitivity and dynamic range of the detector for the analyte.

Preparation: Limited or extensive sample prep may be required as defined by the relative complexity of the sample. Sample preparation may include any of the following steps dilution, preconcentration, filteration, extraction, ultrafilteration or derivatization.

Analysis time : Analysis time is in a range from 5 min to 2 hr. (generally 10-25 min). Sample preparation differs from sample to sample. Sample preparation may be extensive and require more time than the analysis.

Applications of HPLC

1. Separation of a wide variety of compounds, organic, inorganic and biological compounds, organic, inorganic and biological compounds, polymers, chiral compounds, thermally labile compounds and small ions to macromolecules.

2. Analysis of impurities.
3. Analysis of both volatile and nonvolatile compounds.
4. Determination of neutral, ionic or zwitterionic molecules.
5. Isolation and purification of compounds.
6. Separation of closely related compounds.
7. Ultratrance to preparative and process.
8. Nondestructive method.
9. Qualitative and quantitative method.

Limitations :

1. Compound identification may be limited unless high PLC is interfaced e mass spectrometry.
2. Resolution can be difficult to attain e complex samples.
3. Only one sample can be analyzed at a time.
4. Requires training in order to optimize separations.
5. Time analysis can be long (compared e capillary electrophoresis).
6. Sample preparation of often required.

BAMBOOS IN WORLD

Bamboo is monocotyledonous woody grass belonging to the sub-family *Bambusoideae* of the family *Poaceae*.Bamboos are the fastest growing plant in the world (60 cm/day). Worldwide there are m They occur across East Asia, from 50°N latitude in Sakhalin through to Northern Australia, and west to India and the Himalayas.

They also occur in sub-Saharan Africa, and in the Americas from the Mid-Atlantic United States, south to Argentina and Chile, reaching their southernmost point anywhere, at 47°S latitude. Major areas with no native bamboos include Europe and Antarctica.India is very rich in bamboo diversity. More than 1,250 species under 75 genera of bamboo, which are unevenly distributed in the various parts of the humid tropical, sub-tropical and temperate regions of the earth (Subramaniam, 1998).

BAMBOOS IN INDIA

India is the seventh largest country in the world covering an area of 328.78 million ha. It lies entirely in the northern hemisphere and extends between 8ºN to 37ºN latitudes and 68ºE to 97ºE longitudes. The forest cover is over an area of 63.3 million ha which is 19.27 per cent of the total geographical area. Overall six percent of world species are found in India. It is one of the twelve mega-biodiversity countries. (Status of bamboo and rattan in India Jk rawat and dc khanduri, 1. forest research institute India and 2. ministry of environment and forest India). Table Distribution of main bamboo species in India (ICFRE 1998) :

Species	States / UTs
Bambusa arundinacea	Arunachal Pradesh, Karnataka, Orissa, Maharashtra, Himachal Pradesh, Andhra Pradesh and Gujarat
Bambusa balcooa	Arunachal Pradesh, Mizoram
Bambusa pallida	Arunachal Pradesh, Nagaland, Mizoram, Tripura
Bambusa tulda	Arunachal Pradesh, Assam, Mizoram, Nagaland, Tripura
Bambusa polymorpha	Tripura
Dendrocalamus hamiltonii	Arunachal Pradesh, Assam, Mizoram, Nagaland
Dendrocalamus longispathus	Mizoram
Dendrocalamus strictus	Andhra Pradesh, Assam, Gujarat, Maharashtra, Himachal Pradesh, Madhya Pradesh, Manipur, Orissa, Karnataka, Uttar Pradesh, Rajasthan
Melocanna bambusoides	Assam, Mizoram, Nagaland, Tripura, Manipur, Meghalaya
Neebenzia balcooa	Nagaland
Oxytenanthera nigrociliata	Tripura, Assam
Oxytenanthera parviflora	Assam
Pseudostachhys polymorphium	Arunachal Pradesh

There are 124 indigenous and exotic species, under 23 genera, found naturally and/or under cultivation (Naithani, 1993). This natural resource plays a major role in the livelihood of rural people and in rural industry. This green gold is sufficiently cheap and plentiful to meet the vast needs of human that is why sometimes it is known as *"poor man's timber.*

India is one of the leading countries in the world in bamboo production. Because of the versatile uses of bamboos there is great demand for this resource throughout India.

Annual production of bamboos in India is about 13.47 m tons a year is far short of the 26.69 mt. demand a year. Till recently the area under bamboo is confined to the 12.8% of forest cover; two third of the growing stock (80.42mt) located in the north east (Latest press information release Govt. of India).

An estimated 8.96 million ha forest area of the country contains bamboo (Rai and Chauhan, 1998). It is found to grow practically all over the country, particularly in the tropical, sub-tropical and temperate regions where the annual rainfall ranges between 1,200 mm to 4,000 mm and the temperature varies between 16°C and 38°C.

BAMBOOS IN MADHYA PRADESH

Bamboo is also found at places in M.P. forests. Normally *Dendrocalamus strictus* is the main bamboo species found. It is distributed over Balaghat, Seoni, Chhindwara , Betul ,Mandala ,Shahdol and Sehore (near Budni railway station).In M.P. alone 40000 basods depend entirely for their livelihood on bamboo.(Singhal and Gangopadhyaya 1999).

Distribution : In India, it is found in the states of Assam, Bihar, Meghalaya, Mizoram, Nagaland and Tripura. Cultivated in Arunachal Pradesh, Karataka and Bengal. The species is extensively grown in low hills of central Assam.

It is also occurs in Bangladesh, Myammar and Thailand. It is one of the major species of Bangladesh. This species life-span is 25-40 years.

Climate & Soil : Frequently found to grow as an under growth sporadically or in patches in the mixed semi-deciduous forests. Grows well in moist and moderately high rainfall (4000 – 6500 mm) area with temperature range from 4-37 or 40°C. It commonly grows on the flat alluvial deposits land along water courses up to 1500 m. attitude. Soils under this species contained reserve of organic matter, nitrogen, Ca, K, P.

Description : This species is a evergreen or deciduous, tufted, gregarious bamboo.

Culms : Culms usually 7-23 m high and 5-10 cm in diameter, glabrous, green when young, gray-green on maturity, nodes slightly thickened, lower ones have fibrous roots, internodes 40-70 cm long.

Culm sheaths : It is 15-25 cm long and broad, attenuate upwards and rounded or truncate at top, deciduous, adaxial surface smooth and often with whitish powder, abaxial surface sometimes covered with appressed brown hairs.

Leaves : Leaf 15-20 cm long and 2-4 cm broad, linear and lanceoalate, alternate on opposite sides leaf – sheath striate, glabrous, 2.5 mm long hairy petiole.

Inflorescene : Its occur on leafless branches and spikelets variable in length from 2.5 – 7.5 cm long and 5 mm broad, sessile, glabrous, cylindrical and acute at first, after wards divided into many flowers separated by conspicuous rachillae, becoming first 1-2 short bracts, then 2-4 usually gemmiparous empty glumes, 4-6 fertile flowers and 1 or 2 imperfect or male terminal flowers.

Stamens long exerted, anther 7.5 mm, glabrous, blunt at the tip or emarginated, ovary, obovate oblong, white, hairy above, surrounded by a short haring style, divided into 3 long plumose wavy stigmas.

Flowering cycle : Flowering cycle is reported to vary from 30-60 years. It flowers gregariously over considerable areas. Flowering was observed in Bengal during the years 1867-68, 1872, 1884, 1919, 1930 & 1936, in Assam during 1886, 1910 & 1930, in Myanmar during 1892, 1903, 1908, 1911 & 1914 and in Bangladesh in 1876, 1886, 1929-30, 1976-77, 1978-79, 1982-83 & 1983-84.

Recently it flowered at Dehradun in 1986, flowering only once in their lifetime and die after they bloom.

Fruit : Coryopsis type, oblong, 7.5 mm long, hirsute the apex,furrowed.

Propagation : Vegetative propagation using one year old, culm cutting treated with NAA + K or IAA + K in July gave maximum rooting.

Planting in summer season was better (Adarsh Kumar *et al.*, 1988). An efficient protocol for *invitro* propagation through shoot proliferation is developed (Saxena, 1990). About 80% survival is reported when the seedlings are transferred to soil after hardening. It takes 6-10 years for the new seedling to mature after gregarious flowering.

Uses : The species is used through out North-East India for covering the houses and scaffolding. The tender shoots are used for making excellent pickles. It is suitable for the manufacture of wrapping, writing and printing paper.

Used in Tripura for making toys, mats, screens, wall plates, wall hangers, hats, baskets, food grain containers etc.

In Arunachal Pradesh this species is used for flute, locally "Eloo" and used for priests during "Dree" festival with the belief that the sound will keep the evil spirits away.

In Northern Thailand, it is one of the two most important edible species until half a century ago.

It has long been exported to Europe and the USA under the names "Calcutta cane" or "East India Brown Bamboo". It can be used as reinforcement in cement concrete.

The succulent shoots are rich in phytosterols and the fermented shoots can be used for production of sterol drugs.It is mainly used by the Indian paper pulping industry.

SPECIES – B

Classification	:	Kingdom	-	Plantae
		Sub-Kingdom	-	Tracheobionata
		Division	-	Magnoliophyta
		Class	-	Liliopsida
		Sub-class	-	Commelinideae
		Order	-	Cyperales
		Family	-	Gramineae
		Genus	-	Dendrocalamus
		Species	-	Longispathus
Vernacular name	:	Rupai		

Distribution : The species is distributed in Mizoram and Tripura and generally found in the village area of Dhalbhum tract of Singhbhumi district of Bihar.

The species has been introduced to Orissa and Western Peninsula. It is cultivated in Calcutta and Malabar. Also reported from Bangladesh and Myammar (Banik 1987a, Prasad 1965 and Gamble, 1986).

Description : It is a large tufted bamboo.

Culms : Usually 10-18 m high, glaucous green when young, grayish – green on maturity, nodes-slightly swollen, internodes – 25 to 60 cm long and 6 to 10 cm diameter, covered by long papery remnants of sheaths and dark brown pubescence.

Culm sheaths : 35-50 cm long and 10-20 cm broad, inner surface glabrous and outer surface clothed densely with patches of stiff dark – brown hair, margin light straw colored in the upper half. Young shoots spear – shaped. Culm sheth ligulate.

Leaves : 10-30 cm long and 2.5 – 3.5 cm broad, oblong – lanceolate and linear – lanceolate, short stalked, margin rough, leaf sheath ligulate covered with brown pubescence and margin ciliate.

Inflorescence : A large panicle of interruptedly spicate clusters of spikelets. Sometimes few flowers are blunt in spikelets heads. Stamens – short, Anther-yellow, short, ending in a black mucronate point, filaments – short, ovary – broadly avoid, somewhat acute, hairy, ending in a rather short style and short purple stigma.

Flowering : flowering cycle is reported to vary from 30-45 years. Flowering has been reported from Bangladesh during the year 1876, 79, 80, 85, 1930 & 1977-79, from Myammar during 1862, 71, 75, 87, 91, 1912 & 1913.

Flowering was observed in the clumps planted at Nilambur and Wynad (Kerala) in 1990.

Fruiting : Caryopsis type, 7-8 mm long, oblong and furrowed.

Propagation : Vegetative propagation by two nodded culm cuttings, rhizome cuttings gives good response. Miropropagation through shoot proliferation is developed (Saxena & Bhojwani 1993). The species can be propagated by seeds.

Uses : It is generally used for the manufacture of paper. In Tripura it is used for making baskets and containers. This is found as an idea for the manufacture of good quality tooth picks. This being an elegant species is grown in gardens.

Medicinal Plants

A medicinal plant is any plant which in one or more of its organs, contains substance that can be used for therapeutic purpose of which is a precursor for synthesis of useful drugs.

The plants that posses therapeutic properties or exert beneficial pharmacological effects on the animal body are generally designated as "Medicinal plants".

Although there are no apparent morphological characteristics in the medicinal plants growing with them, yet they posses some special qualities or virtues that make them medicinally important. It has now been established that the plants which naturally synthesis and accumulate some secondary metabolites, like alkaloids, glycosides, tannins, volatile oils and contain minerals and vitamins possess medicinal properties.

Medicinal plants constitute an important natural wealth of a country. They play a significant role in providing primary health care services to rural peoples. they serve as the therapeutic agents as well as important row materials for the manufacture of traditional and modern medicine. In India medicinal plants widely used by all sections of the population and it has been estimated that in total over 7500 species of plants are used by several ethnic communities.

Secondary metabolites

Plants are the source of a large variety of biochemicals, which are metabolites of both primary and second metabolism. But secondary metabolites are of much greater interest since they have impressive biological activities like antimicrobial, antibiotic, insecticidal, molluscicidal, hormonal properties and valuable pharmacological and pharmaceutical activities, in addition, many of them are used as flavours, fragrances, etc. The tem secondary metabolite is ill-defined but convenient, it is applied to all those compounds, which are not directly involved in the primary metabolite processes, eg. photosynthesis, respiration protein and lipid biosynthesis etc. Secondary metabolites include a wide variety of compounds.

Higher plants are the source of a large number of pharmaceutical important biochemicals, about 25% of the prescribed medicines are solely derived from plants.

Medicinal Plant - *Rauwolfia serpentine*

Classification :

Kingdom - Plantae

Division - Magnoliophyta

Class - Magnoliopsida

Order - Gentianales

Family - Apocynaceae

Genus - *Rauwolfia*

Species - *serpentine*

Common name : Snake root, serpentine root, sarpgandha etc.

Habitat : It is grown in India, Pakistan, Srilanka, Burma and Thailand. In India, it is widely distributed in the sub-Himalayan track from Punjab to Nepal, Sikkim & Bhutan. It is also found in the lower hills of Gangetic plains, eastern and Western Ghats and Andamans. It is mostly found in moist deciduous forests at altitudes ranging from sea level to an altitude of 1,200 m high. In the Deccan it is associated with bamboo forests.

Morphology description : It is an evergreen, perennial, glabrous and erect undershrub grows up to height of 60 cm (rarely more than it) roots are tuberous with pale brown cork. leaves are in whorls of three, elliptic to lanceolate or obovate, bright green above, pale green below, tip acute or acuminate, base tapering and slender, petioles long.

Flowers are in many flowered irregular corymbose cymes. Peduncles long but pedicles stout flowers white, often has violet color. Calyx glabrous bright red and lanceolate, corolla is longer than calyx, tube slender, swollen a little above the middle, lobes 3 and elliptic oblong. Disc is cup shaped. Drupes are slightly connate, obliquely avoid and purplish black in color.

Reserpine is an indole alkaloid formerly used in treatment of schizophrenia and hypertension (it's still rarely used for hypertension therapy today). Alkaloids often classified on the basis of their chemical structure. For example, those alkaloids that contain a ring system called indole are known as indole alkaloids. On this basis, the principal classes of alkaloids are the pyrrolidines, pyridines, tropanes, pyrrolizidines, isoquinolines, indoles, quinolines, and the terpenodis and steroids.

Molecular Formula : $C_{33}H_{40}N_2O_9$

Molecular mass : 608.68 g/mol

Uses : This plant is used medicinally both in the Modern Western Medical system and also in Ayurveda, Unani & folk medicine. It helps to reduce blood pressure, depresses activity of central nervous system and acts as a hypnotic snake root depletes catecholamines and serotonin from nerve in central nervous system.

Refined snakeroot has been used extensively in recent years to treat hypertension. It is used as an antidote to the bites of poisonous reptile like snakes.It is also used to treat dysentery and other painful affections of the intestinal canal.

2

Review of Literature

PLANT TISSUE CULTURE : A HISTORICAL INTRODUCTION

The science of plant cell and tissue culture is really not more than five decades old. It was conceived and enunciated by Haberlandt in 1902. Haberlandt visualized the idea of growing plant cells in artificial media in the hope of rejuvenating a quiescent cell and triggering it into division and growth, to form a tissue and eventually, regenerate a whole new plant. But in this, he himself was unsuccessful. Robbins (1922a, b) was the first to develop a technique for the culture of isolated roots. He conducted a series of experiments using maize roots capable of being subcultured, and demonstrated the efficiency of yeast extract (YE) for growth, indicating the necessity for vitamin requirements.

However, his cultures did not survive indefinitely, perhaps because the selection of material was not good. In 1939 some more progress was reported in the successful culture of organized structures such as tomato roots, storage roots of carrot. Street and his co-workers carried out extensive studies on isolated root tips of several plants for organ culture, to understand the factors concerned with their growth. Gautheret, Heller and Camus (1939-1957) of the French School of Tissue Culture, examined the histo-physiological changes brought about in explanted tissues by substances such as B-vitamins, cysteine HCl, glucose and Indole acetic acid (IAA) in the basic media. Experiments on the induction of vascular tissues by grafting of shoot buds into callus, gave the clue to the influence of growth hormones in cyto-differentiation and morphogenesis. Studies by Wetmore and sorokin (1955). Wetmore and Rier (1963) and others in USA confirmed the role of auxins and vitamins as controlling factors in growth.

Skoog and Miller (1957) demonstrated that regulation and differentiation of roots and shoots (orgnogenesis) in tobacco pith cultures depended on the relative concentration of auxin / cytokinin. The stimulatory effect of coconut mil (CCM) in plant embryo nutrition *in vitro* was established by van Overbeek (1941b) through his experiments with Daturu embryos. Later, Steward, Caplin and Miller (1952) emphasized the importance of coconut milk in nutrition, callus growth and embryogenesis or carrot, followed by Reinert (1958) and Pilet (1961) who indicated their development on a purely synthetic medium without the addition of the liquid endosperm or other plant extracts. Culture of excised root tips of tomato (an example of organ culture), indicated the need for vitamins of the B-group as growth supplements in the medium (White, 1943).

Between 1939 and 1956, tissue culture studies were in a state of flux. It was a period of exploration and innovation in approach and technique, using such plants as carrot, tobacco and Helianthus tuberosus (Jerusalem artichoke). By then considerable progress had been made on the question of tissue nutrition. It soon came to be realized that no one single medium was satisfactory for the growth of all tissues, and this led to the formulation of different media to suit different tissues. A balanced solution which served as a basic medium for a wide spectrum of plant tissues is that of Murashige-Skoog (MS) (1962) and several modifications.

The demonstration of the development of somatic embryos (embryoids) from carrot cells in suspension by Reinert in Germany and Steward in USA (1958, 1959) and subsequently of leaf mesophyll cells of Mc Cleaya cordata by Kohlenbach (1966, was another in the history of cell culture technology).

Isolation and culture of shoot meristems and nodal meristems of plants resulted in regeneration of multiple shoots and of plants free of virus and other pathogens, widely applicable to breeding to true-to-type progenies, an offshoot of the technique developed by Morel (1960) with orchids. Single cell culture were developed by Muir (1953) and Muir *et al.* (1958) by the paper-raft nurse technique, by Torrey (157) and Jones *et al.* (1960) by the micro-chamber method (hanging drop culture), and by Bergmann (1960) through the agar-planting method as for bacteria. By the 1960s, tissue culture techniques had become common place the world over. Subsequently, some very exciting technical developments in the manipulation of individual cells led to the isolation and release of cell protoplasts, by treating the cell with cell wall degrading enzymes, through the pioneering efforts of Edward Cocking at the University of Nottingham, UK in the 1970s.

The successful growth *in vitro* of ovary, ovule and embryo parts in fruitset and seed development has been highlighted, as response to exogeneous hormones, in a series of publications in the 1960s. A fascinating outcome of tissue culture studies initiated at the University of Delhi has been the spectacular demonstration for the first time of the development of pollen embryoids and plantlets from another culture of Datura innoxia by Guha and Maheshwari (1964, 1967).

Tissue cultures of elite forest tree genera such as *Santalum album* (andalwood), Eucalyptus, teak (Tectona grandis) and *Dalbergia latifolia* (East Indian rosewood), even from tissues isolated from mature 100-year-old trees and from the oil palm, have been made at the Plant Bio-Technology Division of Bhabha Atomic Research Centre (BARC), Bombay, the Indian Institute of Science, bangalore, the National Chemical Laboratory, Pune, Central Plantation Crop Research Institute, Kasaragod, Kerala, India and at the Indian Institute of Horticultural Research, Bangalore, India. *In vitro* culture of grain legumes, arboreal forms of Gramineae and of several conifers are also being pursued at the Department of Botany, University of Delhi, India.

Yet another fruitful area has been recognized in the manipulation of cultured cells for the increased production of high value secondary compounds using industrial fermentors and bio-reactors. Lindsey and Yeoman (1986) envisaged the application of the principle of aggregation and passive immobilization of small groups of plant cells in a fixed bed reactor for augmenting the biosynthetic potential of cell cultures and training cells to produce and accumulate the desired compound. Technical advances in recent years in cell culture have been tremendous and unique in their application as commercial tools to horticulture, silviculture, agriculture, biochemistry and plant pathology. Dramatic strides have been made over the years in the step-by-step evolutionary progress in the culture and manipulation of the plant cell.

TISSUE CULTURE RESEARCH ON BAMBOO

The first paper on successful tissue culture is with Alexander and Rao (1968) who described embryoculture. In the eighties there was a considerable increase with propagation of seedlings in tissue culture (Nadgir *et al.*, 1984), the induction of somatic embryogenesis in bamboo seeds of tropical species (Rao *et al.* 1985), clonal propagation of *Guadua angustifolia* (Manzur, 1988) and other induction of somatic embryogenesis in bamboo seeds of tropical species (Rao *et al.* 1985), clonal propagation of *Guadua angustifolia* (Manzur, 1988) and other species (Prutpongse and Gavinlertvatana, 1992), and the induction of organogenesis (caulogenesis) in mature bamboos (Huang *et al.*, 1989).

The plants obtained through micropropagation based on methodologies using seeds and seedlings are similar to the seedling material, juvenile in appearance with "weedy" stems, and progress through growth phases akin to seedlings. However, plantlets of *Dendrocalamus latiflorus*, obtained adventitiously from callus generated from rhizome and internode calli, shifted toa culm growth habit similar to cutting-derived planting material within a year in the greenhouse (Zamora *et al.* 1991). The number of papers about this subject however is much less, and this is solely due to lack of success. Indeed, technically the propagation of adult plants via axillary branching is much more difficult than with seedlings of tropical bamboos. (Zomora, 1994 , Nadgauda *et. al.*, 1997).

For bamboo different propagation techniques are available, such as seed propagation, clump division, rhizome and culm cuttings (Banik, 1994). But these methods suffer from serious drawbacks when one talks about large or mass scale propagation.

For tissue culture of bamboo the use of starting material (seeds or adult plants) and the choice of the propagation method are crucial (Gielis, 1999). The two major advantages of using seedlings are that seedlings establish a new generation, and that the technology is easier. But the disadvantages are considerable : (1) insufficient or no knowledge of genetic background, (2) restricted availability of seeds for most species and rapid loss of germination capacity, and (3) comparison of *in vitro* to *in vivo* performance has not been thoroughly evaluated. In addition there is a huge variability in responsiveness in tissue culture (Saxena and Dhawan, 1994).

For bamboo different propagation techniques are available, such as seed propagation, clump division, rhizome and culm cuttings (Banik, 1994, Banik, 1995). But these methods suffer from serious drawbacks for large or mass scale propagation. For mass scale propagation (> 500 000 plants per year) classical techniques are largely insufficient and inefficient, and tissue culture is the only viable method. Indeed, the order of magnitude of the demand for bamboo planting materials indicate that micropropagation will inevitably be necessary for mass scale propagation (Subramanlam, 1994, Gielis, 1999).

One of the main problems with bamboo is that it has been regarded as a resource, which is simply there to take, as has been done for thousands of years by people in rural economies. However, in industrial economies such practice leads to considerable overexploitation and rapid depletion of bamboo resources in the vicinity of the paper mills and factories. Up to the point that transportation costs have become too high for bamboo to be economical (indeed transportation of culms is a lot of air). Estimates regarding future use of bamboo all indicate that there will be an huge shortage for bamboo planting material in medium and long term (Subramanlam, 1994, Nadgauda, 1997).

Indeed, the order of magnitude of the demand for bamboo planting materials indicates that micropropagation will inevitably be necessary for mass scale propagation (Subramanlam, 1994, Gielis, 1995). Classical techniques alone can never solve this problem.

The propogation of bamboos is done with seeds, clump divisions, and rhizome and culm cuttings. However, gregarious flowering, low seed viability, high costs, problems facing long-distance transportation of vegetative propagules, and poor efficiency of plant production, compdelled development of alternative propagation methods (Gielis et al., 2001).

Gielis and Oprins (2002), this *invitro* micro-propogation will be of choice for mass scale propagation of bamboos because the regenerated plants are genetically uniform. Since the diversity of bamboos is so vast, it is difficult to present a unique step-by-step protocol for micropropagation of all plants classified within this group.

In vitro micropropagation constitutes a feasible alternative to mass-propagate individuals in this plant group. Somatic embryogenesis (Lin *et al.*, 2004 and references therein) and propagation using axillary buds (Jimenez *et al.*, 2006, Ramanayake *et al.*, 2006 and references therein) have effectively been used to multiply bamboos *in vitro*.

Research on *Bambusa tulda* :

Saxena (1990) given *in vitro* propagation of the *Bambusa tulda* through shoot prolieration shoots from 3-week-old aseptically grown seedlings were used to initiate cultures. Multiple shoots were obtained on liquid MS medium supplemented with benzyladenine (8 x 10-6 M) and kinetin (4 x 10-6 M). Continuous shoot proliferation at a rate of 4-5 fold every 3 weeks was achieved through forced axillary branching. More than 90% of shoots were rooted on a modified MS medium containing IAA (1 x 10-5 M) and cournarin (6.8 x 10-5 M). Following simple hardening procedures, the *in vitro* raised plants were transferred to soil with an > 80% success rate.

Banik (1980) given propagation of bamboos by clonal methods and by seed. Techniques of bamboo propagation with special reference to pre-rooted and prerhizomed branch cuttings and tissue culture discussed in proceedings of a Workshop on Bamboo Research in Asia held on 28-30 May, 1980 in Singapore.

Raina and Prasad in 1988 given effect of nutrients on the growth behaviour of *Bambusa tulda* in the nursery.

Kumar and Dhawan, *et al*. in 1988 given vegetative propagation of *Bambusa tulda* using growth promoting substances.

The communication describe standardization of an efficient *in vitro* propagation and hardening procedure for obtaining plantlets from field grown culms of *Bambusa tulda*. Administration for 10 min of 0.05 and 0.1% mercuric chloride to explants collected in winter and summer seasons, respectively facilitated optimum culture establishment and bud break, 0.1-0.2% mercuric chloride in rainy season enhanced aseptic culture establishment but inhibited bud break due to toxicity to explants. MS liquid medium enriched with 100 mM glutamine, 0.1 mM indole-3-acetic acid and 12 mM 6-benzylaminopurine supported maximum *in vitro* shoot multiplication rate of two-fold. The proliferated shoots were successfully rooted on MS liquid medium supplemented with 40 mM coumarin resulting in a maximum of 98% rooting. The procedure requires 45 days cycle for the *in vitro* clonal propagation (15 days for shoot multiplication and 30 days for root induction) and 80 days for acclimatized plantlet production (Yogeshwar *et al*. 2008).

Research on *Dendrocalamus longispathus*:

Rooting percentages for adult bamboos ranged from very low percentages to 73% for adult Dendrocolamus longispathus (Saxena and Bhojwani, 1993).

When using adult bamboos main problems are : (1) endogenous contamination, (2) hyperhydricity and instability of multiplication rates, and (3) many problems with rooting also in bamboos that root readily in nature. Rooting percentages for adult bamboos ranged from very low percentages of 10% for Bambusa vulgaris to 73% for adult *Dendrocalamus longispathus* (Saxena and Dhawan, 1994). A rooting percentage of 77% was obtained for adult *Dendrocalamus giganteus* in 3 or 4 weeks (Ramanayake and Yakandawala, 1997). Low rooting frequencies are the major bottleneck to developing commercially viable protocols (Saxena, 1993). The combination of photomixotrophic *in vitro* multiplication and photoauthtrophic *in vitro* rooting stages resulted in improved transplanting success (Watanabe *et al.*, 2000). Improvement of rooting percentages and transplanting has been achieved in various commercial laboratories.

Another recent study examining micropropagation of 4 years old plant of *Dendrocalamus longispathus* has also found that the nature of the explant and the season are important determinants of micropropogation success.(Saxena and Bhojwani 1993).

3

Materials and Method

ROTARY EVAPORAT OR (ROTAVAP)

The rotary evaporator was invented by Lyman C. Craig, while it was first commercialized by Swiss company Buchi. The Buchi Rotavapor continues to be the most widely used rotary evaporator, and Rotavapor has become a synonym for such instruments. It is a device used in chemical and biochemical laboratories for the efficient and gentle evaporation of solvents. The main components of a rotary evaporator are a vacuum system, consisting of a vacuum pump and a controller, a rotating evaporation flask that can be heated in a heated water bath, and a condenser with a condensate-collecting flask. The system works because lowering the pressure lowers the boiling point of liquids, including that of the solvent. This allows the solvent to be removed without excessive heating.

The Rotavapor is essentially a distillation unit incorporating a rotating evaporation flask. The rotavapor will evaporate solvent at a much faster rate than systems using stationary evaporation flasks.

The rotation transfers a thin film of the liquid sample to the whole of the inner surface of the flask, markedly increasing evaporation rate and assisting heat transfer from the heating bath. The rotating flask and vapor duct have a sealing system, which allows operation under vacuum, further accelerating the evaporation process because of the reduction in boiling point of the solvent and efficient removal of the vapor phase. Vacuum operation also permits heat labile materials to be successfully concentrated without degradation. A typical rotary evaporator has a heatable water bath to keep the solvent from cooling or even freezing during the evaporation process. The solvent is removed under vacuum is trapped by a condenser and is collected for reuse or disposal.

SOXHLET

Soxhlet extractor is a piece of laboratory apparatus invented in 1879 by Franz von Soxhlet. It was originally designed for the extraction of a lipid from a solid material. However, a Soxhlet extractor is not limited to the extraction of lipids. Typically, a Soxhlet extraction is only required where the desired compound has only a limited solubility in a solvent, and the impurity is insoluble in that solvent. If the desired compound has a high solubility in a solvent then a simple filtration can be used to separate the compound from the insoluble substance.

The sample is placed in a thumblet. Normally a solid material containing some of the desired compound is placed inside a thumblet made from thick filter paper, which is loaded into the main chamber of the Soxhlet extractor. The Soxhlet extractor is placed into a flask containing the extraction solvent. The Soxhlet is then equipped with a condenser.

The solvent is heated to reflux. The solvent vapour travels up a distillation arm, and floods into the chamber housing the thumblet of solid. The condenser ensures that any solvent vapour cools, and drips back down into the chamber housing the solid material.

The chamber containing the solid material slowly fills with warm solvent. Some of the desired compound will then dissolve in the warm solvent. When the Soxhlet chamber is almost full, the chamber is automatically emptied by a siphon side arm, with the solvent running back down to the distillation flask. This cycle may be allowed to repeat many times, over hours of days.

During each cycle, a portion of the non-volatile compound dissolves in the solvent. After many cycles the desired compound is concentrated in the distillation flask. The advantage of this system is that instead of many portions of warm solvent being passed through the sample, just one batch of solvent is recycled.

MILLIPORE-SUCTIOIN FILTERATION PORE

Nitrocellulose filters or cellulose nitrate and cellulose acetate filters are used that consist of a close network of fibers providing very small pore size that allows separation of very fine particles. Because of both the pore size and surface tensions, liquids do not easily pass through these filter with gravity as the driving force so that pressure or suction is usually employed. Filters of various pore sizes are used.

The pores of filter are not circular but irregularly shaped and account for roughly 80% of the surface area. The filters are sufficiently thin that are retained parties.

ULTRASONICATOR

It is used for degassing. This instrument is based on sound to agitate particles in a sample for various purposes.

HPLC

The instrument is an assemblage of a pressure pump, solvent delivery system that is connected to the chromatography column through an injection port (for loading sample). The column is kept in chromatographic oven that is further connected to detector, which is in turn linked to a recorder.

Chemical used in HPLC for the extraction of reserpine

- o Acetonitrile
- o Hexane
- o 3% HCl
- o 10% NH_3
- o Sodium sulphate
- o Chloroform
- o Dragondroff's reagent

Media Preparation and Sterilization

The *invitro* growth of the plant cells occurs in a suitable medium containing all the requisite elements. The ingredients of the medium effect the growth and metabolism of cells.

Murashige and Skoog's growth medium referred to as MS medium was used and supplemented with 100 mg/l of myo-inositol and 3% sucrose as carbon source.

- Plant growth regulators – Auxin IAA (0.5 – 1.0 mg/l) and cytokinin (1.0 – 5.0 mg/l) were used.
- pH – pH was adjusted to 5.7 to 5.8 with 1N HCl & 1N NaOH.
- Solidifying agent – Solid growth medium prepared by supplementing 0.8% agar.

Table : Composition of MS medium (Murashige & Skoog 1962) **:**

S.No.	Compound	Amount (mg/l)
1.	NH_4NO_3	1650
2.	KNO_3	1900
3.	$MgSO_4.7H_2O$	370
4.	$CaCl_2.2H_2O$	440
5.	KH_2PO_4	170
6.	KI	0.83
7.	H_3BO_3	6.2
8.	$MnSO_4.4H_2O$	22.3
9.	$ZnSO_4.7H_2O$	8.6
10.	$NaMoO_4.2H_2O$	0.25
11.	$CuSO_4.5H_2O$	0.025
12.	$CoCl_2.6H_2O$	0.025
13.	$FeSO_4.7H_2O$	27.8
14.	$Na_2EDTA.2H_2O$	37.3
15.	Inosited	100

16.	Nicotinic acid	0.5
17.	Pyridoxine HCl	0.5
18.	Thiamine HCl	0.1
19.	Glycine	2

PGR: As per need

Sucrose: 30% (30 mg/l)

Ph: 5.7 – 5.8 (using 1 HCl or 1N NaOH)

Agar: 0.8% (8 mg/l)

Table : Stock solutions :

	Compound	Amount mg/l
A.	Stock I (20x) – Macronutrients	
	NH_4NO_3	33000
	KNO_3	38000
	$CaCl_2.H_2O$	8800
	$MgSO_4$	7400
	KH_2PO_4	3400
B.	Stock II (200 x) – Micronutrients	
	KI	166
	H_3BO_3	1240
	$MnSO_4.4H_2O$	4460
	$ZnSO_4.7H_2O$	1720
	$NaMoO_4.7H_2O$	50
	$CuSO_4.5H_2O$	5
	$CoCl_2.6H_2O$	5
C.	Stock III (200 x) – Iron	
	$FeSO_4.7H_2O$	5560
	$Na_2EDTA.2H_2O$	7460
D.	Stock IV (200 x) – Vitamin	
	Inositol	22000
	Nicotinic acid	100

Pyridoxine HCl	100
Thiamine HCl	20
Glycine	400

For the preparation of stock solutions, each component should be separately dissolved to the last particle and then mixed with the others.

- All components were dissolved separately in some amount of double distilled water, mixed with each other and final volume is made up.
- Stock solutions were stored in refrigerator and iron stock stored in a amber coloured bottle (to prevent photoxidation).

Volume of stock solution		Volume of Media	
	2000 ml	1000 ml	500 ml
Stock I	100 ml.	50 ml.	25 ml.
Stock II	10 ml.	5 ml.	2.5 ml.
Stock III	10 ml.	5 ml.	2.5 ml.
Stock IV	10 ml.	5 ml.	2.5 ml.

Explant

Tissue culture is started from pieces of whole plants. The small organs or pieces of tissue that are used are called explants.

The part of the plant from which explants are obtained, depends on :

- o The type of culture to be initiated
- o The purpose of the proposed culture
- o The plant species to be used

Collection time of explant

The time of explant affects the success of plant tissue culture. The explant is favoured for tissue culture as it is less susceptible contamination as compared to large sized explants.

Preparation of explant - A

Explant collection - Explant was collected from Bamborium/ Bambusetum of SFRI, Jabalpur.

Criteria for clump selection :

- Clump should be phenotypically superior
- Clump should be healthy and disease free.
- Number of culms should be more.
- Culm shows maximum branching.

Criteria for explant selection (collected from mature culms)

- Nodal part having unsprouted bud was taken as explant.
- Nodal part should be free from dust & contamination.
- The size of explant would be ranging from few mm to few inches.
  - o Explant was UV sterilized for 45 min in laminar air flow cabinet.
  - o Washing of explant was performed 3-4 times with sterilized double distilled water.
  - o Explant was treated with 0.1% $HgCl_2$ for 8-12 min. for surface sterilization and again washed with sterilized double distilled water (3-4 times).

Inoculation

- o Fresh culturing : The treated explant was inoculated in sterilized medium test tubes and sealed with cellophan tape and inoculation date and accession number was marked. This procedure was performed under aseptic condition in Laminar Air Flow cabinet.
- o Subculturing : The *in-vitro* grown shoots explants were cut above (transverse cutting) and below (slant cutting) nodal region and transferred in sterilized medium (in bottles) for further growth.
- o Maintenance of culture : Inoculated culture vessels were transferred to the culture rocks for growth (at 16 hrs. of photoperiod and 8 hours dark at 25 + 2°C temperature).

o Observation :

- Cultures were timely observed for growth and contamination.
- Contaminated cultures were immediately removed.

Preparation of explant : B

Explant collection : Explant was collected from bamborium / bambusetum of SFRI ,Jabalpur. The plant was tissue cultured , which was recently flowered in Dec 08- Jan 09.

Criteria for seed selection : Seed should be healthy and disease free.

Treatment of explant during inoculation (under aseptic condition)

o Explant was UV – sterilized for 45 min in Laminar Air Flow cabinet.

o Washing of explant (seeds) was performed 3-4 times with sterilized double distilled water.

o Explant was treated with 0.1% $HgCl_2$ for 5-10 min for surface sterilization and again washed with sterilized double distilled water (3-4 times).

Inoculation

o Fresh culturing : The treated explant was inoculated in sterilized medium test tubes and sealed with cellophan tap and inoculation date & accession number was marked. This procedure was performed under aseptic condition in Laminar Air Flow cabinet.

o Sub culturing : Seeds were removed from *in-vitro* grown plants and transferred in sterilized medium (in bottles) for further growth.

- Maintenance of culture : Inoculated culture vessels were transferred to the culture racks for growth (at 16-18 hrs. of photoperiod and 6-8 hrs. dark at 25 + 2°C temperature).
- Observation :

- o Cultures were timely observed for growth and contamination.
- o Contaminated culture was immediately removed

PREPARATION OF SAMPLE FOR HPLC :-

Procedure : Soxhlet process

- o Collect the material and wash them.
- o Keep for 15-25 days for drying.
- o Take 2 gm. of dried powdered material.
- o Perform solubility test.
- o Refluxing in soxhlet apparatus for 8 hrs.
- o Sample should be concentrated and recovery of solvent by rotary vapor.
- o Then undergo for purification.

Dipping process :

- o Take the 2 gm. of sample.
- o Dipped into 150 ml. of acetonitrile (solvent).
- o Kept in conical flask into water bath for 8 hrs.
- o Filter the sample by Whatt's man filter paper.
- o Heat (again left for 8 hrs.).
- o Load the collected sample in rotary vapor.
- o Solvent was extracted out.
- o Then undergo for purification.

Purification process :

1. Collect the concentrated sample and treat with equal amount of hexane times.
2. Use pellet as a sample and add equal amount of 3% HCl mix properly and filter it.
3. Take supernatant as a sample and adjust the pH 7-7.2 with the help of 10% NH_3.
4. Filter it and treat with chloroform (3 times).

5. Take the supernatant as a sample and add 1 gm. of sodium sulphate and dissolve it.
6. Test with dragondroff's reagent for alkaloid sample is filtered through Millipore suction filter.
7. Take 5 ml solution for injection into HPLC.
8. Sample injected into HPLC system through injector and loaded peak is obtained after retention time.

Precautions :

1. Flushing : To cleanup column flushing is required for this run the solvent for at least half an hour, when switch on the unit and half an hour before switch off the unit.

4

The Hydraulic Limitation Hypothesis

Foresters have known for a long time that as trees mature their growth reaches a peak, at which point further increases in height and diameter begin to decrease (Smith et al., 1997; Bond-Lamberty et al., 2004; Litvak et al., 2003). It has also been noted that in very old trees of species such as Douglas-fir and coastal redwoods, height growth is significantly reduced when compared to shorter trees of the same species (McDowell et al., 2002a, Koch et al., 2004). There are several possible reasons why forest growth and tree height in particular would begin to decline as trees get older and taller. One possibility is that larger trees have larger respiratory demands leaving less carbon available for growth (Ryan and Yoder, 1997). However, Ryan and Waring (1992) found that maintenance respiration of woody tissues was only slightly and insignificantly higher in a 245 yr old lodgepole pine (*Pinus contorta*) stand compared to a 40 yr old stand. Another possibility is that as trees get taller, they also become older and that growth is reduced in older tissues relative to younger ones.

However, a study done by Mencuccini et al. (2005) found that when shoots from the tops of old ash (*Fraxinus excelsior*), sycamore (*Acer pseudoplatanus*), poplar (*Populus* sp.), and Scots pine (*Pinus sylvestris*) trees were grafted onto young rootstock, their relative growth rates and net photosynthetic rates recovered to values similar to that of younger, smaller trees. It is also possible that limitations in phloem loading at the tops of tall trees and phloem transport across long distances may limit height growth in trees (Koch and Fredeen, 2005; Zimmermann, 1973). Another possibility is that as trees grow taller, the mechanical stresses on the stem increase, making trees more susceptible to uprooting and wind damage. Meng et al. (2006) found some evidence for this by tethering tall lodgepole pines to reduce their bending moment. They found that six years of tethering resulted in a 40% increase in height growth relative to the previous period when the trees were not tethered.

With experimental evidence disproving many of these previous hypotheses, the hydraulic limitation hypothesis remains as a viable explanation for height growth rates declines in very tall trees (Ryan and Yoder, 1997, Koch et al., 2004). Hydraulic limitations could begin to impact taller trees because, as trees grow in height, the gravitational potential increases as well as the path length of water travel. This means that taller trees are, by virtue, less efficient at transporting water to their leaves relative to shorter trees. In order to overcome this inefficiency, taller trees require a more negative leaf water potential to move the same quantity of water as shorter trees. Since trees of a given species also tend to exhibit representative minimum leaf water potentials in order to protect their water conducting conduits, the tallest trees of a given species will reach their minimum leaf water potential sooner than shorter trees, causing stomatal closure, and reduced photosynthesis and carbon gain (Ryan and Yoder, 1997). This phenomenon is thought to then act as a negative feedback on further height growth in very tall trees and would tend to set characteristic maximum heights for given tree species growing in given environmental conditions.

Since its proposal, several studies have found evidence in support of the hydraulic limitation hypothesis. For example, in a study of European beech (*Fagus sylvatica*), Schäfer et al. (2000) found that at similar environmental conditions, stomatal conductance, and in turn, the amount of carbon dioxide available in the leaf for photosynthesis was decreased by 60% for a given 30m increase in tree height. Ryan et al. (2000) found that water flux and whole tree stomatal conductance was half as much in

36m tall ponderosa pines (*Pinus ponderosa*) as in 12m tall trees. Additionally, Hubbard et al. (1999) found that old ponderosa pines had 53% lower whole tree sapflow per unit leaf area than younger trees. In maritime pines (*Pinus pinaster*), Phillips et al. (2003a) found that not only did taller Oregon white oaks (*Quercus garryana*) have decreased sapflux compared to shorter trees, but they also had more leaf area for a given sapwood area, compounding the effects of hydraulic limitation to carbon gain. Another consequence of the hydraulic limitation hypothesis may also include decreased turgor pressure at the tops of tall trees which could limit cell expansion unless osmotic adjustment occurs (Koch et al., 2004; Woodruff et al., 2004; Meinzer et al., 2008). Decreased turgor represents another way in which height growth could be limited in tall trees because, although not affecting stomatal conductance, decreases in total leaf area will reduce carbon gain by decreasing the area of leaf tissue available for photosynthesis. If osmotic adjustment does occur to maintain turgor, this represents an additional carbon requirement in tall trees relative to shorter ones.

Although hydraulic limitation seems reasonable given the physical laws of water transport in tall trees, there are also data which seem to contradict or a least complicate this issue. For example, in their study of old-growth Douglas-fir trees, McDowell et al. (2002a) found that stomatal conductance, photosynthetic assimilation and leaf-specific hydraulic conductance were not significantly different among trees of different heights and Barnard and Ryan (2003) also found that taller Eucalyptus trees had similar photosynthetic assimilation, sapflux per unit leaf area and whole tree stomatal conductance than their shorter counterparts. Additionally, West et al. (1999) propose that if conduits taper sufficiently, hydraulic resistance can become independent of path length, because hydraulic resistance is inversely proportional to the fourth power of conduit radius, but only linearly related to length (Becker et al., 2000, Zimmermann, 1983).

Tall trees can also make alterations to their anatomy and physiology in order to alleviate some of the affects of hydraulic limitations on photosynthesis and carbon gain. One way in which taller trees can move as much water as their shorter counterparts is by increasing the tension the water is under and exhibiting more negative leaf water potentials. In fact, both Barnard and Ryan (2003) and McDowell et al. (2002a) saw this adjustment in leaf water potential made in the trees they studied. According to the hydraulic limitation hypothesis, taller trees should not exhibit more negative water potentials (Ryan and Yoder, 1997) because more negative water potentials increase the risk of disfunction of the water conducting vessels or tracheids in terms of embolism formation(Zimmermann, 1983). Embolisms occur when air is pulled into a water conducting conduit that is under a large negative pressure (the air-seeding hypothesis) or when the water column itself freezes in the vascular tissues of plants (freeze-thaw embolism) (Zimmermann, 1983; Tyree and Sperry, 1989). These embolism events reduce conductivity (Zimmermann, 1983) and cause reductions in transpiration and photosynthesis (Sperry et al., 1993; Hubbard et al., 2001). However, taller trees could sustain more negative water potentials if they construct conduits that are more resistant to embolism formation. This phenomenon was seen in old growth Douglas-fir trees by Woodruff et al. (2007) and Domec et al. (2008).

There is some contradictory information about whether the conductivity in taller trees will increase to offset the path length and gravitational effect, or decrease as a result of increased resistance to embolisms. Increases of sapwood conductivity with height have been seen in several studies of conifer trees (Pothier et al., 1989; Domec and Gartner, 2003; Burgess et al., 2006). However, it is generally assumed that there is a tradeoff between conductivity and embolism resistance. This trade-off is described for vessels by Hacke et al. (2006) in that vessels with smaller pit pore areas are more embolism resistant but limited in length and diameter, leading to lower conductances. One way that tall trees could sustain more negative water potentials than shorter trees, but avoid any tradeoffs between embolism resistance and conductivity may be efficient refilling of conduits that embolize. Recent study has shown that trees may be able to reverse embolisms that have formed in their conduits, in many cases while the leaves are still transpiring and the water column is still under tension (Zwieniecki and Holbrook, (1998; Bucci et al., 2003; Stiller et al., 2005).

Tall trees can also make biometric adjustments in leaf area to bole area ratios in order decrease the water demanding to water supply area and increase their capacity for bole water storage. Leaf area to sapwood area ratios have generally been found to decrease as trees grow taller (Schäfer et al., 2000; Phillips et al., 2001; Sterck and Bongers, 2001; McDowell et al., 2002b; Barnard and Ryan, 2003). However, the DESPOT model which optimizes carbon gain in trees predicts that leaf area to sapwood area ratios should increase with tree height (Buckley and Roberts, 2006). Even though lowering leaf area for a given sapwood area can alleviate restrictions on stomatal conductance in tall trees, this can still be considered a "hydraulic" limitation because taller trees would need to put more of a carbon investment into water conducting tissues over leaf tissue serving to further limit their carbon gain ability (Phillips et al. 2003a). Taller trees have also been shown to have a greater reliance on stored water in their boles than shorter trees (Goldstein et al., 1998; Phillips et al., 2003b). However, Meinzer et al. (2004) found that although larger tropical trees had greater use of stored water, they also had greater daily water use than smaller trees. Therefore, the contribution of stored water to daily water use was equivalent across tree size.

It is obvious that trees are very complex organisms and the study of physiological phenomena can be difficult. With regard to validating the hydraulic limitation hypothesis, the complicated branching patterns of many species mean that each leaf on the tree will have a different path length from the ground. Additionally, the hydraulic architecture of many trees is designed in such a way that branches receiving more sunlight are hydraulically favored over lower branches (Protz et al., 2000). Much of this complexity could be avoided by focusing on tree species that have a much simpler form. Palms have all the criteria to make them a model organism because, compared to other tree species, they are structurally, very simple with a relatively fixed crown size and vascular system (Zimmermann et al., 1982; Tomlinson, 1987). In particular, palms are a good tree form to use because unlike most trees, palms lack complex branching patterns making the path length of water flow easily measurable. In addition, their small, compact crowns allow for a very accurate estimate of leaf area.

DISTINCTIVE PHYSIOLOGICAL FEATURES OF PALMS

Palms are very distinctive members of the plant world in many ways. They are one of the few members of the monocot class that are able to reach significant heights with the tallest palm species (*Ceroxylon quinduiense*) reaching 60m in height (Henderson et al., 1995). In doing so, they are able to transport water very long distances, matching many dicotyledonous species. However as monocots, palms lack a vascular cambium and therefore do not have any secondary woody growth for vascular transport. All vascular transport and mechanical support is accomplished through thousands of vascular bundles which are comprised of primary xylem vessels, phloem sieve tube cells and fibers. This makes the boles of palms very heterogenous in nature where they have been shown to encompass an entire range of published wood density values within a single stem (Rich, 1987b). Although the crowns of palms are very simple compared with many other tree species, they are unique in many ways. One important difference between palms and dicotyledonous trees is that vertical growth in palms is directly tied to leaf production by the apical meristem (Rich, 1986). Palm leaves are extraordinary within the plant world holding records for both the longest pinnate self-supporting leaf in *Raphia regalis* Becc. at 25m as well as the largest palmately compound self-supporting leaf in *Corypha umbraculifera* L. at 8m in leaf diameter (Tomlinson, 2006). Also, because tall palms generally hold between 5 and 30 palm fronds depending on the species, study of just one frond can represent up to 1/5 of the total photosynthetic area of the individual.

Another important difference between palms and dicotyledonous trees is that palms lack dormancy mechanisms and without secondary growth mechanisms, are largely excluded from habitats exhibiting extensive freezing temperatures (Tomlinson, 2006). Species of palms can be found growing in a wide range of biomes from tropical montane regions to dry forests to savannas and desert oases (Tomlinson, 2006). However the majority of palm species (about 75%) are found growing in rainforests biomes (Dransfield, 1978). Although a large proportion of palms grow in tropical rainforests, they are still exemplary of the flexibility of this plant group, as they can occupy a wide range of niches from shaded understories to dominant canopies (Dransfield, 1978), many times within the life cycle of a single individual. Many species of palms including *Mauritia flexuosa* dominate perpetually inundated sites making aerial roots in order to withstand the anoxic soil conditions (Tomlinson, 1979).

Although palm trees lack dormancy mechanisms and continue apical growth thoughout their lifetimes, many species have been found to exhibit maximum heights. Waterhouse et al. (1978) found that *Archontophoenix cunninghamiana* palms seemed to reach maximum heights of between 23 to 25 meters but ascribed this to possible biomechanical senescence. Zimmermann (1973) also observed that palms seem to reach maximum heights, but hypothesized that these were limited by mechanical rather than hydraulic costs, because tall palms tended to be broken off or uprooted as opposed to exhibiting wilting leaves. Indeed, Rich et al. (1986) report that palms at their maximum height have a lower margin of safety against mechanical failure than shorter palms.

Younger palms are also overbuilt for mechanical safety with respect to diameter while older palms are underbuilt with respect to diameter when compared to both younger palms and with angiosperm and conifer species (Rich, 1987a). However, instead of exhibiting large increases in diameter, palms increase the stiffness and strength of their stem tissues in order to make themselves more mechanically stable (Rich, 1987a). The upper region of palm stems also becomes increasingly flexible (Rich, 1987a) and the crown becomes narrower (Rich et al., 1986) in order to make tall palms less susceptible to wind damage.

However, Gale and Barfod (1999) found that many *Iriartea deltoidea* palms (47%) died standing, while 45% died from being snapped and 8% were uprooted (although all of the palms that were snapped or uprooted were pushed over by other trees).

Palms also appear to exhibit decreases in height growth as they get older/taller. Homeier et al. (2002) found that *Iriartea deltoidea* reaches its maximum height growth rates at about 10-12m when the palm reaches reproductive age, at which point vertical growth rates decrease. Lugo and Rivera Batlle (1987) also found that dominant *Prestoea montana* palms grew fast in height when they are small, but height growth slowed once they reached the canopy. Palms also provide a unique opportunity to study vulnerability to embolism and embolism repair because they lack the capacity to make new conducting tissues. Therefore, their vascular conduits either need to efficiently avoid embolisms or efficiently reverse embolisms that were to occur in their vascular tissues if they are to remain functional over a lifetime. Few studies have looked at the rate of embolism formation and reversal in palm species. A study done by Drake and Franks (2003) found that vascular conductivity was significantly decreased in the dry season compared to the wet season in two species of *Calamus*, a rattan in the Palmae.

A study done by Sperry (1986) on *Rhapis excelsa*, found that large tensions were required to induce xylem embolisms and when embolisms did occur, they were confined to conduits in the petiole with conduits in the bole remaining intact. Bole conduits were protected by the hydraulic architecture of the palm, with most of the resistance to water flow located at the stem to leaf connection and in the leaf itself (Sperry, 1985). If embolisms do occur in palms, then some mechanism of refilling would be necessary, given that palms cannot replace embolized vessels. It also seems plausible that the phloem tissue could be involved in vessel refilling because of its proximity to the xylem vessels in the vascular bundle.

Phloem carries sugars from their origins to locations throughout the plant. When sugars transported through the phloem exit, the osmotic potential of the phloem drops and the surplus water that originally transported the sugars also exits and is recycled by the xylem (Milburn, 1996; Patrick et al., 2001). This surplus phloem water makes up 1 to 3% of xylem transport and could make up much of the water used to refill embolized vessels (Milburn, 1996). Measurements of xylem tensions and changes in phloem turgor suggest that there is a close association of radial water movement from the phloem to the xylem (Sovonick-Dunford et al., 1981). Several studies have found that inactivating the phloem by girdling significantly impairs embolism repair (Salleo et al., 1996; Zwieniecki et al., 2000; Salleo et al., 2004).

DISSERTATION STRUCTURE

Chapter 2 describes a test of the hydraulic limitation hypothesis in *Washingtonia robusta* palms growing in Southern California. Relationships of sapflux per unit leaf area, stomatal conductance, maximum photosynthetic rates, leaf water potentials, stomatal densities, guard cell lengths, leaf dry mass per unit area were evaluated with palm height to determine whether photosynthesis in taller palms was more hydraulically limited. As well bole water storage and leaf epidermal cell sizes, and total leaf areas were compared in palms of differing heights to determine whether any physiological compensations were occurring to overcome hydraulic limitations.

Chapter 3 describes a study comparing wet season and dry season transpiration in a tropical rainforest palm, *Iriartea deltoidea*. Atmospheric data, soil moisture data and sapfluxes were compared in order to determine if transpiration was more stomatally limited in the dry season compared to the wet season and if so, was that driven more by atmospheric vapor pressure deficits or soil moisture availability. Additionally, based on published tree abundances in this area, measured sap fluxes in *Iriartea deltoidea* were scaled up to the hectare level.

Chapter 4 tests the hydraulic limitation hypothesis in two species of tropical rainforest palms, *Iriartea deltoidea* and *Mauritia flexuosa*. Height growth rates, sapfluxes per unit leaf area and total leaf areas were compared within species across palms of differing heights to determine if hydraulic limitations were occurring. Additionally, physiological comparisons were made between *Iriartea deltoidea* and *Mauritia flexuosa* because all though they experience similar atmospheric conditions, they differ markedly in edaphic conditions (terra firme vs swamp), leaf type (pinnate vs. palmate) and ontogenetic bole development. This comparison led to speculation as to whether sustained stem lengthening can occur in *Iriartea deltoidea*.

Chapter 5 focuses specifically on comparing the hydraulic characteristics of petioles from these three palm species (*Washingtonia robusta, Iriartea deltoidea* and *Mauritia flexuosa*) across an ontogenetic gradient as well as across an atmospheric moisture gradient. Comparison of leaf area to conducting area ratios, petiole conductivity, anatomic properties, and vulnerability to embolism shed light on any hydraulic compensations to increased height that were occurring at the petiole level. As well, comparison of P_{50} values (point at which 50% of hydraulic conductivity is lost) with measurements of midday leaf water potentials, as well as a double-dye staining experiment, allowed for estimation of the magnitude of daily embolism formation in these palm petioles. This led to speculation about whether palms avoid embolisms through tight stomatal control, or refill embolisms that occur on a daily basis.

5

Comparative Hydraulic and Anatomic Properties in Palm Trees

INTRODUCTION

It has been frequently observed that as trees mature, height growth reaches a peak, at which point rates begin to decrease (Barnes et al. 1998; McDowell et al. 2002a; Litvak et al. 2003; Bond-Lamberty et al. 2004; Koch et al. 2004). There have been several proposed hypotheses regarding forest growth decline and, in particular, why tree height growth may begin to decline as trees get older and taller, including increased respiration (Ryan and Waring, 1992), differences in the vigor of older tissues relative to younger ones (Mencuccini et al. 2005; Bond et al. 2007; Vanderklein et al. 2007) and increased mechanical stresses (Meng et al. 2006).

However, there are several promising studies that suggest that hydraulic limitation may not only explain why height growth in tall trees is limited (Ryan and Yoder 1997) but could be used to predict maximum heights of a given tree species growing under given environmental conditions (Koch et al. 2004; Burgess and Dawson 2007).

The hydraulic limitation hypothesis is built upon the idea that as trees get taller, not only does the hydrostatic gradient due to gravity increase, but the path length of water travel increases, with taller trees overcoming more friction in water transport than shorter trees.

This means that taller trees are, by virtue of their height, less efficient at transporting water to their leaves relative to shorter trees. This lower efficiency could lead to lower stomatal conductance and, therefore, reduced photosynthesis and carbon gain (Ryan and Yoder 1997). Additionally, the turgor pressure at the tops of these trees will decrease, unless osmotic adjustment occurs, making cell expansion more difficult in developing leaves (Koch et al. 2004; Woodruff et al. 2004). Decreased turgor at the tops of the largest palms could therefore lead to decreases in leaf cell sizes and increases in leaf mass per unit area (LMA).

Studies in species ranging from ponderosa pine (*Pinus ponderosa* Dougl. ex C. Lawson) (Hubbard et al. 1999; Ryan et al. 2000), European beech (*Fagus sylvatica* L.)(Schäfer et al. 2000), eucalyptus (*Eucalyptus saligna* Sm.) (Barnard and Ryan 2003), Oregon white oak (*Quercus garryana* Dougl.) (Phillips et al. 2003a) and the tallest trees in the world, coastal redwoods (*Sequoia sempervirens* (D. Don) Endl.) (Koch et al. 2004) have found evidence that the hydraulic cost of increased frictional resistance reduced stomatal conductance in tall trees relative to shorter ones (reviewed in Ryan et al. 2006).

However, there are other studies that suggest that the hydraulic costs that taller trees face can be offset by alterations in their architecture (Becker et al. 2000a). Also, theoretical models (West et al. 1999; Becker et al. 2000b) as well as empirical measurements show that hydraulic resistance due to path length can be significantly reduced (Weitz et al. 2006, Coomes et al. 2007), but in very tall trees not completely overcome (Anfodillo et al. 2006; Petit et al. 2008), by the tapering of vascular conduits along the length of trees. However, these compensatory features of taller trees are, in fact, consistent with the presence of hydraulic constraints to water transport in taller trees.

About 60 to 70% of studies that have measured one or more of the components of the hydraulic limitation hypothesis have found results that were consistent (Ryan et al. 2006), although several studies have provided some contradictory data (McDowell et al. 2002a; Barnard and Ryan 2003). One reason for the conflicting information could be the complexity of most tree systems. Their complicated branching patterns mean that each leaf on the tree will have a different path length from the ground. Also, the hydraulic architecture has been shown to be designed in such a way that branches receiving more sunlight are hydraulically favored over lower branches (Protz et al. 2000). Much of this complexity could be avoided if a simpler tree species such as palms were used to study hydraulic limitation. Palms represent a desirable tree form to use because, unlike most trees, they lack complex branching patterns and exhibit relatively fixed crown sizes (Zimmermann et al. 1982; Tomlinson 1990) making the path length of water flow as well as leaf area easily measurable.

Additionally, hydraulic limitations in palms become especially important considering they lack secondary growth and may exhibit decreased functioning of xylem and phloem tissues with age (Zimmermann, 1973). This is especially relevant for a palm species such as *Washingtonia robusta* where older, taller palms are likely to have experienced more frost episodes over their lifetime than younger, shorter palms and may not be able to refill embolized conduits (Sperry, 1986). If vessels are able to refill, multiple freeze-thaw episodes have been shown to negatively affect the functioning of xylem tissues through cavitation fatigue, which may or may not be reversible (Hacke et al. 2001; Stiller and Sperry, 2002).

We studied hydraulic limitation in Mexican fan palms, *Washingtonia robusta* (H. Wendl.), a species that is naturally distributed throughout southern and central Baja California and western Sonora, Mexico along streams and canyons or near springs (Uhl and Dransfield 1987; Bullock and Heath 2006). Bullock and Heath (2006) studied *Washingtonia robusta* in the Baja California desert and estimate that they reach reproductive maturation at approximately 8 m tall with the tallest palms in their study being 32 m. They also estimate the potential longevity of these palms to exceed 500 years.

We hypothesize that hydraulic constraints on leaf gas exchange will increase with height in *Washingtonia robusta* with taller palms having lower sap flux per unit leaf area and lower stomatal conductance than shorter palms. Additionally, we are interested in any alterations in physiology or hydraulic architecture that tall palms exhibit in order to compensate for an increased path length of water flow relative to shorter palms; including changes in minimum leaf water potential, maximum photosynthetic rates, and leaf area to conducting area ratios. Not only could this research shed light on the physiological costs of increasing size in palms, but, because the biophysical variables we studied are also shared by woody plants, it may shed light on the physiological costs and compensations in tree species, in general, as they grow taller.

MATERIALS AND METHODS

Site Description

This study was performed from July 23 to August 3, 2007 on 10 individuals of *Washingtonia robusta* (H. Wendl.) growing at the Los Angeles County Arboretum & Botanic Garden (34° 8' 29.43"N, 118° 3' 15.15"W) in Arcadia, California. The site contained several open-grown palm individuals scattered throughout a lawn with palms varying in height from 1 m tall to approximately 35 m tall. The site is adjacent to a natural aquifer; therefore, the water table is elevated in this location. Also, the area was sprinkler irrigated approximately three times per week for one to two hours at each interval, and plants, therefore, should not have experienced soil moisture stress during the experimental period.

Measurements of solar radiation were made using a pyranometer (Apogee Instruments, Roseville, CA, USA) located on an open lawn. Diurnal measures of temperature and relative humidity were made using a Campbell Scientific (CS215) temperature and relative humidity sensor (Campbell Scientific Inc., Logan UT, USA) located approximately 5 m above the ground in an exposed area. Atmospheric and radiation data were captured at intervals of 30 sec and logged every 2 min using a CR10X datalogger and an associated AM16/32A multiplexer (Campbell Scientific Inc., Logan, UT, USA). For the 10 day measurement period, daily maximum temperatures ranged from 29 to 34°C and nightly minimum temperature ranged from 17 to 20°C. Daily minimum humidity ranged from 21 to 50% and nightly maximum humidity ranged from 82 to 90%. Daily maximum vapor pressure deficits (VPD) ranged from 2 to 4 kPa. Maximum daily solar radiative flux densities ranged from 850 to 1060 W m^{-2}.

Palm Height Estimation

Palm heights were estimated, with the aid of a tape measure, from the ground to the point at which the lowest leaves of the crown attached to the bole. Tall palms were accessed using a bucket lift. For shorter palms, height was estimated by making a mark on the bole 1 m above the ground, then estimating height by eye based on this mark. Because shorter palms tended to have more leaves, height was measured from the ground to the midpoint of the crown of leaves. The palm reported to be 2 m tall was a juvenile that did not possess a trunk; therefore its height was measured from the top of its leaves to the ground.

Sap Flux Measurement

Sap flux was measured in a total of 10 palms in this study, ranging in height from 2 m to 34 m. Sap flux sensors were distributed as follows: Sap flux sensors were installed in the *boles* of eight palms ranging from 7 m to 34 m tall using 2 cm long Granier heat dissipation sensors (Granier 1987). Sap flux was also measured in the *petioles* in five palms ranging from 2 m tall to 34 m tall, in each of which two sap flux sensors were installed in two separate petioles.

In boles, the leaf bases (if any) were removed from the base of the palm and two sensors were installed on either side of the bole directly beneath the pseudobark, with this position indicated by a color change that was indicative of wet, conductive bole material. An additional sensor was also installed at a depth of 2 cm below the pseudobark, giving a total of three sensors per palm bole. Sensors were connected to a CR10X datalogger and an associated AM16/32A multiplexer that captured data at intervals of 30 sec and logged every 2 min (Campbell Scientific

Inc., Logan, UT, USA). The boles were wrapped with reflective insulation to prevent external temperature fluctuations. Data from outer bole sensors and the 2 cm depth sensor were pooled because statistical analysis indicated that they were not significantly different (p-value = 0.25). Sap flux data (g m^{-2} s^{-1}) were scaled up to the whole tree level by multiplying by the cross-sectional area of the bole minus the area of the pseudobark (approximated to be 1 cm thick) giving sap flux units of kg day^{-1} and then divided by total palm leaf area to give units of kg day^{-1} m^{-2} leaf area. We are assuming that sap flux is more or less constant across the radius of the bole (and indeed we found no significant differences between outer bole and 2 cm depth sensors). This assumption is also validated by work done by Roupsard et al. (2006) who found a constant pattern of sap flux throughout the stem of coconut palms (*Cocos nucifera* L.) up to a 12 cm radius. Likewise, Sellami and Sifaoui (2003) found that the sap flow in date palms (*Phoenix dactylifera* L.) did not differ significantly between the 3 cm and 6 cm depth sensors.

For the petiole sap flux, 1 cm long Granier sensors were only used in the petioles of the 2 m tall palm. All other petioles had 2 cm long Granier sensors. The shape of the petiole cross-section is approximately a semi-circle and sensors were inserted in the flat portion of the petiole (adaxial side). Petioles were then wrapped with reflective insulation to minimize external temperature fluctuations. Sap flux data (g m^{-2} s^{-1}) were scaled-up by multiplying by the cross-sectional area of the petiole, giving sap flux units of kg day^{-1} and then divided by individual frond leaf area to give units of kg day^{-1} m^{-2} leaf area.

Stem water storage was also investigated in order to ascertain contributions of stored water in the bole to overall sap flux. Palms that are more reliant on stored bole water will tend to lag behind palms that have less stored bole water. To evaluate this, diurnal time courses of bole sap fluxes (g m^{-2} s^{-1}) in two short palms (7 m and 8 m) were compared with diurnal time courses of bole sap fluxes (g m^{-2} s^{-1}) in three tall palms (28 m to 34 m) using cross-correlation analysis. In addition, two of the ten palms (8 m and 28 m tall) had simultaneous bole and petiole sap flow data. In these individuals, stem water storage was estimated by pairing diurnal time courses of sap flux made in the bole with that of corresponding petioles using cross-correlation analysis. The time lag corresponding to the maximum degree of correlation between the petiole sap flux and the bole sap flux represented the approximate amount of water storage in the bole of the palm.

Stomatal Conductance and Photosynthesis

Stomatal conductance and photosynthetic assimilation were measured diurnally on five palms ranging from 8 m to 34 m tall using a LiCor 6400 photosynthesis system (Licor, Lincoln, NE, USA) fitted with a red-blue LED light source. Five palms were chosen from among the 10 total palms to span a large range in height of reproductively mature individuals, and to maintain reasonable sampling time intervals throughout the day. Measurements were made over a four day period at intervals of approximately 1.5 h (from approx. 7 am to 5 pm) with a light level of 1500 μmol m^{-2} s^{-1} and a CO_2 level of 400 mmol mol^{-1}.

Two leaf segments from different fronds were measured per palm during each time period. Measurements were taken when both stomatal conductance and photosynthetic assimilation had stabilized. Measurements from the two leaf segments were averaged per time period. Polynomial equations were then fit to the diurnal stomatal conductance and photosynthetic assimilation data and were used to calculate maximum daily stomatal conductance and maximum daily photosynthetic assimilation rate (both calculated by setting the first derivative equal to zero) for each palm measured. With few exceptions, the rankings of maximum photosynthetic assimilation and maximum stomatal conductance across tree height were the same whether values were obtained from the polynomial equations or from the raw data.

Water Potential Measurement

Diurnal measures of leaf water potential were made on five palms ranging from 2 m to 28 m tall using a Scholander type pressure chamber (Soil Moisture Equipment Corp., Santa Barbara,

CA, USA)(Scholander et al. 1965). These individuals were selected from among the ten total palms to cover a large range in palm height but to maintain a manageable diurnal sampling schedule. Leaf water potentials were measured over a four day period at intervals of approximately 1.5 h (from approximately 6 am to 5 pm).

Water potential measurements were made by removing two individual segments from the leaf. Leaf segments were immediately placed in a plastic bag and covered in order to promote stomatal closure and prevent further leaf dehydration. An approximately 1 cm length of leaf tissue was removed from either side of the midrib, and the remainder of the segment was placed in the pressure chamber with the midrib exposed to the outside environment.

Measurements from the two leaf segments were averaged to give one measurement per palm at a given time period. Polynomial equations were then fit to the diurnal leaf water potential data and were used to calculate minimum leaf water potential and the time of minimum leaf water potential (both calculated by setting the first derivative equal to zero) for each palm. The rankings of minimum leaf water potential across tree height were the same whether values were obtained from the polynomial equations or from the raw data.

Leaf Characteristics

Leaf areas were estimated for the same two leaves used to measure petiole sap flux in four of the ten study palms ranging from 8 m to 34 m tall. These palms represented a range of heights and could be accessed using the bucket lift or ladder. Leaves were harvested after sap flux measurement had been completed and an overhead digital photo was taken of each leaf with a known scaling factor. Image analysis software (Image J, Scion Image, Frederick, MD, USA) was then used to measure leaf area. Measurements of the two leaves were pooled to give an average leaf area for each palm. In order to measure leaf dry mass per unit area (LMA), three leaf segments from each leaf were removed and their individual areas measured. These leaf segments were allowed to air dry for one week, then their dry weight was obtained. Additionally, live leaf counts were made on each individual.

Leaf epidermal cell sizes, stomatal density and guard cell length were measured by making hand sections of leaf material. To begin, individual leaf segments were gathered from palms 2 m to 34 m tall, and then thin sections were cut with a razor blade from the adaxial side of two individual leaf segments tangential to the midrib. Sections were then stained with a solution of 1% Toluidine Blue O and mounted on slides using Permount. The slides were viewed at 200X magnification using a compound light microscope (Nikon Alphaphot-2, Melville, NY, USA) and photographs were taken with digital camera (Fuji FinePix F700 Valhalla, NY, USA). These photographs were imported into image analysis software (Image J, Scion Image, Frederick, MD, USA) for measurement. Leaf epidermal cell areas were measured by tracing around the perimeter of approximately 20 to 30 cells per photograph and calculating the area of this traced section.

Approximately 2 to 5 photographs per palm were used for this measurement giving a total of approximately 50 to 150 cells measured per palm. Stomatal densities were calculated by counting the number of stomata within a field of view, then calculating the area of that field of view. Approximately 15 to 20 different fields of view were used per palm. Guard cell lengths were calculated by measuring the distance between the two points where the guard cells meet. Approximately 50 and 100 stomata were measured per palm in order to calculate average guard cell length.

Statistical Analyses

Means, standard errors and Tukey HSD tests were calculated using JMP 7.0 statistical software (SAS Institute, Cary, NC, USA). All linear and polynomial regressions were fitted using SigmaPlot 2000 Version 6.1 (SPSS Inc. Chicago, IL, USA) software. R^2 and p-values for all regressions were also calculated using SigmaPlot 2000.

RESULTS

Palms were found to range in height from 2 m tall to 34 m tall. Due to its significant lean, the crown of one of the palms reported to be 34 m tall was only 27 m about the ground. However, because hydraulic limitation is concerned with friction imposed on water travel as well as hydrostatic gradients in water potential, trunk length is as important in this study as actual crown height above the ground. All other palms did not possess a significant lean. The palm reported to be 2 m tall was a juvenile that did not possess a trunk therefore, because this individual differed so greatly in development from the other individuals, only petiole sap flux, water potentials and leaf epidermal cell areas were compared with taller palms, and only to make limited inferences (in discussion).

Representative diurnal time courses of bole sap flux (g m^{-2} s^{-1}) in palms ranging in height from 7 m to 34 m tall are presented with corresponding VPD and solar radiation time data. Daily minimums, maximums, means and standard errors for the palms studied are presented in Table 2.3. There is a slight positive relationship between palm height and daily bole sap flux per unit leaf area ($p=0.06$, $r^2 = 0.46$) due to the decrease in leaf area with increases in palm height, but no relationship between palm height and daily petiolar sap flux per unit leaf area (Fig 2.2b; p-value= 0.54). Variability in *Washingtonia robusta* sap flux both within and between palms was considerable with bole sap flux per unit leaf area differing by up to a factor of about 3 and petiole sap flux per unit leaf area differing by almost a factor of about 6. Roupsard et al. (2006) also found large variability in coconut palms with sap flow varying by up to a factor of 3 between palms.

Investigation of stem water storage using between-palm cross-correlation analysis indicated that bole sap flux in large palms lagged behind bole sap flux of small palms by 30 min (n= 4 palms; maximum $r^2 = 0.68$). Similarly, within-palm cross-correlation analysis indicated a larger petiole-bole time lag in a larger palm (44 min lag in a 28m tall palm; maximum $r^2 = 0.87$) than a shorter palm (28 min lag in an 8 m tall palm; maximum

$r^2 = 0.8$). These lags correspond to approximately 16 and 22% of daily water use respectively according to procedures and assumptions described in Phillips et al (2003b).

Maximum daily stomatal conductance showed no discernable relationship with tree height (p-value = 0.36). Additionally, there was no observable relationship between tree height and either stomatal density (p-value = 0.82) or guard cell length (p-value = 0.86)(data not shown). Maximum daily photosynthetic assimilation rate exhibited a positive linear correlation with tree height (r^2=0.80, p-value=0.041) with taller palms exhibiting higher photosynthetic rates than shorter palms. There was no observable relationship between LMA and tree height (p-value = 0.19) and individuals did not differ significantly from one another.

Minimum leaf water potentials were significantly and non-linearly correlated with tree height (r^2=0.97, p-value=0.0234) with taller palms generally having more negative minimum leaf water potentials than shorter palms; although the slope of the curve decreases with increasing height. Also, the time of minimum leaf water potential was negatively correlated with tree height (r^2=0.61, p-value=0.12) with taller palms reaching a minimum leaf water potential earlier in the day than shorter palms. Because all individuals were open grown, it is unlikely that differences in the timing of minimum leaf water potential were the result of differences in solar radiation throughout the day. The earliest minimum leaf water potential (in the tallest palm) was reached at approximately 13:42 PDT and the latest minimum leaf water potential (in the shortest palm) was reached at 16:36 PDT (mean = 14:42 PDT, SE = 29 min). Although the 2 m tall palm was still a juvenile and therefore differed developmentally from the other individuals, we feel that comparisons of leaf water potential are still valid.

Leaf areas were significantly and negatively correlated with tree height. Taller palms had fewer leaves (r^2=0.6, p-value=0.026) and leaves with smaller areas (r^2=0.99, p-value = 0.058) than shorter palms; although both of these relationships were non-linear with the slope of the curve decreasing as tree height increased. Leaf epidermal cell sizes were found to remain constant in palms 2 m tall to 22 m tall with Tukey HSD tests confirming that cell sizes in these palms did not differ significantly from one another at a 95% confidence level. On the other hand, leaf epidermal cell sizes in both 28 m tall palms and 34 m tall palms were found to be significantly smaller (p-values < 0.05) than in palms 2 m to 22 m tall. Additionally, leaf epidermal cells from the 34 m tall palm were found to be significantly smaller than cells from the 28 m tall palm (p-value < 0.001).

DISCUSSION

The hydraulic limitation hypothesis states that as trees grow taller, greater friction to water flow causes taller trees to reach minimum leaf water potentials sooner in the day than shorter trees causing stomatal closure that decreases carbon gain (Yoder et al. 1994; Ryan and Yoder 1997). However, *Washingtonia robusta* palms showed no discernable decrease in daily bole sap flux per unit leaf area, daily petiolar sap flux per unit leaf area, maximum stomatal conductance, stomatal densities or stomatal sizes with an increase in tree height suggest that taller palms are not experiencing the effects of hydraulic limitation. Barnard and Ryan (2003) also found that taller *Eucalyptus* trees had similar sap flux per unit leaf area and whole tree stomatal conductance compared to their shorter counterparts. McDowell et al. (2002a) found similar results in old-growth Douglas-fir trees, in that stomatal conductance, photosynthetic assimilation and leaf-specific hydraulic conductance were not significantly different among trees of different heights.

Although hydraulic limitation was not observed in *Washingtonia robusta* in terms of lower stomatal conductance in taller palms, we found several alterations in physiology with height including decreasing leaf area, decreasing leaf cell sizes and more negative midday leaf water potentials suggesting that tall palms face, and in turn compensate for, some degree of hydraulic path length constraint. For example, taller palms reached a minimum leaf water potential sooner in the day than shorter palms. Because all individuals were open grown, it is unlikely that differences in the timing of minimum leaf water potential were the result of differences in solar radiation throughout the day.

The timing of minimum leaf water potential may have been even more disparate had all palms exhibited the same minimum leaf water potential. However, as with many other studies of trees across a height gradient (McDowell et al. 2002a; Barnard and Ryan 2003; Woodruff et al. 2007), taller palms also exhibited more negative minimum leaf water potentials than shorter trees. It is interesting that taller palms would be able to withstand more negative water potentials than shorter palms and it begs the question; Why don't shorter palms keep their stomata open longer and reach the minimum water potentials that tall palms do? One reason could be that the petiole xylem of taller palms is more resistant to cavitation than petioles of shorter palms. Woodruff et al. (2007) found minimum leaf water potentials were highly correlated with the water potential at which leaves lost hydraulic conductance along a height gradient. Their finding implies that not only do the leaves at the top of tall trees keep their stomata open at more negative leaf water potentials, but stomatal closure could be correlated to a loss of leaf hydraulic conductance.

Lower leaf water potentials were one way in which taller palms compensate for a longer path length of water travel. However, in order to sustain these more negative water potentials, leaf cells in taller trees may have had to increase their osmotic potential in order to maintain turgor (Meinzer et al., 2008). This additional carbon requirement in taller palms could negatively affect increased height growth.

It is also interesting to note that differences in minimum leaf water potential between the 8 m tall palm and the 28 m tall palm are approximately 0.4 MPa, and we would expect the taller palm to exhibit, at minimum, a decrease of 0.2 MPa, simply due to the hydrostatic gradient alone (i.e. if there were zero frictional resistance). Therefore, about half of the difference in leaf water potential between the 8 m tall palm and the 28 m tall palm is a consequence of moving water against gravity with the other half likely resulting from the added friction to the water column given the increased path length.

Another compensation that trees can make to offset hydraulic limitation is to alter their hydraulic architecture so that they have less leaf area for a given unit of sapwood area that needs to be supplied with water. For many palm species including *Washingtonia robusta,* bole diameters remain more or less constant across various heights once their stems reach maximum diameter and begin to elongate vertically. Likewise, palm species do not lose conducting area of their boles through the formation of heartwood. Therefore, any changes in hydraulic architecture in this and many other palm species occur mainly through changes in leaf area. In our study, not only did taller palms have fewer leaves than shorter palms, but the leaves they had were smaller in area.

This is unlikely to be influenced by light environment since all individuals were open-grown. Decreases in leaf area to sapwood area ratios across height has been seen in several other studies (Schäfer et al. 2000; Phillips et al. 2001; McDowell et al. 2002b; Barnard and Ryan 2003), although there are some exceptions to this trend (Phillips et al., 2003a). Specifically, Buckley and Roberts (2006) predict that leaf area to sapwood area ratios should increase with height growth (until height growth tapers off) in order to maximize carbon gain. Of course, these decreases in leaf area may also be the result of a mechanical limitation and not a hydraulic one since a smaller crown would put less strain on the bole than a larger, heavier one.

Not only do taller trees face an increased path length to water flow but the turgor pressures at the tops of these trees will also decrease unless osmotic adjustment occurs (Koch et al. 2004; Woodruff et al. 2004). This decreased turgor pressure could lead to more limited cell expansion at the tops of tall trees relative to shorter ones (Woodruff et al. 2004) and increased LMA (Marshall and Monserud 2003; Koch et al. 2004). However, we found no significant differences in LMA between palms of different heights.

LMA may be consistent across palm height because all palms were open-grown and it has been observed that LMA is affected by light availability (Bond et al. 1999) as well as tree height. We did, however, find that the tallest palms (28 m and 34 m tall) had smaller epidermal cells than shorter palms, potentially due to a decreased turgor pressure in these cells during expansion. It is also interesting to note that although epidermal cells were significantly smaller in taller palms than shorter ones, guard cell sizes showed no pattern of decrease with height. In addition, although taller palms had less leaf area than shorter palms, their leaves increased in photosynthetic capacity, exhibiting higher maximum daily photosynthetic assimilation rates than did those of shorter palms. This higher photosynthetic capacity could offset some of the carbon gain lost by having smaller leaf areas.

Taller palms also appeared to exhibit greater stem water storage, both in cross-correlation analysis of basal bole sap flux between taller and shorter palms and in cross-correlation analysis between petioles and boles and this trend has been seen in other studies as well (Goldstein et al. 1998; Phillips et al. 2003b). Specifically for palms, Holbrook and Sinclair (1992) found that water storage per unit leaf area within the stem increased linearly with palm height in *Sabal palmetto* ((Walt.) Lodd). However, this pattern may not hold true in all palm species with Rich (1987) finding that wet density of the central tissue in *Iriartea gigantea* (H. A. Wendl. ex Burret) palms decreased with individual height and that water content decreased from 90% to 25% by weight in peripheral tissues and from 95% to 90% in the central tissues as tree height increased. For most tree species, increases in stem water storage occur mainly through increases in diameter. However in palms, which exhibit more or less constant bole diameters, increases in stem water storage can still be achieved through increases in height and changes in stem tissue properties.

In summary, although *Washingtonia robusta* palms in this study were some of the tallest known palms of this species in the Los Angeles area, we found no evidence that hydraulic limitation was impacting stomatal conductance, at least on a per unit leaf area basis. There was a large amount of variability in bole and petiole sap flux that could be masking any trends in sap flux with height, however our sap flux data agrees with independently measured stomatal conductance data in finding no negative relationship in stomatal conductance with height. One reason that palms may not exhibit hydraulic limitations with height could be due to their hydraulic architecture.

The bole-frond junction is a point of large resistance because only the small vessels of the protoxylem connect the bole with the frond (Tomlinson, 1990). Because the major point of hydraulic resistance in palms exists at this bole-frond connection, palms may be able to increase the length of their boles without incurring the costs of increased friction normally associated with hydraulic limitation with height (Noel Michele Holbrook, pers. comm.). We did find, however, that taller palms had lower minimum leaf water potentials that occurred earlier in the day than in shorter palms.

Also, taller palms had both fewer, smaller leaves that were more photosynthetically efficient than did shorter palms. Therefore, although carbon gain was not more stomatally limited in taller palms than in shorter palms, they did exhibit lower leaf areas than shorter palms which could limit their overall carbon gain (Phillips et al. 2003a) and therefore limit subsequent increases in height. Alternatively, decreased height growth rates in tall palms could be a response to mechanical limitation.

Palms at their maximum height have been shown to have a lower margin of safety against mechanical failure than both shorter palms as well as angiosperm and conifer species (Rich et al.1986; Rich 1987). Although not studying palm species, Meng et al. (2006) found that by tethering tall lodgepole pines (*Pinus contorta* Dougl.) to reduce their bending movement, the trees increased their height growth by 40% relative to the previous, untethered period. Lower leaf areas in taller palms may, in fact, be a response to mechanical limitation as well as hydraulic limitation with one or both of these factors explaining the decreased height growth rates exhibited by tall *Washingtonia robusta* palms.

6

Wet Versus Dry Season Transpiration in an Amazonian Rainforest Palm

INTRODUCTION

Although not as pronounced as the seasonality in temperate forests, tropical rainforests also exhibit seasonality in precipitation, soil moisture and irradiance. There is, however, some disagreement as to whether the differences in precipitation between wet and dry seasons are enough to affect the physiology of the plants growing there. Carswell *et al.* (2002) found no difference in carbon dioxide exchange between seasons in a tropical rainforest near Pará, Brazil. However, other studies have found that soil water content is lower during the dry season (Bonal *et al.* 2000, Malhi *et al.* 2002, Harris *et al.* 2004) and, in turn, evapotranspiration higher in the wet season. However while the shallow soil layer may dry out, deeper layers remain hydrated year round (da Rocha *et al.* 2004, Nepstad *et al.* 1994).

Even though precipitation is reduced during the dry season, other studies have found that evapotranspiration is actually higher than in the wet season (Carswell *et al.* 2002, da Rocha *et al.* 2004). Evapotranspiration may be greater in the dry season because of the increased irradiance rainforests receive due to reduced cloudiness (Malhi *et al.* 2002). In fact, Saleska *et al.* (2003) found that light limitations due to clouds may be so substantial that net ecosystem carbon is lost during the wet season because of increased soil respiration, but sequestered during the dry season in a tropical forest near Santarém, Brazil. Additionally, Graham *et al.* (2003) found that sap flow was 28 percent greater in branches that were experimentally illuminated on cloudy days compared to controls. Myneni *et al.* (2007) found that seasonal fluctuations of leaf area in Amazonian rainforests were timed with seasonal changes in solar radiation in such a way that net increases in leaf area corresponded with the beginning of the cloud-free, dry season and net leaf losses corresponded with the beginning of the cloudy, wet season.

Climatic and soil moisture differences between the wet and dry season are important because they could potentially determine rates of stomatal conductance in rainforest species, with consequences for both water and carbon cycling. It has been shown that stomata respond to soil moisture availability through the transfer of abscisic acid from the roots to the shoots (Zhang *et al.* 1987, Zhang & Davies 1989, Jones & Sutherland 1991). It has also been shown that humidity and vapor pressure deficit (VPD) affect stomatal conductance (Fanjul & Jones 1982, Meinzer *et al.* 1997) possibly through the alteration of transpiration rate (Franks *et al.* 2007). Stomata may also be sensitive to changes in hydraulic conductance, which can indicate embolisms in the hydraulic pathway (Nardini & Salleo 2000, Domec *et al.* 2006). For example, Sperry *et al.* (1993) and Hubbard *et al.* (2001) found that experimentally decreasing stem hydraulic conductivity reduced stomatal conductance.

This study seeks to determine if differences in sap flux are evident between *Iriartea deltoidea* (Ruíz & Pavón) palms measured in the wet season and the subsequent dry season due to differences in irradiance, evaporative demand and/or soil moisture. Additionally, since published tree species abundances are available, sap fluxes measured in these palms can be scaled up to the hectare level and their contribution to total rainforest transpiration estimated. *Iriartea deltoidea* is an important species to monitor because it is distributed widely over the lowlands of western Amazonia and into Central America (Montufar & Pintaud 2006). *Iriartea deltoidea* is also an important tree for indigenous populations (Macía 2004) as well as many rainforest animal species (Henderson 1990, Beck 2006). The study of an arborescent palm in this context is also important because palms, unlike dicotyledonous trees, lack a vascular cambium and, therefore, cannot produce new vascular tissue. This means that stomata should be especially sensitive in order to prevent embolisms in the irreplaceable conductive tissue (Sperry 1986), which should result in sap flux differences between seasons.

METHODS

SITE LOCATION

This research was conducted at Tiputini Biodiversity Station (0° 36′ S, 76° 27′ W), a 650 ha research facility located within Yasuní National Park in eastern Ecuador. The site receives approximately 2860 mm of rainfall annually and has an average temperature of 25.5°C (Macía 2004). Research was conducted in May and June, 2006 corresponding to the wet season in this part of the Amazon and January and February, 2007 corresponding to the dry season. During the wet season, this site receives about 395 mm of rain per month (May, June, July) and during the dry season about 107 mm per month (December, January, February; data courtesy of Dr. Jaime Guerra). The closed canopy forest reaches about 30 m in height, with numerous tree fall gaps. Small palms within this forest were located in the understory, medium-sized palms were, for the most part, codominant and large palms were dominant trees in the canopy. In a study of species abundance in the Amazonian rainforests of Yasuní National Park in Ecuador and Manu National Park in Peru, *Iriartea deltoidea* was the most common tree species in both sites at between 45 and 49 individuals/ha (Pitman *et al.* 2001).

MICROMETEOROLOGICAL DATA

Air temperature and humidity were measured using a Vaisala HMP45C temperature and relative humidity sensor (Vaisala, Helsinki, Finland) located approximately 20 m above ground and attached to a canopy tower. At this height the sensor was approximately midway between the medium-sized palms and the large palms. This sensor was attached to a Campbell CR-10X datalogger (Campbell Scientific, Logan, Utah, USA) that collected data every 30 min. These data were then used to calculate vapor pressure deficit (VPD, kPa). Values of photosynthetic photon flux density (PPFD, mmol/m^2 sec) were measured using a Li-Cor LI190SB quantum sensor (Licor, Lincoln, Nebraska, USA) located at the top of a 30 m tall tower. This sensor was attached to a Campbell CR-10X datalogger that collected data every 30 min. Photosynthetic radiation data from the first three weeks of the wet season were unrealistically high, and values were rescaled so that the maximum PPFD readings did not exceed 2000 mmol/m^2 sec. After this period, the datalogger program was altered to correct this bias.

SOIL MOISTURE DATA.

In the dry season, soil moisture data were collected by sampling, daily, approximately 10 to 20 g of soil from approximately 5 cm below the soil surface. This region was representative of the upper soil (A-B horizon) profile in terms of bulk density (based on information from the SOTERLAC database; Dijkshoorn *et al.* 2005) with the top 30 cm of soil containing 70% of root biomass in evergreen tropical forests (Jackson *et al.* 1996). These daily soil samples were then weighed, placed in a drying oven for one week at a minimum, and reweighed. Dry-season soil water content was calculated using the following equation:

$$\theta = \frac{(M_{field} - M_{dry}) / \rho_w}{M_{dry} / \rho_T} \tag{1}$$

where è is volumetric soil water content, M_{field} is the fresh mass of the soil, M_{dry} is the dry mass of the soil, r_w is the density of water, and r_T is the bulk density of the soil (0.976, calculated from soil cores). In February 2009, soil cores from the top 6 cm of the soil (below the organic layer) were collected from the site and returned to the lab. Using these cores, soil water release curves were obtained. To begin, samples were saturated fully overnight then put into Tempe Cells (SoilMoisture Equipment Corp. Santa Barbara, CA) and pressures from 2 to 1000 cm were applied. Samples were then placed in a drying oven at 105°C overnight. A soil water release curve was made by plotting the effective saturation, q_E ($q_{saturated}$-$q_{residual}$/q-$q_{residual}$), vs. the applied pressure. A van Genuchten model (van Genuchten 1980) was fitted to the soil water release data based on the following equation:

$$\theta_E = \left[1 + (\alpha[h]^n\right]^{-m} \qquad (2)$$

where a, n and m are curve fitting parameters.

This curve was then used to determine the average soil water potential at our site during the dry-season field campaign. Once parameters a, n and m were estimated, they were then used to calculate relative soil hydraulic conductivity at the measured dry-season soil water potential (K_r) using the following equation (van Genuchten 1980):

$$K_r = \theta_E^{1/2}[1-(1-\theta_E^{1/m})^m]^2 \qquad (3)$$

where m = 1-1/n.

In the wet season, we assumed that the soils were more or less saturated and soil hydraulic conductivity (K) at a maximum, close to saturated condition. Our assumption that wet-season soils were at or near saturation was also supported by our visual observations of apparently saturated soils over the duration of our data collection in the wet season, which was due to a total of 542 mm of rainfall distributed over 60 days of our field campaign (based on TRMM 2b31-Based Rainfall Climatology data courtesy of King's College London).

In order to determine if this dry-season soil moisture could be limiting transpiration in our palms, soil resistance to water flow during the dry season was estimated based on an Ohm's law analogy as follows:

$$J = \frac{\Psi_{soil} - \Psi_{leaf}}{R_{soil} + R_{plant}} \quad (4)$$

where J is peak midday dry-season sapflux, Y_{soil} is soil water potential, Y_{leaf} is minimum leaf water potential (measured during the 2009 dry season at -1.2MPa) and R_{plant} is the resistance to water flow in the palm. In order to calculate R_{plant}, wet-season midday sapflux (J) and minimum leaf water potential (Y_{leaf} = -0.5 MPa) were used to calculate R_{plant} with the assumption that R_{soil} in the wet season is negligible.

Sap Flux Measurement

Sap flux was measured during both the wet season and dry season using one cm long, Granier-style heat dissipation sensors (Granier 1987). Briefly, this methodology works by measuring the amount of heat dissipated by water flow around a heated sensor relative to a reference sensor that are both radially inserted into the tree about 10 cm apart. Sap fluxes are estimated by measuring the difference in temperature between the heated and reference sensor, assuming that, at night, no sap is flowing and the temperature difference is maximal.

Sensors were installed in both the petioles and the boles of three small palms (between 2.3 and 3.2 m tall) and in the boles and stilt roots of four medium-sized palms (between 6.7 and 14.7 m tall) and three large palms (between 30.9 and 32.2 m tall). Before installing sensors into the boles or stilt roots, the outer tissue ("bark") was scraped away until the vascular fibers were just visible. Sampling and biometric information are summarized in Table 3.1. For petioles, sensors were installed in the base slightly above the point where the petiole attaches to the bole. After sensor installation, aluminum insulating wrap was stapled around the sensors to shield them from sun flecks. The heat dissipation sensors were attached to a Campbell CR-10X datalogger and AM-32 multiplexer (Campbell Scientific, Logan, Utah, USA) that collected data every 30 min. The program, Baseliner version 2.4.2 (C-H20 Ecology Group, Duke University,

Durham North Carolina, USA) was used to convert the millivolt signal from the datalogger into sap fluxes (g/ m^2 sec). During the wet season some of the sensors failed, likely due to moisture condensation on equipment. Table 3.1 summarizes the number of functioning sensors from each season that were used for comparisons.

SAP FLUX SENSOR CALIBRATION

Because Granier heat dissipation sensors have been used mainly to measure sap flux in conifer and angiosperm trees, it was important to evaluate these sensors in tissue from *Iriartea deltoidea,* especially considering how different palm "wood" is from dicot wood (Smith and Allen 1996). A calibration was performed in a 0.5 m long, 5 cm in diameter excised piece of bole from a small *Iriartea deltoidea* palm. Both ends of the palm piece were recut using a very sharp razorblade and a heated and reference sensor were installed at approximately the midpoint in length and attached to a CR10X datalogger (Campbell Scientific, Logan, Utah, USA). A rubber fitting was then attached tightly to the top end of the palm piece and placed in a ring stand in order to keep it vertical. About 1 m of pipe (4 cm in diameter) was attached above the palm piece to the other end of the rubber fitting. An electronic balance was placed below the palm piece in order to measure the amount of throughflow. To begin, approximately 50 mL of water was added to the pipe and the mass of water exiting the palm piece was measured every minute. Every ten minutes another 50 mL of water was added until the water level had reached the top of the pipe. In order to achieve a baseline value with no water flow, the palm piece was placed horizontal.

Using these data, a graph was produced with sap flux density through the palm piece on the x axis (u, m^3/ m^2 s $*10^6$) vs. sap flux index (K) on the y axis where:

$$K = \frac{\Delta T(0)}{\Delta T(u)} - 1 \tag{5}$$

where DT(0) represents the temperature difference between the sensors at zero flow and DT(u) represents the temperature difference between the sensors at a given sap flux (u). Because the calibration provided by Granier fits within the 95% confidence interval of the present equation, the Granier equation was used to convert the millivolt signal into sap flux densities.

STATISTICAL AND DATA ANALYSES

All data were plotted and regression lines and 95% confidence intervals calculated using SigmaPlot 2000 Version 6.1 (SPSS Inc. Chicago, IL, USA). Significance tests between wet-season and dry-season data were performed using R version 2.5.1 (The R Foundation for Statistical Computing, http://www.R-project.org.). In order to calculate daily sap flux values, sap flux measured by the sensors were scaled up to the entire cross section of the organ being measured assuming sapflux is constant throughout the cross-section (Roupsard *et al.* 2006, Sellami and Sifaoui 2003). Sap fluxes from individual sensors were scaled up by summing 30 min averaged sap flux readings throughout a day, and multiplying by the respective cross-sectional area. For each palm size category and location, daily values were averaged. In order to compare sap fluxes based on VPD conditions, daily sap flux values were divided by the integral of the daytime VPD curve. This parameter provides a measure of daily conductance, or the daily amount of flow per atmospheric driving force (daily VPD) (Phillips and Oren 1998).

To calculate the contribution of *Iriartea deltoidea* palms to total transpiration, sap flux (kg/d) was scaled up to the hectare level by multiplying by the number of stems per hectare (45; based on Pitman *et al.*, 2001). Since sap flux was not constant with palm height, data from Svenning (1999) was also used to distribute the 45 individuals into height categories. Sap flux (kg/d) was non-linear with height ($r^2 = 0.78$; sap flux = -0.112 + 0.527*height – 0.00844*height^2) and this equation was used to calculate sap fluxes for *Iriartea deltoidea* palms of given heights. These sap fluxes were summed across the 45 individuals distributed across a range of heights yielding total sap flux in m^3 water / d. Dividing by 10,000 m^2 (or 1 ha) provided an estimate of transpiration in mm/ d.

RESULTS

MICROMETEOROLOGICAL DATA

Both average daily maximum and average daily minimum temperatures differed between the wet and dry season. Average daily minimum humidities were higher in the wet season than the dry season. The temperature and humidity data yielded daily vapor pressure deficit (VPD) maximums ranging from 0.2 to 2.2 kPa in the wet season and 0.1 to 3.4 kPa in the dry season. Average daily maximum vapor pressure deficits were lower in the wet season than the dry season. Daily maximum measurements of photosynthetic photon flux density (PPFD) ranged from 156 to 2083 mmol/ m^2 sec in the wet season and from 284 to 2248 mmol/ m^2 sec in the dry season. When PPFD values were integrated over whole days, they yielded averages that were higher in the dry season than the wet season.

SOIL MOISTURE

Volumetric soil water contents during the dry season were found to be around 0.38 which corresponds to an effective saturation (q_E) of about 0.64. Based on the soil water release curve, dry-season soils had a water potential of around -378 cm or -37 kPa. Our soil water release curve also yielded a saturated volumetric water content of 0.60 (SE 0.04) for these soils, and we assume this value during the wet season. At a soil water potential of -37 kPa, soil hydraulic conductivity (K_r) was calculated to be about 33% of that in saturated soils. Soil resistance (R_{soil}) was calculated to represent about one third of the total resistance in the soil to leaf pathway during the dry season, while during the wet season we assume that R_{soil} is negligible.

SENSOR CALIBRATION AND SAP FLUX DATA

The calibration of the Granier heat dissipation sensors in the bole of *Iriartea deltoidea* yielded the following equation:

$$u = 192.3 \times 10^{-6} K^{1.3} \tag{6}$$

where u = sap flux density (m^3/m^2 s) and K = [DT (0)/DT(u)-1]. Our calibration had larger a and b values than the Granier equation (a = 119 x 10^{-6}, b = 1.23) however the Granier equation was within the 95% confidence intervals of our equation.

Both average total daily sap flux and average total daily sap flux per VPD were not significantly different between the wet season and the dry season in the petioles of small palms. Although average total daily sap fluxes did not differ significantly in the wet season vs. the dry season for medium-sized palms, average total daily sap fluxes per VPD were significantly lower in the dry season compared to the wet season. In the stilt roots of tall palms, neither average total daily sap flux nor average total daily sap flux per VPD differed significantly in the wet season compared to the dry season. Although average total daily sap flux did not differ significantly, average total daily sap flux per VPD was significantly lower in the dry season compared to the wet season. When sap fluxes were scaled up to the hectare level, it yielded a transpiration value of 0.03 mm /d for *Iriartea deltoidea* palms.

The average wet-season and dry-season sap flux (g/ m^2 sec) exhibited at given vapor pressure deficit ranges . Sap flux in the petioles of small palms displayed a non-linear, asymptotic relationship (r^2 = 0.53) with VPD in the wet season and an approximately linear relationship (r^2 = 0.86) with VPD in the dry season). For the boles of medium-sized palms, the relationship between sap flux and VPD was approximately linear in the wet season (r^2 = 0.97) but non-linear (r^2 = 0.87) in the dry season with sap flux having a positive, asymptotic relationship with VPD. Sap flux in both the stilt roots and boles of large palms had an approximately linear relationship with VPD in the wet season (r^2 = 0.92 and 0.96 respectively) and a non-linear, asymptotic relationship in the dry season (r^2 =0.78 and 0.96 respectively).

As with VPD, average wet-season and dry-season sap flux (g/ m^2 sec) exhibited at given PPFD ranges are presented. Sap flux in the petioles of small palms displayed a non-linear, asymptotic relationship (r^2 = 0.47) with PPFD in the wet season and an approximately linear relationship (r^2 = 0.95) with PPFD in the dry season similar to the relationships between sap flux and VPD for small palms. For the boles of medium-sized palms, the relationship between sap flux and PPFD was non-linear in the wet season (r^2 = 0.71) and the dry season (r^2 = 0.76) with sap flux having a positive, asymptotic, nearly identical relationship with PPFD in both seasons. Sap flux in both the stilt roots and boles of large palms had a non-linear asymptotic relationship with PPFD in the wet season (r^2 = 0.78 and 0.69 respectively) as well as the dry season (r^2 =0.90 and 0.93 respectively) with curves being very similar in both seasons in both the boles and roots of large palms.

DISCUSSION

Climate was found to differ significantly between the wet and dry season with higher PPFD, higher VPD and lower soil water contents in the dry season and this led to significantly lower daily sap flux per daytime VPD in the dry season compared to the wet season in both medium and large palms. Likewise, sap fluxes in the boles of medium and large palms in the dry season reach an asymptote with increasing VPD that is not seen in the wet season, providing evidence for stomatal closure at larger VPD in the dry season. We saw no differences in the patterns of sap flux with increasing PPFD between seasons, suggesting that the larger VPD in the dry season is causing stomatal closure that overrides any opening that would be induced by high PPFD. Therefore, transpiration and subsequent carbon gain are stomatally limited in the dry season compared to the wet season in *Iriartea deltoidea*. Similar results were found by O'Brien *et al.* (2004) who found sap flux in ten rainforest tree species to reach an asymptote with increases in light and evaporative demand and by Repellin *et al.* (1997) as well as Roupsard *et al.* (2006) who found that stomatal closure was triggered by high vapor pressure deficits even in well-watered plants. Several other studies have found evidence for stomatal closure in coconut (*Cocos nucifera* L.) during the dry season compared to the wet season (Kasturibai *et al.* 1988, Prado *et al.* 2001, Gomes & Prado 2007). However, Fisher *et al.* (2006) found that sap flow was 44 percent higher in the dry season compared to the wet season, but 15 percent lower when rainfall was excluded from plots (presumably the result of soil moisture deficits).

In addition to large vapor pressure deficits, *Iriartea deltoidea* palms may also be closing their stomates in the dry season in response to reduced soil moisture availability. Soil water content during the dry season was found to be approximately 20 percent lower than saturation. This may not always reflect seasonal differences, but based on water release curves for these soils, soil water potential in the dry season was found to be around -37 kPa in the upper soil layers. This alone is unlikely to lead to stomatal closure, however drying soils not only mean lower matric water potentials, but also to increased resistance of water flow to the roots (Pettijohn *et al.* 2009). In the dry season, soil resistance (R_{soil}) was calculated to represent approximately one third of the total resistance of water flow from the soil to leaf pathway whereas during the wet season, it is presumed to be negligible. Similar results were found in a tropical rainforest near Manaus, Brazil where soil to root hydraulic resistance was significantly larger during the dry season (Williams *et al.* 1998).

Additionally, soil hydraulic conductivity in the dry season (K_r) has also been calculated to be about 33% of values during the nearly saturated wet season. It is interesting to note that these two widely differing methods for estimating soil hydraulic resistance were remarkably consistent in terms of predicting significantly greater soil resistance during the dry season. Also, for the dry-season soil water contents seen in this study, the slope of the curve with soil water potential begins to increase dramatically and these large changes in soil water potential with relatively small changes in soil water content may trigger stomatal closure as well. If climate change causes decreased precipitation, soil water content could decrease dramatically with relatively small decreases in soil water content (Phillips *et al.* 2001).

Given the principles of the hydraulic limitation hypothesis

(Ryan & Yoder 1997), it may be expected that the larger palms would be more adversely affected by high VPD in the dry season and exhibit greater stomatal closure than smaller trees. Several studies have found that taller trees exhibit reduced stomatal conductance relative to shorter trees in similar environmental conditions (Andrade *et al.* 1998, Ryan *et al.* 2000, Schäfer *et al.* 2000). Consistent with the hydraulic limitation hypothesis, medium-sized palms showed a greater slope of sap flux vs. VPD in the wet season compared to tall palms (5.8 vs. 5.1 respectively, std error = 0.24 for both) meaning that in the wet season, stomates were more open at a given VPD in medium-sized palms than tall palms.

Oren *et al.* (1999) also report that individuals with a high stomatal conductance at low vapor pressure deficit (VPD) show greater stomatal sensitivity to VPD than individuals with lower stomatal conductance. Indeed the difference in sap flux at a given VPD between seasons was larger in medium palms than large ones (4.25 and 3.14 g/ m^2 '" sec respectively at a VPD of 2 kPa). There are also several reasons why larger palms would be less adversely affected by dry-season conditions than smaller palms including deeper roots (Irvine *et al.* 2002) and larger reserves of stored water within boles (Holbrook and Sinclair 1992).

In order to investigate whether bole water storage was playing a role in the daily water use in *Iriartea deltoidea,* lag analysis between bole sap flux and environmental variables was performed. A lag between lower bole sap flux and VPD and/or PPFD (depending on the trigger for stomatal opening) would indicate that leaves were drawing water from stored sources within the bole before pulling water from the ground where it would be detected by the sap flux sensor. We did not detect lags between basal sap flux and VPD in any palm, but did detect lags between basal sap flux and PPFD (and between PPFD and VPD). Therefore, if stomatal opening is being driven primarily by PPFD, bole water storage may play a role in the daily water use, whereas if it is primarily driven by VPD, then bole water storage is a minor part of daily water use. Regardless, storage of water within the boles of these palms may still be important over longer timescales (Chapotin *et al.*, 2006). This study is one of the few to perform a calibration of Granier heat dissipation sensors on palm material whose structure differs greatly from dicot wood. In a calibration of sap flux in coconut palms (*Cocos nucifera* L.), a was also found to be higher (315 x 10^{-6}) than the Granier equation with the b value being similar (Roupsard *et al.* 2006). Additionally, because sap fluxes were measured in three separate plant organs (stilt roots, boles and petioles), comparison of these values can yield information about the hydraulic architecture of this palm species. Sap velocities increase from the roots to the boles to the petioles, suggesting that conducting area is decreasing from the bottom of the palm to the top (McCulloh and Sperry 2005).

This fits with the idea of conduit tapering seen in many tree species (West *et al.* 1999). It is also interesting to note in this study that sap fluxes in the petioles of small palms behaved much differently from that seen in boles of medium-sized and larger palms, showing larger sap fluxes at larger vapor pressure deficits and PPFD values in the dry season compared to the wet season. This is presumably the result of a very different microclimate for the small palms, where VPD may not be as large near the forest floor, compared to larger palms which are higher in the canopy. Additionally, small trees growing in the forest understory are most likely ultimately light limited and, therefore, would benefit from the higher irradiance of the dry season. Additionally, Meinzer & Grantz (1989) found that stomata control of transpiration is determined by the magnitudes of stomatal and boundary layer conductances, and because small trees are located in the understory, they may exhibit much smaller boundary layer conductances than larger trees.

In summary, the present research provides important evidence that *Iriartea deltoidea* palms exhibit greater stomatal closure in the dry season compared to the wet season. This stomatal closure seems to result from larger vapor pressure deficits and possibly reduced soil moisture. Even though irradiance was marginally larger in the dry season than the wet season, *Iriartea deltoidea* would be limited in the degree to which it could increase photosynthesis because of stomatal closure and hydraulic limitations to carbon gain. These results could also have implications for tropical rainforests in the future as it has been shown that, although global warming should not alter the climate of the Amazon significantly, decreased annual rainfall and longer dry seasons are predicted (Hulme & Viner 1998).

Additionally, it is important to note that *Iriartea deltoidea* palms were estimated to contribute 0.03 mm/d to transpiration in this Amazonian rainforest region. Transpiration from an Amazonian rainforest in Brazil was estimated to be between 2 and 4 mm/d (Roberts *et al.* 1993). Therefore, if this estimate of total rainforest transpiration is similar in Ecuador, then *Iriartea deltoidea* represents about 1 percent of total rainforest transpiration. Although this seems like a small percentage for a single species, it becomes significant considering that based on leaf area data for *Iriartea deltoidea* provided by Rich *et al.* (1995) and LAI data from Myneni *et al.* (2007) for the Amazon basin (peak LAI of approximately 5.5), *Iriartea deltoidea* represents about 0.5 percent of the leaf area of an Amazon rainforest. Therefore, per unit leaf area, *Iriartea deltoidea* contributes significantly more transpiration than the average leaf found in the rainforest.

7

Development and Growing Environment

INTRODUCTION

Iriartea deltoidea (Ruiz & Pav.) and *Mauritia flexuosa* (L.) are two prominent palm species growing in the lowland rainforests of the Western Amazon. While growing in fairly close proximity to one another, they differ greatly in their growing environment. *Mauritia flexuosa* is found primarily growing in permanently flooded soils where it forms nearly monospecific stands called morichales or aquajales (Rull, 1998). *Iriartea deltoidea,* on the other hand, grows on terra firme and varsea (occasionally flooded) soils where it has been found to be the most common tree species in several locations in Western Amazonia (Pitman et al., 2001, Montufar and Pintaud, 2006).

Therefore, while they share a similar atmospheric growing environment, their habitats differ greatly edaphically. Besides growing environment, *Iriartea deltoidea* and *Mauritia flexuosa* have different anatomic features and life histories. *Iriartea deltoidea* has pinnate leaves while *Mauritia flexuosa* has costapalmate leaves (Uhl and Dransfield, 1987). *Iriartea deltoidea* also has a large cone of stilt roots at its base that allows the species to grow rapidly in height (Schatz et al., 1985), while *Mauritia flexuosa* palms have specialized roots called pneumatophores that allow for respiratory exchange under flooded soil conditions (de Granville, 1974). Finally, *Iriartea deltoidea* and *Mauritia flexuosa* differ greatly in their ontogenetic development. The trunk of *Mauritia flexuosa* increases in diameter underground until it reaches its final size, at which point the trunk emerges from underground, growing vertically while maintaining diameter. Waterhouse and Quinn (1978) refer to this as Type A development. Type B development, on the other hand, is exhibited by *Iriartea deltoidea,* in that all palms past the seedling stage exhibit aboveground trunks that increase in diameter substantially over an extended period of time (Waterhouse and Quinn, 1978).

These differences in palm type, anatomy and growing environment will affect both of these palm species as they develop ontogenetically. Rich (1987b) found that palm stems are more heterogenous and undergo more changes in structure and density ontogenetically than dicotyledons or conifers, many times encompassing an entire range of published wood density values within a single stem. Ontogenetic differences with regard to trunk diameter formation could lead to significant differences in vertical height growth rates between *Iriartea deltoidea* and *Mauritia flexuosa.*

As well, differences in trunk size with height could lead to differences in water storage capacity. Reliance on stored water is correlated with trunk diameter (Meinzer et al., 2004) and has been shown to be significant in palms including the Cuban belly palm, *Gastrococos crispa* ((Kunth) H.E. Moore)(Fisher et al., 1996) and *Sabal palmetto* ((Walt.) Lodd.) (Holbrook and Sinclair, 1992). Because *Iriartea deltoidea* has a Type B development, increases in stored water with age and height should be more dramatic than in *Mauritia flexuosa,* a Type A palm. Also, differences in leaf type may lead to interesting relationships between leaf size and leaf life span both ontogenetically and between species. Kikuzawa and Ackerly (1999) have found that leaf life spans generally increase with plant size but are unrelated to overall leaf size when compared within plant groups (Ackerly and Reich, 1999).

Leaf production in palms is also tied to height growth with new stem tissue made to support new leaves (Rich, 1986). Therefore, although additions cannot be made to the vascular structure at the base (however its orientation may change as in the trunk expansion seen in *Iriartea deltoidea*), new vertical stem tissue may differ ontogenetically as palms grow taller and their hydraulic needs and constraints change. The hydraulic supply system of trees often becomes challenged as they grow taller and the frictional resistance increases (Ryan and Yoder, 1997) and changes in the vascular system with height have been shown to mediate this (West et al. 1999; Becker et al. 2000a; Becker et al. 2000b).

The objectives of this study were to determine how intrinsic hydraulic factors such as vascular and stomatal anatomy and bole water storage affect extrinsic factors such as vertical growth rates, leaf turnover rates, sapfluxes and leaf areas in *Iriartea deltoidea* and *Mauritia flexuosa*. Additionally, because these two palm species have differing growing environments, leaf structures and aboveground growth patterns comparison of these intrinsic and extrinsic factors between species was also of interest. Finally, because palms of varying heights were studied, information about how both intrinsic and extrinsic factors change or remain constant across height as also determined.

Not only will the information gained from this study help to better understand these two palm species across ontogeny, but these data can be used to better understand palms as a plant group; one that has been shown to be both economically and environmentally important (Plotkin and Balick, 1984; Kahn, 1988; Kahn, 1991; Salm et al., 2005; Tomlinson, 2006; Walther et al., 2007). Palms as arborescent monocots possess a very unique growing habit in terms of have columnar boles and a relatively simple crown of leaves that allowed for the effective measurement of various physiological (growth rates, sapflux rates, leaf areas) and anatomical variables (stomatal properties, conduit properties) that are much more difficult in dicotyledonous, arborescent species (Phillips et al., 2008a; Phillips et al. 2008b). Furthermore, even though the vascular anatomy of palms differs greatly from dicotyledonous trees, because the same physical laws that govern the movement of water through trees apply to palms, this research can shed light on the features and trade-offs that may be universal and those that may differ between arborescent monocots and dicots.

MATERIALS AND METHODS

Site Description

This research was performed at Tiputini Biodiversity Station (0æ% 36′ S, 76æ% 27′ W), a 650 ha research facility located within Yasuní National Park in eastern Ecuador. The site receives approximately 2860 mm of rainfall annually and has an average temperature of 25.5æ%C (Macía, 2004).

Research was conducted in May and June of 2006 (the wet season) and January, February and March from 2007 to 2009 which is the driest part of the year in this region of the Amazon rainforest receiving about 107 mm of rain per month (data courtesy of Dr. J. Guerra). *Iriartea deltoidea* palms were found growing in the terra firme forest where the canopy reaches about 30 m in height, with numerous tree fall gaps. *Iriartea deltoidea* is one of the most common tree species in this area (Pitman et al., 2001). *Mauritia flexuosa* palms were found in a nearby, permanently inundated swamp. This site had a more open canopy than the rest of the terra firme forest with *Mauritia flexuosa* palms being the dominant tree species. *Astrocaryum* sp. palms were also present at all stages of development in this area.

Growth Rates and Leaf Turnover Rates

Because both *Iriartea deltoidea* and *Mauritia flexuosa* have distinct leaf scar nodes, height growth rates could be determined by measuring the distance between these nodes. All measurements were performed in February and March, 2008. In small palms (1 m tall), internode distances were measured with a measuring tape. In all other palms, internode distances were measured using digital pictures of the palm boles. Successive pictures of an individual bole were taken then "stitched together" using image software (ArcSoft PhotoStudio 5.5, Fremont, California, USA) with internode distances measured using image analysis software (Image J, Scion Image, Frederick, Maryland,

USA). The height of the palm to the base of the live crown as well as the horizontal distance between the photographer and the palm were measured using a TruPulse 200 hypsometer (Laser Technology Inc., Centennial, Colorado, USA). On a nearby canopy tower, flagging tape was tied every 0.5 m from the base to 30 m. Standing the same distance from the tower as from the palms, digital pictures were taken of this tower "scale" and these were used to correct for the angle at which the pictures were taken as well as to scale the measurements in meters. Internode distances were also measured opportunistically on a 20 m tall *Iriartea deltoidea* treefall and these measurements matched well with those calculated from the bole photographs.

Because internode distances represent the time between production of successive leaves, leaf production rates are important in order to interpret the internode distances as height growth rates. Therefore, leaf turnover rates were determined for various-sized *Iriartea deltoidea* and *Mauritia flexuosa* palms with the assumption that turnover rates and production rates are approximately equal. For *Iriartea deltoidea,* the method for determining leaf turnover rates was similar to that of Tomlinson (1963).

In February and March, 2008 four small palms (ca. 1 m tall), two medium sized palms (12 and 14 m tall) and one tall palm (24 m tall) were marked by hammering an aluminum tag on the most recently produced leaf scar node. Medium palms were accessed using a palm climbing apparatus (www.nif.org.in/bd/node/125) and the tall palm was accessed using ropes. For two additional medium sized palms (6 m and 11 m) and three additional tall palms (24 to 26 m tall), digital pictures of the crowns were taken from a canopy tower and the location of the photographer was tagged.

In February, 2009 digital pictures were taken from the same location and compared with the previous year to determine the number of leaves lost and newly made. Additionally, the leaf node scars above the tagged scar were counted on the aluminum tagged palms. Because the leaves of *Mauritia flexuosa* palms do not drop once they desiccate and this species is not found growing near the canopy towers, another methodology was required. Therefore, in February and March, 2008, two juvenile palms that lacked an aboveground trunk (0 m tall), two medium sized palms (6 and 7 m tall) and two tall palms (18 and 24 m tall) were marked for leaf turnover by tying flagging tape around all green leaves. The following February, 2009, these palms were revisited and the number of flagged and dead leaves, flagged and living leaves, and unflagged, living leaves were counted.

Sapflux and *Mauritia Flexuosa* Bole Water Storage Estimation

Sapflux was measured in the boles of three small *Iriartea deltoidea* palms (ca. 1 m tall), four medium *Iriartea deltoidea* palms (between 6 and 14 m tall) and three tall *Iriartea deltoidea* palms (between 24 and 26 m tall) during May and June, 2006 (wet season) and January and February, 2007 (dry season) using one cm long, Granier-style heat dissipation sensors (Granier, 1987). One cm long sensors were used due to the difficulty of installing the sensors into *Iriartea deltoidea* boles. For *Mauritia flexuosa*, sapflux was measured in the boles and/or petioles of two juvenile palms (no aboveground trunk), two medium palms (6 to 7 m tall) and two large palms (18 and 22 m tall) during January and February, 2007, February and March, 2008 and January and February 2009 using two cm long, Granier sensors.

In order to install sensors in the petioles of medium and tall *Mauritia flexuosa*, palms were climbed by passing a rope through the crown of the intended palm then securing it at both ends. Heavy gauge nylon wire was first shot through the crown using a bow and arrow then the heavier climbing rope was passed through the crown. The rope was then climbed using single rope ascenders and crown access was gained. The Granier sensor methodology involves measuring the amount of heat dissipated by water flow around a heated sensor relative to a reference sensor that are both radially inserted into the palm.

When water flows past the heated sensor, it dissipates some of the heat produced, with the amount of dissipation being related to the rate of sapflux. After sensor installation, aluminum insulating wrap was stapled around sensors to shield them from temperature variation due to sun flecks. The heat dissipation sensors were attached to a Campbell CR-10X datalogger and AM-32 multiplexer (Campbell Scientific, Logan, Utah, USA) that collected data every 30 min for *Iriartea deltoidea* and every 2 min for *Mauritia flexuosa*. The program, Baseliner version 2.4.2 (C-H20 Ecology Group, Duke University, Durham, North Carolina, USA) was used to convert the millivolt signal from the datalogger into sapfluxes (g '" m^{-2} '" sec^{-1}) using the Granier equation (Granier, 1987). We performed a calibration of the Granier style sensors in the bole of a small *Iriartea deltoidea* palm and found that the Granier equation was within the 95% confidence limits of our calibration (Renninger et al, in press). Solar panels located on the top of a canopy tower provided power for the data logger and sensor heating in the *Iriartea deltoidea* site. For the *Mauritia flexuosa* site, a solar panel located in the understory provided some of the power for the system, however batteries also needed to be shuttled back and forth to the field camp generator in order to be recharged and supply the site with power.

In order to calculate daily sapflux values for *Iriartea deltoidea,* we used vascular bundle densities in the central and peripheral bole region reported in Rich (1987a) and assumed that metaxylem vessels are more or less constant across the bole radius. According to Rich (1987a) vascular bundle densities in the central core are approximately half that of the outer periphery. We used our own observations of fallen *Iriartea deltoidea* palms to estimate the proportion of the bole area considered "central" which yielded the following equation: $y = 0.8013e^{-0.036x}$ where x = palm height and y = proportion of dbh occupied by the central region.

These data were then used to scale our sapflux values measured in the bole periphery to the entire cross sectional area of the *Iriartea deltoidea* palms. For *Mauritia flexuosa* we did not have access to vascular bundle density data, therefore we assumed that flux was more or less constant throughout the cross-section. This assumption is supported by Roupsard et al. (2006) who found a constant pattern of sapflux throughout the stem of coconut

(*Cocos nucifera* L.) palms up to a 12 cm radius, Sellami and Sifaoui (2003) who found that sap flow at 3 cm depth and 6 cm depth did not differ significantly in date palms (*Phoenix dactylifera* L.) and Renninger et al. (2009) who found that sapflux at 2 cm and 4 cm did not differ significantly in Mexican fan palms (*Washingtonia robusta* H.Wendl.). For *Mauritia flexuosa* petiole sapflux, we multiplied individual petiole sapflux by the number of fronds to get an estimate of whole palm sapflux.

For *Mauritia flexuosa,* because concurrent measurements of sapflux in the base of the bole as well as in the petiole were taken, it allowed for the examination of evidence of daily usage of water stored in the bole by palms. In palms that are more reliant on stored water in the stem, sapflux in the lower bole will tend to lag behind sapflux in the petiole (i.e. initiation of morning sapflux, peak midday sapflux and nighttime decline will occur later). Cross-correlation analysis of the sapflux time series data was performed in the 6 m, 7 m, 18 m and 22 m tall palms. The time lag corresponding to the maximum degree of correlation between the petiole sapflux signal and the bole sapflux signal, therefore, represented the approximate amount of daily usage of stored water in the bole of the palm.

Leaf Anatomical Properties

Leaflets were collected from *Iriartea deltoidea* and *Mauritia flexuosa* palms both opportunistically and by climbing them. For *Iriartea deltoidea* leaflets were collected from medium sized palms (6 to 14 m tall) by climbing the bole using a palm climbing apparatus (www.nif.org.in/bd/node/125) to the base of the live crown and a pole saw was then used to cut leaflets down. Large *Iriartea deltoidea* palms could not be accessed this way; therefore, leaflets were collected opportunistically when they or the entire frond had fallen from a tall *Iriartea deltoidea*. For *Mauritia flexuosa,* leaflets were collected from palms when the petiole sapflux sensors were being installed.

For other palms, dead leaflet material (no longer green) was collected by either climbing the boles to the dead fronds or collecting from fronds that had recently fallen to the ground.

These fronds retained all of their microscopic anatomical features even though they were no longer green. Once leaflets were obtained, they were returned to the lab where they were hand sectioned with a razor blade taking thin sections of epidermal tissue from the abaxial side of the leaf. *Mauritia flexuosa* posed some difficultly as stomata were concentrated on the main parallel ribs; therefore, hand sectioning was concentrated in these regions. Sections were then stained with a solution of 1% Toluidine Blue O and mounted on slides using Permount (Fisher Scientific, Pittsburgh, Pennsylvania, USA).

The slides were viewed at 200X magnification using a compound light microscope (Leica CME, Bannockburn, Illinois, USA) and photographs were taken with a digital camera (Olympus SP-550 UZ, Center Valley, Pennsylvania, USA). These photographs were imported into image analysis software (Image J, Scion Image, Frederick, Maryland, USA) for measurement. Leaf epidermal cell areas were measured by tracing around the perimeter of approximately 300 to 500 cells per palm distributed across 20 to 30 photographs. Stomatal densities were calculated by counting the number of stomata within a field of view, then calculating the area of that viewfield. Approximately 20 to 30 different fields of view were used per palm. Guard cell lengths were calculated by measuring the distance between the two points where guard cells meet. Approximately 50 and 150 stomata were measured per palm in order to calculate average guard cell length. Total stomatal pore area index (SPI) was then calculated as (stomatal density ''' guard cell length^2) (Sack et al., 2003).

Iriartea Deltoidea Bole and Stilt Root Anatomical Properties

Bole material was collected from two *Iriartea deltoidea* palms (14 m and 20 m tall) that had been pushed over in a storm. Material was collected from midheight and from the base of the live crown. The bole sections were split into four quadrants and samples were taken from both the inner (center) and outer (peripheral) bole region of each of the four quadrants. Additionally, five small *Iriartea deltoidea* palms (1 to 5 m tall) were harvested, split in half, and inner and outer bole material from each half was collected as well as samples from the stilt roots. Stilt roots were also collected from five medium-sized *Iriartea deltoidea* palms (10 to 15 m tall) and from five large *Iriartea deltoidea* palms (20 to 25 m tall). Samples were hand sectioned with a razorblade on the transverse (cross-sectional) plane.

Sections were stained with a solution of 1% Toluidine Blue O and mounted on slides using Permount. The slides were viewed at 40X magnification using a compound light microscope (Leica CME, Bannockburn, Illinois, USA) and photographs were taken with a digital camera (Olympus SP-550 UZ, Center Valley, Pennsylvania, USA). These photographs were imported into image analysis software for measurement of vessel diameters and vascular bundle densities. Approximately 50 to 100 metaxylem vessels were measured for each palm height/location category. Vascular bundle densities were calculated by counting the number of bundles within a field of view, then calculating the area of that viewfield. Approximately 10 to 20 different fields of view were used per palm. These same fields of view were then used to calculate Hagen-Poiseuille conductivities (k_{HP}) using the following equation:

$$k_{HP} = \frac{\sum \frac{\pi r^4}{8\eta}}{A_s}$$

where r is the radius of metaxylem vessels, ç is the viscosity of water, and A_s is the cross-sectional area of the field of view, with the summation over all metaxylem vessels in the field of view. Hagen-Poiseuille conductivities are ideal maximums and do not include any resistances that would be introduced by vessel end walls (Zimmermann, 1983).

In order to quantify the capacity for water storage in both the inner and outer regions of the bole in *Iriartea deltoidea*, percentages of the cross-sections that were occupied by parenchyma tissue were calculated. For this calculation, only parenchyma cells that were outside of the vascular bundles were included. Approximately 20 to 30 fields of view were used for each height/location category.

To begin, vascular bundles and any area not to be included in the field of view were blacked out using image analysis software (Image J). Then, using the thresholding technique, the area of parenchyma was selected and measured. This was compared with the total area being evaluated to determine the percent area occupied by parenchyma capable of storing water within the bole.

STATISTICAL ANALYSES

r^2 and p-values for all regressions were calculated using SigmaPlot 2000 Version 6.1 (SPSS Inc. Chicago, Illinois, USA).

RESULTS

Growth Rates and Leaf Turnover Rates

In all *Iriartea deltoidea* height categories, internode lengths initially increase, reach a maximum that is sustained to differing degrees, then decrease towards smaller and smaller values. For *Iriartea deltoidea,* leaf turnover rates decrease as palms get taller ($r^2 = 0.57$, $P = 0.033$). Therefore, internode lengths represent increasing lengths of time from the bottom of the *Iriartea deltoidea* palms to the top, meaning that height growth rates at the tops of tall palms are even slower than the internode distances would make it appear due to the decrease in leaf turnover.

For *Mauritia flexuosa,* small and medium sized palms exhibit constant internode lengths after an initial increase in internode length. In large *Mauritia flexuosa,* internode lengths initially increase, remain constant over an extended length of the bole then decrease sharply to very low levels. However unlike *Iriartea deltoidea,* in *Mauritia flexuosa,* leaf turnover rates increase with palm height ($r^2 = 0.997$, $P = 0.0002$). Therefore internode lengths represent decreasing lengths of time from the bottom of *Mauritia flexuosa* palms to the top, which would tend to decrease the growth rates suggested by the large internode lengths at midheight, and suggest slightly faster growth rates at the tops of tall *Mauritia flexuosa* than is suggested by the internode lengths alone.

Leaf Properties

Iriartea deltoidea and *Mauritia flexuosa* exhibit opposing but complimentary relationships between the number of live fronds per palm and individual frond leaf area with height. In *Iriartea deltoidea*, individual frond leaf areas increase linearly with height ($r^2 = 0.97$, $P < 0.0001$), while the number of live fronds per palm increases non-linearly approaching an asymptote in taller palms ($r^2 = 0.76$, $P = 0.0005$). However in *Mauritia flexuosa*, the individual frond leaf area increases *non-linearly* reaching an asymptote in taller palms ($r^2 = 0.80$, $P < 0.0001$) while the number of live fronds per palm increases *linearly* with height ($r^2 = 0.83$, $P < 0.0001$). Putting these two variables together, both *Iriartea deltoidea* and *Mauritia flexuosa* show a similar linear increase in total leaf area with height ($r^2 = 0.91$, $P < 0.0001$) with neither the slopes nor y-intercepts of the individual species linear regressions differing significantly at a = 0.05.

The leaves of *Iriartea deltoidea* palms had significantly larger epidermal cells than leaves of *Mauritia flexuosa*. Leaf epidermal cell sizes decreases with height in both species with *Iriartea deltoidea* exhibiting a non-linear relationship ($r^2 = 0.74$, $P = 0.018$) and *Mauritia flexuosa* exhibiting a linear one ($r^2 = 0.93$, $P = 0.0021$). Stomatal densities and guard cell lengths showed opposing, complimentary relationships with height in *Iriartea deltoidea* and *Mauritia flexuosa*.

In *Iriartea deltoidea*, stomatal densities increased nonlinearly with height ($r^2 = 0.85$, $P = 0.0005$), while guard cell lengths decreased nonlinearly with height ($r^2 = 0.9$, $P = 0.0012$). On the other hand in *Mauritia flexuosa* stomatal densities *decreased* nonlinearly with height ($r^2 = 0.68$, $P = 0.0063$), while guard cell lengths *increased* nonlinearly with height ($r^2 = 0.94$, $P = 0.0038$). Stomatal pore area index (SPI) was constant for leaves from *Iriartea deltoidea* palms of different heights. However, for *Mauritia flexuosa*, SPI decreased nonlinearly in leaves from taller palms ($r^2 = 0.90$, $P = 0.001$).

Sapflux

For both *Iriartea deltoidea* and *Mauritia flexuosa*, there was no relationship between bole cross-sectional area and sap-flux per unit area of outer bole material (kg '" m^{-2} '" day^{-1}; data not shown). However, when sapflux data were scaled up to the total bole cross-sectional area (kg/day), both *Iriartea deltoidea* and *Mauritia flexuosa* showed greater sapflux rates in taller palms than shorter ones. As well, for *Iriartea deltoidea*, sapflux measured in the boles of palms showed the same relationship with height during the wet season (May-June) and the following dry season (Jan-Feb) as the slopes and y-intercepts were not significantly different at a = 0.05 and a single line was fitted to the data (r^2=0.79, $P < 0.0001$). In *Mauritia flexuosa*, sapflux measured in the base of the bole showed the same relationship with palm height as sapflux measured in a petiole and scaled up to the whole palm level as the slopes and y-intercepts did not significantly differ at a = 0.05 and a single line was fitted to the data ($r^2 = 0.80$, $p < 0.0001$).

This degree of overlap lends a certain degree of confidence to the assumptions that were made in scaling total sapflux from the single sensor values. In order to determine if sápflux per unit leaf area also differed in palms of differing heights, daily sapflux (kg/day) was divided by the total leaf area of the palm being measured. Since total leaf area also increases with palm height, there was no relationship between daily sapflux per unit leaf area and palm height, for either *Iriartea deltoidea* ($P = 0.1983$) or *Mauritia flexuosa* ($P = 0.1583$). Sapflux per unit leaf area was approximately four times higher in *Mauritia flexuosa* palms than in *Iriartea deltoidea* palms.

Bole Water Storage

Cross correlation analysis between petiole and lower bole sapflux in *Mauritia flexuosa* revealed differences in bole water storage in palms of different heights. For a 6 m and 7 m tall *Mauritia flexuosa* palm an average lag of 14.4 min (SE = 3.1) corresponded to the highest correlation between petiole and bole sapflux over a ten day period. This value represents about 11.8%

(SE = 1.0%) of the total daily water use for these palms. For an 18 m tall *Mauritia flexuosa* palm, an average lag of 20.5 min (SE = 5.3) corresponded to the highest correlation over a 9 day period which represents about 12.2 % (SE = 1.6%) of the total daily water use for this palm.

For a 22.5m tall *Mauritia flexuosa* palm an average lag of 48.6 min (SE = 8.3) corresponded to the highest degree of correlation over an 8 day period. This represents about 19.4 % of the total daily water use for this palm. The lags corresponding to a maximum degree of correlation are higher than the mean lags for each palm, but they show the same trend of increasing lags and therefore increasing reliance on stored bole water in taller palms.

For *Iriartea deltoidea,* cross correlation analysis between petioles and boles could not be performed, therefore the percent area occupied by parenchyma cells in the inner and outer bole was quantified. Only parenchyma cells external to the vascular bundles were quantified since this is a likely location for bole water storage. Parenchyma in the inner bole region occupied 48% (SE = 2.6) of the area with large lacunae present. In the outer bole region, parenchyma occupied 25% (1.5%) of the area with no lacunae present. Therefore, the inner bole of *Iriartea deltoidea* palms has approximately twice the water storage capacity as the outer bole region. Additionally, the percent area occupied by parenchyma tissue remains relatively constant across height in both the inner and outer bole. However, bole cross-sectional areas increase as palms get taller thus increasing the size of the inner bole and outer bole region in taller palms.

Bole Anatomical Properties

In the boles of *Iriartea deltoidea* palms, vessels diameters increase non-linearly with increasing height above ground (r^2 = 0.65, P = 0.0002). Vessels from the inner bole and the outer bole showed statistically similar curves between vessel diameter and palm height. Unlike boles, vessel diameters in stilt roots were constant across height classes and were therefore pooled. Vascular bundle densities showed the opposite relationship as vessel diameter in the boles of *Iriartea deltoidea* with bundle densities decreasing non-linearly in taller palms. Vascular bundle densities in the inner bole decreased more sharply ($r^2 = 0.95$, $P < 0.0001$) with increasing height than bundle densities in the outer bole ($r^2 = 0.85$, $P = 0.0012$). As with vessel diameters, vascular bundle densities in the stilt roots were constant across height classes and were pooled. Vessel diameters and vascular bundle densities were used to calculate Hagen-Poiseuille conductivities.

Calculated conductivities increased with palm height more sharply in the outer bole ($r^2 = 0.74$, $P = 0.006$) than in the inner bole ($r^2 = 0.38$, $P = 0.1058$). Stilt root conductivities remained constant across height categories and were pooled. Vessel diameters varied non-linearly with vascular bundle densities ($r^2 = 0.63$, $P < 0.0001$) with smaller vessels exhibiting greater vascular bundle densities. Likewise, the relationship between vessel diameter and vascular bundle density from the outer bole, the inner bole, and the stilt roots from *Iriartea deltoidea* palms ranging in height from 1 m to 25 m tall all converged on a single line.

DISCUSSION

In both *Iriartea deltoidea* and *Mauritia flexuosa*, height growth rates based on internode distances were significantly reduced at the tops of the tallest palms compared to growth rates at the midheight range. The tallest palms we studied were near the tallest reported for each species (Henderson, 1995). A similar relationship was found in coconut palms (*Cocos nucifera*) where internode length also decreased with height (Friend and Corley, 1994). However, the pattern of internode length along the trunks of *Iriartea deltoidea* and *Mauritia flexuosa* differs with *Mauritia flexuosa* exhibiting fairly constant internode distances with significant decreases only at the top of the tallest palms.

This is similar to a pattern found by Lugo and Rivera Batlle (1987) in *Prestoea montana* ((Graham) Nicholson) where the fastest height growth rates were found when palms were young. *Iriartea deltoidea,* however, exhibited increasing internode lengths until reaching a maximum in approximately the mid-trunk region and then decreases in internode length occur at the tops of all palm boles. Homeier et al. (2002) describe a similar pattern for *Iriartea deltoidea* palms growing in Costa Rica and, although they did not investigate leaf turnover rates, they attribute the decreases in height growth at the tops of tall palms to higher energy requirements needed for reproduction.

Differences in the pattern of internode length with height between *Iriartea deltoidea* and *Mauritia flexuosa* may be related to their differing growth types. *Mauritia flexuosa* has a Type A design, and therefore, does not increase in diameter once it creates an aboveground trunk. *Iriartea deltoidea,* with its Type B design, has a bole that increases substantially in diameter after it has been formed (Waterhouse and Quinn, 1978). With a Type A design, internode sizes appear to be relatively fixed in *Mauritia flexuosa.* However in *Iriartea deltoidea,* it seems plausible that if stems can increase in girth after formation, internodes may be able to lengthen as well. That could explain how the internode lengths at the tops of mid-height palms could be so much shorter than at a similar height on tall palms. This strategy could be important in the terra-firme rainforest where plasticity in height growth rates and rapid height growth would be important in taking advantage of short-lived forest gaps.

Waterhouse and Quinn (1978) argue that it is anatomically impossible for internodes to lengthen after leaf fall due to the fact that metaxylem vessels are differentiated at that point and therefore could not lengthen. However, it is also known that vascular bundles follow a spiral pattern through the bole (Zimmermann and Tomlinson, 1965; Zimmermann and Tomlinson, 1972). Therefore, vascular bundles could lengthen in a similar way that a spring lengthens (without the addition of new material).

Likewise, stem expansion in girth could then be accomplished through sustained increases in parenchyma cell size and intercellular distance (Rich, 1987a; Niklas, 1992). Of course, an alternative hypothesis would be that these medium-sized palms are approaching their maximum height and will never achieve the heights of very tall palms of the same species because of their growing environment. However, the medium-sized palms measured in our study were not shaded from above and had started flowering in the time period of this study. More research is needed to reconcile these differing height growth patterns in *Iriartea deltoidea* palms of differing heights.

One interesting aspect of palms is that their height growth rates are directly tied to their leaf production rates. Therefore, although internode lengths are important in determining height growth rates, leaf turnover rates also need to be incorporated. According to Lugo and Rivera Batlle (1987), studies that have not incorporated both pieces of information may be limited in their interpretations of growth.

Iriartea deltoidea and *Mauritia flexuosa,* in addition to displaying differing patterns of internode lengths along their boles, also have differing leaf turnover rates with height. In *Iriartea deltoidea* leaf turnover rates slow down in taller palms, whereas in *Mauritia flexuosa* they speed up.

It makes sense that leaf turnover rates would slow in *Iriartea deltoidea* palms with height as taller palms have significantly larger fronds with greater leaf area than shorter palms. Rich (1986) found that leaf production rates increased with height in *Iriartea deltoidea,* but only palms up to 13 m tall were studied. In *Mauritia flexuosa,* slower leaf turnover rates in shorter palms may be a response to the increased stem tissue increments that are made by shorter palms relative to the tops of taller palms, where much less of an investment in stem tissue is made.

Additionally, Lugo and Rivera Batlle (1987) found that *Prestoea montana* exhibited higher rates of leaf production in dominant palms and De Steven et al. (1987) found that palms with larger crowns produce more leaves per year than those with fewer leaves. However, de Carvalho et al (1999) did not find differences in leaf production rates in *Euterpe edulis* (Mart.) palms across different ontogenetic stages, although they focused on pre-reproductive individuals. Finally, frond turnover rates in palms may be related to soil nutrients with Beard et al. (2005) finding that palms in plots that had a wood addition treatment had greater frond turnover rates than control or wood removal plots and that differences in frond turnover rates were not associated with droughts or hurricanes.

In both *Iriartea deltoidea* and *Mauritia flexuosa,* leaf areas increase as palms get taller. However, the level of overlap in the leaf area between the two species across all ranges of height is very interesting, with a single line fitting data from both species. Increases in leaf area with height in these two rainforest palm species contrasts sharply with the patterns seen in a subtropical species, *Washingtonia robusta,* which exhibited both smaller and fewer leaves in taller palms relative to shorter ones (Renninger et al., 2009).

It is intriguing that not only do *Iriartea deltoidea* and *Mauritia flexuosa* exhibit the same pattern of leaf area increase with height, but they also exhibit contrasting strategies for increasing leaf area. *Iriartea deltoidea* shows significant increases in individual frond leaf area in taller palms with more or less constant number of fronds per palm (Rich et al., 1995), while in *Mauritia flexuosa,* individual frond leaf areas remain more or less constant while the number of live fronds increases significantly in taller palms.

These differing strategies may be a function of their differing leaf shapes with *Iriartea deltoidea* possessing pinnately compound leaves and *Mauritia flexuosa* possessing palmate leaves. The ability to dissipate heat may set an upper limit to the size *Mauritia flexuosa* leaves can achieve (Parkhurst and Loucks, 1972), while not affecting the pinnate leaflets of *Iriartea deltoidea* (Balding and Cunningham, 1976).

The design of *Iriartea deltoidea* leaves may also be important during periods of high wind as it has been shown that pinnately compound leaves can close in around the rachis forming a cylinder that has very low drag in high winds (Vogel, 1989). This would be important for tall *Iriartea deltoidea* palms that are frequently emergent trees in the canopy. However, for *Mauritia flexuosa* palms found growing mainly in lowland swamps, topography should make wind a much weaker driver of leaf architecture. It is also interesting to note that *Mauritia flexuosa* is the only palmate species in its subtribe, with Horn et al. (2009) finding that palmate leaves evolved twice in the palm family, with *Mauritia flexuosa* representing one of those occurrences. *Mauritia flexuosa* dominates the permanently flooded areas where it is found and it is interesting to speculate whether the palmate leaf habit contributes to that.

Although total leaf areas increased dramatically in both *Iriartea deltoidea* and *Mauritia flexuosa*, palm sapflux increased in the same proportion yielding similar sapflux rates per unit leaf area across height in both species. *Mauritia flexuosa* did, however, have significantly higher sapflux per unit leaf area than *Iriartea deltoidea* which could be a function of its constant supply of water but also could be necessary in leaf cooling through transpiration, as trees growing in swamps typically encounter low wind, high irradiance, and high humidity (Vogel, 2009). In both *Iriartea deltoidea* and *Mauritia flexuosa*, stomatal densities and sizes differ between palms of different heights.

In *Iriartea deltoidea*, taller palms have smaller but more frequent stomata, resulting in a constant stomatal pore area index (SPI) across height. This is consistent with the constant sapflux per unit leaf area across height and well as with observations from Sack et al. (2003, 2005) that leaf hydraulic conductance (K_{leaf}) is strongly correlated with SPI.

However, *Mauritia flexuosa* exhibits an opposite pattern with larger but less frequent stomata in leaves from taller palms and, in turn, SPI values decrease non-linearly with height. This may be the result of the manner in which the stomata were distributed across the leaf with them being found almost exclusively near midveins, especially in leaves from taller palms (H. Renninger, pers. obs.).

Because sapflux per unit leaf area remains relatively constant across height in both *Iriartea deltoidea* and *Mauritia flexuosa*, it appears that neither palm is showing evidence for hydraulic limitations in taller palms relative to shorter ones (Ryan and Yoder, 1997). Mechanical constraints may play a central role in the maximum heights palms can achieve because, in many cases (Type A design), final bole size is achieved long before lengthening of the bole occurs (Niklas, 1992). Furthermore, Niklas (1993) found that estimates of stem height composed of sclerenchyma matched closely with mean heights seen in palms, while the same was not true for woody stems.

However, Gale and Barfod (1999) found that most *Iriartea deltoidea* palms (with a Type B design) either died while standing or where snapped off by other treefalls. This would suggest a biological mechanism as the primary driver of height growth reductions in *Iriartea deltoidea*. Increased respiration costs may be a possibility, as palms accumulate parenchyma tissue as they grow taller. We also observed that leaf epidermal cell sizes decreased with palm height in both *Iriartea deltoidea* and *Mauritia flexuosa*, which may be due to height related decreases in turgor pressure that may limit cell expansion in leaves from taller palms (Woodruff et al., 2004, Meinzer et al., 2008).

The variation in conduit sizes and densities in the boles of various sizes of *Iriartea deltoidea* palms may provide a clue as to why taller palms do not show evidence for hydraulic limitation in terms of decreased sapflux per unit leaf area. In *Iriartea deltoidea* boles, the metaxylem vessel diameters increase nonlinearly from the lower to the upper portions of the boles seeming to reach an asymptote.

Tapering of hydraulic conduits along a stem length was hypothesized to compensate for the increased frictional path length resistance (West et al., 1999; Becker et al., 2000a) and was experimentally shown in sycamore (*Acer pseudoplatanus* L.) (Petit et al., 2007) to partially compensate for an increased resistance in tall trees. West et al (1999) also hypothesize that vessel diameters reaching a theoretical maximum at the tops of tall trees may ultimately determine maximum heights and we see some evidence of this in that vessel diameters appear to be reaching an asymptote with height in *Iriartea deltoidea* boles.

We also observed that vascular bundle density declines with height more drastically in the inner region of the bole than in the peripheral region (Rich, 1987a). However, calculated Hagen-Poiseuille conductivities increase along the length of the bole do to the increases in vessel diameter. We also observed a coordinated pattern of vessel diameter and vascular bundle density across various regions of the *Iriartea deltoidea* boles and stilt roots where values tend to fall on a single line. The decreases in vascular bundle density in the inner boles were a direct consequence of increases in both the size of ground parenchyma cells and the lacunae diameters (Rich, 1987a).

We hypothesize that the increased size of parenchyma cells as well as the larger bole diameters allow taller *Iriartea deltoidea* palms to have greater water storage capacity which would also tend to mitigate any increased resistance in water flow due to the increased path length resistance (Goldstein et al., 1998; Phillips et al., 2003). Likewise, the increase in lacunae allow for large changes in parenchyma cell water content without incurring additional pressure forces within the bole (Holbrook and Sinclair, 1992). To evaluate the reliance of *Mauritia flexuosa* palms on bole water storage, we performed time lag analysis of sapflux measured in the lower bole and petioles, and found that daily sapflux in taller palms was more reliant on stored bole water than shorter palms. This may seem counterintuitive considering *Mauritia flexuosa* grows in inundated swamps; however reliance on stored water would, again, decrease the resistance of water flow to the leaves compared to pulling water from the inundation zone.

Therefore, although *Iriartea deltoidea* and *Mauritia flexuosa* are both palm species that are found in the western Amazonian rainforest, they exhibited interesting differences in intrinsic and extrinsic properties that were related, to varying degrees, with their differences in edaphic growing environment, differences in leaf habit, and differences in their ontogenetic bole development (Type A or Type B habit). We were also able to compare these two palm species individually across a range of heights in order to determine how growth rates, leaf area, sapflux rates and intrinsic anatomic properties changed as palms grew taller.

These findings have helped to elucidate the various strategies that these palms utilize to move water ever increasing distances to support increasing leaf areas as they get taller (capacitance, changes in conduit properties). Of course, this research has also introduced some still unanswered questions including the possible sustained lengthening of the boles in *Iriartea deltoidea*, as well as the significance of the palmate leaf habit in *Mauritia flexuosa*. Overall, the unique growing habit of these two palm species in terms of their columnar boles and relatively simple crown of leaves has allowed for the elucidation of many physiological (growth rates, sapflux rates, leaf areas) and anatomical aspects (stomatal properties, conduit properties) that would have been much more difficult in dicotyledonous, arborescent species.

8

Hydraulic Properties and Vulnerability to Embolism

INTRODUCTION

Palms are very distinctive members of the plant world in many ways. They are one of the few members of the monocot class that are able to reach significant heights. In doing so, they are able to transport water very long distances, matching many dicotyledonous species, without many of the features shared by almost all dicot trees including significant secondary growth and highly branched crowns. Although the crowns of palms are very simple compared with many other tree species, they are unique in many ways. For example, palm species hold records for both the longest pinnate self-supporting leaf in *Raphia regalis* Becc. at 25m as well as the largest palmately compound self-supporting leaf in *Corypha umbraculifera* L. at 8m in leaf diameter (Tomlinson, 2006). Not only do these records make the study of the hydraulics of palm petioles interesting, but they also allow for a significant proportion of the palm crown to be evaluated. Because tall palms generally hold between 5 and 30 palm fronds depending on the species, study of just one frond can represent up to 1/5 of the total photosynthetic area of the individual.

This study focuses on the hydraulics of palm petioles from three species; *Iriartea deltoidea* Ruiz & Pav. a species that grows in the northwest Amazon, *Mauritia flexuosa* L. a species that grows in swamps in the northwest Amazon and *Washingtonia robusta* H.Wendl., a species that grows in northwestern Mexico and southwestern United States (Uhl and Dransfield, 1987). These three species grow in widely different environments and represent the broad range of habitats where palms are found. Although about 75% of palms grow in habitats classified as rainforests (Dransfield, 1978), species are also found growing in tropical montane regions, dry forests, savannas and desert oases which include *Washingtonia robusta* (Tomlinson, 2006).

The only ecotype in which palms are largely excluded is one exhibiting extensive freezing temperatures due to the absence of secondary growth and dormancy mechanisms in palms (Tomlinson, 2006) although *Washingtonia robusta* is found growing where temperatures can drop below freezing. Even though a large proportion of palms grow in tropical rainforests, they are still exemplary of the flexibility of this plant group, as they can occupy a wide range of niches from shaded understories to dominant canopies (Dransfield, 1978), many times within the life cycle of a single individual as in the case of *Iriartea deltoidea.* Many species of palms including *Mauritia flexuosa* dominate perpetually inundated sites making aerial roots in order to withstand the anoxic soil conditions (Tomlinson, 1979).

Because various species of palms are able to grow and thrive in such varied habitats, it stands to reason that, as a group, they should exhibit interesting physiological mechanisms that allow them to deal with water stresses including low soil moisture and high evaporative demand. Several studies have focused on water relations in oil palms (*Elaeis guineensis* Jacq.), a species that grows in seasonally dry habitats, and found that stomatal closure is influenced by both soil water and atmospheric vapor pressure deficit (*D*)(Smith, 1989).

For example, Rees (1961) report midday stomatal closure at the end of the dry season due to both low soil moisture and high air temperature, with no stomatal closure during the wet season. Focusing only on the atmosphere, Dufrene and Saugier (1993) found that increased *D* induced rapid stomatal closure as well as increases in water use efficiency. Stomatal closures may be evidence that palms are avoiding embolism formation in their vascular conduits.

Embolisms are thought to occur when air is pulled into the water conducting conduits that are under a large negative pressure (Zimmermann, 1983; Tyree and Sperry, 1989; Cochard et al., 2007). These embolism events cause disruption in the water conducting pathways reducing conductivity (Zimmermann, 1983) and causing reductions in transpiration and photosynthesis (Sperry et al., 1993; Hubbard et al., 2001). Additionally, embolisms can also form in vascular conduits if the sap freezes and thaws under tension (Zimmermann, 1983). This could be especially important for a palm species like *Washingtonia robusta* which grow in places where freezing temperatures occasionally occur. Also, because palms lack significant secondary growth, they cannot replace conducting tissues every year. Therefore, their vascular conduits either need to efficiently avoid embolisms or efficiently reverse embolisms that were to occur in their vascular tissues if they are to remain functional over a lifetime.

This study seeks to measure hydraulic properties in palm fronds including leaf area to conducting area ratio, petiole conductivity, conduit anatomical properties and vulnerability to embolism. One objective of this study deals with comparing these hydraulic properties in fronds gathered from palms occurring over a range of heights. Palm fronds have been shown to differ significantly in leaf area across height (Rich et al., 1995); however, it is unknown if and how hydraulic properties of the petioles differ across height.

Additionally, petioles from taller palms may face additional challenges as the distance of water travel increases from the ground to the leaves (Ryan and Yoder, 1997). Another main objective of this study is to compare these hydraulic properties and their relationships with palm height between species growing in habitats that impart varying degrees of water stress and freezing stress on the plants found there. *Mauritia flexuosa*, growing in swamps in the tropical rainforest, faces the least water stress in terms of soil moisture and evaporative demand, *Iriartea deltoidea* like faces slightly more water stress growing in *terra firme* and *varzea* sites in the tropical rainforest, and *Washingtonia robusta,* growing in very dry habitats where palms tap groundwater sources (Uhl and Dransfield, 1987), faces the most water stress in terms of both soil moisture and evaporative demand.

Additionally, the two tropical rainforest species face no stress in terms of freezing temperatures, whereas *Washingtonia robusta,* would encounter freezing temperatures, albeit rarely, over the lifetime of a typical palm. Information gathered from this study will help elucidate how palms deal with water stress both from the external environment and from an increased path length of water travel as they grow taller.

MATERIALS AND METHODS

Site Descriptions

Iriartea deltoidea and *Mauritia flexuosa* palms were measured growing in Tiputini Biodiversity Station (0° 36′ S, 76° 27′ W), a 650 ha research facility located within Yasuni National Park in eastern Ecuador. The site receives approximately 2860 mm of rainfall annually and has an average temperature of 25.5°C (Macía 2004). *Mauritia flexuosa* was found growing in inundated conditions and measurements were made during February and March, 2008 and *Iriartea deltoidea* palms were found growing in terra firme sites and measurements were made during January and February, 2009. *Washingtonia robusta* palms were measured during July and August, 2008 on the campus of the University of Western Sydney in New South Wales Australia (33°36' S, 150°45' E) were they had been planted.

This site receives about 860 mm of rain per year with average monthly temperatures ranging from 3°C to 17°C in the winter and 17°C to 29°C in the summer (www.weather.com). This site also experiences freeze-thaw episodes with minimum temperatures ranging from -1°C to -7.2 °C for winter months from 1965 to 1975. Likewise the number of days with temperatures below 0°C ranged from 1 to 8.6 days per month for the same period (http://www.bom.gov.au/climate/averages /tables/

cw_067021). Leaf areas, petiole cross-sectional areas, and Huber values (petiole cross-sectional area/leaf area) from *Washingtonia robusta* palms growing at the Los Angeles County Arboretum & Botanic Garden (34° 8' N, 118° 3' W) in Arcadia, California (Renninger et al., 2009) were also included to compare with individuals growing in Australia.

As with Australia, this site also experiences occasional freeze-thaw events with record low temperatures ranging from -1 °C to -6 °C for winter months from 1940 to 2003 (http://www.weather.com/outlook/travel/businesstraveler/wxclimatology/ daily/USCA0040?climoMonth=3).

Frond Collection

For *Iriartea deltoidea,* fronds were collected from palms ranging in height from 1m to 15m tall measured from the ground to the base of the live crown. Palm fronds were collected by throwing a high limb rope chain saw™ (Green Mountain Products Inc., Norwalk, CT) over one of the lower fronds of a palm. This rope contains a section of chain saw links with teeth that allow the rope to grip into the palm petiole without slipping. Sufficient pulling on the rope ends would break the frond from the trunk of the palm allowing it to fall to the ground where it could be further processed.

For *Mauritia flexuosa,* fronds were collected from palms ranging in height from 0m (palms lacking an aboveground trunk) to 22m tall measured from the water surface to the base of the live crown. Since fronds were too stiff to be pulled down with ropes, palms were climbed by passing a rope through the crown.

The rope was secured on both sides and climbed using ascenders. Petioles were then cut using a machete and dropped to the ground where they could be processed. For *Washingtonia robusta,* fronds were collected from palms ranging in height from 1m to 16m tall measured from the ground to the base of the live crown. Depending on the height of the palms, fronds were cut down either with a 6m long pole saw, or with the aid of a bucket lift and the pole saw.

Leaf And Petiole Cross-sectional Area

For *Iriartea deltoidea,* leaf areas were measured by removing most of the leaflets from the petiole/rachis (two or three leaflets were left on the petiole/rachis for measuring water potential for the vulnerability curves, but their area was accounted for). Leaflets were weighed and then one leaflet was weighed singly and an overhead photograph of it taken with a known scaling factor so that total leaf weight in grams could be converted to m^2 leaf area. For *Mauritia flexuosa,* leaf areas were measured by taking an overhead photograph of the entire frond with a known scaling factor and then measuring its area using image analysis software (Image J, Scion Image, Frederick, MD, USA).

For *Washingtonia robusta,* leaf areas were measured by passing all leaflets through a Li-Cor leaf area meter (LI-3100C, Lincoln, NE). For all species, petiole cross-sectional areas were measured by tracing the end of the petiole on a piece of paper with a known scaling factor, taking an overhead photograph, then measuring its area using image analysis software. For *Iriartea deltoidea,* cross-sectional petiole area was measured at the point just below where the first leaflet was attached (i.e. where the petiole ends and the rachis begins) because leaves were pinnately compound. For *Mauritia flexuosa* and *Washingtonia robusta* both with palmate leaves, cross-sectional petiole area was measured at a point between 50 and 70 cm from the leaf lamina on the petiole.

Conductivity Measurement

For *Iriartea deltoidea,* specific conductivity (K_S) was measured using a gravity driven pressure apparatus. All fronds were removed from palms during rain events in order to prevent significant embolisms in the petioles. In addition, approximately 1m of the petiole was removed from the cut (proximal) end by recutting the petiole under water and subsequently the cut end was kept in water and the remaining leaves bagged to prevent embolism formation. Most leaflets were removed however approximately 4-5 were kept attached to the rachis so that the water potential of the petiole xylem could be measured for the vulnerability curves (see *Vulnerability curves* section).

There is some discrepancy as to where the majority of the hydraulic resistance in the leaf lies and whether it is within the leaf vasculature (Sack et al., 2004) or outside of it (Cochard et al., 2004); however removal of the majority of leaflets should alleviate all of the leaf resistance outside the vascular tissue and most of the resistance from the leaf lamina xylem (other than the junction between the petiole xylem and midribs). The cut end of the petiole was inserted into a compression fitting designed for use with the high pressure flow meter (HPFM; Dynamax, Houston, TX) and Blu-tack (Bostik, Thomastown, Victoria, Australia) was inserted into the spaces between the petiole and the rubber stopper to ensure a waterproof fit. The compression fitting was then attached to tubing that was fitted to a pipette raised approximately 0.5m above the sample. Specific conductivity (K_S) (kg m^{-1} s^{-1} MPa^{-1}) was calculated as follows:

$$K_s = \frac{Q \times l}{A \times \Delta P} \tag{1}$$

where Q is the volume flow rate (kg s^{-1}) of water through the sample measured by timing the drop of the meniscus through the pipette, l is the length of the petiole/rachis (m), A is the petiole cross-sectional area (m^2) and DP is the gravity induced pressure head (MPa).

Leaf specific conductivity (K_L) (kg m^{-1} s^{-1} MPa^{-1}) was then calculated by multiplying specific conductivity by the Huber value.

For *Mauritia flexuosa,* specific conductivity was measured using a similar pressure driven flow as used for *Iriartea deltoidea* except that instead of using the entire petiole, two subsamples approximately 1cm^2 and 10 cm long were cut from the petiole and used to make the measurements. After these samples were cut, they were placed under a vacuum to remove all embolisms from the vessels. Specific conductivity (K_s) was measured using a pressure sleeve apparatus where the sample is placed in a chamber containing a latex membrane (Spicer and Gartner 1998). A very low pressure was applied to the chamber to press the membrane against the sample to prevent water leakage from its cut sides. Flow rate through the subsamples was measured and specific conductivity and leaf specific conductivity were calculated using the equations described for *Iriartea deltoidea*.

For *Washingtonia robusta*, specific conductivity was measured on the entire petiole as with *Iriartea deltoidea*. Similarly, the petiole cut end was inserted into a compression fitting for the HPFM and Blu-tack was inserted for a waterproof fit. All vessels were refilled by attaching the petiole to the HPFM and pushing water through with a maximum pressure of 200 kPa ensuring that all embolisms were removed. Specific conductivity was noted so that it could be compared to the vacuum driven method (as follows) (Kolb et al., 1996). Petioles were then attached to an apparatus that used slight (< 50 kPa) negative pressures generated using a vacuum pump (instead of gravity driven positive pressures) to measure conductivity. Leaves remained attached to the petioles however they were folded over the petiole so that they could fit into the vacuum chamber.

This procedure broke many of the main midribs but left some of the smaller leaflets intact for use in measuring xylem water potentials of the petioles for the vulnerability curves (see *Vulnerability curves* section). Again, this should have removed most of the resistance outside the leaf xylem and within the leaf xylem other than the resistance in the junction from the petiole to the leaf midribs. Petioles were placed inside a chamber, and tubing attached to the HPFM compression fitting was inserted through a seal in the chamber lid and attached to a pipette. A vacuum pump was used to draw a vacuum on the chamber that provided the gradient to pull water from the pipette through the petiole (Prior and Eamus, 2000).

Flow rate was measured by timing the drop in the meniscus of water through the pipette. Flow rates were measured at five different negative pressures (DP = -15, -20, -25, -30, -40 kPa) with the slope of a relationship between flow rate (kg s^{-1}) and negative pressure (MPa) representing hydraulic conductance (K_h) of the sample. This value was multiplied by the length of the petiole and divided by the cross sectional area of the petiole to give a value of specific conductivity (K_S). This value was then multiplied by the Huber value to provide an estimate of leaf specific conductivity (K_L). Several studies have found no significant differences between hydraulic conductance measured with vacuum driven tensions, positive pressures, and evaporative methods even though they all use different driving forces (Kolb et al. 1996; Nardini et al., 2001; Sack et al., 2002) therefore comparisons of specific conductivity between palm species should be appropriate.

Vulnerability Curves

Vulnerability curves were made for both *Iriartea deltoidea* and *Washingtonia robusta.* After initial specific conductivities were measured, petioles were allowed to bench dry. Parafilm was wrapped around the cut end of the petiole to keep it moist and remaining leaflets were put in an opaque plastic bag so their stomata would close and their water potential would equilibrate with the petiole. After *ca.* 2 hours, a piece of leaf containing a prominent vein was removed and its water potential measured using a Scholander type pressure chamber (PMS Instruments, Corvallis, Oregon). The cut end of the petiole was refreshed using a razor blade and specific conductivity was again measured with either gravity driven pressure in the case of *Iriartea deltoidea* or negative pressure in the case of *Washingtonia robusta.* This process was repeated until at least 80% of the conductivity in the petiole was lost to embolism. Vulnerability curves were made by plotting petiole water potential vs. percent loss of conductivity (PLC) calculated as follows:

$$PLC = \frac{K_S - K_\psi}{K_\psi} \quad (2)$$

where K_S is the maximum conductivity and K_Y is the conductivity at a given water potential. Sigmoid functions were fit and used to find P_{50}, the water potential at which 50% of the conductivity was lost.

Petiole Conduit Properties

Vessel lengths were measured in the petioles of both *Iriartea deltoidea* and *Washingtonia robusta.* For *Iriartea deltoidea* vessel lengths were determined using a similar air injection methodology as Zimmermann and Jeje (1981). The petiole end was attached to tubing that was inserted into the pressure chamber (PMS Instruments, Corvallis, Oregon).

The chamber was then pressurized with low pressure (less than 0.5 MPa) and the opposite end of the petiole was placed in water to check for the presence of bubbles. Pieces 10cm long were cut from the end until bubbles were seen. For *Washingtonia robusta* maximum vessel length was determined using the HPFM (Dynamax, Houston, TX). To begin, the petiole was attached to the HPFM and resistance to flow was logged. 5cm long pieces were cut from the opposite end corresponding to decreases in resistance. Once the point of maximum vessel length was reached, removal of 5cm long pieces corresponded to larger decreases in resistance. Plots of resistance vs. length of the sample confirmed this transition and signified the maximum vessel length of the petiole.

Vessel diameters and vascular bundle densities were measured in all three species. Before conductivity was measured a small piece of the petiole (approximately 5cm long) was removed. Thin cross-sections were cut by hand with a razorblade and stained with 1% Toluidine Blue O. Sections were then destained in water and placed on a slide. Water was removed from the slide, permount™ (Fisher Scientific, Fair Lawn NJ) was applied and a coverslip was attached. Slides were then placed under a compound light microscope (Olympus BX60 with Jenoptik C14 ProgRes Camera) and photographs were taken at 20X magnification in the case of *Mauritia flexuosa* and *Washingtonia robusta* and at 40X magnification in the case of *Iriartea deltoidea* (on a Leica CME compound light microscope). Photographs were then imported into image analysis software (ImageJ, Scion Image, Frederick, MD, USA) and vessel diameters and vascular bundle densities (counts of vascular bundles per area) were measured.

Only metaxylem vessels were measured for vessel diameters since they are significantly larger than protoxylem vessels and account for the majority of flow through petioles/rachises.

Leaf Water Potentials

Leaf water potentials were measured in *Iriartea deltoidea* and *Washingtonia robusta*. For *Iriartea deltoidea*, leaf water potentials were measured around midday (between 1100 and 1400) on January 16 and 17, 2009, both of which were clear days with blue skies and little cloud cover. Leaflets were collected from palms of varying heights and their water potentials measured with a Scholander type pressure chamber (PMS Instruments, Corvallis, Oregon). For palms that were too tall to be reached from the ground a pole saw was used to cut leaflets. Palms between 6m to 13m tall were growing near each other, so the tallest palm (13 m) was climbed using a palm climbing apparatus (www.nif.org.in/bd/node/125) to the base of the live crown and a pole saw used to cut leaflets from all three palms. The 23 m tall palm was located next to a canopy walkway, and the pole saw was used from the walkway to remove a leaflet from this palm. For *Washingtonia robusta*, leaf water potentials were measured around midday (between 1130 and 1430) on June 25th, 2008 which was a clear day with blue skies and little cloud cover. Leaflets were collected from palms of varying heights and their water potentials measured with a Scholander type pressure chamber (PMS Instruments, Corvallis, Oregon). For palms that were too tall to be reached from the ground, a bucket lift was used to access the crowns.

DOUBLE-DYE EXPERIMENT

For small *Washingtonia robusta* palms, approximately 1m tall, a double-dye staining experiment was performed similar in methodology to Zwieniecki and Holbrook (1998) in order to determine if vessels in the petioles embolize and refill on a daily basis. To begin, a 0.1% solution of basic fuchsin was introduced to petioles around 1400h through a syringe needle that was attached via tubing to a reservoir of the dye. In order to introduce the dye without causing embolisms, a piece of large tubing (approx. 5cm in diameter) was cut to a length of approximately 5cm. Blu-tack (Bostik, Thomastown, Victoria, Australia) was pressed to the end of the tubing and once the tubing was placed on the flat (adaxial) side of the petiole, it created a water-tight seal. The tubing was filled with water, and a probe was used to create a hole in the petiole under the water layer.

The tip of the syringe was then placed in this hole and the flow of dye into the petiole commenced. The dye was allowed to be drawn into the petiole via the transpiration stream until around sunset (approximately 1800h) at which point water was fed into the syringe. The following morning around sunrise (600h) a 0.1% solution of Toluidine Blue O was introduced through the same hole in the petiole and was allowed to be drawn into the petiole until around 1000h. The frond was then cut from the palm and returned to the lab. The petiole was cut into 5cm long pieces from the point of dye insertion to the point of leaf attachment. Vessels that were functional in the afternoon were stained purple from both dyes or simply red from the basic fuchsin (as the basic fuchsin has a greater absorption to the cell walls (Zweiniecki and Holbrook, 1998)), vessels that had embolized in the afternoon and refilled overnight were stained blue and vessels that are unstained were not in the conducting path where the dye was introduced.

Because of a larger evaporative demand in the afternoon the basic fuchsin traveled farther up the stem than the Toluidine blue. Therefore locations fairly close to the site of dye insertion (approximately 10-15 cm away) were chosen for analysis. Pieces were then viewed with a dissecting scope (Leica MZ12 with JVC KY camera) and hand sections were cut with a razor blade, placed on slides and viewed at 20X magnification with a compound light microscope (Olympus BX60 with Jenoptik C14 ProgRes Camera). Using images from 8 separate petioles viewed under the dissecting scope, counts of vascular bundles stained blue, red and purple were made and percentages of the total number of stained vascular bundles were calculated.

Statistical Analyses

Correlation and significance (r^2 and p-values) for all regressions were calculated using SigmaPlot 2000 Version 6.1 (SPSS Inc. Chicago, IL, USA). Least square analysis and Tukey HSD tests were also performed using R version 2.5.1 (The R Foundation for Statistical Computing, http://www.R-project.org) to determine whether means in each category were significantly different from one another.

RESULTS

Leaf And Petiole Cross-sectional Areas

Individual frond leaf areas showed contrasting patterns relative to height. *Iriartea deltoidea* leaf areas linearly increased with height ($r^2 = 0.69$, $p = 0.0005$); *Mauritia flexuosa* leaf areas initially increased then reached an asymptote in tall palms ($r^2 = 0.97$, $p = 0.0053$) and leaf areas in *Washingtonia robusta* initially increasing with height, reaching a maximum then decreasing in taller palms ($r^2 = 0.61$, $p = 0.0021$). Individual frond leaf areas and Huber values from *Washingtonia robusta* palms growing in Los Angeles match closely with those from Australia.

Averaged across height, individual frond leaf areas did not differ significantly between *Iriartea deltoidea* and *Mauritia flexuosa,* but were three times higher than that of *Washingtonia robusta.* Petiole cross-sectional areas for all three species followed similar patterns as leaf areas with regard to height (data not shown). Petiole cross-sectional areas did not differ significantly between *Iriartea deltoidea* and *Washingtonia robusta.* However, they were significantly greater in *Mauritia flexuosa* by almost a factor of ten. Except for fronds from small palms, Huber values remained constant across height for *Iriartea deltoidea, Mauritia flexuosa* and *Washingtonia robusta* (p-values = 0.71, 0.46 and 0.34 respectively when 0 and 1m tall palms are excluded). When averaged across height, Huber values for *Washingtonia robusta* were significantly larger than *Iriartea deltoidea* by about a factor of two, but significantly smaller than *Mauritia flexuosa* by about a factor of two.

Conductivity

There were no significant patterns between specific conductivity (K_S) and height in *Iriartea deltoidea* (p = 0.18), *Mauritia flexuosa* (p = 0.82), or *Washingtonia robusta* (p = 0.80). Averaged across height, specific conductivities in *Iriartea deltoidea* petioles were significantly greater by a factor of two or more compared to *Mauritia flexuosa* and *Washingtonia robusta* (which did not differ significantly)(Table 5.1). Likewise, there was no pattern between leaf specific conductivity (K_L) and height in *Iriartea deltoidea* (p = 0.97) or *Mauritia flexuosa* (p = 0.88). However, there was a slight, but significant relationship between height and leaf specific conductivity in *Washingtonia robusta* ($r^2 = 0.57$, p = 0.0007), with leaf specific conductivity in petioles decreasing slightly in taller palms.

Averaged across heights, leaf specific conductivities of *Iriartea deltoidea* and *Washingtonia robusta* petioles were not significantly different from each other, but were significantly smaller than *Mauritia flexuosa* petioles by about a factor of two.

Vessel And Vascular Bundle Properties

For both *Iriartea deltoidea* and *Washingtonia robusta*, maximum vessel lengths in petioles initially increased with height, reached a maximum then remained constant in taller palms ($r^2 = 0.72$, p = 0.078 and $r^2 = 0.45$, p = 0.028 respectively). Averaged across height, maximum vessels lengths in *Iriartea deltoidea* were significantly longer than in *Washingtonia robusta* but about a factor of two. Average metaxylem vessel diameters differed in all three species with height, with *Iriartea deltoidea* exhibiting a linear increase across height ($r^2 = 0.41$, p = 0.014), *Mauritia flexuosa* exhibiting no relationship with height (p = 0.46) and *Washingtonia robusta* exhibiting a weak curvilinear relationship where vessels initially widened with height, reached a maximum at *ca.* 9 m palm height, then were smaller in petioles from taller palms ($r^2 = 0.25$, p = 0.16).

Averaged across heights, metaxylem vessels were significantly wider by about a factor of two in *Mauritia flexuosa* compared to *Iriartea deltoidea* and *Washingtonia robusta* which did not differ significantly from one another. Vascular bundle densities showed opposing patterns with height than vessel diameters in *Iriartea deltoidea* and *Washingtonia robusta*. Vascular bundles were more frequent with height showing a linear increase in both *Washingtonia robusta* ($r^2 = 0.52$, $p = 0.0015$) and *Mauritia flexuosa* ($r^2 = 0.68$, $p = 0.0009$), but decreasing nonlinearly in frequency with height in *Iriartea deltoidea* ($r^2 = 0.33$, $p = 0.11$). Averaged across height, vascular bundle densities were slightly but significantly higher in *Washingtonia robusta* than *Iriartea deltoidea* and both differed significantly from *Mauritia flexuosa* having higher vascular bundle densities by about a factor of five.

Vulnerability to Embolism

P_{50} values did not differ significantly across height in *Iriartea deltoidea* ($p = 0.61$), while P_{50} values became increasingly more negative in taller *Washingtonia robusta* palms ($r^2 = 0.66$, $p = 0.0001$). Despite the different relationships with height, when averaged across height, P_{50} values for *Iriartea deltoidea* and *Washingtonia robusta* were not significantly different. Midday leaf water potentials showed no significant relationship with height in either *Iriartea deltoidea* ($p = 0.17$) or *Washingtonia robusta* ($p = 0.2$). For *Iriartea deltoidea* the regression was performed by excluding the 1m tall palms as they were more shaded than taller palms, which may have given them less negative leaf water potentials. Averaged across height, midday leaf water potentials were significantly more negative in *Washingtonia robusta* than in *Iriartea deltoidea*.

Double-dye Experiment

The double-dye staining experiment in petioles from 1m tall *Washingtonia robusta* palms showed evidence that vessels were embolized and non-functional in the afternoon and had refilled the following morning. Across eight different petioles, an average of 37% (SE = 0.07) of stained vessels were blue (the morning dye), 30% (SE = 0.07) of the stained vessels were red (the afternoon dye) and 0.33% (SE = 0.05) of the stained vessels were purple (representing both colors). Therefore 37% of the vessels in contact with the dye were embolized in the afternoon and refilled the following morning while 63% remained functional.

DISCUSSION

We found some interesting differences as well as similarities in the hydraulic properties of petioles both within a species across palm height and between species that grow in widely differing climate regimes. With regard to vulnerability to embolism, it is interesting to note that the average P_{50} value for both *Iriartea deltoidea,* a tropical rainforest species, and *Washingtonia robusta,* a subtropical species growing in a drier climate, were not significantly different from one another at around -1.3 MPa. It does appear that these palms are fairly vulnerable to embolism however other tropical tree species are fairly vulnerable as well with *Schefflera morototoni* ((Aubl.) Maguire, Steyerm. & Frodin) having a P50 value of -1.5 MPa (Tyree et al., 1991) and *Ochroma pyramidale* (Cav. ex lamb) and *Pseudobombax septenatum* (Jacq.) both being at least 50% embolized at -1 MPa (Machado and Tyree, 1994). However, our palms were significantly more vulnerable to embolism than *Rhapis excelsa* (Thunb.) A. Henry, where embolisms occurred only below -2.9 MPa (Sperry, 1985; Sperry 1986). While P_{50} values were consistent across height in *Iriartea deltoidea,* there was a significant relationship in *Washingtonia robusta* where taller palms had significantly more negative P_{50} values. When comparing P_{50} values with leaf water potentials taken in the field, it would appear that petioles from both species experience fairly considerable daily embolisms.

For *Iriartea deltoidea,* P_{50} values matched fairly well with midday leaf water potentials for a cloudless, high VPD day meaning that 50% of petiole conductivity could have been lost to embolisms on that particular day. In *Washingtonia robusta,* the differences are even more disparate where average midday leaf water potentials were around -2.2 MPa on a sunny, high VPD day. This corresponds to about 50% loss of conductivity in taller palms and significantly more in shorter palms. Of course, it is important to point out that comparison of leaf water potentials with P_{50} values of the petiole xylem could be misleading if there is a large resistance, and therefore large difference in water potential, between the petiole and leaf attachment (Meinzer, 2002).

We have estimates of the resistance of the petiole and leaf attachment zone as well as the resistance of the petiole with leaves removed from our estimates of maximum vessel length in *Washingtonia robusta*. These measurements show that approximately 32% (SE =0.04) of the total resistance resides in the leaf attachment zone with the petiole comprising approximately 68%. Therefore, even if the bole resistance was minimal, petiole water potential would still be around -1.5 MPa which is similar to the P_{50} values of medium height *Washingtonia robusta* palms but still well above the P_{50} values of the shortest palms. This calculated value could vary between both individuals and between differing species.

For example, Sperry (1985) reported that the pressure potential difference between the stem and leaf lamina in *Rhapis excelsa* was between -0.7 to -1.5 MPa. In *Cocos nucifera*, petiole xylem water potentials (measured on bagged leaves) were between -0.2 and -1.3 MPa depending on environmental conditions (Milburn and Zimmermann, 1977), which are significantly lower than the leaf water potentials we measured in *Washingtonia robusta*, a similar subtropical species, but with the maximum being similar to our calculated value for petiole water potential.

It is apparent from the comparison of leaf water potentials and P_{50} values and the double-dye staining experiment in *Washingtonia robusta* that some degree of embolism is occurring daily in the petioles of *Iriartea deltoidea* and *Washingtonia robusta*. One might expect that a monocot species with little ability for secondary growth would be especially resistant to embolisms in order to preserve its conducting tissues. However, Canny (2001) report that large metaxylem vessels in maize leaves embolized during the day, and Neufeld et al. (1992) found that some sugarcane clones lost between 50 and 80% conductivity during the day with both studies finding refilling overnight. As for palms, Drake and Franks (2003) found that specific conductivity was significantly reduced in two species of climbing palms (*Calamus sp.*) during the dry season, and Sperry (1985) found evidence for embolisms in the petioles of *Rhapis excelsa* during dry periods. Also, several studies have found petioles to be more vulnerable to embolism than stems, and that cavitation in the petioles may act as a signal for stomatal closure (Tyree et al., 1993; Tsuda and Tyree, 1997; Salleo et al., 2001).

Also, if the main resistance to water transport in the frond is located in the leaf lamina, then significant cavitation in the petiole may not have a large impact on whole frond conductance (Nardini et al., 2003). In a situation that can be viewed as analogous to whole palm fronds, Meinzer (2002) calculated that if shoot resistance is partitioned equally between stems and leaves, a 50% loss of conductivity in the stem will only decrease total shoot resistance by 25%. If leaf resistance is much larger than petiole resistance, cavitation in the petiole will have even less of an impact on total frond resistance. Additionally, in a modeling exercise, Hölttä et al. (2008) found that cavitation may actually be beneficial to plants because the water freed by cavitation will increase water potentials providing a "capacitive effect".

This effect may allow stomata to remain open for a longer period of time in conditions that are conducive to photosynthesis (but also to embolism formation). They also calculate that this capacitive effect will be larger the closer the conduits are to the leaves, meaning that cavitation in petiole xylem of palm fronds may benefit leaf gas exchange in this regard. Of course, this effect is only beneficial if cavitations can be repaired as discussed below. Therefore, evidence is mounting that daily embolism formation and nightly reversal may be a more frequent occurrence than first thought (Zwieniecki and Holbrook, 1998; Bucci et al., 2003).

Although we focused on measuring vulnerability to water stress induced cavitation, freeze-thaw induced embolism may also be important for *Washingtonia robusta*, a species that grows in places that experience occasional freezing temperatures that are likely to occur over the lifetime of a palm. Although minimum temperatures are not severe (from -1°C to -6°C) xylem sap contains little solutes and therefore freezes at temperatures just under 0°C (Ball et al., 2006). Freeze-thaw embolisms occur when the liquid xylem freezes, forcing air out of solution. When the sap thaws, these bubbles can dissolve back into solution or expand to cavitate the conduit. Cavitation depends both on the size of the bubble (which is directly related to the size of the conduit) and the degree of tension in the water column during thawing (Zimmermann, 1983)

Several studies report vessels sizes at which trees are sensitive to freeze-thaw embolisms even at relatively minor tensions which range from 15mm (Feild and Brodribb, 2001), to 22mm (Stuart et al., 2007), to 40mm (Davis et al., 1999). Vessel diameters in the petioles of *Washingtonia robusta* range from between 80mm and 120 mm with a mean of 105 mm across a range of heights. Therefore, even very minor tensions in the petiole during the thawing process will cause vessels to cavitate. Langan et al. (1997) found that *Rhus laurina* with vessels that range from 40-80 mm in diameter embolized at all tensions measured during a freeze-thaw treatment, and Sperry and Sullivan (1992) found that *Quercus gambelii* with vessels that range from 10 to 110 mm became 90% embolized by freeze-thaw treatment at the moderate tension of 0.2 MPa. Of course, in *Washingtonia robusta* palms that can reach 30m tall in their lifetime, tensions of 0.3 MPa will be found in petioles of the tallest palms, simply due to the gravity component.

Since monocot stems cannot produce new vessels to replace embolized ones, efficient refilling of embolized vessels to restore conductivity is necessary. Positive pressures generated by the roots may be one way in which palms can refill embolized vessels. Davis (1961) measured positive pressures ranging from 0.003 to 0.12 MPa in 10 palm species and Milburn and Davis (1973) hypothesize that because cavitation occurred relatively easily in palms subjected to leaf water stress, positive root pressures could serve to refill embclized vessels overnight. This could prove to be particularly important in the short *Washingtonia robusta* palms that were found to be exceptionally vulnerable to embolism but within a height range that root pressures could function in refilling. However, root pressure is unlikely to be responsible for refilling of vessels at the tops of tall palms and can only function when the plant is not actively transpiring.

Two other theories for refilling of embolisms suggest the either osmosis or reverse osmosis is responsible for xylem refilling with either sugar secretion into embolized vessels providing the driving force to refill them or sugar buildup in surrounding parenchyma cells (causing an increase in turgor and a pressure buildup) that would force water into embolized conduits (McCully, 1999; Lovisolo and Schubert, 2006). Kasturi Bai and Rajagopal (2000) found that coconut palms accumulated more sugars in their leaves during periods of water stress compared to non-stressed periods with more drought tolerant palms accumulating significantly more.

Currently, the reverse osmosis mechanism has more experimental evidence with Canny (1997) and McCully (1999) presenting images showing that embolized vessels are refilled by liquid extruded through pits shared with parenchyma. Additionally, Salleo et al. (1996) found that externally applied positive pressures sped up conduit refilling compared with unpressurized stems.

There is also promising research that suggests that phloem may play a role (Salleo et al., 1996; Zwieniecki et al., 2000; Salleo et al., 2004) in repairing embolisms. Phloem carries sugars from their origins to locations throughout the plant and could serve as the source for the sugars that generate the osmotic potential to refill vessels.

Additionally, when sugars exit the phloem, the osmotic potential of the phloem drops and the surplus water that originally transported the sugars also exits the phloem and is recycled by the xylem (Milburn, 1996; Patrick et al., 2001). This surplus phloem water makes up 1 to 3% of xylem transport and could make up much of the water used to refill embolized vessels (Milburn, 1996). Several studies have found that inactivating the phloem by girdling significantly impairs embolism repair (Salleo et al., 1996; Zwieniecki et al., 2000; Salleo et al., 2004).

Salleo et al. (2006) suggest that both the amount of active phloem and the intra-phloem pressure are important to embolism refilling because girdled stems that were mechanically pressurized refilled similarly to stems with intact phloem. Because palms are monocots their "woody" tissue is made up of thousands of vascular bundles that contain both xylem and phloem elements. Therefore, the phloem tissue in palms is in very close proximity to xylem conduits, making it plausible that the phloem could play a direct role if xylem conduits were to become embolized. This is in contrast with dicotyledonous trees in which the phloem is located adjacent to the vascular cambium and is, therefore, only in close proximity to the newest formed xylem conduits.

In addition to the vulnerability to embolism, several interesting comparisons arise between leaf and petiole traits both across species and within species of differing palm heights. For example, the three palm species studied show wide variation in leaf area as well as opposing patterns of leaf area with height. These patterns appear to be related to their environment with the tropical rainforest palms, *Iriartea deltoidea* and *Mauritia flexuosa,* maintaining significantly higher frond leaf areas than *Washingtonia robusta,* a species that grows in relatively dry, subtropical locations. Likewise, in both tropical rainforest species, leaf areas increase with palm height, whereas in *Washingtonia robusta,* leaf areas decrease with height after an initial increase.

These findings are consistent with work done by Calvo-Alvarado et al. (2008) which shows that in 5 rainforest species, leaf areas increase exponentially with height and contrary to most temperate species which exhibit decreases in leaf area to sapwood areas with height (McDowell et al., 2002). The smaller leaf areas seen in *Washingtonia robusta* as well as the decrease in leaf area with height may be related to leaf temperature as well with larger leaves having higher resistances to heat dissipation through convection than smaller leaves (Parkhurst and Loucks, 1972) which becomes important when stomata close and latent heat exchange is reduced (Knoerr and Gay, 1965) or when wind speed is reduced (Vogel, 2009). Smaller leaf areas in taller *Washingtonia robusta* palms may also be a function of increased exposure to wind with Niklas (1996) finding that open grown *Acer saccharum* (L.) saplings had smaller leaves than that of sheltered saplings.

Although none of our palm species showed changes in Huber values (petiole area to leaf area ratio) with height, they differed widely in their Huber values. *Washingtonia robusta* exhibited significantly more petiole area per unit leaf area than *Iriartea deltoidea* and Huber values in *Mauritia flexuosa* were far greater than either palm species. *Washingtonia robusta* may exhibit higher Huber values due to its windy growing environment, as Watt et al (2005) found that radiata pines (*Pinus radiata* D.Don) had larger branch diameter when they were exposed to wind compared to sheltered environments. Widening branches increases the second moment of area and would make the branches more stable as well as adding conducting area that would make up for low conductivity, compression wood in stems (Watt et al., 2005). Although palms do not exhibit compression wood, larger conducting areas could make up for an increased proportion of fibers in petioles. However, *Mauritia flexuosa,* a palm species that grows in tropical rainforest swamps and is exposed to little wind, has by far the highest Huber values.

These large Huber values may be needed to support high rates of transpiration needed for latent heat loss (Niinemets et al., 2007; Vogel, 2009). It is also interesting to note that both *Mauritia flexuosa* and *Washingtonia robusta* have palmate leaves while *Iriartea deltoidea* has pinnate leaves and these differences could explain the difference in Huber values. Zobel and Liu (1980) found that fan palms have much larger conductances than pinnate palms and this may be due to a need for greater evaporative cooling of the large, undivided palmate leaves. Additionally, in their study of pinnate and palmate leaves, Niklas (1993) found that the tapering of petioles of nine pinnate leaves is consistent with their principle of "economy in design" in terms of providing uniform strength with the least amount of construction material, as opposed to six palmate leaves which did not follow this design principle. Therefore, pinnate leaves may be more efficient not only structurally, but in providing water to leaves.

As with Huber values, petiole specific conductivity showed no relationship with palm height in any of the species studied, although there were differences between species. *Washingtonia robusta,* which grows in the driest climate had the lowest petiole specific conductivity and is consistent with findings from Preston and Ackerly (2003) that more xeric adapted species generally have lower stem specific conductivity. Likewise, maximum vessel lengths were significantly longer in *Iriartea deltoidea* than in *Washingtonia robusta*. This may be a reaction to greater water stress in *Washingtonia robusta* as shorter vessels provide more redundancy if a vessel is lost to embolism and may be more easily refilled (Zimmermann, 1983), but has decreased conductivity because of greater end wall resistance (Sperry et al., 2005).

Also, although *Iriartea deltoidea* and *Washingtonia robusta* overlap broadly in vessel diameter and vascular bundle densities, they each exhibit opposing relationships in terms of these two variables with palm height that allow them to maintain specific conductivities in the petioles from palms of differing heights. This pattern of a tradeoff between conduit size and density is reported by Sperry et al. (2008) finding that there is a universal trend in hydraulic architecture for a decrease in conduits per area with increasing conduit diameter.

This also would explain why *Mauritia flexuosa,* which has, by far, the largest vessels also has, by far, the lowest vascular bundle density. *Mauritia flexuosa* may exhibit such large vessels because it grows predominantly in swamps with little risk of soil moisture stress and embolism. It is also possible that the contrasting patterns in vascular bundle density and vessel diameter with height in *Iriartea deltoidea* could be driven by structural mechanics instead of hydraulics. As petioles get larger and heavier, vascular bundles with more fibrous bundles may be needed lowering the overall bundle density but necessitating larger diameter vessels to maintain conductivity.

Despite wide variation in leaf areas, Huber values, specific conductivities and vascular anatomy both across height within petioles of a given species and between the three palm species grown in contrasting environments, leaf specific conductivities in petioles of *Iriartea deltoidea* and *Washingtonia robusta* are surprisingly similar; both within and between species. Other studies have found similar results with Brodribb and Feild (2000) finding convergence in leaf specific conductivity in several species of vessel and vessel-less angiosperms as well as a conifer in rainforests of New Caledonia and Tasmania. Likewise, Vander Willigen et al. (2000) grew five subtropical tree species from contrasting environments in a common garden and found that branch specific conductivities and Huber values varied conversely resulting in similar maximum leaf specific conductivity values.

Therefore, although the palm individuals studied differed significantly in height and growing environment, they all exhibited similar capacities for water transport per unit leaf area. *Mauritia flexuosa* exhibited slightly higher leaf specific conductivities than the other two species, possibly because it grows in swamps and is therefore not subjected to soil moisture stress.

In summary, we found significant differences in leaf area, Huber values, specific conductivity and petiole vascular anatomy in three palm species studied due in part to their widely differing growing environments. Despite large differences in leaf area within a given species in fronds from palms of different heights and the large differences in leaf area, Huber values and specific conductivity between species, *Iriartea deltoidea* and *Washingtonia robusta* displayed surprisingly similar leaf specific conductivities both within species in fronds from palms varying widely in height and leaf area and between species even though they grow in widely differing environments.

It was also interesting to note that both species had similar average P_{50} values in petioles subjected to water stress induced embolism, although a significant relationship between P_{50} and palm height was found in *Washingtonia robusta* but not *Iriartea deltoidea*. We also present evidence that water stress induced embolisms may occur on a daily basis and be refilled nightly in the petioles from these species. Likewise, *Washingtonia robusta* is vulnerable to freeze-thaw induced cavitation because of its growing location. These results on embolism formation and reversal warrant more study in both the daily dynamics of embolism formation and refilling in palms as well as the mechanism by which refilling occurs.

9

Fungal Diseases

DAMPING OFF OF SEEDLINGS

Causal organism: Phythium debaryanum

Symptoms: Damping off may appear as pre-emergence or post-emergence

1) In case of pre-emergence damping off , the young seedlings are killed even before they reach the surface of soil. They may be killed before hypocotyl has broken the seed coat. The radical & plumule, when come out of seed under go complete rotting.
2) The post emergence damping off is very conspicuous:
    i) It is characterized by toppling over of infected seedling any time after they emerge from soil.
    ii) Infection usually occurs at or below ground level.
    iii) Infected tissues appear water soaked and soft.
    iv) As the disease advance the stem becomes constricted at base & plant collapse
    v) Generally cotyledons & leaves slightly wilt before seedling fall on ground.
    vi) Finally the fallen seedling loses its colour & rots away.

Control measures:

(1) Seed treatment with fungicides provides good control for pre emergence damping off. The common fungicides are Thiram , Captan , Metalaxyl.

(2) Seed coating with spores of Trichoderma harzianum & penicillium oxalicum have been found effective as *biological control* method of damping off .

3) Treatment of nursery soil is also very important. Sprinkling Formalin over lose soil in sufficient amount to soak it to depth of at least 10cm & sowing should be done after several days when formalin disappear .

4) Drenching of soil with 1% Bordeaux mixture , 0.5% Perenox , 0.1% Ceresan , 0.2% Fytolon is useful for disinfection of soil &control of post emergence D.O.

5) Additional precautions such as :

   i) Thin sowing to avoid crowding.

   ii) Light sandy soils for nursery.

   iii) Well decomposed manure should de used.

   iv) Raised nursery beds to drain excess water.

   v) Light but frequent irrigation.

   vi) Sterilizing soil by burning a 30cm thick stack of farm thrash on nursery beds. are useful for control of disease.

Disease cycle: The pathogen is a natural inhabitant of soil where it may grow saprophytically or in parasitic form on fibrous roots.

The *primary infection* occur through oospores which serves as over wintering or over summering organs . Under favorable conditions , the oospores germinate to produce zoospores which come in contact with host & germinate by givibg out germ tube , which penetrates the cell wall of hypocotyl & becomes established in intercellular space of cortical tissues.

Soon the fungus grows inter or intra cellularly in the parenchymatous tissues where it begins to reproduce by formation of sporangia .

The sporangia get detached & are dispersed by wind & water to other locations where they germinate and cause infection. Thus acting as secondary source of infection.

LATE BLIGHT OF POTATO

Causal organism: Phytophthora infestans

Host: Potato plant (Solanum tuberosum)

Symptoms:

(1) First symptom of disease appears as hydrotic spots at margins and tips of lower leaves. These spots later become necrotic & turn brown to black in colour .

(2) In moist weather these spots spread & cover the whole plant, the host plant decays and produces fowl smell.

(3) The potato tubers are also infected while in field or during harvest or storage. The first sign of tuber infection is that the upper skin of tuber becomes brown & then turns black.

4) The diseased tubers are some what depressed and wrinkled.

5) Later on rusty spots develop below the tuber skin and the tubers decay before harvest and turn pulpy

Control measures:

(1) Disease free tubers obtained from uninfected field should be used.

(2) Use of resistant varieties.

(3) Diseased plant should be destroyed & burnt before harvesting.

4) Sanitation of field by destroying straws and weeds

5) Disease can be controlled by foliar spray of fungicides like Dithane M-45, Brestan , Diflotan 80WP . Bordeaux mixture has been most popular & effective.

6) Harvesting of diseased crop should be delayed until plants are fully mature , this will kill the spores present on the foliage and thus avoid infection of harvested tuber

7) Tubers should be dug in dry weather and only healthy potato tubers should be collected first & kept for cold storage.

8) The tubers should be given 90minute dip in 1:1000 mercuric chloride solution before storage.
9) The tubers should be properly stored i.e. at temperature of 4-5 C

Disease cycle: The primary infection occur through tubers used as seed , which are stored in cold storage fungus produces sporangia as means of sexual reproduction . The secondary infection occurs by means of sporangia. The sporangia are disseminated by wind and germinate on healthy host. The germinate by producing biflagellate zoospore. Under favorable conditions the zoospore infect the new host , the zoospores , encyst & infect the plant by penetrating germ tube . The germ tube directly penetrates through epidermal cells or enters host leaf through stomata.

WHITE RUST OF CRUCIFERS

**It is also known as White blisters of crucifers

Causal organism : Albugo candida

Host : Mustard { Turnip , Cauliflower , Cabbage , Radish }

Symptoms :

(1) The first symptom of the disease is seen in the form of white shining patches or blisters on the leaves & stem.

(2) Infection is of 2 type (a) Local (b) Systemic

a) In case of local infections isolated pustules develop on stem & leaves. These pustules are raised, shiny white areas and are variable in shape & size. They may arise in close proximity and later on merge to form larger patches. The host epidermis ruptures before or after the pustules are fully formed and these exposed pustules show a lot of white powder mass.

b) The fungus becomes systemic when young stem and inflorescence are infected & result into hypertrophy. Blisters may also appear on inflorescence and floral parts. Due to hypertrophy (increased cell size) and hyperplasia (increased cell division) twisting of stem, deformation, swelling & distortion of tissues of the floral parts & inflorescence takes place.

Control measures: The white rust is economically not so important to justify expensive fungicidal treatment.

Important control measure are:

(1) Priority should be given to clean cultivation, use of clean seeds and destruction of weeds in destruction of weeds in & around the field.

(2) Soil borne primary inoculum can be avoided by crop rotation.

(3) Destruction of weeds and infested crop refuse.

4) Use of dil. Solution of copper sulphate mixed with saw dust & applying it at base of seedling.

5) Spraying of Bordeaux mixture at regular interval.

Disease cycle: Primary inoculum persists in the form of oospores in plant debris or in the form of mycelia in perennial host. Infection occurs by germination of oospores on the leaves of host. They germinate to produce zoospores which encyst & germinate by giving out germ tube. The germ tube enters into host leaf through stomata. The fungus reproduces asexually by production of sporangia which are blown by wind & cause secondary infection on healthy host plant.

POWDERY MILDEW OF CUCURBITS

Causal organism: Sphaerotheca fuliginea

Host: Most of cucurbitaceous. Specially bottle gourd

Symptoms:

(1) First visible symptom of disease appear on the leaves and stem in the form of small white to dirty grey spots which become powdery as they enlarge. Gradually the powdery mass covers the entire host surface.

(2) In later stages of the disease , small black pin head like structure called clesitothecia , appear on the white powdery mass.

(3) Due to severe infection the leaves fall of prematurely.

4) The fruits remain undersized & often deformed.

Control measure:

(1) Dusting with colloidal sulphur & thiram are effective in controlling the disease.

(2) Foliar spray of benomyl is effective in controlling the disease in bottle gourd.

(3) Diseased plant refuse should be collected and burnt.

4) Use resistant varieties

5) Field sanitation is also recommended.

Disease cycle: The fungus has wide range of host & survives throughout the year on collateral host. Thus the primary infection occurs by germination of conidia on host surface which come from collateral host. The cleistothecia are rarely formed & therefore not effective in disease recurrence.

POWDERY MILDEW OF PEAS

**The disease appears in epidemic form in January & Feb when condition are dry. It causes great loss in pod no: as well as in pod weight.

Causal organism: Erysiphe polygoni

Host: The common host is Pea

Symptoms:

(1) Symptoms of disease appear first on leaves in the form of white irregular powdery patches over the upper surfaces. Gradually these patches enlarge and cover the leaves, petioles, stem and even pods.

(2) Leaves turn yellow and shed.

(3) Yield also reduces considerably

Control measure:

(1) Beat protection against the powdery mildew is a fungicidal cover of the foliage. Sulphur fungicides are most commonly recommended.

(2) Dusting with sulphur at rate of 25-30kg/ha is very effective for control of disease.

(3) Elasol, Morocide, Kararhane, Cosan are also effective against it

4) Diseased plant refuse should be collected and burnt.

5) Field sanitation is also recommended.

6) Use of resistant varieties.

Disease cycle: The disease is soil borne. The fungus perennates in the soil in the cleistothecia stage. Primary infection occurs through ascospores released from cleistothecia. Secondary spread occur through conidia.

PEACH LEAF CURL

Causal organism: Taphrina deformans

Host: Peach plant

Symptoms:

** The symptoms of disease appear in early spring.

(1) Soon after the leaves are well out of bud some of them appeared twisted, thickened, curled and distorted.

(2) In some leaves only a part of lamina may be affected but more often the entire leaf is malformed.

(3) In the beginning the affected leaves are pale green or yellowish but finally they turn reddish purple.

4) The affected leaves are fleshy & thicker than the normal green leaves.

5) The reddish velvety surface of lamina soon becomes covered with a whitish bloom which represents the fungal fructification.

6) Young shoots attacked by the fungus are swollen & distorted. Even flowers and fruits are sometime attacked.

7) The affected leaves fall off early & heavy infection lead to premature defoliation, which may lead to small fruit and fruit drop.

Control measure:

(1) Tree & orchard sanitation is important.

(2) Tree should be kept free from diseased leaves

(3) All fallen & diseased leaves, twigs should be collected and burnt.

4) Spraying trees with lime sulphur and copper fungicides gives good result . a no: of copper fungicides such as Bordeaux mixture, Perenox, Blitox-50 are also effective. Captan gives the best control over the disease.

5) Some varieties like Bed Will's Early , July Elberta etc are tolerant to disease.

6) Late blooming varieties generally escape the cool wet weather condition conductive for disease, so these should be grown.

Disease cycle: The fungus has no definite body. The asci are produced in a naked layer of host surface. The mycelium is intercellular , subcuticular. The hyphae develop below the cuticle of affected leaves.

It produces large no: of ascogenous cells which grows vertically rupturing the epidermis. These develop into asci which are naked. Each ascus contain eight or less ascospores. Yeast like budding of ascospores with in ascus is common. The resulting spores are called sprout conidia & represent asexual or conidia stage of fungus.

The ascospores & conidia are discharged from ascus & are carried away by wind or rain.

These spores germinate by producing short germ tube and causes infection on surface of host.

APPLE SCAB

Causal organism: Venturia inaequalis

Host: Apple plant

Symptoms:

** Typical symptoms of disease appear on leaves & fruits and are distinct from each other.

** Symptoms on leaves and flower buds:

(1) The first symptoms are seen on young leaves and flowering buds in spring. Light brown (or olive green) irregular spots appear on the lower surface of leaf.

(2) Later on more pronounced spots are seen on the upper surface of leaves which have velvety grayish dark surface and are more circular in outline.

(3) Soon these lesions become even more circular and metallic brown in colour, the tissues surrounding these spots are often thickened and sometime bulged upward.

4) In severe infection leaf may become dwarf & curly and there is premature fall of leaves & flower buds.

** Symptoms on fruit:

(1) On fruits scab spots are usually well defined in shape & appearance and vary with host variety & stage of development of fruit at time of infection.

(2) The spots are initially dull in appearance, brownish-black and becomes almost black with passage of time.

(3) Early scab infection results in splitting of the fruits skin in the area of spot. Later on this forms corky layer with deep cracks.

4) When the infection occurs early near the stem end the fruits are often deformed.

Control measures:

(1) Collection & burning of fallen leaves in winter is helpful for elimination of spurce of primary inoculum.

(2) Pruning of infected twigs.

(3) Cultivation of resistant varieties.

4) Spraying of tree with 5% urea in autumn period prior to leaf fall and again 2% urea just before bud burst not only reduces ascospore no: but also prevent release of ascospore from perithecia in the remaining leaves , thus controlling infection.

5) Use of fungicides is also helpful for control of disease, a large no: of fungicides have been found effective against apple scab pathogen. These fungicides are Polyram, Difolatan, Captan, Bavistin.

6) Ground spray of Elgetol reduces amount of inoculum from over wintering leaves.

7) Phenyl mercuric compound are also effective when applied to foliage in the autumn.

GREEN EAR DISEASE OF BAJRA

**It is also known as Downy Mildew of Bajra.

Causal organism: Sclerospora graminicola

Host: Bajra plant (Pennisetum typhoides)

Symptoms: These can be studied in 2 stages:

(1) Downy mildew stage : which is prominent on leaves

(2) Green ear stage : which infects the ears

(1) Downy mildew stage:

i) The diseased plant remain stunted and dwarf due shortening of internodes and excessive tillering.

ii) The leaves lose their chlorophyll and plant looks pale yellow and gives sick appearance.

iii) Leaves also becomes twisted, distorted and splits into threads.

iv) The leaves show chlorosis in streaks on the upper surface, below these streaks on the lower surface fine downy fungal growth may be seen.

(2) Green ear stage: Gradually the symptoms appear in ear:

i) Ears get transformed into leafy bearded structure.

ii) The various floral parts including glumes, palea, stamens and pistil are transformed into green leafy structure.

Control measures:

(1) Crop rotation is very effective means of controlling the disease.

(2) Treatment of seeds with organo-mercurial fungicides like Agrosan, Thiram etc.

(3) Uprooting of infected plant before the formation of oospores.

4) Use of resistant varieties like PHB-47, PHB-10, PHB-14 etc.

Disease cycle: The disease is soil borne. The oospores present in the diseased leaves fall on the ground and perennate during summer. They germinate when come in contact with young seedlings and cause infection. The disease spread from one plant to another by means of zoospores produced from sporangia.

ERGOT OF BAJRA

Causal organism: Claviceps fusiformis

Host: Bajra

Symptoms:

(1) The disease becomes evident from small droplets of pink or light honey coloured fluid which keep excuding from spikelet.

(2) Later on these droplets becomes darker and cover larger area of cob.

(3) In advanced stage small dark brown sclerotia can be seen projecting from between the glumes.

Control measure:

(1) Crop rotation help in avoiding soil borne inoculum.

(2) Repeated deep ploughing especially during summers reduces the viability of sclerotia which cause infection.

(3) The best mean of managing ergot disease in bajra is through the use of resistant varieties.

4) Use of clean seeds also helps to control disease. Seeping the seeds in 20-32% salt solution floats the sclerotia which can be removed by hand.

5) Intercropping of bajra with mug beans also reduces incidences of ergot disease.

6) Spraying of Ziram , Copper oxychloride + zineb and Sulphur is also effective incontrol of ergot.

LOOSE SMUT OF WHEAT

Causal organism: Ustilago tritici

Host: Wheat (Triticum aestivum)

Symptoms:

(1) The fungus is present in the form of secondary mycelium in the whole plant but external symptoms appear only at the flowering stage.

(2) The disease is evident first when the blackened ears emerge from the leaf sheath.

(3) Diseased ears emerge out of boot leaf earlier than the healthy ones.

4) Blackened ears contain smut spores, when these are blown off only the central rachis of the spikelet is left.

5) Spore mass remain covered by a delicate silvery membrane which usually brusts before the emergence of ear to expose the black powdery smut spores.

6) In some varieties of wheat (Sonalika) characteristic yellowing and chlorotic streaks, which later turn necrotic occurs on the flag leaves before emergence of ear. Also significant reduction in height & no: of tillers also occur in this variety due to this disease.

Control measures:

(1) Plucking & burning of the infected ear before the smut spores are sufficiently ripe to be dispersed by wind.

(2) Hot water treatment: This method consist of soaking the grain in ordinary cold water for 4hrs , then dipping in hot water at 55 C for about 10mins kill smut spores.

(3) Solar treatment : During summer when temp. is high before rains the suspected seeds are soaked in water and are exposed to solar heat for 4hrs this kill dormant mycelium present on seeds.

4) Use of systemic fungicides like Thiram, Vitavax, Bavistin, to control infection caused by loose smut.

5) Soaking of seeds in 50% sol. Of CuSO4 for about 2hrs kill spores sticking on grain.

6) Soaking of seeds for 15mins in Formalin sol. also control seed borne infection

7) Soaking of seeds in water at 25 C for 41hrs or at 30 C for 28hrs eliminates fungus completely.

8) Use of resistant varieties.

Disease cycle: The disease is seed borne, once the diseased ear is exposed all the smut spores escape through rain or wind leaving behind the naked rachis. The spores germinate on the stigma of healthy flower. They germinate to produce sporidia. The sporidia fuse with each other and the dokaryotic hypha penetrates into ovary. It grows along the development of seed. The fungus survives in the seed in the form of dormant hypha, which becomes active as soon as the infected grain is swon in the field.

COVERED SMUT OF BARLEY

Causal organism: Ustilago hordei

Host: Barley (Hordeum vulgare)

Symptoms:

** Symptoms of disease appear in the ear.

(1) The grain of the diseased ear are completely filled with black coloured smut spores.

(2) The spores are enclosed inside the persistent membrane of grain.

(3) The defected ear remains shorter and is usually retained with in the sheath for longer period.

4) The diseased ear usually shows fusion of the spikelet in the lower parts.

Control measures:

(1) The disease is controlled by the treatment of seeds with AgrosanCN (2-2.5 g/kg seeds).

(2) By growing resistant varieties of barley for eg C163, BHS4 , HBL1.

Disease cycle: The disease is seed borne. The smut spores are carried on the surface of seed & germinate along the germination of grain. Each smut spores germinate to produce a basidium which develops sporidia. The sporidia of opposite strain fuse to form a dikaryotic infection hypha which penetrates the primary shoot of the host before it comes out of soil level. After infection the fungus grows systemically in the host tissues in the intercellular spaces as well as intracellularly. Sporulation occur inside the ovaries. The sori remained covered with the grain walls which come out at the time of threshing. The spores stick to healthy seeds and remain dormant during the storage of grain.

BLACK OR STEM RUST OF WHEAT

Causal organism: Puccinia graminis tritici

Host: Wheat (Triticum aestivum)

Symptoms:

(1) The first visible symptom of is the formation of elongated brown pustules on the stalk, leaf sheath and leaves. But the stalk is most severely infected.

(2) The symptoms appear in the form of Uredopustules or Teleutopustules.

(3) The Uredosori (or uredia) appear in the form of large, elongated, coalescing pustules or streaks. The reddish brown or rusty red coloured uredospores are exposed by the rupture of host epidermis. The torn epidermis forms a collar like boundary around the sorus.

4) The Teleutosori (or telia) develop later in the same sorus as uredia or independently. They are darker in colour than uredia and burst through epidermis in same manner as uredia , exposing black bed of spores.

5) In case of severe infection the plant looks unhealthy and fails to form normal ears. The grains are shriveled and are lighter in weight.

Control measures:

(1) Use of resistant varieties (eg Sonara 64 , Lerma rao)

(2) Use of fungicides (RH-124 and Plantavax)

(3) Proper drainage of soil and less use of nitrogenous fertilizers.

4) Destruction and eradication of collateral host on which uredospores oversummers.

Disease cycle: The disease is air borne. The annual recurrence of the disease is by uredospores from hills. The uredospores remain viable on the hills and over summer on the out season wheat stubble and grass hosts. They serve as source of primary infection foe wheat plant. The pathogen is heteroecious and requires two host to complete life cycle. The primary host is wheat. The fungus produces uredospores & teleutospores on wheat plants.

The uredospores serve to spread the disease where as teleutospores germinate on the ground near the foot hills. The produce basidia and basidispores. The basidispores germinate on the alternate host – barberry and produce intercellular primary mycelium. It develops spermogonia towards upper epidermis & aecidial cups towards lower epidermis. The aecidial cups produce aecidispores which are disseminated by wind. They germinate on wheat plant to complete life cycle of fungus.

YELLOW RUST OF WHEAT

Causal organism: Puccinia striiformis

Host: Wheat plant

Symptoms:

(1) The disease appears earlier than the black rust and before the grains is formed.

(2) If the attack is mild, then the Uredia are formed mainly on the leaves, but in case the attack is severe, they appear on the leaf sheath, stalk and glumes also.

(3) The green colour of the leaves fades in long streaks on which rows of small uredosori appears. Each row consists of several oval lemon-yellow pustules.

4) The uredospores do not break through epidermis as quickly as in other rusts but do so eventually and a yellow spore mass is exposed for wind dispersal.

5) The telial sori appear as dull black patches or spots mainly on the under surface of leaf.

6) Telia are often arranged in row. They do not break through the epidermis and remain covered by epidermis as a flat black crust.

7) Plants attacked by yellow rust generally show a poorly developed root system, which might be the result of heavy leaf infection which hinders translocation of food from the leaves to roots which are starved.

Disease cycle: The yellow rust of wheat is caused by Puccinia striiformis west. The uredospores are round binucleate. The teleuospores are dark brown oblong smooth and slightly constricted at septum.

When uredospores germinate the germ tube forms a small fragile appresorium over a stomata of leaf and enters through the stomatal opening & forms a large thick walled cylindrical vesicle. From this infection hypha arises. Another short branching hyphae with club shaped haustoria obtain food from the adjoining cells. These hypha collect beneath the epidermis to form the uredosori. The teleutospores are capable of immediate germination when mature. No pycinal and aecial stages are discovered. The basidiospores have not been to infect any known species. This fungus survives through uredopspores formed on the collateral hosts like grasses at high altitudes on hills

Conrol measures: On next page

BROWN RUST OR LEAF RUST OF WHEAT

Causal organism: Puccinia recondita

Host: Wheat plant

Symptoms:

(1) The uredia develop on leaves being rare on sheath and stalk. The burst on upper surface as bright orange points gathered in small clusters or may be irregularly scattered all over the lamina surface.

(2) Pustules are bigger in size and on maturity turn brown in colour.

(3) Sometimes teleutosori may not develop but in case they are formed are similar to those of yellow rust and are on the ventral surface of leaf.

4) Telial sorus is small, oval or linear, dull black and covered by epidermis.

5) These spores interfere with leaf function and increase rate of transpiration. Cause plants to take much longer time to produce mature ears.

6) Grain quality becomes poorer, root system is poorly developed & yield decreases.

Disease cycle: Uredospores are brown and with 7-10 germpores. Infection by germ tubes formed by uredospores occurs through the stomata on either side of leaf.

Over a stoma the germ tube forms an apperssorium. In sub stomatal cavity hyphae branch and invades the leaf tissues and intercellular mycelium is formed. The teleutospores are 2-3 celled smooth and brown.

CONTROL MEASURES FOR RUST DISEASE:

(1) Early sowing of wheat may also prevents the rust outbreak.

(2) Sulphur dusting at rate of 30lbs/acre at interval of 4days during infection periods is a very good control measure.

(3) Dithane , Cycloheximide , Zineb etc are also quite successful in controlling wheat rust.

4) The cultivation of resistant varieties of wheat is one of the most effective method of control eg NP4 , NP52 , PB409 , C13 , C46 etc.

5) Mixed cropping of wheat with suitable crop can also minimize the inoculum for secondary spread of the disease.

6) The reduction in proportion of nitrogen in NPK ratio can also help in reducing incidence in a susceptible variety.

7) Antibiotics like Cycloheximide derivatives plays an imp. Role in rust control.

8) Systemic fungicides like Vitavax & Plantvax plays an imp. role in control. These fungicides are effective in soil treatment, seed treatment as well as foliar spray.

SMUT OF SUGARCANE

Causal organism: Ustilago scitaminea

Host: Sugarcane (Saccharum officinarum)

Symptoms:

(1) Symptoms of disease appear in the inflorescence axis which becomes long , curved and whip like.

(2) Several feet long whip is covered by black dusty smut spores enclosed inside a silvery thin membrane which soon flakes away.

(3) Affected plants usually have slender and thin canes.

4) Affected canes are taller & stand distinctly higher than the rest of crop.

5) The canes may show stem galls and multiple buds.

Control measures:

(1) Smutted whips should be removed from field, this reduces secondary infection of buds.

(2) In susceptible varieties the practice of ratooning should be avoided.

(3) Seed setts should be selected from healthy fields.

4) Use of resistant varieties like CO49, CO527, CO6806, S3-7, S4-7.

5) Seed setts must be disinfected by physical and chemical treatment like:

i) 5mins dip of setts in 0.25% suspension of Agallel.

ii) 5mins dip in 4:4:50 Bordeaux mixture.

iii) 10mins dip in water at 55 C to 60 C before planting.

iv) Dipping of setts in 0.5% Bavistin, Vitavax and Allagel.

GRAIN SMUT OF SORGHUM

Causal organism: Sphacelotheca sorghi

Host: Jowar (Sorghum vulgare)

Symptoms:

**Only grains are attacked by disease.

(1) Each grain is transformed into a dirty grey spore sac which varies in shape and size according to variety of host. The sac is surrounded by the unaltered glumes at the base.

(2) Stamens are absent or are involved in the sorus and being represented by three conical protrusions from sides of sorus.

(3) In some varieties the shape and size of smutted grain is not affected but the grain is full of smut powder.

Control measures:

(1) As the disease is seed borne so seed treatment with suitable fungicides is very effective.

(2) Use of clean seeds from cobs free from smut spores.

(3) Immersion of seeds in 0.5% formalin for 2hrs followed by quick drying and sowing is also very effective control of disease.

4) Soaking of seeds in water at ordinary temperature during summer for 4hrs in the morning and then spread out in sun or shade to dry is also effective control.

5) Use of resistant varieties like PJ7K, PJ23K, CSH-9, SPV-104.

Disease cycle: The fungus is branched septate, grows first intercellular then infect the cells. The mycelium bears spores which are short, oval, dark brown. These are united in loose balls and break up into individual spore when placed in water.

The spores from grains are dispersed by wind spores are generally released during harvest and get lodged on the surface of healthy seeds. They remain dormant until next season. When the seeds germinate the spores also germinate. The promycelium bear sporidia which are spindle shaped, the sporidia germinates to form infection hyphae. In some cases the promycelium directly develops inti an infection hyphae. The infection can only take place during the period between germination & emergence of seedlings above the soil surface.

KARNAL BUNT OF WHEAT

Causal organism: Neovossia indica

Host: Wheat

Symptoms:

(1) The disease becomes evident when the grains have developed.

(2) Due to infection grains have been found to be partially converted into black powdery mass enclosed by the pericarp.

(3) Not all the ears carry the disease and even in the same ear only few grains are smutted.

4) Smutted grains are very irregularly distributed due to the localized infection.

5) Diseased ears are slim compared to healthy ones and remained greenish for longer period.

6) Diseased kernels are off coloured, tending to be grayish brown and finally black powdery mass of spores in the whole kernel with in pericarp.

7) The physiology and growth of host is affected. Host plant growth is stunted. Other important symptoms are abnormal morphology of spikes difference in development of floral parts , increased or decreased tillering and reduction in root development.

8) The presence of fowl smell due to trimethylamine is prominent in this disease. Therefore this disease is also known as Stinking Smut.

Control measure:

(1) Crop rotation: It reduces the severity of bunt when wheat is rotated with some other crop in order to avoid soil borne inoculum.

(2) Use of healthy and clean seeds.

(3) Seed treatment: Seeds carrying infection should be treated with fungicides like

   (a) In Bordeaux mixture for10-15mins

   (b) In CopperSulphate for 10-15mins

   (c) In Formalin for 10mins

   (d) Ceresin & Agrosan GN.

4) Use of resistant varieties : most important control measure to avoid susceptible varieties and grow resistant varieties like HD1907, H1358, PBW 34, PBW154.

5) Cultural practices: Deep ploughing during summers to bury the spores, some modification in date of sowing , amount of fertilizers and no: of irrigations should be adopted to reduce the inoculum load in area.

EARLY BLIGHT OF POTATO

** The disease is called early blight of potato because it appears in potato plants earlier than late blight. It appears 3-4 weeks after crop is sown.

Causal organism: Alternaria solani

Host: Potato (Solanum tuberosum)

Symptoms:

(1) Symptoms of disease first appear on leaves in form of small isolated pale brown irregularly scattered oval angular or irregular spots.

(2) These spots get covered by deep greenish blue growth of fungus.

(3) Leaves near the soil are attacked first and the disease progress upward and gradually the upper leaves are infected.

4) The older spots develop necrotic areas in the centre surrounded by series of concentric ridges giving target board effect. This is most characteristic symptom of early blight.

5) Usually spots are surrounded by narrow chlorotic zone which spread out as the spot enlarges.

6) In severe infection the spots may develop on petioles and stems.

7) The symptoms of disease also appear on underground tubers in the form of dark sunken irregular or circular lesions. The underlying tissues show brown corky rot.

8) In severe attack leaves shrivel and fall off.

Control measures:

(1) Field sanitation and rotation of crop minimize infection as the disease is soil borne.

(2) Regular & timely spray with fungicides effectively controls the disease. The spraying should be started early about a month after planting and should be continued through out the period of plant growth at interval of 10-21 days.

Important effective commercial fungicides are Blitox, Difolatan, Daconil, and

Captan , Bordeaux mixture etc.

(3) Care should be taken to maintain a good plant vigor by suitable cultural practices.

Disease cycle: Fungal mycelium and conidia remain viable but dormant in plant debris and serve as the source of primary inoculum for next season and secondary infection occurs through wind blown conidia from diseased plant. The mycelium consists of septate branched light brown hyphae which becomes dark with age. Initially the hyphae are intercellular later on they penetrate into cells of invaded tissues. Conidiophores emerge through the stomata from the dead centers of spots.

TIKKA DISEASE OF GROUNDNUT

Causal organism: Cercospora arachidicola & Cercospora personata

Host: Groundnut (Arachis hypogaea)

Symptoms:

(1) The symptoms of disease appear in the form of characteristic leaf spot when plants are one to two month old.

(2) First of all the spots appear as small pale area on the surface of older leaves which later on turn brown.

(3) The foliage finally dries up due to excessive heat and results in defoliation.

4) The two species can be identified on the basis of colour spots. If observed from lower surface the spots appear light brown in case of Cersospora arachidicola and carbon black in case of C. personata.

Control measures:

(A) CULTURAL PRACTICES:

(1) Plant debris from the previous crop should be burnt to avoid soil borne primary inoculum.

(2) Rotation & deep burying of debris may also help to destroy the soil borne inoculum.

(3) Alternation in the dates of sowing can help in avoiding the damage by disease.

4) By growing early maturing varieties one can escape the loss caused by disease and also by growing varieties having bushy foliage as they are less liable to damage than erect and less foliage varieties.

5) Disease is favoured by mineral deficiency such as deficiency of MAGNESIUM. Such deficiency in crop should br corrected by use of nutrient thus preventing the disease.

(B) CHEMICAL CONTROL

(1) Seed treatment is essential to eliminate seed borne inoculum.

  i) Disinfection of seeds with shells can be done by using sulphuric acid.

  ii) Seeds without shells are disinfected by half hour dip in 0.5% CuSO4 solution.

  iii) Seed dressing with Agrosan GN

(2) Foliar spray with protectant and systemic fungicides have been recommended and is highly effective in checking the secondary spread of the disease occurring through conidia. Some important fungicides which can check the disease are Bordeaux mixture , Dithane , CuSO4 mixture , Bavistin , Derosol , Agrozim.

RED ROT OF SUGARCANE

Causal organism: Colletotrichum falcatum

Host: Sugarcane

Symptoms:

(1) First symptom of the disease appears after rainy season in the upper leaves which begin to lose colour and drop slightly.

(2) In late stages, the cane becomes shriveled, the rind shrinks and becomes longitudinally wrinkled.

(3) The mid rib region of leaves show dark reddish areas.

4) Infected stem shows longitudinal red streaks crossed by white patches.

5) The symptoms are more clearly visible if the cane is splitted length wise. It shows characteristic red blotches through out the length of plth.

6) The juice often gives a bad colour and does not set well on boiling and has alcoholic smell.

7) Late in season minute velvety dark dots are formed near about the nodes of the diseased canes and also in shrunken areas.

Control measures:

(1) Use of healthy seedsetts , absolutely disease free.

(2) Do not ratoon the diseased crop.

(3) Field sanitation for checking inoculum build up.

4) Crop rotation for 2-3 years is quite effective.

5) Same variety should not be cultivated for several years in the same field.

6) Rouge and burn the diseased canes , uproot the entire clumps and not merely the affected stalks.

7) Best method to control disease is use of resistant varieties such as COJ83, COJ84.

8) Treatment of seeds with Agallol aor Eminsan helps in eradication of superficial inoculum.

MANGO ANTHRACNOSE

Causal organism: Colletotrichum gloeosporioides

Host: Mango plant

Symptoms:

(1) The disease mostly affects the tender parts of mango

plants like young shoots , leaves, panicles, flowers and fruits are liable to attack.

(2) On leaves dark brown necrotic areas appear while on twigs black necrotic patches are observed

(3) Numerous oval or irregular spots may appear on the leaf surface. Under humid condition these spots increase and form irregular dark brown necrotic area.

4) When young shoots are infected the attacked part shows symptoms of die back.

5) Black necrotic areas are formed on the affected twigs which dry from the tip downwards accompanied by defoliation of branch.

6) In blossom blight the inflorescence shows minute black spots on the flower which dry and shed.

7) Fruits may also show small dark brown or black raised areas.

Control measures:

(1) Good plant vigour is important for keeping the infection of twigs down. Proper fertilization and watering of trees during summer must be done to maintain tree vigour .

(2) Tree sanitation is also important.

(3) Diseased twigs and leaves should be pruned and burnt along with fallen leaves.

4) Pruning should be followed by sprays of suitable fungicides such as 6:6:50 Bordeaux , 0.5% Cuprocide, Fytolan or Blitox50. 4to5 sprays between Jan & July gives satisfactory control of disease.

5) A combination of Captan with Zineb for spraying the trees has been found very effective against this disease

ANTHRACNOSE OF GRAPES

Causal organism: Elsinoe ampelina

Host: Grapes (Vitis vinifera)

Symptoms:

(1) Shear small light brown spots appear on young leaves which later turn dark brown and give shot hole appearance.

(2) In severe attack early defoliation occurs.

(3) Dark brown sunken spots with raised margins develop on new shoot / canes leading to their death from tip backwards.

4) Similarly spots appear on laterals of clusters.

5) Under favourable conditions dark brown depressed spots appear on berries also. On berries the disease is referred to as "birds eye spot" because of grey centre surrounded by a reddish brown zone.

Control measure:

(1) Prune the shoots & canes during Jan – Feb and give one dormant spray of Bordeaux mixture after pruning.

(2) Spray with Bordeaux mixture in the last week of march

(3) Spray Bavistin 50WP @ 500g per acre in last week of April using 500litres of water.

CITRUS DIE BACK

Causal organism: Colletotrichum gloeosporioides

Host: Citrus plant

Symptoms:

(1) The disease manifests itself as light green spots which soon turn brown. If the spots have sufficient moisture pinkish mass of spores ooze out of the surface.

(2) The spots may be at the margins or tips of the leaf blades and sometime near the midrib.

(3) The lesions are usually surrounded by concentric rings.

4) In advance stages lesions are found on twigs which start dying back.

Control measure:

(1) Regulation of crop in early years helps in reducing the disease.

(2) Pruning of diseased twigs also helps in reducing the disease.

(3) By spraying fungicides like Bordeaux mixture, Copper oxychloride during March, July and September helps in reducing the disease.

ROOT ROT OF COTTON

Causal organism: Rhizoctonia bataticola & Rhizoctonia solani

Host: Cotton plant

Symptoms:

(1) The disease appear in patches.

(2) Due to disease perfectly healthy plants may wilt within 24hrs with leaves drooping without showing any discolouration.

(3) Root, rots & bark of affected root shreds.

4) The loss in yield due to reduction in plant stands by way of sudden death.

Control measure:

(1) Adopt good crop rotation for 3or 4 years.

(2) With the Ist appearance of root rot, the affected plant should be removed & the soil may be drenched with 0.2% Carbendazim.

(3) Treat the seeds before sowing with conc. Sulphuric acid, Emisan, Streptocycline.

STEM ROT OF RICE

Causal organism: Sclerotium oryzae

Host: Rice (Oryza sativa)

Symptoms:

(1) The affected plant produces light ears.

(2) The affected plant have tendency to throw out green shoots from base when rest of the crop is ripening & turning yellow.

(3) The base of stem is slightly discoloured ate the lowest distinct internode orthe next one or the two above.

4) Inside the clum a dark greyish weft of mycelium is found and the inner surface may be dotted with small round shining black sclerotia.

5) Lower leaf sheaths may also invade and with in their rotting tissues sclerotia are present.

Control measures:

(1) Straw and stubbles of infected crop should be burnt.

(2) Patches of diseased plants should be marked out & should be either uprooted and destroyed or they should not be harvested along with healthy plants. After harvest these can be burnt at spots.

(3) Passage of irrigation water or rain water through or from infected field to healthy field should be checked.

4) Hot weather ploughing helps in decreasing viability of sclerotia.

5) Spray of 0.2% Bavistin or Topsin can reduce the incidence of disease.

6) Use of resistant varieties

7) Less use of Nitrogenous fertilizers and herbicides.

10

Bacterial Diseases

CITRUS CANKER

Causal organism: Xanthomonas citri or Xanthomonas campestris pv citri

Host: Citrus plants

Symptoms:

(1) Symptoms of disease appear on almost all the above ground parts of host plant, especially on leaves, twigs, young branches and fruits.

(2) Infected parts show the presence of crust like lesions and small cankers.

(3) The canker on leaves first appear as small, round, watery , translucent spots on lower surface of leaf with raised convex surface of dark green colour than the surrounding tissues.

4) Later on these spots turn white or greyish and finally rupture exposing corky brown mass surrounded by a yellowish brown to green raised margins and water yellow halo.

5) Spots occurring on petioles & midrib are like those on leaves and cause premature defoliation.

6) Cankers on fruits are similar to those on leaves except that the yellow halo is absent and depression in the centre is more prominent.

7) The injury to fruit is only skin deep and no effect on pulp or juice is noticed.

Control measures:

(1) Effective method of control of citrus canker is complete destruction of affected trees by burning.

(2) Pruning of affected twigs & spraying with a copper fungicides.

(3) The fallen canker affected leaves & twigs should be collected and burnt.

4) Use of disease free nursery stock for planting in new orchard.

5) Spraying of trees before planting in new orchard with copper fungicides.

6) Spraying of 1% Bordeaux mixture.

7) Control of leaf miners.

8) By spraying antibiotics. Streptomycin sulphate spraying after fortnight is found to be quite effective in aged trees. Phytomycin was also found effective.

9) Spraying of neem cake at rate of 7kg/acre was also found effective.

10) Plant vigor should always be maintained by proper fertilization & irrigation.

Disease cycle: X. ctiri is small rod shaped monotrichous bacterium. It forms chains & capsule but no spores, it is gram –ve and aerobic. It forms colonies which are circular yellow in colour slightly raised & shining. Favourable conditions for disease are mild temp. and wet weather.

Optimum temp. is 20-35 C. Diseased twigs & leaves serves as source of infection and provides inoculum year after year. The bacterium enters host through stomata and wounds. Bacterium multiplies rapidly in host intercellular spaces dissolving middle lamella and establishing itself in the cortical region. The disease is disseminated by wind rain or insects. The bacterium do not survive in soil or in infected plant parts fallen on ground due to antagonism of other soil micro-organism to this bacterium under natural condition.

TUNDU DISEASE OF WHEAT

** It is also known as Bacterial Rot of Wheat Ear or Yellow ear rot/ Ear cockle disease.

Causal organism: Corynebacterium tritici & Angunia tritici

Host: Wheat

Symptoms:

(1) First visible symptom of disease is wrinkling of lower leaves which is followed by twisting of central leaves.

(2) Entire ear is enveloped by exudates of blight (Yellow sticky slime) which binds the glumes stem & leaf sheath as a result further plant growth is checked.

(3) The stem shows distortion.

4) If the weather is wet then the slime trickles down but in dry weather it becomes deep yellow, dry & hard.

5) When the crop is fully mature the symptoms of disease are visible only then.

6) The whole of infected ear is full of black galls (mamni) instead of normal grains.

Control measure:

(1) The best control measure is to use wheat seeds free from nematode galls.

(2) Removal of galls by flotation after dipping them in brine.

(3) Use of those seeds which have been obtained from places where this disease does not occur.

4) Deep ploughing of soil in the month of May – June when temp. is high to destroy nematodes.

5) Uprooting & burning of diseased plant.

6) Good drainage of fields.

Disease cycle: The bacterium is rod shaped, motile, monotrichous and gram +ve . Disease spreads from soil having both bacteria and nematodes. Nematodes mechanically transmit the disease. Bacterium is carried on the surface of the galls formed by nematodes. When such seeds with cockle or galls are sown the galls swell and liberate larvae of nematodes which infect wheat plants and carries bacterial cells along with them.

BACTERIAL BLIGHT OF RICE

Causal organism: Xanthomonas oryzae

Host: Rice (Oryza sativa)

Symptoms:

** Symptoms of disease vary considerably with the stage of infection & prevailing weather conditions. So the symptoms of disease are divided in to 3 distinct phases.

(1) LEAF BLIGHT PHASE:

i) It is most commonly seen phase of disease which is characterized by linear yellow to straw coloured strips with wavy margins which appear on leaves. This is followed by drying & twisting of leaf tips.

ii) Blightening may extend to leaf sheath, clum and glumes killing tillers or the whole clum.

iii) Bacterial mass ooze & dry on the surface of lesions.

iv) the blight phase of disease usually appear after 4-6 weeks after transplanting.

(2) WILT/ KRESEK PHASE:

The second phase of disease is called wilt phase, which is most destructive. It results in completer rolling & drooping of leaves which turn yellow or grey. If the attack is severe the whole plant is killed.

(3) PALE – YELLOW LEAF PHASE

The third phase is called pale yellow leaf phase. Some of young leaves in a clum turn pale yellow or whitish. These leaves later turn yellowish brown and withers away.

Control measure:

(1) Crop rotation should be followed to control the disease.

(2) Use of chlorinated water for irrigation or application of bleaching powder to the standing water in the field reduces disease incidence.

(3) Spray of certain chemicals & antibiotics have been used to control the disease. The antibiotic Streptocycline has been most commonly used for seed treatment and foliar spray against bacterial blight of rice.

4) Soaking of seeds for 12hrs in 0.02% Agrimucin & 0.05% Ceresan , followed by hot water treatment at 52-54 C for half an hour helps in 95% eradication of infection in seeds.

5) Spray of Agrimycin prevents secondary spreading of disease.

6) Use of resistant varieties like PR111, PR113, PR115 etc.

7) Do not transplant before 10th June and apply recommended dose of fertilizers.

Disease cycle: Bacterium is rod shaped, occurs singly and forms no capsule. It is gram-ve , monotrichous and optimum temp. for growth is 25-30 C. The disease is seed borne , the bacterium also survives on crop stubbles and plant body of cynodon dactylon , cypreus rotundus and acts as primary source if inoculum. Irrigation water contaminated with bacterium flowing through field to field also provides the primary source of inoculum. Secondary spread is brought about through wounds and stomata by bacterial cells disseminated by wind borne rain splash. The leaf hoppers and grasshoppers can transmit bacterium mechanically. After entry the bacterium multiplies in the intercellular spaces of the host parenchyma and is again released through stomata.

ANGULAR LEAF SPOT OF COTTON

It is also known as Blight of cotton or Black Arm of cotton

Causal organism : Xanthomonas malvacearum

Host: Cotton plant

Symptoms:

The bacterium attacks all aerial parts of plants at different stages of plant growth. The disease has 4 distinct phases depending upon the plant part affected

(1) Angular leaf spot (leaf infection)

(2) Black arm (stem infection)

(3) Boll rot (boll infection)

4) Seedling blight (seedling infection)

(1) SEEDLING BLIGHT: The earliest symptoms of the disease are seen in the cotyledons of germinating seeds. Minute water soaked spots appear on the surface of cotyledons, later on these increase in diameter turn brown to black and form irregular patches causing them to dry. The disease may spread to new leaves formed or the seedling may die.

(2) ANGULAR LEAF SPOT: The disease appears first on the seed leaves as they come above the ground. On the leaves similar water soaked spots appear on the undersurface first and then on the upper surface.

* They increase in size becomes angular bound by small vienlets of leaf& turn brown to black.

* Most of such plants die. If the infection is less severe spots on petioles & stem becomes water soaked and enlarges into angular spots.

* These spots often coalescence and the leaf gradually turns yellow & droops

(3) BLACK ARM: Lesions on stem, petioles and fruiting branches are dark brown to black. They are elongated and sunken. The affected stem shows cracks or these may be girdling and the death of affected organs. These are black arm symptoms.

4) BOLL ROT: On bolls the disease is characterized by the

appearance of water soaked lesions on the surface. These lesions later turn brown & finally black and are invariably sunken. Young infected bolls may fall down prematurely. If the bolls mature lint is of no commercial use.

Disease cycle : Xanthomonas campestris pv malvacearum bacterium is rod shaped. It occurs singly or in pairs. It is capsulated but no spore formation is there. The organism has 1-4 flagella. It is of gram –ve strain. The main source of primary inoculum is seed. The bacterium may be present as slimy mass on the fuzz or inside the seed. On germination of such seed the bacterium moves to cotyledons and then maintain population on 1st and 2nd leaf. In favourable weather the inoculum from this source spread to new leaves and further spread continues. Infected cotton bolls leaves and twigs present on the soil surface also forms important source of carry over of bacterium. Leaves are infected mainly through stomata secondary spread is through wind splashed rain and dew.

Control measure:

(1) Removal and destruction of diseased plant debris to reduce the soil borne inoculum.

(2) Deep ploughing after harvest buries the infected parts and thus reduces survival ability of bacterium in soil.

(3) Crop rotation, late sowing, early thinning, good tillage, early irrigation and addition of Potash to soil help in reduction of disease incidence.

4) Seed treatment with Vitavax & Plantvax also helps in eradication of inoculum.

5) Hot water treatment of seeds at seeds at 56 C for 10 mins destroys the external as well as internal inoculum.

6) The secondary spread of disease can be checked by regular spray with copper fungicides at different intervals.

7) Most effective control measure is use of resistant varieties like HC-9, BTA-592, and T-12.

8) Seed borne inoculum can be eliminated by seed treatment:

** External inoculum on seed is destroyed by delinting of seed with conc. Sulphuric acid. Seeds are immersed in acid for 10-15mins then rinsed in water thoroughly and finally dried. And treating them with organo mercurial compounds such as Agrosan-GN, Ceresan etc.

** Internal seed borne inoculum can be eradicated by treatment with antibiotics like Streptomycin.

BRINJAL LITTLE LEAF

Causal organism: Mycoplasma

Host: Brinjal (Solanum melongena)

Symptoms:

(1) The leaves and nodes of diseased plants greatly reduced in size.

(2) The petioles become so reduced in size that the leaves appear sticking to stem.

(3) Infected leaves are narrow, soft, smooth and yellow.

4) Plant gives bushy appearance.

5) Plants having severe infection fail to produce flowers and fruits.

6) The flower commonly becomes phylloid.

Control measure:

(1) Tetracycline therapy is an effective control measure.

(2) Spraying with Ledermycin at 550ppm is also found to be effective.

(3) Eradication of weed hosts and diseased brinjal plants.

4) Control of insect vectors.

SESAMUM PHYLLODY

Causal organism: Mycoplasma like organisms transmitted by Leaf Hopper

Host: Sesamum (Sesamum indicum)

Symptoms:

(1) The disease becomes evident at flowering stage of crop. One or more floral organs are transformed fully or partially into green leafy structures followed by abundant vegetative growth.

(2) Heavily infected plants produce abnormal growth, small leaves, short internodes and abnormal branching.

(3) Transformation of top portion of infected plant into heavy bunches tend the branches to bend downwards.

4) Partially infected plant may produce capsules on lower portion but seed in such capsules are light in weight and low in oil content.

Control measure:

(1) Eradication of diseased plants.

(2) Spread of disease under field conditions should be checked by killing hoppers by foliar application of Oxydemeton methyl (Metasystox 25 EC) at rate of iml per liter of water.

PHYSIOGENIC DISEASES

Black Tip of Mango

Black tip, tip rot or mango necrosis locally known as KOELI is peculiar in India.

Causes for disease: The black tip disorder of mango fruit is very serious problem in mango orchard located in vicinity of brick kilns. The flumes that come out of brick kiln as a result of burning of coal contains sulphur dioxide , ethylene and carbon monoxide. All these gases are toxic to young developing fruits of mango and these gases cause necrosis of tissues of fruits.

Symptoms:

(1) The disease is characterized by a depressed spot of yellowing tissue (or necrosis) at the distal end of fruit.

(2) First symptom is the development of small etiolated area at the distal end which gradually increases in size with

time and also changes colour to brown and finally black and cover the tip completely.

(3) The tip is flattened without skin turning hard and sunken.

4) The inner portion is soft and yield dark brown liquid.

5) The disease commonly occurs when fruits are about 6-8 weeks old. Black tip affected fruit almost stop growth and after premature ripening such fruit becomes soft and drop down earlier.

Control measure:

(1) Shifting the site of existing brick kilns to two km on east & west and one km on north & south.

(2) The operation of existing brick kilns should be avoided from feb to 4th week of may.

(3) Telescopic chimneys should be used.

4) The appearance of disorder can be checked by spraying of 0.6% Borax three times i.e. before flowering, during flowering and after fruit setting along with Bordeaux mixture. Or 1.5kg Copper oxychloride per 500litres of water

KHARIA DISEASE OF RICE

Cause: Disease is caused by zinc deficiency

Symptoms:

(1) It usually appears in nursery but may appear in patches after 10-15 days of transplanting.

(2) Growth of diseased plant is stunted.

(3) High yielding varieties shows chlorosis between veins of new leaves where brown spots are formed.

4) On lower leaves a large no: of small brown to bronze spots appear which later on forms bigger spots & ultimately the entire leaf turns bronze coloured and dries.

5) Root growth is also restricted & usually the main roots turn brown & finer roots are destroyed.

6) Plants fail to grow further & produce no ears.

Control measures :

(1) Spray mixture of 5kg Zinc sulphate & 2.5 kg lime in 1000 litres of water after 10days of sowing in nursery.

(2) Give 2nd spray as above on 20th day in nursery.

(3) Give 3rd spray as above in fields after 15-20 days of transplanting if symptoms appear in field.

PHARNEROGENIC PARASITES

Cuscuta

It is also known as Dodder, Love vine or Amarbel. It is a stem parasite and is holoparasite (i.e. entirely dependent on host)

General characters:

- These are non chlorophyll bearing leafless, twining, parasitic seed plant which attach their yellow, orange or pink thread like stems to the stem or other parts of cultivated or wild plant.
- The general characters of different species of cuscuta are very similar which are:
- They first appear as small masses of branched thread like, leafless stems which are devoid of chlorophyll and twine around the stem or leaves of host.
- The leaves are represented by minute functionless scales which are evident on close look.
- When stem comes in contact with host minute root like organs (haustoria) penetrate the host cortex reaching into vascular bundles. They serve as an anchor as well as organ of food absorption.
- The tiny white, pink or yellowish flowers occur in clusters. The fruit is a capsule producing tiny grey or reddish brown, slightly rough seeds.

Clover, Berseem, Flax and many oil seed crops are commonly attacked. The common dodder (Cuscuta gronovii) attacks garden ornamentals and hedge plants.

** The parasite may be introduced into field and spread by any of following means:

i) As impurity in the crop seeds. Seeds of dodder often go undetected in seeds of crops like berseem.

ii) As seeds and stem pieces moved by irrigation water.

iii) As stem piece present on the dry straw from infested field.

iv) As seed in manure

v) As stem piece transported by cattle, birds strong wind and farm implements.

Control measures:

(1) The crop seeds should be free from dodder seeds.

(2) Dodder infested cattle fodder should not be used, grazing animals should not be allowed to move through infested area.

(3) Badly infested crop should be burnt before the parasite produces seeds.

4) If dodder is already present in field scattered patches may be sprayed with herbicides such as Diesel oil fortified with DNBP , PCP (pentachlorophenol) or 2-4D.

5) When dodder infestation in a field is wide spread, frequent tillage burning and use of soil herbicides like Chloroprophan DCPA, Dinoseb or Pronamide have been recommended.

6) The herbicide Glyphosate is effective even after dodder has established connection with the host.

OROBANCHE

It is also known as Broomrape. It is total root parasite affecting tobacco, brinjal, tomato, cabbage and many other solanaceous and crucifer plants.

Plants attacked by orobanche usually occur un small patches in field and look stunted.

General characters

(1) The parasite consists of a stout, fleshy stem 15-20cm tall.

(2) The stem is pale yellowish or brownish red in colour and is covered by small thin brown scaly leaves.

(3) Flowers are white and tubular and appear in axil of scale leaves.

4) The seeds are produced in ovoid pods about 5cm long and are very small and black.

The parasite perennates through seeds, these seeds germinate only when roots of certain plants grow near them. On germination the seed produces a radicle which grows towards the root of host plants and attaches it and produces a shallow disc or cup like appressorium, which surrounds the host root and absorb nutrient and water from it

Control measure:

(1) The best way to eliminate broom rape is to destroy it before seed formation if seeds are formed and shed on soil it is difficult to eradicate the parasite for several years.

(2) Long crop rotations also help in eradication of parasite.

(3) Spraying of soil with 25% Copper sulphate solution destroys parasite.

4) Herbicides Glyphosate is also very effective to control the parasite.

STRIGA

It is also known as Witchweed. It is a well known semi root parasite of sugarcane, cereals, maize and millets. The attacked plants remain stunted and chlorotic. Heavily infected plants wilt & die.

General characters :

- The parasite is small plant 15-30cm tall with bright green slightly hairy stem and leaves.

- Usually these plants develop in clusters around the stem of the host.
- The parasite stem appear branched. Leaves are narrow, long and in opposite pairs.
- The flowers are small and usually brick red or scarlet, although some may be yellowish-red, yellowish or almost white always having yellow centre.
- Flowers appear just above the leaf attachment to the stem and are produced throughout the season.
- Seeds are formed in pods or capsule each containing thousands of tiny brown seeds.

** Striga is obligate root parasite dependent on host from germination to flowering and reproduction. After establishment of vascular connections with the host the parasite grows underground for 4-8weeks prior to emergence above the ground.

- The underground stem contains buds in the axils of leaves. The parasite produce more roots from initial rootlet which moves parallel to host root and send more haustoria into them.
- As soon as the striga rootlets come in contact with host roots, its tips swells into conical or bulb shaped haustorium.
- The haustorium dissolves host cells by enzymic secretion and penetrates the host roots within 8-24 hrs.
- Finally striga's leading cells usually tracheids reach the vessel of host roots. The walls of host vessels are dissolved and the tracheids of parasite enter the host vessels from which they absorb water and nutrient.

Control measures:

(1) Weeding and interculture can be successful only when practiced in early stages of parasitic growth , with in 2months . 4-6 weedings may be needed.

(2) Keeping the field flooded for sometime and then draining out water also helps in control of parasite.

(3) Catch crops consisting of host plants may be planted to force the germination of witchweed seed & the parasite then can be destroyed by ploughing or by use of weedicides such as 2-4D.

4) Soaking of soil upto a depth of 10-15cm with 2-3% $CuSO4$ can control witchweed.

5) Spraying Fernoxone at rate of 400g chemical in 500liter water is very effective against Striga. Application of Tetrachlorodimethyl phenoxyacetic acid also kills the parasite.

PERSEA AMERICANA

Avocado

Constituents

Fruit: fixed oil, 6-10%; protein 1.3-6%.

Parts used: Bark, fruit, leaves and seeds.

Medicinal properties: Digestive, emmenagogue, antibacterial, antioxidant, antifungal, pectoral, stomachic, anthelmintic, antiperiodic, antidiarrheal.

Uses

Nutritional

- A good source of vitamins A, some B, C and E, potassium (higher than bananas) and fiber ; fair source of iron; low in calcium. A fruit with high-energy producing value, each edible pound allegedly provides an average of 1,000 calories.
- High in fat, about 25-35 gms on average. however, about 65% of it is health-promoting monosaturated fat, particularly oleic acid.

Folkloric

- The pulp is thought to promote menstruation.
- Decoction of pulverized seeds used as gargles for toothaches.

- The leaves and bark promote menstruation; the tea has been used to expel worms.
- Used for diarrhea and dysentery.
- Rheumatism and neuralgia: Pulverize seeds or bark, mix with oil and apply on affected area as counterirritant.
- Beverage: Take decoction of leaves as tea.
- Pulp is applied to shallow cuts, prevents infection.
- Flesh of ripe fruit is soothing to sunburned skin.
- In different parts of the world, has been recommended for anemia, exhaustion, high cholesterol, hypertension, gastritis and duodenal ulcers. The leaves have been reported effective as antitussive, antidiabetic, antiarthritic and antiinflammatory.

Others

- Juice from seeds used to make permanent ink for fabric lettering.

BAMBUSA SPINOSA ROXB.

Bamboo

Parts utilized: Stems, roots, leaves.

Constituents and Properties: Emollient, diuretic and diaphoretic, emmenagogue, astringent.

Leaves are considered stimulant, aromatic, tonic, emmenagogue, anthelmintic and aphrodiasiac.

The bark is astringent and used in hemorrhoids, nausea and vomiting.

Leaves are rich in hydrocyanic and benzoic acids.

Uses

Folkloric

- Decoction of leaves as emmenagogue, to induce lochia after childbirth.

- Decoction (20 gms for 1 liter ofwater; 3 cups daily) of stems of young shoots applied externally for inflammed joints.
- Decoction of leaves used to stimulate menstruation; also used for intestinal worms.
- Poultice of young shoots used for dislodgement of worms from ulcers.
- Decoction of roots used for anuria.
- Decoction of shoots taken for respiratory ailments.
- Poultice of tender shoots used for cleaning wounds. Decoction or juice of leaves applied to wounds.
- Decoction of tender shoots used as abortifactient in the first month and in the last month, to induce labor, and to facilitate placental expulsion.
- In India, decoction of leaves used for diarrhea.

Nutrition

The young shoots (labong) are edible as vegetables, the seasonal ingredient in atchara preparations.

Others

- Bambusa spinosa is the most commonly used specie of bamboo in the Philippines.
- Used in the building of bamboo houses, furniture and household utensils.

MUSA SAPIENTUM LINN.

Banana

Constituents and properties: Demulcent, nutrient, cooling, astringent, antiscorbutic, antifebrile, restorative, emmenagogue, cardialgic, styptic.

The ripe fruit is laxative.: Juice of the flower-stem contains potash, soda, lime, magnesia, alumina, chlorine, sulfuric anhydride, silica and carbon anhydride.

Insert

Bunch of bananas with "puso" - male inflorescence. Young growth.

Parts used

Leaves, fruit.

Uses

Nutritional: The "puso" (male inflorescence) of saba is used as a vegetable.

Unripe fruit is sugared and candied.

Rich in vitamins A, B, and C; a fair source of iron.

Others: Plant fibers used in the manufacture of paper and clothes.

Leaves used for wrapping food.

Folkloric

- Young leaves used for cool dressing of inflammed and blistered surfaces and as cool application for headaches.
- Thinning hair: Apply the juice of the trunk to scalp.
- Cooked flower used for diabetes.
- Sap of the flower used for earaches.
- In traditional medicine in India, used for diabetes.
- In South-Western Nigeria, green fruits used for diabetes.

MOMORDICA CHARANTIA LINN.

BITTER GOURD / BITTER MELON

Properties: Considered astringent, antidiabetic, abortifacient, antirheumatic, contraceptive, galactagogue, parasiticide, anthelmintic, purgative, emetic, antipyretic, febrifuge, emmenagogue, cooling , tonic, vulnerary.

Parts utilized: Leaves, roots and fruits.

Uses

Folkloric: Astringent powdered leaves or root decoction can be applied to hemorrhoids.

Leaf juice for cough and as a purgative and anthelminthic to expel intestinal parasites, and for healing wounds.

Seeds also used to expel worms.

Juice from fruit used for dysentery and chronic colitis.

The vine or the juice of leaves used as mild purgative for children.

In large doses, the fresh juice is a drastic purgative.

Decoction of roots and seeds used for urethral discharges.

Pounded leaves used for scalds.

Infusion of leaves or leaf juice used for fevers.

In Jamaica, leaf decoction or infusion is taken for colds, as laxative and blood cleanser. Warm tea infusions also used for toothaches and mouth infections. Also used as a bath/wash for skin eruptions and acne.

Used for eczema, malarial, gout, jaundice, abdominal pain, kidney (stone), leprosy, leucorrhea, piles, pneumonia, psoriasis, rheumatism, fever and scabies.

In China, used as hypoglycemic and antidiabetic.

Nutritional: The leaves and fruit - used as vegetables - are excellent sources of Vit B, iron, calcium, and phosphorus. It has twice the amount of beta carotene in broccoli and twice the calcium content of spinach. Characteristically bitter-tasting, slight soaking in salty water before cooking removes some of the bitter taste of the fruit.

Recent use

Diabetes Mellitus: A Philippine herb that has recently gained international recognition for its possible benefits in the treatment of diabetes mellitus. Despite its bitter taste, it has also become a popular nutritional drink for a boost of vim and vigor. In fact, the more bitter, the better, as it is believed that the bitterness is proportionate to its potency.

Studies have suggested that ampalaya contains a hypoglycemic polypeptide, a plant insulin responsible for its blood sugar lowering effect. Other benefits suggested were body detoxification (including removal of nicotine), strengthening of the immune system and fertility regulation.

It is increasingly recommended as an adjunct or supplement to traditional therapeutic regimens for diabetes mellitus.

BRASSICA OLERACEA

CABBAGE

Parts utilized: Seeds, leaves.

Chemical constituents and properties: Contains a considerable amount of sulfur.

Contains significant amounts of the amino acid glutamine with its antiinflammatory properties.

Seeds are diuretic, laxative, stomachic and antihelminthic.

Leaf considered digestive and tonic.

Red cabbage is emollinet and pectoral: Possibly cholesterol-lowering, anticancer, antifungal.

Uses

Folkloric

- Juice of red cabbage used for chronic coughs, bronchitis, asthma.
- Juice of white cabbage used to treat warts.
- Bruised leaves of the common white cabbage used for blisters.
- In European folk medicine, leaves are used for acute inflammation, the paste of raw cabbage are placed on a cabbage leaf and applied to the affected area.

Nutrition: Excellent source of vitamin C; good source of vitamin B; fair source of vitamin A.

DAUCUS CAROTA L.

CARROT

Parts used and preparation: Roots, seeds.

Uses

Nutritional: Roots contain vitamin A. B, C, E, the minerals phosphorus, potassium, calcium.

Folkloric: Believed to be beneficial for cancers and kidney problems.

For coughs and chest afflictions, the roots are boiled in milk; the milk is drunk and a poultice of the root is applied to the chest.

For burns and infected ulcers, grated carrots are applied to the affected parts.

Poultice of carrots also used for ulcers, carbuncles, infected woounds.

Seeds of the plant when ground to powder and taken as tea for colic and to increase urine flow.

Tea of carrot blossoms has been used for treatment of dropsy.

In European folk medicine, used for jaundice and hepatic disorders.

ANACARDIUM OCCIDENTALE

CASHEW

Parts used and preparation: Bark, leaves, and ripe fruit.

Uses

Folkloric

- Astringent and mouth wash: Gargle dilute infusion of bark and leaves and retain in mouth for a few minutes to relieve toothache, sore gums, or sore throat. Do not swallow.

- Decoction of bark used for diarrhea.

Infusion of bark and leaves is astringent, used to relieve toothaches and sore gums, and as a lotion and mouthwash.

- In Guyana, decoction of bark used as antidiarrheal. Powdered seeds used as antivenom for snake bites. Nut oil used as antifungal and for healing cracked heels.
- In western Nigeria, used for anrthritis and other inflammatory conditions.

Nutrition: Ripe fleshy portion of fruit may be eaten.

Young leaves eaten as vegetable.

Others

Oil from the pericarp effective against white ants.

Oil from the kernel is a chemical antidote for irritant poisons and a good vehicle for liniments and other external applications.

The bark yields a gum that repels insects.

Cardole, the oil from the shell of the nut, is effective for preserving wood, books; also, against white ants.

Cardanol, from anacardic acid, is used for resins, coatings and frictional materials.

MANIHOT ESCULENTA CRANTZ

CASSAVA, TAPIOCA PLANT

Properties and constituents

- Two well-known varieties: bitter and sweet.
- The bitter, more robust and planted for its starch; the roots containing hydrocyanic acid, considered poisonous but easily dissipated by heat. It is the source of tapioca.
- Sweet cassava is not as good a starch producer as the bitter kind, but is non-poisonous, tasty and grown for use as vegetable.

- Mandiocin, a glucoside, has been isolated from the leaves.
- Most of the poisonous hydrocyanic acid from the cortical layers of the roots is removed by thorough peeling of the tubers.

Parts used and preparation: Tuber, leaves.

Uses

Folkloric : Leaves used for measles, small pox, chicken pox, and/or skin rashes.

Used as flour for starch bath.

Remove peelings and grate the tuber. Extract the juice, add enough water for a baby tub bath and boil.

Poultice of fresh rhizome used for ulcers.

Leaf sap latex used for eye conditions.

Decoction of trunk bark used for rheumatism.

In west tropical Africa, compress of powdered leaves used for fevers and headaches.

In Cambodia, pounded tubers used for ulcerated wounds.

In Brazil, ointment useful for ulcers of the cornea; also used to preserve meat.

Others

Source of tapioca.

The bitter variety is planted for the production of starch. The roots contain hydrocyanic acid and poisonous: the hydrocyanic acid is dissipated by heat.

The root, harmless when fresh, becomes poisonous when stale. Thorough peeling of the tubers before cooking removes the chance of poisoning. The sweet variety is grown for use as a vegetable.

In Brazil, the indians use the tender leaves as food; fruit used as fish poison.

CINNAMOMUM MINDANAENSE

MINDANAO CINNAMON

Properties / Constituents: Diaphoretic, parasiticide, antispasmodic, aphrodisiac, analgesic, diuretic.

Bark is carminative, stimulant, astringent, aromatic, antiseptic, antifungal, antiviral.

The medicinal element is the oil extracted from the bark, especially from young trees, and the leaf. Cinnamaldehyde, an essential oil that accounts for 65% to 80% of the herb possesses analagesic, antifungal, and antidiarrheal effects. The essential oils from the bark are active against Aspergillus parasiticus growth. (Professional Guide to Complementary & Alternative Therapies)

Parts used and preparation: Bark, leaves.

Uses

Preparation

- Decoction: - One heaping teaspoon of powdered bark to a cup of boiling water; or, 0.5 to 1 g of bark to 7 oz of boiling water fir 5-10 minutes, then steep.
- Tincture: Moisten 200 parts of cinnamon bark evenly with ethanol and percolate to produce 1,000 parts of tincture. Use 3-4 cc three times daily.

Folkloric

- Decoction or infusion of the bark used for loss of appetite, bloating, vomiting, flatulence, toothache, headaches, rheumatism, dysentery, to help expel flatus and to facilitate menses; colds, fevers, sinus infections and bronchitis.
- Powdered bark: one heaping teaspoon to a cup of boiling water, 4 cups daily. For flatulence, stronger doses used, 2 tbsp for adults, 1 tsp for children.
- Decoction of leaves also used for expeling gas.
- Used for diarrhea, menorrhagia, dysmenorrhea.

- Paste prepared from the bark is applied locally for neuralgic pains and severe headaches.
- Candida and other yeast infections.
- Used for treatment of scabies and lice.

Others

- A popular spice and flavoring agent.

Studies

- Diabetes: A search for ways to help keep blood sugars normal have led finding MHCP (methylhydroxy chalcone polymer) in cinnamon. MHCP is a chalcone, a type of polyphenol or flavanoid, found to imake cells more sensitive to insulin in the test tube. It was also found to have antioxidant properties that can slow down various other complications in diabetes. MHCP is water soluble and is not found in the spice oils or oil extracts sold as food additives. (New Scientist, Aug 2000)
- A USDA research also found that daily cinnamon supplements reduced blood sugars by 20-30%. It also reduced total cholesterol, LDL cholesterol and triglycerides from 13-30 percent in a study of 60 patients with type 2 diabetes, an effect comparable to that obtained from statin drugs. The author suggested that it may also be useful for healthy people. The spice has no known risks and negligible calories. Half a teaspoon a day seems to be beneficial. Avoid the oils as the phenophenols are removed in processing.
- Suggested use: 1/4 teaspon of cinnamon a day added to coffee, fruit juice or cereal. It may also delay the onset of type of diagetes.
- Trans-Cinnamaldehyde from Cinnamomum zeylanicum Bark Essential Oil Reduces the Clindamycin Resistance of Clostridium difficile in vitro: The essential oil of C Zeylanicum bark enhanced the bactericidal activity of clindamycin. The active fraction from the oil was identified aqs trans-cinnamaldehyde.

- Antidiabetic effect of Cinnamomum cassia and Cinnamomum zeylanicum in vivo and in vitro: Study showed the cassia extract has a direct antidiabetic potency.
- Inactivation of Escherichia coli O157:H7 by essential oil from Cinnamomum zeylanicum: Study suggests the essential oil of CZ tobe bactericidal against E. coli.

COFFEA ARABICA LINN.

ARABIAN COFFEE

Chemical constituents

- The alkaloids of coffea arabica are caffeine, adenine, xanthine, hypoxanthine, guanosine and proteids.
- Leaves contain an alkaloid, caffeine, 1.15 to 1.25 percent.
- The pericarp of the fruit contains caffeine, mallic acid, mannite, invert sugar and saccharose.
- The seeds contain caffeine, gallic acid, citric acid, legumin, glucose, dextrine, fat, and volatile oil (caffeol).
- Caffeine is medically known as trimethyl xanthine, $C_8H_{10}N_4O_2$.

Properties

Respiratory, gastric and renal stimulant; diuretic, antilithic, digestive, peristaltic, febrifuge.

Increases reflex action and mental activity. More stimulatiing than cocoa.

Roasted coffee believed to have disinfectant and deodorant properties.

A strong infusion of coffee is antisoporific.

Parts used and preparation

Seeds and leaves.

Roasted coffee considered in Indian medicine as disinfectant and deodorant.

Uses

Folkloric : Infusion or decoction of roasted coffee leaves as a stimulant. Some prefer the leaf to the berry.

An important alkaloid used as a stimulant for the nervous system and circulation.

- In traditional Indian medicine, coffee is a palliative in spasmodic asthma, whooping cough, delirium tremens.
- Used as a diuretic in dropsy.

COCOS NUCIFERA

COCONUT

Constituents: Fixed oil, 57.5 - 71%; volatile oil, wax containing the myricyl ester of cerotic acid.

Meat: potein, 6.3%; vitamins A, B, and C; nonyl alcohol; methyl heptyl ketone; methyl undecyl ketone; capronic, decylic, caprylic, lauric and myristic acids; lecithin; stigmasterin, phytosterin; choline; globulin; galactoaraban; galactomannan.

Water, 93%; protein, 0.5%; ash, 1%; saccharose; oxidase; catalase, diastase.

Parts used and preparation: Roots and bark.

- Young and mature fruit.

Uses

Folkloric

- Myriads of use in the traditional systems worldwide: abscesses, asthma, baldness, burns and bruises,, cough and colds, kidney stones, scabies, ulcers, among many others.
- Constipation: Take 1 to 2 tablespoons of gata (cream).
- Dandruff: Massage oil on scalp, leave overnight, and wash hair.
- Diarrhea and/or vomiting: Drink water of young fruit, as tolerated. Water from the young coconut has been used

as a substiture for dextrose infusion in emergent situations during World War II.

- Dry skin: Apply oil and massage into affected area.
- Young roots astriingent for sore throats.
- Ash of bark used for scabies.
- In New Guinea, young leaves chewed to a past and applied to cuts to stop the bleeding.
- Water is fed to infants with diarrhea.
- In emergencies, water has been used as intravenous drips.

Food

- Use oil for cooking; take meat and/or gata (cream) as food.
- The ubod part is a delicacy used in a variety of preparations: lumpia, achara, salads. A good source of iron and calcium.

Others

- Most versatile of all palms with its wide range of utility : as lumber, food, drink, alcohol, vinegar, thatching material, manufacture of baskets, rope, hats, brooms; shell for making charcoal and utensils as cups, bowls, spoons; oil for food, massage, and as base for medications for external use; cooking, illumination, , soap making; decorative for celebrations and religious rituals.
- Lauric acid, the dominant fatty acid in coconut oil, finds application in cooking, detergents, soaps and cosmetics.

Dandelion: Chemical constituents and properties

- Aperient, depurative, diuretic, laxative,stomachic, tonic.
- Root is milky and bitter.
- Plant contains inosit, asparagine, a reducing sugar, a bitter principle, saponin, tyrosinase, palmitic acid, oleic acid, linoleic acid, resinic acids, cholin.
- The flowers contain inulin and a bitter alkaloid, taraxacin. The milky juice contains taraxin, inosit, and taraxacerin.
- Contains an antioxidant, luteolin.

Parts used and preparation: Roots, leaves.

Uses

Nutritional: Used by some as salad component.

A rich source of vitamins A, B, C and D as well as minerals.

Folkloric

- Its multiplicity of uses rates it a herbal cure-all, especially for the treating hepato-biliary disease and as a diuretic.
- in Europe, widely used for gastrointestinal ailments. It is taken as broth with leaves of sorrel and egg yolk for chronic liver congestion.
- Used for its gently laxative effect and as bitter tonic in atonic dyspepsia.
- Promotes appetite and digestion.
- Root preparation used for a variety of conditions: fevers, diabetes, eczema, scurvy, bowel inflammation.
- Pounded poultice of leaves applied to wounds and cuts.
- As a drink: 20 gms of root to a cup of boiling water, take 3-5 glasses a day.
- Juice of the stalk used to remove warts.
- Powdered dried roots used with coffee, and a substitute for coffee when roasted and powdered.
- Extract of dandelion used as remedy for fevers and chills.
- Infusion used to treat anemia, jaundice and nervousness.
- Decoction of root herb taken for scrofula, eczema, scurvy and various skin eruptions.
- Used for eczema and acne.
- Native American Indians have used infusions and decoctions of the root and herb for kidney diseases, dyspepsia and heartburn.
- Traditional Arabian medicine has used it for liver and spleen diseases.

- Chinese medicine used it for hepatitis,bronchitis, pneumonia, as a topical compress for mastitis.

Others: Dandelion wine.

Durio zibethinus Murr.

LIU LIAN

DURIAN

Properties and constituents

- Fruit is considered tonic, operative, depurative, and vermifuge.
- The odor of the flesh believed to be dues to indole compounds which are bacteriostatic.
- Study identified the three strongest sulfury durian odorants and one non-sulfurous odorant with the highest odor impact.

Parts used and preparation

Fruit. leaves and root.

Nutritional Facts

- Serving size: 1 - cup, chopped or diced (8.6 oz)
- Calories 357
- Total Fat 13.0 g
- Cholesterol 0 mg
- Total Carbs 65.8 g
- Fiber 9.2 g
- Protein 3.6 g
- Calcium 14.6 mg
- Potassium 1059.5 mg

Uses: Folkloric

- Decoction of root and leaves taken for fevers.
- Leaves are used in medicinal baths for jaundice.

- The juice is used in a solution for bathing the head of a patient with fever.
- Fruit walls used externally for skin problems.
- In Malaya, decoction of leaves and roots used as febrifuge.
- Leaf juice applied on head for fever.
- Leaves used in medicinal baths for jaundiced patients.
- Decoction of leaves and fruits used for swelling and skin diseases.
- Flesh used as aphrodisiac.
- In China, decoction of leaves and roots used for fever. Used for colds, phlegm. Leaves used in medicinal baths for patients with jaundice. Ash of burned rind taken after childbirth. Used to improve sexual function.
- In Malaysia, leaf juice applied to head for fever.
- A Malay prescription for fever is a decoction or poultice of boiled roots of Hibiscus rosa-sinensis, Durio zibethinus, Nephelium longan, Nephelium mutabile and Artocarpus integrifolia. source

Others

- Dried rinds burned as fuel and used to smoke fish>
- Ash used to bleach silk.

SOLANUM MELONGENA L.

EGGPLANT

Parts used and preparation

Fruits, roots.

Uses: Nutritional: Fruit is an excellent vegetable and popular in the rural day-to-day cuisine.

A good source of vitamins A, B, and C.

A good source of calcium, phosphorus, and iron.

Folkloric: Decoction of roots taken internally for asthma and as a general stimulant.

Leaves are used for piles.

The boiled root of the wild plant, mixed with sour milk and grain porridge has been used for the treatment of syphilis.

Decoction of roots, dried stalk, and leaves is used for washing sores, exudative surfaces.

The juice of leaves used for throat and stomach troubles.

The fruit, bruised with vinegar, is used as a poultice for abscesses and cracked nipples.

In Taiwan folk medicine, roots are used for rheumatism, inflammation and foot pain.

EUCALYPTUS GLOBULUS

EUCALYPTOS

Distribution

Usually planted as a garden plant.

Chemical Constituents and Properties

- Volatile oil, 0.01 - 1.96% - cineol, 80%, d-alpha pinene, camphene, fenchene, butyric and caprionic aldehydes, ethyl and iso-amyl alcohols, acetic acid, cymol, sesquiterpene, eudesmos, 1-pinocarveol.
- There are more than 300 species. The species with the highest yield of volatile oils are E. globosus, E. tereticornis, E. polyanthemos and E. citriodora.
- Volatile oil: phellandrene, aldehydes and ketone, 33%, phenol, 9%.
- Oils are in classified into: (1) medicinal, containing eucalytol or cineol (2) industrial, containing terpenes, used in mining operations, and (3) aromatic, as in E. citriodora.
- Considered anesthetic, antiseptic, antispasmodic, diuretic, febrifuge, rebefacient, analgesic, stimulant.
- Cooling, antiinflammatory, antirheumatic, antiviral, insellect repellent, antiparasitic.

Parts used: Mature leaves.

Uses

Folkloric: Antiseptic and deodorant: Apply crushed leaves on affected area.

Decoction of leaves as tea for cough, asthma, hoarseness, fevers.

Pure eucalyptus oil, two drops in a tsp of warm water, for coughs, whooping coughs, asthma and bronchitis.

Infusion of leaves used for asthma, catarrh, bronchits, whooping cough, coryza, dysentery, diabetes, fevers and colds, malaria, rhinitis, tuberculosis.

For sinusitis, breathing of vapor of decoction of leaves.

Decoction of leaves used for washing and cleaning wounds.

Other uses: Diabetes, lumbago, sciatica, toothaches, tuberculosis, dysentery, gout.

In China, used for promote eschar formation.

In France, leaf extract used as hypoglycemic.

In Guatemala, leaf decoction for fever. Hot water extract of dried leaf used for ringworm, wounds, ulcers, pimples and as vaginal douche.

In India, as moquito repellant and insecticide.

In Italy, as inhalation therapy for asthma; also for diabetes.

In Kenya, for snail infestation.

In Mexico, for urethritis, laryngitis, cystitis, gastritis, enteritis; as antipyretic and antimalarial.

In Tunisia, for branchiol conditions and cough.

In Spain, for colds, catarrh, diabetes.

Preparation for use: Gather the leaves, dry in the sun for 5-6 hours. Place in a paper bag, tie and hang in the shade for a week. Decoct 50 gms of the dried leaves in a pint of boiling water;

drink 6 glasses daily. For fresh leaves, use 60 to 70 gms to a pint of boiling water, drink the same amount.

Other: Insect repellant: Burn leaves.

Extract used to kill fleas.

Extraction of oil: Boil mature leaves in water, condensing the vapor to recover the oil. Eucalyptus globulus yields less oil than the other varieties used for commercial production of medicinal grade oils.

Studies

- Antibacterial Activity of Three Medicinal Plants: Eucalyptus Globulus, Aristolochial Latas and Vitex Negundo against Enteric Pathogens: The medicinal plants tested showed varying degrees of antibacterial activity with the maximum zone of inhibition obtained with E. globulus.
- Antihyperglycemic Actions of Eucalyptus globulus (Eucalyptus) are Associated with Pancreatic and Extra-Pancreatic Effects in Mice: The study suggests that E. globulus may be an effective antihyperglycemic dietary supplement for the treatment of diabetes. The study also showed pancreatic protection or regeneration following exposure to streptozotocin.
- Antibacterial activity of leaf essential oils of Eucalyptus globulus and Eucalyptus camaldulensis: Study suggested the potential usefulness of the two Eucalyptus species as a micobiostatis, antiseptic or as a disinfectant agent.

ALLIUM SATIVUM

SUAN

GARLIC

Characteristics and constituents: Saponins; tannins; sulfurous compounds; prostaglandins; alkaloids; volatile oils; allicin (bulb).

The antihelminthic property is due to allyl disulphie content.

Antibacterial, antihelminthic, antimycotic, antiviral, antispasmodic, diaphoretic, expectorant, fibrinolytic, hypotensive, promiting leucocytosis, lowering lipids and inhibiting platelet aggregation

The most important chemical constituents are the cysteine sulfoxides (alliin) and the nonvolatile glutamylcysteine peptides which make up more than 82% of the sulfur content of garlic. Allicin, ajoenes and sulfides are degradation products of alliin.

Bulb: allicin; volatile oil, 0.9% - allyl disulfide, allypropyl disulfide; inulin; protein; fat, 1.3%; carbohydrates, 0.2%; ash, 9.4%; choline, 0.7%; myrosinase.

Leaves: Protein, i.2%; fat, 0.5%; sulfides.

Parts utilized: Bulbs: Features prominently as a condiment and flavor in Filipino cuisine.

Herbalists, with concerns that cooking diminishes medicinal potency, recommends eating raw garlic cloves.

Uses

Folkloric : Arthritis, rheumatism, toothaches: Crush several cloves and rub on affected areas.

Headaches: Crush one clove and apply to both temples as poultice.

Insect bites: Crush garlic or cut clove crosswise and rub directly to affected area.

Athlete's foot.

Decoction of leaves and bulbs for fever and as hypotensive, carminative, expectorant, and antihelmintic.

Juice from freshly crushed garlic used for colds, cough, sore throat, hoarseness, asthma and bronchitis.

Decoction use for tonsillitis.

For nasal congestion - a steam inhalation of chopped garlic and a teaspoon of vinegar in boiling water.

Fresh garlic has been used as a complement to INH therapy for tuberculosis.

Also used for menstrual cramps.

Digestive problems and gastrointestinal spasms.

For gas pains, drink an infusion of a peeled broild clove.

ALLIUM SATIVUM

GARLIC

Characteristics and constituents: Saponins; tannins; sulfurous compounds; prostaglandins; alkaloids; volatile oils; allicin (bulb).

The antihelminthic property is due to allyl disulphie content.

Antibacterial, antihelminthic, antimycotic, antiviral, antispasmodic, diaphoretic, expectorant, fibrinolytic, hypotensive, promiting leucocytosis, lowering lipids and inhibiting platelet aggregation

The most important chemical constituents are the cysteine sulfoxides (alliin) and the nonvolatile glutamylcysteine peptides which make up more than 82% of the sulfur content of garlic. Allicin, ajoenes and sulfides are degradation products of alliin.

Bulb: allicin; volatile oil, 0.9% - allyl disulfide, allypropyl disulfide; inulin; protein; fat, 1.3%; carbohydrates, 0.2%; ash, 9.4%; choline, 0.7%; myrosinase.

Leaves: Protein, i.2%; fat, 0.5%; sulfides.

Parts utilized: Bulbs: Features prominently as a condiment and flavor in Filipino cuisine.

Herbalists, with concerns that cooking diminishes medicinal potency, recommends eating raw garlic cloves.

Uses

Folkloric : Arthritis, rheumatism, toothaches: Crush several cloves and rub on affected areas.

Headaches: Crush one clove and apply to both temples as poultice.

Insect bites: Crush garlic or cut clove crosswise and rub directly to affected area.

Athlete's foot.

Decoction of leaves and bulbs for fever and as hypotensive, carminative, expectorant, and antihelmintic.

Juice from freshly crushed garlic used for colds, cough, sore throat, hoarseness, asthma and bronchitis.

Decoction use for tonsillitis.

For nasal congestion - a steam inhalation of chopped garlic and a teaspoon of vinegar in boiling water.

Fresh garlic has been used as a complement to INH therapy for tuberculosis.

Also used for menstrual cramps.

Digestive problems and gastrointestinal spasms.

For gas pains, drink an infusion of a peeled broild clove.

CITRUS DECUMANA LINN.

GRAPEFRUIT / POMELO

Constituents

- Leaves - volatile oil, 1.7% - dipentene, 25%; linalool, 15%; citral, 3.5%; a-pinene, 0.5-1.5%; d-limone, 90-92%.

Pericarp - saccharose, reducing sugar; organic acid.

- Juice - insulin like substance; lycopene; vitamin C; peroxidase; sugar, 14.3%; acid, 1.1%; fat, 0.33%; cellulose, 1.3%; nitrogenous substances, 1.6%
- Rind - crystalline glycosidal bitter principle, naringin (peviously reported as hesperidin), 0.2-1.6% ;, 10%; pectin, 10%; peroxidase.
- Phytochemical studies of various Citrus spp. yielded naringin, hesperidin, diosmin and naringenin.
- Phytochemical study of the peel of the grapefruit isolated

five compounds: friedelin, b-sitosterol, limonin, cordialin B, and a previously unreported compound, 7(3',7',11',14'-tetramethy)pentadec-2',6',10'-trienyloxycoumarin. source

Parts used and preparation: Leaves and fruit.

Uses

Nutritional: Food - Fresh fruit and preserved rind.

Fresh fruit ia good source of vitamin B, iron and calcium.

Folkloric: Nausea and fainting: Squeeze rind near nostrils for patient to inhale.

Aromatic baths: Boil leaves in water.

Infusion or decoction of flowers and leaves for nervous affections, coughs, ulcers.

Peel or rind, dried or in decoction, for dyspepsia.

Boiled seeds in a gallon of water can be used for sitz-baths.

In the Himalayas, fruit juice recommended for ulcers; used in diabetes; and mixed with black pepper and a littlc rock salt, used for malaria. Fruit juice with its pulp, with honey, is given to improve urinary flow.

PSIDIUM GUAJAVA LINN.

GUAVA

Parts utilized

Leaves: Chemical constituents and properties

Fixed oil, 6%; volatile (essential) oil, 0.365%; eugenol; tannin 8-15%; saponins; amydalin; phenolic acids; malic acid; ash, aldehydes.

Contains catequinic components and flavonoids.

Major constituents of leaves are tannins, ß-sitosterol, maslinic acid, essential oils, triterpenoids and flavonoids.

Andiarrheal, antiseptic, antispasmodic, antioxidant

hepatoprotective, anti-allergy, antimicrobial, antigenotoxic, antiplasmodial, cardioactive, anticough, antidiabetic, antiinflammatory, antinociceptive.

Uses

Nutrition: Very high in vitamin C(80 mg in 100 gm of fruit) with large amounts of vitamin A. Fruit can be eaten raw or canned, jellied, juiced or powdered.

Folkloric: Astringent, antispasmodic, anthelminthic and antiseptic properties.

Leaves used for wounds and toothache must always be fresh.

Decoction or infusion of fresh leaves used for wound cleaning to prevent infection and to facilitate healing.

Warm decoction of leaves for aromatic baths.

For diarrhea, boil for 15 minutes 4 to 6 tablespoons of chopped leaves in 18 ounces of water. Strain and cool. Drink 1/4 of the decoction every 3 - 4 hours.

For toothache, cew 2-3 young leaves and put into the tooth cavity;

For gum swelling, chew leaves or use the leaf decoction as mouthwash 3 times daily; chewed leaves.

For skin ulcers, pruritic or infected wounds: Apply decoction of leaves or unripe fruit as wash or the leaf poultice on the wound or use the decoction for wound cleansing. It is also popularly used for the wound healing of circumcision wounds.

Nosebleeds: Densely roll the bayabas leaves and place into the nostril cavity.

Vaginal wash: Because of antiseptic properties, warm decoction of leaves as vaginal wash (after childbirth) or douche.

Cosmetic: Leaf extract used in skin whitening products.

Dental: Toothbrush au-natural: Bayabas twigs, chewed at the ends until frayed, used as alternative for toothbrushing with whitening effect.

Others: Wood is suitalbe for carpentry, turnery, fuel or charcoal.

A favorite rural use for tool handles.

LAUREL

PLUMBAGO ROSEA

Constituents and Medicinal Properties: Contains plumbagin, sitosterol glucoside.

Roots are the highest source of plumbagin.

Considered vesicant, stimulant, sialagogue.

Parts used and preparation: Roots, bark.

Uses

Folkloric: Poulticed bark scrappings for headaches.

Bark plaster applied to spine for fevers; antidyspeptic.

In india, root is used as abortifacient.

Juice of leaves with oil, for rheumatism, glandular swelling.

Roots also used for dyspepsia, piles, diarrhea, and to improve the appetite.

In Myanmar, used for leprosy and syphylis.

Studies

- Uterotrophic, Fetotoxic and Abortifacient Effect of Malaysian Variety of Plumbago rosea L. on Isolated Rat Uterus and Pregnant Mice: Pronounced fetotoxic and mild abortifacient potential supports its traditional use.
- A simple method for isolation of plumbagin from roots of Plumbago rosea
- In vivo tumor inhibitory and radiosensitizing effects of an Indian medicinal plant, Plumbago rosea on experimental mouse tumors: Study shows PE to have a weak antitumore effect, but may have a potential use in enhancing the tumor-killing effect of radiation.

- Antimicrobial Activity in Vitro of Plumbagin Isolated from Plumbago Species: PR was shown to exhibit activitiy against yeast and bacteria suggesting the naphthoquinone plumbagin as a promising antimicrobial agent.

NELUMBO NUCIFERA LINN.

SACRED LOTUS

Parts utilized: Whole plant.

Chemical constituents and characteristics

Nelumbine is present in dried seeds, cotyledons and young leaves.

- Seed contains flavonoids and alkaloids.

All parts of the plant are used: – astringent, cardiotonic, febrifuge, hypotensive, resolvent, stomachic, styptics, tonic and vasodilator.

The rhizomes contain asparagin.

Seeds are demulcent and nutritive.

Filaments and flowers are cooling, sedative, astringent, bitter, refrigerant and expectorant.

Roots are demulcent; used as emmenagogue.

Leaves are antifebrile and antihemorrhagic.

Roots are considered by some as aphrodisiac.

Uses

FOLKLORIC

- Roots, rhizomes, and flowers are used as astringent.
- The leaves and seeds are used in poultices.
- Flowers, filaments and juice of flower-stalks are used in diarrhea, cholera, liver complaints, and fevers.
- A syrup made from the flowers used in coughs, beeding piles, menorrhagia and dysentery.

- Stamens are used for bleeding piles and parturition.
- Nodes of the rhizome used to stop bleeding.
- Astringent petals used for syphilis.
- Seeds used in leprosy and skin diseases; for spermatorrhea and erotic dreams.
- Roots and young leaves used for piles.
- The milky juice of leaves and flower stalks used in diarrhea.
- Leaves used as deterrent for skin maladies.
- Pounded leaves applied to the body for high fevers, mucous membranes and skin irritation, and over the forehead for headaches.
- Rhizome root used as rejuvenating tonic.
- Receptacle/.flower stalk used in Chinese medicine to stop internal bleeding caused by gastric ulcers; menorrhagia or parturient hemorrhage.
- Decoction of flowers used for premature ejaculation.
- Decoction of floral receptacle used for abdominal cramps, bloody discharges.
- Flower stalk used for bleeding gastric ulcers, excessive menses, post-partum hemorrhages.
- Paste of root starch used for ringworm and other skin ailments.
- There is folkloric use in the treatment of cancer.
- In Chhattisgarh, India, the oil prepared from the roots is applied to the genitals to increase retention time.
- In Japan, the leaf of NN has been used for home remedy of the summer heat syndrome.
- In China, leaf used to treat obesity.

Nutrition

- Lotus is a food plant. The unripe seeds are eaten boiled, raw, or roasted; the ripe seeds, boiled or roasted. The rhizomes, sliced, are eaten raw or cooked. The petioles, without the rough outer layer, and the leaves are boiled and eaten. The pollen and stamens are used to perfume tea.

- Roasted seed used as coffee substitute.

MAHOGANY

SWIETENIA MAHOGANI JACQ.

Constituents and properties

- The bark contains tannin.
- Two new tetranortriterpenoids, mahonin and secomahoganin were isolated from the cotyledons of SM. (Source)
- Leaves contain seven phragmalin limonoids.
- Study yields 6-Desoxyswietenine, a tetranortriterpenoid from Swietenia mahogani
- Considered astringent, depurative.

Uses

Folkloric : Bark is antipyretic, tonic and astringent.

Decoction of seeds used as abortifacient.

Used for hypertension, amoebiasis, chest pains, parasitism, cancer.

Used by Ifugao migrants for malaria, cough and miscarriage.

In India, bark extracts used as astringent for wounds.

Used for malaria, anemia, diarrhea, fever and dysentery.

Others : In India, wood is a popular material for making of furniture, musical instruments, boats, caskets.

Studies

- The Effect of Swietenia Mahogani (Mahogany) Seed Extract On Indomethacin-Inducd Gastric UlcersI in Female Sprague-Dawley Rats: Study found a potential effect on the healing of gastric ulcers, probably through inhibition of gastric bacterial metabolism and providing an attractive possibility for H. pylori therapy.

- Hypoglycemic / Hypolipidemic: Hypoglycemic effect of Swietenia macrophylla seeds against type II diab: In India, Swietenia macrophylla is a folk-medicinal tree known as mahogany. Study concludes that the ME of seeds of Swietenia macrophylla has hypoglycemic as well as hypolipidemic effect.

MANGIFERA INDICA

MANGO

Chemical constituents and properties: Mangiferin; mangin; piuri-yellow dye; benzoic acid; citric acid; tannin, 10%.

The leaves contain 43-46 percent euxanthin acid and some euxanthon.

Seed contains a fixed oil, oleostearin.

The bark exudate yields a resin, gun, ash, and tannin.

Mangostine, 29-hydroxymangiferonic acid, mangiferin and flavonoids have been isolated from the stem bark. Leaves and flowers yield an essential oil containing humulene, elemene, ocimene, linalool and nerol.

Properties

- Root, diuretic; bark, astringent; seeds, astringent and mifuge; leaves, pectoral.
- Considered antiseptic, antibacterial, antiinflammatory, diaphoretic, stomachic, vermifuge, cardiotonic and laxative.

Insert: Young unripe mangos.

Parts used and preparation: Leaves, kernel, bark and fruit.

Uses

Nutritional: Good source of iron (deficient in calcium);

excellent source of vitamins A, B, and C. Fruit contains citric, tartaric and mallic acids.

Food: As fruit or mango-ade.

Folkloric: Decoction of root is considered diuretic.

Bark and seeds are astringent.

Resin is used for aphthous stomatitis.

Cough: Drink infusion of young leaves as needed.

Diarrhea: Take decoction of bark or kernel as tea.

Hot lotion from bark used for rheumatism.

Gum resin from bark, mixed with coconut oil, used for scabies and other parasitic skin diseases.

Juice of leaves used for dysentery.

Tea of leaves with a little honey used for hoarseness and aphonia, 4 glasses daily.

Powdered dried leaves, 1 tbsp to a cup of warm water, 4 times daily, used for diabetes.

Ashes of burned leaves used for scalds and burns.

Infusion of young leaves used in asthma and cough.

Tea of powdered dried flowers, 4 times daily for diarrhea, urethritis.

Juice of peel of unripe mangoes used for skin diseases.

Seed is vermifuge and astringent.

Infusion of powdered dried seeds used fir asthma, diarrhea, dysentery, menorrhagia, bleeding piles, round worms.

Studies

- Antibacterial: Antibacterial activity of Mangifera indica (L.): Study showed that leaf extracts of M. indica possess some antibacterial activity against S aureus, E coli, P aeruginosa and provides a basis for its medical use in Uganda.

- Hematologic benefits: Effects of Aqueous Extract of Mangifera indica L. (Mango) Stem Bark on Haematological Parameters of Normal Albino Rats: Stem bark extracts of MI showed positive effects on the haemopoietic system of test rats.
- Antiinflammatory, Analgesic and Hypoglycemic: Anti-inflammatory, analgesic and hypoglycaemic effects of Mangifera indica Linn. (Anacardiaceae) stem-bark aqueous extract: Results of the study support the folkloric use of the plant for painful arthritic and other inflammatory conditions, as well as T2DM.
- Anti-Clostridium tetany activity: The activity of Mangifera indica L. leaf extracts against the tetanus causing bacterium, Clostridium tetani: Study showed anti-clostridum tetany activity.
- Anti-asthmatic: Mangifera indica stem bark effect on the rat trachea contracted by acetylcholine and histamine: Study showed MI blockage of histaminic and muscarinic receptors, supporting the traditional use of MI stem back in the treatment of asthma.
- Immunostimulant: Immunomodulatory activity of alcoholic extract of Mangifera indica L. in mice: Study showed increased humoral antibody titer and delayed type hypersensitivity in mice suggesting a potential for a drug with immunostimulant properties.
- Antihyperglycemic: Antihyperglycaemic effect of Mangifera indica in rat: Study showed leaf extract of MI possess hypoglycemic activity, possibly due to reduction in intestinal absorption of glucose.

GARCINIA MANGOSTANA

MANGOSTEEN

Chemical constituents

- Rind contains 5.5% tannin, and a resin.
- Also from the rind, a bitter principle, mangostin.

- Fruit flesh (aril) contains saccharose 10.8%; dextrose, 1%; and kerrelose 1.2 %.
- Acidity of fruit due to malic acid.
- Recent studies have isolated a new xanthone from the pericarp, mangostinone, and a new polyoxygenated xanthone, mangostanol, from the fruit hulls.
- From the green fruit hulls, 3 new xanthones: mangostenol, mangostenone A and mangostenone B.

Parts utilized: Pericarp (peel) and seeds.

Pericarp which is used as medicine is separated from the edible portion and is sliced into desired sizes immediately after the fruit is opened. The pericarp pieces are strung and dried (air-drying, sun-drying, and "tapahan" method where the pericarp is dried by smoking) immediately to avoid fungi infestation. Sun-dried pericarp yield the highest tannin concentration of 5.5%.

Uses

Folkloric: Abdominal pain and diarrhea.

Decoction of roots used for dysmenorrhea and genitourinary ailments.

Bark and young seeds used in diarrhea, dysentery, and GI problems; also, a wash for stomatitis.

Decoction of leaves and bark used as febrifuge and to treat thrush.

Decoction of powdered rind used for external astringent application.

In Cambodia, the bark and fruit rind are used for diarrhea and dysentery.

In Malaya, infusion of leaves mixed with unripe banana and benzoin used for the circumcision wound.

New Rage - 2004

Now, it is XANTHONES, an ingredient in the mangosteen fruit that is being touted as the new "miracle" supplement-drink.

As much hype and fanfare as the "Noni" juice craze that spawned a short-lived industry that flooded many a distant shore. See: Xanthones.html

Others: In Malaya, a black dye is obtained from the shell.

In Ghana, mangosteen twigs used as chewsticks.

Studies

- Antifungal activity: Antifungal activity of xanthones isolated from the fruit hulls of GM.
- Antibacterial: Extracts of GM showed inhibitory effects against S aureus.
- Antioxidant: The methanol extract of fruit hulls was found to possess potent radical scavenging effect.
- Acne vulgaris: Effect of Garcinia mangostana on inflammation caused by Propionibacterium acnes: Study showed that G mangostana possess significant antioxidant activity – highly effective in scavenging free radicals and suppressing the production of pro-inflammatory cytokines. It suggests a potential source of an agent for the treatment of acne vulgaris.
- A Geranylated biphenyl derivative from Garcinia mangostana: Extracts of root bark, stem bark and latex yielded compounds with antibacterial, anti-inflammatory and antifungal activities supporting its use in indigenous medicine.
- Antiproliferation, antioxidation and induction of apoptosis by GM (mangosteen) on SKBR3 human breast cancer cell line: Study suggests a potential use for cancer chemoprevention.
- Tuberculosis: Antimycobacterial Activity of Prenylated Xanthones from the Fruits of Garcinia mangostana: Prenylated xanthones, alpha- and beta- mangostins and garcinone B showed strong inhibitory activity against M tuberculosis.
- Antioxidant and Cytoprotective Activities of Methanolic

Extract from Garcinia mangostana Hulls: Study suggests GM extract possess antioxidant and chemoprotective activities through a reducing mechanism and inhibition of intracellular oxidative stress.

BRASSICA INTEGRIFOLIA O. E. SCHUTZ.

MUSTARD

Constituents and medicinal properties

- Counterirritant, emmenagogue, rubefacient.
- Seed contains the mustard oil, the active principle. Pure mustard oil is pale yellow, faintly smelling of mustard with a shard and pungent taste.
- Considered analgesic, antibacterial, antifungal, diuretic, emetic, galatagogue, stimulant.
- Purification and properties of phenylalanine ammonia-lyase from leaf mustard.

Uses

Nutritional: Leaves eaten as green leafy vegetable.

Excellent source of calcium, phosphorus, iron and vitamin B.

Folkloric: Counterirritant, leaves applied externally for pleurodynia and pleuritis, neuralgia, lumbago.

Hot-foot bath of mustard (seeds or leaves) for headaches, common cold, and fevers.

Hip-bath of mustard used as emmenagogue.

Poultice of mustard leaves or seeds used for neuralgic and rheumatic complaints.

Pure fresh oil taken from seeds used as external counterirritant.

Combined oil of mustard and camplor used for muscle pains,

As an emetic, 4-5 tsp in a cup of warm water.

COLEUS AROMATICUS BENTH.

OREGANO

Chemical constituents and Medicinal Properties

Aromatic, carminative, emmenagogue, diaphoretic, tonic, stimulant.

In India, considered antilithiotic, chemopreventive, antiepileptic, antioxidant.

Fresh leaves yield 0.055 volatile oil, largely carvacrol.

Parts utilized: Leaves

Uses

Folkloric : The juice of the leaves for dyspepsia, asthma, chronic coughs, bronchits, colic, flatulence, rheumatism. The dose is one tablespoonful of the fresh juice every hour for adults and one teaspoonful every two hours, four times daily, for children. As an infusion, 50 to 60 grams to a pint of boiling water, and drink the tea, 4 to 5 glasses a day. For chilldren, 1/2 cup 4 times daily.

For otalgia (ear aches), pour the fresh, pure juice into the ear for 10 minutes.

For carbuncles, boils, sprains, felons, painful swellings: Apply the poultice of leaves to the affected area, four times daily.

For sore throats, a decoction of two tablespoonfuls of dried leaves to a pint of boiling water, taken one hour before or after meals.

Decoction of leaves is given after childbirth.

In India, leaves are used traditionally for bronchitis, asthma, diarrhea, epilepsy, nephro-cystolithiasi, fever, indigestion and cough.

Recent uses and preparations

Respiratory ailments like cough, asthma and bronchitis: Squeeze juice of the leaves. Take one teaspoon every hour for adults. For children above 2 years old, 3 to 4 teaspoons a day.

ALLIUM CEPA L.

TRUE ONION

Properties: Carminative, demulcent, diuretic, emmenagogue, expectorant, rubefacient, stimulant.

Juice is disinfectant, rejuvinative, antispasmodic.

Parts used: Bulb

Uses

Folkloric: Bulb is emmenagogue, stimulant, diuretic, expectorant; externally, is rubefacient.

Mixed with common salt, is used for fever, catarrh, chronic bronchitis.

Bulb applied as cooling poultice for boils, bruises, and wounds.

Juice or slices of raw onion is applied to insect bites and stings or burns.

Juice of the bulb mixed with mustard oil or coconut oil is used for rheumatic and inflammatory swellings.

Onion and garlic juice used for nervousness, insomnia, and rheumatism: 3 tbsp daily.

Juices of onion, garlic carrot, radish, garlic and lemon: Used for bronchitis, asthma.

Others: Peeled and eaten raw, powdered, juiced, infused or decocted as tea, infused.

Okra

Medicinal Properties: Demulcent, emollient, sudorific, cooling, carminative, stimulang, cordial, antispasmodic

Parts utilized: Roots, leaves, young pods, seeds.

Nutrition: Contains vitamins A and C. A good source of iron and calcium. Also contains starch, fat, ash, thiamine and riboflavine.

Uses

Folkloric : Decoction of roots and leaves as a tea or for washing.

Decoction of young fruit useful for catarrh, urinary problems.

Syrup from mucilaginous fruit used for sore throat.

Poultice of roots and leaves for wound healing.

Young pods for fevers, difficult urination and diarrhea.

Decoction of roots for headaches, varicose veins, arthritis, fevers.

Decoctions of leaves for abdominal pain.

Leaves also useful as emollient poultice.

Seeds used a coffee substitute. Paste of seeds, mixed with milk, used for pruritic skin lesions.

SETARIA PALMIFOLIA STAPF.

PALM GRASS

Parts used and preparation: Leaves, seeds.

Uses

Folkloric: A compound decoction taken for ireegular menses.

Others: Grain of the grass sometimes used as rice substitute.

In Malaya, tender shoots are eaten as vegetable.

Feed for cattle.

CARICA PAPAYA

MELON TREE

Properties: Antirheumatic, emmenagogue, anthelmintic.

Constituents and properties

- Leaf, fruit, stem and root: Papain; phytokinase; malic acid; calcium maleate.
- Fresh latex: chymopapain.

- Leaves: Carpaine (alkaloid); carposide (glucoside); saccharose, 0.85%; dextrose, 2.6%; levulose, 2.1%; citrates.
- Seeds: Volatile oil.
- Seeds are considered antiinflammatory, anthelmintic, analgesic, stomachic and antifungal.
- Leaves are used as tonic, stomachic and analgesic.
- Roots are analgesic.

Parts used and preparation: Leaves, fruit and latex of trunk.

Uses

Nutritional: Source of calcium, iron; good source of vitamins A and B; excellent source of vit C.

Folkloric: · Debridement (removal of purulent exudate and blood clots from wound and ulcer): Apply latex (dagta) of unripe fruit or trunk on the wound or ulcer.

Laxative: Eat ripe fruit liberally. (May cause harless yellowing of the skin, specially palms and soles but not the eyes.)

Cystitis: Boil cup of chopped fresh leaves and 1 cup chopped green fruit in glasses of water for 15 mins; taken 1 cu 3 times daily.

Acne: Mix 3 tablespoons of mashed ripe papaya with a tablespoon of kalamansi juice; apply the mixture to face for 30 minues, then wash face with warm water.

Worm infestation: 1 cup of dried seeds, pulverized and mixed with 1 cup of milk or water; 1 teaspoon 2 hours after supper.

Poultice of bruised papaya leaves for rheumatic complaints.

Tea decoction of dried leaves for variety of stomach troubles.

Decoction of boiled flowers or powdered seeds promote menstruation.

Infusion of male flowers (left insert) with honey used for cough, hoarseness, bronchitis, laryngitis and tracheitis: a spoonful every hour.

Poultice of roots used for centipede bites.

In India and Sri Lanka, green papaya is used as contraceptive and abortifacient.

In southern Nigeria, aqueous extract of unripe papaya taken by sickle cell patients for its "antisickling" activity.

Others

Meat tenderizer: Mix the peelings of the unripe fruit or latex with raw meat before cooking. The enzyme "papain" is a main ingredient in commercial meat tenderizers.

- Papain is also the main ingredient of an ointment populaly used as a topical application for cuts, rashes, stings and burns.

Food: Eat unripe or ripe fruit.

- Young leaves of papaya are sometimes steamed and eaten like spinach.
- Seeds are edible, sharp and spicy.

PIPER NIGRUM

BLACK PEPPER

Properties and chemical constituents : The dried fruits furnish the black pepper of commerce. When the outer shell is removed, the product is white pepper.

The pepper contains an active resin (oleoresin) responsible for the known pungent taste and aromatic odor. Contains an alkaloid piperine, 5 - 9%; piperidine, 5%; mesocarp contains chavicine.

Considered acrid, rubifacient, stimulant, counterirritant, stomachic, carminative.

Parts utilized: Roots, leaves, seeds.

Uses

Folkloric: Decoction used as mouthwash for toothache; rubifacient in alopeicia and skin diseases.

Liniment used in rheumatism.

Infusion used as gargle for afflictions of the throat.

Juice of leaves boiled and applied externally for scabies.

Ointment mixed with lard used againsst Tinea capitis.

Mixed with brandy and anise, used as a febrifuge in malaria.

Used in shellfish and mushroom poisoning.

Mixed with honey and ginger, used by Malay as abortifacient.

Roots used as antihelmintic.

In Iraian traditional medicine, used to relieve menorrhagia in women.

In Ayurveda, paste of black pepper is used for boils, piles, rheumatic pains, headache, prolapsed rectum, toothaches. Pepper is given for dyspepsia, flatulence, diarrhea, cholea, cough, gonorrhea and malarial fever.

Others: Culinary: A kitchen essenntial; a condiment and spice since early times.

SOLANUM TUBEROSUM

POTATO

Constituents and Properties

- Antiscorbutic, aperient, diuretic, galactagogue, stimulant, emollient, antidote, antispasmodic.
- Study isolated putrescine N-methyltransferase, a calystegine,a nortropane alkaloid with glycosidase inhibitory activity.

Uses

Nutritional: Good source of fiber, vitamins B and C, and minerals.

Peels are high in potassium.

Folkloric: Gently laxative, but non-purging.

Promotes milk.

Useful for gout.

Potato-peel tea for hypertension.

Poultice of leaves as a tonic.

Used for scurvy, dyspepsia, hyperacidity, gout and arthritis.

Decoction of leaves for chronic cough.

Poultice of grated raw potato used for light burns, arthritis, itching, etc

RAPHANUS SATIVUS

RADI8H

Parts utilized

Whole plant.

When seeds are ripe, harvest the whole plant, sun-dry, remove the seeds and dry again. Crush on use. Roots can also be sun-dried for use.

Properties

Considered anthelmintic, antifungal, antibacterial, antiscorbutic, diuretic, laxative, tonic, carminative, corrective, stomachic, cholagogue, lithotriptic, emmenagogue.

The juice of the fresh root is considered powerfully antiscorbutic.

Uses

Nutritional: Edible: Leaves, flowers, roots, seed.

A vegetable, eaten raw or cooked.

Excellent source of iron and good source of calcium; also a source of vitamin B.

Folkloric: For diarrhea: boil the fresh leaves to concentrated decoction and drink.

Juice of leaves increaes the flow of urine and promotes bowel movements.

Root is used for piles and stomach pains.

Juice used to expel wind from the bowels.

Poultice of roots used for burns, scalds, or fetid smelling feet.

Decoction of root used for fevers.

Coughs: Decoction of flowers; or, boil 6 to 15 gms seed preparation to decoction and drink.

Seeds promote the flow of urine, bowel movements, and menstruation.

For patients with edema, bloated belly (ascites), pale yellowish face, and oliguria: used dried root preparation with citrus rind preparation (5:1 proportion). Boil to a concentrated decoction and drink.

Others: Repellent

ROSMARINUS OFFICINALIS

ROSEMARY

Properties: Antispasmodic, emmenagogue, stimulant, bitter tonic, astringent, carminative, diaphoretic, aromatic, nervine, stomachic, febrifuge.

Constituents: Volatile oil, 1.2 - 2% - alpha-pinene, cineol, borneol, camphene, rosemarin.

Parts used : Herb.

Uses

Culinary: As condiment in flavoring and preserving meat.

Folkloric: Used to ward off evil.

Cough: Inhale steam of strong decoction of herb.

Diuretic: Take decoction of herb as needed.

Gas pains: Take decoction of herb as needed.

Rheumatism: Make decoction of herb and soak affected area.

Conjunctivitis: Infusion of leaves used as an eyewash, 4 to 5 times daily.

Vapor baths, using 30 to 40 gms of leaves in boiling water for rheumatism, catarrh.

Juice of leaves applied to areas of thinning hair and dandruff; also, as rosemary vinegar.

Rosemary tea also used as conditioning hair rinse,

Infusion of leaves as tea for dyspepsia, flatulence.

Decoction of leaves as mouthwash for gums disease, halitosis, sore throat.

Aromatic bath: Use decoction of herb.

Infusion with oil for massages.

Daily use of rosemary tea believed to prevent cataracts.

For Hair wash: Steep 25 g of rosemary in 2 pt of cider vinegar for two weeks, shaking occasionally; strain. In hair washing, put 1-2 tsp in the final rinse.

For dandruff, massage rosemary vinegar thoroughly into scalp, 20 mins before washing.

Postpartum bath: Boil a head of petals in a quart of water). (Related article: Suob)

FICUS ELASTICA

INDIAN RUBBER TREE

Chemical constituents and characteristics

The latex contains caoutchouc, 10-30 per cent; a bitter substance; albuminoid. The wax contains cerotic acid.

Parts utilized: Rootlets and bark.

Uses

Folkloric

Skin eruptions and dermatitis: Boil one cup of chopped bark in 1/2 gallon of water for 10 mins; use decoction to wash involved areas, twice daily.

Decoction of aerial rootlets used for wounds, cuts and sores.

Bark is astringent and used as styptics for wounds.

ecoction of latex for parasitic worms (trichuris trichura).

In northern Cameroon, used as fertility enhancement. source

Plant that Detoxify the Air : Of the ficus plants tested, the rubber plant is the best for removing chemical toxins from the indoor environment, especially formaldehyde.

GLYCINE MAX (L.) MERR.

SOYBEAN

Constituents and properties

- Considered astringent, carminative.
- Dried sprout considered laxative, resolvent, and constructive.
- Contains a fixed oil, 14-22&; protein, 50%; carbohydrates, 16.2%; diastase, urease, lipase, allantoinase, peroxidase, pentosan, sojasterol, sitosterin, and phasin.
- The two primary isoflavones are daidzein and genistein; others are puerarin, genistin and daidzin.
- Soybean proteins have two major components: beta-conglycinin (vicilin class) and glycinin (legumin class), accounting for 390-40% of total seed proteins.

Parts used: Leaves, flowers, oil.

Uses

Nutritional: One of the world's most useful plant.

Typically consumed as a protein drink, soy flour, soy protein, extract, fiber, cereal or milk beverage.

Staple article of food in China and Japan.

"Tokua" as food and" toyo" as flavoring are made from the beans.

Soy milk is considered a substitute for human milk, and used in making ice-cream and flan.

Soybean is a good source of vitamins A and B; the sprouts have good vitamin C content.

Soybeans and soy foods are considered the best dietary sources of isoflavones.

Folkloric

- Bruised leaves applied to snake bites.
- Flowers used for blindness and corneal opacities.
- Green bean hulls chewed to a pulp are applied to smallpox ulcers, corneal ulcers and excoriations in children from urine
- Dried sprouts believed to be beneficial for hair growth and curative for ascites and rheumatism.
- Oil used for ulcers and skin diseases:

TETRAGONIA EXPANSA MURR.

NEW ZEALAND SPINACH

Parts utilized: Leaves, stems, tops and seeds.

Characteristics and Constituents

Pleasant tasting.

Excellent source of vitamin C, E, K and nitrates.

Contains saponins, including oxalic acid.

Antiscorbutic.

Anticancerous.

Juice of leaves and stems is tonic, diuretic, laxative, depurative.

Raw leaves as salad are digestive and cleansing of the GI tract; also calmative and appetizer.

Uses

Nutritional: A common vegetable.

Folkloric: Used for pulmonary and intestinal afflictions.

Gastrointestinal complaints and fatigue.

Used for scurvy and anemia.

Useful for suppressed menses, anthritis, intestinal catarrh, and diarrhea.

Seeds in infusion are laxative in dose of 30 grams in 1 liter of water.

In Brazil, used as an antiscorbutic and for treatment of pulmonary and intestinal afflictions.

Other possible benefits: Consumption of fresh leaves associated with decreased risk of stomach cancer.

CHRYSOPHYLLUM CAINITO LINN.

STAR APPLE

Chemical constituents and characteristics: Seed contains saponin, pouterin, and a bitter principle (lucumin) and a fixed oil.

Leaves contain an amorphous bitter principle, some alkaloids and no saponin.

Pectoral, tonic, stimulant.

Bark is rich in tannin.

Seed is tonic, diuretic and febrifuge.

Parts used and preparation

Seeds, leaves, bark, fruit.

Uses

Folkloric

- Dysentery: Decoction of the bark.
- Tonic: Infusion of the bark is tonic and refreshing.

- Latex is used for abscesses.
- Dried latex used as antihelminthic.
- In some countries, the fruit is used for diabetes.
- Bitter seed sometimes used as tonic, for diarrhea and fevers.
- Fruit eaten for inflammation in laryngitis and pneumonia.
- Used for diabetes.
- Decoction used for angina.
- In Venezuela, unripe fruit used for intestinal problems.
- Decoction of bark used as tonic and stimulant; used for diarrhea, dysentery, hemorrhages and treatment of gonorrhea.
- Cubans in Miami reported to use the leaf decoction for cancer treatment.
- In Brazil, bark latex used on abscesses; and as a potent vermifuge when dried and powdered.

FRAGARIA VESCA LINN.

WILD STRAWBERRY

Parts utilized: Whole plant.

Constituents and properties

Studies have yielded ellagic acid, flavonoids, carotenoids and terpenoids responsibe for antioxidant activity.

Leaf and fruit yield flavonoid, tannin, borneol and ellagic acid.

Considered alterative, astringent, depurative, diuretic, laxative and refrigerant.

Uses

Folkloric: The leaf tea claimed to improve the appetite; also as a mild astringent for diarrhea and digestive upsets and a cleansing diuretic.for rheumatic disorders

The leaf decoction also used for chronic diarrhea.

The roots has same medicinal properties.

Fruit used for intestinal worms, gout, arthritis, jaundice, liver and stomach problems.

For bladder stones, the juice of fresh strawberry is taken before breakfast; also, preventive.

Also used for podagra.

Dyspepsia.

In Campania, Italy, leaf infusion used as appetizer. Leaves used topically on wounds. source

In folk medicine elsewhere, for diabetes, cancder, hypertension, tuberculosis, tumores, and urogenital problems.

HELIANTHUS ANNUUS

SUN FLOWER

Parts used and preparation: Seeds, flowers, roots, bark.

Constituents and properties: Decoction of seed considered diuretic and expectorant.

Seeds and flowers considered febrifuge and stomachic.

Also considered as aphrodisiac, emollient, anti-malarial and anti-cancer.

Plant contains an oleic acid and triacyl glycerol, alkaloids, cyanogenic glycosides, saponins, cardiac glycosides, tannins, fixed oils, phenolics.

Uses

Folkloric: Tea from flowers, dried or fresh leaves is used for facilitating expectoration, relieving coughs, colds.

For whooping cough, an infusion of the brown seeds, drink the tea 4 to 5 times daily.

For asthma, an infusion of the leaves.

For diabetes, tea from decocted roots (10 gms to half a glass of water).

When flowers and leaves are mixed with oil, let stand for 5-10 days before using.

Seeds are diuretic, used to increase the flow of urine.

The bark (boiled) and flowers (steeped) used for fevers, 3-4 tbsp 3-4 times daily.

Poultice of leaves used for sores, insect bites and snake bites.

Elsewhere, flower decoction used for malaria and lung problems.

IPOMOEA BATATAS LINN.

SWEET POTATO

Parts utilized: Tops, leaves and edible roots.

Constituents and properties

- Source of polyphenolic antioxidants.
- Leaves have a high content of polyphenolics - anthocyanins and phenolic acids, with at least 15 biologically active anthocyanins with medicinal value.
- Polyphenols have physiologic funtions, radical scavenging activity, antimutagenic, anticancer, antidiabetes and antibacterial activity in vitro and vivo.
- Considered hemostatic, spleen invigorating.

Uses

Nutritional: Edible: Leaves and roots.

Has a higher nutritional value than the common potato.

Good source of vitamins A, B and C, iron, calcium and phosphorus.

High in complex carbohydrates and dietary fiber; deficient in protein.

Leafy tops eaten as vegetables.

A component of many traditional cuisines.

A staple food crop in some countries.

Industrial: Starch and industrial alcohol production.

Folkloric: Tops, especially purplish ones, used for diabetes.

Crushed leaves applied to boils and acne.

For diarrhea: Boiled or boiled roots.

LYCOPERSICUM ESCULENTUM

TOMATO

Constituents and properties: 100 gm of tomato contains: Water 94%, protein 1 gm; fat 0,3%, carbohydrate 4%, fiber 0.6%, vitamin A 1,100 IU, Vit B 0.2mh. vitamin C 23 mg, nicotinic acid 0.6%, pantothenic acid 0.31 mg, vitamin E 0.27 mg, biotin 0.004 mg, malic acid 150 mg, citric acid 390 mg, oxalic acid 7.5 mg, sodium 3 mg, potassium 268 mg, calcium 11 mg, magnesium 11 mg, iron 0.6 mg, copper 0.1 mg, manganese 0.19 mg, phosphorus 27 mg, sulfur 11 mg, chlorine 51 mg.

Uses

Nutritional: It's both fruit and vegetable.

Good source of iron, phosphorus, calcium, vitamins A and B, and excellent source of vitamin C.

Tomatoes are loaded for vitamin C, a potent antioxidant that mops up free radicals.

Tomatoes also contain lycopene, p-coumaric acid and cholorogenic acid, all possibly helpful in reducing cancer risks.

Folkloric

Pulp and juice are mild aperient.

Juice used for asthma and bronchitis.

TAMARINDUS INDICA LINN.

TAMARIND

Properties: Astringent, tonic, digestive, antiasthmatic, febrifuge, carminative, antiscorbutic, antibilious.

Constituents: Fixed oil, 15-20%; citric, acetic, butyric and oxalic acids; tannin; pectin.

Parts used and preparation: Leaves, fruits, flowers, and bark.

Gather fruits from March to June when fruits ripen.

Remove rind, dry under the sun.

Uses

Folkloric

- Fever: Macerate pulp or ripe fruit in water, sweeten to taste, and drink.
- Laxative: Eat pulp of ripe fruit liberally and follow with plenty of water.
- Asthma: Bark; chop and boil a foot-long piece of bark in 3 glasses of water for 10 minutes. Adults, 1 cup after every meal and at bedtime; children, 1/2 cup 4 times daily; Babies, 2 tbsps 4 times daily.
- Aromatic bath: Use decoction of leaves, especially after childbirth and during convalescence.

Decoction of ash: For colic, indigestion; as gargle for sore throats, aphthous sores.

Ash preparation: Fry the bark with common salk in an earthen pot until it turns to white ash; heaping teaspoon of the ash to half-cup of boiling water; cool and drink.

Poultice or lotion from bark applied to ulcers, boils, and rashes.

Poultice of leaves to inflammatory swellings of ankles and joints.

Decoction of leaves as postpartum tea; also used as a wash for indolent ulcers.

Flowers for conjunctival inflammation. Internally, as decoction or infusion, for bleeding piles (4 glasses of tea daily).

Pulp surrounding the seeds is cooling and laxative.

Culinary / Nutrition: As a souring condiment.

Source of vitamins B and C.

Sweetened, candied.

ANANAS COMOSUS LINN.

PINEAPPLE

Chemical constituents and properties: The native variety has a much higher carbohydrate content than the Cayenne variety. Both are fair sources of calcium and iron, good sources of vitamins A and B, and excellent sources of vitamin C. Contains citric acid, phosphoric and sulfuric acid, lime, magnesia, iron, silica, sodium and chlorides of potassium. Anthelmintic, vermicide, diuretic, aperient, antiscorbutic, diaphoretic, refrigerant, digestive, styptic, emmenagogue. Antihelminthic property of fresh fruit juice attributed to its constituent, bromelin, a proteolytic ferment, that is toxic to Ascaris lumbricoides and Macracanthorynchus hirudinaceous.

Uses

Nutritional: Fair source of calcium and iron; good source of vitamins A and B; excellent source of vitamin C.

Folkloric: Juice of leaves: anthelmintic; used for intestinal animal parasites (decoction of fresh young leaves, 4x daily).

Ripe fruit good for acid dyspepsia and aids digestion,.

Juice of ripe fruit increases urine flow, gently laxative, cooling and digestive.

11

Plants: Diversity and Reproduction

VASCULAR PLANT

Vascular plants (also known as tracheophytes or higher plants) are those plants that have lignified tissues for conducting water, minerals, and photosynthetic products through the plant. Vascular plants include the ferns, clubmosses, flowering plants, conifers and other gymnosperms. Scientific names for the group include *Tracheophyta* and *Tracheobionta,* but neither name is very widely used.

Characteristics

Vascular plants are distinguished by two primary characteristics:

1. Vascular plants have vascular tissues, which circulate resources through the plant. This feature allows vascular plants to evolve to a larger size than non-vascular plants, which lack these specialized conducting tissues and are therefore restricted to relatively small sizes.
2. In vascular plants, the principal generation phase is the *sporophyte,* which is usually diploid with two sets of chromosomes per cell. Only the germ cells and gametophytes are haploid. By contrast, the principal generation phase in non-vascular plants is usually the *gametophyte,* which is haploid with one set of chromosomes

per cell. In these plants, generally only the spore stalk and capsule are diploid.

One possible mechanism for the presumed switch from emphasis on the haploid generation to emphasis on the diploid generation is the greater efficiency in spore dispersal with more complex diploid structures. In other words, elaboration of the spore stalk enabled the production of more spore and the ability to release it higher and to broadcast it farther. Such developments may include more photosynthetic area for the spore-bearing structure, the ability to grow independent roots, woody structure for support, and more branching.

Water transport happens in either xylem or phloem: xylem carries water and inorganic solutes upward toward the leaves from the roots, while phloem carries organic solutes throughout the plant. Group of plants having lignified conducting tissue (xylem vessels or tracheids)

NUTRIENT DISTRIBUTION

Photographs showing xylem elements in the shoot of a fig tree (*Ficus alba*): crushed in hydrochloric acid, between slides and cover slips.

Nutrients and water from the soil and the organic compounds produced in leaves are distributed to specific areas in the plant through the xylem and phloem. The xylem draws water and nutrients up from the roots to the upper sections of the plant's body, and the phloem conducts other materials, such as the sucrose produced during photosynthesis, which gives the plant energy to keep growing and seeding.

The xylem consists of tracheids, which are dead hard-walled hollow cells arranged to form tiny tubes to function in water transport. A tracheid cell wall usually contains the polymer lignin. The phloem however consists of living cells called sieve-tube members. Between the sieve-tube members are sieve plates, which have pores to allow molecules to pass through. Sieve-tube members lack such organs as nuclei or ribosomes, but cells next to them, the companion cells, function to keep the sieve-tube members alive. The movement of nutrients, water and sugars is affected by transpiration, conduction and absorption of water.

Transpiration

The most abundant compound in all plants, as in all life, is water which serves an important role in the various processes taking place. Transpiration is the main process a plant can call upon to move compounds within its tissues. The basic minerals and nutrients a plant is composed of remain, generally, within the plant. Water is constantly lost from the plant through its stomata to the atmosphere.

Water is transpired from the plants leaves via stomata, carried there via leaf veins and vascular bundles within the plants cambium layer. The movement of water out of the leaf stomata creates, when the leaves are considered collectively, a transpiration pull. The pull is created through water surface tension within the plant cells.

The draw of water upwards is assisted by the movement of water into the roots via osmosis. This process also assists the plant in absorbing nutrients from the soil as soluble salts, a process known as absorption. Surprisingly, the movement of water upwards requires very little or no energy from the plant. Hydrogen bonds exist between water molecules, which cause them to line up, as the molecules at the top of the plant evaporate, they pull the next one up to replace it, which in turn pulls on the next one in line.

Absorption

Xylem vessels allow the movement of water and nutrients upwards towards the shoots and leaves through the roots and fine root hairs from the soil. Living root cells passively absorb water in the absence of transpiration pull via osmosis creating root pressure. It is possible for there to be no evapotranspiration and therefore no pull of water towards the shoots and leaves. This is usually due to high temperatures, high humidity, darkness or drought.

Conduction

Xylem and phloem tissues are involved in the conduction processes within plants. Sugars are conducted throughout the plant in the phloem and other nutrients through the xylem. Conduction occurs from a source to a sink for each separate nutrient. Sugars are produced in the leaves (a source) by photosynthesis and transported to the roots (a sink) for use in cellular respiration or storage. Minerals are absorbed in the roots (a source) and transported to the shoots to allow cell division and growth.

Pteridophyte (fern)

The pteridophytes are vascular plants (plants with xylem and phloem) that produce neither flowers nor seeds, and are hence called vascular cryptogams. Instead, they reproduce and disperse only via spores.

Pteridophyte classification

They do not form a monophyletic group but consist of two groups:

- the Lycopodiophyta (club mosses, spike mosses, and quillworts),
- Ferns:
    - o Marattioid ferns,
    - o Equisetophyta (horsetails),
    - o Psilotophyta (whisk ferns) and Ophioglossophyta (adder's tongues and grape ferns),
    - o Leptosporangiate ferns (the largest group of ferns).

In addition to these living groups of pteridophytes are several groups now extinct and known only from fossils. These groups include the Rhyniophyta, Zosterophyllophyta, Trimerophytophyta, and the progymnosperms.

Modern studies of the land plants agree that all the pteridophytes share a single common ancestor. However, they are not a clade (monophyletic group) because the seed plants are also descended from within this group—probably close relatives of the progymnosperms.

PTERIDOPHYTE SEXUALITY

These plants are generally sporophyte-oriented; that is, the normal plant is the diploid sporophyte, with the only haploid structure being the gametophyte (prothallium) in season. This basic pattern is like that found in the seed plants but with an important exception. Unlike the seed plants, the pteridophytes have a gametophyte stage that is free-living. As a result, pteridophyte sexuality is more complicated than that of the seed plants.

There are several basic categories of sexuality in pteridophytes. The terms distinguish between types of gametophyte sexuality:

- Dioicous pteridophytes produce only antheridia (male organs) or archegonia (female organ) on a single gametophyte body.
- Monoicous pteridophytes produce both antheridia and archegonia on the same gametophyte body.

Protandrous pteridophytes produce the male antheridia first, and then their female archegonia.

Protogynous pteridophytes produce the archegonia first, followed by the antheridia.

Notice that these terms are *not* the same as monoecious and dioecious, which refer to whether or not a sporophyte plant bears one or both kinds of gametophyte. Those terms apply only to seed plants.

Spermatophyte (seed)

The spermatophytes (also known as phanerogams) comprise those plants that produce seeds. They are a subset of the embryophytes or land plants. The living spermatophytes form five groups:

- cycads, a subtropical and tropical group of plants with a large crown of compound leaves and a stout trunk,
- *Ginkgo,* a single living species of tree,
- conifers, cone-bearing trees and shrubs,
- gnetophytes, woody plants in the genera *Gnetum, Welwitschia,* and *Ephedra,* and
- angiosperms, the flowering plants, a large group including many familiar plants in a wide variety of habitats.

In addition to the taxa listed above, the fossil record contains evidence of many extinct taxa of seed plants. The so-called "seed ferns" (Pteridospermae) were one of the earliest successful groups of land plants, and forests dominated by seed ferns were prevalent in the late Paleozoic. *Glossopteris* was the most prominent tree genus in the ancient southern supercontinent of Gondwana during the Permian period. By the Triassic period, seed ferns had declined in ecological importance, and representatives of modern gymnosperm groups were abundant and dominant through the end of the Cretaceous, when angiosperms radiated. Another Late Paleozoic group of probable spermatophytes were the gigantopterids.

RELATIONSHIPS AND NOMENCLATURE

Seed-bearing plants were traditionally divided into angiosperms, or flowering plants, and gymnosperms, which includes the gnetophytes, cycads, ginkgo, and conifers. Older morphological studies have shown a close relationship between the gnetophytes and the angiosperms, in particular based on vessel elements. However, molecular studies (and some more recent morphological and fossil papers) have generally shown a clade of gymnosperms, with the gnetophytes in or near the conifers. For example, one common proposed set of relationships is known as the *gne-pine hypothesis* and looks like:

The relationships between these groups should not be considered settled. A traditional classification grouped all the seed plants in a single division, with classes for our five groups:

- Division Spermatophyta
  - o Cycadopsida, the cycads
  - o Ginkgoopsida, the ginkgo
  - o Pinopsida, the conifers, ("Coniferopsida")
  - o Gnetopsida, the gnetophytes
  - o Magnoliopsida, the flowering plants, or Angiospermopsida

A more modern classification ranks these groups as separate divisions (sometimes under the Superdivision Spermatophyta):

- Cycadophyta, the cycads
- Ginkgophyta, the ginkgo
- Pinophyta, the conifers
- Gnetophyta, the gnetophytes
- Magnoliophyta, the flowering plants

Bryophyte

Bryophytes are all embryophytes ('land plants') that are non-vascular: they have tissues and enclosed reproductive systems, but they lack vascular tissue that circulates liquids.They neither have flowers nor produce seeds, reproducing via spores. The term *bryophyte* comes from Greek *âñýïí - bryon,* "tree-moss, oyster-green" and" plant".

Bryophyte classification

The bryophytes (or non-tracheophytes) do not form a monophyletic group but consist of three groups, the Marchantiophyta (liverworts), Anthocerotophyta (hornworts), and Bryophyta (mosses). Originally the three groups were brought together as the three classes of division Bryophyta. However, since the three groups of bryophytes form a paraphyletic group, they now are placed in three separate divisions

Bryophyte sexuality

These plants are generally gametophyte-oriented; that is, the normal plant is the haploid gametophyte, with the only diploid structure being the sporangium in season. As a result, bryophyte sexuality is very different from that of other plants. There are two basic categories of sexuality in bryophytes:

- Dioicous bryophytes produce only antheridia (male organs) or archegonia (female organs) on a single plant body.
- Monoicous bryophytes produce both antheridia and archegonia on the same plant body.

Some bryophyte species may be either monoicous or dioicous depending on environmental conditions. Other species grow exclusively with one type of sexuality.Notice that these terms are *not* the same as monoecious and dioecious, which refer to whether or not a sporophyte plant bears one or both kinds of gametophyte. Those terms apply only to seed plants.

Bryophyte life cycle

Dispersal in bryophytes is via spores; they neither have flowers nor produce seeds. Bryophytes do produce gametes that fuse to form a zygote, which in turn develops into an embryo, but this is not contained in a seed as in gymnosperms and angiosperms.

Angiosperms

The flowering plants or angiosperms (Angiospermae or Magnoliophyta) are the most diverse group of land plants. The flowering plants and the gymnosperms are the only extant groups of seed plants. The flowering plants are distinguished from other seed plants by a series of apomorphies, or derived characteristics.

The ancestors of flowering plants diverged from gymnosperms around 245–202 million years ago, and the first flowering plants known to exist are from 140 million years ago. They became widespread around 100 million years ago, but replaced conifers as the dominant trees only around 60-70 million years ago.

ANGIOSPERM DERIVED CHARACTERISTICS

- Flowers: The flowers, which are the reproductive organs of flowering plants, are the most remarkable feature distinguishing them from other seed plants. Flowers aid angiosperms by enabling a wider range of adaptability and broadening the ecological niches open to them. This has allowed flowering plants to largely dominate terrestrial ecosystems.
- Stamens with two pairs of pollen sacs: Stamens are much lighter than the corresponding organs of gymnosperms and have contributed to the diversification of angiosperms through time with adaptations to specialized pollination syndromes, such as particular pollinators. Stamens have also become modified through time to prevent self-fertilization, which has permitted further diversification, allowing angiosperms eventually to fill more niches.
- Reduced male parts, three cells: The male gametophyte in angiosperms is significantly reduced in size compared to those of gymnosperm seed plants. The smaller pollen decreases the time from pollination — the pollen grain reaching the female plant — to fertilization of the ovary; in gymnosperms fertilization can occur up to a year after pollination, while in angiosperms the fertilization begins very soon after pollination. The shorter time leads to angiosperm plants setting seeds sooner and faster than gymnosperms, which is a distinct evolutionary advantage.
- Closed carpel enclosing the ovules (carpel or carpels and accessory parts may become the fruit): The closed carpel of angiosperms also allows adaptations to specialized pollination syndromes and controls. This helps to prevent self-fertilization, thereby maintaining increased diversity. Once the ovary is fertilized, the carpel and some surrounding tissues develop into a fruit. This fruit often serves as an attractant to seed-dispersing animals. The resulting cooperative relationship presents another advantage to angiosperms in the process of dispersal.
- Reduced female gametophyte, seven cells with eight nuclei: The reduced female gametophyte, like the reduced

male gametophyte, may be an adaptation allowing for more rapid seed set, eventually leading to such flowering plant adaptations as annual herbaceous life cycles, allowing the flowering plants to fill even more niches.

- Endosperm: Endosperm formation generally begins after fertilization and before the first division of the zygote. Endosperm is a highly nutritive tissue that can provide food for the developing embryo, the cotyledons, and sometimes for the seedling when it first appears.

These distinguishing characteristics taken together have made the angiosperms the most diverse and numerous land plants and the most commercially important group to humans. The major exception to the dominance of terrestrial ecosystems by flowering plants is the coniferous forest.

FLOWERS

The characteristic feature of angiosperms is the flower. Flowers show remarkable variation in form and elaboration, and provide the most trustworthy external characteristics for establishing relationships among angiosperm species. The function of the flower is to ensure fertilization of the ovule and development of fruit containing seeds. The floral apparatus may arise terminally on a shoot or from the axil of a leaf (where the petiole attaches to the stem). Occasionally, as in violets, a flower arises singly in the axil of an ordinary foliage-leaf. More typically, the flower-bearing portion of the plant is sharply distinguished from the foliage-bearing or vegetative portion, and forms a more or less elaborate branch-system called an inflorescence.

The reproductive cells produced by flowers are of two kinds. Microspores, which will divide to become pollen grains, are the "male" cells and are borne in the stamens (or microsporophylls). The "female" cells called megaspores, which will divide to become the egg-cell (megagametogenesis), are contained in the ovule and enclosed in the carpel (or megasporophyll).

The flower may consist only of these parts, as in willow, where each flower comprises only a few stamens or two carpels. Usually other structures are present and serve to protect the sporophylls and to form an envelope attractive to pollinators. The individual members of these surrounding structures are known as sepals and petals (or tepals in flowers such as *Magnolia* where sepals and petals are not distinguishable from each other). The outer series (calyx of sepals) is usually green and leaf-like, and functions to protect the rest of the flower, especially the bud. The inner series (corolla of petals) is generally white or brightly colored, and is more delicate in structure. It functions to attract insect or bird pollinators. Attraction is effected by color, scent, and nectar, which may be secreted in some part of the flower. The characteristics that attract pollinators account for the popularity of flowers and flowering plants among humans.

While the majority of flowers are perfect or hermaphrodite (having both male and female parts in the same flower structure), flowering plants have developed numerous morphological and physiological mechanisms to reduce or prevent self-fertilization. Heteromorphic flowers have short carpels and long stamens, or vice versa, so animal pollinators cannot easily transfer pollen to the pistil (receptive part of the carpel). Homomorphic flowers may employ a biochemical (physiological) mechanism called self-incompatibility to discriminate between self- and non-self pollen grains. In other species, the male and female parts are morphologically separated, developing on different flowers.

Flower structure

Flowers form at the end of a specialized branch of a plant. The tip of the branch is called receptacle. Attached to the receptacle are four parts: sepals, petals, stamens and carpels. The outermost part of the flower is made of the sepals and petals. Both of these kinds of structures appear leaf like. Sepals usually green; petals are usually white or brightly colored. Sepals being the outermost part commonly enclose the flower before it opens. A stamen is the male reproductive part of a lower. It usually consists of a long filament topped with an anther. Inside the anther are numerous sacs in which pollen grains are produced. In the middle of the flower is the female reproductive structure called the carpel. At the base of the carpel is the ovary. The ovary sectioned into compartments that contain ovules. These are the structures that develop into seeds. Above the ovary is the tubular structure called the style. On the top o the style is the stigma, the place where pollen first collects.

Flowers vary in the number, color, shape, and arrangement of their parts. Most flowers have both male and female parts. Such flowers are referred to as perfect. In contrast, some flowers have only male or female parts are termed imperfect. Some plants like oak trees have male and females flowers on the same plant. Other plant species have male and female flowers on separate plants.

The arrangement of flowers also varies among different kinds of plants some plantshave flowers that occur singly, like tulips. Others have flowers in a cluster called an inflorescence.

The characteristics of flowers are used to classify them. Monocots and dicots can be distinguished easily by differences in flower structure. Monocots usually have flower parts in multiples of three. For example, lilies usually have six sepals, six petals, and six stamens. Flower parts of dicots usually are in multiples of four and five.

Fertilization and embryogenesis

Double fertilization refers to a process in which two sperm cells fertilize cells in the ovary. This process begins when a pollen grain adheres to the stigma of the pistil (female reproductive structure), germinates, and grows a long pollen tube. While this pollen tube is growing, a haploid generative cell travels down the tube behind the tube nucleus. The generative cell divides by mitosis to produce two haploid (*n*) sperm cells. As the pollen tube grows, it makes its way from the stigma, down the style and into the ovary. Here the pollen tube reaches the micropyle of the ovule and digests its way into one of the synergids, releasing its contents (which include the sperm cells). The synergid that the cells were released into degenerates and one sperm makes its way to fertilize the egg cell, producing a diploid (2*n*) zygote. The second sperm cell fuses with both central cell nuclei, producing a triploid (3*n*) cell. As the zygote develops into an embryo, the triploid cell develops into the endosperm, which serves as the embryo's food supply. The ovary now will develop into fruit and the ovule will develop into seed.

Fruit and seed

As the development of embryo and endosperm proceeds within the embryo-sac, the sac wall enlarges and combines with the nucellus (which is likewise enlarging) and the integument to form the *seed-coat*. The ovary wall develops to form the fruit or pericarp, whose form is closely associated with the manner of distribution of the seed.

Frequently the influence of fertilization is felt beyond the ovary, and other parts of the flower take part in the formation of the fruit, *e.g.* the floral receptacle in the apple, strawberry and others.

The character of the seed-coat bears a definite relation to that of the fruit. They protect the embryo and aid in dissemination; they may also directly promote germination. Among plants with indehiscent fruits, the fruit generally provides protection for the embryo and secures dissemination. In this case, the seed-coat is only slightly developed. If the fruit is dehiscent and the seed is exposed, the seed-coat is generally well developed, and must discharge the functions otherwise executed by the fruit.

Gymnosperm

The gymnosperms are a group of seed-bearing plants that includes conifers, cycads, *Ginkgo* and Gnetales. The term "gymnosperm" comes from the Greek word *gymnospermos* (*ãõìíüóðåñìïò*), meaning "naked seeds", after the unenclosed condition of their seeds (called ovules in their unfertilized state).

Their naked condition stands in contrast to the seeds or ovules of flowering plants (angiosperms) which are enclosed during pollination. Gymnosperm seeds develop either on the surface of scale- or leaf-like appendages of cones, or at the end of short stalks (*Ginkgo*).

The gymnosperms and angiosperms together comprise the spermatophytes or seed plants. By far the largest group of living gymnosperms are the conifers (pines, cypresses, and relatives), followed by cycads, Gnetales (*Gnetum*, *Ephedra* and *Welwitschia*), and *Ginkgo* (a single living species).

Classification

In early classification schemes, the gymnosperms (Gymnospermae) were regarded as a "natural" group. There is conflicting evidence on the question of whether the living gymnosperms form a clade although according to some recent analyses of molecular data the living gymnosperms do appear to be monophyletic.. The fossil record of gymnosperms includes many distinctive taxa that do not belong to the four modern groups, including seed-bearing trees that have a somewhat fern-like vegetative morphology (the so-called seed ferns or pteridosperms.) When fossil gymnosperms such as Bennettitales, *Caytonia* and the glossopterids are considered, it is clear that angiosperms are nested within a larger gymnosperm clade, although which group of gymnosperms are their closest relatives remains unclear.

Seeds

For the lower vascular plants the important evolutionary development was in the water and food conducting tissues of the sporophyte. As we move on through the plant kingdom the next important development was the seed. The free living gametophyte is a vulnerable phase of the life cycle. Reproduction by seeds is a less chancy procedure and has other advantages for plant survival and dispersal. Seeds can be remarkably tolerant of environmental extremes heat, cold and drought. Unlike free-living gametophytes seeds can postpone their development until conditions are right. And, of course, we find them very convenient for plant propagation. Already in the coal-measure forests there were plants that reproduced by seeds. Some were the so-called "seed ferns". none of which survive. Others were the ancestors of the plants we now know collectively as "gymnosperms". In these plants the seeds are not enclosed in an ovary, as in the flowering plants; they grow on the surface of a modified leaf in a strobilus or cone. "Gymnosperm" means naked seed.

Alternation of generations is still involved in the reproduction of these plants. They are all heterosporous: the microspores are shed as pollen, whereas the megaspore germinates in the strobilus to produce the female gametophyte. The archegonia in this gametophyte get fertilized by sperm from the male gametophyte and the zygote grows to produce an embryo which is enclosed in a seed coat of tissue from the parent plant.

Gymnosperms were the dominant land plants in the age of dinosaurs, the Cretaceous and Jurassic periods. The surviving gymnosperms in the Coniferophyta, Cycadophyta and Ginkgophyta are similar in their woody habit and pattern of seed development but are not closely related.

Coniferophyta

Conifer leaves are needle or scale-like. They result from the downsizing of true megaphylls and unlike the microphylls of lower plants they are connected to the vascular system of the stem. Conifers are often large and can dominate the plant life in some ecosystems because their stems continue to expand in width as well as length throughout the life of the plant. The older parts of the stem become woody, which provides a further distinction from the seedless vascular plants of which there are no surviving woody representatives.

Cycadophyta

Cycads or similar plants were the food of herbivorous dinosaurs and the fate of both of these groups of organisms was probably closely linked. They survive as a few species of tropical palm-like trees, including one which is native to the USA, *Zamia pumila* the cardboard palm. This is found on sandy soils in Florida and is sometimes grown as a foliage plant. *Cycas* species are larger and are often used as ornamentals in tropical areas. The cycads can be viewed as beneficial as they form symbiotic associations with nitrogen fixing bacteria, but they have also been the subject of extermination programs since they are highly toxic to livestock.

Ginkgophyta

This is a monotypic division, a single species of a single genus, *Ginkgo biloba* the maidenhair tree. Several relatives are known as fossils dating back to Pennsylvanian times. *Ginkgo biloba* was preserved in the gardens of Buddhist monasteries in

China and Japan where it was encountered by Westerners in the eighteenth century. It has turned out to be a valuable street tree because of its unusual foliage and tolerance of pollution.

Life cycle

Gymnosperms are spore-bearing plants (sporophytes), with a sporophyte-dominant life cycle; as in all other vascular plants the gametophyte (gamete-bearing phase) is relatively short-lived. Two spore types, microspores and megaspores, are generally produced in pollen cones or ovulate cones, respectively. A short-lived multicellular haploid, gamete-bearing phase (gametophyte) develops inside the spore wall. Pollen grains (microgametophytes) mature from microspores, and ultimately produce sperm cells; megagametophyte tissue develops in the megaspore of each ovule, and produces multiple egg cells. Thus, megaspores are enclosed in ovules (unfertilized seeds) and give rise to megagametophytes and ultimately to egg cells.

During pollination, pollen grains are physically transferred between plants, from pollen cone to the ovule, being transferred by wind or insects. Whole grains enter each ovule through a microscopic gap in the ovule coat (integument) called the micropyle. The pollen grains mature further inside the ovule and produce sperm cells. Two main modes of fertilization are found in gymnosperms. Cycads and *Ginkgo* have motile sperm that swim directly to the egg inside the ovule, while conifers and gnetophytes have sperm with no flagella that are conveyed to the egg along a pollen tube. After fertilization (joining of the sperm and egg cell), the zygote develops into an embryo (young sporophyte). More than one embryo is usually initiated in each gymnosperm seed. Competition between the embryos for nutritional resources within polyembryonic seeds produces programmed cell death to all but one embryo. The mature seed comprises the embryo and the remains of the female gametophyte, which serves as a food supply, and the seed coat (integument).

Bibliography

Brandwein, P.F.: *Sourcebook for the Biological Sciences*, San Diego, Harcourt Brace JOvanovich, 1986.

Chrispeels, Maarten : *Plants, Genes and Crop Biotechnology*, Sudbury MA, Jones and Barlett Publishers, 2003.

David Sadava: *Plants, Genes and Crop Biotechnology*, Sudbury MA, Jones and Barlett Publishers, 2003.

Fransman M, Junne G, Roobeek A: *The Biotechnology Revolution?*, Oxford, Blackwell, 1995.

George S. Paul: *Beyond Humanity: Cyber Evolution and Future Minds*, Roackland, Charles River Media, 1996.

Goodsell, David S.: *Bionanotechnology: Lessons From Nature*, Hoboken, Wiley-Liss, 2004.

Moravec, Hans: *Mind Children: The Future of Robot and Human Intelligence*, Cambridge, Harvard University Press, 1988.

Murray, David: *Seeds of Concern: The Genetic Manipulation of Plants*, Sydney, University of New South Wales, 2003.

Postman, Neil: *Technopoly: The Surrender of Culture to Technology*, New York, Vintage Books, 1992.

Retzer, W.J.: *Biotechnology Workbook*, Englewood Cliffs, Prentice Hall, 1991.

Shetty, Kalidas: *Food Biotechnology*, New York, Dekker/CRC Press, 2005.

Smith, John E.: *Biotechnology*, Cambridge, Cambridge University Press, 2004.

Towle, Albert: *Modern Biology*, Austin, Holt, Rinehart and Winston, 1988.

Walden, Richard: *Genetic Transformation in Plants*, England, Open University Press, 1988.

Index

□□□